Studies in Development Economics and Policy

Series Editor: Finn Tarp
UNU WORLD INSTITUTE FOR DEVELOPMENT ECONOMICS RESEARCH

(UNU-WIDER) was established by the United Nations University as its first research and training centre and started work in Helsinki, Finland, in 1985. The purpose of the institute is to undertake applied research and policy analysis of structural changes affecting the developing and transitional economies; to provide a forum for the advocacy of policies leading to robust, equitable and environmentally sustainable growth; and to promote capacity strengthening and training in the field of economic and social policy-making. Its work is carried out by staff researchers and visiting scholars in Helsinki, and through networks of collaborating scholars and institutions around the world.

UNU World Institute for Development Economics Research (UNU-WIDER)
Katajanokanlaituri 6 B, FIN-00160 Helsinki, Finland

Titles include:

Tony Addison and Alan Roe (*editors*)
FISCAL POLICY FOR DEVELOPMENT
Poverty, Reconstruction and Growth

Tony Addison, Henrik Hansen and Finn Tarp (*editors*)
DEBT RELIEF FOR POOR COUNTRIES

Tony Addison and George Mavrotas (*editors*)
DEVELOPMENT FINANCE IN THE GLOBAL ECONOMY
The Road Ahead

Tony Addison and Tilman Brück (*editors*)
MAKING PEACE WORK
The Challenges of Social and Economic Reconstruction

George G. Borjas and Jeff Crisp (*editors*)
POVERTY, INTERNATIONAL MIGRATION AND ASYLUM

Ricardo Ffrench-Davis and Stephany Griffith-Jones (*editors*)
FROM CAPITAL SURGES TO DROUGHT
Seeking Stability for Emerging Economies

David Fielding (*editor*)
MACROECONOMIC POLICY IN THE FRANC ZONE

Basudeb Guha-Khasnobis and George Mavrotas (*editors*)
FINANCIAL DEVELOPMENTS, INSTITUTIONS, GROWTH AND POVERTY
REDUCTION

Basudeb Guha-Khasnobis, Shabd S. Acharya and Benjamin Davis (*editors*)
FOOD INSECURITY, VULNERABILITY AND HUMAN RIGHTS FAILURE

Basudeb Guha-Khasnobis and Ravi Kanbur (*editors*)
INFORMAL LABOUR MARKETS AND DEVELOPMENT

Basudeb Guha-Khasnobis (*editor*)
THE WTO, DEVELOPING COUNTRIES AND THE DOHA DEVELOPMENT AGENDA
Prospects and Challenges for Trade-Led Growth

Aiguo Lu and Manuel F. Montes (*editors*)
POVERTY, INCOME DISTRIBUTION AND WELL-BEING IN ASIA DURING
THE TRANSITION

George Mavrotas and Anthony Shorrocks (*editors*)
ADVANCING DEVELOPMENT
Core Themes in Global Economics

George Mavrotas and Mark McGillivray (*editors*)
DEVELOPMENT AID
A Fresh Look

George Mavrotas (*editor*)
DOMESTIC RESOURCE MOBILIZATION AND FINANCIAL DEVELOPMENT

Mark McGillivray (*editor*)
ACHIEVING THE MILLENNIUM DEVELOPMENT GOALS

Mark McGillivray (*editor*)
HUMAN WELL-BEING
Concept and Measurement

Mark McGillivray, Indranil Dutta and David Lawson (*editor*)
HEALTH INEQUALITY AND DEVELOPMENT

Mark McGillivray (*editor*)
INEQUALITY, POVERTY AND WELL-BEING

Robert J. McIntyre and Bruno Dallago (*editors*)
SMALL AND MEDIUM ENTERPRISES IN TRANSITIONAL ECONOMIES

Vladimir Mikhalev (*editor*)
INEQUALITY AND SOCIAL STRUCTURE DURING THE TRANSITION

E. Wayne Nafziger and Raimo Väyrynen (*editors*)
THE PREVENTION OF HUMANITARIAN EMERGENCIES

Wim Naudé (*editor*)
ENTREPRENEURSHIP AND ECONOMIC DEVELOPMENT

Machiko Nissanke and Erik Thorbecke (*editors*)
THE IMPACT OF GLOBALIZATION ON THE WORLD'S POOR
Transmission Mechanisms

Machiko Nissanke and Erik Thorbecke (*editors*)
GLOBALIZATION AND THE POOR IN ASIA

Matthew Odedokun (*editor*)
EXTERNAL FINANCE FOR PRIVATE SECTOR DEVELOPMENT
Appraisals and Issues

Amelia U. Santos-Paulino and Guanghua Wan (*editors*)
THE RISE OF CHINA AND INDIA
Impacts, Prospects and Implications

Laixiang Sun (*editor*)
OWNERSHIP AND GOVERNANCE OF ENTERPRISES
Recent Innovative Developments

Guanghua Wan (*editor*)
UNDERSTANDING INEQUALITY AND POVERTY IN CHINA
Methods and Applications

Studies in Development Economics and Policy
Series Standing Order ISBN 978–0333–96424–8 hardcover
Series Standing Order ISBN 978–0230–20041–8 paperback
(*outside North America only*)

You can receive future titles in this series as they are published by placing a standing order. Please contact your bookseller or, in case of difficulty, write to us at the address below with your name and address, the title of the series and the ISBNs quoted above.

Customer Services Department, Macmillan Distribution Ltd, Houndmills, Basingstoke, Hampshire RG21 6XS, England

Economies in Transition

The Long-Run View

Edited by

Gérard Roland

Professor of Economics and Political Science, University of California, Berkeley, USA

WITHDRAWN

In association with United Nations
University-World Institute for Development
Economics Research (UNU-WIDER)

First published 2012 by
PALGRAVE MACMILLAN

Palgrave Macmillan in the UK is an imprint of Macmillan Publishers Limited,
registered in England, company number 785998, of Houndmills, Basingstoke,
Hampshire RG21 6XS.

Palgrave Macmillan in the US is a division of St Martin's Press LLC,
175 Fifth Avenue, New York, NY 10010.

Palgrave Macmillan is the global academic imprint of the above companies
and has companies and representatives throughout the world.

Palgrave® and Macmillan® are registered trademarks in the United States,
the United Kingdom, Europe and other countries.

ISBN 978–0–230–34348–1

This book is printed on paper suitable for recycling and made from fully
managed and sustained forest sources. Logging, pulping and manufacturing
processes are expected to conform to the environmental regulations of the
country of origin.

A catalogue record for this book is available from the British Library.

A catalog record for this book is available from the Library of Congress.

10   9   8   7   6   5   4   3   2   1
21 20 19 18 17 16 15 14 13 12

Printed and bound in the United States of America

Contents

Figures and Tables

Figures

Tables

Annexes

Acknowledgements

We would like to thank Tony Shorrocks, who had the original idea of putting together the conference Reflections on Transition: Twenty Years after the Fall of the Berlin Wall, in Helsinki in September 2009. We are grateful to Finn Tarp, who, in late 2009, took over as director of UNU-WIDER and pushed the project forward. We would also like to thank Luc Christiaensen and Neha Mehrotra for their input. And last but not least, we are truly grateful to Lorraine Telfer-Taivainen at UNU-WIDER who took charge of all the details of the conference, the project and the manuscript, seeing each stage through from beginning to end, making it a very successful conference and, indeed, a great book.

Gérard Roland
Berkeley, California

Foreword

This book is the result of a project initially conceived by my predecessor, Tony Shorrocks, who, 20 years after the fall of the Berlin Wall, considered the time was ripe for scholarly assessment of transition economies and how they fared in the somewhat heady days following the crumbling of the centrally planned economy model.

Gérard Roland was appointed project director and brought together a top team of transition scholars at a research conference in Helsinki in September 2009, to discuss and review the experiences of transition countries during the past two decades and to draw out possible lessons for the future. The conference keynote paper was delivered by Hungarian economist and elder of transition studies János Kornai, someone well known for his critique of the command economies in Eastern Europe. This fascinating keynote was reworked and now comprises the first chapter of the book. The academic debate was set off at a very high calibre by Václav Havel, the former President of both Czechoslovakia and the Czech Republic, who was an invitee to the conference but was unable to travel. We were, thanks to modern technology, still able to have him present by video to give the opening address.

A selection of the studies presented at the Helsinki conference were honed and developed further, following extensive and frank peer review, to comprise this distinctive book. They tell a multifaceted, multilayered story of economic transition. The text looks at institutional change and geopolitical evolutions along with their socioeconomic implications. Privatization and liberalization are put under the microscope in the transitioning country context, with predictions about their longer-term trajectories and impacts for the country and citizens alike. Economic growth and decline, poverty, ethnic tensions, nostalgia for the past, changing demographics, increasing crime rates, and changing health and fertility patterns are all painted onto the colourful canvas. This book will therefore be of interest not only to transition researchers and policy makers but also to professionals in other areas and to laypersons interested in following the transition literature with a comparative analysis of what has happened, rightly or wrongly, with hints as to what also might have happened given different political and economic backdrops.

Finally, I would like to express my sincere thanks to Gérard Roland for his top-rate academic and professional skills in bringing this project successfully to fruition.

Finn Tarp, Director
UNU-WIDER Helsinki

Notes on Contributors

Erik Berglöf is Chief Economist and Special Adviser to the President at the European Bank for Reconstruction and Development. He has been Director of SITE at the Stockholm School of Economics, has taught at the Université Libre de Bruxelles, and has held visiting positions at Harvard, Stanford, and MIT. He is a non-resident senior fellow of the Brookings Institution in Washington, DC. He has published widely on financial development, corporate governance, and transition economics. His interests have been particularly oriented towards policy issues in emerging economies, but he has also contributed extensively to the debate on regional and global institutional architecture.

Elizabeth Brainerd is the Susan and Barton Winokur Professor of Economics and Women's and Gender Studies. Her research focuses on labour and health economics, with particular interest in understanding the social and health consequences of the transition to capitalism in formerly socialist countries. Her work has examined changes in the gender wage gap and wage inequality in Eastern Europe, the impact of the Second World War on marriage and fertility in Russian women, and the impact of economic transition on mortality in post-socialist countries.

László Bruszt is Head of the Department of Political and Social Sciences at the European University Institute in Florence. His more recent studies focus on the interplay between transnationalization, institutional development, and economic change, with one of his latest publications focusing on the comparative study of transnational integration regimes.

Lise Bruynooghe is an analyst at the European Bank for Reconstruction and Development. Prior to her current role in the Agribusiness Banking Team, she participated in the bank's research programmes on small and medium-sized businesses and the assessment of transition processes in Eastern Europe and Russia. She has co-written chapters in the bank's flagship publication, *The Transition Report*, and in joint EBRD publications with the EC and the OECD.

Nauro F. Campos is a professor of economics and finance at Brunel University, London. His research interests include political economy and economic growth in developing and transition countries.

Giovanni Andrea Cornia teaches economics at the University of Florence. Previously he was Director of UNU-WIDER in Helsinki. His research has mostly focused on macroeconomics, inequality, public economics, and health–mortality–human development issues in developing and transitional economies.

Lire Ersado is a senior economist at the World Bank and works within the Europe and Central Asia region on issues of human development, poverty reduction, project design and implementation, and analytic and advisory services. He holds a PhD in economics from Virginia Polytechnic Institute and State University.

Jan Fidrmuc is a senior lecturer in economics at Brunel University, London, and Research Fellow at the CESIfo Institute, Munich. He has published numerous research articles on issues relating to political economy, transition economics and economic development, institutional economics, labour, and economics of languages.

Heike Harmgart is a principal economist at the European Bank for Reconstruction and Development. She received her PhD in economics from University College London. Her main research interests include industrial organization, behavioural and experimental economics, and agricultural and development economics.

János Kornai is Professor of Economics Emeritus at Harvard University. His research has focused on critical analysis of the socialist system and post-socialist transition. Recently he has been working on a series of papers comparing the real and observable advantageous and disadvantageous, attractive and repulsive features of the socialist and capitalist systems, soon to appear as a collection of papers in Hungarian (*Gondolatok a kapitalizmusról*— 'Thoughts about Capitalism').

Charles S. Maier is the Leverett Saltonstall Professor of History at Harvard University and a member of its Center for European Studies, which he directed from 1994 to 2001. He has published numerous articles on the history of the Cold War, contemporary Europe, and modern Germany, with his most recent study being 'The Cold War and the World Economy' in *The Cambridge History of the Cold War*, published in 2010.

Branko Milanovic is a lead economist in the World Bank Research Department and adjunct professor at the School of Public Policy, University of Maryland. He has written numerous articles on methodology and empirics of global income distribution, effects of globalization, and social policy in transition economies. His most recent book, *The Haves and the Have-nots: A Short and Idiosyncratic History of Global Inequality*, was published in 2010.

Gur Ofer is Professor Emeritus at the Department of Economics at the Hebrew University of Jerusalem. His main research interests have been the Soviet economy, the socialist economic system, comparative economic systems, and, of late, the economics of transition—on all of which he has published extensively during the last four decades. He was one of the founders of the New Economic School in Moscow and served as the chair of its international advisory board during 1991–2004.

Katharina Pistor is the Michael I. Sovern Professor of Law at Columbia Law School. Her teaching, research, and writing focus on comparative law, corporate and financial governance, law and development, and global legal transformation.

Leonid Polishchuk is Professor of Economics at the Higher School of Economics, National Research University, in Moscow. His research interests, on which he has published widely, include political economy, public choice, institutional reform and the role of social capital in governance, development and institutional performance.

Richard Pomfret is Professor of Economics at the University of Adelaide and Associate Fellow at Centre d'Économie de la Sorbonne (Axe Développement et Mondialisation). His research interests are in international economics and economic development, with a focus on Central and East Asia. His most recent book is entitled *The Age of Equality: The Twentieth Century in Economic Perspective*, published in 2011.

Vladimir Popov is an adviser in the UN Department of Economic and Social Affairs and a professor at the New Economic School in Moscow. He has written extensively on growth and development and on transition economies. His latest book, *Strategies of Economic Development*, was published in 2011.

Gérard Roland is Professor of Economics and Political Science at the University of California at Berkeley and Editor of the *Journal of Comparative Economics*. Previously he taught at the Université Libre de Bruxelles. His areas of research include political economics, and comparative and institutional economics.

Peter Sanfey is a lead economist at the European Bank for Reconstruction and Development, where he analyses economic developments and reforms in Southeast Europe and participates in the bank's research programmes. He has published widely in international journals on various topics, including the link between reforms and growth, informal labour markets, measures of subjective well-being, and migration, and he is the co-author, with Christopher Cviic, of *In Search of the Balkan Recovery*, published in 2010.

Helena Schweiger is a principal economist at the European Bank for Reconstruction and Development, where she works on management, organization and innovation surveys, and on business environment and enterprise performance surveys. She also participates in the bank's research programmes. Her research interests lie in applying micro to macro empirical analysis to try to understand the causes of the differences in productivity and growth across countries, businesses and time, and their policy implications.

Daniel Treisman is Professor of Political Science at the University of California, Los Angeles, and a visiting fellow at the Institute for Human Sciences, Vienna (2010–11). His research focuses on comparative political economy and on the politics and economics of post-communist Russia. His latest book, published in 2011, is entitled *The Return: Russia's Journey from Gorbachev to Medvedev*.

Milica Uvalic is Professor of Economics at the University of Perugia, President of the Italian Association for Comparative Economic Studies, and a member of the UN Committee for Development Policy. She has published extensively on transition economies, particularly on the Balkans, and on issues related to macroeconomic policies, privatization, corporate governance, regional co-operation, trade liberalization, and EU enlargement.

Jeromin Zettelmeyer is Deputy Chief Economist and Director of Research at the European Bank for Reconstruction and Development. In this capacity, he headed the teams writing the EBRD flagship publication, *the Transition Report*, in 2009 (*Transition in Crisis?*) and 2010 (*Recovery and Reform*). From 1994 until mid-2008, he worked at the International Monetary Fund, mainly in the research department. His research and policy interests include financial crises, international financial architecture, and economics of transition.

Introduction

Gérard Roland

Twenty years after the fall of the Berlin Wall, many celebrations of this important milestone of recent history were held. Conferences were organized, and books were written to look back at the events, reminisce, commemorate and comment. As part of the tributes, United Nations University-World Institute for Development Economics Research (UNU-WIDER) organized a conference in Helsinki in September 2009 on the theme 'Reflections on Transition: Twenty Years after the Fall of the Berlin Wall'. This event gathered a group of top scholars who had been involved in the research on the process of transition from socialism to capitalism over the last 20 years. This volume puts together most of the presentations made at that conference.

Contrary to many other commemorations, instead of looking back and reflecting one more time on transition policies from two decades ago, the conference focused instead on the long-run view of transition. What is the long-run trajectory of transition countries? Did particular reform policies affect those long-run trajectories or not? What trace did communism leave on institutions and behaviour in transition countries? Are their institutions going to change much in the coming decades? If so, in what direction? What are the long-run economic prospects of particular countries or groups of countries? What will be their role in the global economy in the twenty-first century?

One of the major facts that immediately stands out when looking at the transition experience is the divergence of the institutional and economic trajectories of post-communist countries. Central European and Baltic countries appeared for many years to epitomize the success of the transition to markets and democracy. They adopted the institutions of the European Union (EU) and went on to become full-blown members. However, they were also badly hurt by the global economic crisis of 2008. How stable is their success? How real are the dangers of political instability? Might they be tempted by forms of nationalist experiments? How dangerous is the emergence of authoritarian extreme-right nationalist parties?

1

Countries of the former Soviet Union (FSU) and of most of former Yugoslavia were generally less successful than the early reformers of Central Europe. Democratization was somewhat imperfect as various countries replaced communist dictatorships with new autocratic regimes. Many countries, like Russia, became stuck in a strange no-man's land between democracy and dictatorship—elections take place but there is massive fraud. Freedom of the media remains relative and abuse of power by incumbent governments goes unpunished. The effect of economic reforms has been disappointing in many of those countries, even though rich endowments of natural resources have brought substantial export revenues to some, such as Russia. Will those countries follow the path of Central European countries with some delay? Will they remain stuck in their current institutional settings? Might they even reverse some of the transition reforms, as has been the case with the many renationalizations in Russia? Will they grow or stagnate?

China has experienced an extremely successful economic transition, with more than 30 years of very strong economic growth, lifting hundreds of millions of people out of poverty. However, the Communist Party keeps tight control over the country and there is no sign of any evolution towards democracy. It is an ironic paradox that the most successful transition to the market, in terms of growth, has happened under communist rule. The state sector keeps a strong place in the economy and market reforms have been put on hold for many years already. China's economic success and the severity of the global economic crisis of 2008 are seen as justifications for halting the reform process. How will China evolve in the coming years? Will the growth slow down? Will the Communist Party keep control over Chinese society as strongly as in the last few decades?

These very divergent evolutions were not predicted by researchers working on transition. Moreover, their causes are still not well understood. Scholars of the transition process have tended to analyse evolutions in transition countries in reference to the benchmark of advanced market democracies. Countries get ranked and rated in terms of their observed progress towards democracy and the market. This way of thinking is not very helpful to understand the real evolution of transition countries. How can we explain this strong divergence? Answering that fundamental question should offer a better clue to understanding the long-run evolution of transition countries rather than their position relative to some transition benchmarks. Most of the action in terms of economic and political reforms took place in the first five to ten years after the beginning of transition. We would be fooling ourselves if we thought that the observed evolutions from the next ten years reflect nothing else than temporary hurdles in an otherwise long-run gravitation to the economic and political model of Western societies. Instead of continuing to read events in post-communist countries through the lens of transition benchmarks, we need to take a fresh look and try to detect and understand the logic of their long-run evolution.

The studies gathered in this volume, written by top scholars on transition, provide a unique and comprehensive set of contributions to better understand these evolutions. More than half of the chapters address important issues analysed in a comparative perspective across transition countries: innovation, demographic trends, inequality, the evolution of political and financial institutions, the role of culture, differences in civil society development and the legacy of communism. Some studies look back at policies of governments and international institutions, and provide a long-run evaluation. Finally, a third set of studies documents and interprets evolutions in particular countries and regions: Russia, East Germany, South Eastern Europe and Central Asia.

János Kornai, the most prominent scholar of the socialist economic system and its transition to capitalism, gave the keynote lecture at the conference. He chose to revisit one of the fundamental flaws of the socialist economy: its inferiority to capitalism in generating technical progress and innovation. Even in the absence of Gorbachev or the collapse of the Berlin Wall in 1989, capitalism would have eventually proved its superiority due to its dynamism in generating innovation. This characteristic of capitalism was outlined by Schumpeter more than half a century ago. Kornai documents 87 major innovations in the world economy since 1917, the year of the Russian Revolution. A good third of them are related to computers and information technology. It is remarkable to observe that socialist countries do not feature on Kornai's list—only in the military sector was the socialist system comparable to the capitalist system in generating innovation. The Soviets invented Sputnik, while the US military invented email. The main culprit for the absence of socialist innovation was not the lack of fundamental research but the systemic inability of socialism to diffuse innovations. Adam Joffe, a Soviet physicist who was quite ahead of his time, was one of the pioneers of semiconductors in the 1930s, but industrial applications were not developed in the Soviet Union until after the USA and Asia had. Jacek Karpinski, a Polish engineer, invented the first mini-computer in 1971–73, but it was never used on Polish soil. The famous Rubik's cube—developed by Hungarian Ernö Rubik—was commercialized by a US toy company. The floppy disk was first invented in Hungary but not used; it was later reinvented in Japan. The list of such examples is long. Innovation under socialism was stymied by the bureaucratic centralization of the research process, the lack of rewards for innovators, and the absence of competition, experimentation and flexible capital allocated to innovation. After the collapse of socialism, innovation started to blossom in transition countries. Skype was registered initially in Estonia. Graphisoft, a successful three-dimensional graphic design for architects, was developed in Hungary. Kornai thinks that the comparison between socialism and capitalism clearly illustrates the fundamental dynamism of capitalism in its capacity to generate innovation. Behind this dynamism lies the capacity of capitalism to improve living standards. Transition has brought dissatisfaction in many countries and sometimes nostalgia for socialism, but Kornai considers that academics and politicians alike are guilty of not educating the public about capitalism's fundamental capacity to generate innovation, and socialism's dismal record in that sphere. The key role of innovation under capitalism is still cruelly absent from the main economics textbooks and even more so in speeches by politicians.

Demographic trends related to the transition process are analysed very systematically by Elizabeth Brainerd, the well-known expert on demographic trends and health issues in transition. A very important trend that is observable everywhere is the decline in fertility and the shift in the age of childbearing. For example, in Hungary until the 1990s, the highest rates of births occurred when women were between the ages of 20 and 24 years. With transition, the highest rates of birth are between the ages of 30 and 34—a shift of ten years. Note that these changes can be seen as a movement of convergence with demographic trends observed in Western Europe. Another sign of convergence is the increase in extramarital births. Overall, Brainerd notes that the increased childrearing age and declining fertility rates have been associated with a better use of contraception compared with the communist period. They have not been associated with any increase in the number of abortions. The research Brainerd surveys shows that a higher education level is a significant determinant of lower fertility. At the beginning of the transition when fertility rates started plunging, increased uncertainty about one's economic and life environment was mentioned as a major cause of this decline. However, research done over the transition period shows mixed results for uncertainty being a cause of lower fertility rates.

Another major demographic trend of the transition period is the large decline in life expectancy in the FSU, including the Baltic countries. Male life expectancy was as low as 61.3 years in 2007 in Russia. During the same time however, it increased in Central Europe and mortality rates fell. Improvements in diet and medical care are behind this trend. The decline in life expectancy in Russia and other transition countries appeared puzzling at first, but today the phenomenon is better understood. The large increase in mortality rates of middle-aged males is related to increases in circulatory diseases that are best explained by excessive alcohol consumption and binge-drinking, which are linked to lower relative prices of alcohol. The economic consequences of the fall in life expectancy in the FSU are not yet clear. However, they do induce a drastic decline in population.

One remarkable but puzzling trend that is concentrated in the Caucasus is the increase in sex ratios at birth. Azeri official statistics give a ratio of 1:1.168 in 2008, and this was significantly above 1:1 in Armenia (in 2001) and Georgia (in 2002). These figures are comparable to sex ratios at birth observed in China and India, which are considered quite dramatic. No such trend has, however, been observed in Central Asia.

The evolution of income inequality in the transition process has always been a matter of concern because scholars believed that the introduction of the market economy would inevitably lead to an increase in inequality. The question was how strong that trend would be. Branko Milanovic, one of the world's experts on income inequality, presents in his contribution the latest findings on trends in inequality in transition countries in a chapter written with Lire Ersado. They do this using a new database for 26 countries covering the period between 1990 and 2005, compiled from household survey data. Milanovic and Ersado show that the most dramatic changes in income inequality occurred in the very first years of transition, between 1990 and 1995. In that period, the income share of the top decile increased from 20 to 25 per cent while the bottom decile lost out from 4.5 to 3 per cent. That picture remained pretty stable during the following 15 years. They then portray a comprehensive picture of the trends and policies, and their effects on the rich and the poor in transition countries. Contrary to the view that growth benefits the poor via a trickle-down process, Milanovic and Ersado find that growth has been beneficial to the top decile but not to the bottom decile. Similarly, inflation has hurt low incomes but not top incomes. Reforms have overall not been favourable for the poorest 50 per cent (the lowest five deciles) while they were definitively favourable for the top two deciles. Government expenditures have been on the whole neutral and did not really benefit the poor in a redistributive manner. Democracy, on the other hand, proved favourable for the bottom six deciles, neutral for the next three, and bad for the top decile. Small-scale privatization and policies favouring the entry of small businesses has benefited the bottom five deciles but had a negative effect on the top three. The latter finding is rather surprising. Large-scale privatization, unsurprisingly, did not benefit the poor but was good for the top decile. Infrastructure reform was found to be bad for the poor because it was related to privatization and the introduction of fees, while it benefited the top two deciles. The effects of infrastructure reform counterbalance the pro-poor effects of small-scale privatization. To summarize, growth, inflation, democracy, economic reforms, privatization and infrastructure reform are the main variables that have affected inequality in one way or another. Only democracy and small-scale privatization benefited the poor; all the rest benefited the rich and hurt the poor.

The divergence in political institutions is one of the major long-run phenomena observed in transition countries. Dan Treisman—a well-known Russia observer and one of the most famous political scientists studying transition processes—reviews the evolution of political systems since the collapse of communism. He argues convincingly that the Polity scores give us a more nuanced and realistic measure of the evolution of political institutions in transition countries compared with the Freedom House indexes, which are also very popular among researchers. Freedom House ranks, for example, Russia only one step away from a pure autocracy like the United Arab

Emirates. However, Russia has elections, a democratic constitution and some freedom of the press, even though all these are obviously imperfect. Estonia is seen as a perfect democracy in the Freedom House rankings but not in the Polity score because of well-known discrimination against Russians living in Estonia. Looking at the evolution of various countries across time, Treisman distinguishes between the following groups. Central Europe and the Baltic countries sprinted towards democracy. Central Asia never really entered the race. The Balkans started with a sprint but then jogged on. Croatia and Serbia did a late sprint. A final group, including Russia, Ukraine, Georgia and Armenia, sprinted to the edge and then stalled. How do we explain these differences? The distance of a country from Düsseldorf accounts for 58 per cent of the variation in Polity scores. However, this geographical explanation stops being significant when one includes in the regressions dummy variables for the FSU and the proportion of Muslims in a country. These variables affect democracy scores negatively. The most convincing explanation for the FSU effect is the length of life under a communist regime that was longer in the FSU (more than 70 years) than in Central Europe (slightly more than 40 years). Many other variables are not significant, such as being an oil exporter, having belonged to a former empire, ethnic fractionalization, and the percentage of Catholics or Protestants. To summarize, the main determinants in the variation of Polity scores in former communist countries are the length of time under communism and the percentage of Muslims in the country. There is so far no generally accepted theory for why these variables matter, a topic that requires further research.

The introduction of financial systems was one of the most difficult reforms in transition countries. Katherina Pistor—one of the world's most renowned experts in legal institutions and a very keen observer of institutional reforms in transition countries—does not redo the whole history of financial reforms but instead assesses some of their main current weaknesses in the light of the 2008 crisis, which has challenged much of our thinking on financial systems. She points to the fact that in transition countries, financial liberalization was associated with the delegation of the role of ultimate guardian over the financial system to supranational authorities. The standards of the EU and of the International Monetary Fund were adopted. The privatization of banks to foreign-owned banks meant a surrender of monitoring to foreign regulators. This created a stark trade-off. On the one hand, drastic liberalization led to a strong development of the financial sector. On the other hand, national governments abdicated and surrendered the governance of their financial markets to supranational and foreign governments. In an ideal world, such an abdication should not pose big problems. However, national regulators are rarely independent of political pressure. Such pressure would lead them to favour the home bank and its jobs over foreign subsidiaries, especially if they are located in small transition countries.

One solution to this problem would be the creation of one central European regulator for financial markets. Proposals in this direction have, however, been blocked by several European countries. A second option would be to adopt an effect-based regulatory power, as is the case, for example, in anti-trust law. Effect-based regulatory power means that domestic law can apply abroad as long as the decisions of foreign entities broach domestic laws. This is how, for example, Microsoft, a US company, can be sued in Europe for anti-competitive behaviour. However, Europe is not ready for such regulations. Pistor fears that the costs of abdicating governance over one's own financial system will become clearer over time despite trends towards more harmonization of financial regulation.

The effects of culture have not been taken into account much in transition debates. Gérard Roland takes up the theme of cultural inertia in the context of transition. Using various questions from the World Values Survey over the last 20 years, he shows that despite the massive institutional changes taking place in transition countries, values and beliefs of citizens in those countries have not changed much. Comparing the USA, the EU and transition countries on a number of indicators of attitudes towards less government intervention in the economy and towards more democracy, he finds a remarkable stability of the three regions over time. In the USA, there are strong preferences for democracy and against authoritarian government, as well as strong preferences for little government intervention in the economy. The picture is similar for EU countries except that there is more preference for government intervention in the economy. A stark finding is that, for transition countries, there are stronger preferences for authoritarian forms of government and for more government intervention in the economy. These preferences have hardly changed since the fall of communism and they are not necessarily the result of life under communism. Indeed, new research documents long-run cultural effects of living together under a former empire. Interestingly, if one were to make extrapolations a hundred years ago of where China, Russia and Central Europe would stand today in terms of their economy and institutions, the picture might be quite accurate. The question is raised as to whether communism was a historical anomaly disturbing the low frequency evolution of countries. Cultural inertia is certainly one important factor in these low frequency movements.

Leonid Polishchuk takes a close look at the discrepancy between institutions prima facie and how they work in reality. This discrepancy between reality and formal institutions is quite strong in some countries. Formal institutions are often misused and abused. For example, in Russia bankruptcy law has been exploited by unscrupulous creditors to raid companies that are otherwise financially sound. Intermediaries that are supposed to facilitate transactions have been used as cover to hide corrupt activities and make them more difficult to detect. Courts and subnational governments have been captured by powerful interest groups. How can one explain the misuse of institutions? The public may be indifferent to it because of weaknesses in collective action, low social capital or a limited history in non-despotic government in their country. Formal laws, often imported from abroad, might contradict existing social norms and culture. Government reaction against the misuse of institutions in Russia has been particularly blunt. After media reports of abuse by non-governmental organizations serving as tax shelters, there was a strong crackdown on them. Gubernatorial elections were cancelled to fight subnational capture but Russia turned instead into a unitary state.

The topic of collective action and civil society is taken up in the chapter by Bruszt, Campos, Fidrmuc and Roland. They show that under communism in the 1980s, protest activities were much more widespread and repression less strong in Central Europe, and to a certain degree South Eastern Europe, compared with the FSU. They have built an original database based on dissident activities and their repression across transition countries, the content of which is used to measure the variation in strength of civil society across countries. The authors find that this can explain the choices of political regimes. Countries having a more vibrant civil society opted for parliamentary regimes, as opposed to presidential regimes with strong executive powers in countries where civil society was less developed. These differences account also for the stronger support for and progress of transition reforms. Differences in civil society development can thus have far-reaching and long-run institutional consequences.

Convergent with previous studies of the institutional picture of transition is the contribution by Gur Ofer, a well-known veteran observer of socialism and transition, who analyses the institutional legacy of communism in Russia. He argues that authoritarianism opened the door to corruption. The tradition of opposition to government has been turned against post-communist governments and no culture of civil duty has emerged. The new elites have developed a general mentality of shirking and cynicism, and a widespread hypocrisy. There is a lack of moral outrage against government capture, as was clear in the privatization process, but this cynicism and passivity have become widespread. The new regime inherited, among the negative inheritance from communism, a high level of human capital and a strong national research capacity. However, the low level of trust and social capital and the bad institutional environment are ruining even these meagre positive inheritances.

Various studies look back not only at institutions but also at economic policies and economic performance. Erik Berglöf, the current chief economist of the European Bank for Reconstruction and Development (EBRD) and an important contributor to transition debates, presents with Lise Bruynooghe, Heike Harmgart, Peter Sanfey, Helena Schweiger and Jeromin Zettelmeyer, also from the EBRD, an assessment of the progress in transition in various regions. The EBRD currently takes a broader view of transition, looking more than before at the quality of institutions supporting markets. In this assessment, Central Asia seriously lags behind in all sectors of the economy in terms of its reform process. In Russia, Eastern Europe and the Caucasus, market development is seriously hampered by strong state interference in various sectors, the lack of an adequate legal framework (or its effective implementation) and an unfavourable business environment. In South Eastern Europe, there is a mixture of small, medium and large challenges, with smaller ones in two EU countries: Bulgaria and Romania. Despite gradual alignment of regulation with EU standards, further work is needed in most countries to implement international best practice and strengthen the implementation capacity of regulatory authorities. In Central Europe and the Baltics, transition gaps are by now mainly small, with the exceptions of sustainable energy, transport and financial institutions, where medium-sized gaps remain. All countries have aligned their institutional frameworks with EU norms, and the remaining challenges relate mainly to improving efficiency, productivity and competition. There are sectoral differences, with industry being usually more problematic than agri-business, for example. The study provides a comprehensive review of the transition gaps remaining in different sectors in different countries. An interesting aspect of the chapter is that transition countries are not only compared among themselves but also with other developed and developing countries. For example, the institutional quality in Central Europe and the Baltics is higher than in China and India. The obstacles to business in the FSU (tax rates, political instability and access to finance) are higher than the average for developing countries, which is not the case for Central Europe. Russia, Romania, Kazakhstan and even Romania rank very low in terms of management practices—lower than China. Central European countries have caught up with EU management practices but are still behind Germany. The chapter highlights strong divergences among the evolution of transition countries in new areas that were less the subject of research previously.

Giovanni Andrea Cornia—a former director of UNU-WIDER, who took many initiatives on research in transition—examines the structural changes that have taken place in transition economies. Some common trends are detectable in all countries. The share of agriculture and industry went down whereas the share of services went up. Similarly, all countries have experienced a significant reduction in energy consumption per capita. He identifies four clusters of countries. The first consists of countries specializing in exports of manufacturing products. Roughly half the countries were in this category in 1996 but many of them have joined the second cluster—that of tertiarized economies reflecting the general deindustrialization in transition countries. The third cluster comprises oil- and ore-exporting countries and includes Azerbaijan, Kazakhstan, Turkmenistan and Russia. This is the group that has seen the fastest economic growth since 2000. The last cluster comprises countries dependent on remittances from emigrant workers and aid. It includes Albania, Armenia, Kyrgyzstan, Macedonia, Tajikistan and Uzbekistan. This group has been relatively stable over the last ten years. Vladimir Popov has studied the transition process in Russia since the beginning and has been critical of many of the policies followed. In his chapter, he delivers his analysis of its evolution. He does not accept the notion of Russia as a 'normal country', comparable to Mexico or Brazil. Russia sent the first man into space, has had 20 Nobel Prize winners, has 8 out of 40 Fields Medal winners, has had a relatively good education system, and even had a reasonable level of life expectancy before the transition started. The reason Russia did not fare well in the transition period is, according to Popov, due to larger initial distortions but mostly to an institutional collapse that was worse than in other transition regions and led to a lower institutional capacity as a consequence. Existing institutions were thoroughly destroyed, in contrast with China. However, the new ones that were imported did not take root for various reasons. Democracy was introduced rapidly in a context where there was no rule of law. Without the underpinning of the rule of law, Popov argues, Russia was doomed to have low institutional capacities.

Harvard historian Charles Maier has contributed a study on transition in the former German Democratic Republic. It can easily be argued that East Germany should have had the easiest economic transition. It was the economic powerhouse of the Soviet Bloc. Its transition happened under unification. In effect, it inherited overnight from Germany's institutions. Nevertheless, transition in East Germany is not seen as a success. As of today, unemployment there is still double that in West Germany, with 13.1 per cent in the former compared to 6.1 per cent in the latter. Nowhere was shock therapy worse than in East Germany. In firms privatized in the 1990s, 70 per cent of jobs were lost. The industrial sector lost 60 per cent of its initial jobs. East German wages were too high compared with its Central European neighbours, but the skills of the labour force were not on a par with those in West Germany. Massive transfers from West Germany to compensate for such losses considerably strained the German economy in the 1990s, which led to cutbacks in the welfare state, leading to a split among the German left. East German labour became the vanguard of an insecure workforce. The huge pains of transition and the *de facto* colonization of East Germany by the rich West Germans fuelled a strong bitterness in East Germany that led to support for the extreme left—a situation that would have seemed highly unlikely at the time of the fall of the Berlin Wall.

Milica Uvalic, a well-known specialist on Balkan economies, gives us an overview of the transition period in South Eastern Europe, a region that includes countries from former Yugoslavia, Albania, Romania and Bulgaria. Former Yugoslavia was also thought to have great initial conditions for transition. Self-management and far-reaching reforms towards the market economy had already been introduced as early as 1965. The Yugoslav regime was one of the most open and liberal among socialist countries. Since the early 1950s it had been completely independent from the Soviet Union. Unfortunately, the cruel war unleashed after the disintegration of Yugoslavia in mid-1991 changed the situation completely. Military conflicts in Slovenia (1991), Croatia (1990–91), Bosnia and Herzegovina (1992–95), Kosovo (1998–99) and the Former Yugoslav Republic of Macedonia (2001) left very deep scars. The newly created states tended to pursue nationalistic and inward-oriented policies with authoritarian regimes, in particular in Croatia and Serbia. Whereas Romania and Bulgaria received aid from the EU early on, this was not the case for countries from former Yugoslavia, with the important exception of Slovenia. Transition reforms were considerably delayed in countries entangled in military conflicts, but there has been a lot of catching up since. Trade integration with Europe has made big advances in the last ten years. Regional trade has also been booming, despite the wars. There has, nevertheless, been slow progress in restructuring and competition policy, and also in financial reform and infrastructure.

Well-known development economist Richard Pomfret gives us a comprehensive overview of landlocked Central Asia, a region too often neglected in transition studies. Transitions in Central Asia have been very diverse, ranging from rapid transition in Kyrgyzstan to very hesitant, and under Nyazov non-existent, reforms in Turkmenistan. Kyrgyzstan, despite strong early liberalization, stopped its reform process after 1998 and the growth performance of its economy has been disappointing. Kazakhstan experienced an evolution similar to that of Russia, with private interests capturing the reform process. Its decline in the 1990s was at least as bad. Uzbekistan was also a timid reformer, protecting its cotton industry and keeping strong foreign exchange controls until at least 2003. Tajikistan had a civil war until 1997. Overall, Pomfret argues, endowments play a bigger role in the fate of Central Asian economies than reforms. Uzbekistan benefited from good cotton prices in the early 1990s. Turkmenistan also benefited from its endowments and from high gas prices. The same is true for Kazakhstan, whose fate has been strongly linked to oil prices, low in the 1990s but higher in the following decade. Kyrgyzstan and Tajikistan are the only resource-poor countries, but they are developing their hydro-resources. Overall, Central Asia is an important energy route, although the countries in the region have failed to co-operate to take advantage of this.

As we can see, this book offers a very rich set of contributions from a large group of well-known experts on transition, offering an analysis of long-run developments in those countries. Kornai's chapter reminds us of the basic differences between socialism and capitalism in relation to an economic system's capacity to generate innovations. Issues that matter for long-run development are also covered: demographics (Brainerd), inequality (Milanovic and Ersado), financial institutions (Pistor), political institutions (Treisman), and cultural values and beliefs (Roland). The various geographical regions are very well covered, with chapters not only on Russia (Ofer, Popov) but also on Central Asia (Pomfret), South Eastern Europe (Uvalic) and East Germany (Maier). Moreover, various contributions, such as those by Berglof et al. and Cornia, cover broadly the economic performance in the transition world as a whole. Many chapters go beyond comparisons within the group of transition countries and make comparisons with both developed and developing countries. This gives a better idea of where transition countries stand and is more fruitful than the comparison to the 'ideal market economy' benchmark that has been used ad nauseam (though for understandable reasons) during the early years of transition.

Not surprisingly, and this is one of the most important contributions of this volume, the various chapters offer different perspectives on different paths adopted through the institutional changes in these countries. The differences in democratization paths described by Treisman play a key role in understanding divergences in institutional paths as well as the determinants of these differences. Among these, the length of the communist regime in a country appears to be an important factor. What are the mechanisms that could explain why a longer life under communism makes a country less successful at democratizing? Here, the other contributions offer a helpful perspective. Ofer suggests that life under an authoritarian regime has engendered more private cynicism and a lesser sense of civic morality. For him, this explains more generally the institutional weakness observed in Russia today, since formal institutions need to be complemented by the appropriate social norms to make them work. Polishchuk's perspective is very similar. Institutions that look good on paper can be misused in reality when people are passive and when collective action is too weak to fight abuses by elite interest groups. The analysis by Bruszt et al. echoes this idea by showing empirically the link between strength of collective action and dissent under communism and the type of political institutions that emerged in transition countries after the fall of the Berlin Wall.

The legacy of communism in transition countries is, however, not the only factor explaining institutional divergence. Contributions by Popov and Roland look at more long-run explanations. According to Popov, China had a successful transition because it adopted institutions for the market economy that are adapted to its traditional pre-communist collectivist values. Central European countries had already achieved major progress in adopting modern Western values, whereas this was not the case in Russia. In the latter, old institutions were destroyed at a frantic speed before the new ones could mature. Attempts to establish the rule of law in Russia were thus less successful because values had not yet evolved sufficiently along the Western modernization path. Roland explores at greater length the theme of values and cultural inertia. Countries' economic structures and geopolitical borders evolve in the long run in line with their geographical endowments and comparative advantage, but cultural beliefs play a key role in the establishment of institutions that in turn affect economic performance. It is difficult to understand the origin of various cultures in the world, but cultural inertia is an important phenomenon, rooted in a country's long-term history. Because of its inertia, culture affects institutional change and its direction. Given the very diverse histories of countries that lived under communism, this interaction between culture and institutions might play a key role—possibly a larger role than the communist path itself—in explaining the differences in trajectories observed in former communist countries.

Overall, this book presents both very informative and very stimulating reading and will be seen as a milestone in reflections on the long-run consequences of transition. It is hoped that it will trigger further research and scholarship, and affect policy discussions.

1

Innovation and Dynamism: Interaction between Systems and Technical Progress

János Kornai

1 Introduction

The essence of post-socialist transformation can be easily summarized in a few words—a large set of countries moved from socialism to capitalism. This shift itself is the strongest historical evidence of the superiority of capitalism over socialism. Nevertheless, it is our obligation to continue the impartial and unbiased comparison of the two systems. All the more so since we are living in difficult times, and nostalgia for the failed old regime can be felt by a significant portion of the population. We must convince our fellow citizens that we are heading in the right direction. There are several arguments to support this optimistic belief. I would like to spell out only one virtue of capitalism: its innovative and dynamic nature. In the first part of this study, I argue that rapid innovation and dynamism are not a random phenomenon that may or may not occur, but a deeply rooted system-specific property of capitalism. The same can be said about its opposite, the socialist system. Its inability to create great revolutionary new products and delay in other dimensions of technical progress are not due to some errors in policy but are a deeply rooted system-specific property of socialism. Unfortunately, this highly visible great virtue of capitalism does not get the appreciation it deserves. It is completely ignored by most people and even by most professional students of alternative systems, and I feel angry and frustrated watching that neglect, motivating me to choose the theme of this study.

Entering the world of capitalism creates the conditions of innovative processes and faster technical progress, and also increases the chances that the country will take this opportunity. But it does not guarantee full success immediately. The second and third parts of my study will discuss problems of the transition period.

The 'Great Transformation' is an ensemble of several processes. First, there were changes in the political domain: the transition from a single-party dictatorship to a multi-party democracy. This transformation put an end to the state-protected privileges of the Marxist-Leninist ideology and gave the green light to the competition of various schools of thought. Then there were changes in the economic domain: the predominance of state ownership was replaced by the predominance of private ownership. Associated with the transformation of ownership forms, the relative influence of various co-ordination mechanisms also went through radical changes. The impact of centralized bureaucratic control became much smaller, and the influence of market co-ordination and other decentralized procedures increased dramatically. These profound political and economic changes associated with several other changes jointly mean the change of the system, that is, the transition from socialism to capitalism.

The post-socialist region has experienced another class of changes in the domain of technical progress as well. Although, due to its familiarity, I apply the term 'technical progress', in my interpretation it is a much wider phenomenon. Based on the stream of new products and new technologies, its effects go far beyond the technical aspects. It is a part of modernization, generating profound changes on our lives. This meaning of technical progress will unfold in the context of my study. It was going on, of course, all the time, also before 1989, but following 1989 it has accelerated spectacularly.

In our profession, or sub-profession, all the experts on post-socialist transition have been concentrating their attention on the study of political, economic and social changes as part of the Great Transformation. Let us confess frankly that we perhaps briefly mention technical progress once in a while, but we have not studied thoroughly the interaction between changing the system, on the one hand, and changing our profile in generating and using new products and new technologies, on the other. I myself have certainly missed this point before. I have written two studies summarizing the main consequences of the changes after 1989, but discussing only political and economic changes and their interaction (Kornai 2001, 2006). I now start to catch up on what I missed before. Thus, the subject of the second and third parts of my study is the interaction between the post-1989 change of the system and the acceleration of technical progress.

2 Capitalism, socialism, and technical progress

2.1 Revolutionary new products

The complex process of technical progress is composed of several subprocesses. Let us begin with the great, breakthrough, revolutionary innovations, illustrated by 89 examples given in Table 1.1.[1] As we take a look at the role of socialist countries in creating revolutionary new products, we

Table 1.1 Revolutionary innovations

Innovation	Year	Country	Company
Computer, information, communication			
Integrated circuit	1961	USA	Fairchild
Touch-tone telephone	1963	USA	AT&T
Fax	1966	USA	Xerox
Optical fibre cable	1970	USA	Corning
Pocket electronic calculator	1971	USA	Bowmar
Word processing	1972	USA	Wang
Microprocessor	1974	USA	Intel
Laser printer	1976	USA	IBM
Modem	1978	USA	Hayes
MS-DOS operating system	1980	USA	Microsoft
Hard disk drive	1980	USA	Hard disk drive
Graphical user interface	1981	USA	Xerox
Laptop	1981	USA	Epson
Touch screen	1983	USA	Hewlett-Packard
Mobil telephone	1983	USA	Motorola
Mouse	1984	USA	Apple
Web search engine	1994	USA	WebCrawler
Pendrive	2000	USA	IBM
Skype (peer-to-peer phone)	2003	Estonia	Skype
Facebook 'social network'	2004	USA	Facebook
YouTube video sharing website	2005	USA	YouTube
iPhone, smartphone suitable for internet connection and multimedia services	2007	USA	Apple
Household, food, clothing			
Tea bag	1920	USA	Joseph Krieger
Hair dryer, hand-held, electric	1920	USA	Hamilton Beach
Wall plug	1920	UK	Rawlplug Co.
Spin dryer	1924	USA	Savage
Automatic pop-up toaster	1925	USA	Waters Genter Co.
Steam electric iron	1926	USA	Eldec
Electric refrigerator	1927	USA	General Electric
Air-conditioning, home	1928	USA	Carrier Engineering Co.
Neon light	1938	USA	General Electric
Instant coffee	1938	Switzerland	Nestle
Electric clothes dryer	1938	USA	Hamilton Manufacturing Co.
Nylon	1939	USA	DuPont
Espresso machine (high pressure)	1946	Italy	Gaggia
Microwave oven	1947	USA	Raytheon

Drive-through restaurant	1948	USA	In-n-Out Burger
Saran plastic wrap	1949	USA	Dow Chemical
Polyester	1953	USA	DuPont
Tefal kitchenware	1956	France	Tefal
Hook-and-loop fastener (Velcro)	1957	USA	Velcro
Athletic shoe	1958	UK	Reebok
Halogen lamp	1959	USA	GE
Food processor	1960	USA	Roboot-Coupe
Tetra Pak	1961	Sweden	Tetra Pak
Beverage can	1963	USA	Pittsburgh Brewing Co.

Health, cosmetics

Adhesive bandage (Band-aid)	1921	USA	Johnson & Johnson
Facial tissue (Kleenex)	1924	USA	Kimberley-Clark
Paper towel	1931	USA	Scott Paper Co.
Electric shaver	1931	USA	Schick
Aerosol container	1947	USA	Airosol Co.
Disposable diaper	1949	USA	Johnson & Johnson
Transistor hearing aid	1952	USA	Sonotone
Roll-on deodorant	1955	USA	Mum
Disposable razor	1975	USA	BIC
Liquid detergent	1982	USA	Procter & Gamble

Office

Adhesive tape (pressure-sensitive Scotch tape)	1930	USA	3M
Ball-point pen	1943	Argentina	Biro Pens
Correction fluid	1951	USA	Mistake Out
Copy-machine	1959	USA	Haloid Xerox
'Post-it'	1980	USA	3M

Transport

Escalator	1921	USA	Otis
Parking meter	1935	UK	Dual Parking Meter Co.
Scooter	1946	Italy	Piaggio
Jet-propelled passenger aeroplane	1952	USA	Comet
Black box (for aeroplanes)	1958	UK	S. Davall & Son

Leisure

Drive-in cinema	1933	USA	Hollingshead
Instant camera	1948	USA	Polaroid
TV remote control	1956	USA	Zenith

Table 1.1   (Continued)

Innovation	Year	Country	Company
Plastic construction toy	1958	Denmark	Lego
Barbie doll	1959	USA	Mattel
Quartz wristwatch	1969	Japan	Seiko
Video cassette recording	1971	Netherlands	Philips
Walkman	1979	Japan	Sony
Rubik's cube	1980	USA	Ideal Toys
CD	1982	Netherlands, Japan	Sony, Philips
Portable video-game	1989	Japan	Nintendo
Digital camera	1991	USA	Kodak
Book trade on the internet	1995	USA	Amazon
DVD	1996	Japan	Philips, Sony, Toshiba
Commerce, banking			
Supermarket	1930	USA	King Kullen
Shopping cart	1937	USA	Humpty Dumpty Supermarket
Shopping mall	1950	USA	Northgate Mall
Charge card	1950	USA	Diners Club,
Credit card	1958	USA	Bank of America
Automated teller machine	1967	UK	Barclays Bank
Express shipping	1973	USA	Federal Express
Barcode	1974	USA	IBM
e-commerce	1998	USA	eBay

Note: Entries are selected out of a larger set of innovations surveyed in various collections and lists of relevant inventions and innovations. The main inclusion criterion was the relevance for large groups of users, well-known to the majority of people and not only to small groups of experts. Some of the criteria of exclusion are discussed in the text: (i) The list contains only Schumpeterian-type innovations. Accordingly, innovations initiated and financed mainly by the military are excluded. (ii) New products and services used for medical care, that is, medicines, diagnostic equipment and so on are not included, simply because of the difficulty of selection of the greatest innovations out of hundreds or thousands of new drugs and new medical instruments (perhaps at a later stage of research this sector might be included).
Source: The sources of several entries were Ceruzzi (2000) and Harrison (2003, 2004). The source of each entry is on record and is available from the author on request.

have to go back in time to the birth of the Soviet Union, the first socialist state. Therefore the period covered by the list starts in 1917.

Since then, many innovations of great significance have been born. It is debatable why exactly these 89 are included in the table, as we could perhaps find 20 or 50 additional ones of no less significance. The selection is arbitrary, yet the list seems to be apt to demonstrate that all the innovations mentioned here in a narrower or wider scope fundamentally change the everyday practice of people's lives, work, consumption, recreation, and relationships with others.[2] The office and the factory, transportation, shopping, housework, and education have all changed. The tie between the home and the workplace differs, travel has changed as well—and we could continue listing, at great length, the effects of innovation causing permanent upheaval and the reorganization of life. The modern world is made dynamic by the perpetual flow of innovations. We consider our times more dynamic compared with earlier periods because many more innovations are being introduced, and these are generating much deeper changes in our everyday life.

Of the 89 innovations, about 25–30 are related to computers, digital equipment and information. This subset attracts the most intensive attention of the public and the academic world. A large and fast-growing literature is studying the social effects of the information society.[3] My study cannot penetrate deeply in this exciting subject because I would like to cover a wider set of innovations. Around 60 of 89 in the list are innovations unrelated, or not closely related, to the revolution in the information–communication sphere. Admitting wholeheartedly the extraordinary importance of information and communication, there have been, and will be, innovations in many areas outside this area. For the poorest inhabitants of a poor Albanian or Siberian village, the introduction of the refrigerator or the appearance of a supermarket might contribute to relevant changes in lifestyle—the use of the computer might come later. I would like to discuss certain issues of technical progress as a whole, that is, the technical change related and unrelated to the revolution of information and communication.

Innovation is preceded by invention. The first step is made by the inventor: the professional or amateur researcher, the academic scholar or the company's engineer is the one to whom the new idea occurs. However, the originality of the idea, its novelty, and its ingenuity are not at all enough. In the second step, the invention becomes an innovation; the practical introduction begins, that is, the organization of production and the diffusion of the new product, or the application of a new organizational form. If we turn our attention towards this second phase, to the practical execution of the change (Table 1.1 indicates the country in which the innovator company is operating), we will, without exception, read the names of capitalist countries here. As the time period captured in the table includes the entire era during which the socialist system existed, it is clear that in no instance did the innovation occur in a socialist country.[4]

2.2 Following the pioneers, the diffusion of innovation

While revolutionary innovation is the most important component of technical progress, there are other components as well. The pioneer has followers. Beside the first innovator, after some time-lag, various other organizations participate in minor quality improvements, in the implementation of small but not negligible inventions, and in the process of diffusion. The innovation appears first in a certain country but then followers show up in other countries as well.

The socialist system in numerous spheres followed the pioneering inventions born in a capitalist country, and took diverse forms. Sometimes it was just imitation. The mere reproduction of the model, perhaps its makeshift copying, was simple. Breaking up the secret was a relatively more difficult task. The reinvention of the innovations protected by patents and business privacy virtually developed into an art in socialist economies. Industrial espionage—the stealing of intellectual property—was a further possibility.[5] However, despite the diverse attempts, regarding these processes the socialist economy sluggishly trudged behind the capitalist economy.

Let me draw your attention to two details. First, in the socialist countries this delay—the followers lag behind the pioneers—was significantly greater in magnitude than in the capitalist countries; see, for example, the data given in Tables 1.2 and 1.3. Examining a longer time period, the lag measured in years was mostly growing instead of shrinking.

And second, the diffusion of new products and new technologies was much faster in the capitalist economies than in the socialist ones; for example, see Table 1.4 and Figure 1.1 (the table is shown

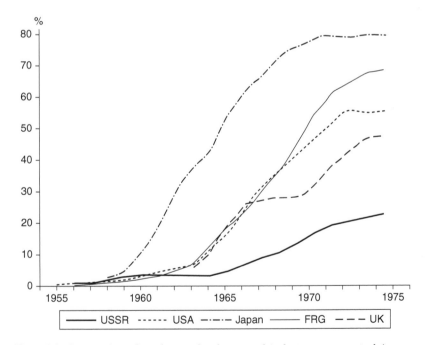

Figure 1.1 Penetration of modern technology: steel industry, oxygen steel (oxygen steel as a proportion of total steel output, percentage of total)
Source: Amann et al. (1977: 97).

Table 1.2 Time-lag in following the leaders of innovation: plastic materials

Product	Innovator		First follower		Second follower		Soviet Union	Delay behind innovator (years)
Cellophane	France	1917	USA	1924	Germany	1925	1936	19
Polystyrene	Germany	1930	USA	1933	Italy	1943	1955–9	25–9
PVC	Germany	1931	USA	1933	Japan	1939	1940	9
Silicon polymers	USA	1941	Germany	1950	Japan	1951	1947	6*
Epoxy resins	Switzerland	1936	USA	1947	Germany	1955	1957–9	21–3
	USA	1957			UK	1955		
Polypropylene	Germany	1957	UK	1959	France	1960	1970	13
	Italy	1957						

Note: *In this case the Soviet Union followed the pioneering country faster than the capitalist economies.
Source: Amann et al. (1977: 272–85).

Table 1.3 Time-lag in following the leaders of innovation: controlled machine tools

	Reached by USSR in	USSR (+ in advance; − behind) in relation to			
		USA	UK	Japan	FRG
Start of research	1949	−2	−1	+4	+6
First prototype	1958	−6	−2	−	−
Start of industrial production*	1965	−8	−2	+1	−1
First machining centre	1971	−12	(−10)	−5	−10
First third-generation control system	1973	−7	(−5)	(−5)	(−5)
First use of computer for control	1973	−6	(−4)	−5	(−4)

Note: Values in parentheses represent estimates. *Fifty units or more per annum.
Source: Amann et al. (1977: 41).

Table 1.4 Percentage penetration of modern technology: steel industry, continuous casting

Country	Continuous casting per total production		
	1970	1980	1987
Socialist countries			
Bulgaria	0	0	10
Czechoslovakia	0	2	8
East Germany	0	14	38
Hungary	0	36	56
Poland	0	4	11
Romania	0	18	32*
Soviet Union	4	11	16
Capitalist countries			
France	1	41	93
Italy	4	50	90
Japan	6	59	93
Spain	12	49	67
UK	2	27	65
USA	4	20	58
West Germany	8	46	88

Note: *1986.
Source: Finansy i Statistika (1988: 109).

only as an illustration). The large amount of empirical evidence in the comparative economic literature also supports the proposition that the socialist system was sluggish in following the pioneering innovations.[6]

2.3 Innovative entrepreneurship under capitalism

Thus, capitalism produced all the breakthrough innovations and was much faster in other aspects of technical progress—historical experience grants irrefutable evidence. Nevertheless, let us add the causal explanation of that crucial systemic difference. In capitalism, the entrepreneur plays a distinguished role.[7] My study adopts this term in the sense used by Joseph Schumpeter (1912/1934). Beyond terminology, Schumpeter's theories about development and the nature of capitalism leave their mark on the message of this study.[8]

Innovative entrepreneurship is a function, a role, that can be fulfilled by an individual alone or by teaming up with one or more partners, or with the support of a small firm. Or even a large firm can function as an entrepreneur. The main point is that the entrepreneur is the one who brings together the necessary financial and personal conditions that the innovation calls for—the human resources, the physical instruments and the financial resources essential to the activity. They are the one finding the place of application, and they direct the execution of the change. Often a long time passes before a promising invention is taken up by a true entrepreneur.[9] Probably it is a frequent occurrence that an invention or discovery and an entrepreneur do not find each other. Fortunately, it is quite frequent that the match is made. From Table 1.1 it emerges how many different types of innovation are possible—not only new products, or new production technologies, but new organizational forms as well.

In most cases the Schumpeterian entrepreneur drives the innovation process during the first realization of the revolutionary innovation. Diffusion, that is, the process following the pioneering innovation, is also mostly driven by entrepreneurs. At the beginning of the sequence the initiative appears. For example, in 1996 Larry Page, a PhD student at Stanford, was searching for a dissertation topic. Some specific issues about browsing the internet attracted his attention. He teamed up with another student, Sergey Brin, and they developed a 'search engine'. On the Stanford homepage it is named 'google.stanford.edu'. In this story these two men unite the two usually separated roles: they are the inventors and at the same time they are the innovators. Skipping over all the intermediate stages, let us jump to where we are right now. Google is one of the world's largest and wealthiest companies.[10] Its worldwide network is using about 450,000 servers. I would not like to play lightly with words, but the influence of Google has proved to be of revolutionary significance.[11] I will return to the Google story, but only to illustrate the general characteristics of the innovation process taking place in the capitalist environment.

Let me summarize the specific characteristics of the capitalist economy not only making the innovation process possible but also inducing, constantly developing and propelling it:

(A) *Decentralized initiative.* Larry Page and Sergey Brin did not receive any orders from their superiors to solve a specific innovational task. They did not have to ask for permission from their superiors to work on a special direction of an innovative action. The individuals and the decision makers of small firms, or the chief executives of large companies—in other words, the separate entities functioning inside the entire system—determine for themselves what they want to do.[12]

(B) *Gigantic reward.* Today Page and Brin are among the richest people in the world.[13] It is not the task of this study to analyse the difficult ethical dilemmas of income distribution. How large is the reward that is 'proportional' to performance? One point is certain: the most successful innovations usually (not always, but very often, with a high probability) result in enormously large rewards.[14] The range of the reward spreads rather unevenly. At the end of the scale one can find the owners of gigantic wealth; people like Bill Gates, or in the older generations the Fords or the Duponts. The entrepreneur leading the technical progress is able to gain a huge monopolistic rent. It is worth being the first, even temporarily, because it creates a monopolist position. The enormous financial reward is usually accompanied by prestige, fame and reputation.

(C) *Competition.* This is inseparable from the previous point. Strong, often ruthless competition is taking place to attract the customers. The faster and more successful innovation is not the exclusive instrument for that purpose, yet a highly important one to gain advantage over one's competitors.

(D) *Extensive experimenting.* There must have been hundreds, perhaps thousands, of entrepreneurs wanting to find suitable tools to search the internet. Only a few achieved almost as great a breakthrough as the founders of Google. However, others have also been able to realize innovations with fairly large, medium or small success. And there must have been many who tried but failed. Moving beyond the example, so far no one has assessed the volume of innovational attempts constantly occurring in all spheres under capitalism and the distribution of their success and failure. Those gaining an impression about this highly important activity can only intuitively sense the huge number of attempts, compared with the rare spectacular successes like the stories of Google, Microsoft, Tetra Pak, Nokia, or Nintendo. Many highly talented people are motivated precisely towards innovation, because—although with quite a small probability—a phenomenal success is promised, and even with a larger probability a more moderate yet still substantial success materializes, and that is why it is worth taking up the risk of failure.[15]

(E) *Reserve capital waiting to be invested: the flexibility of financing.* The two founders of Google gained access to financial resources enabling them to launch the innovative activity, the distribution. Successful researcher and innovator Andy Bechtolsheim (who happened to also be a wealthy businessman) at the very beginning of the process signed a cheque for US$100,000.

An innovative enterprise is rarely realized solely from the innovator's own resources. Although there are examples of this, resorting to outside resources is much more common.[16] The diverse forms of opening up resources include a bank loan, investors willing to take part in the business, and 'venture capital' institutions specialized in particularly high-risk and, in case of success, high-reward projects (Bygrave and Timmons 1992). Basically, flexible disposable capital is needed to realize the pioneering introduction and quick diffusion of innovations, which includes wide range experimenting, some of which is ultimately unsuccessful.

I do not claim that Schumpeterian-type entrepreneurship is the only way to generate innovative processes in a capitalist system. Let me mention three of the several non-Schumpeterian frameworks:

(i) In several instances an important innovation is initiated, financed and implemented by the military. For example, in the 1960s there was a strong demand expressed by the Pentagon to generate a completely decentralized mailing service to assure that the destruction of the centre of the postal system would not lead to a breakdown of written communication. This requirement of the military and the generous financial support of research in that direction led to a revolutionary innovation, the creation of email, a completely decentralized 'invisible hand' device for communication. Although at a later stage the free-of-charge, non-profit email system, intertwined with more commercial profit-oriented activities, is still a classical example of a non-Schumpeterian innovation.

While under socialism competition was eliminated in the centralized, bureaucratically managed civilian economy, the Soviet Union and its allies were deeply involved in the military race with the West, primarily with the USA. This competition put the innovative process under sufficient pressure for generating great innovation. The first satellite, Sputnik, was created by the Soviet Union. The sluggishness of technical progress in the civilian sector was overruled by the overall objectives of the leadership, to keep pace with, or even ahead of, the development of the Western military forces. But when it came to the civilian utilization of a military innovation, the inferiority of the socialist system showed up again. In the USA, pioneering military applications were followed by the use of satellites for civilian use, leading to rapid quality and efficiency improvements in all areas of telecommunication. In the Soviet Bloc, civilian application followed only after a long delay. The example of the satellites demonstrates that focused action in a highly centralized bureaucratic system might produce spectacular results, but without the same strong spillover effect as great innovations appearing in a decentralized, entrepreneurial capitalism.

(ii) In certain instances, important research and, later, the diffusion of the invention are initiated and financed by civilian, non-military sectors of the government; for example, the agencies in charge of medical care. There are good examples when intelligent, competition-friendly government policy is promoting targeted innovation (e.g. to protect the environment).

(iii) In several instances, important innovations are initiated, and also executed, by an ad hoc ensemble of researchers, or by an association, or by a non-governmental and non-profit organization. That is how one of the most significant and truly revolutionary innovations, the World Wide Web started (see the memoirs of the pioneer Berners-Lee (1999)). Many other important innovations (e.g. SMS, Linux) in the sphere of computers, digital applications, information and communication started in this civilian, non-profit, associative way of the non-Schumpeterian innovation.

Notwithstanding the relevance of non-Schumpeterian processes, most breakthrough innovations follow the Schumpeterian path. That is certainly true of the innovations targeted at the market of consumer goods and services for practical use in everyday life. And even the non-Schumpeterian starts are followed typically by many profit-oriented applications, and innovators with a commercial orientation execute the larger share of wide diffusion.

2.4 The impossibility of innovative entrepreneurship under socialism

Moving on to socialism, let us begin by stepping back to the preceding phase of innovation, namely invention. Creative minds also lived in socialist countries. Excellent scientists and engineers worked there, and made important discoveries and created inventions that were of revolutionary significance, with potential to be applied in industry and commerce. The first example is the Soviet physicist Abram Joffe, who is regarded as one of the pioneers of semiconductors, which today play a fundamental role in the electronics industry. He had already come forward with his discoveries during the 1930s but the economic environment simply did not allow for the introduction of their industrial applications. Much later, the manufacture of semiconductors became dominated by the USA, Japan, Taiwan, and South Korea; the Soviet Union trailed behind the leaders.[17]

Jacek Karpinski, a Polish engineer and scientist, invented the first mini-computer between 1971 and 1973. His name is recognized among the great pioneers of computer technology. However, his invention did not become a widely dispersed innovation while he lived on Polish soil. Karpinski later emigrated, and his invention, in competition with similar discoveries, became a widespread innovation in the capitalist world.

The most famous Hungarian example is the story of Rubik's cube. The inventor, Ernö Rubik, tried to initiate worldwide distribution after seeing the enthusiastic reaction of everyone getting familiar with this intellectual masterpiece, but with a rather moderate effect. Later it became a fantastic success when a well-known, truly entrepreneurial American toy company bought it and started worldwide marketing.

Even in Hungary, only a few know that the floppy disk, the plastic covered simple data storage device for personal computers used by millions, was invented by a Hungarian engineer, Marcell Jánosi. After inventing it in 1974, Jánosi offered the well-functioning prototype to the Hungarian industry and exporters in vain; the leaders of the socialist industry did not see the great business opportunity in the invention. They felt reluctant to risk mass production and worldwide distribution, and did not even support the extension of its patent protection. The inventor was not allowed to take the marketing of his intellectual product into his own hands. In the end, a Japanese firm 'reinvented' it and it was in Japan that the innovative process of mass introduction developed.[18]

After these sad stories of frustrated inventors, we turn to the innovation phase. Surely, even in the socialist system, many individuals had entrepreneurial talent, albeit dormant. Perhaps a project's leader could to a certain extent unfold his talent, provided that he was picked for his position because of his abilities and not his party connections. Still, the inherent characteristics of the system did not allow the development of a Schumpeterian-type entrepreneurship.[19] Let us return, one by one, to the conditions reviewed earlier when discussing capitalism and study the situation under the socialist system.

(A) *Centralization, bureaucratic commands and permissions.* The plan of technical innovation is one chapter in the state plan. The central planners set key changes to be carried out regarding the composition and the quality, together with the production technology, of the products. What follows is the disaggregation of the central plan into plans for sectors, sub-sectors and, at the end to companies. The 'command economy' means, among others things, that firms receive detailed orders about when they should replace one product with a new one, and which old machinery or technology should be replaced. Before the final approval of the plan, company managers are allowed to make suggestions, so among other things they can initiate the adaptation of a new product or a new technology; that is to say, they can join in the process of innovation diffusion. However, they must ask for permission for all significant initiatives. If an action happens to be large scale, even their immediate superiors cannot decide by themselves but must turn to the higher levels of the hierarchy for approval. The more extensive an initiative is, the higher one has to go for the final decision and the longer the bureaucratic process preceding the actual action.[20]

As opposed to the above, if in capitalism a very promising innovation is rejected by the first company, another one may be willing to embrace it. This is made possible by decentralization, private property, and the market. In the centralized socialist economies, the innovative idea follows the official pathways, and in case of a declared negative decision, no appeal can be made.

(B) *No or only insignificant reward.* If the higher authority deems a technical innovation in a factory unit successful, the manager and perhaps his immediate colleagues receive a bonus, an amount equal to one or two months' salary at best.

(C) *There is no competition between producers and sellers.*[21] Production is strongly concentrated. Many companies enjoy monopolist positions, or at least a (regional) monopoly, in producing an entire group of products. The chronic shortage of products creates monopolist behaviour even where many producers operate in parallel. The shortage economy, one of the strongest system-specific properties of socialism, paralyses the forceful engine of innovation, the incentive to fight for the favours of the customer (Kornai 1970, 1980, 1992: chapters 11–12.) The producer/seller is not compelled to attract the buyer by offering him a new and better product, since the latter is happy to get anything in the shop, even an obsolete and poor-quality product. There are examples of inventive activities motivated by chronic shortages: ingeniously created substitutes for missing materials or machinery parts (Laki 1984–5). These results of the inventor's creative mind, however, do not become widespread, commercially successful innovations in the Schumpeterian sense.[22]

(D) *The tight limits of experimenting.* Capitalism allows for hundreds or thousands of barren or barely fruitful attempts, so that afterwards perhaps one out of the hundreds or thousands will succeed and bring immense success. In the socialist planned economy, actors are inclined to avoid risks. As a result, the application of revolutionarily significant innovations are more or less excluded, since those always mean a leap into the dark, as success is necessarily unpredictable. As far as followers are concerned, some economies follow up quickly, others slowly. The socialist economies belong to the group characterized by the slowest pace. They prefer to maintain the familiar old production procedures and produce the old, well-tried products—new technologies and new products have too many uncertain characteristics, making planning difficult.

(E) *There is no capital waiting to be utilized, investment allocation is rigid.* Central planning is not miserly with the resources devoted to capital formation. The share of investment carved out from the total output is typically higher than in the capitalist economies. However, this enormous volume is appropriated ahead of time to the last penny. Moreover, most of the time, over-allocation takes place; in other words, the ensemble of all project plans prescribes the requisition of more resources than the required amount to execute the plan. It never happens that unallocated capital is waiting for someone with a good idea. The allocators do not search for an entrepreneur waiting to step forward with a proposal for innovation. Flexible capital markets are unknown. Instead, the rigid and bureaucratic regulation of project activities takes place. And to devote capital resources to activities with possibly uncertain outcomes is unconceivable. No foolish minister of industry or factory manager could be found who would demand money for ventures, admitting in advance that the money may be wasted and the innovation may not succeed.[23]

At this point, it is worth running again through the points from A to E about the description of the mechanisms of innovation since these are actually the consequences of the basic characteristics of the capitalist and the socialist systems. The reviewed phenomena are direct results of private property and market co-ordination in one system and of public property and bureaucratic co-ordination in the other.

I do not claim that a country's pace of technical progress solely depends on its being governed by a capitalist or a socialist system. Numerous other factors play significant roles: the country's state of economic development; the level of education, including the training of researchers; the level and the institutional framework of financing academic research and industrial R&D activity; research financed by the military; and so on. Luck undeniably also plays a role. It was a matter of luck that it is in Finland, and not Denmark or Norway, that a company like Nokia has appeared and reached unparalleled success in the diffusion of mobile phones. Following the pioneering work by Zwi Griliches (1957), there is rich recent literature discussing the problems of diffusion, leaders and followers in the innovation process (see, e.g., Davila et al. 2006; Freeman 1982; Rogers 1995).[24] Admitting the relevance of all other explanatory factors, I maintain the proposition: the system-specific effect is quite strong.[25]

2.5 Political factors and technical progress

The decisive factor explaining the nature of the innovative process is the influence of the system-specific features of the economy, which is, of course, ultimately determined by the political structure of the system. There are, however, several direct links between the political structure and technical progress, and I will briefly touch upon a few.

Communist dictatorship aggressively promoted innovations in the information–communication sphere when it provided efficient technology for political propaganda and, more generally, the spreading of the official ideology. Lenin was among the first political leaders to understand the relevance of cinema for propaganda purposes. Also, the USSR was among the fastest countries in introducing television broadcasting, since it was a highly centralized medium in the first period, concentrated in a single or only a few studios, and subject to the tough political control of the party. Also, the programme of the radio stations could be easily controlled, and transmitted through loudspeakers even to remote villages.

Radio and television were supported by the communist regime as long as tough central control was feasible. Luckily, as the integrated circuit (IC) technology developed further, complete centralization and censorship became technically impossible. The Berlin Wall stopped people crossing between the two worlds, but no wall could be built to stop radio and TV waves, and jamming was a poor device to stop the destabilizing impact of Western broadcasts. Among the numerous factors leading to the collapse of the socialist system, one was the technical impossibility of isolating socialist countries from voices coming from the rest of the world.

The final turmoil in the socialist bloc occurred in the period when Xerox machines, email, and the internet became available. Gorbachev called for *glaznost* (openness), and through the open doors of new communications technology, information flowed from abroad. It had a devastating effect on old dogmas, frozen beliefs and misleading party propaganda, liberating the minds of people (Shane 1994; Kedzie 1997a, 1997b; Stolyarov 2008). Let me come back to the relationship between political structure and technical progress later.

2.6   First summary: systems and technical progress

Assume for a moment that the vision of Marx, Lenin and Trotsky had materialized, and the world revolution was victorious without a spot of capitalism left. In such a case, we would never have the computer and the transistor radio, the refrigerator and the supermarket, the internet and the escalator, the CD and DVD, digital photography, the mobile phone and all the other revolutionary technical changes. Our way of life, at least with respect to the use of various devices and equipment, would more or less stagnate at the standard taken over from the last spots of capitalism before its final defeat.

We arrive here at fundamental issues of understanding and explaining the long-lasting trends of human history. The technologies utilized in all activities (not only in goods production but also in other individual and social activities) are developed in a complex social process—what we call technical progress. The speed and other properties of technical progress are determined by several factors. The general philosophy underlying this study (and my other writings) is as follows. One of the strongest explanatory factors is the system. A strong causal relationship is working between the type of system (capitalism or socialism) as one of the causes, and the speed and other properties of technical progress as the effect.

I am using the concept of technical progress generally accepted by the economics profession. We must be aware that 'progress' has an appreciative or even laudatory sound, as it reflects a value judgment: it is better to live in a world with dishwashers, mobile phones and CDs, than in a world without those products. But is it really? Nobody, even the most enthusiastic fans of modern technology, would reply with a simple 'yes' without qualifications and reservations. Since the invention of the fire and the knife, all new instruments and technologies have been used for both good and evil. It is a trivial, but still extremely important, fact of life that the latest great wave of technical progress, namely the headlong development in the sphere of computers, electronics, and digital instruments—modern technologies of information and communication—can serve criminals, sex offenders, terrorists, and extremist political movements alike, also opening up the new technology for tricky advertisement to mislead or at least to bother people. The substitution of the work of human beings by robots can lead to the 'dehumanization' of various activities and contacts. Sitting in front of the screen of a computer or TV day and night can distract children and adults from more worthy pursuits. Technical progress has been, and will be, used not only for peaceful but also for military activities, and not only for the defence of the homeland but also for aggression. Yet, the majority of people, myself included, call the direction of technical changes 'progress' because it brings many more benefits than drawbacks or dangers (find survey results that prove this to be the majority opinion below).

Based on this value judgment, I regard the promoting impact of capitalism on technical progress as one of the greatest virtues of that system, and the retarding impact of socialism on technical progress as one of the greatest vices of that other system. This observation alone could be a good reason to celebrate the fall of the socialist system.

3 Transformation and the acceleration of technical progress

Entering the world of capitalism, all post-socialist countries have opened the door for entrepreneurship, path-breaking innovations, and the fast diffusion of new products and new technologies. The change in the basic features of the economy has created the conditions for the acceleration of technical progress in this part of the world.

When formulating the above sentences, I tried to be cautious. Capitalism has a built-in tendency for entrepreneurship, innovation and dynamism. However, this is just a tendency, an inclination, a disposition—and no more than that. It is not like a law of physics, which must materialize.

The earlier section discussing innovation under capitalism underlines that beside the decisive impact of system-specific factors, other circumstances also exert a significant influence. The diversity of these other, non-system-specific factors explains the differences in the speed of the innovative process between various transition economies. As entrepreneurship, innovation and dynamism come to life through human action, it is the social, political and legal environments created by human beings that influence how far and how quickly the tendency breaks through. It depends on the business climate, and it depends to a large extent on the courage, inspiration and competence of individuals who might become entrepreneurs.

3.1 New innovator entrepreneurs

Let us start with innovations introducing revolutionary new products. The first example is Skype, listed among the great revolutionary innovations in Table 1.1. Its two inventors are Niklas Zennström, who is Swedish, and Janus Friis, who is Danish, but the software was elaborated in Estonia. The company launching the worldwide distribution was also founded and registered in Estonia. Therefore, following the criteria applied in this study, it could be regarded as an Estonian innovation. It was so successful that the USA-based eBay paid almost €2 billion for the pioneering company when it took over and continued the innovative process.

A second, less spectacular but still remarkable example is the story of the Hungarian high-tech company Graphisoft. The inventor–innovator, Gábor Bojár, a former senior fellow in an academic research institute, created a programme for three-dimensional design targeted for utilization mainly by architects (Bojár 2007). While not unique in the field, compared with other products, this software is elegant and efficient, and thus commercially successful, and it is marketed worldwide. This is a classic example of a Schumpeterian entrepreneurial career. What a difference there is between the two Hungarians: floppy disk inventor Jánosi not succeeding in the pre-1989 era, remaining poor and virtually unknown, and Graphisoft creator Bojár gaining fame and fortune.

The third story, about data recovery from damaged hard disks, starts also in Kádár-era Hungary, characterized by half-way market reforms. At the time there were already quite a few computers around, but these were rather expensive in the Hungarian context. If a computer breaks down, the most valuable part, the hard drive, should not be dumped but rather restored for use in another computer. Two brothers, János and Sándor Kürti, acquired special skills in the restoration of hard drives. And then comes the creative idea: the same skill can be used if the data stored on the hard disk gets lost. Everybody knows the traumatic feeling of losing valuable information on their computer. The Kürtis learnt the technique, or, more precisely, 'the art' of conjuring data believed to be lost forever from the damaged disk. After 1989, this very specialized knowledge became a marketable service, so the

Kürti brothers founded a company, and trained several experts in their art. Today they have customers from all over the world (Kürti and Gábor 2008; Laki 2009), making theirs another story of highly successful Schumpeterian innovators.

Although two of the three examples come from Hungary, due to my personal connections with people familiar with those cases, I am convinced that there are similar stories in many other post-socialist countries.

3.2 The acceleration of follow-up and diffusion

As post-socialist economies were moving forward in enlarging the private sector and creating the institutions of market co-ordination, technical progress accelerated in many ways, including the faster follow-up of innovations introduced elsewhere. The need for access to a telephone line has been self-evident to everyone in the West in recent decades, but not in the least so for citizens of socialist countries, where it was a service in very short supply, reserved for the privileged and provided for others only after a waiting period of several years. There were not enough lines because planners had assigned the service a low priority and allocated resources to other sectors. As long as socialism prevailed, the idea of changing the relationship between supply and demand in the telephone service seemed hopeless. Then followed changes to the system and as a result the situation completely reversed in the telephone sector. Table 1.5 shows that in a relatively short time, the old-style cable phone service became accessible to everyone. In addition, a revolutionary new product, the mobile phone, appeared and conquered the phone market[26] (see Tables 1.6–1.8). The penetration of these services occurred at great speed (Cooper 2009). As the use of the phone has become unconstrained on the supply side, nowadays only the demand constraint is effective.

Table 1.5 Telephone lines: comparative data*

Year	Bulgaria	Hungary	Poland	Romania	Soviet Union	Germany	Greece	Italy
1979	91	53	53	67	67	308	226	216
1980	102	58	55	73	70	332	235	231
1985	167	70	67	88	103	416	314	305
1990	242	96	86	102	140	441	384	387
1995	305	210	148	131	169	514	494	434
2000	353	372	283	174	218	610	536	474
2005	323	332	307	203	280	661	567	431

Note: *Number of lines per 1,000 people.
Source: United Nations Statistics Division (2009).

Table 1.6 Penetration of modern communication technology in EU countries: 15 old EU member states (EU15) versus 10 new post-socialist member states (EU10)

Indicator	Unit of measurement	Group	1995	2001	2007
GDP	per capita, constant 2000 US$	EU15	19,706	23,747	26,781
		EU10	3,469	4,425	6,295
GDP	per capita, PPP, constant 2005 US$	EU15	25,831	31,134	35,058
		EU10	9,758	12,286	17,570
Personal computers	per 100 people	EU15	16	35	37
		EU10	3	12	33
Internet users	per 100 people	EU15	3	32	64
		EU10	1	14	48
Broadband subscribers	per 100 people	EU15	NA	2	24
		EU10	NA	0	12
Mobile phone subscriptions	per 100 people	EU15	7	77	116
		EU10	1	40	118

Notes: Figures are simple means for each country group. For missing data (NA), see source.
Source: World Bank (2008).

The clear causal relationship between capitalism and the abundant supply of the phone service is present on several levels. The transition to private ownership based on the liberalized market economy put an end to the shortage economy. A phone service is supplied because domestic or foreign entrepreneurs profit from this business. Because of the close substitutability of the cable-connected telephone by mobile phones, the first cannot remain a monopoly. On the contrary, we witness a fierce rivalry between phone companies. Some 30 years ago in the Soviet Union or in Eastern Europe, the would-be-customer begged the bureaucracy for a phone line. Nowadays, phone companies are bidding for the favour of the customer.

I, for one, remember well my own troubles due to the lack of a home phone line, and I am grateful to post-socialist transition and to capitalism for the fact that now I and all my family members have a home phone. I am grateful for the improved chances of technical progress due to the change of the system. I know that 'gratitude' is a word missing from the vocabulary of economics and political science. Yet, I want to use exactly that term because it clearly reflects not only my rational understanding of a positive causal relationship between capitalism and innovation in general, and the shift towards capitalism and the availability of phone services in particular, but also a strong emotion towards the post-1989 changes. In spite of all short-comings and lost battles, I genuinely celebrate the anniversary and it is one of the important reasons to celebrate the advent of capitalism that all the

Table 1.7 Penetration of modern communication technology in EU countries: five Visegrád countries versus three South European countries

Indicator	Unit of measurement	Group	1995	1997	1999	2001	2003	2005	2007
GDP	per capita, constant 2000 US$	S3	10,406	11,020	11,847	12,642	13,054	13,623	14,289
		V5	3,865	4,194	4,435	4,756	5,108	5,635	6,338
GDP	per capita, PPP, constant 2005 US$	S3	18,620	19,721	21,200	22,618	23,345	24,357	25,545
		V5	11,550	12,535	13,228	14,176	15,237	16,821	18,956
Personal computers	per 100 people	S3	5	7	9	14	15	17	28
		V5	4	6	9	12	18	23	39
Internet users	per 100 people	S3	1	3	10	16	26	33	41
		V5	1	2	6	13	29	39	50
Broadband subscribers	per 100 people	S3	NA	NA	0	1	3	8	14
		V5	NA	NA	0	0	1	5	11
Mobile phone subscriptions	per 100 people	S3	3	12	40	74	88	100	115
		V5	1	4	14	46	72	92	113

Notes: Figures are simple averages for each country group. V5, Visegrád countries: the Czech Republic, Hungary, Poland, Slovakia and Slovenia; S3, South European countries: Greece, Portugal and Spain.
Source: World Bank (2008).

Table 1.8   Penetration of modern communication technology in Russia and some other countries

Indicator	Unit of measurement	Country	1995	2001	2007
GDP	per capita US$	Russia	1,618	1,870	2,858
		Brazil	3,611	3,696	4,222
		Mexico	4,892	5,864	6,543
GDP	per capita PPP	Russia	7,853	9,076	13,873
		Brazil	7,727	7,910	9,034
		Mexico	9,949	11,927	13,307
Personal computers	per 100 people	Russia	2	8	NA
		Brazil	2	6	NA
		Mexico	3	7	NA
Internet users	per 100 people	Russia	0	3	21
		Brazil	0	5	35
		Mexico	0	7	23
Broadband	per 100 people	Russia	NA	0	3
		Brazil	NA	0	4
		Mexico	NA	0	4
Mobile phone subscriptions	per 100 people	Russia	0	5	115
		Brazil	1	16	63
		Mexico	1	22	63

Source: World Bank (2008).

products of technical progress are finally available also for us, the citizens of the post-socialist region.

Tables 1.6–1.8 show similar results for quite a few other, not less important, diffusion processes: the use of computers, access to the internet and so on. The speed of following the pioneering countries has accelerated quite spectacularly.

Numerous entrepreneurs take the example of a pioneer, adapt the idea to actual local circumstances and achieve great successes. One of these great Schumpeterian innovators is the Chinese businessman Ma Yun, the founder and leader of the Alibaba Group. The main activity of the companies belonging to his group is business-to-business trade over the internet, especially trading between small companies. The Alibaba Group is now the largest company of that sector in China and one of the largest in the world. Ma Yun started as a high-school teacher and became a multibillionaire.[27] (The story of Alibaba is a spectacular success story, but hundreds of other impressive innovation stories have evolved in the post-socialist world.) To sum up, the gap between the most developed countries and the post-socialist countries has not disappeared, but it is narrower now than it was in the socialist era when the gap was typically increasing over time.[28]

3.3 Creative destruction

The process of innovation and the dynamics of firms' entry and exit are closely associated. Schumpeter coined the name 'creative destruction' for the latter, describing concisely and precisely the two inseparable sides of fast technical progress. It is easy to appreciate happy arrivals to the business world, especially if they appear in the form of successful innovators. But there is no fast progress without the sad events of bankruptcies, business failure, exits, and the accompanying bitter phenomena of lay-offs and unemployment.

Transition economies have had the bad fortune of experiencing two big waves of creative destruction. I called the first one 'transformational recession' in an earlier study (Kornai 1993). It caused trauma in all post-socialist countries, leading to a huge number of exits and creating the first shock of mass unemployment after decades of over-employment and job security. The present recession is not yet over, but—looking with some degree of optimism into the near future—it will probably lead to a smaller fall in production than the decline of output under the transformational recession. That was probably one of the deepest recessions in economic history, but the world paid less attention to it than to the present crisis because we, the citizens of the former communist region, were the only victims of the transformational recession, and the rest of the world did not share the painful experience.

The transformational recession carried a dreadfully high price tag of suffering, but it created benefits as well. It compelled quick adjustments to a radical shift in the composition of the internal and external market, and also cleared the way for more dynamism, more innovation, and higher productivity. Many obsolete production lines, rusty factories, and poorly supplied shops disappeared, and brand-new production units located in modern buildings equipped with the latest technology, and new supermarkets and shopping centres appeared. Well-organized data are available on entry and exit in the post-socialist area. The article by Bartelsman et al. (2004) provides a careful report and analysis, based on firm-level data, of the process of creative destruction across 24 countries, including several transition countries—Estonia, Hungary, Latvia, Romania and Slovenia (see Figure 1.2 as an illustration).

In the first years of transition, the number of entries was much larger than the number of exits, which was different from more mature market economies where the difference in these two flows is usually smaller, or is negative. Many large (formerly state-owned) companies went out of business, and small businesses entered in huge numbers. Total firm turnover (exit + entry rate) was between 3 and 8 per cent in most industrial countries, and more than 10 per cent in some of the transition economies in the 1990s. The turbulence caused by the fast turnover and short lifespan of newly created firms later calmed down. By the end of the 1990s, the characteristic

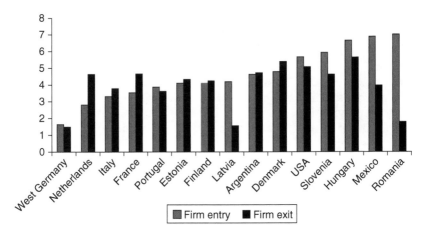

Figure 1.2   Firms' entry and exit rates in the 1990s

Note: Columns in light grey show the entry rates, defined as the number of new firms divided by the total number of incumbent and entrant firms in a given year. Columns in dark grey show the exit rates, defined as the number of firms exiting the market in a given year divided by the population of origin; that is, the incumbents in the previous year.

Source: Bartelsman et al. (2004: 16, panel C).

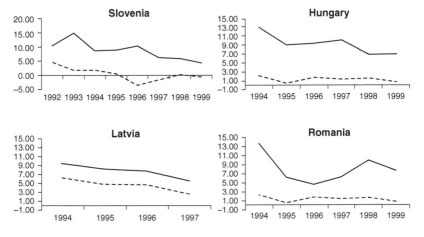

Figure 1.3   The evolution of gross and net firm flows in transition economies

Notes: The calculations cover the whole business sector. The black line shows the total turnover (entry rate plus exit rate) and the grey line the net flow (entry rate minus exit rate).

Source: Bartelsman et al. (Scarpetta 2004: 17, figure 2, panel B).

demographic data of the firm population came fairly close to those observed in other countries. Figure 1.3 shows the trend towards a more balanced ratio between entry and exit. The dashed line is approaching the zero position, where the numbers of employee-weighted entry and exit rates cancel each other out. It took several years to get over the worst phase of the destructive side of the Schumpeterian process. Post-socialist economies started to grow with increased efficiency, producing a much more up-to-date output mix, when suddenly a new external shock, the impact of the global recession, shook the economy. The people of our region are going through a second painful recession. It is quite understandable that nowadays the word 'capitalism' does not resonate pleasingly in the ears of the citizens of post-socialist countries.

It is too early to ask whether the present recession—beside causing disturbance and suffering—has a cleansing effect in the Schumpeterian sense. Does the destruction clear the way for more construction in the post-socialist region? Ten or more years from now will provide sufficient evidence to answer that question. It would require a separate detailed study to discuss the policy implications of the positive description provided above. What I can do here is just offer a few hints at policy options and the dilemmas associated with the choice between these options.

1. Accepting the basic Schumpeterian idea of creative destruction does not imply an automatic approval of all specific manifestations of destruction. If blind market forces lead to the exit of a firm, some organizations (the central or local government, the financial sector or some other entities) might consider a bailout. Here, we are in the middle of a huge area of theoretical and practical problems discussed in the literature on the soft budget constraint and moral hazard. I have discussed this issue previously (Kornai et al. 2003; Kornai 2009). At this point I want to add only one remark: the Schumpeterian process of innovation is accompanied by the spectacularly rapid growth of exactly the sectors and sub-sectors that are the most promising and most 'fashionable' (remember the mass entry and tumultuous growth of 'dot.com' firms). This process has inevitably two sides: many projects are needed for the few great successes, and at the same time we get too many of them. But then 'natural selection' follows, and we must not fight for the survival of each species destined for extinction. Policy makers might posit strong arguments in favour of certain bailouts; for example, to protect the economy as a whole from far-reaching serious macroeconomic damage caused by an excessive numbers of exits. However, the counter-arguments must also be carefully considered.

2. The debate about the causes of the recent recession is ongoing. A well-known train of thought refers to the easy-going lending policy of the financial sector and is calling for much more rigorous, more conservative lending rules in the future. I do not reject this line of thinking but I must add a warning. The Schumpeterian process of innovation requires relatively easy access to capital for risky projects that might fail, or might lead to the fantastic achievements of technical progress (see conditions D and

E in the above survey of circumstances necessary to the Schumpeterian process of innovation). The general mood calls for caution and stronger risk aversion than before the recession. I agree that more caution is needed than before, but it would be a fatal mistake to apply a very conservative attitude blindly. Lending criteria should be carefully differentiated so as to leave the chances of financing risky but promising innovative projects open.

3. We hear loud calls for regulation and warnings against the unfettered rule of market forces. These calls and warnings are legitimate, up to a certain point. Beyond that, we might enter the area of over-regulation, the bureaucratic obstacles of starting businesses that can dampen the vigour of the entrepreneurial spirit. Moreover, in quite a few post-socialist countries, it is still a difficult obstacle race to start a business (see the report of the World Bank and the International Finance Corporation (2009), *Doing Business*). Policy makers should avoid both types of mistake: going too far in deregulation and introducing too much (and/or ill-targeted) regulation.

4. The public mood is upset because of sky-rocketing earnings of many business people and top managers. We hear calls for practical measures against this phenomenon. Although the anger is morally justified and psychologically understandable, an (unpopular) caveat is needed. One of the conditions of the Schumpeterian process (condition B in the above listing) is the gigantic reward in the case of success—not simply a large, but a huge reward. Only that encourages the would-be innovators to take the large risk of failure. Let us remember that in this context not only do the pioneers of introducing great breakthrough inventions deserve the name 'innovators', but also the entrepreneurs who are quick to follow the (domestic or foreign) pioneers. On the other hand, how difficult it is to imagine the work of an honest and competent jury able to draw the line between a well-deserved and an undeserved large reward. I am not prepared to propose a feasible procedure but just want to draw the attention to the two (mutually contradictory) aspects of very high business income.

4 Reflection of historical reality in people's minds

4.1 The basic phenomenon: lack of understanding

In the previous parts of this study, I described the historical reality of the interaction between the Great Transformation, that is, the change of the system, and technical progress. Allowing for errors in the description, I am convinced about its basic accuracy, supported by sufficient evidence. We have to separate the description of historical reality and the reflection of that reality in people's minds. The reflexive process works differently in different people. The reality described in the earlier sections is perceived,

Table 1.9 Evaluation of technical progress

	Scientific and technological progress will help to cure diseases such as AIDS and cancer	Thanks to science and technology, there will be greater opportunities for future generations	Science and technology make our lives healthier, easier and more comfortable	Science and technology will help eliminate poverty and hunger around the world	The benefits of science are greater than the harmful effects it could have
AT	82	71	71	33	48
FIN	89	77	77	21	50
IT	82	73	76	50	57
SP	79	66	73	37	57
PL	89	93	83	45	65
HU	94	81	79	34	63
CZ	85	74	70	35	44

Notes: The following question was asked: 'Do you agree with the following statements?' The table shows the proportions of positive answers in percentages of the total number of respondents. AT = Austria, FIN = Finland, IT = Italy, SP = Spain, PL = Poland, HU = Hungary, CZ = Czech Republic.
Source: Eurobarometer (2005).

understood and evaluated differently by each individual, depending on their social status, education, personal history, and character.

The first question we must raise is about the evaluation of technical progress. Do people regard the past and future appearance of inventions and innovations, new products and new technologies as advancement, or are they afraid of the process and regard it as harmful or dangerous? The question has been asked in some international surveys: Tables 1.9 and 1.10 give us interesting insights. Considering benefits and harms caused by technical progress, two-thirds of Polish and Hungarian respondents find the positive effect stronger than the negative. In that respect, a larger proportion of citizens of these two post-socialist countries are in favour of technical progress than in Austria, Finland, Italy, and Spain, and in the post-socialist Czech Republic. The proportion of respondents approving technical progress is much higher when the question is about the future impact (see the fifth column of Table 1.9 and the first column of Table 1.10).

The second question aims not at evaluation but causality. I take the risk and start with a bold general conjecture. The majority of citizens in the post-socialist region do not understand the basic causal relationship between capitalism and technological progress. Although the innovations of the last 50–100 years, and in particular the revolutionary change in information and communication technology, have dramatically changed people's lives, people do not attribute this great change to capitalism.[29] On the contrary, a large part of the population has moderate or even vehement

Table 1.10   Expectations concerning the impact of new technologies

Country	Solar energy	Computers and information technology	Biotechnology and genetic engineering	The internet	Mobile phones	New energy sources to power cars	Air transport
EU15	90	85	63	77	67	90	79
EU10	84	87	64	81	70	86	79
Germany	95	89	65	75	57	92	72
UK	91	92	65	81	61	90	80
Hungary	87	87	74	78	67	81	75
Poland	89	92	63	86	80	88	88
Romania	78	86	65	82	75	84	85

Notes: The following question was asked: 'Do you think the following new technologies will have positive negative or neutral effects?' Only the percentages of positive answers are shown.
Source: Eurobarometer (2005).

anti-capitalist feelings—while taking advantage of the mobile phone, the internet, the barcode in the supermarket, the plastic materials and synthetic fibres, the modern household appliances, the Xerox copier and so on, without acknowledging that all of them, without exception, are creations of the (despised) capitalist system. This is conjecture. And to my regret, I cannot refer to one single survey, public opinion poll or value survey supporting, correcting, or refuting that conjecture.[30] Among the hundreds of more or less relevant questions asked of the informants, nobody ever asked in any form the question formulated here: What do you think and how do you feel about the interaction between the overall system (capitalism, socialism, transition from socialism to capitalism) on the one hand and technical progress on the other?

Let me maintain the conjecture until we get the first survey data providing a reliable insight into people's minds concerning these questions, and the results call for the modification of the conjecture. The lack of surveys seems, in some strange way, an indirect support of my conjecture. If professional researchers studying the understanding of social change and people's sentiments vis-á-vis the changes completely ignore this set of questions, then what can we expect from the average citizen? The complete lack of surveys related to these vital issues is a clear indication of intellectual indifference towards the understanding of the relationship between the political and economic sphere and the acceleration of technical progress. Public opinion is shaped by a complex social process. Everyone is taking part: the parents and teachers in kindergartens and primary schools, our neighbours and colleagues. I would make a few remarks about professional groups carrying special responsibility for shaping public opinion.

4.2 The responsibility of the economic profession

What do we teach students? The exciting and important new current of growth theory, inspired to a large extent by Schumpeter (Aghion and Howitt 1998; Grossman and Helpman 1991), is acknowledged by the rest of the profession, and usually respect is expressed in a polite footnote but without profoundly penetrating the way of thinking in mainstream economics. Highly distinguished economists (Baumol et al. 2007; Phelps 2008: 77–98) put a heavy emphasis on entrepreneurship in explaining the virtues of capitalism. The recent representatives of the Austrian school (see, e.g., Kirzner 1985: 119–49) never tire of drawing attention to the innovative nature of spontaneous market forces. Economists specializing in comparative economics and the study of socialist and post-socialist economies draw attention to the strong causal relationship between the specific properties of a system and the characteristics of technical progress. An excellent example is in Balcerowicz (1995: Chapter 6). Nevertheless, these valuable ideas do not penetrate, via courses on microeconomics, to the routine education of young economists.

There is a simple but decisive test; let us check the most influential introductory textbooks. Take Gregory Mankiw's (2009) book, which is one of the most widely used and has been translated into several languages. It is a masterpiece in didactics, well written, and full of interesting illustrations of the main propositions. Yet, not a single sentence on the Schumpeterian innovative process can be found! There are several dozen names in the index, but Schumpeter's name does not appear. There are a few pallid paragraphs about the increase in factor productivity and technical progress, but that does not compensate for the lack of the vivid description of the innovative process and the profound explanation of the dynamism of capitalism.[31]

Let me add a few reservations. I focus here only on introductory texts because they play a crucial role in the formation of the thinking of students—they do the 'imprinting' of the conditional reflexes and automatisms of the thought process.

I have cited names of distinguished economists who are perfectly aware of the role of entrepreneurship and the Schumpeterian approach. If these scholars (and a few others accepting a similar view of the capitalist economy) are teaching microeconomics, they certainly ignore the innovative process and the role of the capitalist system in generating breakthrough innovations.[32] Our small sample is, of course, not representative. It is beyond the limits of my present research to analyse a large and representative sample of textbooks and draw the appropriate conclusions. But until I meet well-substantiated refutation, I maintain the hypothesis claiming that a large (probably dominant) part of the higher education introducing the students to the principles of economics does not explain this highly important system-specific property of capitalism sufficiently. Mainstream economics is often accused of advertising the favourable properties of capitalism. If so, it is doing a rather poor job in teaching, lacking the mention of one of the main virtues of the system: its inclination towards unstoppable innovation.

The GDP has become the dominant indicator when it comes to the measurement of growth—it is a great achievement of economists and statisticians to have an operational definition and methodology for measuring GDP, uniformly accepted all over the world. But this important success has generated some kind of laziness in evaluating the successes and failures of the development process. Attention is focused on GDP growth rates to an exaggerated extent. Perhaps a few other indicators should also get attention: inflation, fiscal balance, the current account, measures of inequality, and a few more. But there are no widely accepted and regularly observed indicators of measuring success or failure, acceleration or slowdown of technical progress (understanding this term in the spirit of this study). Post-socialist economies in East Central Europe reached the pre-1990 level of GDP in around 1994–2000, and the successor states of the Soviet Union followed even later, or are still below that level. In the meantime, everyday life has completely changed for the majority of people due to accelerated use of new products and technologies created by the capitalist innovative process. We lament problems with the level of GDP, but a large part of the population is now connected to the rest of society by phone and the internet, and a much larger number of people have cars and modern household appliances, and use several other new products that were formerly available in the West only. We should elaborate appropriate indicators and measurement methods to reach a more correct observation and demonstration of the effects of technical progress on everyday life.

The need to complement the measurement of GDP with other indicators to reflect other aspects of welfare and development is well known to every economist and statistician. Important new initiatives are emerging to improve the measurement of growth, and they are complementing the data on aggregate output with various indicators of health, education, income distribution, and so on.[33] I am worried that the aspect highlighted in this study—the impact of technical progress on the way of life—may again be left out of efforts to reform statistics and may not receive the attention it deserves.

4.3   The responsibility of politicians

Politicians are, self-evidently, in charge of governmental policy. Everything mentioned above with respect to the policy implications of the analysis belongs to the competence of political decision makers. Right now, however, I will make a few remarks about another aspect of political activity: political leaders are also educators of their nation.

With the help of a few colleagues, we read some public speeches of political leaders of the following countries: Bulgaria, Croatia, the Czech Republic,

Hungary, Poland, Serbia, Slovakia and Slovenia. In each country, we chose the speeches or writings of the head of state and/or the prime minister, and the leader(s) of the most influential opposition party (or parties). We tried to select speeches or statements offering a general overview of a country's successes and failures, such as the State of the Union address in the USA. In some cases we were able to find a speech celebrating the 20th anniversary of the 1989 events and providing an overall evaluation of the post-socialist transition.[34] The general finding is easy to summarize. Of 53 speeches and political statements, there was not a single one explaining the causal linkage between capitalism and technical progress and the impact of this progress on people's lives. This virtue of capitalism was not spelt out in order to convince the people that moving from socialism to capitalism meant a shift to the world of innovation, modernization and dynamism. Some political leaders say a few words about technical progress, and the same politicians speak favourably of the capitalist system, but we did not find the argument just explained in their speeches. The sample of 53 statements is large enough to speak out loudly—that is a shocking and disappointing observation. We observe here not the conduct of radical anti-capitalist political figures from the extreme Right or the extreme Left, but of leaders of the political 'establishment' in Eastern Europe. They are either in government or the opposition, but they are certainly friends and not enemies of capitalism, and yet they miss one of the best arguments in favour of the system. Let us add immediately that very few are ready to take a stand for capitalism. It is becoming quite common among politicians (on both the Left and the Right) to emphasize the dark side of the system, and to speak out against it.

Certainly, more political speeches and statements should be checked. I would welcome any counter-examples, that is, speeches by politicians underlining the role of capitalism in generating innovation, and adding the acceleration of technical progress to the list of successes achieved in the era of transition. However, as long as it is not refuted, I maintain the proposition: politicians at all points of the political spectrum carry heavy responsibility for neglecting the explanation of the causal relationship; capitalism→innovation→changes in the way of life. Understanding this crucial linkage would be an effective antidote against anti-capitalist sentiments—and our political leaders do not provide that antidote.

Neglect is, of course, the milder sin. What I find most irritating is populist demagoguery against capitalism by those who make practical use of all the discoveries and innovations generated by capitalism. It is morally repulsive to see political activists mobilizing people for an extremist anti-capitalist meeting or protest demonstration using a personal computer, mobile phones and communication channels provided by satellites and optical fibre. That is happening in the post-socialist region. Political activists, denying even the simple fact that the system change has already happened, put their populist anti-capitalist slogans on a blog or an internet site, give inflammatory speeches to a mob through electronic loudspeakers and communicate with each other via mobile phones, thus exploiting technologies generated by capitalism.

4.4 Interconnectivity and democracy

Although we know practically nothing about the comprehension and evaluation of the 'capitalism→innovation→changes in the way of life' causal linkage in people's minds, we have some insights into the opposite direction of interaction, namely, the effect of technical progress (more precisely, progress in the information–communication sector) on the political views of people in post-socialist countries. Tables 1.11–1.13 summarize survey data on post-socialist area respondents' attitudes towards democracy, capitalism and the former socialist system. In the tabulations presented here, the population was divided into two classes: people using and not using the internet frequently. The difference is quite impressive.[35] Those connected to the world of modern information technology hold more favourable views on democracy and capitalism, and are more critical of the past regime. The users of the internet are more immune to sentiments of nostalgia for the old socialist order—a feeling strengthened in many, especially since the recent economic crisis. The empirical results reported above fit well into the findings of another line of study: research on 'interconnectivity'. The intuitive meaning of the term is clearly indicated by the name: individuals are connected to each other by various technical instruments and procedures. Email

Table 1.11 Satisfaction with democracy: population divided into users and non-users of the internet

Country	Internet users		Non-users	
	Mean	%	Mean	%
Central Eastern Europe	2.6	30	2.8	70
Czech Republic	2.5	42	2.8	57
Hungary*	2.2	23	2.4	77
Poland	2.7	34	2.9	66
Russia	3.0	14	3.1	86
Slovenia	2.2	57	2.1	43

Notes: The second and fourth columns contain the percentages of users and non-users of the internet, respectively. The following question was asked: 'How satisfied are you with the way democracy works?' Answers were expected on a 4-degree scale: 1 = completely satisfied; 2 = somewhat satisfied; 3 = not very satisfied; 4 = completely dissatisfied. The table shows the mean (not weighted).
*I have reservations concerning the Hungarian data on internet users; the figure seems to be too low compared with other statistics (JK).
Source: Rose (2004).

Table 1.12 Evaluation of the capitalist economic system: population divided into users and non-users of the internet

Country	Internet users		Non-users	
	Mean	%	Mean	%
Central Eastern Europe	1.9	30	0.4	70
Czech Republic	2.5	42	0.7	58
Hungary*	0.7	23	−0.5	77
Poland	1.1	34	−0.9	66
Russia	0.9	14	−0.8	86
Slovenia	1.6	57	0.7	43

Notes: The second and fourth columns contain the percentages of users and non-users of the internet, respectively. The following question was asked: 'How satisfied are you with the capitalist system?' Answers were expected on a 21-degree scale: −10 = worst, 0 = neutral, +10 = best. The table shows the mean (not weighted). *I have reservations concerning the Hungarian data on internet users; the figure seems to be too low compared with other statistics (JK).
Source: Rose (2004).

Table 1.13 Evaluation of the socialist economic system: population divided into users and non-users of the internet

Country	Internet users		Non-users	
	Mean	%	Mean	%
Central Eastern Europe	1.1	30	3.7	70
Czech Republic	−2.6	42	0.6	58
Hungary*	0.2	23	3.0	77
Poland	−0.4	34	3.4	66
Russia	1.6	14	4.4	86
Slovenia	3.0	57	4.0	43

Notes: The second and fourth columns contain the percentages of users and non-users of the internet, respectively. The following question was asked: 'How satisfied were you with the former socialist system?' Answers were expected on a 21-degree scale: −10 = worst, 0 = neutral, +10 = best. The table shows the mean (not weighted). *I have reservations concerning the Hungarian data on internet users; the figure seems to be too low compared with other statistics (JK).
Source: Rose (2004).

plays a particularly important role in this respect. The more people are technically able to send email to others, the tighter the network of connections becomes. That phenomenon is certainly observable and measurable.

I rely here on an exciting study by Kedzie (1997a), who refers to a metric measuring 'interconnectivity'. Not being an expert in that field, I cannot judge whether the metric used in Kedzie's study is the best available for the purpose he is using it. Conditionally accepting his choice, the basic results of his study are certainly worth mentioning. He looked, beside other calculations, on the correlation between 'democracy' (measured by various indicators) and 'interconnectivity'. This correlation turns out to be 0.73, stronger than the correlation of democracy with per capita GDP (0.57). I report the proposition with some reservation, due to my lack of knowledge in the area utilized by the interconnectivity index. A more recent study by Frisch (2003), however, supports Kedzie's findings. Hopefully, research in that direction will continue.

Let me recall my earlier remark on the role of modern information–communication technology in dismantling the monolithic power of the communist party and the official Marxist-Leninist ideology. There, I looked at events that happened twenty years ago in the former Soviet Union and in the socialist countries of East Central Europe. The problem is, however, not outdated at all. There are two small countries, Cuba and North Korea, where not much has changed in the economy, and heavy-handed communist dictatorship still prevails. And then there are two large countries, China and Vietnam, where far-reaching reforms have been introduced and have moved the economy close to capitalism while the political structure has changed very little, remaining a single-party dictatorship. How will modern information–communication technology influence those countries? The two large countries eagerly utilize all advantages provided by the revolutionary achievements of technical progress, and at the same time they are scared of the consequences. These two objectives of the leadership—maximum gain from technical progress and maximum protection of the monopoly of power—diametrically contradict each other, resulting in hesitation, steps forward and backward, and ambivalence.

Another major problem to analyse is the prospects: What is the future of the interaction between the forthcoming waves of innovation and the way of life? On my pessimistic days I foresee various evil scenarios. Even without a special talent for prophecy, we can easily predict the misuse of technical achievements. I have read several reports about efforts of the Chinese government to apply political censorship to the internet, block the transmission of certain TV channels or shut down outspoken blogs.[36] Since an ever-growing share of all computers used in China is produced domestically, it is easy to enforce the incorporation of centrally controlled censorship software into the operating system. Sadly, large Western corporations, scared of losing the huge Chinese market, are willing to co-operate with the officials in their efforts to introduce political censorship.

When Orwell (1949/1950) wrote his book *Nineteen Eighty-Four*, 'Big Brother' did not have the equipment envisaged in the novel. But nowadays there would be no technical difficulty involved in the installation of cameras and listening devices in every home and office. Imagine a Stalin of the future with the latest observation gadgets, resolved to using them to watch all citizens. But then, on my more optimistic days, I escape these nightmarish visions and hope that modern technology gives birth time and again to decentralization, whatever efforts dictatorships devote to assure or even further strengthen centralization. If the centralizator invents a new way of blocking information, there will be hundreds and thousands of decentralizators who break through the blockades and barriers.[37]

5 Concluding remarks

My study has covered a vast array of topics. I did not intend to limit it to one or two issues. We are looking at a huge white area on the otherwise colourful map of research in comparative economics and post-socialist 'transitology'. The purpose of my study was to give a general overview of that area. Among the great number of valuable studies on several topics, some are mentioned here. Unfortunately, each topic has its own large body of literature, but they are sharply separated from each other and lacking cross-references. The emphasis of my study was not the detailed description and analysis of one or other linkage but to give an impression of the totality of interactions. And there are also dozens of themes deserving penetrating research, empirical observation and theoretical analysis, barely touched upon or not even mentioned here. The study of technical progress and its relationship to society is going on in a multidimensional space. The points discussed in my study are located in a sub-space, and I am aware that there are relevant dimensions outside my sub-space.[38]

I wish I were younger, with all the energy needed for the careful exploration of the white area as a whole. What an exciting and intellectually challenging subject for research! I hope that my study will encourage others to enter this largely under-researched field. In any case, I would like to continue the study of the interaction between the change in the political and economic spheres of the system and the properties of technical progress.

Acknowledgements

This study is an updated version of a paper presented at the UNU-WIDER conference Reflections on Transition: Twenty Years after the Fall of the Berlin Wall, held in Helsinki on 18–19 September 2009. I express my gratitude to Philippe Aghion, Julian Cooper, Zsuzsa Dániel, Zsolt Fekete, Thomas Geodecki, Philip Hanson, Jerzy Hausner, Judit Hürkecz, László Karvalics, Zdenek Kudrna, Mihály Laki, Lukasz Mamica, Tibor Meszmann, Gérard Roland, Dániel Róna, András Simonovits, Katalin Szabó and Chenggang Xu for their valuable comments and their devoted help in collecting data and readings, and to Collegium Budapest and the Central European University for permanent support and a stimulating research environment. I highly appreciate the help I got from Hédi Erdős, Rita Fancsovits, Katalin Lévayné Deseő, Anna Patkós, Ildikó Pető, Andrea Reményi and László Tóth in editing this paper.

Notes

1. The literature on technical progress and innovation distinguishes new products and new technologies, although the appearance of these two categories is often intertwined. For example, while the Xerox machine is a new product, it has also introduced a new technology of printing. Table 1.1 lists new products because of their salience in everyday life.
2. Certain classes of innovation were excluded in the selection. Criteria of exclusion are explained partly in the note at the bottom of the table and partly in later sections of the study.
3. Perhaps the most influential work in this area is Castells (1996–8). See also Fuchs (2008).
4. Table 1.1 excludes innovations initiated in the military sector of the economy. The military sector produced innovations appearing first in a socialist country. I will return to that point later.
5. Stealing Western intellectual property in the high-tech sphere was hindered by various barriers; for example, strictly enforced prohibition of exporting certain products to communist countries—the so-called Co-ordinating Committee for Multilateral Export Controls list of products used for military purposes. In spite of strict prohibitions, the co-operation of smart spies and technical experts was successful enough to slip through the holes in the barriers.
6. The most important empirical works on the subject are the books by Amann and Cooper (1982) and Amman et al. (1977). See also Berliner (1976), Hanson (1981) and Hanson and Pavitt (1987).
7. Not all entrepreneurs are innovators (Baumol and Schilling 2008). This study focuses on one extremely important class: the entrepreneurs engaged in the process of innovation.
8. On Schumpeter's contributions to social science, see Heertje (2006) and McCraw (2007). See also Baumol (2002); the title of his book catches the real essence of the phenomenon I will discuss: *The Free-Market Innovation Machine: Analyzing the Growth Miracle of Capitalism*.
9. One can find numerous examples of this delay in the 1995 book of Rogers. See also Freeman (1982: 111–12).
10. For a concise introduction to the Google story, see the company's own brief summary (Google 2009) and the entry on Google in Wikipedia (2009a).
11. Based on my personal experience, I admit that it has changed my research habits as well. It is different to be a researcher in the Google age than it was earlier, in the Gutenberg era.
12. Acemoglu et al. (2007) argue in a recent paper, both theoretically and empirically, that pioneering innovation requires decentralization.
13. According to the well-known ranking of *Forbes* magazine, they tie for fifth rank in the USA.
14. The Google story can be considered a unique case, where the pioneering inventor and the role of the innovator are played by the same people. In the more frequent instance of these roles being separated, the inventor in some cases does, in others does not, attain benefits from the invention or the discovery. The latter was the fate of the computer mouse. The inventor, Douglas Engelbart, has received no financial reward for his ingenious invention. Apple, the innovator company pioneering the mass introduction, has produced enormous profit on this innovation.

15. On the importance of experimentation, see Thomke (2003).
16. Undoubtedly, there is a connection between the economic booms of the great innovative periods and the increase in the available amount of credit. Easily accessible money helps technical progress, but also entails the danger of a bubble formation. It is timely to reread Schumpeter when analyzing the history preceding the current crisis (Schumpeter 1939, especially Chapter IV.) The great temptation to discuss this aspect is regrettably limited by the available space.
17. Joffe was first showered with the highest state awards, and he received high academic honours, but during the last years of Stalin's terror he was removed from his high positions as a 'Zionist'. Whether up or down, his discoveries never turned into a revolutionary innovation.
18. The Hungarian inventor is still alive. Since his retirement he has been living on a very modest pension. See the story of the floppy in Kovács (1999) and Drávucz (2004).
19. For empirical studies see the references in endnote 7. For a theoretical explanation, see Berliner (1976), Gomulka (1983), Kornai (1980, 1992).
20. For a powerful theoretical analysis of the relationship between centralization and innovation, see Qian and Xu (1998).
21. As mentioned before, the defence industry was an exception, because in this area the Soviet empire was in truly fierce competition with the West.
22. The socialist system is not alone in suffering from chronic shortages. During wars, shortages occur in capitalist economies as well. During the Second World War, the shortage of raw materials spurred innovating activities to develop 'ersatz' (substitute) raw materials.
23. For the analysis of the relationship between flexibility of financing, centralization and innovation, see Huang and Xu (1998).
24. Rogers (1995) is perhaps the most quoted work in the literature written for businessmen and managers interested in the practical issues of innovation. In this otherwise excellent and very carefully written book, the name Schumpeter is not even mentioned, nor is any other economic theory of innovation.
25. The experience of the divided Germany is especially instructive. East Germany, beside Czechoslovakia, was the most developed country in the socialist region. It started with an excellent research infrastructure and devoted generous resources to higher education, and academic and industrial research. Yet it was not able to step forward with even one breakthrough revolutionary innovation. In spite of having first-rate, highly skilled experts at its disposal, the rate of following the pioneering innovations was in most sectors slower than in West Germany (Bauer 1999; Stokes 2000).
26. In some countries (e.g. Hungary), it has not only stopped the further increase of cable-connected phone service but has actually started to replace it in many households.
27. See http://www.alibaba.com (company information).
28. According to the Information Society Index, reflecting the development of various aspects of 'information society' in a synthetic way, several post-socialist countries (e.g. the Czech Republic, Hungary, and Slovenia) have achieved a decent position in the ranking (Karvalics 2009). The whole group of countries observed is moving ahead and is getting higher values each year, though it takes strong efforts just to hold the rank achieved today.
29. In an earlier section, talking about the shortage of telephone lines under socialism and the abundant supply after 1989, I made a subjective remark that I am grateful

to capitalism for this change in my life. Perhaps I am not the only one who has this feeling, but I am afraid we are a small minority.

30. With the help of my assistant Dániel Róna, we tried to check the most respected surveys carefully. We checked the four best-known transnational surveys looking for the question formulated above in the text and did not find anything resembling the content of that question. The results of these surveys are on record and are available from the author.

31. With the help of my research assistant, Judit Hürkecz, we checked seven more popular introductory textbooks, which are widely used for teaching in the USA and Europe, including post-socialist countries. Every remark made on Mankiw's book applies exactly to six books as well. Out of the small sample of eight books, there is only one exception. (I come back to that exception in note 32.) The list of these textbooks is on record and is available on request from the author.

32. Small wonder that the exception in our sample is the work of Baumol and Blinder (2009). William Baumol is one of the intellectual leaders advocating a Schumpeterian approach in understanding capitalism.

33. The president of the French Republic has invited a group of economists and statisticians, chaired by Joseph Stiglitz, Amartya Sen, and Jean-Paul Fitoussi, to work on new proposals for improving the measurement of growth and development. At the moment the group is circulating the first drafts of the report (Stiglitz et al. 2009).

34. The list of documents studied is on record and is available from the author.

35. We touch here upon a highly relevant question of whether the appearance of high-tech communication expands social inequality. The search for an answer reaches beyond the limits of this study.

36. See Chao (2009) and Timmer (2009) on Chinese efforts to apply political censorship. For a general overview, see the entry on internet censorship in Wikipedia (2009b).

37. In note 37, I referred to an article by Timmer (2009) published on the internet. The editor asked for comments. Here is the first comment: 'So what is there to keep Chinese citizens from reformatting their hard drives and installing pirated copies of Windows?'

38. Let me mention a few dimensions not appearing in my study:

- What is the effect of the new technology of information and communication on the relationship between individuals, social groups, settlements, countries, and states? What can be expected concerning the relationship between high-tech information and communication, on the one hand, and the nation-state and globalization, on the other? (Castells 1996–8; Nyíri 2004; Webster et al. 2004).
- The future of capitalism. Does the new age of information lead to a radical change in the basic properties of capitalism? Or does it create a new system that cannot be called capitalism any more? Two Hungarian economists, Szabó and Hámori (2006), wrote an interesting book with the following subtitle *Digital capitalism or a new economic system*; see Haug (2003). How does the revolutionary change in information and communication technology affect the practical mode of running a business, especially in the financial sector?
- What are the implications of the new information age concerning property rights, especially with respect to intellectual property?

A quite different direction of thought is to reconsider at a more abstract philosophical level our general understanding of human history. What is the role of the changes in the technology of production and human interaction on the institutions of society, and on the functions of the government?

References

Acemoglu, D., P. Aghion, C. Lelarge, J. Van Reenen and F. Zilibotti (2007) 'Technology, Information, and the Decentralization of the Firm', *The Quarterly Journal of Economics*, 122(4): 1759–99.
Aghion, P. and P. Howitt (1998) *Endogenous Growth Theory* (Cambridge, MA: MIT Press).
Amann, R., J. Cooper and R.W. Davies (1977) *The Technological Level of Soviet Industry* (New Haven and London: Yale University Press).
Amann, R. and J. Cooper (1982) *Industrial Innovation in the Soviet Union* (New Haven and London: Yale University Press).
Balcerowicz, L. (1995) *Socialism Capitalism Transformation* (Budapest: CEU Press).
Bartelsman, E., J. Haltiwanger and S. Scarpetta (2004) 'Microeconomic Evidence of Creative Destruction in Industrial and Developing Countries'. Mimeo. (Washington, DC: World Bank).
Bauer, R. (1999) *Pkw-Bau in der DDR: Zur Innovationsschwäche von Zentralverwaltungswirtschaften* (Frankfurt am Main: Peter Lang).
Baumol, W.J. (2002) *The Free-Market Innovation Machine: Analyzing the Growth Miracle of Capitalism* (Princeton, NJ: Princeton University Press).
Baumol, W.J. and A.S. Blinder (2009) *Economics: Principles and Policy* (Mason, IA: South-Western Cengage Learning).
Baumol, W.J., R.E. Litan and C.J. Schramm (2007) *Good Capitalism, Bad Capitalism, and the Economics of Growth and Prosperity* (New Haven and London: Yale University Press).
Baumol, W.J. and M.A. Schilling (2008) 'Entrepreneurship', in S.N. Durlauf, and L.W. Blume (eds) *The New Palgrave Dictionary of Economics*, 2nd edn. (London: Palgrave Macmillan).
Berliner, J. (1976) *The Innovation Decision in Soviet Industry* (Cambridge, MA: MIT Press).
Berners-Lee, T. (1999) *Weaving the Web* (San Francisco, CA: Harper).
Bojár, G. (2007) *The Graphisoft Story: Hungarian Perestroika from an Entrepreneur's Perspective* (Budapest: Manager Könyvkiadó).
Bygrave, W. and J. Timmons (1992) *Venture Capital at the Crossroads* (Boston, MA: Harvard Business School Press).
Castells, M. (1996–8) *The Information Age: Economy, Society, and Culture*, Vols. I–III. (Oxford: Blackwell).
Ceruzzi, P.E. (2000) *A History of Modern Computing* (Cambridge, MA: MIT Press).
Chao, L. (2009) 'China Squeezes PC Makers', *The Wall Street Journal*, 8 June. http://online.wsj.com/article/SB124440211524192081.html#mod=todays_us_page_one.
Cooper, J. (2009) 'Russia as a Populous Emerging Economy: A Comparative Perspective'. Mimeo.
Davila, T., M.J. Epstein and R. Shelton (2006) *Making Innovation Work: How to Manage it, Measure it, and Profit from It* (Philadelphia, PA: Wharton School).
Drávucz, P. (2004) 'Ez nagyobb dobás lesz a floppinál' ('This is gonna be a greater hit than the floppy') *Magyar Hírlap*, 20 March.
Eurobarometer (2005) Special survey on science and technology (fieldwork: January–February 2005) http://ec.europa.eu/public_opinion/archives/eb_special_240_220_en.htm

Finansy i Statistika (Finance and Statistics) (1988) *SSSR i zarubezhnye strany* 1987 (The USSR and foreign countries 1987), Moscow.

Freeman, C. (1982) *The Economics of Industrial Innovation* (Cambridge, MA: MIT Press).

Frisch, W. (2003) 'Co-evolution of Information Revolution and Spread of Democracy', *Journal of International and Comparative Economics*, 33: 252–5.

Fuchs, C. (2008) *Internet and Society* (New York: London: Routledge).

Gomulka, S. (1983) 'The Incompatibility of Socialism and Rapid Innovation', *Millennium: Journal of International Studies*, 13(1): 16–26.

Google Corporate Information (2009) *Google Milestones*, www.google.com/corporate/history.html.

Griliches, Z. (1957) 'Hybrid Corn: An Exploration in the Economics of Technical Change', *Econometrica*, 25(4): 501–22.

Grossman, G.M. and E. Helpman (1991) *Innovation and Growth in the Global Economy* (Cambridge, MA: MIT Press).

Hanson, P. (1981) *Trade and Technology in Soviet-Western Relations* (London: Macmillan).

Hanson, P. and K. Pavitt (1987) *The Comparative Economics of Research Development and Innovation in East and West: A Survey* (Chur, London, Paris, New York and Melbourne: Harwood).

Harrison, I. (2003) *The Book of Firsts* (London: Cassell Illustrated).

Harrison, I. (2004) *Book of Inventions* (London: Cassell Illustrated).

Haug, W.F. (2003) *High-Tech-Kapitalismus* (Hamburg: Argument).

Heertje, A. (2006) *Schumpeter on the Economics of Innovation and the Development of Capitalism* (Cheltenham: Elgar).

Huang, H. and C. Xu (1998) 'Soft Budget Constraint and the Optimal Choices of Research and Development Projects Financing', *Journal of Comparative Economics*, 26: 62–79.

Karvalics, L. (2009) *The Information (Society) Race* (Budapest: BKE).

Kedzie, C.R. (1997a) 'Democracy and Network Interconnectivity', in S. Kiesler (ed.) *Culture on the Internet* (Mahwah, NJ: Erlbaum).

Kedzie, C.R. (1997b) 'The Case of the Soviet Union: The Dictator's Dilemma', *Communications and Democracy: Coincident Revolutions and the Emergent Dictators*. Rand. www.rand.org/pubs/rgs_dissertations/RGSD127/sec2.html

Kirzner, I.M. (1985) *Discovery and the Capitalist Process* (Chicago, IL: University of Chicago Press).

Kornai, J. (1970) *Anti-Equilibrium* (Amsterdam: North-Holland).

Kornai, J. (1980) *Economics of Shortage*. Vol. A-B. (Amsterdam: North-Holland).

Kornai, J. (1992) *The Socialist System* (Princeton, NJ and Oxford: Princeton University Press and Oxford University Press).

Kornai, J. (1993) 'Transformational Recession: A General Phenomenon Examined through the Example of Hungary's Development', *Economie Appliquée*, 46(2): 181–227.

Kornai, J. (2001) 'Ten Years after The Road to a Free Economy: The Author's Self Evaluation', in B. Pleskovic and N. Stern (eds) *Annual Bank Conference on Development Economics 2000* (Washington, DC: World Bank).

Kornai, J. (2006) 'The Great Transformation of Central and Eastern Europe: Success and Disappointment', *The Economics of Transition*, 14(2): 207–44.

Kornai, J. (2009) 'The Soft Budget Constraint Syndrome and the Global Financial Crisis: Some Warnings of an East European Economist', published on the blog of Willem Buiter associated with *Financial Times* with the introduction by

Willem Buiter (14th October) http://blogs.ft.com/maverecon/2009/10/kornai-on-soft-budget-constraints-bail-outs-and-the-financial-crisis/.

Kornai, J., E. Maskin and G. Roland (2003) 'Understanding the Soft Budget Constraint', *Journal of Economic Literature*, 61(4): 1095–1136.

Kovács, G. (1999) 'Egy elpuskázott találmány: Jánosi Marcell és a kazettás "floppy" (A messed up invention: Marcell Jánosi and the cassette floppy)'. Exhibition poster. Budapest.

Kürti, S. and F. Gábor (eds) (2008) *20 éves a KÜRT, az Infostrázsa (20 Years of KÜRT, the Info-Guard)* (Budapest: Kürt Információmenezsment).

Laki, M. (1984–5) 'Kényszerített innováció' (Forced innovation), *Szociológia*, 12: 45–53.

Laki M. (2009) 'Interjú a Kürti-fívérekkel' (Interview with the Kürti brothers). Mimeo. (Budapest: MTA Közgazdaságtudományi Intézet).

Mankiw, G.N. (2009) *Principles of Economics* (Mason, IA: South-Western Cengage Learning).

McCraw, T.K. (2007) *Prophet of Innovation: Joseph Schumpeter and Creative Destruction* (Cambridge, MA and London: Harvard University Press).

Nyíri, K.J. (2004) 'Review of Castells, the Information Age', in F. Webster and B. Dimitriou (eds) *Manuel Castells*, Vol. III (London: Sage).

Orwell, G. (1949/1950) *Nineteen Eighty-Four* (New York: Penguin).

Phelps, E. (2008) 'Understanding the Great Changes in the World: Gaining Ground and Losing Ground since World War II', in J. Kornai, M. László and G. Roland (eds) *Institutional Change and Economic Behaviour* (Basingstoke: Palgrave Macmillan).

Qian, Y. and C. Xu (1998) 'Innovation and Bureaucracy under Soft and Hard Budget Constraint', *Review of Economic Studies*, 65(1): 151–64.

Rogers, E.M. (1995) *Diffusion of Innovations* (New York: The Free Press).

Rose, R. (2004): *Insiders and Outsiders: New Europe Barometer 2004*, University of Aberdeen fieldwork from 1 October 2004 to 27 February 2005, http://www.abdn.ac.uk/cspp/view_item.php?id=404 (Aberdeen: Centre for the Study of Public Policy).

Schumpeter, J.A. (1912/1934) *The Theory of Economic Development: An Inquiry into Profits, Capital, Credit, Interest, and the Business Cycle* (Cambridge, MA: Harvard University Press).

Schumpeter, J.A. (1939) *Business Cycles* (New York and London: McGraw Hill).

Shane, S. (1994) *Dismantling Utopia: How Information Ended the Soviet Union* (Chicago, IL: Ivan R. Dee).

Stiglitz, J.E., A. Sen and J.-P. Fitoussi (eds) (2009) Report by the Commission on the Measurement of Economic Performance and Social Progress, http://www.stiglitz-sen-fitoussi.fr/documents/rapport_anglais.pdf.

Stokes, R.G. (2000) *Constructing Socialism: Technology and Change in East Germany, 1945–1990* (Baltimore, MD: Johns Hopkins University Press).

Stolyarov, G. (2008) *Liberation by Internet*, www.mises.org/story/3060 (Auburn,AL: Ludwig von Mises Institute).

Szabó, K. and B. Hámori (2006) *Információgazdaság: Digitális kapitalizmus vagy új gazdasági rendszer? (Information Richness: Digital Capitalism or New Economic System?)* (Budapest: Akadémiai Kiadó).

Thomke, S. (2003) *Experimentation Matters: Unlocking the Potential of New Technologies for Innovation* (Boston, MA: Harvard Business School Press).

Timmer, J. (2009) 'China to Mandate Web Filtering Software on All New PCs', *Ars Technica*, http://arstechnica.com/tech-policy/news/2009/06/china-to-mandate-web-filtering-software-on-all-new-pcs.ars.

United Nations Statistics Division (2009) Industrial Commodity Statistics Database (radio, television and communication equipment and apparatus), http://data.un.org/Data.aspx?d=ICS&f=cmID%3a47220-1, accessed 16 July 2009.

Webster, F., R. Blom, E. Karvonen, H. Malin, K. Nordenstreng and E. Puoskan (eds) (2004) *The Information Society Reader* (London: Routledge).

Wikipedia (2009a) *Google*, accessed 23 July 2009.

Wikipedia (2009b) *Internet Censorship*, accessed 19 August 2009.

World Bank (2008) *World Development Indicators* (Washington, DC: World Bank).

World Bank (2009) *Doing Business 2009*, World Bank International Finance Corporation (Washington, DC: Palgrave Macmillan).

2

The Demographic Transformation of Post-Socialist Countries: Causes, Consequences, and Questions

Elizabeth Brainerd

1 Introduction

In May 2006, Russian leader Vladimir Putin announced a radical new package of pronatalist policies designed to halt, and possibly reverse, the steep decline in Russia's birth rate over the past 15 years. The package included increased child benefits, longer maternity leave, and a payment of over US$9,000 to each woman who has a second child. While economists and demographers have long debated the efficacy of such pronatalist government policies in raising birth rates, the intention of this package of measures was clear—to stop the large declines in population that have affected Russia since the early 1990s.

The abrupt fall in fertility in Russia during the transition from socialism is not unique: virtually every country in Eastern Europe (EE) and the former Soviet Union (FSU) experienced significant declines in birth rates in the 1990s, and depressed levels of fertility continued in many countries well into the 2000s. Many countries also recorded a dramatic increase in mortality in the early 1990s; when combined with declining fertility, this led to significant population declines across the region since the start of transition, particularly in the countries of the FSU.

This study reviews these changes in fertility, family formation and mortality in EE and the FSU during the transition period, and discusses what is currently known about the causes of the demographic processes that have been underway in the region since 1989. As will be evident, the demographic transformation of the region has been remarkable in its speed and scope. Many East European countries now resemble Western Europe in their fertility and marriage patterns, and, after decades of low and stagnant levels of life expectancy under socialism, they are now recording rapid gains in life expectancy to levels nearly convergent with those of the West. This demographic transformation has progressed more slowly in the FSU but appears to be well underway nevertheless. The changes in fertility and mortality documented here will likely have far-reaching consequences for each country's population size and age structure, and may influence the region's long-term economic growth prospects. The study concludes with a discussion of some of the possible consequences of this fundamental transformation of society in post-socialist countries.[1]

2   Fertility and family formation

2.1   Changes in birth rates by age and marital status

The formerly socialist countries were characterized by a distinctive pattern of fertility and family formation—marriage and childbearing took place at relatively young ages (compared with Western Europe) and were near-universal. In Russia, for example, the average age at first marriage for women in 1989 was 22.1 years, compared with 25.3 in France. Rates of childlessness were near the biological limit of about 5 per cent; in the 1989 census, only 8 per cent of Russian women aged 40–49 had not had children. Aside from some of the less-developed republics of the USSR with high fertility levels, in all other transition countries, fertility rates had stabilized at about the replacement level of fertility (2.1 children per woman) in the period from 1965 to 1989. As is well known, in many countries, abortion rates were high, with abortion being used as the primary means of birth control in many countries of the FSU.

All of these patterns have changed markedly since the start of the transition. As noted above, virtually every country in EE and the FSU experienced a steep decline in fertility beginning in the late 1980s or early 1990s. This is illustrated in Figure 2.1, which shows the total fertility rate (TFR) in selected countries since 1970.[2] The TFR declined to well below the replacement rate in many countries in the early years of the transition, and the pattern is remarkably similar across countries. In fact, fertility levels in Bulgaria (TFR of 1.09 in 1997) and Ukraine (TFR of 1.086 in 2001) fell below the lowest fertility level ever recorded in a European country during peacetime, that of Spain in 1997, with a TFR of 1.10. Fertility rates have increased slightly in most countries in recent years but remain depressed both historically and in comparison with other developed countries.

Demographers have argued that two distinctive fertility patterns have emerged in the region—a rapid shift toward later (first) childbearing that characterizes EE, and continued early and near-universal first births in the FSU (particularly Russia and Ukraine) but with the postponement of second- and higher-order births.[3] However, recent data (discussed below) indicate that while fertility patterns shifted several years earlier and more dramatically in EE than in the FSU, the countries of the former USSR appear to be moving toward later childbearing and marriage as well.

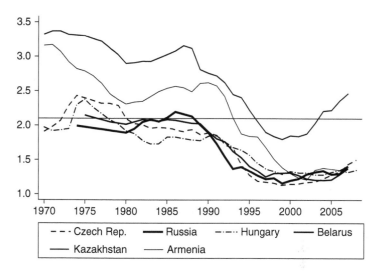

Figure 2.1 Total fertility rate, selected countries
Source: Author.

A key question is whether the fertility decline represents a permanent transition to below-replacement fertility levels or a temporary decline driven by women deciding to delay rather than forego childbearing. One approach to answering this question is to examine changes in age-specific birth rates: Did younger women who postponed childbirth in the early 1990s have children a decade later? Figures 2.2a and 2.2b illustrate age-specific birth rates

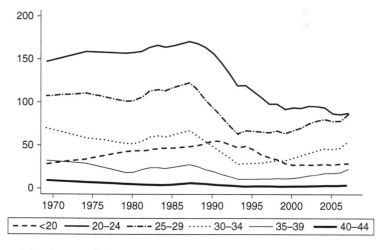

Figure 2.2a Age-specific birth rates, Russia
Source: Author.

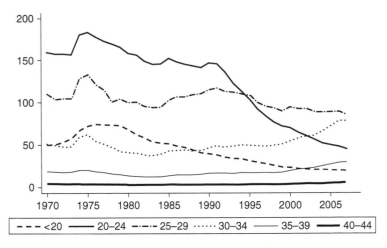

Figure 2.2b   Age-specific birth rates, Hungary
Source: Author.

for Russia and Hungary from 1970 to 2007. Russia's pattern is characteristic of many countries in the western Soviet Union, such as Ukraine and
Belarus, while Hungary's pattern is typical of many East European countries.
Both figures illustrate that until the 1990s, women aged 20–24 had by far
the highest birth rates in both countries, followed by women aged 25–29.
The decline in fertility rates in the 1990s was exceptionally steep for women
aged 20–24 in both countries. In Hungary, birth rates have increased among
women aged 30–39; if current trends continue, the highest birth rates in
Hungary will be for women aged 30–34. This is a fundamental change in
the age structure of fertility, becoming much like the West European pattern
where the majority of childbearing is postponed until the early thirties. Later
childbearing is also occurring in Russia, but women aged 20–24 continue to
have the highest birth rates. The increase in birth rates among older women
indicates that some of the fertility decline in formerly socialist countries was
due to the postponement of births. But in the absence of other changes, this
increase in births is unlikely to compensate for the decline in births during
the 1990s. At least for the cohort of women in their prime childbearing years
during early transition, completed fertility will likely be below that of earlier
cohorts.

The decline in birth rates for younger women is reflected in a sharply
increasing age at first birth in many countries (Figures 2.3a and 2.3b). The
increase in age at first birth has been large and rapid across EE and appears
to have converged with West European levels (age at first birth is shown
for France in Figure 2.3b). Age at first birth has also increased in the FSU,

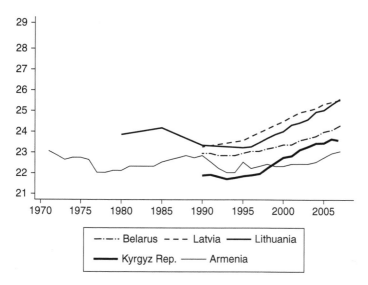

Figure 2.3a Age at first birth, FSU, 1970–2007
Source: Author.

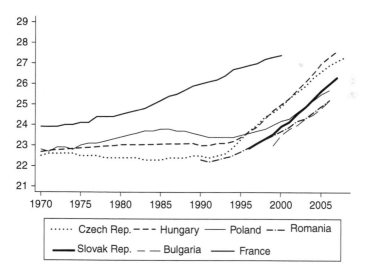

Figure 2.3b Age at first birth, EE and France, 1970–2007
Source: Author.

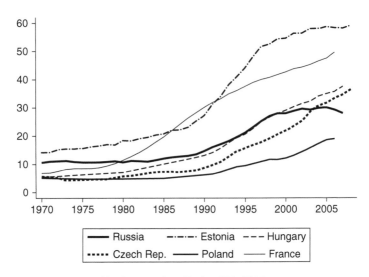

Figure 2.4   Percentage of births out of wedlock, 1970–2007
Source: Author.

although the increase has not been as steep or dramatic as in EE. Age at first marriage shows a similar pattern and appears to be approaching that of Western Europe. While the increase in age at first birth has occurred more slowly in Belarus, it is a clear trend, suggesting that the long-established pattern of early childbirth and marriage in the more slowly reforming countries of the FSU is beginning to change.

A further sign of demographic 'convergence' with Western Europe is the rapid increase in out-of-wedlock births experienced in most countries. As shown in Figure 2.4, the share of extramarital births increased across the region beginning in the early-to-mid 1990s; the highest rate is in Estonia (nearly 60 per cent of all births), which rivals the out-of-wedlock birth rates of Scandinavian countries. The contribution of extramarital births to changes in overall fertility varies across countries. In most countries, a decline in marital births accounted for the large drop in overall fertility rates in the early 1990s; in some countries, like the Czech Republic and Estonia, the increase in out-of-wedlock births has more than compensated for the decline in marital fertility and is the main reason for the slight increase in fertility rates since 2000.

Figure 2.5 shows that the decline in birth rates was not achieved through increasing abortion rates. On the contrary, the very high abortion rate in Russia plummeted from over 100 abortions per 1,000 women aged 15–49 in 1990 to 50 by the year 2000. While abortion rates remain high compared with Western countries, the decline is significant and appears to be due at least in part to the increased availability of modern contraceptive methods in

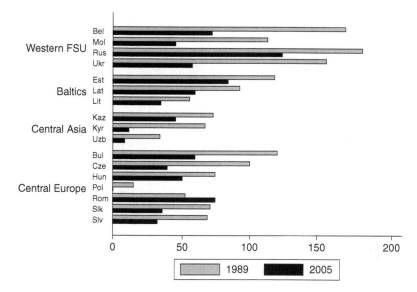

Figure 2.5   Abortions per 100 births, 1989 and 2005
Source: Author.

the 1990s and a resulting substitution of contraception for abortion.[4] Survey evidence also suggests that the financial cost of abortion has increased in many countries (Agadjanian 2002), which is a further reason for the decline in the abortion rate.

Most of the changes in the patterns of fertility and family formation described above represent a potential improvement in the welfare of children in formerly socialist countries. Later marriage and childbearing may result in parents who are better prepared—financially and otherwise—to raise a family; the increase in the use of modern contraception leads to better timing of childbirth and possibly fewer 'unwanted' children. The increase in out-of-wedlock births may be a negative trend, but even this may not be highly detrimental if the increase in extramarital births reflects a shift from registered marriage to cohabitation rather than an increase in single parenthood. This appears to be the case in Russia (see Heleniak 2005) and is likely true in other countries as well.

But there is one fertility trend in the region that is unambiguously negative—an increase in sex ratios at birth in the Caucasus. The sex ratio in the Soviet Union had always fluctuated around the biological norm of 1.05 males to 1 female; normal sex ratios also characterized the more traditional, less industrialized Soviet republics in Central Asia and the Caucasus. But since the dissolution of the Soviet Union, there has been a striking upward trend in the sex ratio of children aged 0–4 in all three Caucasian republics. Azeri official statistics indicate a sex ratio of 1.168 in 2008; the 2001 Armenian census reveals a sex ratio of 1.145; and the 2002 Georgian census shows a sex ratio of 1.104. In contrast, the sex ratio in Russia in the 2001 census is 1.049. According to these figures, excess female mortality in Armenia, Azerbaijan and Georgia appears to be at a level similar to that of China and India, where the most recent sex ratios for children aged 0–4 are 1.145 and 1.106, respectively.

Given the Soviet state's longstanding efforts to promote the secularization of the less developed republics and equal treatment of women, including compulsory education for both boys and girls beginning in the 1930s, that such strong evidence of son preference has emerged so rapidly is surprising and difficult to explain. It is even more perplexing given the diverse cultures and religions of the three Caucasus countries. Most Armenians and Georgians are Christians (but belong to two distinct orthodox churches), while Azerbaijan is a predominantly Muslim country. One should also note that no indication of son preference has emerged in Central Asia, despite evidence that son preference characterized all of the Central Asian countries in the twentieth century (Brainerd 2011). Demographers have concluded that the trends are real and not an artefact of inconsistencies in birth registration (Meslé et al. 2007).

2.2   Explaining fertility change in post-socialist countries

The standard neoclassical theory of fertility was developed by Gary Becker and is described in his influential *A Treatise on the Family* (1981). One of the key insights from this work is that income and fertility may be negatively related—while children are considered to be a 'normal' good (when income increases, couples desire more children), the time-intensive nature of childrearing also represents a significant opportunity cost for parents, particularly women. As women's wages have risen over the last century, the opportunity cost of having children has increased, leading to declines in fertility rates and a negative relationship between income and fertility rates. Women's relative wages have increased in many East European countries (Brainerd 2000; Grajek 2003; Jolliffe and Campos 2005); this increased opportunity cost of children is likely a factor in explaining the fertility decline in the region.[5] Women have fared less well in Ukraine and Russia, however, so the increase in female wages does not provide a universal explanation for the trend across countries. A related explanation is the increase in the return to education, which has occurred across nearly all transition countries, in turn inducing large increases in tertiary enrolment rates.[6] As in the USA, women in many formerly socialist countries now enrol in tertiary education at a higher rate than men. In Hungary, for example, 24 per cent of women aged 25–29 have higher education, compared with only 16 per cent of men of the same age; this difference in the higher education gap has increased markedly since 1990 (see Figure 2.6). This increase

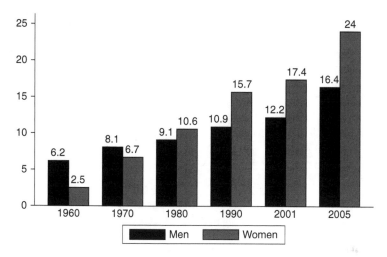

Figure 2.6 Share of men and women aged 25–29 with higher education, Hungary
Source: Author.

in higher education for women further delays marriage and childbearing among the younger generation. Despite problematic econometric issues, a recent study indicates that there is a causal relationship between education and fertility; an additional year of female education appears to reduce early fertility by 0.26 births (Osili and Long 2008).

Figure 2.7 illustrates the cross-country relationship between changes in the return to education and changes in fertility between 1990 and 2002. While a crude test of the theory, the relationship is negative and suggests that strong incentives to gain higher education have played a role in the fertility decline in EE and the FSU. Two country-level studies of fertility change also provide evidence of a negative relationship between fertility and education in the region. Perelli-Harris (2005), using data from the Ukrainian Reproductive Health Survey, finds that higher levels of education are significantly associated with later ages at first birth. Klasen and Launov (2006) use data from the Fertility and Family Survey of 1998 in the Czech Republic to compare the timing of births by cohort to infer the effects of education on fertility decisions under socialism versus transition. The results indicate a negative relationship between education levels and the timing of the first birth, and that the strength of this education effect has increased significantly since the start of transition. Women with more education are also more likely to be childless than women with less education.

This traditional neoclassical view of fertility does not explicitly include a role for economic uncertainty in fertility decisions, which is sensible if one is trying to explain long-term changes in fertility rates. In the context of the

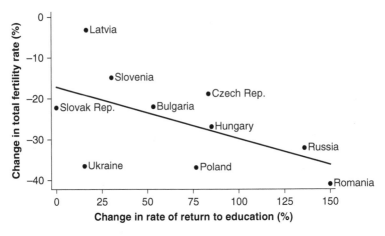

Figure 2.7   Changes in fertility and returns to education, 1990–2002
Source: Author.

transition countries, however, it is likely that the uncertainty surrounding the change from a socialist system to capitalism influenced couples' decisions to have children. As is well known, workers in the socialist countries did not enjoy a high standard of living but were entitled to stable employment and income, guaranteed pensions, universal medical care and free education. With the transition to a market economy, this social contract was broken and workers had few guarantees, facing uncertainty at the individual level regarding how well they would survive the shift and at the national level regarding the growth or stagnation of the economy under such a transition. The economic theory of investment under uncertainty offers clear predictions about the optimal course of action in an uncertain climate; for investments that are irreversible (e.g., children) and that can be postponed, there is an option value to waiting to make the investment (Dixit and Pindyck 1994; Grogan 2006).

Several papers examining the fertility declines in the FSU and EE have focused on the role of economic uncertainty in this decline. Bhaumik and Nugent (2005) study the large fertility decline in eastern Germany between 1992 and 2002 and find a significant effect of unemployment uncertainty— particularly that of women—on the probability of childbirth. Chase (2003) examines fertility in the Czech and Slovak republics, comparing fertility in the two countries and in the pre-transition (1981–84) and post-transition (1989–93) periods. While he finds no evidence of a relationship between economic uncertainty and fertility behavior for these samples, the measure of economic uncertainty used in the paper—whether the respondent changed jobs in the past four years—is a tenuous measure of job insecurity, given that some of the respondents undoubtedly changed jobs voluntarily. Kohler and Kohler (2002) use the Russian Longitudinal Monitoring Survey to assess birth outcomes in the early period of reform, 1994–96, and find few relationships in the data between the decision to have a child and measures of labour market uncertainty. Overall, the econometric evidence for the effect of uncertainty on fertility behavior is mixed.

A number of other factors may have accelerated the decline in fertility in EE and the FSU during the 1990s. One of these is the decrease in the number of state-supported nurseries and pre-school facilities, and the near-disappearance of daycare facilities provided at enterprises. For example, in Russia the share of children in kindergarten and nurseries declined by over 55 per cent between 1989 and 1997; the price of such care also rose sharply in this period (Lokshin 2005). An additional factor is simply the decrease in the number of middle-aged men; as described below, many former Soviet countries experienced a dramatic increase in mortality rates among men aged 25–54 in the 1990s. If women are reluctant to raise a child as a single mother, this too would be expected to account for at least part of the decline in fertility over the period.

To summarize, the formerly socialist countries have experienced a remarkably rapid change in fertility and family formation in the two decades since 1989. On many dimensions the region now looks like Western Europe, with low fertility rates, later marriage and childbearing, and high and rising out-of-wedlock birth rates. Some of the changes appear to be driven by changes in returns to education and economic uncertainty, but to date there is a paucity of research seeking to explain these fundamental shifts in behavior.

3 Mortality

Between 1990 and 1994, the death rate among working-age men in Russia increased by 70 per cent, from 759.2 to 1323.7 deaths per 100,000 population. Male life expectancy at birth fell from 63.7 years to 57.4 years during that period, while female life expectancy at birth fell from 74.3 years to 71.1 years. A similar increase in mortality rates occurred in many other countries of the FSU in the early 1990s, in particular in Belarus, Ukraine, and the three Baltic countries. Although some of the declines in life expectancy were reversed in Russia and many of its neighbours in the late 1990s, the magnitude of the declines and the large and erratic swings of this usually slowly evolving indicator are unprecedented in the twentieth century for countries at peace and in the absence of major famines and epidemics.

The timing of this demographic crisis coincided with the introduction of market reforms in the FSU, suggesting that rising mortality was related to the transition to a market economy. But mortality trends in the transition countries of EE differ markedly from those of the FSU; despite declining GDP and sharply rising unemployment rates in many East European countries in the early-to-mid 1990s, mortality rates fell and life expectancy rose throughout the region. The unprecedented increase in cardiovascular mortality in the FSU in the early 1990s was nearly matched by an unprecedented decrease in cardiovascular mortality in EE. Why did mortality trends differ so markedly between the two regions? This section explores some of the possible explanations. However, as will become evident, a clear answer to the question remains elusive.

3.1   Trends in life expectancy and age- and cause-specific mortality

The change in male life expectancy at birth is shown in Figure 2.8 for selected countries.[7] This illustrates the differing mortality experiences of the FSU and EE. In the FSU, changes in life expectancy are erratic and appear to be sensitive to macroeconomic fluctuations; in EE, every country has experienced a sustained increase in life expectancy since the early-to-mid 1990s.[8] Despite the recent improvements in life expectancy in the FSU since the mid-1990s, male life expectancy remains extremely low, both historically and in comparison with other developed countries. In Russia, for example, male life expectancy at birth in 2007 was 61.39 years; this represents a decline of 1.60 years from the level of male life expectancy in Russia in 1958, and a difference of over 16 years with male life expectancy in France (77.6 years in 2007). In 1958, male life expectancy in France exceeded that of Russia by only 3.81 years. East European countries are, in contrast, slowly closing the life expectancy gap with Western Europe; the difference in male life expectancy between France and the Czech Republic in 1989 was 4.38 years, falling to 3.93 years by 2007.

The mortality crisis in the FSU primarily affected middle-aged men. The groups traditionally most vulnerable to the health effects of economic crisis—children and the elderly—avoided large increases in mortality during transition. In fact, infant and child mortality declined in almost all countries across the region during the 1990s.

Changes in death rates by five-year age groups for Russia, Estonia, and Hungary are shown in Figure 2.9. In Estonia and Russia (and many other former Soviet countries), the increase in death rates for men aged 25–54 between 1989 and 1994 was astonishing. In Estonia, for example, the death rate for men aged 40–44 increased from 5.93 deaths per 1,000 men in this age group in 1989 to 13.19 deaths per 1,000 in 1994, an increase of 122 per cent. Over the entire transition period (right panel of Figure 2.9), the increase in death rates among middle-aged men remained high in Russia but had begun to decline in Estonia and the other Baltic republics.

Even in some East European countries, the death rate among middle-aged men increased during the early years of transition. This increase was most prominent in Hungary, where the age-specific death rate for men aged 40–44 increased from 6.82 per 1,000 population in 1989 to 9.08 in 1994, and in Romania, where the death rate increased by over 43 per cent for these men

Former Soviet Union, selected countries

Eastern Europe

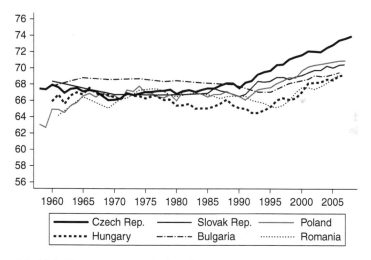

Figure 2.8 Male life expectancy at birth in formerly socialist countries
Source: Author.

between 1990 and 1997. However, by 2007 all age groups experienced significant declines in mortality rates in Hungary, with the largest declines among younger men (right panel of Figure 2.9). This pattern of large declines in mortality rates across most age groups by 2007 is similar for all East European

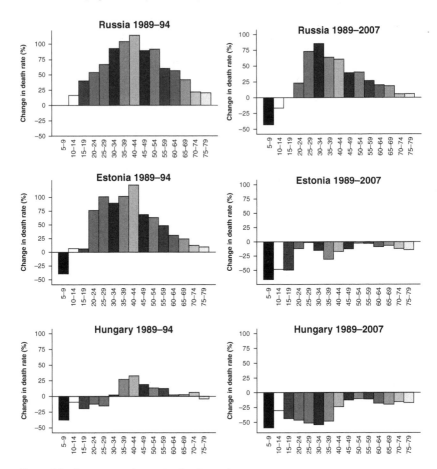

Figure 2.9   Percentage change in death rate by age group, men
Source: Author.

countries for which data are available, including the Czech Republic, Poland and Romania.

The increase in death rates in the FSU in the early 1990s was primarily due to a tremendous increase in deaths due to circulatory diseases (heart disease and strokes) and due to external causes. Changes in the age-standardized death rate for men aged 25–64 due to circulatory diseases are shown in Figure 2.10. In the FSU, the death rate from both of these broad categories of death was much higher than in other developed countries, even prior to the transition. All former USSR countries experienced a significant increase in circulatory disease and external cause deaths between 1989 and 1994. The external cause deaths include an epidemic of homicide and suicide across

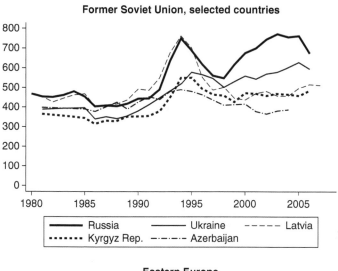

Former Soviet Union, selected countries

Russia — Ukraine — ----- Latvia
••••••• Kyrgyz Rep. — · — · · — Azerbaijan

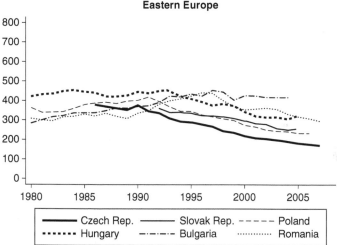

Eastern Europe

Czech Rep. — Slovak Rep. — ----- Poland
•••••• Hungary — · — · · — Bulgaria ············ Romania

Figure 2.10 Standardized death rate, circulatory diseases, men aged 25–64
Source: Based on WHO Mortality Database (January 2009 version) data.

the region, peaking around 1994 and again primarily affecting working-age men. For example, in Lithuania the death rate due to suicide among men aged 45–54 increased from 109 deaths per 100,000 population in 1985— already extremely high compared with Western countries—to 160 deaths per 100,000 population in 1995. After the mid-1990s, these death rates declined but remain at least as high as in the pre-transition period in most countries.

The Russian mortality pattern differs somewhat from that of other former Soviet countries, as cardiovascular disease (CVD) and external cause deaths spiked again following the 1998 financial crisis until finally beginning to decline in 2005.

The pre-transition rates of circulatory diseases were also significantly higher in EE than in Western Europe across the region, and they increased by 17 per cent and 33 per cent, respectively, among men aged 25–64 in Bulgaria and Romania between 1989 and 1994. In the other EE countries, deaths due to circulatory diseases for men in this age group declined substantially between 1989 and 2007. In the Czech Republic, for example, deaths due to CVD fell from 354 to 170 deaths per 100,000 population between 1989 and 2007 for men aged 25–64. While nearly all developed countries have recorded significant declines in circulatory disease mortality in recent decades, the speed and magnitude of the decline in EE may be unprecedented. Deaths due to external causes were always much lower in EE than in the FSU (although about twice as high as in Western Europe), and these causes of death have changed relatively little during the transition period.[9] The one cause of death with negative trends in some East European countries is chronic liver disease and cirrhosis, which has increased significantly in Hungary, Romania and Moldova; this trend, along with a small increase in deaths due to CVD, likely accounts for the increase in deaths among men aged 40–44 noted above.

3.2   Did Russians drink themselves to death?

Deaths due to chronic liver disease and cirrhosis also increased in Russia and the Baltics in the 1990s, but the death rates from these diseases are far too low to account for the increase in mortality in the region.[10] Nevertheless, most analysts believe that alcohol consumption is one of the major causes of the large swings in mortality in western FSU in the 1990s. Brainerd and Cutler (2005) analyse the cross-country differences in mortality in EE and the FSU, and they identify alcohol consumption, stress, and possibly diet, as contributing factors. This study, like many others in this area of research, concludes that a significant share of the change in mortality in the FSU remains unexplained.[11] Limited data combined with the widespread nature of the crisis across regions, cohorts and types of death has frustrated efforts to identify the causes of the mortality crisis, and this in turn has hampered the efforts of governments, health care providers, and international donors to identify and implement policies to reduce premature adult mortality.

One puzzle in attempting to explain the swings in cardiovascular mortality in the FSU is that the prevalence of the principal risk factors for CVD—smoking, hypertension, and high cholesterol levels—in former Soviet countries is somewhat lower than in the Western countries that have much lower rates of CVD, and that trends in these risk factors were mildly favourable during the 1990s (Puska et al. 1993; Kristenson et al. 1997;

Stegmayr et al. 2000; Averina et al. 2003). On this basis, most researchers have concluded that conventional CVD risk factors fail to explain the high levels and large increases in cardiovascular mortality in the FSU. Some argue instead that non-traditional risk factors account for high CVD mortality in this region, in particular that the style of drinking (binge drinking) negates the protective effect of alcohol on the heart and leads to increased arrhythmias and heart attacks (McKee and Britton 1998). Recent research provides supportive evidence of this idea; for example, a small case-control study of adult male deaths in Udmurtia (the Urals) confirmed that cardiovascular deaths are strongly associated with periods of heavy drinking among adult men (Shkolnikov et al. 2001). Another study of 25–64-year-old men in Novosibirsk (Siberia) found an increased risk of CVD and external cause mortality among frequent heavy drinkers (Malyutina et al. 2002).

Evidence also suggests that the high number of deaths in Russia classified as due to 'other' or 'unspecified' ischaemic heart disease may be overstated and that 'these are more properly classified as deaths from alcohol poisoning. An analysis of nearly 25,000 autopsies conducted in Barnaul (Siberia) between 1990 and 2004 indicated that 21 per cent of all autopsied adult male deaths attributed to circulatory diseases had lethal or near-lethal levels of ethanol in the blood (Zaridze et al. 2009a). A further study of 48,000 deaths in three Siberian cities led the authors to conclude that alcohol consumption may be responsible for more than half of all adult male deaths in Russia from 1990 to 2001, and a third of adult female deaths (Zaridze et al. 2009b).

Recent research has also highlighted the important role that the consumption of 'surrogate' alcohol has played in the mortality crisis in Russia. A significant amount of alcohol is consumed in the form of either home-made alcohol (*samogon*), which has high ethanol concentrations, or 'non-beverage' alcohol, such as aftershave, antifreeze and lighter fluid, which contain high concentrations of ethanol and toxic ingredients (McKee et al. 2005; Leon et al. 2007). These forms of alcohol are untaxed and, per litre of pure alcohol, are much cheaper than the vodka sold in retail stores. The combination of high ethanol concentration and toxic ingredients also makes these surrogate alcohol products much more lethal than commercially sold vodka.

The autopsy and surrogate alcohol studies provide persuasive evidence that alcohol consumption played an even more important role than previously thought in the increase in deaths due to both cardiovascular and external causes in Russia. But there are still many unanswered questions regarding the role of alcohol consumption in the mortality crisis. First, does alcohol consumption also explain the large swings in mortality in the countries of the FSU besides Russia? Evidence for other countries is much more limited since most of the epidemiological research has focused on the mortality crisis in Russia. A study by Chenet et al. (2001) shows that the pattern of alcohol consumption and CVD mortality in Lithuania is similar to that of Russia; another study indicates that binge drinking of grain-based alcohol is characteristic of Ukraine and the Baltics but not of EE (Popova et al. 2007). This evidence suggests that alcohol consumption explains much of the increase in mortality across the FSU in the early 1990s but is far from conclusive. Additional research is needed on the mortality experiences of other countries to establish this conclusion. A second question is: Why did drinking become so lethal in the 1990s? Did alcohol consumption increase a great deal, or the frequency of binge drinking? Given the difficulty of measuring alcohol intake at either the national or the individual level, this question may be impossible to answer. It is clear that the price of alcohol relative to the price of food fell dramatically in the early years of transition in Russia, which likely exacerbated the tendency to consume alcohol.[12]

A key piece of information needed to better understand the effects of such price changes on alcohol consumption is the price (and income) elasticity of demand for alcohol in former Soviet countries, as well as the cross-price elasticity of demand between store-bought vodka and surrogate alcohol consumption. One approach to the drinking problem is to raise taxes on alcohol. Studies of the US population, for example, indicate that higher alcohol prices reduce binge drinking among youth.[13] But it is quite possible that higher alcohol prices would worsen mortality in the FSU; higher prices for alcohol sold through official outlets may induce individuals to substitute low-quality surrogate alcohol and homemade alcohol for higher quality alcohol, which in turn could lead to increased deaths from accidental alcohol poisoning. To date, however, studies of the price and cross-price elasticity of demand for alcohol in the FSU have not been conducted.

Turning to EE, researchers have devoted even less attention to explaining changes in mortality rates in this region. It is clearly of interest, however, to understand why the mortality outcomes in this region have been so different from that of the FSU, especially given that the improvement in cardiovascular mortality in some of these countries has been so remarkable and unexpected.

The few studies that have examined mortality trends in EE have identified changing diet as the most likely explanation for the rapid improvement in CVD mortality rates. The end of state subsidies for meat and the greatly increased availability of fruits and vegetables led to a radical change in the diet of much of the population in the region in the early 1990s. Foremost among the changes was a shift in the consumption of animal fat to vegetable fat, and an increase in the intake of antioxidants. This dietary shift occurred in the Czech Republic (Dzúrová 2000) and in Poland (Zatonski et al. 1998). Bobak et al. (1997) document a decrease in cholesterol levels among Czech men and women after 1988, which they attribute to the increase in consumption of vegetable fats. As an example, per capita consumption of butter in the Czech Republic fell from 9.4 kg in 1989 to 5.4 kg in 1992. Zatonski et al. (2008) further argue that a shift from the use of sunflower oil to rapeseed oil in many East European countries contributed to the decline in CVD mortality in EE; rapeseed oil is relatively high in fatty acids, which are beneficial to cardiovascular health, while sunflower oil lacks these. Researchers argue that the health effects of dietary change can occur relatively quickly, appearing within two to three years from the change in diet (Zatonski et al. 1998).

A secondary reason for the reduction in mortality rates in EE may be an improvement in the quality of medical care. Evidence on this factor is very sparse, however. The study by Dzúrová (2000) identified improvements in the supply of cardiovascular medicines and medical equipment, and an increase in cardiovascular operations, as major reasons for improved cardiovascular mortality in the Czech Republic. And it is likely that the substantial reductions in infant and child mortality are also attributable to improvements in medical care. Given the lack of evidence, however, the contribution of improved medical care to increasing life expectancy in EE remains speculative.

4 Consequences of demographic change in Eastern Europe and the FSU

Declining fertility and rising mortality have combined to produce significant decreases in population size across most countries of the FSU in the last two decades. In Russia, the population stood at 147 million in 1989 but had fallen to 142 million by 2008, a drop of 3.4 per cent. The population decline is even more dramatic if one excludes the substantial net immigration inflows that Russia experienced over the period; over 6 million (net) immigrants arrived between 1989–2008, indicating that the number of native Russians fell by 11 million in those years. As shown in Figure 2.11, the population loss in Russia was small compared with other countries of the western part of the FSU: the population fell by nearly 20 per cent in Moldova and Georgia, by nearly 15 per cent in Estonia and Latvia, and by 4–10 per cent in Kazakhstan, Armenia, Lithuania and Ukraine. Bulgaria and Romania experienced similar population declines. The only countries with growing populations over the period were the Central Asian countries (besides Kazakhstan), Azerbaijan and Hungary.

What are the economic consequences of population declines of this magnitude? Few countries have experienced a sustained decrease in population size like that recorded in the western FSU, so there is scant historical evidence on which to rely to make predictions. One should also recognize that population declines are likely to continue in many countries due to the much smaller cohorts of women entering their childbearing years. In Russia there were 12 million women aged 20–29 in 2008; this number will fall to only 7 million by 2020 (Heleniak 2005). Even if Putin's fertility 'bonus' spurs an

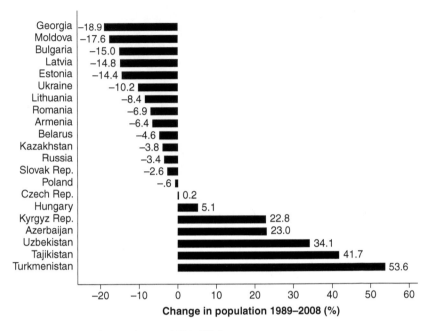

Figure 2.11   Population change, 1989–2008
Source: Based on TransMONEE database (2009 version) data.

increase in fertility in Russia, mechanically it is nearly impossible for such an increase to compensate for the small cohort of women of childbearing age. Recognizing this, the Russian statistical agency forecasts that the population will decrease from 142 million in 2008 to 137.5 million in 2025 (Federal State Statistics Service 2008). The pace of negative population growth may be mitigated in some countries by increasing life expectancy, however, and the actual outcomes will be strongly affected by the immigration policies enacted by each country.

Assuming that population declines continue in some of the formerly socialist countries, the canonical Solow growth model predicts that this decrease can be beneficial for economic growth: the smaller population leads to an increase in the capital:labour ratio, thus increasing productivity and growth. Young (2005) uses this basic insight to calibrate a growth model for South Africa, showing that the AIDS tragedy could lead to higher wages and economic growth among survivors through this mechanism. A related question is how changes in population health, as proxied by life expectancy, affect economic growth. While much of the literature on this issue has shown a positive relationship between life expectancy and economic growth across countries, the likely reverse causality between growth and health (and omitted variable bias) has hindered efforts to demonstrate that the relationship between the two is causal. Acemoglu and Johnson (2007) use an instrumental variables approach to demonstrate that the health improvements in the post-war period had an inconsequential or a slightly negative effect on growth. In a reply to that paper, Bloom et al. (2009b) show that, allowing for a lagged (rather than instantaneous) effect of health on growth, there is a positive and statistically significant relationship between life expectancy and economic growth across countries. Given that even the sign of the relationship between life expectancy and growth remains in dispute, it is difficult to predict how changing life expectancy in EE and the FSU will affect long-term economic growth. If the relationship is positive (and causal), the rapid gains in life expectancy in EE will enhance the region's growth prospects.

Another route through which the demographic changes will affect growth is via the changing age structure of the population. Almost all countries in the region experienced an increase in the share of the population older than working age in the last 20 years. In Bulgaria, for example, the elderly dependency ratio[14] reached 37.4 per cent in 2008, as compared with 30.9 per cent in 1989. In all three Baltic countries, the elderly dependency ratio is at nearly 35 per cent. This trend is likely to continue given declining fertility and rising life expectancy in most countries. Increases in the elderly dependency ratio pose a threat to government-funded retirement programs that rely on contributions from current workers to maintain solvency. And as emphasized by Bloom et al. (2009a), changing age structure of the population is a crucial mechanism through which changing fertility (and mortality) can affect economic growth. These authors argue that while declining fertility can lead to an increase in economic growth in the short run through the standard Solow effect, in the long run the increase in the inactive share of the population will have negative effects on economic growth.

Further consequences of the mortality changes in the region will likely operate through changes in human capital. In the FSU, the steep death rates of men aged 25–54 represent a massive loss of human capital among a segment of the population in their most productive working years. To the extent that this human capital was transferable from the socialist economic system to the market economies of the region, this loss likely represents a negative shock to economic growth. The high adult mortality rates of the region also shorten individuals' time horizons and will lead to lower investments in human and physical capital, further depressing the economic growth prospects of the region.[15] The opposite effect may boost the economic growth prospects of the EE countries—as adult mortality rates continue to decline, changing time horizons and improved health should induce individuals to increase their investment in human and physical capital.

5 Concluding remarks

Rarely in modern history has a population experienced such a fundamental transformation of life circumstances in such a short period of time as that experienced by the people of EE and the FSU in the last two decades. Women in the region now postpone marriage and childbirth and have children out of wedlock in patterns similar to that of Western Europe. Men in EE are much less likely to die of CVD than they were 20 years ago, while the opposite is true of men in the FSU. These trends and patterns are clear, but much remains unknown about the underlying reasons for them. There is a dearth of convincing research explaining the decline in fertility and marriage in formerly socialist countries. Few studies have examined the relationship between changing labour market opportunities for women and changing fertility behavior in the region. And little is known about the causes and consequences of the decline in abortion as a mode of contraception in the FSU, or of the impact of Poland's near-ban on abortion in the early 1990s.

The need for more research is perhaps even greater on the mortality side of the ledger. Without a clear understanding of the causes of the mortality crisis, it is difficult to design policies to mitigate premature mortality in these countries. As discussed above, there are large gaps in the current research relating to the responsiveness of alcohol consumption to price changes, and to the causes of the mortality crisis in FSU countries other than Russia. In addition, an improved understanding of the reasons for the decrease in cardiovascular mortality in EE has the potential to provide new insights into the underlying causes of cardiovascular mortality that would benefit at-risk populations in all countries. As has long been the case even before the fall of communism, the unique and puzzling demography of EE and the FSU presents a myriad of questions for researchers to investigate.

Acknowledgements

This study was prepared for the UNU-WIDER conference Reflections on Transition: Twenty Years after the Fall of the Berlin Wall, Helsinki, 18–19 September 2009. The author thanks Giovanni Andrea Cornia, Mario Nuti, Vladimir Popov, Gérard Roland, Daniel Treisman, and conference participants for helpful comments and suggestions.

Notes

1. Albania, Tajikistan, Turkmenistan and the countries of the former Yugoslavia are excluded from the analysis due to data limitations.
2. The TFR is calculated based on current age-specific birth rates and represents the average number of children a woman can be expected to have during her lifetime. The fertility and mortality data used in this study are from the most

recent national statistical or demographic yearbooks published by each country. When such data are missing, data from the TransMONEE database (www. transmonee.org), the WHO Health for All database (www.euro.who.int/HFADB), or the WHO Mortality database (www.euro.who.int/InformationSources/Data/ 20011017_1) are used.

3. See, for example, Kharkova and Andreev (2000), Sobotka (2003), Barkalov (2005), and Perelli-Harris (2005, 2006).

4. See Westoff (2005) for a survey of trends in abortion and contraceptive prevalence in some of the former socialist countries. The decline of abortion in Poland is due to stringent restrictions imposed on abortion in that country in the early 1990s. See Levine and Staiger (2004) for an overview of the legislative changes to abortion laws in transition countries in the 1990s.

5. While women's real wages have declined in many countries, the increase in female wages relative to male wages represents an increasing opportunity cost of fertility within the household and will still lead to the prediction of reduced fertility.

6. See Flabbi et al. (2008) and Fleisher et al. (2005) for surveys of returns to education before and after transition. Campos and Jolliffe (2007) find that returns to higher education increased significantly in Hungary between 1986 and 2004, and the gains were larger for women than for men.

7. Life expectancy trends for women are similar in all countries to those of men, although the decline in life expectancy in the FSU is less dramatic for women than for men. For studies of mortality in individual countries, see Badurashvili et al. (2001) on Georgia; Shkolnikov et al. (2001) and Denisova (2010) on Russia; Dolea et al. (2002) on Romania; and Becker and Urzhumova (2005) on Kazakhstan.

8. The quality of mortality statistics in the formerly socialist countries is considered to be reasonably reliable. A few exceptions include the likely underestimation of infant mortality rates in the Caucasus and Central Asia (Aleshina and Redmond 2005); questionable adult mortality data for Armenia and Georgia (Badurashvili et al. 2001; Stillman 2006); and possible over-reporting of deaths due to 'ill-defined conditions' and under-reporting of deaths due to external causes in Russia (Gavrilova et al. 2008).

9. One exception to the statement is Hungary, where suicide rates have declined from high levels in the pre-transition period to much lower rates in recent years: the suicide rate for men aged 45–49 fell from 104 deaths per 100,000 population in 1989 to 73 deaths per 100,000 population in 2007.

10. For example, in Russia the male death rate from cirrhosis increased from 14.2 to 27.1 deaths per 100,000 population between 1989 and 1994, while the overall male death rate increased from 1,629.5 to 2,290.5 deaths per 100,000 population over the same period.

11. Chen et al. (1996) give an insightful summary of hypotheses and evidence on the causes of Russia's mortality crisis. Edited collections of papers on mortality in transition include Bobadilla et al. (1997), Becker and Bloom (1998), and Cornia and Paniccià (2000). Stillman (2006) provides a comprehensive survey of the literature on health and mortality in transition countries. Stuckler et al. (2009) argue that mass privatization contributed to increased mortality rates in post-communist countries, but the evidence presented is not robust; see Earle and Gehlbach (2010) and Gerry et al. (2010) for a comprehensive assessment.

12. Treisman (2008) analyses the effects of the decline in the price of vodka on mortality in Russia; see also Denisova (2010) for further evidence on alcohol prices and mortality in Russia.

13. See Cook and Moore (2000) for reviews of this literature.
14. Defined as the population aged 60 and over divided by the population aged 15–59 years.
15. Lorentzen et al. (2008) show that high adult mortality reduces economic growth across countries due to shortened time horizons and increased risky behavior.

References

Acemoglu, D. and S. Johnson (2007) 'Disease and Development: The Effect of Life Expectancy on Growth', *Journal of Political Economy*, 115(6): 925–85.

Agadjanian, V. (2002) 'Is "Abortion Culture" Fading in the Former Soviet Union? Views about Abortion and Contraception in Kazakhstan', *Studies in Family Planning*, 33(3): 237–48.

Aleshina, N. and G. Redmond (2005) 'How High is Infant Mortality in Central and Eastern Europe and the Commonwealth of Independent States?', *Population Studies*, 59(1): 39–54.

Averina, M., O. Nilssen, T. Brenn, J. Brox, A.G. Kalinin and V.L. Arkhipovsky (2003) 'High Cardiovascular Mortality in Russia Cannot Be Explained by the Classical Risk Factors: The Arkhangelsk Study 2000', *European Journal of Epidemiology*, 18: 871–8.

Badurashvili, I., M. McKee, G. Tsuladze, F. Meslé, J. Vallin and V. Shkolnikov (2001) 'Where There Are No Data: What Has Happened to Life Expectancy in Georgia Since 1990?', *Public Health*, 115: 394–400.

Barkalov, N.B. (2005) 'Changes in the Quantum of Russian Fertility During the 1980s and Early 1990s', *Population and Development Review*, 31(3): 545–56.

Becker, C.M. and D. Bloom (eds) (1998) 'The Demographic Crisis in the Former Soviet Union', *World Development*, 26(11): 1957–75.

Becker, C.M. and D.S. Urzhumova (2005) 'Mortality Recovery and Stabilization in Kazakhstan, 1995–2001', *Economics and Human Biology*, 3: 97–122.

Becker, G.S. (1981) *A Treatise on the Family* Harvard University Press: Cambridge, MA.

Bhaumik, S.K. and J.B. Nugent (2005) 'Does Economic Uncertainty Affect the Decision to Bear Children? Evidence from East and West Germany', *IZA Discussion Paper* No. 1746.

Bloom, D.E., D. Canning, G. Fink and J.E. Finlay (2009a) 'The Cost of Low Fertility in Europe', *NBER Working Paper No. 14820*.

Bloom, D.E., D. Canning and G. Fink (2009b) 'Disease and Development Revisited', *NBER Working Paper No. 15137*.

Bobadilla, J.L., C.A. Costello and F. Mitchell (eds) (1997) *Premature Death in the New Independent States* National Academy Press: Washington, DC.

Bobak, M., Z. Skodova, Z. Pisa, R. Poledne and M. Marmot (1997) 'Political Changes and Trends in Cardiovascular Risk Factors in the Czech Republic, 1985–1992', *Journal of Epidemiology and Community Health*, 51: 272–7.

Brainerd, E. (2000) 'Women in Transition: Changes in Gender Wage Differentials in Eastern Europe and the Former Soviet Union', *Industrial and Labor Relations Review*, 54(1): 138–62.

Brainerd, E. and D.M. Cutler (2005) 'Autopsy on an Empire: Understanding Mortality in Russia and the Former Soviet Union', *The Journal of Economic Perspectives*, 19(1): 107–30.

Brainerd, E. (2011) 'Missing Women in the Former Soviet Union? Son Preference and Children's Health in Central Asia and the Caucasus during Transition', mimeo.

Campos, N. and D. Jolliffe (2007) 'Earnings, Schooling and Economic Reform: Econometric Evidence from Hungary (1986–2004)', *World Bank Economic Review*, 21(3): 509–26.

Chase, R.S. (2003) 'Household Fertility Responses Following Communism: Transition in the Czech Republic and Slovakia', *Journal of Population Economics*, 16: 579–95.

Chen, L.C., F. Wittgenstein and E. McKeon (1996) 'The Upsurge of Mortality in Russia: Causes and Policy Implications', *Population and Development Review*, 22(3): 517–30.

Chenet, L., A. Britton, R. Kalediene and J. Petrauskiene (2001) 'Daily Variations in Deaths in Lithuania: The Possible Contribution of Binge Drinking', *International Journal of Epidemiology*, 30: 743–8.

Cook, P.J. and M.J. Moore (2000) 'Alcohol', in A.J. Culyer and J.P. Newhouse (eds) *Handbook of Health Economics* Elsevier: Amsterdam.

Cornia, G.A. and R. Paniccià (eds) (2000) *The Mortality Crisis in Transitional Economies* Oxford University Press: Oxford.

Denisova, I. (2010) 'Adult Mortality in Russia: A Microanalysis', *Economics of Transition*, 18(2): 333–63.

Dixit, A.K. and R.S. Pindyck (1994) *Investment under Uncertainty* Princeton University Press: Princeton, NJ.

Dolea, C., E. Nolte and M. McKee (2002) 'Changing Life Expectancy in Romania after the Transition', *Journal of Epidemiology and Community Health*, 56(6): 444–9.

Dzúrová, D. (2000) 'Mortality Differentials in the Czech Republic during the Post-1989 Socio-Political Transformation', *Health & Place*, 6: 352–62.

Earle, J.S. and S. Gehlbach (2010) 'Did Mass Privatisation Really Increase Post-Communist Mortality?' *The Lancet*, 375: 372.

Federal State Statistics Service of Russia (2008) *Demographic Yearbook of Russia 2008* Federal State Statistics Service of Russia: Moscow.

Flabbi, L., S. Paternostro and E.R. Tiongson (2008) 'Returns to Education in the Economic Transition: A Systematic Assessment Using Comparable Data', *Economics of Education Review*, 27: 724–40.

Fleisher, B.M., K. Sabirianova and X. Wang (2005) 'Returns to Skills and the Speed of Reforms: Evidence from Central and Eastern Europe, China, and Russia', *Journal of Comparative Economics*, 33: 351–70.

Gavrilova, N.S., V.G. Semyonova, E. Dubrovina, G.N. Evdokushkina, A.E. Ivanova and L.A. Gavrilov (2008) 'Russian Mortality Crisis and the Quality of Vital Statistics', *Population Research and Policy Review*, 27(5): 551–74.

Gerry, C., T.M. Mickiewicz and Z. Nikoloski (2010) 'Did Mass Privatisation Really Increase Post-Communist Mortality?' *The Lancet*, 375: 371.

Grajek, M. (2003) 'Gender Pay Gap in Poland', *Economics of Planning*, 36(1): 23–44.

Grogan, L. (2006) 'An Economic Examination of the Post-Transition Fertility Decline in Russia', *Post-Communist Economies*, 18(4): 363–97.

Heleniak, T. (2005) 'The Causes and Consequences of Fertility Decline in the Former Soviet Union and Central and Eastern Europe', mimeo.

Jolliffe, D. and N.F. Campos (2005) 'Does Market Liberalisation Reduce Gender Discrimination? Econometric Evidence from Hungary, 1986–1998', *Labour Economics*, 12(1): 1–22.

Kharkova, T.L. and E.M. Andreev (2000) 'Did the Economic Crisis Cause the Fertility Decline in Russia: Evidence from the 1994 Microcensus', *European Journal of Population*, 16(3): 211–33.

Klasen, S. and A. Launov (2006) 'Analysis of the Determinants of Fertility Decline in the Czech Republic', *Journal of Population Economics*, 19: 25–54.

Kohler, H.-P. and I. Kohler (2002) 'Fertility Decline in Russia in the Early and Mid 1990s: The Role of Economic Uncertainty and Labour Market Crises', *European Journal of Population*, 18: 233–62.

Kristenson, M., B. Zieden, Z. Kucinskiene, et al. (1997) 'Antioxidant State and Mortality from Coronary Heart Disease in Lithuanian and Swedish Men: Concomitant Cross Sectional Study of Men Aged 50', *British Medical Journal*, 314: 629–33.

Leon, D.A., L. Saburova, S. Tomkins, E. Andreev, N. Kiryanov, M. McKee and V.M. Shkolnikov (2007) 'Hazardous Alcohol Drinking and Premature Mortality in Russia: A Population Based Case-Control Study', *The Lancet*, 369: 2001–9.

Levine, P.B. and D. Staiger (2004) 'Abortion Policy and Fertility Outcomes: The Eastern European Experience', *Journal of Law and Economics*, April: 223–43.

Lokshin, M. (2005) 'Household Childcare Choices and Women's Work Behavior in Russia', *The Journal of Human Resources*, 39(4): 1094–115.

Lorentzen, P., J. McMillan and R. Wacziarg (2008) 'Death and Development', *Journal of Economic Growth*, 13: 81–124.

Malyutina, S., M. Bobak, S. Kurilovitch, V. Gafarov, G. Simonova, Y. Nikitin and M. Marmot (2002) 'Relation between Heavy and Binge Drinking and All-cause and Cardiovascular Mortality in Novosibirsk, Russia: A Prospective Cohort Study', *The Lancet*, 360: 1448–54.

McKee, M. and A. Britton (1998) 'The Positive Relationship Between Alcohol and Heart Disease in Eastern Europe: Potential Physiological Mechanisms', *Journal of the Royal Society of Medicine*, 91: 402–7.

McKee, M., S. Süzcs, A. Sárváry, R. Ádany, N. Kiryanov, L. Saburova, S. Tomkins, E. Andreev and D.A. Leon (2005) 'The Composition of Surrogate Alcohols Consumed in Russia', *Alcoholism: Clinical and Experimental Research*, 29(10): 1884–8.

Meslé, F., J. Vallin and I. Badurashvili (2007) 'A Sharp Increase in Sex Ratio at Birth in the Caucasus. Why? How?', in I. Attané and C.Z. Guilmoto (eds) *Watering the Neighbour's Garden: The Growing Demographic Female Deficit in Asia* Committee for International Co-operation in National Research in Demography: Paris.

Osili, U.O. and B.T. Long, (2008) 'Does Female Schooling Reduce Fertility? Evidence from Nigeria', *Journal of Development Economics*, 87(1): 57–75.

Perelli-Harris, B. (2005) 'The Path to Lowest-Low Fertility in Ukraine', *Population Studies*, 59(1): 55–70.

Perelli-Harris, B. (2006) 'The Influence of Informal Work and Subjective Well-Being on Childbearing in Post-Soviet Russia', *Population and Development Review*, 32(4): 729–53.

Popova, S., J. Rehm, J. Patra and W. Zatonski (2007) 'Comparing Alcohol Consumption in Central and Eastern Europe to Other European Countries', *Alcohol & Alcoholism*, 42(5): 465–73.

Puska, P., T. Matilainen, P. Jousilahti, et al. (1993) 'Cardiovascular Risk Factors in the Republic of Karelia, Russia, and in North Karelia, Finland', *International Journal of Epidemiology*, 22(6): 1048–55.

Shkolnikov, V., M. McKee and D.A. Leon (2001) 'Changes in Life Expectancy in Russia in the mid 1990s', *The Lancet*, 357: 917–21.

Stegmayr, B., T. Vinogradova, S. Malyutina, M. Peltonen, Y. Nikitin and K. Asplund (2000) 'Widening Gap of Stroke Between East and West: Eight-Year Trends in Occurrence and Risk Factors in Russia and Sweden', *Stroke*, January: 2–8.

Stillman, S. (2006) 'Health and Nutrition in Eastern Europe and the Former Soviet Union during the Decade of Transition: A Review of the Literature', *Economics and Human Biology*, 4: 104–46.

Stuckler, D., L. King and M. McKee (2009) 'Mass Privatisation and the Post-Communist Mortality Crisis: A Cross-National Analysis', *The Lancet* 373: 399–407.

Sobotka, T. (2003) 'Re-Emerging Diversity: Rapid Fertility Change in Central and Eastern Europe After the Collapse of the Communist Regimes', *Population* (English Edition), 58(4/5): 451–85.

Treisman, D. (2008) 'Pricing Death: The Political Economy of Russia's Alcohol Crisis', mimeo.

Westoff, C.F. (2005) 'Recent Trends in Abortion and Contraception in 12 Countries', *Demographic and Health Surveys Analytical Studies*, 8: 27–105.

Young, A. (2005) 'The Gift of the Dying: The Tragedy of AIDS and the Welfare of Future African Generations', *Quarterly Journal of Economics*, 120(2): 423–66.

Zaridze, D., D. Maximovitch, A. Lazarev, V. Igitov, A. Boroda, J. Boreham, P. Boyle, R. Peto and P. Boffetta (2009a) 'Alcohol Poisoning is a Main Determinant of Recent Mortality Trends in Russia: Evidence from a Detailed Analysis of Mortality Statistics and Autopsies', *International Journal of Epidemiology*, 38: 143–53.

Zaridze, D., P. Brennan, J. Boreham, A. Boroda, R. Karpov, A. Lazarev, I. Konobeevskaya, V. Igitov, T. Terechova, P. Boffetta and R. Peto (2009b) 'Alcohol and Cause-Specific Mortality in Russia: A Retrospective Case-Control Study of 48,557 Adult Deaths', *The Lancet*, 373: 2201–14.

Zatonski, W.A., A.J. McMichael and J.W. Powles (1998) 'Ecological Study of Reasons for Sharp Decline in Mortality from Ischaemic Heart Disease in Poland since 1991', *British Medical Journal*, 316(4): 1047–51.

Zatonski, W.A., H. Campos and W. Willett, (2008) 'Rapid Declines in Coronary Heart Disease Mortality in Eastern Europe are Associated with Increased Consumption of Oils Rich in Alpha-Linolenic Acid', *European Journal of Epidemiology*, 23: 3–10.

3

Reform and Inequality during the Transition: An Analysis Using Panel Household Survey Data, 1990–2005

Branko Milanovic and Lire Ersado

1 Inequality in Europe and Central Asia: literature review

Inequality considerations are important to policy makers because they are linked not only to the economic state of affairs but also to social and political conditions of a given country. This is even more the case in the countries of Eastern Europe (EE) and the former Soviet Union (FSU) that underwent transition from state-controlled to market economy in the era of globalization. However, there are a limited number of rigorous empirical studies on the evolution of inequality in the transition economies. Although there is a lack of consensus on the impact of inequality on economic growth, the limited empirical evidence that has recently become available for the transition countries shows that the effect of inequality on growth can be negative and robust (e.g., Ferreira 1999; Ivanova 2006; Sukiassyan 2007). We start with a brief review of the literature on the determinants of inequality in transition countries, with particular emphasis on the role of institutions and government policies pursued under the new economic order following transition. The study then attempts to investigate the causes of, and establish some stylized facts about, the changes in inequality using a rich database of household surveys collected over the period 1990–2005.

Empirical studies on inequality in the transition countries are relatively few in number despite the importance of the topic. There are only a handful of studies that attempt to systematically and empirically investigate inequality in the transition countries and to provide some possible explanations for its evolution since the beginning of transition (Mitra and Yemtsov 2006; Ferreira 1999; Milanovic 1999; Ivaschenko 2002; Giammatteo 2006). These studies on the distribution of income immediately before, during, and after transition show that there has been an appreciable increase in inequality in most EE and FSU countries, albeit at varying degrees of magnitude and pace. A widespread view is that the transition to market economy, which entailed several transformations—including liberalization of capital, goods and services, and labour markets, and their integration into regional and world markets; privatization of state-owned enterprises; and the formation of new institutions to serve the market economy—has invariably led to a significant shift in the distribution of income.

Mitra and Yemtsov (2006) provide a summary of the findings of many studies. After careful review of the existing literature, they conclude that all EE and FSU countries experienced an increase in inequality but with considerable variations. A rapid increase in inequality took place in the middle-income and low-income Commonwealth of Independent States (CIS)[1] countries, whereas the new member states of the European Union (EU) appear to have experienced a smaller and more gradual increase in inequality. For example, in Russia, the Gini coefficient increased from 25.9 in 1989–90 to 40.9 in 1994, showing a very rapid increase immediately after the dismantling of the old communist system. In contrast, in Poland, despite a similar level of inequality in 1989–90 (Gini of 25.5), the level of inequality increased to only 32 by 1995.

Milanovic (1999) argues that the observed increase in inequality in the transition countries is driven mainly by higher inequality in wage distribution following the dismantling of the state sector with its compressed wage structure, and its replacement by the newly emerging private sector with its much broader wage distribution. He also finds the effects of social transfers to have varied widely, in some cases halting further increases in inequality (Poland), and in others (e.g. Russia during the early years of transition) having the perverse effect of contributing to inequality. Ivaschenko (2002) looks at the determinants of changes in income inequality using a panel of inequality estimates for 24 EE and FSU countries for the period 1989–98. His is the first panel analysis of inequality during transition. His main conclusion is that increases in inequality are associated with privatization and deindustrialization (often the two facets of the same phenomenon). Ivaschenko also finds that there was no significant impact of unemployment rate and the size of government spending on income distribution. Another interesting finding of the study was the contrast between EE and FSU country-groups in the relationship between income inequality and per capita GDP. While there was no association between the GDP per capita level and changes in inequality in EE, Ivaschenko notes a significant U-shaped relationship (the increase in inequality was smallest among middle-income countries) between the two variables for FSU countries.

A study by Ivanova (2006) highlights the effect of government policies on inequality using evidence from Hungary, Poland, and Bulgaria. She shows that government policies prompted by the trend towards liberalization and privatization, such as reducing social spending, limiting access to social assistance through strong selectivity and conditionality criteria, and introducing market-regulated (fee-based) access to many social services, have had a profoundly negative impact on socioeconomic equality and contributed to inequality's getting embedded in the transforming societies. According to this study, inequality was not only a by-product of macroeconomic policies but also a natural outcome of the particular model of society chosen by the transition economies; for instance, the choice of the minimalist safety net approach as opposed to the universalistic welfare state approach of the European social market economies.

While inequality increased in the transition region overall, country-specific studies provide a clearer trend of changes in inequality within each country. A study of Poland's income distribution before and during the transition (Keane and Prasad 2002) reveals significant increases in inequality as measured by wages from formal employment. Keane and Prasad also find that the reallocation of workers from a public sector with a compressed wage distribution to a private sector with much higher wage inequality accounts for the bulk of increased earnings inequality during transition. They highlight the role that increased social transfers had in limiting the increase in inequality. The unemployment benefits, pensions, family and child allowances that provided economic protection for the most vulnerable citizens prior to the transition underwent major transformations. Giammatteo (2006) looks at the impact of state transfers (and taxes) and market-oriented reforms on gross and disposable income inequality. His study uses the Luxemburg Income Study (LIS) data for Poland, Hungary, and Russia and concludes that these changes led to an increase in inequality in these countries during 1990–2000. He shows that Russia had the most unequal market and disposable income distribution, followed by Hungary and then Poland. The study concludes that the redistribution policies in some countries played a key role during the transition period, allowing the government to contain inequality during the period of profound economic and social reforms. The inequality-decreasing effects of state transfers were robust and continued to be effective during the latter part of the 1990s, particularly in Poland and Hungary.[2] More recently, Gorodnichenko, Peter, and Stolaryov (2010), using 10 years of panel data (1995–2004) from the Russian Longitudinal Household Survey, record decreasing (but still high by international standards) inequality in Russia, which they ascribe to reduced volatility in income (and hence in consumption as well).

2   Main trends

In this study, we use a newly created database of inequality statistics for 26 transition economies. This has three important characteristics: (i) it is the largest database because it includes detailed inequality data for more than 200 country/years covering the 16-year period of 1990–2005; (ii) it is overwhelmingly calculated from micro (household-level) survey data; and (iii) we are therefore able to go, in the empirical analysis (sections 3 and 4), beyond the use of synthetic inequality statistics (such as the Gini coefficient) and to use decile shares. The advantage of the last point is that it allows us to make many more observations and, more importantly, presents a much more nuanced and accurate picture of the entire distribution than a single number can, be it a Gini, a Theil, or any other synthetic inequality indicator. Household surveys of income or expenditure (or consumption) are of course the most common tool for the study of income distribution.

The issue has been raised recently (Atkinson et al. 2011) that surveys may systematically underestimate top-of-income distributions because rich households refuse to participate in surveys or under-report their incomes, particularly so property incomes. This is almost certainly the case in many post-communist countries where new millionaires or billionaires ('the oligarchs') are thought unlikely to agree to participate in surveys even if selected to be part of the random sample taken among the population. This is, for example, one of the reasons why we have decided to omit data from Azerbaijan, which show an unrealistically low inequality in all years. However, when discussing the possible omission of the rich and thus the downward bias to inequality, one has to keep in mind that (i) in all countries studied here, the super-rich are a tiny proportion of the population and that even if their refusal rates were not different from the rest of the population, a random sample would seldom include them anyway, and (ii) their omission may influence the average income of the top decile but would leave the rest of the income distribution unchanged. Thus most of our analysis is unaffected.

Figure 3.1 summarizes the evolution of inequality in the transition countries over the period 1990–2005. The top line shows the share of the top decile in total income, the bottom line the share of the lowest decile. The biggest distributional changes occurred between 1990 and 1995, and since then the distributions have, on average, been stable. Between 1990 and 1995, the share of the top decile increased from about 20 per cent of total income to about 25 per cent (and it has been remarkably stable since), while the share of the bottom decile dropped from about 4.5 per cent of total income to 3 per cent. The top and bottom deciles registered the biggest swings: positive by about a quarter of its previous share for the top decile and negative by almost a third for the bottom decile. In contrast, the shares of the middle deciles did not change much: the share of the fifth decile dropped from about 8.6 to 8.1 per cent and the share of the sixth from 9.6 to 9.3 per cent, and so on. This is consistent with other evidence, which shows that the biggest difference (in cross-country studies) between the relatively unequal and relatively equal countries is observed in their top and bottom decile shares, whereas middle-class income shares are relatively stable (Milanovic

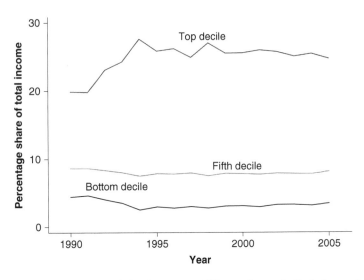

Figure 3.1 The evolution of the bottom, middle, and top deciles' share of total income (percentage of total income)

Note: The unweighted (unbalanced panel) average for 26 economies.

Source: Computed by the authors based on data from household surveys (see Annexe 3.1).

2008; Palma 2006). One can thus expect that a temporal change in inequality, as here, would involve most important swings for the two extreme deciles.

The total number of inequality observations we have is 209. At the beginning of the period (1990 and 1991), we have observations for only six and seven countries, respectively, and at the very end of the period (2005) for nine countries.[3] For all other years in between, the number of countries included ranges between 15 and 21. This is because annual data for each of the 26 countries are not available, either because the surveys were not conducted or (less frequently) because we did not have access to them. The list of countries with their number of observations and the average top and bottom decile shares is given in Annexe 3.1. We therefore have an unbalanced panel where the number of observations ranges from 16 (i.e. available for all years) for Poland to only 2 (for Bosnia, Croatia, and Montenegro). The average number of observations per country is about eight (209 divided by 26 countries). Among our explanatory variables, the one that we are most interested in is a set of policy variables as defined and numerically estimated by the European Bank for Reconstruction and Development (EBRD). We shall use these variables as an indicator both of the average intensity of reforms (taking an unweighted average of all nine EBRD reform indexes) and of each reform separately.[4] Other right-hand side variables are pretty straightforward. They include annual real growth rate, government expenditure as percentage of GDP, and annual inflation rate as measured by the change in the consumer price index (all three obtained from World Development Indicators). It may be worth briefly mentioning their evolution in time since all three are reflective of the transition process.

The growth rates are available annually for 24 countries.[5] The average unweighted rate at the onset of transition, in 1991 and 1992, was −13 and −19 per cent, respectively.[6] Beginning with 1995, the average unweighted growth rate turned positive, almost monotonically increasing from about 1 per cent in 1995 to more than 6 per cent at the end of the period. This is a remarkable turnaround, although the depth of the early depression means that the GDPs per capita for the 11 countries are still below their 1990 levels.[7] The population-weighted area's average GDP per capita is now only 2 per cent above its 1990 level, and total real GDP of the area is exactly the same as it was 16 years ago. However, illustrating the recent turnaround we note, for example, that since 2000 there have been only five observations of negative (and mildly so) growth rates while there were 18 observations of growth rates in excess of 10 per cent per annum. At the beginning of the period the situation was exactly the reverse: in the years 1991 and 1992 there were no fewer than 30 observations of double-digit negative growth.

The evolution of inflation is very similar to that of growth: years of low growth were also the years of high inflation, and vice versa. The average unweighted inflation rate for the transition countries decreased from its peak of more than 1,000 per cent in 1992 and just below 1,000 per cent in 1993 to around 6 per cent in both 2004 and 2005. Again, from 1993 the decline in the unweighted inflation rate was monotonical: each successive year saw a lower average rate. The evolutions of unweighted growth rate and inflation are shown in Figure 3.2. The situation is just slightly different with respect to government expenditure as a share of GDP. Government spending was inelastic, both when incomes dropped severely at the onset of the transition and when they kept on increasing later. Thus, the unweighted government spending as a share of GDP reached its peak of 42 per cent in 1992 and more or less dropped continuously to under 30 per cent by the end of the period.

The broad contours of the changes in our key variables during the transition are remarkably clear. Of course, this holds for the sample as a whole—the evolution for each individual country is bound to show peculiarities of its own. On average, inequality grew between 1990 and 1995, and has remained stable since; growth was negative over the same period and after 1995 increased steadily year after year; inflation peaked in 1992 and 1993 and has since steadily gone down; and government expenditure as a share of GDP peaked around the point where the average output hit the bottom (1993 and 1994) and has gone down ever since.

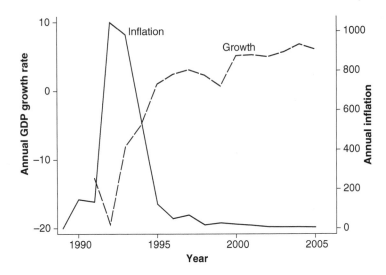

Figure 3.2 Average (unweighted) growth rate and inflation during transition, 1990–2005

Note: GDP growth in percentage per annum (broken line; left axis). Inflation in percentage per annum (right axis). Data are the unweighted average of 26 transition economies.

Source: Computed by the authors based on data from the World Bank's World Development Indicators.

With regard to transitional reforms, most transition countries have made significant progress over the past decade and half (see Figure 3.3 and Annexe 3.2), but two broad patterns have emerged. In the more advanced countries, such as Poland and Estonia, rapid liberalization and sustained macroeconomic stabilization laid the basis for gradual institutional change. The bulk of these changes have been driven by the process of European integration. By 2005 the countries with the highest average EBRD index were Hungary, with a value of almost 4 (out of a maximum of 4.33), and Estonia and the Czech Republic (around 3.8). At the beginning of the transition in 1989, Estonia and the Czech Republic had a reform index at the very minimum level of 1, and Hungary at 1.3. Overall, as Figure 3.3 shows, EE countries remained ahead of CIS countries and the difference has even increased recently. As for the least advanced countries, such as Turkmenistan, Belarus, and Uzbekistan, progress in liberalization and privatization has been slow and uneven and stabilization has been jeopardized by the persistence of soft budget constraints. In 2005, Turkmenistan's mean reform index stood at 1.3, Belarus's at 1.8 and Uzbekistan's at 2.1. Thus, reform-wise, they seem to be almost where many of the advanced countries were after one or two years of the transition. For both the EE and particularly CIS countries, the intensity of reforms was greater up to

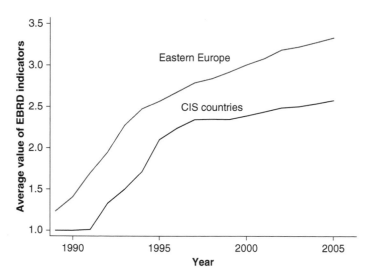

Figure 3.3 The evolution of average EBRD reform indicators in EE and the CIS, 1990–2005

Note: Unweighted average.
Source: Computed by the authors based on EBRD data.

the mid-1990s than afterwards (shown by the steepness of the line in Figure 3.3 and a flexion point around 1995). This is as expected since the reform index is bounded from above (as are, in a more substantive sense, reforms too).

3 What explains change in inequality?

An explanation of the increase in inequality during the transition has to rely on very little theory. The reason to some extent is obvious, namely that the transition from communism to capitalism took place quickly and unexpectedly, so no *a priori* theory was developed. After the beginning of transition, and faced with the often dramatic increases in inequality, several studies tried to formalize the factors and mechanisms associated with the increase. These were reviewed earlier in this chapter. Milanovic (1999) saw increased inequality arising from the transfer of labour force from an egalitarian public sector to a much more inegalitarian private sector. In his view, the structural, or rather ownership, transformation was the primary force behind increased inequality. Similarly, Ivaschenko (2002) links privatization and structural change, expressed as 'deindustrialization', to increased inequality. But, as discussed in the review of the existing litera-ture, other factors were, in a heuristic fashion, also associated with changes in inequality. Noticing smaller increases in Central European countries whose welfare systems 'survived' the first wave of transition much better than those of the former Soviet republics, Keane and Prasad (2002) argue that maintaining social expenditure provided a strong cushion against runaway inequality. In an early article on the political economy of reforms, Hellman (1988) links high levels of inequality to non-completed reforms. In his simple cross-section, both the more advanced reformers in Central Europe and the non-reformers in Central Asia had lower levels of inequality than reformers that stopped 'halfway', like Russia and Ukraine. He ascribes these developments to the entrenched role of the new oligarchic elites.

Following on from some of these insights, we estimate a country fixed-effect model where inequality is associated with the growth rate of the economy (measured by the annual GDI increase), inflation rate (measured by the annual increase in the consumer price index), intensity of structural reforms (measured as the unweighted average value of nine EBRD reform indices), government spending as a share of GDI, and the level of a country's democracy (as measured by the Polity database). In addition, we control for the type of survey instrument used (income or expenditure) and the survey reference period (whether monthly, quarterly, semi-annual, or annual). From the existing literature, both transition-based and non-transition-based, we can derive assumptions regarding the role of some of the explanatory variables. For example, inflation is generally found to be positively associated with inequality (Bulir 2001). Social expenditure, as already mentioned, is expected to dampen the rise in inequality. Democracy is also generally found to be anti-inequality although the evidence is not very robust (see, e.g., Bollen and Jackman 1985; Li et al. 1998; but see also Rodrik 1999). But for a couple of variables we lack strong priors based on theory or existing empirical evidence. For example, different types of reform may be assumed to affect inequality differently. While there is little disagreement that privatization is likely to increase inequality (see in particular Ivaschenko 2002: 155–98), other reforms may have the opposite effect. Thus, financial liberalization, associated with financial deepening and easier access to credit, could be thought to be pro-equality as indeed some influential papers argue (e.g. Li et al. 1998). For this reason, in addition to reforms overall whose effects are explored in this section, we shall look in due course at the effect of each individual reform. Even less *a priori* obvious is the effect of the growth rate of the economy. Its effect cannot even be postulated in advance since some growth-inducing policies may be pro-poor and others anti-poor. Therefore, whether the growth process as such has been pro- or anti-poor, should emerge as result of empirical analysis rather than be hypothesized in advance.

The regressions are run across each decile share defined as the share of *i*-th decile (deciles running from 1, the poorest, to 10, the richest) in total survey income (or total survey expenditure, depending on what the survey instrument is). We use the method of seemingly unrelated regressions (SUR), where each individual left-hand side variable is regressed on the same set of explanatory variables.[8] Since the decile shares sum to 1, we impose constraints on the coefficients such that the sum of products of coefficients associated with a given variable and decile shares be equal to 0. In other words, we want to guarantee that an infinitesimal increase in an explanatory variable leaves the sum of income shares unchanged, that is, equal to 1. The regression is written as

$$D_{ijt} = \beta_0 + \beta_1 G_{jt} + \beta_2 INF_{jt} + \beta_3 REF_{jt} + \beta_4 EXP_{jt} + \beta_5 DEM_{jt} + \beta_6 DIj_t$$
$$+ \beta_7 DS_{jt} + \beta_8 DD_j + e_{ijt}$$

where subscripts i, j and t denote, respectively, decile, country, and time (year), D = decile share,[9] G = real growth rate, INF = annual inflation, REF = the average unweighted EBRD reform index, EXP = total government expenditure as percentage of GDI, DEM = value of Polity2 variable from the Polity database (ranging from –10 for complete dictatorship to +10 for full democracy), DI = dummy variable for whether survey is income- or expenditure-based, DS = dummy variable for survey reference period (monthly, quarterly, semi-annual, annual), DD = country dummy and e_{ijt} = error term.[10] To control for inter- and intra-country heteroscedasticity the regressions are run with robust (Huber-White) standard errors.[11] Since reforms were, in almost all cases, influenced or imposed from abroad, being at first mostly of the Washington consensus type favoured by the World Bank, the EBRD and the IMF, and later of the milder type favoured by the EU, their exogeneity seems patent—it is very unlikely that they were responding to domestic income distribution concerns.

The results are shown in Table 3.1. As can be seen, there are 177 surveys giving a total of 1,770 data points (for all ten deciles).[12] Each regression is run over 177 points belonging to a given decile. The panel is unbalanced as some countries have many more observations than others. However, since we adjust for unobserved fixed country effects, this should not affect the estimated values of the coefficients. The R-square runs between 0.5 and 0.6 for the bottom six deciles and the top decile. For the four upper-middle deciles, R^2 is lower, ranging between 0.2 and 0.38. We will consider the results one by one. Growth rate is strongly anti-poor as the coefficients on the two bottom deciles are statistically significantly negative and, likewise, the coefficients on the top two deciles are significantly positive. Across the rest of the income distribution, the higher growth rate is neutral, that is, it does not affect the decile shares. The implication is that the acceleration of growth has generally left the income share of the poor lower. This does not imply, however, that their average income had gone down since a smaller share might have

Table 3.1 Explaining decile shares in transition countries (with the overall EBRD index)

Decile	First	Second	Third	Fourth	Fifth	Sixth	Seventh	Eighth	Ninth	Tenth
Growth rate	-0.265	-0.066	-0.010	0.001	0.002	-0.011	-0.004	-0.003	0.135	0.221
	(2.80)**	(0.81)	(0.13)	(0.01)	(0.03)	(0.20)	(0.08)	(0.05)	(1.34)	(0.58)
Inflation	-0.019	-0.019	-0.016	-0.011	-0.008	-0.005	-0.001	0.005	0.021	0.052
	(3.43)**	(3.89)**	(3.47)**	(2.83)**	(2.33)*	(1.59)	(0.48)	(1.75)	(3.60)**	(2.33)*
EBRD_total	-0.067	-0.072	-0.059	-0.038	-0.025	-0.013	-0.003	0.018	0.084	0.176
	(3.16)**	(3.90)**	(3.40)**	(2.51)**	(1.83)	(1.09)	(0.29)	(1.51)	(3.67)**	(2.04)*
Exp_gdp	-0.001	0.0003	0.0003	0.001	0.0004	0.0001	-0.0002	0.00001	0.002	-0.002
	(0.85)	(0.36)	(0.41)	(0.94)	(0.78)	(0.16)	(0.50)	(0.02)	(2.17)*	(0.62)
Polity2	0.008	0.008	0.007	0.006	0.005	0.004	0.002	-0.001	-0.005	-0.034
	(3.01)**	(3.45)**	(3.37)**	(3.19)**	(3.00)**	(2.63)**	(1.73)	(0.77)	(1.78)	(3.20)**
Dincome	-0.013	-0.001	0.007	0.013	0.015	0.016	0.016	0.025	0.040	0.012
	(0.96)	(0.06)	(0.60)	(1.27)	(1.46)	(1.67)	(1.65)	(2.13)*	(1.69)	(0.21)
Quarterly	-0.005	-0.015	-0.012	-0.016	-0.018	-0.018	-0.013	-0.005	0.013	0.155
	(0.09)	(0.29)	(0.25)	(0.36)	(0.42)	(0.43)	(0.31)	(0.09)	(0.13)	(0.64)
Semi-annual	0.030	-0.004	-0.010	-0.021	-0.020	-0.038	-0.052	-0.065	-0.040	0.153
	(0.47)	(0.08)	(0.19)	(0.42)	(0.43)	(0.84)	(1.14)	(1.17)	(0.36)	(0.59)
Annual	-0.005	-0.010	-0.011	-0.013	-0.009	-0.006	-0.001	0.007	0.038	0.091
	(0.39)	(0.95)	(1.02)	(1.33)	(0.93)	(0.67)	(0.16)	(0.67)	(1.70)	(1.78)
Constant	0.577	0.721	0.764	0.793	0.860	0.937	1.058	1.187	1.202	1.901
	(6.71)**	(9.61)**	(10.91)**	(12.67)**	(15.01)**	(18.28)**	(21.98)**	(21.36)**	(11.19)**	(5.44)**
No. of obs	177	177	177	177	177	177	177	177	177	177
R^2	0.546	0.606	0.604	0.589	0.510	0.379	0.200	0.280	0.312	0.539

Note: Statistically significant coefficients (at 1 and 5 per cent levels) denoted by, respectively, ** and *. z values in brackets. Dincome is a binary variable taking a value of 1 if the survey is income-based and 0 if expenditure- or consumption-based. Quarterly, semi-annual, and annual are binary variables for the survey reference period (the omitted variable is monthly). The inflation rate is expressed in natural logs. All regressions include country dummies.
Source: See text for explanation.

been counterbalanced by a higher overall income, but it does highlight the concern that advantages of growth were unbalanced and tended to accrue mostly to higher-income groups. While statistically significant, the absolute amount of the effect seems to be small. For the bottom decile, acceleration of 1 per cent in growth is associated with a decrease in its income share by 0.026 percentage points. The average income share of the bottom decile is 3.2 percentage points. Thus, to keep the absolute real income of the bottom decile from falling, the growth acceleration needs to be greater than 0.8 per cent,[13] which, as we have seen, is the case by assumption. For the second decile, the outcome is even stronger, as the implicit growth rate needed to keep its absolute income from falling is only 0.13 per cent. We conclude that higher growth tended to increase absolute incomes also of the poorest but did so proportionally less than the rest (see Figure 3.4, left panel).

The effect of inflation is clear. It tended to influence negatively (in a statistically significant way) the income shares of the bottom five deciles, and positively the top two (see Figure 3.4, right panel). This result, as mentioned before, corresponds with our expectations and with earlier findings in the literature. Similar is the effect of structural reforms measured by the EBRD index. A greater level of reforms is strongly negatively associated with the income shares of the four lower deciles, and positively with the shares of the top two deciles. For example, one standard deviation increase in the reform index (0.84 EBRD points) is associated with about

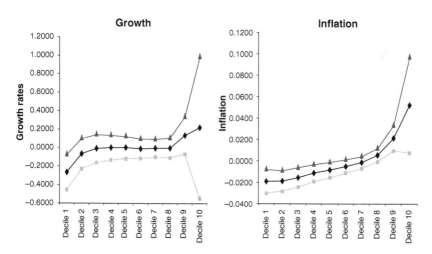

Figure 3.4 The regression coefficients on growth and inflation variables (by decile)
Note: The broken line around the coefficient gives the spread of two standard deviations.

1.1 percentage point share increase for the top decile. Note that the top decile receives, on average, 25 per cent of total income, hence the gains from the reforms are not negligible for the top income group. For the bottom decile, on the other hand, one standard deviation increase in reforms reduces the share by 0.4 per cent. Their (bottom decile's) average share in the sample is 3.2 per cent of total income. Accordingly, in order for greater reforms to increase the absolute income of the bottom decile, the increase in total income generated by reforms must be in excess of 12.5 per cent (0.4 divided by 3.2). This is, of course, extremely high growth on a yearly basis and reforms in the short term are therefore very unlikely to be pro-poor in an absolute sense as far as the bottom income decile is concerned.

A somewhat surprising finding is that greater government expenditure seems to be distribution-neutral. In effect, for no decile, except weakly for the ninth decile, does greater expenditure (as a share of GDI) show either a positive or a negative statistically significant coefficient. The effect is generally very strong (including here regressions not shown in the text) when the run in a cross-country setting dissipates in a model where we control for country effects. In other words, the conclusion that the difference between inequality in (say) Poland and Russia may be related to their governments' spending does not seem to be warranted. Once we control for unobserved country characteristics, we cannot argue that greater government spending in Russia (or in Poland) would result in less inequality. It seems that all of the identification of this variable's effect on inequality comes from cross-country variation. Part of the problem may lie, however, in the fact that government expenditure includes all kinds of expenditure, all of which may not be directed towards the poor or lower middle classes. If one could isolate the social component of total government expenditure (which unfortunately is not possible with the data) it could be that the effect would cease to be insignificant.

The effect of democracy is very interesting. Its pro-equality effect cuts very deeply because it raises the income shares of the bottom six deciles, is neutral for the following three deciles, and is then strongly anti-top decile. The increase by one democracy point on the 21-point Polity scale increases the share of the bottom decile by 0.08 percentage points, which seems small in absolute amounts but not so when we reflect that the average share of the bottom decile is only 3.2 percentage points. In other words, a one-point increase in the democracy indicator is equal to a distribution-neutral growth rate of some 2.5 per cent (0.08 divided by 3.2). The effect is similar for the following two deciles (second and third). An intriguing result is that a combination of modest democratization (increase by 1 Polity point) and modest acceleration in growth (1 per cent) will, on average, increase absolute incomes of the bottom deciles even if growth per se has a disequalizing effect. However, a very strong negative effect of reforms on bottom decile share cannot be so easily offset by democratization. As a robustness check, we also introduce the ratio between exports of some key natural resources (oil, natural gas, diamonds, gold) and GDI.[14] This is done to test the hypothesis that natural resource exports tend to be associated with more unequal distributions. In this case, however, the coefficient on the natural resource exports variable is insignificant throughout, while coefficients on the other variables are not affected. Finally, the effects of the survey instrument (income or expenditure) or reference period are statistically insignificant throughout.

4 The role of individual EBRD reform indicators

In the previous section the intensity of structural reforms in transition countries was measured by the unweighted average of the nine EBRD transitional indicators. However, as already mentioned, it is highly likely that these various components of the EBRD transition index could have different, and even opposing, effects in the evolution of inequality. For example, while large-scale privatization may likely lead to an increase in inequality (Ivaschenko 2002), financial liberalization could have the opposite effect (Li et al. 1998). Hence, in this section we analyse the effect on decile shares of each of the nine EBRD transitional indicators separately.

Table 3.2 presents the coefficients from a seemingly unrelated regression equation (SURE) of the share of deciles where all nine EBRD transition indicators are used as explanatory variables. Before discussing the results, it is worth mentioning that the other key explanatory variables stayed robust despite introducing a new set of explanatory structural reform variables. For example, both the signs and the significance of growth, inflation, government expenditure, and democracy variables remained robust; that is, the same as they were in the previous regressions (Table 3.1). Therefore, this section discusses the effects on inequality of the EBRD transition indicators only.

Large- and small-scale privatization schemes appear to have opposing effects on the evolution of inequality in the transition countries. The statistically significant and positive coefficients on the bottom five deciles suggest that progress in small-scale privatization is strongly pro-poor. This observation is further strengthened by the statistically significant negative coefficients on the top three deciles. On other hand, large-scale privatization tends to worsen inequality as implied by the negative coefficients (albeit not significant at conventional level) on the bottom deciles' income shares.

Table 3.2 Explaining decile shares in transition countries (with individual EBRD indexes)

Decile	First	Second	Third	Fourth	Fifth	Sixth	Seventh	Eighth	Ninth	Tenth
Growth	-0.332	-0.133	-0.068	-0.047	-0.039	-0.040	-0.006	0.034	0.185	0.446
	(3.50)**	(1.63)	(0.89)	(0.69)	(0.63)	(0.75)	(0.13)	(0.65)	(1.76)	(1.16)
Inflation	-0.021	-0.021	-0.018	-0.014	-0.012	-0.009	-0.004	0.004	0.025	0.068
	(3.68)**	(4.14)**	(3.87)**	(3.26)**	(3.11)**	(2.65)**	(1.48)	(1.39)	(3.95)**	(2.91)**
Large-scale privatization	-0.017	-0.022	-0.010	-0.004	0.002	0.002	0.002	0.012	0.039	-0.004
	(1.15)	(1.72)	(0.82)	(0.35)	(0.23)	(0.23)	(0.30)	(1.44)	(2.32)*	(0.06)
Small-scale privatization	0.036	0.037	0.033	0.027	0.021	0.014	-0.002	-0.024	-0.034	-0.108
	(2.44)*	(2.94)**	(2.77)**	(2.56)*	(2.17)*	(1.71)	(0.21)	(2.96)**	(2.08)*	(1.82)
Governance and enterprise restructuring	-0.028	-0.021	-0.024	-0.022	-0.023	-0.023	-0.017	-0.016	-0.010	0.183
	(1.38)	(1.22)	(1.52)	(1.56)	(1.82)	(2.03)*	(1.67)	(1.42)	(0.44)	(2.27)*
Price liberalization	0.029	0.024	0.018	0.013	0.006	-0.000	-0.006	-0.009	-0.002	-0.073
	(1.69)	(1.60)	(1.27)	(1.06)	(0.52)	(0.03)	(0.70)	(0.90)	(0.10)	(1.04)
Trade and foreign exchange liberalization	-0.017	-0.005	-0.002	-0.003	-0.004	-0.004	-0.006	-0.011	0.009	0.043
	(1.27)	(0.43)	(0.18)	(0.33)	(0.48)	(0.51)	(0.80)	(1.50)	(0.62)	(0.78)
Competition policy	0.022	0.003	-0.003	0.002	0.009	0.019	0.021	0.013	-0.021	-0.065
	(1.31)	(0.23)	(0.20)	(0.15)	(0.79)	(1.98)*	(2.50)*	(1.36)	(1.12)	(0.95)
Banking system liberalization	-0.015	-0.012	-0.013	-0.009	0.001	0.008	0.018	0.030	0.018	-0.025
	(0.85)	(0.81)	(0.91)	(0.74)	(0.06)	(0.86)	(2.01)*	(3.09)**	(0.91)	(0.36)

	(1)	(2)	(3)	(4)	(5)	(6)	(7)	(8)	(9)	(10)
Infrastructural reform	-0.039	-0.044	-0.045	-0.034	-0.034	-0.030	-0.020	0.005	0.054	0.187
	(2.32)*	(3.06)**	(3.32)**	(2.85)**	(3.12)**	(3.22)**	(2.29)*	(0.58)	(2.91)**	(2.74)**
Capital market reform	-0.011	-0.012	-0.005	-0.004	-0.005	-0.005	-0.001	0.008	0.011	0.022
	(0.70)	(0.89)	(0.38)	(0.34)	(0.50)	(0.52)	(0.12)	(0.97)	(0.67)	(0.35)
Exp_gdp	-0.001	-0.000	0.000	0.001	0.000	0.000	-0.000	0.000	0.002	-0.002
	(0.61)	(0.24)	(0.44)	(0.93)	(0.74)	(0.10)	(0.41)	(0.28)	(1.82)	(0.67)
Polity2	0.008	0.009	0.008	0.007	0.006	0.004	0.002	-0.002	-0.006	-0.037
	(3.23)**	(4.08)**	(4.06)**	(3.70)**	(3.43)**	(2.98)**	(1.74)	(1.41)	(2.17)*	(3.52)**
Dincome	-0.011	0.002	0.009	0.014	0.015	0.016	0.017	0.024	0.029	0.015
	(0.80)	(0.13)	(0.71)	(1.25)	(1.42)	(1.67)	(1.76)	(2.17)*	(1.30)	(0.25)
Quarterly	0.008	0.004	0.003	-0.006	-0.010	-0.010	-0.009	-0.013	-0.016	0.116
	(0.13)	(0.08)	(0.06)	(0.14)	(0.24)	(0.25)	(0.23)	(0.26)	(0.16)	(0.49)
Semi-annual	0.048	0.033	0.025	-0.000	-0.010	-0.039	-0.061	-0.082	-0.042	0.061
	(0.69)	(0.53)	(0.43)	(0.00)	(0.20)	(0.82)	(1.29)	(1.50)	(0.38)	(0.21)
Annual	-0.002	-0.006	-0.007	-0.010	-0.007	-0.005	-0.002	0.003	0.029	0.088
	(0.17)	(0.56)	(0.63)	(1.00)	(0.70)	(0.52)	(0.21)	(0.26)	(1.36)	(1.75)
Constant	0.385	0.515	0.602	0.679	0.800	0.920	1.098	1.309	1.336	2.357
	(3.33)**	(5.16)**	(6.45)**	(8.10)**	(10.50)**	(13.75)**	(17.81)**	(19.19)**	(9.76)**	(5.05)**
No. of obs	177	177	177	177	177	177	177	177	177	177
R-square	0.579	0.629	0.622	0.602	0.532	0.413	0.263	0.388	0.364	0.567

Note: Statistically significant coefficients (at 1 and 5 per cent levels) denoted by, respectively, ** and *. z values in brackets. Dincome is a binary variable taking a value of 1 if survey is income-based and 0 if expenditure- or consumption-based. Quarterly, semi-annual, and annual are binary variables for survey reference period (the omitted variable is monthly). The inflation rate is expressed in natural logs. All regressions include country dummies.

Source: See text for explanation.

Another EBRD reform that has significant bearing on the evolution of inequality is progress in reforming infrastructure, which includes electric power, railways, roads, telecommunications, water, and waste. Reforms in these infrastructure and utility sectors have worsened inequality. They appear to benefit mostly those in the top two deciles (that is the richest 20 per cent) of the population. Nearly 70 per cent of the population have seen their share of consumption or income decline as a result of infrastructure privatization and fee changes. This outcome may be partly explained by the fact that infrastructure privatization meant the abolition of monolithic government ownership of these structures that used to provide at times inefficient yet subsidized and/or free services to citizens. The sizes of the two strongly significant effects (pro-poor small-scale privatization and pro-rich infrastructure reform) are such that they almost exactly balance each other out—one point increase in the respective EBRD indexes produces about the same absolute effect.[15]

The rest of the EBRD transition indicators played more or less non-discriminatory roles in the evolution of inequality. Enforcement actions to reduce abuse of market power and to promote a competitive business environment appear to favour those in the middle-income classes, with no significant effect on the poorest and the richest. Improvements in banking laws and regulations, and financial deepening, also benefit more those in the middle- and upper-income brackets. There is some indication that enterprise restructuring tends to favour the very top income class to the detriment of the middle. If job losses following restructuring are concentrated among the middle classes it is not surprising. The rest of the EBRD components are inequality-neutral. But in some cases that neutrality is quite remarkable. Thus price liberalization, and foreign trade and exchange rate liberalization, frequently regarded as anti-poor, at least in the short term, appear to have an entirely neutral effect on income distribution.

5   Conclusions

Using for the first time micro data from household surveys in an unbalanced panel framework covering 26 transition economies over a 16-year period, this study has investigated the correlates of inequality increase in post-communist countries. Another feature of the study has been the use of decile shares, which give a much more detailed picture of changes in the entire distribution than a single inequality index like a Gini coefficient. While the Gini coefficient can remain unchanged, for example, with increases in income shares among both the rich and the poor (and a corresponding decline in the middle), the share-based analysis captures these changes well.

Using the SUR method, run for each decile and fixed (country) effect specification, we find that reforms as measured by the average EBRD index for a given country/year have had a robust negative effect on income shares of the bottom four deciles and a positive effect on income shares of the top two. The intuitive feeling that reforms in post-communist countries were anti-poor (at least in the distributional sense) is confirmed. Breaking down the reform index into its nine EBRD-defined types of reform, we find that the negative effect on income shares of the bottom decile is associated mostly with infrastructural reforms, which included introduction (or increases) of fees for services, and privatization of electricity, railways, roads, water provision, and so on. On the other hand, small-scale privatization is associated with the opposite (pro-poor) effect. Among the other relevant variables, the most important and significant is the role of democracy, which raises the income shares of the bottom and middle deciles. Not surprisingly, we find inflation to be anti-poor: highly significant for the income shares of both the bottom and the top groups. Growth as such has, on the other hand, been disequalizing. However, this effect is sufficiently small so that growth overall is associated with an increase in real income of the bottom deciles (including the lowest)—that is, even if the bottom decile's income share is reduced. In other words, growth was anti-poor in a relative but not in an absolute sense. Finally, once we control for country effects, we find an absence of association between government expenditure as a share of GDI and inequality. Thus, the often-quoted relationship between government spending and inequality in (say) Poland versus Russia (with spending being high in Poland and hence, it is argued, inequality low) seems to get its entire identification from cross-country level regressions.

What policy implications emerge from this work? First, it is important to look at the reform process in a more nuanced and discriminating way. This refers in particular to the negative role played by infrastructural reform that might often have been pushed onto the population too fast and too hard. The result also shows that the attempts to cushion low-income groups from the effects of such reforms have been unsuccessful. Second, it confirms the importance of small-scale privatization in keeping inequality in check—probably by providing much needed jobs. Third, it shows the crucial role played by democratization and control of inflation. Fourth, it leads us to be much more sceptical in using government spending as a means to redistribute resources towards the poorer strata. Fifth, it shows that growth is crucial for real incomes of all people, including the poor, even if it tends to be (in relative terms) disequalizing. Sixth, it shows that price and trade liberalization, often regarded as detrimental to the poor, was not so in the context of post-communist transition—the effect of both is entirely distribution-neutral.

Annexe

Annexe 3.1   Average share of bottom and top decile by country, 1990–2005

Country	Country abbreviation	Bottom decile	Top decile	Top-to-bottom ratio	No. of observations
Albania	ALB	3.63	23.40	6.45	3
Armenia	ARM	3.43	26.53	7.74	7
Bulgaria	BGR	3.07	25.39	8.28	14
Bosnia	BIH	3.72	23.27	6.26	2
Belarus	BLR	3.98	21.66	5.44	9
Czech Republic	CZ	4.50	22.29	4.95	6
Estonia	EST	2.58	27.05	10.46	11
Georgia	GEO	2.30	28.70	12.46	11
Croatia	HRV	3.43	24.98	7.29	2
Hungary	HU	3.51	23.83	6.80	13
Kazakhstan	KAZ	3.26	24.30	7.45	6
Kyrgyz Republic	KGZ	3.59	25.31	7.06	9
Lithuania	LTU	2.94	25.25	8.59	10
Latvia	LVA	3.05	25.70	8.42	11
Moldova	MDA	2.48	29.94	12.05	7
Macedonia	MKD	2.92	24.47	8.37	8
Montenegro	MON	3.21	25.13	7.84	2
Poland	PL	3.01	24.96	8.29	16
Romania	ROM	3.13	24.93	7.96	9
Russia	RUS	2.50	27.52	11.00	12
Serbia	SRB	3.31	24.03	7.26	7
Slovakia	SVK	4.50	21.20	4.71	4
Slovenia	SVN	4.00	20.78	5.20	11
Tajikistan	TJK	3.29	25.70	7.82	3
Ukraine	UKR	3.61	22.45	6.22	11
Uzbekistan	UZB	2.77	27.01	9.77	5
Total		3.21	24.97	7.78	209

Source: See text for explanation.

Annexe 3.2 Evolution of the main EBRD transition indexes

Country code	EBRD index	1990–5	1996–2000	2001–present
ALB	Large-scale privatization	1.14	2.47	3.00
	Small-scale privatization	2.29	4.00	4.00
	Infrastructure	1.05	1.46	2.00
	Restructuring	1.29	2.00	2.00
	EBRD average	1.58	2.58	2.84
ARM	Large-scale privatization	1.14	3.00	3.33
	Small-scale privatization	1.71	3.2	3.8
	Infrastructure	1.14	2.07	2.33
	Restructuring	1.14	2.00	2.26
	EBRD average	1.39	2.61	2.97
AZE	Large-scale privatization	1.00	1.67	2.00
	Small-scale privatization	1.00	3.00	3.6
	Infrastructure	1.00	1.4	1.8
	Restructuring	1.1	1.67	1.87
	EBRD average	1.21	2.21	2.55
BGR	Large-scale privatization	1.52	2.93	3.8
	Small-scale privatization	1.52	3.2	3.67
	Infrastructure	1.14	2.2	3.00
	Restructuring	1.29	2.26	2.53
	EBRD average	1.76	2.81	3.3
BIH	Large-scale privatization	1.00	1.6	2.4
	Small-scale privatization	2.43	2.07	2.93
	Infrastructure	1.00	1.46	2.26
	Restructuring	1.00	1.4	1.87
	EBRD average	1.35	1.84	2.43
BLR	Large-scale privatization	1.29	1.00	1.00
	Small-scale privatization	1.43	2.00	2.2
	Infrastructure	1.00	1.13	1.33
	Restructuring	1.1	1.13	1.00
	EBRD average	1.34	1.62	1.78
CZ	Large-scale privatization	2.29	4.00	4.00
	Small-scale privatization	3.00	4.33	4.33
	Infrastructure	1.62	2.73	3.2
	Restructuring	2.14	3.07	3.33
	EBRD average	2.34	3.49	3.71
EST	Large-scale privatization	1.86	4.00	4.00
	Small-scale privatization	2.29	4.33	4.33
	Infrastructure	1.86	2.8	3.33
	Restructuring	2.00	3.00	3.4
	EBRD average	2.04	3.44	3.77

104

Annexe 3.2 (Continued)

Country code	EBRD index	1990–5	1996–2000	2001–present
GEO	Large-scale privatization	1.14	3.26	3.4
	Small-scale privatization	1.57	4.00	4.00
	Infrastructure	1.00	1.87	2.33
	Restructuring	1.14	2.00	2.07
	EBRD average	1.29	2.73	2.95
HRV	Large-scale privatization	1.71	3.00	3.2
	Small-scale privatization	3.43	4.33	4.33
	Infrastructure	1.43	2.13	2.87
	Restructuring	1.29	2.67	2.8
	EBRD average	2.05	3.07	3.35
HU	Large-scale privatization	2.43	4.00	4.00
	Small-scale privatization	2.19	4.26	4.33
	Infrastructure	2.14	3.33	3.67
	Restructuring	2.29	3.2	3.4
	EBRD average	2.54	3.73	3.88
KAZ	Large-scale privatization	1.43	3.00	3.00
	Small-scale privatization	1.76	3.87	4.00
	Infrastructure	1.1	2.00	2.33
	Restructuring	1.00	2.00	2.00
	EBRD average	1.4	2.76	2.89
KGZ	Large-scale privatization	1.86	3.00	3.27
	Small-scale privatization	2.29	4.00	4.00
	Infrastructure	1.09	1.33	1.6
	Restructuring	1.29	2.00	2.00
	EBRD average	1.63	2.77	2.86
LTU	Large-scale privatization	2.00	3.00	3.67
	Small-scale privatization	2.43	4.13	4.33
	Infrastructure	1.1	2.33	2.67
	Restructuring	1.43	2.74	2.93
	EBRD average	1.84	3.11	3.5
LVA	Large-scale privatization	1.57	3.00	3.47
	Small-scale privatization	2.29	4.07	4.33
	Infrastructure	1.29	2.53	3.00
	Restructuring	1.57	2.74	2.87
	EBRD average	1.87	3.14	3.49
MDA	Large-scale privatization	1.57	3.00	3.00
	Small-scale privatization	1.43	3.27	3.67
	Infrastructure	1.00	1.93	2.2
	Restructuring	1.29	2.00	1.87
	EBRD average	1.53	2.67	2.81

MKD	Large-scale privatization	1.43	3.00	3.13
	Small-scale privatization	3.29	4.00	4.00
	Infrastructure	1.28	1.74	2.13
	Restructuring	1.29	2.07	2.33
	EBRD average	1.94	2.67	2.93
MON	Large-scale privatization	1.00	1.27	2.6
	Small-scale privatization	3.00	2.2	2.8
	Infrastructure	1.19	1.33	1.6
	Restructuring	1.00	1.00	1.67
	EBRD average	1.57	1.5	2.25
POL	Large-scale privatization	2.14	3.26	3.33
	Small-scale privatization	3.43	4.33	4.33
	Infrastructure	1.86	2.93	3.33
	Restructuring	2.29	3.00	3.4
	EBRD average	2.53	3.47	3.68
ROM	Large-scale privatization	1.62	2.74	3.47
	Small-scale privatization	1.71	3.4	3.67
	Infrastructure	1.00	2.2	3.13
	Restructuring	1.43	2.00	2.07
	EBRD average	1.62	2.81	3.13
RUS	Large-scale privatization	2.00	3.26	3.26
	Small-scale privatization	2.14	4.00	4.00
	Infrastructure	1.29	2.13	2.47
	Restructuring	1.24	1.93	2.33
	EBRD average	1.74	2.7	2.88
SRB	Large-scale privatization	1.00	1.00	2.07
	Small-scale privatization	3.00	3.00	3.13
	Infrastructure	1.19	1.67	2.00
	Restructuring	1.00	1.00	1.87
	EBRD average	1.57	1.46	2.33
SVN	Large-scale privatization	1.52	2.93	3.00
	Small-scale privatization	3.43	4.33	4.33
	Infrastructure	1.43	2.4	3.00
	Restructuring	1.62	2.67	2.93
	EBRD average	2.24	3.18	3.36
TJK	Large-scale privatization	1.14	2.13	2.33
	Small-scale privatization	1.57	2.73	3.74
	Infrastructure	1.00	1.00	1.13
	Restructuring	1.00	1.4	1.67
	EBRD average	1.25	1.94	2.25
TKM	Large-scale privatization	1.00	1.6	1.00
	Small-scale privatization	1.1	1.93	2.00
	Infrastructure	1.00	1.00	1.00
	Restructuring	1.00	1.4	1.00
	EBRD average	1.06	1.4	1.3

Annexe 3.2   (Continued)

Country code	EBRD index	1990–5	1996–2000	2001–present
UKR	Large-scale privatization	1.14	2.33	3.00
	Small-scale privatization	1.43	3.26	3.8
	Infrastructure	1.00	1.6	2.00
	Restructuring	1.14	2.00	2.00
	EBRD average	1.31	2.48	2.77
UZB	Large-scale privatization	1.38	2.67	2.67
	Small-scale privatization	1.71	3.00	3.00
	Infrastructure	1.00	1.2	1.67
	Restructuring	1.14	1.93	1.67
	EBRD average	1.4	2.1	2.1

Source: See text for explanation.

Acknowledgements

We are grateful to Ruslan Yemtsov, Cem Mete and participants at seminars where this study was presented: World Bank, School for Advanced International Studies in Washington DC, International Economic Association in Istanbul, and UNU-WIDER in Helsinki, as well as to the two referees and the editor of this volume, for useful comments and suggestions. The opinions expressed here are the authors' and should not be attributed to the World Bank or its affiliated organizations.

Notes

1. It includes all the republics of the FSU except the three Baltic republics and, since September 2008, Georgia.
2. Insignificant, and possibly perverse, effect of social transfers on inequality in Russia coincides with the earlier finding by Milanovic (1999: 316).
3. Azerbaijan and Turkmenistan are not included in the analysis because of the unreliability of their household surveys.
4. The reform areas are the following: large-scale privatization, small-scale privatization, governance and enterprise restructuring, price liberalization, trade and foreign exchange system, competition policy, banking reform and interest rate liberalization, securities markets and non-bank financial institutions, and infrastructure reform. The EBRD indexes come from the EBRD *Transition Report*, reflecting progress in all of these areas. Each of these individual EBRD indexes is reported on a 1 to 4+ scale with higher numbers indicating greater reform progress.
5. We do not have data for Bosnia and Herzegovina, and Montenegro.
6. The average unweighted means that each country/year counts as one observation.

7. GDP per capita (and total GDP) is measured at 2005 international prices.
8. Although ordinary least squares estimators are consistent, SURE provides greater efficiency, and efficiency gains increase as correlation between errors across equations goes up (which is the case here; see Greene 2000).
9. In regressions, decile share is expressed as a multiple of the mean rather than as the percentages of the total. Thus, the bottom decile's share of (say) 3 per cent of total income is translated as 0.3 mean incomes. This can be interpreted as the average income of the bottom decile normalized by the mean.
10. Inflation is defined, as usual, as ln (1 + annual inflation rate); the EBRD index runs from 1 to 4.33. Real growth rate, annual inflation, and government expenditure as a share of GDI are all from the World Bank database (World Development Indicators). *Polity2* variable is from PolityIV database (accessible at http://www.systemicpeace.org/polity/polity4.htm), and EBRD index is compiled from various annual EBRD reports.
11. We perform the Breusch-Pagan test of independence to see whether correlations are zero or not. The null hypothesis of no correlation is rejected.
12. Some of the income distribution (decile) information is lost because of a lack of independent variables for those particular countries and years.
13. Calculated as follows: 1 per cent (0.01) acceleration multiplied by the coefficient of –0.265 and multiplied further by 10 (since decile shares are expressed as the multiples of the mean) and then divided by the average decile share of the bottom (3.2 per cent).
14. The results are not shown here but they are available from the authors on request.
15. Of course, this is merely of econometric rather than real relevance since a one point increase in EBRD index may involve vastly different policies in the case of infrastructure reform compared with the case of small-scale privatization.

References

Atkinson, A.B., T. Piketty and E. Saez (2011) 'Top Incomes in the Long Run of History', *Journal of Economic Literature*, 49(1): 3–71.

Bollen, K. and R.W. Jackman (1985) 'Political Democracy and the Size Distribution of Income', *American Sociological Review*, 50: 438–57.

Bulir, A. (2001) 'Income Inequality: Does Inflation Matter?', *IMF Staff Papers*, 48(1): 139–59.

Ferreira, F. (1999) 'Economic Transition and the Distributions of Income and Wealth', *Economics of Transition*, 7(2): 377–410.

Giammatteo, M. (2006) 'Inequality in Transition Countries: The Contributions of Markets and Government Taxes and Transfers', *LIS Working Papers No. 443*.

Gorodnichenko, Y., K.S. Peter and D. Stolaryov (2010) 'Inequality and Volatility Moderation in Russia: Evidence from Micro-level Panel Data on Consumption and Income', *Review of Economic Dynamics*, 13: 209–37.

Greene, W.H. (2000) *Econometric Analysis*, 5th edn., Prentice Hall: New York and London.

Hellman, J. (1988) 'Winners Take All: The Politics of Partial Reform in Postcommunist Transitions', *World Politics*, 50(2): 203–34.

Ivanova, M. (2006) 'Inequality and Government Policies in Central and Eastern Europe', paper presented at the *Annual Meeting of the International Studies Association, 22 March, San Diego*.

Ivaschenko, A. (2002) 'Growth and Inequality: Evidence from Transitional Economies', in T.S. Eicher and S.J. Turnovsky (eds), *Inequality and Growth: Theory and Policy Implications*, MIT Press: Cambridge, MA and London.

Keane, M. and E. Prasad (2002) 'Inequality, Transfers, and Growth: New Evidence from the Economic Transition in Poland', *Review of Economics and Statistics*, 84(2): 324–41.

Li, H., L. Squire and H. Zou (1998) 'Explaining International and Intertemporal Variations in Income Inequality', *Economic Journal*, 108(446): 26–43.

Milanovic, B. (1999) 'Explaining the Increase in Inequality during Transition', *Economics of Transition*, 7(2): 299–341.

Milanovic, B. (2008) 'Where in the World Are You? Assessing the Importance of Circumstance and Effort in a World of Different Mean Country Incomes and (Almost) no Migration', *World Bank Policy Research Working Papers No. 4493*, World Bank: Washington, DC.

Mitra, P. and R. Yemtsov (2006) 'Increasing Inequality in Transition Economies: Is There More to Come?', *World Bank Policy Research Working Papers No. 4007*, World Bank: Washington, DC.

Palma, J.G. (2006) 'Globalizing Inequality: "Centrifugal" and "Centripetal" Forces at Work', *UNDESA Working Papers No. 35*, UN Department of Economic and Social Affairs: New York.

Rodrik, D. (1999) 'Democracies Pay Higher Wages', *Quarterly Journal of Economics*, 114(3): 707–38.

Sukiassyan, G. (2007) 'Inequality and Growth: What Does the Transition Economy Data Say?', *Journal of Comparative Economics*, 35(1): 35–56.

4

Twenty Years of Political Transition

Daniel Treisman

1 Measuring democracy

To assess the extent of change in the political systems of the former communist states since 1989, some metric is needed. Compiling cross-national indexes of democracy has become something of a new industry in recent decades, and three products have pretty much cornered the market. Since 1973, Freedom House, a non-profit advocacy group, founded in New York in 1941 to promote democracy and expand political and economic freedom around the world, has compiled annual ratings of the extent of political and civil liberties in different countries. These ratings, on a 7-point scale, are based, according to Freedom House, on 'a multilayered process of analysis and evaluation by a team of regional experts and scholars'.[1] The Polity project, begun around the same time by a political scientist, Ted Robert Gurr, also evaluates countries annually on the authority characteristics of their political regimes, rating them on a 21-point scale that runs from -10 (a fully institutionalized autocracy) to $+10$ (a fully institutionalized democracy).[2] Finally, a team at the World Bank has been compiling a dataset of worldwide governance indicators (WGIs), at first biannually and now annually. Among these is an index of perceived 'voice and accountability' in countries around the world. Although this is useful for various purposes, a number of features of the voice and accountability index render it less useful for my analysis here. First, the index is available only from 1996, which reduces its value for assessing the dynamics of post-communist transition. Second, the index aims to capture perceptions of democracy rather than to analyze the objective reality (unlike the Freedom House and Polity democracy ratings). Since it is quite likely that in the post-communist world perceptions diverge from the objective reality, this is a problem. Third, the index is an aggregate of many individual sources, which makes it even harder than in the other two cases to be sure exactly what the differences in scores across countries are measuring. (The voice and accountability index also includes the Freedom House data among its sources, with a very high weight; see Kaufmann et al. 2009: 31.) Consequently, I will not discuss the WGI further.

Two other possible sources are the measures of democracy produced by collaborators of Adam Przeworski and the indexes of legislative and executive electoral competitiveness included in the Database of Political Institutions (DPI), compiled under the leadership of Philip Keefer, also at the World Bank.[3] The Przeworski team operationally defines 'democracy' as a regime in which the chief executive and legislature are elected, in which more than one party is allowed to compete for office, and in which the current incumbents have not won three or more elections in a row. This definition deliberately 'errs on the conservative side', classifying as dictatorships those regimes that enjoy extended popularity, such as the administration of Franklin Delano Roosevelt after 1940, but all definitions run into troublesome cases. The reason I do not use this one here is that it is dichotomous, and so does not tell us much about the paths—gradual and undulating, or direct and rapid—that countries took to reach democracy. The DPI measures are also useful for various purposes. But they do not constitute a continuous measure of the degree of democracy and focus only on the competitiveness of elections, rather than a broader conception of democracy.

Given the availability of two potentially valuable sources of data on the same subject, one might begin in at least three ways. One sensible approach is to conduct analysis using all available sources and emphasize results that prove robust across them (e.g. Pop-Eleches 2007). Another is to examine the methods of data collection and the conceptualizations of the target variables of the different data sources and decide on this basis which is more appropriate for a given project. A third approach is to examine the data themselves, checking whether the ratings are consistent with other sources of information about the countries in question, and whether observed objective differences and similarities among countries show up in the ratings. If such a 'reality check' casts doubt on the ability of a data source to accurately distinguish between countries, then requiring results to be robust to the use of such data is likely to lead researchers astray.

Does the choice between Freedom House and Polity matter? In any given year, the two ratings are correlated (see Figure 4.1 for the 2007 scores). However, as Figure 4.1 shows, the countries to which Freedom House assigns the same score often have widely divergent scores on Polity's rating. Countries given 5s by Freedom House, for instance, are rated everything from −7 (close to consolidated autocracy) to +7 (close to consolidated democracy) by Polity. Similarly, countries given the same ratings by Polity sometimes have quite divergent ratings on the Freedom House index. So which data one chooses may very well affect the results.

On theoretical grounds, the Polity ratings have the advantage of using a 21-point scale that permits finer distinctions than the 7-point Freedom

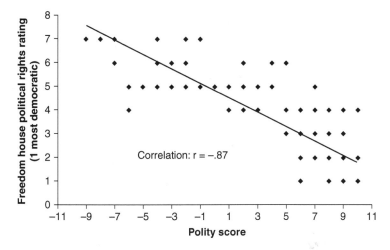

Figure 4.1   Freedom House and Polity democracy ratings, 2007
Source: See text for explanation.

House scale. What makes the decisive difference for me, however, is the results of the reality check. When it comes to the post-communist countries, the Freedom House data contain some curious anomalies. Consider Russia, which from 2005 to 2009 has been rated 6 on Freedom House's political rights scale, one step away from a pure autocracy.[4] This puts it on the same level as the United Arab Emirates (UAE).

Experts agree that Russia's political institutions in the late Putin era fell short of the democratic ideal. Elections were marred by significant falsification; certain candidates were prevented from running; and the state media—which includes all the main national television channels—provided disproportionate and overwhelmingly favourable coverage of the incumbents. In general, direct criticism of the president and prime minister were strongly discouraged on the three main state-owned national television stations. Nevertheless, the country was governed during these years under a democratic constitution by a popularly elected president and parliament. Despite electoral irregularities, most observers agree that the results of national elections did, by and large, reflect popular preferences. Credible polls suggest that the popularity of President, now Prime Minister, Putin was quite genuine. Freedom of the press, although constricted, continued to exist on the internet, in print media, on one national radio station, and on some local and cable television stations. In the 2008 presidential election, a communist, an extreme nationalist, and a centrist ran against the Kremlin-favoured incumbent, and were given hours of free airtime on national television to debate with each other and present their positions.[5]

The UAE, on the other hand, is a federation of seven absolute dynastic monarchs whose appointees make all executive and legislative decisions. The only 'parliament' is a consultative assembly, whose members are either appointed by the emirs or chosen by a college of electors whom the emirs also select. According to Freedom House, there is evidence that 'members of the royal family and the country's police' use 'torture against political rivals'. In Russia, political parties are weak. In the UAE, they do not exist.[6] For a research project that relies on making fine distinctions between countries' political regimes, a rating that equates these two objectively quite different systems is not very useful. In 2007, Polity IV rated Russia 5, on a level with Venezuela and Ecuador, and UAE −8.[7]

Another post-communist country on which the Polity and Freedom House rates differ is Estonia, which received a perfect political rights score of 1 from Freedom House but a 6 (on the scale that runs from −10 to +10) from Polity. The reason Polity did not give the country a perfect score is that the Estonian authorities discriminate against their Russian-speaking minority. In order to acquire citizenship—without which they may not vote in national and EU elections or join political parties—residents must pass a demanding oral and written exam in the Estonian language. As a result, in 2006 a significant part of the population—9 per cent (almost 120,000 people) according to Estonian official statistics—remained without citizenship and thus disenfranchised.[8] Estonia has been criticized for this and for other kinds of discrimination against its ethnic minorities by Amnesty International, the Council of Europe, and the UN's Special Rapporteur on Racism.[9] One can debate the historical context and the politics of the Estonian authorities' decisions, but it is hard to see how the disenfranchisement of almost one tenth of the population is consistent with a rating of perfect democracy.

Since 1996, Freedom House has also published a more fine-grained assessment of democracy in the post-communist countries—the Nations in Transit rating, which is on a continuous scale. The late start, well into the post-communist transition, creates problems in using these data to study the trajectory of change. But even were it not for this, it turns out that the Nations in Transit scores correlate with the simple Freedom House political rights scores at $r = 0.97$. The Nations in Transit scorers evaluate four dimensions of democracy: the competitiveness of the political process, the degree of development of civil society, the independence of the media, and the quality of public administration and governance. Yet, with their more complex methodology, they arrive at almost exactly the same results. Estonia gets the second highest score of all the post-communist countries, surpassed only by Slovenia. Russia is around the level of Tajikistan, which was also in the Freedom House political rights ratings on a level with the UAE. For these reasons, I focus in this study on the Polity data.[10]

2 Transition trajectories

Figure 4.2 shows the average Polity scores for the 26 former communist countries covered by the dataset from 1985 to 2007, the latest year for which data were available. On average, these countries experienced a surge of democratization in 1989–92, reaching the lower borders of what Polity classifies as 'democracy.' There was a slight reversion on average in the mid-1990s, followed by upward movement in the 2000s to something close to the top of the scale. By 2005 the median country had reached a score of 8 on the scale, on which 10 signifies a pure democracy.

The jump in democracy remains impressive if we compare it with what happened in other countries that started towards the bottom of the Polity scale in 1985. That year, the communist countries studied here ranged in Polity scores between −9 (Albania) and −5 (Yugoslavia). The dashed line in Figure 4.2 shows the mean Polity scores in subsequent years for all other countries that had Polity scores of −9 to −5 in 1985. As we see, there was a wave of democratization in the late 1980s and early 1990s outside the communist world as well as within it. However, the communist countries on average reformed much faster and reached a higher level of democracy. The

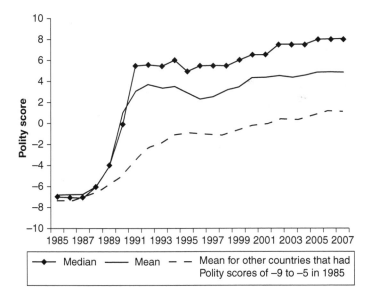

Figure 4.2 The transition from communism: average Polity score of 26 former communist states, 1985–2007

Note: Polity scores: 10 = pure democracy; −10 = pure autocracy.
Source: Based on data from Polity IV, www.systemicpeace.org/polity/polity4.htm; 26 former communist states.

averages, however, conceal a great deal of variation in the transition path. And this variation correlates strongly with geography. Figure 4.3 (panels a–f) shows the average path of countries' Polity scores for six sub-regions of the former communist world.

From studying these graphs and those for individual countries, several patterns of political change emerge. The average pathway in both Eastern Europe (EE) and the Baltic might be called the 'sprint to democracy'. Countries shoot up the Polity scale in the first years of transition, becoming clearly democratic, and then stabilize at a high level, or over time creep even higher. This pattern fits the particular trajectories of Hungary, Poland, the Czech Republic, Slovakia, Bulgaria, Slovenia, Latvia, and Lithuania. At the other end of the spectrum, there is the failure to take off that characterizes the Central Asian states: an initial, relatively weak rise towards democracy, followed in the mid-1990s by reversion to authoritarian government. This pattern fits Kazakhstan, Uzbekistan, Turkmenistan, Azerbaijan, and Belarus. In the case of Belarus, however, the initial rise was very substantial (up to +7), and so was the subsequent fall after the dictator Aleksandr Lukashenko was elected and consolidated control. Between these two polar versions of transition are several more complicated ones. There is the 'sprint, then jog, to democracy' of countries where the initial spurt takes them only part of the way, and which then converge gradually over the course of the

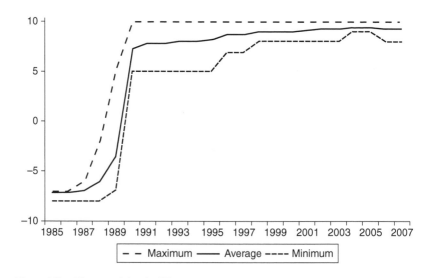

Figure 4.3a   The transition in EE
Note: Polity scores: 10 = pure democracy; −10 = pure autocracy
Source: Based on data from Polity IV, www.systemicpeace.org/polity/polity4.htm; EE: Bulgaria, Czech Republic, Hungary, Poland, Romania, Slovakia.

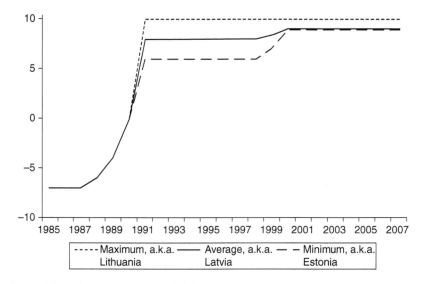

Figure 4.3b The transition in the Baltics

Note: Polity scores: 10 = pure democracy; −10 = pure autocracy.
Source: Based on data from Polity IV, www.systemicpeace.org/polity/polity4.htm; Baltics: Latvia, Lithuania, Estonia.

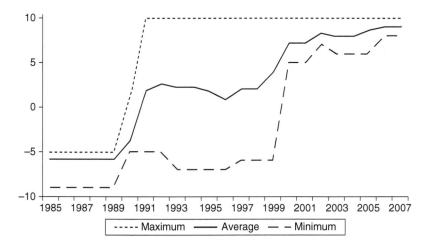

Figure 4.3c The transition in the Balkans

Note: Polity scores: 10 = pure democracy; −10 = pure autocracy.
Source: Based on data from Polity IV, www.systemicpeace.org/polity/polity4.htm; Balkans: Albania, Croatia, Macedonia, Serbia (and Montenegro), Slovenia.

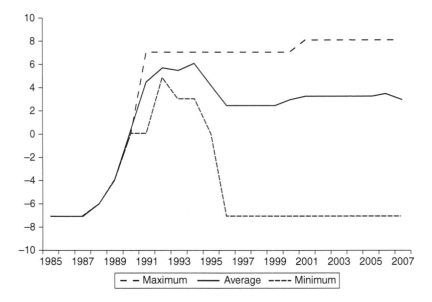

Figure 4.3d   The transition in the European CIS
Note: Polity scores: 10 = pure democracy; −10 = pure autocracy.
Source: Based on data from Polity IV, www.systemicpeace.org/polity/polity4.htm; European CIS:
Belarus, Moldova, Russia, Ukraine.

1990s and 2000s on the high level of democracy achieved by the EE countries. This is illustrated by the average for the Balkan countries, and among
individual cases fits those of Romania, Albania, Macedonia, and Moldova.
Similar in some ways is the 'late sprint to democracy' found in Croatia and
Serbia: very little movement towards democracy occurs in the early 1990s
but then after 1998 both shoot up to +7 or +8 on the scale. This might
have something to do with the war that was taking place in or around their
territories.

In the final two patterns, the country stalls somewhere in the middle
region. In 'sprint to the edge, then stall', countries surge in the early years
to the 5–7 range that marks the border of democracy, and then seem to get
stuck there, bumping up or down a point or two temporarily, but neither
reaching the 8–10 range of consolidated democracy nor falling back into
clearly authoritarian territory. This trajectory is illustrated by the average for
the countries of the European part of the Commonwealth of Independent
States (CIS) and fits the histories of Russia, Ukraine, Georgia, Armenia (if one
disregards a major temporary reversion in 1995–8), and Estonia (which, as
noted, is dragged down below its Baltic peers by its treatment of ethnic
Russian residents). 'Jog half-way, then stop' is a pattern that may turn into

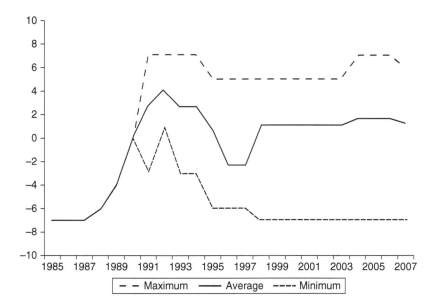

Figure 4.3e The transition in the Caucasus
Note: Polity scores: 10 = pure democracy; −10 = pure autocracy.
Source: Based on data from Polity IV, www.systemicpeace.org/polity/polity4.htm; Caucasus: Armenia, Azerbaijan, Georgia.

either a very slow version of 'sprint, then jog, to democracy' or a slow version of 'failure to take off'. It involves rising modestly to stabilize in the mid-range of −3 to +3. This pattern fits the average for the Caucasus and the individual cases of Tajikistan and Kyrgyzstan.

One final point to note about the trajectories featured in Figure 4.3 is the very different levels of variation in patterns within different geographical sub-regions. At both extremes, variation is relatively low. In EE and the Baltics, all countries travel in a tight cohort, with little difference between the most democratic and least democratic in a given year. To a slightly lesser degree, the Central Asian states also travel together— or rather fail to travel together—almost all staying towards the bottom of the scale. In the Balkans, the dashed lines that show the gap between the most and least democratic countries describe the shape of a snake that has swallowed something large. In the 1990s, countries in the Balkans ranged between 'pure democracies', such as Slovenia, and close to pure autocracies, such as Serbia. Yet this variation disappeared after 2000. All countries converged on relatively high-quality democracy. In the Caucasus and the European CIS, things remain more interesting. After the early years of democratization, the funnel opened up—countries ranged between

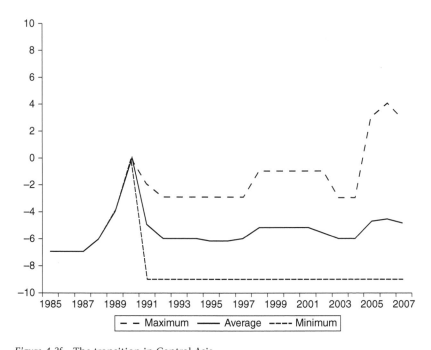

*Figure 4.3*f   The transition in Central Asia

Note: Polity scores: 10 = pure democracy; −10 = pure autocracy.
Source: Based on data from Polity IV, www.systemicpeace.org/polity/polity4.htm; Central Asia: Kazakhstan, Kyrgyzstan, Tajikistan, Turkmenistan, Uzbekistan.

very low and relatively high scores, and the large dispersion remains today.

If there is any conclusion to be drawn from considering these trajectories, it is about the apparent importance of geography. In most EE countries, the Baltics, and the Balkans, one can already say that the transition to democracy has been a success, although it took longer in some countries than in others, and reversions in some are still not ruled out. In Central Asia, attempts to build democracy have so far almost entirely failed, and few will probably be surprised if Kyrgyzstan and Tajikistan, currently in an institutional no-man's land, revert to join their Central Asian neighbours in consolidated autocracy. In between the Baltics and Central Asia—in the European CIS and the Caucasus—the outcomes seem to have been far less strongly predetermined. In these countries, the political future was much more in play. A dictator like Lukashenko could pull his country in a direction different from those followed by Ukraine and Russia.

3 Explaining differences in democracy as of 2007

Why have some of the communist countries become consolidated democracies while others have reverted to authoritarian government? What can explain the noted geographical patterns? To explore this, I ran a number of regressions, seeking to find what factors could both account for the variation in the Polity scores of these countries as of 2007 and steal away the explanatory power of geography. The results are shown in Table 4.1.

Many kinds of factors might have influenced the path of political transition of the communist countries. Some are relatively exogenous, predetermined by forces that were not themselves shaped by the transition itself. Others have to do with particular choices made by participants in the period of change. Since these are the sort of factors that might be reshaped by policy or short-term political conjuncture, it is natural to hope that they are significant so that one can devise ways to quickly reverse undesirable outcomes. Moving from more exogenous to more endogenous factors, I looked for evidence of the influence of countries': geographical location (distance from Western Europe), natural endowments (since oil and minerals are often thought to predispose countries towards authoritarian rule), ethnic heterogeneity and religious traditions, level of economic development and industrialization, political legacy (for how many years the country had lived under communism, what empires had dominated the territory in the period since 1800, whether the country had enjoyed independent statehood between the two world wars), and political institutions in the post-communist era (parliamentary or presidential regime). All of these have been associated by numerous scholars with the quality and durability of democracy. Note first that among the 26 post-communist countries for which data were available, a simple proxy for distance from Western Europe—I use the distance of the country's capital from Düsseldorf, Germany—can account for 58 per cent of the variation (column 1). As was evident in considering trajectories in the previous section, the further east a communist country was, the less likely it was to achieve consolidated democracy by 2007. This relationship is plotted in Figure 4.4. Closeness to Western Europe might matter for at least two reasons: it might increase the diffusion of democratic attitudes and ideas from the West; and it might render the country's future integration into West European institutions, such as the European Union, more plausible (Kopstein and Reilly 2000). However, as will become apparent, the data suggest another interpretation.

Greater endowments of minerals, and in particular oil, have been associated with less democratic government (Ross 2001). To capture such effects, I used a variable measuring the total quantity of oil produced in the country in the years 1970–89, in metric tons, calculated from Michael Ross's dataset on oil and gas. As column 2 shows, this did not have a statistically significant effect, or affect the estimated influence of geography or the

Table 4.1 Correlates of democracy in the post-communist countries, 2007

					Dependent variable: Polity score, 2007					
	(1)	(2)	(3)	(4)	(5)	(6)	(7)	(8)	(9)	(10)
Constant	11.94[c] (1.34)	11.96[c] (2.43)	10.19[c] (2.89)	12.26[c] (1.11)	10.54[c] (2.19)	16.82[c] (5.76)	11.90[c] (1.74)	11.43[c] (2.35)	10.92[c] (1.54)	8.97[c] (1.39)
Geography										
Distance from Düsseldorf, th. km	-3.38[c] (0.62)	-3.41[c] (0.67)	-2.97[c] (0.88)	-2.80[c] (0.93)	-3.09[c] (0.73)	-3.65[c] (0.70)	-3.38[c] (0.68)	-3.26[c] (0.81)	-2.25[b] (0.93)	0.27 (1.36)
Endowments										
Log of oil produced, 1970–89		.011 (.11)								
Historical empire										
Habsburg			1.99 (2.26)							
Ottoman			2.54 (2.08)							
Independent interwar state					2.48 (1.58)					
FSU				-2.77 (2.38)						-3.83 (2.60)
Ethnicity and religion										
Ethnic homogeneity (share of population of largest ethnicity)						-5.53 (6.59)				
Protestant share							-0.002 (0.030)			
Catholic share								0.014 (0.022)		
Muslim share									-0.063 (0.046)	-0.01 (0.02)
Muslim share × former Soviet										-0.14[c] (0.03)
R^2	0.5847	0.5820	0.6038	0.6112	0.6069	0.5911	0.5745	0.5845	0.6203	0.7326
N	26	25	26	26	25	25	24	25	26	26

Dependent variable: Polity score 2007

	(11)	(12)	(13)	(14)	(15)	(16)	(17)	(18)
Constant	15.85[c]	11.55[b]	12.35[c]	21.12[c]	9.75[c]	21.05[b]	19.29[c]	18.13[c]
	(2.29)	(4.19)	(1.22)	(5.44)	(3.19)	(8.21)	(5.49)	(4.61)
Distance from Düsseldorf, th. km	-3.95[c]	-3.11[c]	-3.31[c]	-1.81	-2.89[c]	1.32	1.35	
	(0.71)	(0.88)	(0.82)	(1.32)	(0.90)	(1.97)	(1.78)	
Muslim share						-0.00	-0.01	
						(0.02)	(0.02)	
Muslim share x former Soviet						-0.15[c]	-0.14[c]	-0.11[c]
						(0.03)	(0.03)	(0.04)
Former Soviet republic						0.12		
						(1.67)		
Independent interwar state						0.13		
						(0.66)		
Economic development								
GDP per capita PPP 1989, thousand US$[1]	-0.55							
	(0.37)							
GDP per capita PPP 1990, thousand US$[2]		0.02						
		(0.36)						
Agricultural value added as % of GDP 1990, WDI			-0.024					
			(0.086)					
Political institutions								
Years communist				-0.23		-0.29	-0.27	-0.21[a]
				(0.15)		(0.22)	(0.16)	(0.10)
DPI system: parl = 2, pres = 0, strong pres elected by parl = 1					1.42	-0.46		
					(1.21)	(0.42)		
R^2	0.6058	0.5489	0.5825	0.6618	0.6082	0.7877	0.7881	0.7745
N	25	24	25	26	25	25	26	26

Note: OLS, robust standard errors. [a]$p < 0.10$, [b]$p < 0.05$, [c]$p < 0.01$. [1]Fischer and Sahay (2000); [2]WDI (2009).
Source: Author's calculations; see text.

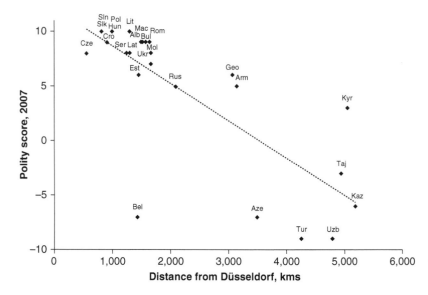

Figure 4.4   Distance from Düsseldorf and Polity rating, 2007
Source: See text for explanation.

amount of variation explained. It might be that countries' pre-communist history affected the extent to which democracy developed in the post-communist years. I classified countries on the basis of which of the three main East European empires—Russian, Ottoman, or Habsburg—had had the greatest influence over the country's current territory during the period after 1800. (I show regressions using dummies for Ottoman and Habsburg domination in Table 4.1, column 3; Russian domination is the excluded category.) Inevitably, this required some perhaps questionable judgment calls. For instance, I classified the dominant influence over Serbia as being the Ottomans rather than the Habsburgs, and the main influence over Azerbaijan as being the Russians rather than the Ottomans. As a check, I also tried classifications that took into account all the empires that had controlled part or all of the territory at some point since 1800. In neither case did the imperial history variables prove statistically significant. I also tried including dummy variables for whether the country had been a for-mer Soviet republic or had had its own independent state in the interwar period. Both variables had the expected sign (negative for the former Soviet republics and positive for interwar statehood), but neither of these was sta-tistically significant (columns 4 and 5). None of these historical variables caused a large drop in the coefficient on distance from Düsseldorf, so they do not seem to explain much of the geographical pattern. To look for the effects of ethnic heterogeneity, I tried including three alternative measures, constructed by Jim Fearon, each of which reflects the distribution of ethnic groups in the population as of 1990: the population shares of the largest and second-largest ethnic groups, and an index of ethnic fractionalization. None of these was statistically significant, and none reduced the explanatory power of geographical location or increased the variation explained by much. In column 6, I show the result for the first of these.

Religious and cultural traditions are often thought to influence the development of political regimes. In these regressions, the proportion of Protestants or Catholics in the population (as of 1980) had no evident effect, but the proportion that were Muslim adherents did.[11] Including a measure of the share of the population that were Muslim adherents reduced the effect of geography by about one third. The Muslim share was not itself significant. However, if one breaks down the Muslims into those that live in the Balkans and Eastern Europe, on the one hand, and those that live in the former Soviet republics, on the other, a clear result emerges. Although the proportion of Muslim adherents in the Balkans and EE is unrelated to the degree of democracy (as we might expect, given the universally high levels of democracy in these regions), states with more Muslim adherents in the former Soviet world were far less democratic (column 10). Including in the regression also a dummy for former Soviet republics (so as to avoid mistaking the effect of Soviet legacy for an effect of Muslim heritage), geographical location is no longer significant and even has a positive sign.

At the start of transition, the communist countries were at very different levels of economic development. The association between economic development and democracy is one of the best known correlations in the social sciences.[12] Did it make a difference here? Answering this is complicated by the great divergence between estimates of what the initial levels of real GDP per capita in these countries were. Consider three relatively authoritative sources of estimates of countries' GDP, adjusted for purchasing power parity—the International Monetary Fund (IMF) (as published in Fischer and Sahay 2000), the World Bank's World Development Indicators (WDIs) (which obtain their data from the International Comparison Program), and the estimates of Angus Maddison of the Organisation for Economic Co-operation and Development (OECD) (Maddison 2003). The estimates of Russia's per capita GDP at purchasing power parity in 1989 or 1990 ranged from US$5,627 (Fischer and Sahay 2000: 36) to US$9,086 (WDIs as of 2009), with the Maddison estimate in between, at US$7,773. The problem is compounded by the fact that the International Comparison Program changes its retrospective estimates of GDP per capita every few years, sometimes by large amounts. Given this, I tried using two alternative measures: those of the IMF and the WDIs, as of 1989–90. Adding these to regressions including just distance from Düsseldorf, neither measure of national income per capita was significant, and neither reduced the estimated effect of location much. I also tried using instead a measure of the agricultural share of GDP in 1990 to pick up effects of initial underdevelopment, but again found no evidence that this mattered (columns 11–13).

Turning to political institutions, whether the country established a presidential, parliamentary, or mixed system, as coded by a team from the World Bank in the Database of Political Institutions (Beck et al. 2001), was not significant and induced only a small drop in the location variable's coefficient (column 15). However, the number of years a country had been communist did appear potentially important; although it was not itself statistically significant, including this reduced the size of the location coefficient by almost 50 per cent (column 14). Based on this preliminary investigation, I show some models including several explanatory variables in columns 16–18. First, in column 16, I show that once we control for the Muslim religion, distinguishing between former Soviet and other Muslims, along with the duration of communism in the country, whether the country had a parliamentary or presidential system and whether the country had had an independent state in the interwar period were completely insignificant, the former now with the 'wrong' sign. We see in columns 16 and 17 that Muslim religion and the number of years under communism can completely account for the effect of location, and actually change the sign of its coefficient. Column 17 drops the dummy for former Soviet states, which is highly correlated with the number of years under communism ($r = 0.84$) and far less significant when the two are included together. Finally, column 18 shows a parsimonious model including just the proportion of Muslims in former Soviet states and the duration of communism. These variables, by themselves, can account for more than three-quarters of the variation in the 2007 Polity scores, including the part correlated with location (adding the distance from Düsseldorf increases the R^2 only slightly, and the variable has a counterintuitive positive sign).

Table 4.2 shows some robustness checks, attempting to weaken the observed relationship between the Polity score, on the one hand, and Soviet Muslim heritage and years under communism, on the other. Column 1 repeats the model from Table 4.1, column 18. Column 2 adds dummy variables for the different regional sub-groups. This actually increases the size of the coefficients on both the Soviet Muslim share and the years communist, although the latter is no longer statistically significant. None of the regional dummies is significantly different from EE, and the proportion of variation explained is only slightly higher. Column 3 controls for current GDP per capita, rather than GDP per capita at the start of transition. Counterintuitively, this turns out to be negatively correlated with democracy (although not statistically significant), after controlling for Soviet Muslim heritage and years under communism. There is no gain in explanatory power, and the coefficients on the two main explanatory variables are the same or slightly larger. In column 4, I try controlling for whether the country experienced a civil war in the transition period.[13] The coefficient on the civil

Table 4.2 Correlates of democracy, robustness checks

Dependent variable	(1) Polity 2007	(2) Polity 2007	(3) Polity 2007	(4) Polity 2007	(5) Polity democracy score 2007	(6) Polity parcomp 2007	(7) Polity 1998	(8) Polity 2007	(9) Polity 2007
Constant	18.13[c] (4.61)	19.20[b] (7.72)	20.43[c] (5.70)	18.38[c] (4.55)	15.66[c] (2.32)	5.84[c] (0.86)	13.02[b] (5.39)	18.63[c] (4.09)	9.18[c] (0.23)
Muslim share* former Soviet	-0.11[c] (0.04)	-0.13[c] (0.03)	-0.11[b] (0.04)	-0.11[c] (0.04)	-0.06[c] (0.02)	-0.02[b] (0.01)	-0.11[c] (0.04)		-0.11[b] (0.04)
Years communist	-0.21[a] (0.10)	-0.23 (0.18)	-0.23[a] (0.11)	-0.22[a] (0.11)	-0.15[c] (0.05)	-0.04[b] (0.02)	-0.14 (0.11)	-0.22[b] (0.09)	
Region dummies (*EE* excluded)									
Balkans		0.18 (0.64)							
Baltic		0.81 (2.03)							
Europeand CIS		-0.13 (1.19)							
Caucasus		2.75 (4.94)							
Central Asia		2.55 (6.16)							
GDP per capita PPP 2007 thousand US$ [1]			-0.08 (0.08)						

Table 4.2 (Continued)

Dependent variable	(1) Polity 2007	(2) Polity 2007	(3) Polity 2007	(4) Polity 2007	(5) Polity democracy score 2007	(6) Polity parcomp 2007	(7) Polity 1998	(8) Polity 2007	(9) Polity 2007
Civil war dummy				1.76 (1.66)					
Central Asia + Azerbaijan								-8.40[c] (2.94)	
Baltics + Moldova									-1.15 (0.80)
Other FSU									-5.63[a] (2.86)
R^2	0.7745	0.7848	0.7434	0.7877	0.8684	0.6111	0.6028	0.7762	0.7705
N	26	26	25	26	26	25	26	26	26

Note: OLS, robust standard errors. [a]$p < 0.10$, [b]$p < 0.05$, [c]$p < 0.01$; [1]WDI (2009).
Source: Author's calculations; see text.

war dummy has an unexpected positive sign, although it is not statistically significant. Soviet Muslim tradition and communist legacy remained significant with coefficients that were not much changed. Column 5 replaces the Polity score, which consists of the sum of Polity's democracy and authoritarianism scores, with just the democracy score (on the 0–10 scale). The results are similar, and now 87 per cent of the variation is explained. Since the dependent variable is now measured on an 11-point, rather than a 21-point, scale, the coefficients are correspondingly somewhat smaller. Column 6 uses as a dependent variable one component of the 2007 Polity democracy score—arguably the one that is least subjective in the coding—the Polity measure of the competitiveness of participation (parcomp). Countries are rated on a five-point scale that runs from 'repressed' (no significant oppositional activity is permitted outside the ranks of the regime and ruling party) to 'competitive' (when stable and enduring political groups compete for national office, without much coercion or disruption). Again, the proportion of Muslims in former Soviet countries and the number of years under communism are significant, and they together explain more than 60 per cent of the variation. Column 7 examines whether the apparent effect of Muslim heritage and years under communism is something new that has emerged in recent years or is a result that would also have shown up in the 1990s. I use as the dependent variable Polity's rating as of 1998. Again, the results are similar, although only 60 per cent of the variation is explained. The Soviet Muslim variable has the same coefficient, but the years under communism variable is somewhat smaller and is no longer statistically significant. This is because of the former Yugoslav states of Serbia and Croatia, which were highly authoritarian in the 1990s despite a relatively shorter time under communism; controlling for the Balkans, one obtains the same coefficient on years under communism as before (–0.21, p < 0.05).

The proportion of Muslims in former Soviet republics variable singles out the Central Asian states plus Azerbaijan (the variable correlates with a dummy for these six states at $r = 0.98$). As might be expected given this correlation, including both in the regression, neither is statistically significant. Replacing the Soviet Muslim variable by the dummy for Central Asia plus Azerbaijan yields a marginally higher R^2. Could there be some factor other than a high proportion of Muslims that unites and distinguishes these six states and that leads to authoritarian government? This is certainly possible, but it is not obvious what that other factor might be. It is not mineral wealth, since countries like Uzbekistan and Kyrgyzstan have little in the way of mineral resources. Nor can it be southern location or agricultural workforce, since Armenia and Georgia are as far south as Azerbaijan, and Georgia and Moldova were as agricultural as the six states in question at the start of transition.

The years communist variable might appear to be picking up just the three-way division between the EE and Balkan states, communized at the end of the Second World War, the Baltics and parts of Moldova, occupied by Stalin's troops in 1940, and the other Soviet republics, incorporated into the USSR in the early 1920s. Including dummies for the Baltics plus Moldova, and for the remaining former Soviet states, yields an R^2 that is slightly lower than that in the column 1 model with years communist. Thus, it is possible that the years communist variable contains more relevant information than is captured by just this three-way division.

To recapitulate, one can account extremely well for the variation across the post-communist countries in levels of democracy as of 2007 with two variables, both of which reflect characteristics of the countries that were strongly correlated with geography and more or less fixed at the start of transition. Countries that had lived under communism for longer and, among the former Soviet republics, those that had more Muslim adherents tended to make a less complete transition to democracy during the years between 1989 and 2007.[14] Choices of political leaders during the transition period appear to have been secondary, or perhaps to have been largely determined by these aspects of the country's cultural and institutional legacies—except, perhaps, in one case. It seems to me that the election of Aleksandr Lukashenko in Belarus, and the determination of this individual to impose autocratic rule, changed the country's course in a quite fundamental way. If this is the case— and if our two explanatory variables, Muslim tradition and years communist, are the right ones—one should expect the relationship between these variables and the Polity score to be even stronger if we drop Belarus from the dataset. This is indeed the case. The R^2 rises from 0.77 to 0.88, and both explanatory variables are much more statistically significant than before.

4 Discussion

But what does all this mean? It is one thing to estimate some regressions, another to believe that what they are telling is 'the truth'. That a Muslim tradition constitutes some sort of obstacle—although by no means an insuperable one—to liberal democracy echoes a result found by scholars who have looked at the determinants of democracy in broader datasets of countries (Fish 2002). Fish presents evidence that the correlation between Islam and authoritarianism is explained in part by the greater prevalence of patriarchal gender relations in the Muslim world, and refers to some other scholars who have argued that 'the unusual tenacity of clan and tribal relations in Muslim societies...are inimical to democracy'. At least in published statistics, the huge gender gaps that Fish demonstrates for many Muslim countries do not show up in the former communist world. There is almost no literacy gap between males and females in the post-communist countries with large Muslim populations—the Central Asian states and Azerbaijan. Nor do these countries have particularly low representation of women in parliament.

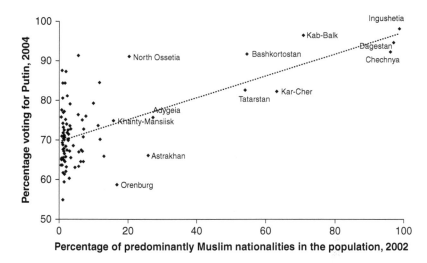

Figure 4.5 Muslim population and very high votes for Putin, 2004
Source: Based on data from Central Electoral Commission and Goskomstat RF.

The tenacity of clan networks may have more to do with it, although how exactly remains unclear. Within Russia, implausibly high electoral turnout and votes for central incumbents have become characteristic of various predominantly Muslim regions. Figure 4.5 shows the relationship for the 2004 presidential election, in which the incumbent, President Putin, won with 72 per cent of the valid vote nationwide. Many of the more egregious reports of electoral irregularities have come from traditionally Muslim regions like Dagestan, Ingushetia, and Chechnya.[15] In these regions, governors have established particularly effective, and repressive, political machines. What role if any Islam played in this is a subject that requires further research. It is also possible that in this region authoritarianism has been fuelled not so much by elements of Islam as by the fear of it, and by the attempts by incumbent regimes to protect against Islamic fundamentalism in anti-democratic ways. In Uzbekistan and Kyrgyzstan in the late 1990s, leaders used arbitrary arrests, imprisonment, and expulsion to crack down on those believed to be potential Islamic extremists (Collins 2002; Luong 2003). Within Russia, this has been one of the justifications for repression in parts of the North Caucasus where 'Wahhabi' terrorist groups have been active.

The second determinant—years under communism—is plausible but vague in its implications. What exactly happened to countries in those additional years of communist rule that reduced the impetus to create effective democratic institutions after communism fell? Whether or not the country had been part of the Soviet Union was not the crucial difference.[16] Nor was past experience of independent statehood (Table 4.1, column 16). Finally,

I tried to see if the level of economic development of the country at the time of communization made a difference. Using Maddison's data, which required huge approximations, such as using Maddison's estimate of average 'USSR' GDP per capita in 1913 ($1,488 1999 international Geary-Khamis dollars) for all the former USSR republics, I found no significant results. Perhaps better data on this would reveal patterns. But it is notable that the Czech Republic, by far the most developed of these countries at the time of communization, with estimated GDP per capita of $3,088 1990 dollars in 1948, was rated slightly less democratic in 2007 than Romania, which had estimated GDP per capita in 1946 of just $816 1990 dollars. There was great variation in the level of economic development among the EE countries at the time of communization, yet they have moved in a pack to high levels of democratic consolidation.

In short, I have no good answer. Countries that were incorporated by the Bolsheviks after 1917 are today the least democratic; those that were incorporated into the Soviet Union during the Second World War come second; and the countries that became communist, but not Soviet, after the end of the Second World War are today the most democratic. Why exactly, I cannot say. In addition, post-Soviet countries where more of the population was traditionally Muslim are today less democratic. Again, why exactly is a question for further research. The strong way in which the data point towards historical legacies—especially in EE, the Balkans, and Central Asia; less decisively in the European CIS and the Caucasus—is striking. It is also disappointing for those who hope, through policy advice, to increase the level of democracy in these countries in the short or medium run. So far, at least, the choices of different policies or of particular configurations of political institutions seem either to have been strongly determined by history and culture or to have mattered less than the historical contexts in which they were chosen.[17]

Acknowledgements

I thank János Kornai, Branko Milanovic, Ivan Szelényi, and other participants at the UNU-WIDER conference, Reflections on Transition: Twenty Years after the Fall of the Berlin Wall, Helsinki, September 2009; Yuliya Tverdova, David Laitin, and other participants at the conference 1989: Twenty Years After, at UC Irvine, November 2009, for helpful comments.

Notes

1. See Freedom House's website at www.freedomhouse.org/template.cfm?page=351&ana_page=354&year=2009.
2. For more details, see the Polity IV site at www.systemicpeace.org/polity/polity4.htm.
3. See Przeworski et al. (2000), the DPI webpage at http://go.worldbank.org/2EAGGLRZ40.

4. Freedom House states on its website that the rating of Russia does not include Chechnya, where political rights are certainly far less than in most other parts of the country.
5. See Treisman (2010: Chapter 10). I draw in this section on my discussion there.
6. The information about the UAE comes from Freedom House's own *Freedom in the World 2009*, available at www.freedomhouse.org/template.cfm?page=445.
7. In September 2009, I contacted Freedom House to ask whether the organization genuinely viewed Russia under Putin to be no more democratic than a federation of absolute autocrats. A representative explained that in Freedom House's finer-grained sub-scores, Russia was rated slightly above the UAE, with a total of 8 out of 40 for political rights, compared with UAE's 5. This is reassuring, as far as it goes. However, the sub-scores themselves raise additional puzzles. On the sum of the political rights sub-scores, Russia is rated lower than Mauritania, a country ruled by a military junta that had just staged a coup, deposing the elected president, arresting officials, and establishing control over the state broadcast media. On 'electoral process', Russia is judged on a level with Oman, where the only elections are for a consultative council without any legislative power.
8. 'Estonia Today: Population by Nationality', Estonian Ministry of Foreign Affairs, http://web-static.vm.ee/static/failid/460/Nationalities.pdf.
9. See Amnesty International, *Amnesty International Report 2009*, 'Estonia', http://report2009.amnesty.org/en/regions/europe-central-asia/estonia, and Freedom House, *Freedom in the World 2008*, 'Estonia', http://www.unhcr.org/refworld/country,,FREEHOU,,EST,4562d8b62,487ca209c,0.html.
10. Even the Polity coders may not be immune from outside pressure. Shortly after I had written the first draft of this study, I thought to check for updates on the Polity website. To my surprise, I found that Polity had indeed 'updated' some of its figures, reducing Russia's Polity score by one point for the entire period from 1992. The coders had also increased Estonia's rating from 6 to 9, close to a perfect score. The only explanation Polity provided for these changes referred to information that had been widely known for years and had already been mentioned in previous Polity reports. The director of the Polity team, when I contacted him to ask the reasons for these changes, explained that an ongoing re-evaluation of democracy scores was in progress. Despite my repeated enquiries, he did not give any specific explanation for the changes to Russia's and Estonia's scores. When I asked if these might have something to do with the fact that since the late 1990s the project has relied on funding from the US government's Political Instability Task Force, itself funded by the Central Intelligence Agency (see the Polity website www.systemicpeace.org/polity/polity4.htm), he replied: 'As regards my response to pressure from our US government supporters, you can be sure that I consider their perspectives as seriously as the many inquiries and criticisms I receive from academics and other experts. There has never been any serious arm-twisting from either side; not that such tactics would be strong enough to induce me to make changes that I did not feel were warranted by the evidence.' I do not doubt the integrity of the project's director. However, I remain baffled by why the project would be unwilling or unable to explain why the scores of these countries had been changed, purportedly on the basis of information that had been well known for years. In this study, I continue to use the original Polity ratings. These are certainly not perfect, but the apparent anomalies in the Polity codings for post-communist countries seem to me smaller than the anomalies in the Freedom House scores.

11. For the proportions of Protestant and Catholic adherents, I used data from Barrett (1982). However, because this source gave non-credible estimates of the proportion of Muslims for some countries (e.g. Albania), I used data from the Association of Religion Data Archives for estimates of the Muslim share of the population (see www.thearda.com/internationalData/countries/Country_3_1.asp).

12. For recent attempts to determine the direction of causation, see Boix and Stokes (2003) and Acemoglu et al. (2008).

13. I coded as 1 the countries Armenia, Azerbaijan, Croatia, Georgia, Russia, Serbia, and Tajikistan; as 0.5 Macedonia, Moldova, and Slovenia; and all others as 0. Bosnia was not in the dataset because of missing data.

14. Pop-Eleches (2007) finds similarly that a Muslim religious tradition and a history of pre-Second World War Soviet statehood correlate with lower democracy ratings.

15. For a review of reports of such irregularities, see Fish (2005).

16. See Table 4.1, column 16. Adding the dummy for the former Soviet republic to a model with just years communist and Soviet republic times Muslim adherents, the Soviet dummy was not significant and the R^2 was only 0.0004 higher.

17. Another question not addressed here is how economic performance during the transition period influenced the evolution of political regimes. In Treisman (2011), I argue that fluctuating performance of the Russian economy in the 1990s and 2000s helps explain the rises and falls in the ratings of presidents Yeltsin and Putin. Similar effects are likely to be found in other post-communist countries. The consequences for democratization, however, are complicated, since better economic performance will tend to entrench both democratically oriented and autocratically inclined incumbents. Thus, the impact on a country's political system will probably depend on what type of leader happened to be in charge in the years when the transitional depression turned into recovery.

References

Acemoglu, D., S. Johnson, J.A. Robinson and P. Yared (2008) 'Income and Democracy', *American Economic Review*, 98(3): 808–42.

Barrett, D. (ed.) (1982) *World Christian Encyclopedia*, Oxford University Press: New York.

Beck, T., G. Clarke, A. Groff, P. Keefer and P. Walsh (2001) 'New tools and new tests in comparative political economy: the database of political institutions', *World Bank Economic Review*, 15: 165–76.

Boix, C. and S. Stokes (2003) 'Endogenous Democratization', *World Politics*, 55: 517–49.

Collins, K. (2002) 'Clans, Pacts, and Politics in Central Asia', *Journal of Democracy*, 13(3): 137–52.

Fischer, S. and R. Sahay (2000) 'The Transition Economies after Ten Years', *IMF Working Paper* WP/00/30, IMF: Washington, DC.

Fish, M.S. (2002) 'Islam and Authoritarianism', *World Politics*, 55(1): 4–37.

Fish, M.S. (2005) *Democracy Derailed in Russia: the Failure of Open Politics*, Cambridge University Press: New York.

Kaufmann, D., A. Kraay and M. Mastruzzi (2009) 'Governance Matters VIII'. *World Bank Policy Research Working Papers No. 4978*.

Kopstein, J. and D. Reilly (2000) 'Geographic Diffusion and the Transformation of the Post-Communist World', *World Politics*, 53(1): 1–37.

Luong, P.J. (2003) 'The Middle Easternization of Central Asia', *Current History*, October.

Maddison, A. (2003) *The World Economy: Historical Statistics*, OECD Development Centre: Paris.

Pop-Eleches, G. (2007) 'Historical Legacies and Post-Communist Regime Change', *The Journal of Politics*, 69(4): 908–26.

Przeworski, A., M.E. Alvarez, J.A. Cheibub and F. Limongi (2000) *Democracy and Development: Political Institutions and Well-Being in the World, 1950–1990*, Cambridge University Press: Cambridge.

Ross, M. (2001) 'Does Oil Hinder Democracy?', *World Politics*, 53(3): 325–61.

Treisman, D. (2010) *The Return: Russia's Journey from Gorbachev to Medvedev*, The Free Press: New York.

Treisman, D. (2011) 'Presidential Popularity in a Hybrid Regime: Russia under Yeltsin and Putin', *American Journal of Political Science*, 55(3): 590–609.

5
Into the Void: Governing Finance in Central and Eastern Europe

Katharina Pistor

1 Introduction

This chapter traces the evolution of the financial system in the former socialist countries of Central and Eastern Europe (CEE) as they prepared themselves for entry into the European Union (EU). While it has often been asserted that EU accession has provided these countries with an important outside anchor (Berglöf and Bolton 2002), the analysis presented here suggests that the integration process also put these countries at great financial risk—one that materialized during the global financial crisis. Using the crisis as a starting point this chapter reflects on twenty years of transition in CEE and the governance void in matters of finance that it has created.

A functioning market-based economy depends on a well-working financial system—that is, on organizations that intermediate between savings and investments and allocate resources, as well as on institutional arrangements that mitigate the risk of collapse associated with complex financial systems. The former socialist countries of CEE possessed certain elements of a financial system, such as savings banks and organizations used by the government to store and to channel money; however, intermediation and allocation functions were centrally controlled and not left to autonomous actors. This arrangement was consistent with the organizational features of a centrally planned economy, but it was unsuitable for decentralized economies that relied increasingly on market mechanisms. For such economies to work, a new set of arrangements had to be found that allowed for greater dispersion of financial services combined with effective checks and balances to guard against the risk of systemic failure.

The story of the transformation of the financial sector in CEE from plan to market has often been told (Rostowski 1995; Buch 1996; Tihanyi and Hegarty 2007) so will not be recounted here. Nonetheless, recalling how finances were organized under socialist regimes serves to illustrate that the operation of financial systems is closely intertwined with the organization of the economies and the prevailing governance regime. The organization of finance takes one form under one regime and quite a different form under another. Market economies are commonly distinguished by the organization of their financial systems, whether they are predominantly market- or bank-based (Mayer 1998; Allen and Gale 2001). Both systems have their distinct institutional arrangements designed to address the specific vulnerabilities inherent in them. Market-based systems are vulnerable to the existence of stock market bubbles, which may result in a crash. Bank-based systems have a high probability of suffering from bank failures and from the cyclical nature of credit booms and busts. Most economies have both stock markets and banks (Levine 2003) and thus are, albeit to varying degrees, vulnerable to either shock.

The history of financial markets is a history of crises (Kindelberger 2005; Minsky 1986), but it is equally a history of attempts to mend the institutional arrangements that prevent them. Often overlooked is that crisis management itself is a critical part of the governance regime for financial markets—arguably the most important one. Once one recognizes that financial markets are inherently instable,[1] crisis management becomes an integral part of the governance of finance; it shapes the future behaviour of market participants—a fact that is widely acknowledged in concerns about the moral hazard associated with government bailouts. More importantly, it reveals who is the ultimate guardian of the financial system: whoever has the resources to rescue a financial system and as such is capable of setting the terms of the rescue deal. This role is typically denoted as 'lender of last resort'. In the context of the global crisis, the role has morphed into 'investor of last resort' and even into the all-encompassing 'whatever it takes' (Andrews 2009)—a commitment that is more appropriately labelled as 'ultimate guardian'. Using the guardian metaphor also emphasizes that crisis management is not about the bailing-out of individual banks or other intermediaries but is an attempt to prevent a collapse of the financial system.

This chapter argues that the designation of the ultimate guardian is the result of policy choices about the governance of finance. These include decisions about liberalizing capital accounts or not; building or not building reserves for 'rainy days'; pegging, floating, or managing the domestic currency; allowing foreign bank ownership/dominance, or restricting it; and accepting or rejecting the principle of home country regulation for foreign banks operating on one's territory. These decisions are not necessarily made for the purpose of outsourcing the function of the ultimate guardian. In fact, most made by countries in CEE were predetermined by the regional or global governance regimes they joined. The combined effect of these policies, however, has disabled governments in most CEE countries from protecting their economies against a looming crisis, as evidenced by their ultimately unsuccessful attempts to control the credit boom in the years leading up to the crisis; once the crisis erupted, causing the drying-up of external finance, they were unable to effectively respond to it as their resources were no match against the scale of private funds that had earlier flooded their economies. The key argument developed here is that countries in CEE were encouraged to proactively relinquish self-governance over their financial systems in favour of a regional regime. At the time, this appeared to be a small price to pay for the promise of European integration. Indeed, the EU has undertaken major efforts to Europeanize the governance of finance by standardizing financial regulation and improving co-ordination among national regulators (Corcoran and Hart 2002; Ferrarini 2002). It is in the interest of this collective enterprise for countries to cede some of their sovereignty over finance. Those countries that have joined the European Monetary Union have relinquished their domestic currencies and control over monetary policies (Zilioli and Selmayr 2001). Moreover, the policy advice given to political leaders in the former socialist world regarding the benefits of financial liberalization was motivated by a desire to protect their economies from undue political interference and thereby promote prosperity (World Bank 1995, 1996; Barth et al. 2004). Yet, there is a risk to this strategy; namely, that supranational governance regimes may be ineffective and/or serve ulterior interests, and the risk that in the event of a crisis, a country is forced to depend on an ultimate guardian over whose strategies and policy directions it has little control. In the context of the global financial crisis, many of these risks were realized in countries in CEE. This raises important questions about the costs and benefits of the manner in which not only countries in CEE but also other emerging markets integrated into the global financial system.

2   The role of ultimate guardian in the governance finance

The operation of finance rests on the credibility of a promise for future returns on investment. *Encyclopaedia Britannica* defines 'finance' as 'the process of raising funds or capital for any kind of expenditure',[2] explaining that some need more money today than they have on hand, while others have excess money that they can invest and thereby earn interests or dividends. The willingness of those with excess money to realize gains from parting with their money depends on the other party's ability to invest productively and to commit to pay returns. The regulatory regime for financial markets is primarily concerned with ensuring that the promises made are indeed credible. A range of legal and regulatory tools has been employed over time and across countries to accomplish this task. These include, among others, legal institutions, such as civil and criminal courts, for enforcing contractual and tort claims; entry regulations for entities and persons wishing to offer financial services; prudential requirements for financial intermediaries; agencies charged with monitoring and supervising such intermediaries; and government-sponsored deposit insurances. None of these tools, whether in isolation or in combination, has succeeded in eliminating financial crises.

A possible explanation is that every new legal tool designed to contain risk invariably gives rise to strategies aimed at circumventing it. Even a perfect legal system could not guard against widespread default resulting from broadly shared misjudgments about the future—not only because the future is difficult to predict but also because collective denial about the sustainability of certain strategies is rampant, particularly in financial markets (Avgouleas 2009).

Perhaps even more importantly, the legal and regulatory tools listed above only partly address the supply of money—the very medium of financial transactions (Galbraith 1976/2001). A substantial change in the money supply can destabilize a financial system however well designed laws and regulations might be. The sources of money supply are multiple; they are the government's printing press, the inflow of foreign capital, and the money multiplier effect embedded in the credit system. The relevant policy tools for governing the money supply include inflation targeting, the management of foreign capital inflows through exchange rate policies, capital controls and sterilization efforts, as well as interest rate policies and changes in reserve requirements to affect the costs of lending by the private sector. A comprehensive analysis of the governance of finance must, therefore, include both the credibility problem as well as the supply side of finance. This is all the more important because the two are interdependent. Changes in the money supply can undermine the credibility of financial commitments, and inflation has the potential to undermine parties' trust in the future value of money and increases incentives for borrowers to defect (Wolf 1993). As the subprime mortgage crisis suggests, an increase in the supply of credit reduces lenders' vigilance as they seek to expand their market share in an increasingly competitive environment. Once the credibility of financial promises is undermined—whether for reasons associated with credibility or money supply—and financial markets freeze up, this delicate system built on promises is prone to collapse.

Every financial system is vulnerable to credibility as well as to supply shocks. Available empirical evidence confirms that financial liberalization—which typically leads to greater supply of capital—is positively associated with subsequent financial crises (Reinhart and Rogoff 2008). In the past, the typical response has been to ensure that afflicted countries improve their institutions. This was based on the assumption that financial markets would operate efficiently as long as they could rely on effective institutions. In response to the East Asian financial crisis of 1997–8, for example, the International Monetary Fund (IMF) developed a comprehensive assessment programme for the institutions governing financial markets around the world—the Financial Sector Assessment Programme (FSAP).[3] This uses 'best-practice standards' drawn from the 'most advanced' financial systems, such as the USA and the UK, to guide other countries in reforming their legal and regulatory framework. Ironically, these standards put at risk both the countries in which they originated and the emerging markets to which they were transplanted.

In reality, it is difficult to determine whether a financial crisis is related to bad institutions, that is, the credibility problem of finance, or to excessive supply of capital in search for high returns. Recognizing the latter as a problem is made more difficult by the fact that capital inflows at first tend to have a positive effect on an economy, spurring investment and growth. Thus, policy makers in CEE and advisers at the IMF and elsewhere were very much aware of rapid credit expansion in the region in the years leading up to the crisis but could not decide whether this was a good thing (a much desired catch-up with the West) or a bad thing (a credit boom that would eventually result in a bust). Ideological priorities further complicated a correct diagnosis of what was happening. Advocates of market self-regulation tend to see the major problem of financial crisis not in the behaviour of market participants but in an unwarranted and undesirable 'external' intervention concocted by politicians—if only politicians were able to commit *ex ante* not to intervene in times of crisis, markets would effectively regulate themselves as market participants would fully internalize the costs of their actions. This argument assumes that the root cause of financial crises can always be found in the credibility problem, that is, the inability of private agents to credibly commit only to those obligations that they will be able to fulfil in the future. It largely misses the money supply problem. While banks control part of the money supply through the money multiplier effect associated with the credit system, each bank can do so only for its own lending activities and has no control over the system-wide implications of the rapid expansion, to which it contributes only as one among many. A bank that chose to cut back its own credit expansion would undercut its ability to compete with others. As the former CEO of Citigroup, Chuck Prince, famously quipped, they have little choice but to get up and dance—until the music stops.

Given the indeterminacy of the ultimate causes of a financial crisis and given that the financial system is indispensible for the operation of a market economy, it is not surprising that most governments will try to protect their financial system from collapse. However, individual governments may lack the resources or the credibility to prevent it; the actual ultimate guardian, therefore, is not necessarily the domestic government but whoever rescues a financial system. The ultimate guardian may be one or more domestic agents (i.e. the central banks and treasury in the case of the USA rescue operations in the global crisis), domestic agents in collaboration with their counterparts in other countries (i.e. the Mexican and US governments in the case of the 1994 bailout of the Mexican financial system), or multilateral agencies, such as the IMF, typically at the request of domestic governments (i.e. interventions in most countries afflicted by the East Asian financial crisis in 1997–8 and a series of emerging markets in the ongoing global crisis). Thus, the identity of the ultimate guardian is often revealed only in a crisis, yet close inspection of a country's governance arrangements can help determine the viability (or lack thereof) of domestic agents and thus establish whether ultimate guardianship has been effectively outsourced.

When finance in CEE countries dried up as a result of the global financial crisis, their governments turned out to be unable to protect their financial systems—and ultimately their economies—without outside help. The sudden stop in foreign capital inflows (in fact the extensive reversal of capital inflows in 2008 and 2009) (Nagy 2009) left their economies in freefall and brought their currencies under attack. Luckily for them, help did come from various sides—at the time of writing, the IMF had entered into emergency loans with Belarus, Bosnia-Herzegovina, Hungary, Latvia, and Ukraine, and had concluded standby agreements with Poland and Romania. The European Bank for Reconstruction and Development (EBRD) established a joint action programme together with the World Bank and the European Investment Bank (EIB) in January 2009, committing €24.5 billion to support the banking sector in the region. The EBRD has already invested €1 billion of these funds in Romania and additional funds in Ukraine. In addition, the EU has provided €50 billion for balance-of-payment support to countries in CEE. Finally, the European Central Bank (ECB) has entered into, and recently activated, a swap arrangement with the Central Bank of Sweden (Sveriges Riksbank) to help it weather the storm of the financial crisis in the Baltics, where many Swedish banks are deeply invested (Sweden has not adopted the euro). In addition to similar arrangements with the central bank of Denmark, the ECB announced co-operation with Narodowy Bank Polski (Poland) as well as Magya Nemzei Bank (Hungary) to provide these countries—which had experienced extensive 'euroization' (Feige and Dean 2002) of their economies—with euro liquidity. These interventions benefited countries that received direct assistance, but also other countries, as these actions signalled that the financial systems of these countries would not be allowed to implode. Still, the rescue operations were conducted in an ad hoc fashion and depended on the perception of third parties (the IMF, the EBRD, etc.) that assistance was warranted, as well as their own willingness and endowment with sufficient resources to step in. This uncertainty about the identity of the ultimate guardian and its commitment to an afflicted country creates a governance void.

3 Into the void

Countries in CEE implemented extensive legal and regulatory reforms to improve their financial systems, and, to this end, they received guidance and support from the EBRD (EBRD 1998; Fries et al. 2002), the World Bank (World Bank 1996) and, most importantly, the EU. One of the first major reform projects of the EBRD in the region was to improve the conditions for the development of credit markets by reforming the regime for collateralizing credit.[4] Additionally, the accession process in the EU required countries in the region to adapt their laws and regulations to European standards. Lastly, all countries were regular clients of the IMF's FSAP.[5] Thus, not only on paper but also in practice, these countries have caught up with the institutional standards widely regarded as critical for maintaining financial stability. Against this background, the rapid expansion of credit in most countries since the late 1990s was regarded as a positive response to the institutional reforms that had been implemented (Cottarelli et al. 2005). Whereas as of 1998 most countries in CEE still lagged behind countries at similar GDP levels in terms of the aggregate size of their credit markets, they now reached, if not exceeded, these comparative benchmark data.[6] The speed with which these changes occurred was remarkable. Within a period of only five years (from 2000 to 2005), the credit to GDP ratio doubled or even tripled in several countries (Enoch 2007). Between 2000 and 2004 alone, the average annual credit growth in Bulgaria and the three Baltic states was 20 per cent and in Hungary, Romania, and Croatia the average annual credit growth was over 10 per cent. In Slovenia the average was around 10 per cent. Only in Poland, the Czech Republic, and Slovakia had credit growth been below 5 per cent and at times even negative (Arcalean et al. 2007). The credit growth persisted, and in some countries it even accelerated in the following years. According to Backe et al. (2007), 'at the end of 2006, the annual growth rates of credit to the private sector ranged from 17 per cent to 64 per cent in the countries covered in this study', namely Bulgaria, Croatia, the Czech Republic, Estonia, Hungary, Latvia, Lithuania, Poland, Romania, Slovakia, and Slovenia.[7] These data almost certainly understate the real growth of credit, as they exclude direct cross-border lending by foreign banks to firms and households in these countries (see below). The persistent, if not accelerating, credit growth occurred notwithstanding the fact that many countries actively tried to rein in credit growth in the early 2000s. The means used varied from country to country yet they shared a common fate—they proved largely ineffective.

In principle, countries have a broad menu of choices to respond to excessive credit expansion. Hilbers et al. (2007) have compiled a menu of such choices, which includes macroeconomic policy measures to manage the supply side of money, including fiscal, monetary and exchange rate responses. It also lists prudential, supervisory and administrative measures, which address the core credibility issues.[8] While some countries appear to have had temporary success at least in slowing the rate of credit growth by employing some of these tools—especially Poland, and to some extent Bulgaria—the subsequent renewed expansion of credit suggests that ultimately these tools were not effective. This can, at least in part, be explained by the accession of countries in CEE to the EU. In 2004 the three Baltic states, along with the Czech Republic, Hungary, Poland, the Slovak Republic, and Slovenia, joined the EU; and in 2007 Bulgaria and Romania followed suit. All countries experienced a major post-accession boom, which has been attributed to increases in capital flows.

With the accession to the EU, the countries of CEE relinquished important tools for governing their financial systems that they previously had at their disposal. The restrictions on policy choices imposed by EU law are plenty. With respect to the governance of money supply, most restrictions can be traced to the new member states' commitment to strive towards introducing the euro. Specifically, Articles 3 and 4 of the respective Accession Treaty entered into by each new member state provides that it participates in the monetary union from the date of accession. Yet, the adoption of the euro has been delayed, as membership has been derogated in accordance with Article 122 of the Maastricht Treaty until the relevant convergence criteria have been met. These include fiscal restraint and the reduction of government debt, price and interest rate stability, and exchange rate stability. The ECB monitors convergence and issues annual convergence reports.[9]

Some policies associated with the convergence criteria work towards taming a credit boom. Fiscal restraint is the most obvious one. The implications of interest rate, and price and exchange rate stability requirements are more ambivalent. Hilbers et al. (2007) list greater exchange rate flexibility as an important tool for controlling rapid credit expansion. Indeed, Poland seems to have been quite successful in employing such strategies at times, but the ECB took note of this in its convergence report (ECB 2008).[10] Other countries had their hands bound by pegging their exchange rates or using currency board arrangements that required tight exchange rate management. Among the various macroeconomic tools for taming the credit boom, this left them with only fiscal policies (Hilbers et al. 2007: 101). In addition, the EU has harmonized the financial governance regime across member states as part of the integration of European financial markets. Notably, the free movement of capital was the last of the 'four freedoms' tackled by the EU. After creating the conditions for the free flow of goods, persons, and (most) services, serious attempts to harmonize financial market regulation were made only with the adoption of the Financial Services Action Plan in 1999; the regime that evolved in the subsequent years became part of the *Acquis Communautaire*, which the new member states had to comply with prior to being accepted into the EU. No serious attempts were made to modify the impact of this regime on the new member states despite the fact that their financial systems were still in the early stages of transformation and nowhere nearly as developed as the mature financial systems of old member states at the time they conceded that it was time to liberalize.

The EU governance regime for credit institutions parallels the global financial governance regime developed by the Bank for International Settlement (BIS). However, the Basel Concordat as well as the two Basel Accords (I & II) is 'soft law' and as such not legally binding. In contrast, an EU directive requires member states to transpose the directive into national law. The key governance principles for finance in the EU are home country regulation, bilateral co-ordination among home and host country regulators under the leadership of the home country regulator, and multilateral co-ordination within a three-level system within the EU.[11] Attempts to vest the ECB with centralized regulatory powers over finance or to create an alternative EU-wide regulator have met with stiff resistance by member states, as well as from their respective financial industries. Therefore, a co-ordinative governance regime, the so-called 'Lamfalussy Process', which had originally been developed for the governance of securities markets (Lamfalussy 2001), was extended to credit institutions (Vander Stichele 2008).

The basic idea of this process, named after the chair of the 'Committee of Wise Men' who wrote the report, is a multilevel governance framework for the making and implementation of harmonized standards for governing finance across the EU. In the aftermath of the financial crisis, this framework has been revised but has nonetheless remained national at the core with European level committees guiding the process. Specifically, EU directives (level 1) set forth the general framework for financial market governance. At level 2, the European Banking Committee, and any body run by the European Commission, shall facilitate the implementation of directives by addressing political issues as well as design problems. At level 3, the Committee of European Banking Supervisors (CEBS) brings together regulators from the member states involved in the regulation of banks. CEBS is charged with providing technical advice and ensuring the consistent implementation of the directive by dispersed national regulators. In addition to collecting information, conducting peer review and involving the financial industry through consultation processes, CEBS also functions as mediator in disputes between home and host country regulator. The complexity of the process and the sheer size of the new committees (51 regulators from 27 countries are currently represented in CEBS), as well as the lack of actual enforcement powers, leave key decision making in the hands of domestic regulators—the regulator in the jurisdiction where a credit institution has been authorized (licensed). A bank wishing to establish a branch in another EU member state can do so simply by notifying the regulatory authorities of that country. The same applies if the same bank wishes to offer financial services in another member state without channelling them through either a branch or a subsidiary, thus facilitating direct cross-border lending. This European passport system was designed to promote financial market integration by reducing the regulatory costs of transnational financial intermediaries within the common market. In contrast, for a separately incorporated entity (e.g. a subsidiary), special authorization is still required.

The distinction between branches and subsidiaries can be interpreted to suggest that domestic regulators maintain full regulatory authority over credit institutions incorporated and licensed within their territory, irrespective of their ownership structure. In other words, the fact that 65 to 98 per cent of bank assets in CEE countries are foreign owned should not matter much, as by far the majority of these banks are fully (domestically) incorporated subsidiaries rather than branch offices. However, in practice the distinction between branches and subsidiaries has become blurred. Two factors account for this. First, banks with EU-wide or global operations treat subsidiaries increasingly as branch offices. Second, they have morphed into vertically integrated financial groups with centralized strategies implemented throughout the group in a manner that is oblivious of national borders and formal differences between branch offices and subsidiaries. The latter remains relevant mostly for accounting and tax purposes. The corollary to the changing industry practice has been the consolidation of regulation for financial groups operating in more than one country.[12] Relevant EU directives allocate regulatory oversight over subsidiaries of EU parent credit institutions and financial holdings to the home regulator of the parent. This 'consolidated supervision' entails the 'co-ordination of the gathering and dissemination of relevant or essential information' as well as the 'planning and co-ordination of supervisory activities' for the going concern as well as in emergency situations.[13] Home country regulators of the subsidiaries shall consult and co-ordinate with host country regulators. This division of labour has been re-enforced by the so-called home-host guidelines adopted by CEBS (one of the banking committees established as part of the Lamfalussy framework). Upon consultation with the finance industry, these guidelines emphasize that to reduce regulatory costs, the home country regulators of the subsidiary should seek information not from the subsidiary or its parent but from the parent's home country regulator. The finance industry has made no secret that it would favour comprehensive delegation of supervisory powers to the parent's home country regulator.[14] Technically, this has been feasible since the adoption of the credit institutions directive in 2000, but so far not a single domestic regulator has done so. In light of the dominance of foreign bank ownership of the domestic banking sector in CEE—which implies that virtually all banks in these countries are subject to consolidated supervision by the home country regulator of the parent—the difference between consolidated and delegated supervision is, however, less pronounced than suggested by the law on the books.

The dominance of foreign banks in CEE countries is a result of privatization in the 1990s and the opening of the financial service sector to foreign investors in anticipation of EU membership. As such, it is a direct result of the transition process. The asset share of foreign-owned banks in CEE countries ranges from a low of 36 per cent in Slovenia to a high of 98 per cent in Estonia (ECB 2005). Only in Estonia and Latvia (47 per cent) is the asset share below 50 per cent. In comparison, in Latin America the asset share of foreign-owned banks is, on average, 45 per cent. Only New Zealand and Botswana have financial systems that are dominated by foreign owners to an extent that matches the countries of CEE. This suggests that the financial systems of CEE countries have been integrated into multinational financial groups with headquarters located outside their jurisdiction (De Haas and Van Lelyveld 2010). The home country regulators of the parent banks viewed these developments favourably as they positively affected the growth of 'their' institutions, and regulators in CEE countries still had at least nominal regulatory control over subsidiaries and could seek information about them via the parent's home country regulator. Indeed, regulators in most CEE countries have signed memoranda of understanding with regulators in the home countries of parent banks that own or control banks within their jurisdiction. However, they could do little to enforce their ultimate policy objective, namely to guard the stability of their domestic markets, when the group switched strategies in response to regulatory constraints they tried to impose. In particular, they could not prevent parent companies from lending directly to sidestep constraints imposed on their subsidiaries by CEE regulators. In a recent study, researchers at the Austrian Central Bank revealed that direct lending by the Austrian parent company grew rapidly during 2002–7, amounting to over €36 billion annually in 2007. In countries that joined the EU in 2004, direct lending by Austrian parent banks grew by an annual rate of 20 per cent on average, and in Bulgaria and Romania (both of whom joined in 2007) by 50 per cent (ONB 2009). As it turns out, most of the borrowers in CEE countries were leasing companies affiliated with the same banking group that owned one or more bank subsidiaries in the same country; the critical difference is that as leasing companies rather than banks, they escaped the regulations that CEE countries sought to impose on their domestic banks to counter the effects of an accelerating credit boom.[15] In other words, the group had found an easy mechanism to arbitrage around regulatory constraints. For countries in the region, direct lending came at the additional risk of foreign currency exposure: 85.4 per cent of these direct loans were denominated in foreign currency (ONB 2009). While euro-denominated loans dominated direct lending, the Swiss franc became increasingly common in Croatia, Hungary, and Slovenia.

The combination of financial liberalization within the EU, the dominance of financial groups from other EU member states, and the emphasis on reducing regulatory costs for these groups by consolidating regulatory oversight in the hands of the home country regulator implies that CEE countries have effectively abdicated the governance of their domestic financial markets. Undoubtedly, the integration of CEE banks into multinational banking groups has also benefited these countries. Reforming the financial sector in the post-socialist CEE countries has previously proven itself difficult, and the influx of foreign capital and expertise was widely regarded as critical for their speedy transformation. Moreover, foreign bank ownership shielded banks against downturns in their domestic economy. Empirical analysis of the lending practice of multinational financial groups suggests that they tend to cross-subsidize subsidiaries in countries facing a temporary downturn (De Haas and Van Lelyveld 2010), helping many banks in the region weather the first impact of the global crisis. Yet, the study also suggests that the same intra-group dynamics that operate in a counter-cyclical fashion when the locus of downturn is the economy in which the subsidiary is located turns pro-cyclical when the downturn affects the parent's home economy. Thus, the price for insurance against purely local economic troubles is exposure to problems that originate with the parent company or its home market. The global crisis has revealed that this price can be substantial: in 2008 alone, US$57 billion left the region as banking groups withdrew their capital to protect their home base (Nagy, supra note 5).

4   Whither financial governance in CEE?

The policies designed to accelerate the integration of the former socialist countries of CEE into the EU have effectively outsourced governance of their financial systems and, most critically, the role of ultimate guardian. This conclusion begs the question: To whom? There is no simple answer to this, which is why in crises these countries find themselves devoid of reliable governance. In the end, the most vulnerable countries had to rely on the IMF while others benefited from the announcement of the EBRD and the ECB to stand ready for additional aid if need be (see above).

With respect to crisis prevention in the form of credibility enhancement or management of parts of the money supply, regulatory oversight was transferred to the home countries of the dominant banking groups. As a result, the most important regulators of banks located in CEE countries are those of Austria, Italy,[16] Sweden, and Belgium, as banks from these countries dominate the scene in CEE countries. The new scope of regulatory jurisdiction of Austria and Sweden recalls their spheres of influence in past eras of empire building; yet, the commitment to guard the interests of these countries and protect them against financial crises has been limited. This raises the question whether the concept of co-ordinated governance over financial markets is workable. Clearly, the European financial governance framework is still a work in progress; nonetheless, it is worth asking how this framework will affect different countries in good as well as in bad times. Ultimately this requires an investigation into the interests and purposes the governance regime will serve. The relevant EU directives skirt the issue by assuming that if all credit institutions complied with the standards established therein, and all domestic regulators made sure that they did, financial markets should operate and savings should be protected.[17] In such a conceptualization, there is little room for conflicting objectives of prudential regulation and oversight from the perspective of the home and host country regulators, whether in times of relative stability or in times of crisis. Yet, such conflicts are easily conceivable. As Herring (2007) suggests, from the host country perspective, the 'nightmare scenarios' involve a foreign entity with a large share of local (i.e. host country) markets 'to be systematically important, while at the same time, being so small relative to the parent group that it is not regarded as significant to the condition of the parent company'. In this case, the home country regulator may not see a case for intervention as it is naturally concerned with the stability of the financial group for its own market, not with the stability of the financial system of countries in which that group operates a subsidiary.

For the transition economies of CEE, the basic features of this nightmare scenario are endemic; the combined legacy of socialism and the process of European integration means that not only are their domestic banking systems dominated by foreign financial groups but also the banking system is highly concentrated. As of 2005, the top five banks in key CEE countries had a market concentration ratio[18] ranging from 48 per cent in Poland to 99 per cent in Estonia (Uhde and Heimeshoff 2009). As noted above, foreign-owned banks' asset share in the same countries is between 36 per cent (Slovenia) and 97 per cent (Estonia) (Enoch 2007). Put differently, a few foreign banking groups own most of the banking sectors in any given CEE country. Even for Poland, the largest country among the new member states, the importance of foreign-owned banks to the domestic economy is far greater than the importance of its subsidiaries to the portfolio of the foreign bank that serves as its parent company (Bednarski and Starnowski 2007). In a small country like Croatia, Austrian banks controlled 60 per cent of the banking sector as of 2007 (Gardor 2008), which translates into 14.7 per cent of total Austrian banking assets.[19] This is not trivial, and indeed Croatia features prominently in the annual report of the Austrian Financial Market Authority (FMA) after the Czech Republic and Romania as one of the three 'main countries' among all countries in Eastern Europe and the former Soviet Union in which Austrian banks hold assets. Notably, the ranking employed by the Austrian FMA is by asset value, and not by the systemic effect that Austrian banks' activities might have on the host country's financial system. This clearly reflects the perspective that the home country regulator brings to its role as consolidated regulator. Indeed, the presentation of Austrian bank exposure in CEE both in the annual report of the FMA and in the *Financial Stability Report* of Austria's Central Bank is illuminating. For the FMA, CEE features primarily as a place of expansion and a profit centre:

> The region of Central, Eastern and South-Eastern Europe (CESEE) became even more important to Austria's banks in 2008. The aggregate balance sheet total, following some restructuring, grew by close to 30 per cent during the third quarter of 2008 compared with the same period of 2007 to approximately €272 billion, whilst the result for the period rose by

a disproportionately high amount, up by around 47 per cent to close to €3.45 billion.

(FMA 2008)

The Österreichische Nationalbank (ONB) reported that the 'exposure' of Austrian banks in the region has had negative repercussions for the Austrian banking sector during the crisis, but it downplayed the likely effect on the Austrian financial system as 'the Austrian financial intermediaries are regionally diversified, a factor that reduces the risk of country-specific or sub-regional clustering' (ONB 2009: 46).[20] Whether the countries on the receiving end of Austrian banks' expansion strategies are similarly diversified is not even discussed.

In sum, the focus of home country regulators is on *their* domestic banks and *their* domestic financial system, yet, in the event of a crisis—whatever its cause—someone must assume the role of ultimate guardian for the sake of people living in the countries on the receiving end of capital flows, both for their own sake and to avoid spillover effects for the European or the global system.[21] In the capital exporting countries of Europe and elsewhere, home country governments have stepped in aggressively for the benefit of their own national systems. They have left multilaterals to deal with those countries that served as capital importers during good times. Thus, the ONB reassured readers in its financial stability report in June 2009 that 'in light of recent rescue measure by the IMF and the EU Commission, extreme scenarios have become much less likely' (ONB 2009).

This is good news for everyone, including the people of the CEE countries. However, it also goes to show that countries that have been subjected to unconstrained cross-border capital flows—and, as a result, have lost the ability to rescue themselves—must depend on the IMF and other multilateral organizations to perform the role of ultimate guardian once the risks inherent in such a strategy materialize. The implication of the IMF's governance structure with its peculiar voting system is that most countries on the recipient side of IMF rescue packages have little influence on the design of these policies. The ten CEE countries that recently acceded to the EU, for example, jointly hold 2.75 per cent of the voting rights.[22] At the EBRD they control 5 per cent.[23] The countries that had experienced the East Asian financial crisis learned that lesson ten years ago. They did not like the policies imposed by IMF conditionalities, which let them experiment with their own insurance devices. Some closed their borders to free capital flows, as Malaysia did, however temporarily (Jomo 2006). CEE countries are prevented from exercising this option by EU treaty obligations, which prohibit restrictions on cross-border capital flows within the EU not only vis-à-vis other member states but also vis-à-vis third countries.[24] Alternatively, countries can make provisions for rainy days by ensuring that they will have sufficient resources to conduct their own rescue should the occasion arise again.

Indeed China,[25] Taiwan, Hong Kong, South Korea, and Singapore have doubled their stockpiles of foreign exchange reserves in the years following the East Asian financial crisis, with over US$800 billion collectively controlling 38 per cent of global reserves by the end of 2002 (Aizenman and Marion 2003). This option, however, presupposes a strong export base for earning foreign currency. It would also run counter to the aspirations and obligations of the new member states to join the euro.

The EU has meanwhile put in place a revised regime for governing finance across the region following the recommendations of the De Larosière report (De Larosière 2008). The central theme of these reforms is to strengthen European supervisory and monitoring bodies, including CEBS, which has been renamed the European Banking Authority (EBA), and to ensure that host countries are better represented in the regulation of multinational groups by including them in the colleges of supervisors, which, however, will be led by the home country regulator. The reforms fall short of full centralization yet do little to strengthen the position of host countries to protect themselves against future excessive capital flows. Within the current EU legal framework, that would be difficult in light of the strong commitment to free movement of capital and the substantial degree of harmonization, which effectively limits member states' policy space.

5   Concluding comments

The financial crises that swept emerging financial markets in the 1990s and the early 2000s left the impression that the world could, and should, be divided into two camps: countries with good institutions capable of participating in an increasingly globalized financial system on the one hand and countries with bad institutions that participated at their own peril, if at all, on the other. The global crisis that has engulfed members of both camps and the aftermath of the crisis suggest a different divide: countries that are capable of bailing themselves out and those that are not. This difference implies that the two groups of countries have different demands on the governance regime for global finance. For countries with bailout capacity and sufficient political clout to act independently irrespective of existing regional or international commitments, a global regime serves two critical purposes: it enables the financial intermediaries it houses to expand in good times and it facilitates cross-border workouts for them in bad times. In comparison, countries that have either *de jure* or *de facto* abdicated their role as ultimate guardian for their financial system have greater needs for risk management in good times to reduce the probability of a crisis. They also are more dependent on external help to bail out their financial system in the event of a crisis.

The transition economies of CEE found themselves on the latter side of this divide. This chapter has suggested that this was neither accidental nor inevitable but reflects a series of policy choices made during the transition period. Their goal was to ensure quick integration of CEE into the EU. An unintended side-effect of these policy choices was to leave CEE countries largely at the mercy of financial policies made outside their own borders. The reforms put into place by the EU in early 2011 do not alter these structural differences, which are therefore likely to shape East–West relations in the EU for the foreseeable future.

Notes

1. Clearly, this has not been a core assumption of standard finance theory. See, however, Minsky (1986); see also Sornette (2004).
2. See www.britannica.com under 'finance'.
3. See www.imf.org/external/NP/fsap/fsap.asp for details.
4. A model law on secured transactions for the region was published as early as 1994; see EBRD, available at www.ebrd.com/pubs/legal/secured.htm.
5. For recent FSAP reports on individual countries, see www.imf.org/external/NP/fsap/fsap.asp.
6. This has been the case in Bosnia-Herzegovina and Croatia. See Figure 2.6 in Arcalean et al. (2007: 22).
7. In the USA, a country with a much larger and deeper financial system, credit extended by commercial banks grew by about 11 per cent in 2006; see FRB (2006: 22).
8. In addition, the menu includes two other items, namely 'market development measures' and the 'promotion of better understanding of risks'. The former includes legal institutions for contract enforcement and improved accounting standards, that is, institutions that fall broadly within the category of credibility measures. Other 'market development measures', like hedging instruments as well as 'market based' risk diversification instruments, potentially have implications for the credibility as well as the money supply sides of financial governance. See the country reports in Enoch and Ötker-Robe (2005).
9. The ECB convergence reports are available at www.ecb.int/pub/convergence/html/index.en.html.
10. The ECB (2008) noted that 'in March 2008 the real effective exchange rate for the Polish zloty stood well above and the real bilateral exchange rate against the euro was somewhat above the corresponding ten-year historical averages'. However it did caution not to over-interpret the results in light of Poland's convergence process.
11. Most of these principles are reflected in Directive 2006/48/EC of the European Parliament and of the Council of 14 June 2006 relating to the taking up and pursuit of the business of credit institutions (recast), 30 June 2006, OJ L 177/1 and Directive 2006/49/EC of the European Parliament and of the Council of 14 June 2006 on the capital adequacy of investment firms and credit institutions (recast), 30 June 2006, OJ L 177/201.
12. See Article 129 of Directive 2006/48 op. cit. at 14.
13. See Article 129 Credit Institution Directives 48/2006 EC.
14. See comments by the Federation of European Banks on the home-host-country guidelines issued by CEBS. See www.cebs.eu.

15. See ONB (2009): '… the share of recipient intra-group FIs [financial institutions] increased from 65 per cent to more than 70 per cent of total direct credit to FIs. These growth rates are *inter alia* due to the growing importance of leasing firms affiliated with Austrian firms.'
16. As a result of Unicredit acquiring the Austrian Bank Creditanstalt.
17. Recital 5 of Directive 2006/48/EC lists as one of the objectives 'to protect savings and to create equal conditions of competition between these institutions'.
18. Calculated as the fraction of the total banking system's assets held by the five largest domestic and foreign banks per country. See Uhde and Heimeshoff 2009. The ECB (2005) confirms a high concentration ratio in these countries.
19. According to the FMA (2008), the total assets of Austria's financial markets amount to €1069.3 billion, 44.7 per cent of which is held by banks (ibid., Table 3). Thus, total assets of the Austrian banking sector in 2008 amounted to €478 billion (ibid., Table 6 and accompanying text). €32.26 billion in Croatian bank assets is held by Austrian banks.
20. Translation by author.
21. This threat has been clearly voiced by Erik Berglöf, the EBRD's chief economist, who wrote on the EBRD blog in May 2009 that not only do foreign banks affect CEE countries but CEE countries can invoke policies that might adversely affect the banks located in other EU member states: 'Eastern European governments can also damage the international bank groups by preventing them from transferring profits or adjusting their exposures. The public pressures to interfere are great.' Available at www.ebrdblog.com (7 May 2009).
22. Author's calculation based on information about voting rights available at www.imf.org/external/np/sec/memdir/members.htm
23. Whereas at the IMF voting rights are determined by the size of the economy at the date of entry (with some adjustments made over time), the Basic Document of the EBRD provides that voting rights are determined by the number of subscribed shares in the capital stock of the bank (Article 29). Calculations are based on subscription levels published on the EBRD website.
24. See Article 56 (1) EU Treaty.
25. China did not suffer from the East Asian financial crisis as it still had capital controls in place. However, it responded to the lessons learnt from observing its neighbours.

References

Aizenman, J. and N. Marion (2003) 'Foreign Exchange Reserves in East Asia: Why the High Demand?', mimeo., Federal Reserve Bank of San Francisco: San Francisco.

Allen, F. and D. Gale (2001) *Comparing Financial Systems*, MIT Press: Cambridge, MA.

Andrews, E.L. (2009) ' "Fed Will Do Everything Possible to Meet Crisis", Baernanke Says', *The New York Times*, 19 February.

Arcalean, C., O. Calvo-Gonzales, C. More, A. van Rixtel, A. Winkler and T. Zumer (2007) 'The Causes and Nature of the Rapid Growth of Bank Credit in the Central, Eastern and South-Eastern European Countries', in C. Enoch and I. Ötker-Robe (eds), *Rapid Credit Growth in Central and Eastern Europe: Endless Boom or Early Warning?*, Palgrave McMillan: New York.

Avgouleas, E. (2009) 'The Global Financial Crisis, Behavioral Finance and Financial Regulation: In Search of a New Orthodoxy', *Journal of Corporate Law Studies*, 9(1): 23–61.

Backe, P., B. Egert and Z. Walko (2007) 'Credit Growth in Central and Eastern Europe Revisited', *Focus*, Österreichische Nationalbank: Vienna.

Barth, J.R., G. Caprio, Jr. and R. Levine (2004) 'Bank Regulation and Supervision: What Works Best?', *Journal of Financial Intermediation*, 13(2): 205–48.

Bednarski, P. and D. Starnowski (2007) 'Home and Host Supervisors' Relations: A Host Supervisor's Perspective', in C. Enoch and I. Ötker-Robe (eds), *Rapid Credit Growth in Central and Eastern Europe: Endless Boom or Early Warning?*, Palgrave Macmillan: New York.

Berglöf, Erik and Patrick Bolton (2002) The Great Divide and Beyond: Financial Market Architecture in Transition, *Journal of Economic Perspectives*, 16(1):77–100.

Buch, C.M. (1996) *Creating Efficient Banking Systems: Theory and Evidence from Eastern Europe*, J.C.B. Mohr: Tübingen.

Corcoran, A.M. and T.L. Hart (2002) 'The Regulation of Cross-Border Financial Services in the EU Internal Market', *Columbia Journal of European Law*, 8(2): 221–92.

Cottarelli, C., G. Dell'Ariccia and I. Vladkova-Hollar (2005) 'Early Birds, Late Risers, and Sleeping Beauties: Bank Credit Growth to the Private Sector in Central and Eastern Europe and in the Balkans', *Journal of Banking and Finance*, 29(1): 83–104.

De Haas, R. and I. Van Lelyveld (2010) 'Internal Capital Markets and Lending by Multinational Bank Subsidiaries', *Journal of Financial Intermediation*, 19(1): 1–25.

De Larosière, J. (2008) *Report by the High Level Group of Financial Supervision in the EU*, European Commission: Brussels.

EBRD (European Bank for Reconstruction and Development) (1998) *Transition Report: Financial Sector in Transition*, EBRD: London.

ECB (European Central Bank) (2005) *Banking Structure in the New Member States*, European Central Bank: Frankfurt am Main.

ECB (2008) *Convergence Report*, European Central Bank: Frankfurt am Main.

Enoch, C. (2007) 'Credit Growth in Central and Eastern Europe', in C. Enoch and I. Ötker-Robe (eds), *The Causes and Nature of the Rapid Growth of Bank Credit in the Central, Eastern and South-Eastern European Countries*, Palgrave Macmillan: New York.

FRB (Federal Reserve Board) (2006) 'Monetary Report to the Congress', 19 June, available at www.federalreserve.gov/monetarypolicy/mpr_default.htm.

Feige, E.L. and J. Dean (2002) 'Dollarization and Euroization in Transition Countries: Currency Substitution, Asset Substitution, Network Externalities and Irreversibility', in A. Volbert, J. Melitz and G.M. Furstenberg (eds), *Monetary Unions and Hard Pegs: Effect on Trade, Financial Development and Stability*, Oxford University Press: Oxford.

Ferrarini, G. (2002) 'Pan-European Securities Markets and the FSAP', *European Business Organization Law Review*, 3(2): 249–92.

FMA (Austrian Financial Market Authority) (2008) *Annual Report of the Financial Authority*, FMA: Vienna.

Fries, S., D. Neven and P. Seabright (2002) 'Bank Performance in Transition Economies', *William Davidson Working Paper No. 505*, William Davidson Institute: Ann Arbor.

Galbraith, J.K. (1976/2001) *Money: Whence It Came, Where It Went*, Mifflin: Houghton.

Gardor, S. (2008) *Croatia: Coping with Rapid Financial Deepening*, Österreichische Nationalbank: Vienna.

Herring, R.J. (2007) *Conflicts between Home and Host Country Prudential Supervisors*, Cross-Border Banking and National Regulation, Chicago Federal Reserve: Chicago.

Hilbers, P., I. Ötker-Robe and C. Pazarbasioglu (2007) 'Analysis of and Policy Responses to Rapid Credit Growth', in C. Enoch and I. Ötker-Robe (eds), *Rapid Credit Growth in Central and Eastern Europe*, Palgrave Macmillan: New York.

Jomo, K.S. (2006) 'Pathways through Financial Crisis: Malaysia', *Global Governance*, 12(4): 489–505.

Kindelberger, C. (2005) *Mania, Panics, and Crashes: A History of Financial Crises*, Wiley: New York.

Lamfalussy, A. (2001) *Final Report of the Committee of Wise Men on the Regulation of European Securities Markets*, European Union: Brussels.

Levine, R. (2003) 'Bank-Based or Market-Based Financial Systems: Which Is Better?', *Journal of Financial Intermediation*, 11(4): 398–428.

Mayer, C. (1998) 'Financial Systems and Corporate Governance: A Review of the Evidence', *Journal of Institutional and Theoretical Economics*, 154(1): 144–65.

Minsky, H. P. (1986) *Stabilizing an Unstable Economy*, Yale University Press: New Haven.

Nagy, P. (2009) 'BIS Data on Cross-Border Flows: A Closer Look', EBRD Blog, 11 May, available at www.ebrdblog.com/2009/05/11/bis-data-on-cross-border-flows-a-closer-look/.

ONB (Österreichische Nationalbank) (2009) *Finanzmarkt-Stabilitätsbericht*, Austrian National Bank: Vienna.

Reinhart, C. and K.S. Rogoff (2008) 'Is the 2007 US Sub-Prime Crisis So Different? An International Historical Comparison', *NBER Working Papes No. 13761*, National Bureau of Economic Research: Cambridge MA.

Rostowski, J. (1995) *Banking Reform in Central Europe and the Former Soviet Union*, CEU Press: Budapest.

Sornette, D. (2004) 'A Complex System View of Why Stock Markets Crash', *New Thesis*, 1(1): 5–18.

Tihanyi, L. and H.W. Hegarty (2007) 'Political Interests and the Emergence of Commercial Banking in Transition Economies', *Journal of Management Studies*, 44(5): 788–813.

Uhde, A. and U. Heimeshoff (2009) 'Consolidation in Banking and Financial Stability in Europe: Empirical Evidence', *Journal of Banking and Finance*, 33(7): 1299–311.

Vander Stichele, M. (2008) 'Financial Regulation in the European Union: Mapping EU Decision Making Structures on Financial Regulation and Supervision', available at www.eurodad.org/uploadedFiles/Whats_New/Reports/EUMapping_Financial_Regulation_FINAL.pdf.

Wolf, H.C. (1993) 'Endogenous Legal Booms', *The Journal of Law, Economics, and Organization*, 9(1): 181–7.

World Bank (1995) *Bureaucrats in Business*, World Bank: Washington, DC.

World Bank (1996) *From Plan to Market*, Oxford University Press: Washington, DC.

Zilioli, C. and M. Selmayr (2001) *The Law of the European Central Bank*, Hart Publishing: Oxford.

6
The Long-Run Weight of Communism or the Weight of Long-Run History?

Gérard Roland

1 Introduction

If one were to have made predictions in 1912 about the outlook for Russia, Central Europe and China in 2012, what plausible scenarios could one imagine? Surprisingly, one can well imagine scenarios that are very close to what we are observing today. Prediction is often nothing less than an extrapolation from the past. Russia was modernizing economically but was remaining politically very autocratic. Central Europe was economically very prosperous and well integrated into Western Europe but was experiencing nationalistic tensions. China was waking up from its torpor and opening up to the outside world, searching for modern institutions capable of unifying it, in all likelihood via a unified military command. A hundred years later, some of the trends one could observe in the early twentieth century can still be observed today. The remarkable thing is that during this century, these different regions of the world have all undergone several decades of living under a communist regime, which had mostly not been predicted in 1912. Seen in the very long term, it would seem, however, that these decades of communism have not left a great influence on the long-run trends one observes in these regions of the world. Was the communist experience, in the very long term, nothing more than a minor historical blip in the long-run evolution of these countries?[1]

There are many traits in post-socialist countries that we tend to attribute to the recent communist past, and the piece by Ofer in this volume (Chapter 9) does a good job of analysing these legacies. However, if we take a closer look, many of these traits might have more to do with the pre-communist historical past than with the communist experience itself. Is Putin's autocratic style and reliance on the secret service a communist trait or rather one that was already associated with Russia before the Bolshevik revolution, for example the role of the Okhranka and previous embodiments of the Tsar's secret service in keeping the state apparatus together? We know that communist ideology is mostly only a façade for the Chinese communist party and that it is more driven by the nationalistic ideals of Sun Yat-sen, the Kuomintang leader in 1912, than by the ideas of Karl Marx. The organization of the Chinese bureaucracy, its meritocratic system, even the moralizing campaigns have less to do with 'democratic centralism' and communist ideology than with the millennial mandarinal system that was relatively efficient most of the time throughout Chinese history. While it is very difficult to precisely disentangle the effects of communism versus those of long-run history, it would definitely be wrong to ignore the latter.

In this chapter, I take a closer look at the weight of long-run history in the observed evolution of post-socialist countries and try to understand if past history really seems to influence these evolutions possibly more than the recent communist past, and why this might be. I start with a quite speculative and blunt, though in my view illuminating, exercise consisting of extrapolating the future of Russia, Central Europe and China from the perspective of 1912. I then provide some hard empirical evidence to show the role of long-run history in shaping cultural values in Central and Eastern Europe (CEE). This evidence tends to show that culture—that is, values and beliefs—moves very slowly and thus that the distant past affects countries' historical path via their culture. I then look at the evolution of beliefs in transition countries since the beginning of the transition. While these states have undergone massive institutional change, it is surprising to see how sticky values and beliefs have been in the last twenty years. I argue in the final section that the long-run stickiness of values and beliefs is a major determinant of the institutional and economic evolution of countries.

2   The future of Russia, China, and Central Europe seen from the perspective of 1912

Economics is notoriously bad at making predictions, let alone long-run predictions. People nevertheless cannot resist the temptation to try, however shaky the foundations. In this section, I propose the following thought experiment. Assume we were in 1912 and did not know any of the history of the next hundred years. Assume one would want to make predictions about how Russia, Central Europe and China would look a hundred years onwards. What would the picture look like? This thought experiment must obviously be taken with a pinch of salt because we are not operating behind a veil of ignorance. Moreover, such long-run predictions do not have a scientific basis and are generally nothing more than loose interpolations from the past. I will not pretend to do more. All I want is to produce some 'makeshift predictions' using interpolation that seem plausible from the perspective of 1912. Since it would have been very difficult to predict then that all these countries would spend a great part of the twentieth century under a communist-imposed socialist economy, and since all these countries have since abandoned socialism, it is useful to see how far such simple interpolations could bring us towards understanding where these countries are today. If this is the case, this would mean that we can understand much about those countries based on their long-run past. This thought experiment does not prove anything by itself. However, in the next section we will bring some evidence to bear on the weight of history.

Let us start with Russia. One could imagine in 1912 that it would continue its economic modernization process that started at the turn of the century under Count Witte and that continued vigorously under Prime Minister Stolypin's reforms. Industrialization was encouraged and there was rapid expansion of the steel and oil industries, and rapid construction of a large network of railways. The agrarian reforms that began under Stolypin included the development of solid private property of land in the countryside, lines of credit for private farmers, and dissemination of methods of land improvement. Peasants were encouraged via the Trans-Siberian Railway to migrate eastwards and take land in Siberia. Russia could have been predicted to have partly caught up with Western Europe (see Miller 1927 for a description of pre-1914 Russia). However, given the size of the country, modern industry was concentrated in a few rich urban centres like St. Petersburg, Moscow, Kiev, Kharkov, Vilna and Riga (Hooson 1968). Simultaneously, there remained huge pockets of rural and backward poverty since serfdom had only recently been abolished and peasants were living under forms of communal ownership. The strong growth in heavy industry relied a lot on foreign investment and Western technical assistance. To pay for all this, the Russian economy of the early twentieth century could rely on the export of energy, natural resources and especially agricultural products.

Since its rebirth under both Ivan the Terrible and Peter the Great, the Russian state was very centralized and relied on a strong repressive apparatus to ruthlessly quell any dissent. In the early twentieth century, the famous Okhranka secret police were quite skilled and efficient in chasing anarchists and revolutionaries of all kinds. In their efforts to build a secret organization that could protect them efficiently against the secret police, the Bolsheviks were able to create an organization that would allow them to seize and keep power in Russia in 1917. Throughout the nineteenth century, Russia had been pushing its territory westwards, taking advantage of the weakening of the Ottoman Empire to gain influence and acquire territory in areas formerly controlled by the latter. This explains the push in the Balkans and in the Caucasus. Russia did not have good access to seas at its western borders. It could push geopolitically either in the north west in the Baltics or in the south west by gaining access to the Mediterranean via the Balkans. Under Tsar Nicolas II, both directions were tried without real focus on either.

So, if we would extrapolate from 1912 over the next hundred years the observed tendencies in terms of economic fundamentals, broad institutional characteristics and geopolitical outlook, what could we reasonably expect? A 'reasonable' prediction would be that Russia would continue its economic modernization, and possibly catch up, at least partly, with the other industrialized nations. There would nevertheless remain large discrepancies between the more developed urban centres and a large backward countryside with huge pockets of poverty. Russia's comparative advantage would remain in the export of natural resources and raw materials. The political regime would be a republic or a constitutional monarchy with strong centralized powers and an ever-present strong secret police. One could reasonably predict that Russia would have a stronger geopolitical role, possibly with a strong presence in the Balkans and in former areas of the Ottoman Empire, but probably less in the Baltics and to the east of Prussian Germany. This would have seemed rational at the time, given the rapid modernization of Germany and its strong military build-up.[2]

This picture would seem very much to describe, with broad brushstrokes, Russia in 2012. Russia has industrialized strongly but this was under central planning. There are large discrepancies between the bigger, richer urban centres and a poor countryside. The countryside was killed by collectivization and was never really able to recover despite the privatization drives of the 1990s. Transition in Russian agriculture is a sad story of failures and badly co-ordinated reforms. In 1912, one would most likely have overestimated the state of Russian agriculture in 2012 as well as the extent of its strength in Russian exports. Russia is a republic with centralized powers and the secret service is still the backbone of the state apparatus. When rebuilding the Russian state on the ashes of the disorganized bureaucracy of the Yeltsin years, Putin built directly on his former KGB (Komitet gosudarstvennoy bezopasnosti: Committee for State Security) network, making it possible to weaken the oligarchs and strengthen the power of the *siloviki* (officers of the KGB). Geopolitically, it is not clear whether Russia is more powerful in relative terms compared with the early twentieth century given its strong decline since the end of the Cold War. It has suffered major losses in territory after the break-up of the Soviet Union. Its power in Western Europe is less than it was a hundred years ago and it is having a hard time dealing with local conflict in Chechnya and in the Caucasus. Russia appears more powerful internationally than it was under Yeltsin but it does not fare much better than under the extraordinary lows of the 1990s when it seemed that Russian policy could be directly influenced by Washington.

Let us now turn to Central Europe. Here it is more difficult to draw a consistent picture because the perspective might be different seen from Budapest, Warsaw, or Prague. We will therefore take even more of a bird's-eye view. In 1912, Central Europe was economically very prosperous and integrated into the world economy. Berlin, Prague, Vienna, and Budapest were on equal terms large centres of culture, trade, and economic growth. This large economic prosperity contrasted with the archaic political institutions governing most of Central Europe. The Austro-Hungarian Empire was governed by a weak, conservative and rigid multi-ethnic bureaucracy that was neither admired nor respected. The German Empire had a more efficient state apparatus but was being challenged from inside by a strong workers' movement fighting for democracy and universal suffrage. Geopolitically, nationalism was boiling everywhere, a trend that had started in the nineteenth century with the revolutionary uprisings of 1830 in Poland and in 1848 throughout most of Europe. Nationalism associated with aspirations for more modern political institutions was making the Austro-Hungarian Empire burst at its seams and appear more and more weak and dysfunctional, its army seeming weaker than the Russian Army. Many territories under the control of the Austro-Hungarian Empire could thus appear to be possible prey for Russian westward expansionism building on pan-Slavic movements from Slovakia to Serbia.

If we extrapolate from 1912, one would reasonably expect Central Europe to remain economically very prosperous and integrated into a German and Czech economic powerhouse.[3] Institutionally, one would predict that the empires would be replaced by more modern republican and democratic institutions. The advent of nationalist democratic movements would, however, lead to a break-up of the multi-ethnic Austro-Hungarian Empire. The borders of a future Central Europe would seem very hard to predict in 1912. One possibility is that of a merger between Austria and Germany. To recall, this merger had failed in the nineteenth century since the establishment of the Zollverein because the conservative Austrian monarchy was afraid that the unified country would be governed by progressive forces (Dumke 1978). Another possibility is that of a very powerful Hungary being the big power in Central Europe and controlling large parts of Slovakia and Romania. It was uncertain whether Poland would gain independence, possibly creating a joint state with a greater Lithuania following the dreams of Pilsudski.

Overall, if we compare these plausible predictions with the reality of 2012, Central Europe probably looks today less prosperous than what might have been predicted in 1912. Of course, four decades of socialism are much to blame for this. Nevertheless, in the nineties, observers tended to marvel at how Central Europe was faring better under transition than the former Soviet Union (FSU), and different explanations were put forward for that 'Great Divide' (see, e.g., Berglöf and Bolton 2002). In historical perspective, Central Europe lost many decades of prosperity when it was chained to the Soviet Empire. Politically, all Central European countries have become democracies like in Western Europe, albeit somewhat less stable for reasons we will discuss below (Section 4). Nevertheless, this appears to be a clean break from the situation of 1912. Geopolitically, Central Europe appears more fragmented than it might have been predicted to be. This fragmentation, established after the First World War under the Wilsonian influence, would appear potentially very unstable given the many possible border conflicts and historical claims of some countries over territories of other countries. Nevertheless, the European Union (EU) has brought great stability to the borders of Central Europe by integrating these countries within the union. Without the existence of the EU, the breaking-away of Central Europe from the Soviet Union after 1989 would certainly have exacerbated local nationalisms and nationalist conflicts between Hungary, Slovakia, and Romania, to give just one example.

Let us now turn to China. Early in the twentieth century, the Qing Dynasty seemed moribund. The Opium Wars had forced China to cede territories to the British and to allow them to sell opium within its borders. Various colonizing countries were looking forward to sharing the spoils of the dying Celestial Empire. Internal revolts were further weakening it. The Boxer Rebellion had shaken all of China only a few decades after the Taiping Rebellion. A more structured nationalist and republican movement, the Kuomintang, was expanding fast under the leadership of Sun Yat-sen, a foreign-educated westernizing intellectual who aspired to make China strong again by modernizing its institutions and reviving its economy, which had been the most affluent in the world until the eighteenth century. 1912 is the year of the death of the Qing Dynasty and the birth of the Republic of China with Sun Yat-sen as president. Seen from the perspective of 1912, Sun Yat-sen seemed likely to succeed and win his gamble of modernizing China. The country could then be seen a hundred years down the road as a nationalist republic, plausibly with military characteristics.[4] The south of China could be seen to play a much larger role in the country in the future. Sun Yat-sen himself was from Guangzhou province and he spent several years in Hong Kong. The larger area surrounding the Pearl River Delta had not played any major role in Chinese history but it was expanding very fast as a major locus of trade and commerce. Many of the supporters of Sun Yat-sen also came from that region.

Given its past traditions, China could be seen to become a major player in the world's exports of agricultural goods as well as of agriculture-intensive products, light industry and manufacturing, with foreign trade being a major source of its economic revival. Compared with China in 2012, this extrapolation would seem pretty much on target. China has become a major powerhouse in the world economy due to its vigorous export of light manufacturing goods. Southern China and the coastal regions have played a major role in the country's economic revival and its participation in world trade. China has got rid of the colonizing powers and taken back Hong Kong and Macau from the British and the Portuguese. It has been unified under a nationalist dictatorship with strong domestic military powers. The only difference is that the revival of the Chinese continent has happened not under the auspices of the Kuomintang but under those of the Chinese communist party, after many detours: an internal civil war, Japanese occupation, the communist victory and the disastrous Maoist years of the Great Leap Forward and the Cultural Revolution. It is only in the 34 years before 2012 that China started its economic revival. The communist party today looks, however, closer to a nationalist Kuomintang than to the ideologically fanatical organization that Mao had built between the 1920s and the Cultural Revolution. Today's China seems also closer than ever to Sun Yat-sen's goals of a slowly emerging democracy, even though the goal of democracy is not shared by the communist leadership. One has reasons to doubt that democracy will be established in China for many decades if only because it could jeopardize the unity of China and reinforce secessionist tendencies in various provinces.

What should we conclude from this thought experiment comparing possible extrapolations from 1912 to 2012 for Russia, Central Europe and China? The picture that emerges based purely on the reality of 1912 seems very close in many aspects to today's reality in those regions. Interestingly, if we had made a prediction for 1962 instead, which would probably have looked very similar, we would have been wildly wrong. The difference is that all these countries became socialist economies in the decades after 1912 and socialism as an economic system had all but disappeared by 2012, apart from in North Korea and Cuba. It might thus seem that communism was a giant historical detour and that by 2012 most countries had at least partially recovered from that detour and gone back to the long-run trends of 1912. Thinking of these long-run trends, it seems that the geopolitical evolution is more uncertain than the long-run economic trends and basic domestic political institutional evolution. This is more true for Central Europe, which given its ethnic diversity could have evolved in many different directions. At the margin, the borders of Russia would not have easily been predicted either. The loss of Ukraine in particular, following the break-up of the Soviet Union, would certainly have seemed like a low-probability event. China appears to be an exception but its borders have experienced exceptional stability over recent centuries.

The natural endowments and geography of a country play a big role in shaping its comparative advantage, together with its history. Some of the economic fundamentals would thus appear to be quite stable. None of these regions has been under-developed for all their history and thus they could count on accumulated human capital to grow.

The 'predictions' for the domestic political institutions are generally on target. Long-run trends thus seem to be discernible. How could that be? A hypothesis that comes to mind is that there is some co-evolution of formal institutions and of a country's culture seen as the general set of values and beliefs about how the world works. Central Europe has a shared culture with Western Europe. It went through the Enlightenment in which the modern culture that has shaped democratic institutions has emerged out of the ashes of the Dark Ages. Therefore, one could have thought that there would in the long run be historical convergence with institutions of Western Europe. This is happening despite some caveats to which we will come later. Russia in contrast missed the Enlightenment as it was living under Tatar rule. Modernization, be it under Peter the Great, Empress Catherine, or Stalin, happened under an original mix of violence and centralized repression on the one hand and aspiration towards Western-inspired values on the other, all in a sea of territorial immensity and large backwardness. The traces of this combination are very palpable in today's Russia.[5] China has developed a civilization of its own with a Confucianist culture, a meritocratic and efficient system of administration with an obsession for political stability and a fear of heterogeneity. There is no place here to describe in detail the effects of Confucianist culture but there is no doubt that they are present in today's China, even if they coexist with the legacy of the Cultural Revolution. How can we understand this long-run co-evolution of institutions and culture? Why is the weight of history so large despite the incredible historical detour given by the failed experiment of creating a socialist system? Before understanding this, it is useful to go beyond the impressionistic and speculative reasoning we have provided so far.

3   The weight of long-run history versus the communist past

Very intriguing empirical evidence exists to show that the weight of long-run history matters significantly in transition countries. Grosjean (2009) has used the Life in Transition Survey (LITS) conducted in 2006 by the European Bank for Reconstruction and Development and the World Bank in 28 post-transition countries and in Turkey in order to analyse the determinants of cultural distance using a gravity model. The data include 21,000 households in 1,050 primary sampling units. Since the location of the surveys is known, she was able to build various distance measures based on all pairs of locations.

The basic specification regresses the distance between a pair of locations for a cultural variable against physical distance, taking into account the presence of mountains, as well as other distance measures and other variables. The other distance measures are (1) the dissimilarity in composition of social classes as measured by the proportion of rich, poor and middle income; (2) the dissimilarity in educational achievement; and (3) the dissimilarity in the composition of the main religions (Muslim, Christian, Jewish, atheist, and other). The regression includes location fixed effects as well as a dummy variable for whether the two localities are in the same country, a dummy variable for whether two localities belong to different but adjacent countries and a dummy for whether the two locations belonged to the same empire in the past for at least 100 years. The relevant empires are the Ottoman, the Austro-Hungarian, the Russian, and the Prussian. Given that borders of empires and countries have moved a lot across time, there is rich variation in the data.

The cultural dependent variable used is the question about 'generalized trust' that is also present in the World Values Surveys: 'Generally speaking, would you say that most people can be trusted or that you can't be too careful in dealing with people?' Grosjean also looks at the distance between occupational compositions using the following categories: white collar, blue collar, service worker, farmer, farm worker, unemployed, housewife, pensioner, and student. Interestingly, she finds that two locations that belonged to the same empire in the past tend to have a smaller cultural distance. However, belonging to the same country or to two adjacent countries does not have any significant effect. Having been integrated in the same empire for more than 100 years is the equivalent of reducing the distance between two locations by more than a third (367 km out of an average distance of 1,029 km in the sample). Similar results are obtained when using occupational distance as a regressor. When looking at the effect of time of being together under the same empire, the effect is only significant after 400 years but is always significant for the occupational variable.

These results are very interesting because they point to the long-run inertia of culture. Culture is transmitted vertically from parents to children and horizontally through influences from peers and the outside world. Physical distance reduces the possibilities of horizontal transmission and also channels of vertical transmission as one was less likely to marry people living at a further distance. The effect of living under a common empire in reducing cultural heterogeneity across space is, however, quite remarkable, but this effect required several centuries to operate.[6] Reduction in economic heterogeneity, as measured here by occupational dissimilarities, appears to require substantially less time.

These findings become even more interesting and confirm the long-run inertia of culture when one considers the results obtained by adding to the regressions a dummy for whether two locations jointly belonged to the FSU or former Yugoslavia. The results on cultural distance are not significant for the FSU and only marginally significant in the case of former Yugoslavia. There is a significant effect for occupational distance though. The effect of former empires generally remains strong and very significant. Moreover, the coefficients of former empires are much higher than those associated with the FSU or former Yugoslavia. A convergent finding is present when looking at the effect of having entered the EU; that is, for pairs of locations that have become EU territory. The effect is not significant for cultural distance but is significant for occupational distance. The research by Grosjean on CEE transition countries and Turkey gives very suggestive evidence of the weight of long-run history and the century-long effect of having lived under a common empire on values and beliefs. It is quite remarkable that these effects of the long-run past come out strongly in regressions.

4 Cultural inertia

One can understand cultural inertia better by looking at another set of data on beliefs. The World Values Survey was conducted in five waves and we have data on transition countries in CEE between 1989 and 2005. Since CEE countries went through such large-scale institutional change after 1989 with a complete transformation of the economic and political system, one would be tempted to believe that these enormous transformations would also affect the beliefs and values of the populations of those countries. Moreover, given the fact that this institutional change aimed at establishing the market and democracy, one would think that this would bring values and beliefs closer to those of populations of advanced democracies and market economies. Surprisingly, none of these hypotheses turns out to be verified. There is a specific set of values and beliefs that existed in these countries prior to the transition process that has hardly changed. It is characterized in particular by a more authoritarian view of government and a preference for a larger responsibility of government in the economy. Moreover, these values and beliefs do not appear to have converged towards those existing in advanced democracies and market economies, be it the EU-15 (countries that were members of the EU before the admission of Central European countries) or the USA. I give a few illustrative examples below.

In Figure 6.1, we can see the evolution of attitudes towards public and private ownership in the economy. Two opposing views are formulated— 'Private ownership of business and industry should be increased', and 'Government ownership of business and industry should be increased'— with higher scores meaning support for the latter proposition and lower scores support for the former. It appears quite clearly that support for public ownership is strongly greater in transition countries relative to the EU-15

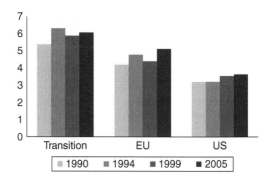

Figure 6.1   Public ownership should be increased
Source: Based on World Values Survey data; see text for explanation.

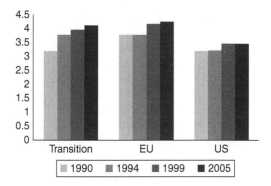

Figure 6.2 Competition is harmful
Source: Based on World Values Survey data; see text for explanation.

or the USA. Moreover, support for public ownership has increased and not decreased since the beginning of the transition process.
Figure 6.2 looks at attitudes towards competition in the economy. The responses refer to a question stating either 'Competition is good. It stimulates people to work hard and develop new ideas', or 'Competition is harmful. It brings out the worst in people.' A high score means agreement with the latter whereas a low score means agreement with the former. As we see, a negative attitude towards competition is more widespread among EU-15 countries than among transition countries, the USA having the most positive attitude. Note, however, that since 1989, views on competition in transition countries have become more negative, not more positive.
Figure 6.3 shows the view on whether nationals should have more right to a job in case of unemployment. The statement was 'When jobs are scarce,

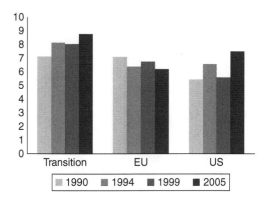

Figure 6.3 Jobs first to nationals over immigrants
Source: Based on World Values Survey data; see text for explanation.

employers should give priority to nationals over immigrants'. A higher score meant agreement with this proposition. As we can see, there is more agreement with this discriminatory proposition in transition countries compared with the EU-15 or the USA.[7] Moreover, positions have not changed very much in the last 20 years—there are even fewer signs of convergence.

Agreement on a proposition to reserve jobs to men relative to women in case of job scarcity is quite a bit higher for transition countries compared to the EU-15 or the USA. A similar response pattern can be observed in response to the following proposition: "When jobs are scarce, older people should be forced to retire from work early.

While the previous questions were about whether there should or should not be discrimination in the job market, Figure 6.4 measures disagreement with the following proposition: 'Hard work doesn't generally bring success, it's more a matter of luck'. This refers to a fundamental belief about the respective roles of effort versus luck in explaining success. As one can see from Figure 6.4, this belief is strongest in the USA and is lower in transition countries and in the EU-15. Note, however, that in transition countries belief in effort appears to have declined since the transition.

Figure 6.5 displays attitudes on an important value: the importance of imagination as a quality for a child. This value can be interpreted in different ways. It can be interpreted as valuing creativity as a product of imagination nurtured in children, but it can also be interpreted as valuing the freedom of thought. Here we see that this value is considerably less important in transition countries compared with the EU and the USA. Some progress can be observed in 2005 but the difference remains quite large.

The next figures illustrate beliefs in government. In Figure 6.6 we illustrate support for the idea that order is the fundamental goal of government.

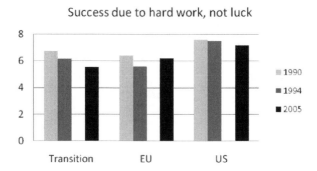

Figure 6.4   Success due to hard work, not luck
Source: Based on World Values Survey data; see text for explanation.

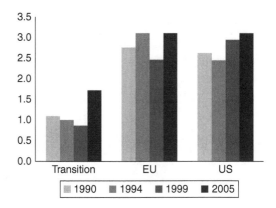

Figure 6.5 Imagination is an important child quality
Source: Based on World Values Survey data; see text for explanation.

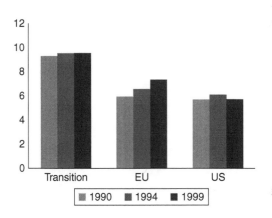

Figure 6.6 Order is the fundamental goal of government
Source: Based on World Values Survey data; see text for explanation.

As one can see from Figure 6.7, there is more support in transition countries compared with the EU and the USA, suggesting that authoritarian values with regard to the role of government are stronger in transition countries. This is confirmed in answers to other questions.

These data do convey both specific values and beliefs in transition countries as well as inertia of these values despite the massive changes that have been taking place in these countries since 1989. If we put these questions together[8] and measure on the horizontal axis (as we do in Figure 6.8) values that favour more government interventionism—in the form of more discrimination, less competition, or more public ownership—and on the vertical axis greater support for authoritarianism, what do we

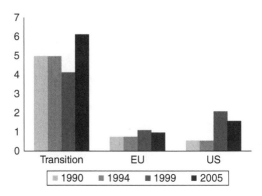

Figure 6.7   Having a strong authoritarian leader is good
Source: Based on World Values Survey data; see text for explanation.

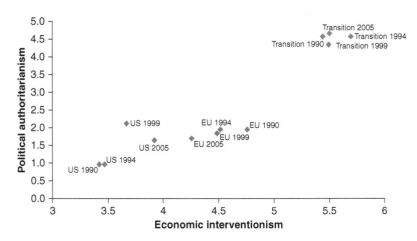

Figure 6.8   Inertia in economic and political values
Source: Based on World Values Survey data; see text for explanation.

get? Figure 6.8 shows a surprising inertia of values in the three groups of countries. In the USA, values have been consistently in favour of less economic interventionism and against authoritarianism. In the EU-15, support for economic intervention of government is somewhat higher but values are also relatively anti-authoritarian. In transition countries, however, there is consistently more support for authoritarianism and economic intervention of government. The inertia in values is quite remarkable. Also notable is that the distance between these three groups of countries is much larger than the distance between values in any group of countries over time.

One might think that Central European countries have values that are closer to the EU-15 compared with East European countries. This is not the case. The European Bank for Reconstruction and Development (EBRD) 2007 report, which contains findings on the LITS, does not show a 'Great Divide' in values between Central Europe and FSU countries. While Central European countries have somewhat less authoritarian views than FSU countries, these are still closer to the latter than to the EU-15. The rapid institutional change that led Central European transition countries to become new member states of the EU has hidden the fact that values in those countries remain more authoritarian and nationalistic, viewing the government more as a repressive law-and-order machine. One should not forget that despite the economic prosperity of Central Europe before the First World War, those countries for the most part never really had experience of democracy before 1989. One can thus predict that there will for quite some time be a tension between values and beliefs in those countries and the EU-style institutions that were adopted. These tensions have already started to appear with strong nationalistic tendencies and signs of political instability in Central Europe after its entry into the EU.

5 The long-run evolution of institutions

Let us step back and try to provide a conceptual framework for understanding the basic facts we have uncovered and highlighted in this study. The post-communist world is a fascinating subject to improve our understanding of institutions and their long-run evolution. Three regions of the world with a very distinct history (Russia, Central Europe, and China) were deeply transformed economically and institutionally in the twentieth century following the beliefs of communist ideology. The communist experiment proved to be a failure and these regions underwent another transformation to replace the socialist economic system with capitalism. The institutions that have emerged from the transition, however, turned out to be very different in these three regions and do not seem to converge in any way. The long-term institutional evolution in these regions seems to follow a path that is very much shaped by a country's long-run history. In contrast, the recent history of communism does not seem to leave as many traces as the long-run history. Seen another way, if communism were the sole determinant of post-transition evolutions, the divergence between these groups of countries would not be as strong as observed.

An important clue to understanding this is the cultural inertia that we documented in the previous section. In Roland (2004), I have argued that culture is a 'slow-moving' institution in contrast with 'fast-moving' institutions. Slow-moving institutions generally change slowly, incrementally and continuously, whereas fast-moving ones are more given to rapid, discontinuous change in large steps. Political institutions, for example, have the potential for centralized decisional changes in large steps. In this sense, they can be fast-moving institutions, which change nearly overnight when there are revolutionary moments. In contrast, social norms are more often an example of slow-moving institutions. While some social norms and values can change very rapidly in historical terms (e.g. a society's tolerance for cigarettes), in general, social norms and values change slowly. Even individual social norms, such as attitudes towards the death penalty or acceptance of corruption, tend to change rather slowly. This may be because many norms are rooted in religions whose basic precepts have changed remarkably little for centuries and even millennia—the major world religions have shaped and still shape the basic values and preferences of individuals, what they consider important in life, and how they expect other people to behave towards them. One can always find examples to the contrary, but values and social norms, seen as a whole, tend to change slowly.

One important reason why culture changes slowly is that many of the beliefs that comprise culture are hard to refute. Metaphysical beliefs are hard to refute, but so are many beliefs about human behaviour and society. We know as social scientists that applying scientific methods to social science is more difficult than applying them to the natural sciences. The obvious reason is that in contrast to the natural sciences, in social science in many, if not most, cases it is difficult to conduct controlled experiments. Moreover, most people do not apply scientific reasoning in their everyday life and tend to follow the beliefs inculcated in them by their parents and environment. The important inertia of culture means that culture must be seen as an important determinant of other institutions in society, such as legal and political institutions. It means that trying to transplant legal and political institutions that are alien to a local culture can only be self-defeating (see the piece by Polishchuk: Chapter 7).

Why do we observe different long-term cultural evolutions in different regions of the world? Cultural evolution should be seen as a combination of autonomous and random emergence of belief systems. Catholicism emerged and became the official religion of the Roman Empire. It is often claimed that it was chosen because its universalism was favourable to cement the unity of the Roman Empire. According to the classic analysis of Gibbon (1776), however, Christianity was the main cause of the decline of the Roman Empire with its emphasis on chastity, otherworldliness and sectarian attitudes towards other religions. Confucianism was first banned when China was unified, when the first emperor, Qin Shi Huang Di, had the books of Confucianist scholars burned and Confucianist scholars executed. It was only in the Han Dynasty that Confucianism became an official religion (or belief system) and it has had a lasting influence ever since. The adoption of

Confucianism with its insistence on social norms and limited and wise government stood in contrast with legalism, the doctrine established under the earlier Qin Dynasty, which justified autocratic rule and subordination to the emperor. However, we can imagine that a doctrine other than Confucianism could have emerged instead. The point is that systems of beliefs such as Christianity and Confucianism emerged in a way that is difficult to explain but, once they were adopted as state religions or systems of beliefs, they had a lasting influence because they shaped the view of the world of citizens living under those empires, and started having a life of their own and persisting long after these empires had disappeared, as is the obvious case for the Roman Empire. It is possible that certain systems of beliefs have a better quality of survival and transmission than others. This is a topic that is clearly not well understood.

6 Conclusions

The transition process from socialism to capitalism has been seen as the elimination of the planned economy and the communist political regime and its replacement by a well-functioning market economy and democratic political institutions. Twenty years after the fall of the Berlin Wall, it appears that the transitions have been very diverse. While Central European countries have embraced democracy and entered the EU, China has not and has instead strengthened the power of the communist party. Russia and many other countries from the FSU have evolved as states with strong autocratic tendencies. While central planning was abandoned everywhere, the economic institutions emerging in the different countries are also quite diverse, reflecting the diversity in political transitions. We have argued in this study that these evolutions can be understood in the light of the long-term historical evolutions of transition countries and their long-run history. Arguably, these evolutions might indeed be better explained by the weight of long-run history than by the long-run weight of communism. Indeed, given the relative similarity in the communist experience in all those regions, how to explain these divergent evolutions?

We have argued that this long-run weight of history can be explained by the inertia of culture understood as the general system of beliefs and values existing in a society. Empirical evidence shows that having lived together in an empire, be it Austro-Hungarian, Russian or Ottoman, explains cultural closeness between locations. We have also shown that values in CEE on a two-dimensional axis measuring preferences for political authoritarianism versus democracy and preferences for economic interventionism versus *laissez-faire* have remained consistently different for EU countries and the USA and have shown no sign of convergence but rather signs of divergence, illustrating the long-run inertia of culture.

Acknowledging and understanding countries' long-run cultural inertia as well as its influence on political and economic institutions is important for various reasons. First, it helps in forming realistic expectations of future reforms in a country as well as the direction of reforms. Developing non-realistic expectations of short- and medium-run evolutions of countries is not very helpful for international collaboration with these countries. Second, one must precisely learn to coexist and collaborate with countries having different sets of core values and beliefs in a spirit of openness, tolerance and respect. Keeping openness not only to trade but also to other ideas, values and beliefs is the best one can do to facilitate cultural exchange. This exchange will not lead to cultural convergence because culture moves too slowly, but it will favour cultural evolution in a positive direction. Most importantly, it will create the basis for collaboration between national elites to jointly work towards the goals of peace, prosperity, and a sustainable environment on our planet.

Acknowledgements

I thank Pauline Grosjean for very illuminating discussions and for sharing her research with me. I also thank Theocharis Grigoriadis and James Zuberi for research assistance.

Notes

1. Four to seven decades is a long time in people's lives but short from a historical perspective.
2. Nicolas II did not make such a choice but focused equally on the Balkans and the Baltic. With hindsight, this seems to have been a mistake of historical consequences since the German push to the East in the First World War eventually led to the downfall of the tsarist regime.
3. The Czech lands of Bohemia and Moravia were among the most prosperous regions of Europe until the Second World War.
4. Sun Yat-sen was in favour of democracy but unifying China was his first goal. Towards that goal, he was in favour of a temporary military dictatorship in order to unify China and prepare it in the longer run for democracy.
5. Popov's chapter in this volume makes a similar point. Because Russia missed the Enlightenment, efforts to impose the rule of law have been more unsuccessful than in Central Europe.
6. Treisman's piece (Chapter 4) looking at the determinants of democratization finds no effect of former empires. This is somewhat orthogonal to Grosjean's results, which are about cultural distance.
7. We weighed the countries by their population for both the EU-15 and transition countries.
8. We also add on the economic interventionism index disagreement with the idea that inequality is needed for incentives. Note that responses to that statement do not differ substantially across the three country-groups.

References

Berglöf, E. and P. Bolton (2002) 'The Great Divide', *Journal of Economic Perspectives*, 16(1): 77–100.

Dumke, R. (1978) 'The Political Economy of German Unification: Tariffs, Trade and Politics of the Zollverein Era', *The Journal of Economic History*, 38(1): 277–8.

EBRD (2007) *People in Transition*, EBRD: London.

Gibbon (1776) *The Decline and Fall of the Roman Empire*, edited by J.B. Bury, 7 volumes (1896–1902), vol. IV: 160–9.

Grosjean, P. (2009) 'The Contributions of Spatial Proximity and History to Cultural Integration: A Gravity Approach', mimeo, University of California: Berkeley.

Hooson, D. (1968) 'The Growth of Cities in Pre-Soviet Russia', in R.P. Beckinsale and J.M. Houston (eds), *Urbanization and its Problems: Essays in Honour of E.W. Gilbert*, Blackwell: London.

Miller, M. (1927) *The Economic Development of Russia: 1905–1919*, Cass and Company Ltd: London.

Roland, G. (2004) 'Understanding Institutional Change: Fast-Moving and Slow-Moving Institutions', *Studies in Comparative International Development*, 38(4): 109–31.

7
Misuse of Institutions: Lessons from Transition

Leonid Polishchuk

> Our institutions and all of that are like birch trees that we've thrust in the ground on the St. Trinity Day to make it look like a forest that grew naturally in Europe...
>
> Birch trees... which are planted need careful treatment... Only those nations have a future that possess a sense of what is important and significant in their institutions, and value those.
>
> Leo Tolstoy, *Anna Karenina*

1 Introduction

The essence and purpose of reforms in transition and developing countries have been to supply institutions that support markets, protect property and contracts, and ensure accountable governance in the private and public sectors and efficient delivery of social services. Such emphasis on institutions is consistent with the massive literature providing evidence of their key role in economic development and welfare (see, e.g., Acemoglu et al. 2002; Easterly and Levine 2003; Kaufman et al. 2005). An equally compelling body of evidence, however, attests to the widespread failure of newly introduced institutions to deliver the expected results. Many economies and societies demonstrate 'institutional invariance' (Acemoglu and Robinson 2008) when reforms do not affect the pre-existing social, economic, and political orders, and newly introduced institutions have little, if any, impact on the *status quo ante*. Such failures blur the link between institutions and development and give rise to the contrarian views that put the causality in reverse; good institutions are outcomes of development, not vice versa (Glaeser et al. 2004). The two decades of post-communist transition provide ample evidence of institutional failures, some of which are documented and explored in this book (e.g. Berglöf et al.: Chapter 10; Milanovic and Ersado: Chapter 3; Ofer: Chapter 9; Popov: Chapter 12; Roland: Chapter 6). Frustration in the outcomes of market reforms in many post-Soviet states and elsewhere in the former Eastern bloc can no longer be ascribed to temporary 'frictions' in the transition process and calls for systemic explanations. Non-performing institutions are often attributed to cultural rejection and 'bad fit' (Cooter 1997; Rodrik 2000; Polterovich 2001; Berkowitz et al. 2003); to inconsistency of a given institution with the rest of the institutional set-up, including a mismatch between newly introduced fast-moving and pre-existing slow-moving institutions (Roland 2004); to incompleteness of reform whereby, due to institutional complementarities (Aoki 2001), absence of essential institutions adversely affects those already in place (Hellman 1998); and to multiplicity of equilibria and 'institutional traps' (Roland 2000; Polterovich 2007).

This study points to yet another commonly observable cause, consonant with the above explanations: institutions could be misused, that is, applied or resorted to for reasons that have little in common with their intended or anticipated purpose. An institution is misused by exploiting the opportunities that it creates in unforeseen ways unrelated to its primary *raison d'être*. Such an institution, when applied destructively (Polterovich 2001), becomes a source of private gains (rent) for opportunistic agents at the expense of the rest of society; it loses its initial value-creation role and capacity, and it is turned into a vehicle for redistribution, often causing aggregate losses of efficiency and welfare. Acemoglu et al. (2002) make a distinction between 'institutions of private property' and 'extractive institutions'. The former serve as public goods/production inputs advancing economic development, whereas the latter are rent-extraction tools that impede development. In terms of this dichotomy, misuse disables a private property-type institution and transforms it into an extractive one.

Institutions are particularly prone to misuse when they have not emerged organically through an evolutionary process in response to grass-roots demand (North 1990) and are supported by norms, conventions, efficient enforcement mechanism, and numerous constituencies of users and beneficiaries, but have been instead 'planted' into often unreceptive soil by way of institutional reform. In the epigraph to this chapter, Leo Tolstoy's character expresses doubts about the sustainability and performance of such 'implants' created by Alexander II's reforms 150 years ago. The recent history of Russia and some of its neighbours gives numerous fresh reasons for such concerns.

The chapter is organized as follows. In the next section, common patterns of institutional misuse are analysed and illustrated by examples drawn primarily from the Russian experience (although also observed elsewhere in transition and developing countries). Causes of institutions' vulnerability to misuse are discussed next, with particular attention to failures of society and state to properly protect institutions. The analysis highlights the role of social capital as a safeguard against misuse of institutions, thus supporting the view that social norms, culture and capacity for collective action are essential for economic development and welfare (Keefer and Knack 2005; Tabellini 2008a). We then look at how without social capital, institutions are left unprotected at the grass-roots level, while unaccountable government is restricted in its enforcement tools and lacks proper incentives, and thus also fails to serve as an institutional guardian. The concluding section discusses implications of the pitfall of misused institutions for economic transition.

2 How institutions can be misused

In a variety of forms in which institutions are misused, several broad patterns are emerging. First, institutions can be manipulated; second, used as a cover to conceal questionable or illicit activities; third, captured and subverted by narrow interests (for more details, see Polishchuk 2008b).

2.1 Manipulation by institutions

Institutions can be manipulated due to laxity of controls of compliance with rules, or to imprecision of such rules that allows behaviour conforming to the letter of institutions but frustrating their spirit and purpose. In the former case an institution loses its ability to reduce uncertainty by sending signals of otherwise unobservable traits and behaviour. The value of such signals depends on the strength of the institution's internal and external control mechanisms. When enforcement mechanisms malfunction, public trust in an institution can be exploited to mislead the society about the true type of an agent and their behaviour. As the number of violators grows bigger, confidence in the institution progressively declines and the institution begins losing its reputation—an asset critically important for the ability to serve as a credible signalling device.

A telltale illustration of this process can be found in the non-profit sector. A major comparative advantage of non-profit over for-profit firms is that the former provide additional assurance to customers of the otherwise uncertain quality of goods and services (credence goods). Since operational surplus (if any) cannot be distributed to non-existent private owners of a non-profit firm, incentives to cut costs by lowering unobservable quality are weaker than in the for-profit case (Hansmann 1980). However, if the non-distribution condition is not properly enforced, unscrupulous operators can take advantage of the statute and reputation of the non-profit sector without following the rules on which such reputation rests. In an ensuing 'pooling equilibrium', credibility of the non-profit sector deteriorates and rent-seekers crowd out *bona fide* non-profits; the latter are forced to reduce the scale of their activities and/or quality of goods and services since the scepticism of customers and donors does not generate sufficient revenues to allow cost recovery at the previously available level (Polishchuk 2008a). The confidence crisis caused by massive misuse disables the institution of non-profits and deprives the society of its benefits and services.

Similar processes recently unfolded in the Russian post-secondary education sector. Uncontrollable proliferation of private universities and colleges,
and commercialization of public institutions of higher education, were
driven to a large extent by profit-seeking motives. Competition between
schools dramatically reduced academic standards and the quality of education, as universities and colleges were luring in prospective students by
promising degrees that would require minimal time and effort. The diminishing premium that such degrees earned in the labour market sustained
the expansion of the post-secondary education sector as long as the willingness to pay for an increasingly worthless diploma still covered the reduced
costs of operating a university (Polishchuk 2010). While the enrolment in
universities and colleges swelled to heretofore unheard of levels (adverse
demographic trends (Brainerd: Chapter 2 in this volume) put the only limit
to this expansion), the ability of such an educational system to enhance
human capital was severely compromised.

Another (but closely related) pattern of manipulation by institutions
exploits imperfections of the laws establishing and upholding formal institutions. Laws are 'incomplete contracts' and often leave grey areas open
to interpretation, which are filled by courts and regulators (Pistor and Xu
2003). When such interpretation is not sufficiently consistent and robust,
the incompleteness of laws makes them vulnerable to misuse whereby the
letter of the law is observed but its intent violated. This can be illustrated by Russian bankruptcy laws (Polterovich 2001; Polishchuk 2008b).
The institution of bankruptcy is expected to protect creditors and improve
the efficiency of corporate governance, but it can also be misused by 'corporate raiders' for takeovers of sound businesses and asset stripping. In the
latter case, application of the bankruptcy law is based on technicalities
while substantive reasons for bankruptcy proceedings are absent. Russia
witnessed a wave of 'contracted bankruptcies' targeting viable companies
that were attractive to corporate raiders, whereas loss-making and debt-
ridden companies—intended targets of the institution of bankruptcy—were
rarely touched. Lack of transparency in the corporate sector and weakness of the court system due to poor judicial quality and political pressure
(Lamber-Mogiliansky et al. 2007) were factors contributing to such practices.

2.2   Institutions as cover

Institutions could be misused to hide activities that cannot be conducted in
the open, and to represent such activities as legitimate and sanctioned. This
pattern can be illustrated by the misuse of corporate social responsibility.
Often, modern corporations voluntarily comply with enhanced environmental, social, ethical and other performance standards in excess of what
is required by laws and regulations, and support various charitable causes.
Such behaviour is motivated by seeking competitive advantages in selling
to socially conscious customers, or is in response to grass-roots societal

pressure that subjects companies to 'civic regulation'. At the same time, corporate social responsibility can be misused by government officials to coerce businesses into financing off-budget projects and programmes, or to accommodate agreements between firms and bureaucrats where corporate support of a government-favoured project is traded for preferential access to markets, resources and procurement contracts, or for tolerance to violations by companies of existing laws and regulations. Although such practices could be detrimental to economic efficiency and social welfare (see, e.g., Shleifer and Vishny 1994), they are legitimized under the guise of corporate social responsibility and as such have become commonplace in modern Russia (Polishchuk 2009). Misused corporate social responsibility creates 'institutional offshores' exempt from controls and oversight that are mandatory in private or public sectors.

Another example of the same pattern is the misuse of the institution of intermediaries. Intermediaries are indispensable in modern market economies as they support exchanges by cutting transaction costs. However, they can also be instrumental in reducing transaction costs of illicit activities; for example, by handling a criminal part of a transaction and disappearing afterwards (Yakovlev 2006). An important role of intermediaries is to assist in meeting legal and regulatory requirements set by governments, where they take advantage of specialization and economies of scale in processing large numbers of similar cases on behalf of their clients. Here, too, there is a dark side: intermediaries can be instrumental in abetting corruption by dramatically reducing its risks and transaction costs. Symbiotic relationships between intermediaries and corrupt officials provide the latter virtual indemnity from prosecution since those who have material evidence of bribery have no incentive to blow a whistle (Lambsdorff 2002). This can aggravate damage caused by corruption (Polishchuk et al. 2008).

2.3   Institutional capture

Capture and subversion are perhaps the best-known patterns of misused institutions. Capture puts an institution under the control of a narrow group that operates the institution or is affected by its performance. Thus, observed practices of economic regulation intended to serve the public interest often better conform to the 'public choice' view (Stigler 1971), where the institution of regulation is controlled by interest groups in the private sector or by government bureaucracy. The public choice view explains broad international variations in the regulation of entry. Taller barriers are not shown to yield higher health and public safety standards, more competition and better protection of consumers' and workers' rights, and so on; rather, they are associated with corruption and the shadow economy (Djankov et al. 2002). The informal sector does not provide an enabling environment for small and medium businesses, and excessive entry barriers, instead of serving public interests, retard economic growth and entail massive efficiency losses (De Soto 2000). The beneficiaries of such a regime, apart from corrupt bureaucracy, are the economic elite that are able to clear the elevated entry barriers and earn higher returns to their assets due to reduced competition in the formal sector (more on this later). As shown by Milanovic and Ersado (Chapter 3 in this volume), reduction of entry barriers for small businesses benefits the bottom half of the society on the income distribution scale but adversely affects the top third.

An institutional alternative to regulation—the courts system—can also be prone to misuse. The intended purpose of courts is to ensure fair and predictable resolution of disputes over torts, property, and contracts. By means of threats, bribes and/or political influence, courts can be misused for expropriation of income and property through legal sanctions obtained from a subverted justice system, or by denying justice to victims of expropriation. Such an outcome is particularly likely against a backdrop of profound economic and political inequality where wealth and power create advantages in influencing courts (Glaeser et al. 2003). Another common pattern of misuse is crossing the line between criminal and civil law, when the threat of opening a criminal case is used in resolving commercial disputes.

Yet another example of misuse by subversion is the capture of subnational governance in a federal system. Well-known advantages of a decentralized system of government, such as greater flexibility of fiscal policies and stronger performance incentives in the public sector, do not materialize automatically, which can be seen from numerous instances of decentralization failures. One reason for such failures is the capture of devolved government prerogatives at regional and local levels. Such risks are aggravated by a greater likelihood of emergence in a smaller jurisdiction of a dominant interest group (Bardhan and Mookherjee 2000; Blanchard and Shleifer 2001). The widespread capture of regional governments that occurred in Russia in the 1990s denied the country the economic benefits of federalism (Polishchuk 2004) and was a contributory factor in the prolonged recession and political instability that continued through most of the decade.

3 Why is misuse unopposed? The role of social capital

Institutions that are supplied exogenously in a process of economic reform differ from those that have evolved endogenously as self-enforcing equilibria (North 1990; Aoki 2001). The anticipated use of the former might not be incentive-compatible, in which case such institutions could be misused. If the correct use of externally established institutions is not an equilibrium outcome, third-party enforcement is required to ensure proper performance (Roland 2004). The scale and scope of institutional misuse observed in Russia and some other transition countries show that such enforcement is often inadequate. Perpetrators of misuse gain at the expense of *bona fide* users who are denied the benefits of the misused institutions. Why are institutions not defended by those who value their legitimate use and thus suffer from misuse? One can offer several plausible explanations, all of which invoke social attitudes and values and find a degree of support in the Russian evidence.

First, a society could be indifferent to misuse if affected institutions are not viewed as valuable and worth protecting; for example, when there is no prior experience of utilizing such institutions that would have demonstrated their value (Ofer: Chapter 9 in this volume). A case in point is social attitudes to political rights and freedoms in countries with a limited history of a non-despotic form of government.[1] Lack of awareness of the importance of such rights for economic well-being makes democratic political institutions shaky and open to misuse.

Pre-existing social values and business practices could be a factor preventing or condoning misuse of newly enacted laws. The effectiveness of such laws depends on whether they are meaningful in the local context, consistent with prevailing norms, and meet the demands of the society and the private sector (Cooter 1997; Berkowitz et al. 2003). Such conditions create an appreciation of the new laws, incentives to use them properly, and willingness of private individuals to assist the state in upholding and enforcing them. Otherwise, laws 'will either not be applied or applied in a way that may be inconsistent with the intention of the rule in the context of which it originated' (ibid.: 174). If a legal system in general is discredited by a history of manipulation in the hands of the powerful (Pistor 1999) or wealthy (Glaeser and Shleifer 2003), continued misuse is tolerated as 'business as usual'.

Social norms and values can themselves be considered as institutions, albeit more inertial and slower-moving than those purposefully established in the process of institutional reform. From this perspective a mismatch between modern institutions and traditional culture (norms, values, beliefs) that allows the former to be misused illustrates possible inconsistency between fast-moving and slow-moving institutions (Roland 2004; see also Ofer: Chapter 9 in this volume).

Public appreciation of institutions and hence willingness (or lack of it) to uphold them at the grass roots could also be strongly affected by events of recent history. If a new institution fails to deliver from the outset and initial positive expectations are frustrated—perhaps due to misuse at an early stage, when the institution is still fragile—public support of the institution will be withdrawn thereafter, and further misuse will continue unimpeded. This can be illustrated by the Russian federal system, which had no solid foundations in the national political culture nor historical precedents of any depth and significance (Polishchuk 1999), and was in part a reaction to the egregious failures of Soviet hyper-centralization, in part a political compromise of the early 1990s crafted to co-opt restive regional elites in a constitutional regime promoted by a weak central government. Absent of social and cultural anchors, federalism Russian-style was prone to the excesses of the early-to-mid 1990s with a nearly disabled federal centre, and succumbed to the subsequent over-centralization when political winds changed direction.

Second, even if an institution is perceived as valuable, its protection against misuse poses a collective action problem typical of grass-roots provision of public goods.[2] Unresolved collective action is a common cause of the persistence of inefficient or dysfunctional institutions (Olson 1982; Roland 2004), including those that are misused. The capacity for collective action is based on social capital—a set of norms, values and networks that facilitate joint efforts for a common cause (Keefer and Knack 2005). Social capital is a potent factor of economic development and welfare (op. cit.), similar in its significance to conventional institutions, such as property rights, markets, and private and public sector governance. Moreover, social capital contributes to economic outcomes largely through institutions. Performance of the latter is shown to depend on trust, mutual respect, co-operation and other values and patterns of behaviour comprising social capital (Tabellini 2008a).

The relationship between (conventional) institutions and social capital continues to be a matter of debate. Data show a degree of substitution between these two factors. In particular, social capital can partially make up for weak or missing institutions (Kranton 1996), in which case the returns to social cohesion, trust, and other ingredients of social capital could be particularly high (Durlauf and Fafchamp 2005). Such substitution, however, appears to be unidirectional: when social capital is in short supply, rampant misuse could debase institutions that are neither trusted nor respected. Thus, sustainable democracy and rule of law are rested on civic culture, a special kind of social capital that includes a broadly shared vision of unalienable political and human rights, and readiness to defend those against transgression and other forms of misuse of democratic institutions (Weingast 1997). Misuse of institutions in the private sector can be similarly prevented by means of self-regulation, which requires, *inter alia*, intensive communication and high-level consensus among the operators and users of an institution (Haufler 2001).[3] These and other examples illustrate complementarity between institutions and social capital—the latter safeguards the former from misuse.

Russia and most other post-communist nations have begun their transition to market democracies with depleted stocks of social capital, which is known to be adversely affected by a political history with a predominantly despotic form of government (Putnam 1993; Tabellini 2008a). Surveys reveal low levels of trust and other indicators of social capital in Russia (Mersijanova and Jakobson 2007). Moreover, the existing social capital often takes anti-modern forms where the purpose of co-operation is to seek joint protection from an adverse institutional environment rather than to fix it (Rose 2000). The dislocation and hardship of often chaotic transition have further eroded social capital across the former Eastern bloc (Aghion et al. 2010).

While the main focus and emphasis of post-communist transition have been on institutional reform, dramatic shortage of social capital has often been downplayed. Concurrency of the two processes—far-reaching institutional transformations and the decline of social capital from initially low bases—jeopardized the outcomes of institutional reforms. In the dynamics that have been set in motion, institutions, values and behaviour are co-evolving (Tabellini 2008b; Aghion et al. 2010), possibly leading to low-level equilibria where social capital remains low and discredited institutions are misused with impunity.

4　Government as institutional guardian

Failure of society to police institutions against misuse calls for involvement of the government, which bears general responsibility for public good delivery. In the case of institutional reform, this role requires not only enactment of new institutions but also enforcement of their rules. More stringent government regulation is a conventional response to low trust and diminished ability to maintain order by private means (Djankov et al. 2002; Aghion et al. 2010), and therefore shifting the burden of institutional protection from a society with low social capital to public agencies would follow this general pattern. Consistent with such a pattern, in Russia and some other transition countries, strong preferences in the society for government involvement and control persisted, if not grew stronger, over the two decades of transition (see, e.g., Denisova et al. 2009) and therefore represent a long-term cultural effect (Roland: Chapter 6 in this volume).

However, government ability to protect institutions on behalf of a society that relinquishes such function is often limited. Popov (Chapter 12 in this volume) points to a low capacity of the Russian state as one of the key reasons for Russia's low institutional scores. Indeed, government performance in low-trust societies usually receives low marks (Putnam 1993; Aghion et al. 2010) due to two overlapping reasons: first, incompetence and poor traits of public servants; and second, weak government accountability to a society that is disorganized and lacks civic culture. Thus in Russia, the government response, if any, to misuse of institutions has been almost invariably to restrict access to the institution both to those attempting misuse and to *bona fide* users alike. Such blunt regulatory tools often suppressed the institution instead of protecting it. For example, abuse of the non-governmental organization (NGO) status for tax evasion and money-laundering purposes (as well as allegedly for political means) resulted in a steep increase in reporting and regulatory requirements for Russian non-profit organizations (prior to which they were also denied tax benefits that are normally accorded to such organizations). The remedy proved to be too radical as it led to a dramatic decline in the ranks of Russian non-profit organizations as they found the cost of compliance with new rules prohibitively high. It is unclear whether the measure indeed contained the misuse of the NGO status, since there was a 'negative selection' at play—pseudo-NGOs that were able to successfully manipulate the old rules obtained comparative advantages over *bona fide* non-profits in navigating through the newly introduced stricter requirements. An equally heavy-handed reaction to the misuse in the 1990s of the Russian federal system was the cancellation of direct elections of regional governors, which essentially turned Russia from a federation into a unitary state.

Perhaps the most striking example of the limited ability of the Russian government to prevent misuse of institutions is the history of Russian bankruptcy law. When such law was first introduced in the early 1990s, it was rarely used due to excessively stringent pre-qualifications for bankruptcy proceedings. To facilitate the badly needed restructuring of Russian firms, the threshold was lowered but that triggered a massive response, mainly from corporate raiders misusing the institution of bankruptcy. The grim choice between an institution that is either defunct or vulnerable to massive misuse was resolved in yet another revision, which again tightened the requirements that had to be met to initiate a bankruptcy. This attempt was not entirely successful as it led to delays in bankruptcy cases initiated with good reasons, whereas raider attacks continued unabated, albeit by resorting to other chapters of the corporate law (Radygin and Simachev 2005).

Such reaction illustrates a common pattern of response to regulatory attempts to stop misuse of an institution by simply shifting misuse onto other institutions. This is a 'seesaw effect' (Acemoglu et al. 2008; see also Polterovich 2007)—when a policy reform imposes constraints on some questionable actions, affected agents sidestep such restrictions by deploying alternative means to the same ends. Another illustration of this phenomenon is the increased reliance on intermediaries in dealing with government agencies, as observed in Russia over the last several years. Demand for intermediary services went up in the aftermath of regulatory and administrative reforms that were expected to simplify and streamline official procedures and increase transparency and accountability of bureaucracy. An important objective of those reforms was to reduce corruption by increasing its risks. In response, corrupt officials resorted to intermediaries that offered 'institutional protection' by hiding bribes as flow-through in their fees (Polishchuk et al. 2008). As a result, the reforms were defused and corruption continued unabated.

A seesaw effect involving a misused institution was also present in the proliferation of corporate social responsibility after a reform of intergovernmental finance that has reduced fiscal discretion and tax revenues of Russian regional governments. As argued earlier in this study, Russian firms are often coerced by government officials into making social investments, and the misused institution of corporate social responsibility *de facto* restored fiscal discretion and revenue bases that regional governments were officially denied by the fiscal reform. However, such quick fixes are questionable surrogates of conventional fiscal tools as they violate basic principles of wholeness (earmarked revenue sources are disallowed) and accountability of modern public finance, and 'soften' budget constraints of subnational governments. For private firms, arbitrary informal levies collected under the guise of corporate social responsibility frustrate the main objectives of the Russian tax reform (to make taxes transparent and predictable, and lower tax rates while broadening tax bases). Finally, ad hoc agreements between businesses and bureaucrats also represent a seesaw effect, bypassing the public administration reform that reduces government officials' discretion and subjects them to clearly stated rules.

The above examples illustrate limited ability of the government to prevent the misuse of institutions by misguided application of blunt regulatory tools. Moreover, institutions are often misused in response to government regulations. Another common cause of the failures to protect institutions from misuse is low accountability of government to society. According to Acemoglu et al. (2008), restrictive regulations produce desired results in the middle range of political accountability—fully accountable officials refrain from questionable actions and properly perform their functions due to political incentives alone, whereas in the case of low accountability, reform fizzles due to the seesaw effect. Insufficiency of social capital adversely affects government accountability (Putnam 1993; Tabellini 2008a), and therefore when the misuse of institutions is not resisted at the grass-roots level, one should not expect government interventions to adequately fill the void. Government actions (or lack thereof) are more likely to be driven by organized interests in the bureaucracy and private sector, and a political economy analysis provides further insight into the origins of institution misuse.

5   Political economy of misused institutions

Organized interests could be misusing captured institutions by transforming them from open-access private property-type institutions to extractive ones that earn rent for a group of the privileged elite. When institutions of private property function as expected, they reduce the elite's rents (North 1990) and hence become targets of subversion. Established elites rely on exclusive (inegalitarian) institutions to protect their privileges (Przeworski 2004) and, since private property-type institutions are egalitarian in their nature, elites attempt to subvert them (see, e.g., Rajan and Zingales 2003; Polishchuk and Savvateev 2004; Acemoglu and Robinson 2008). A useful way to think of this well-known phenomenon is to distinguish between 'fixed costs' of accessing an institution and 'rents' that such an institution affords once the 'entry fee' has been paid. For institutions of private property, fixed costs are kept minimal to ensure universal access, and consequently no rent accrues. Extractive institutions, in contrast, maintain high fixed costs, thus allowing access only to the wealthy, but earn high rent for those qualified as 'club members'. The rent is transferred from the rest of society and a deadweight loss makes such institutions socially inefficient.

Consider an institution (s, r), where s is the fixed cost and r the rate of return that accrues to assets of the institution's user. Assuming no income effect, if K is the capital endowment of an agent, their utility equals $U(s, r; K) = rK + u(s)$, where $u(s)$ is the pay-off to non-capital assets, net of the fixed cost; function u is monotonically decreasing. For two institutional set-ups (s_1, r_1) and (s_2, r_2), such that $s_2 > s_1, r_2 > r_1$, sufficiently wealthy agents will always prefer the latter; furthermore, agents' preferences over (s, r) meet the single-crossing property and thus if an agent with capital K prefers (s_2, r_2) to (s_1, r_1), so will all other agents with $K' > K$. Capital thus serves as a sorting factor that tilts preferences of the elite in favour of inefficient institutions and creates incentives for misuse.[4]

When the institution is not misused, fixed cost is at its minimal (and socially optimal) level, $s_0 \geq 0$, and the rate of return equals r_0. Misuse consists of raising fixed cost s above s_0 in order to increase r and earn rent of $r - r_0$. Suppose a two-class society consists of the elite and the non-elite, where the former comprise share α of the unit continuum of agents and have per capita endowments of capital K_1, and the non-elite's share of the population is $1 - \alpha$ and their capital endowments are $K_2 < K_1$ each. The total stock of the capital in the economy equals $K = \alpha K_1 + (1 - \alpha)K_2$. A misused institution (s, r) with $s > s_0, r > r_0$ entails aggregate welfare losses,

$$\Delta \equiv r_0 K + u(s_0) - rK - u(s) > 0. \tag{1}$$

If the elite prefer misuse, their valuation of the two institutional regimes runs in the opposite direction,

$$rK_1 + u(s) > r_0 K_1 + u(s_0). \tag{2}$$

These two conditions can be restated as

$$(r - r_0)(K_1 - K) > \Delta > 0. \tag{3}$$

In other words, the elite prefer misuse if the rent they earn on their capital in excess of the economy-wide average per capita level exceeds average per capita losses of welfare caused by the misuse (Figure 7.1).

The above theory of misuse can be illustrated by the subversion of entry regulation mentioned earlier, where the purpose of high barriers is to deter entry by holders of small capital assets and thus increase pay-offs to the

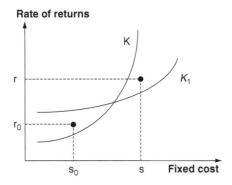

Figure 7.1   Preferences over institutional regime
Source: Author's illustration.

capital of the wealthy.[5] As in De Soto (2000), we assume that those unable to afford high entry costs deploy their assets in the informal sector where returns are much lower; for simplicity, nil. Suppose that the economy's production function, $Y = F(K, L)$, satisfies the standard neoclassical properties, and that in addition to capital assets each agent possesses one unit of labour. If the fixed cost is set at the socially optimal level,[6] all capital is invested in the official sector of the economy,

$$K_2 F_K(K, 1) > s_0. \qquad (4)$$

If the purpose of misuse is to keep small resource owners out, then s should be set equal to $K_2 F_K(\alpha K_1, 1)$, in which case the entry cost cancels out the returns to the capital endowment of a small owner, and entry to the official sector does not produce any economic benefits. After the exclusion of small owners, those in the elite earn the pay-off $(K_1 - K_2)F_K(\alpha K_1, 1) + F_L(\alpha K_1, 1)$, whereas when $s = s_0$, their pay-offs are $K_1 F_K(K, 1) + F_L(K, 1) - s_0$. One can check (invoking concavity of the technology) that due to (4), social welfare decreases when s goes up from s_0 to $K_2 F_K(\alpha K_1, 1)$,

$$\Delta = F(K, 1) - s_0 - (F(\alpha K_1, 1) - \alpha K_2 F_K(\alpha K_1, 1)) > 0, \qquad (5)$$

and the condition (3) in the present context is

$$(K_1 - K)(F_K(\alpha K_1, 1) - F_K(K, 1)) > \Delta. \qquad (6)$$

Notice that the condition (3) (as well as its special case (6)) holds only if distribution of the capital in the economy is sufficiently inequitable. (Figure 7.2 illustrates this for the Cobb–Douglas technology $F(K, L) = \sqrt{KL}$; the horizontal axis shows the share α of the elite in the total population, and the

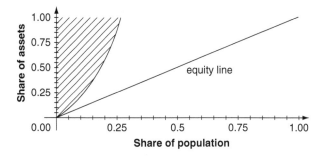

Figure 7.2 Incentives to misuse entry barriers
Source: Author's illustration.

vertical one the share $\alpha K_1/K$ of the elites' assets in the total capital stock of the economy; the shaded area comprises combinations of the above parameters for which the elite would favour excessive entry barriers.) Indeed, misuse of private property-type institutions could benefit a particular interest group only in unequal societies—otherwise every group will bear its share of aggregate welfare losses and will thus be opposed to the misuse.[7]

A remarkably similar logic set forth in Polishchuk and Savvateev (2004) explains the failure of the Russian privatization to establish a secure property rights regime in the country. The privatization strategy implemented in the early 1990s was predicated on the assumption that a massive transfer of capital assets to private hands would create a constituency of private owners naturally interested in effective property rights protection, and hence the institution of property rights would emerge in response to powerful grass-roots demand created by the privatization (Boycko et al. 1995). Arguably the same grass-roots demand of the economically powerful would protect the new institution from misuse. In fact, deep inequality of asset ownership produced by the privatization gave rise to an economic 'oligarchy', which made misuse of private property rights an instrument of choice in further asset accumulation.

These cases are consistent with the general conclusion that extractive institutions (often obtained by misuse through capture of institutions intended to enhance economic efficiency) are likely to emerge and be sustained in societies with profound economic inequality (see, e.g., Engerman and Sokoloff 2000). With a weak civil society, the elite are likely to prevail in shaping government policies due to their advantages in resolving the collective action problem (Olson 1965) and the ability to deploy for lobbying purposes vast resources that they control. Elite dominance in public policy-making explains not only the above-described misuse through capture directly benefiting the elite but also other kinds of misuse at the grass-roots level to which the elite—and hence the government—are simply indifferent.

Indeed, various individuals value the same institution to different extents. For some the institution could be nearly vital; for others, barely noticeable and almost never used. Thus, immediate needs of elites in services provided by NGOs (social programmes and safety nets, protection of social, political and economic rights, and so on) are obviously not particularly acute. The same is true about domestic institutions of post-secondary education and health care, which the powerful and wealthy ignore by sending their children to foreign universities and obtaining treatment at clinics abroad. Similarly the elite can also find (with some caveats) foreign and/or private alternatives to domestic courts and financial markets.

Furthermore, even if general-purpose institutions that are valued by the society at large are also of some value to the elite, the latter have more immediate and overarching needs in club goods that are essential for them but are of little immediate significance to the rest of society. Thus, economic assets controlled by the elite could require specialized public factors of production; one can think, for example, about an economy with a large resource sector dominated by the elite. The latter would thus be concerned about pipelines and other components of the resource industry infrastructure.

To make the discrepancy between institutional needs of the elite and the rest of society particularly stark, assume, as in Acemoglu and Robinson (2008), that the elite and the non-elite take utility in different and non-overlapping types of public goods. In that case, the elite would not waste their political resources on policing institutions that they do not value and will instead use their influence to maximize the supply of club goods. As a result, general-purpose institutions will be misused with impunity because the elite influence leads to the redeployment of public resources, including government oversight capacity, from open-access institutions to club goods.

A menu auction model (Grossman and Helpman 2001) could be used to describe the outcome of such bias. Let G_1 and G_2 be supplies of institution club goods and institution public goods, respectively, which are funded from tax revenues collected at flat rate t. Aggregate social welfare is as follows, $W(t, G_1, G_2) = (1-t)[Y_1(G_1)+Y_2(G_2)]$, where the part $Y_1(G_1)$ accrues (before taxes) to the elite and depends on club goods; G_1, and $Y_2 G_2$ accrue to the non-elite and depend on the availability of the public goods, G_2. Government policy (t, G_1, G_2) must satisfy the budget constraint $G_1 + G_2 \leq t(Y_1(G_1) + Y_2(G_2))$. If there is no lobbying, the government chooses its policy by maximizing W subject to the budget constraint, and it supplies both production inputs at socially optimal levels G_1^0, G_2^0 such that $Y_i'(G_i^0) = 1$, $i = 1, 2$. Suppose now that the elite are organized in a lobby and offer the government a contribution $C(t, G_1, G_2)$ depending on a policy choice, whereas the non-elite are unable to solve a collective action problem and stay unorganized. In that case, the government chooses its policy by maximizing $W + aC$ with some $a > 0$ (characterizing government susceptibility to influence), subject to the same budget constraint. In equilibrium, the lobby's contribution function is locally truthful (Grossman and Helpman 2001), that is, it has the same marginal rates of substitution between policy instruments as in the lobby's utility function $W_1 = (1 - t)Y_1(G_1)$. Equilibrium quantities of production inputs G_1^*, G_2^* immediately follow from this property, and since the elite's preferences now by proxy enter the government's objective function, one can easily check that inequalities $G_1^* > G_1^0, G_2^* < G_2^0$ hold. This means that the elite's club goods compete with general-purpose institutions for tax revenues (which proxy in the model government resources available to supply and sustain an institutional set-up) and thus crowd out the latter. This translates into a lack of protection from misuse of the private property-type institutions.

Similar conclusions are obtained under a different assumption, when the elite do not lobby the government from without but are part of the ruling class and choose from within government policies with regard to institutions in accordance with their economic interests (Polishchuk 2008b). A model based on McGuire and Olson (1996) shows that if the ruling class has its economic assets concentrated in a part of the economy that shows low sensitivity to the supply of institutions-public goods, and requires specific club goods-type production inputs, this too distorts the choice of the government away from the social optimum and leaves private property-type institutions neglected and open to misuse.

A noteworthy result of such analysis concerns the impact of market interests of the ruling class on choices made by a politically unaccountable government. If the ruling class has no direct ownership of economic assets and considers the private sector only as a tax base, public production inputs (including institutions) will usually be undersupplied in comparison with the social optimum, and tax rates will be excessively high. McGuire and Olson (1996) show that when the ruling class directly owns some production assets, it has the ability to improve government policies, leading to lower tax rates and increased provision of the public goods. However, in the present two-sector context, this conclusion is not the case. When the assets of the ruling class are only in the first sector, the tax rate will indeed go down and provision of the club goods, G_1, will increase but the provision of the public goods, G_2, will be lower than in the benchmark case of the ruling class without market assets. The intuition behind this result is as follows. The ruling class still considers the part of the economy that it does not own as merely a tax base and the reduction of the tax rate (out of concern about the ruling class's own market assets) diminishes the incentives to spend public funds on production inputs that expand such a tax base. This conclusion corroborates the findings in Robinson et al. (2006) that 'resource booms' prompt ruling elites to vigorously pursue the 'extraction path' in a close to socially efficient pattern while misallocating resources in the rest of the economy; in our case, by withdrawing support from open access institutions, thus making them vulnerable to misuse.

Notice finally that the incentives of ruling elites to protect general-purpose open-access institutions from misuse (e.g. by maintaining independent judiciary) grow stronger when there is sufficient government turnover and hence non-negligible likelihood that those currently in power might themselves need court protection and other similar public services once they leave the office (Polishchuk and Syunyaev 2011). The tendency of unlimited political tenures and transfer of power, if any, to handpicked successors, which has spread over many successor states of the former Soviet Union, considerably weakens such immediate incentives to protect institutions from misuse, which is yet another explanation for the proliferation of this pathology.

6   Implications for reforms

Massive misuse of newly established institutions was an unexpected outcome of reforms, not unlike 'other surprises' of transition (Roland 2000). A major reason for such an outcome was the complementarity between institutions and culture: the dearth of social capital in post-communist societies left institutions unprotected at the grass-roots level and failed to produce strong demand for government enforcement of rules preventing misuse. Politically organized and influential groups among the elite were either indifferent to the misuse of many institutions or, worse yet, perpetrated it.

While early on in the transition misuse of institutions was perhaps inevitable due to the overall disorganization in the economy and society, and general proliferation of opportunistic behaviour and rent-seeking (Polterovich 2007), in some countries, including Russia, such deviations became chronic, developed their own momentum, and were subsequently reinforced. Misuse of institutions was sustained by the continued decline of social capital, increasing distrust and atomization in the society, growing disappointment in the new institutions, and indifference to their fate. This dynamic refuted the expectations that globalization would force societies to adopt modern culture, which is 'no longer a matter of choice' (Porter 2000: 27). Instead, it proved that norms and values comprising social capital exhibit strong inertia and are susceptible to short-term negative shocks (Tabellini 2008b).

Another aggravating trend was deepening socioeconomic inequality, which was conducive to degeneration of private property institutions into extracting ones. Finally, a powerful contributory factor was incomplete reform. Indeed, misuse of institutions is often facilitated by gaps in the institutional set-up—missing institutions could have provided checks and balances preventing misuse of those institutions that are already in place. Thus, well-established corporate governance and effective and impartial court systems prevent misuse of the institution of bankruptcy. A strong and yet constitutionally constrained federal government is required to maintain 'market-preserving federalism' and prevent misuse of decentralization at the subnational level, such as beggar-thy-neighbour-type policies detrimental to economic growth (Blanchard and Shleifer 2001; Polishchuk 2001). A well-developed system of political parties works to the same end. Political competition, free media and other transparency-enhancing institutions serve to prevent institutional capture by vested interests, and so forth.

An incomplete institutional regime could emerge in a process of gradual reform where new institutions are supplied in a particular sequence and over a significant period of time. Gradual reforms present an alternative to radical ones, when the required institutions are established quickly and nearly simultaneously. Both strategies have their strengths and weaknesses, which are extensively debated in a vast literature on the subject (see, e.g., Roland 2000; Polterovich 2007). Gradualism is usually justified by difficulties of implementation of multiple reforms across a broad front, as well as by benefits of learning and, if necessary, adjustment of earlier blueprints. One of the dangers of a gradual approach is that in the interim it could create opportunities for misuse of institutions already in place. Hellman (1998) argues that political and business elites are better able to extract rent from unfinished reform and thus stay in the way of reform completion, protracting an institutional hiatus. Our analysis shows that rent from half-reformed economies can be extracted through misuse of earlier institutions. In fact, misuse of institutions and incomplete reform feed on each other. This can once again be illustrated by the mistreatment of corporate social responsibility—poor protection of property rights, typical for incomplete reforms, makes businesses susceptible to government coercion. In contrast, unfounded expectations that socially responsible companies should maintain their workforces irrespective of market conditions are likely to delay economic restructuring and modernization of social safety nets (Polishchuk 2009).

Once the misuse of institutions has become entrenched it is difficult to reverse. One can hope that development itself creates more enabling conditions for institutions to function properly; for example, through accumulation of human capital (Lipset 1960; Glaeser et al. 2004). This kind of scenario, however, cannot be assured, given the danger of 'institutional traps' (Polterovich 2007) and commonly observed 'invariance' to reforms of institutional set-ups adverse to development (Acemoglu and Robinson 2008). It is noteworthy that such invariance can be sustained precisely through the misuse of institutions that are expected to eliminate *ancien régime*. Furthermore, social capital is known to be difficult to instil and nurture by government and donors who at best could support and augment 'bottom-up production of norms and networks in non-distorting ways' (Keefer and Knack 2005: 772).

If the damage caused by misuse exceeds the benefits that the institution still produces, and if no reliable means to prevent misuse are available, then not introducing such an institution is the second-best choice (Glaeser and Shleifer 2003). A palliative solution could be to design institutions as 'misuse-proof' so that '[they do] not depend on absent or weak institutions and [are] insulated from or adapted to perverse institutions as far as possible' (Shirley 2005: 630). This reinforces the general dictum that best-fitting institutions for transition and developing countries should be designed to reflect local idiosyncrasies, including the danger of misuse.

Notes

1. Recent opinion polls in Russia reveal a high level of appreciation for social and economic rights, which are valued by a majority of respondents, whereas the percentage of those who value political rights and freedoms is several times smaller (VTSIOM 2009).
2. In the present context, individuals contribute towards a public good by refraining from misuse themselves and preventing it by others through self-regulation, whistle-blowing, and demanding greater accountability from government officials, regulators, and other institution guardians, and so on.
3. A failure to prevent misuse through self-regulation is evident in Russia's post-secondary education, where the academic community has been notoriously unable to endorse and enforce a common stance on educational policies and remains deeply divided over higher education reform strategy in the country.
4. This can be interpreted as increasing returns to scale in rent-seeking (Murphy et al. 1993); see also Rajan and Zingales (2003) and Polishchuk and Savvateev (2004).
5. Djankov et al. (2002) consider two possible patterns of the regulation of entry capture: by the bureaucracy operating the entry process (a 'tollbooth' view) and by vested interests that are based outside the government but can influence the latter. Our analysis follows the second view.
6. Arruñada (2007) cautions about the push to reduce entry barriers below what is required to serve their intended purposes.
7. For more on the role of inequality in shaping preferences in favour of inefficient institutions, see Polishchuk and Savvatev (2004).

References

Acemoglu, D., S. Johnson and J. Robinson (2002) 'Reversal of Fortune: Geography and Institutions in the Making of the Modern World Income Distribution', *Quarterly Journal of Economics*, 117: 1231–94.

Acemoglu, D., S. Johnson, P. Querubin and J. Robinson (2008) 'When Does Policy Reform Work? The Case of Central Bank Independence', *Brookings Papers on Economic Activity No. 2008–1*.

Acemoglu, D. and J. Robinson (2008) 'Persistence of Power, Elites, and Institutions', *American Economic Review*, 98(1): 267–93.

Aghion, P, Y. Algan, P. Cahuc and A. Shleifer (2010) 'Regulation and Distrust', *Quarterly Journal of Economics*, 125(3): 1015–49.

Aoki, M. (2001). *Toward a Comparative Institutional Analysis*, MIT Press: Cambridge, MA.

Arruñada, B. (2007) 'Pitfalls to Avoid When Measuring Institutions: Is Doing Business Damaging Business?', *Journal of Comparative Economics*, 35(4): 729–47.

Bardhan, P. and D. Mookherjee (2000) 'Capture and Governance at Local and National Levels', *American Economic Review*, 90(2): 135–9.

Berkowitz, D., K. Pistor and J.-F. Richard (2003) 'Economic Development, Legality, and the Transplant Effect', *European Economic Review*, 47(1): 165–95.

Blanchard, O. and A. Shleifer (2001) 'Federalism with and without Political Centralization: China versus Russia', *IMF Staff Papers No. 48*.

Boycko, M., A. Shleifer and R. Vishny (1995) *Privatizing Russia*, MIT Press: Cambridge, MA.

Cooter, R. (1997) 'The Rule of State Law and the Rule-of-Law State: Economic Analysis of the Legal Foundations of Development', in *Annual World Bank Conference on Development Economics*, World Bank: Washington, DC.

Denisova, I., M. Eller and E. Zhuravskaya (2009) 'What Do Russians Think About Transition? Evidence From RLMS Survey', *Economics of Transition*, 18(2), 249–80.

De Soto, H. (2000) *The Mystery of Capital: Why Capitalism Triumphs in the West and Fails Everywhere Else*, Basic Books: New York.

Djankov, S., R. La Porta, F. Lopez-de-Silanez and A. Shleifer (2002) 'The Regulation of Entry', *Quarterly Journal of Economics*, 117(1): 1–37.

Durlauf, S. and M. Fafchamp (2005) 'Social Capital', in P. Aghion, S. Durlauf (ed.), *Handbook of Economic Growth*, 1: 1639–99.

Easterly, W. and R. Levine (2003) 'Tropics, Germs and Crops: How Endowments Influence Economic Development', *Journal of Monetary Economics*, 50(1): 3–39.

Engerman, S. and K. Sokoloff (2000) 'Institutions, Factor Endowments, and Paths of Development in the New World', *Journal of Economic Perspectives*, 14(3): 217–32.

Glaeser, E. and A. Shleifer (2003) 'The Rise of the Regulatory State', *Journal of Economic Literature*, 41(2): 401–25.

Glaeser, E., J. Scheinkman and A. Shleifer (2003) 'The Injustice of Inequality', *Journal of Monetary Economics*, 50(1): 199–222.

Glaeser, E., R. La Porta, F. Lopez-de-Silanez and A. Shleifer (2004) 'Do Institutions Cause Growth?', *Journal of Economic Growth*, 9(3): 271–303.

Haufler, V. (2001) *A Public Role for the Private Sector: Industry Self-Regulation in a Global Economy*, Carnegie Endowment for International Peace: New York.

Grossman, G. and E. Helpman (2001) *Special Interest Politics*, MIT Press: Cambridge, MA.

Hansmann, H. (1980) 'The Role of Non-Profit Enterprise', *Yale Law Journal*, 89: 835–901.

Hellman, J. (1998) 'Winners Take All: The Politics of Partial Reform in Postcommunist Transitions', *World Politics*, 50(2): 202–34.

Kaufman, D., A. Kraay and M. Mastruzzi (2005) 'Governance Matters IV: Governance Indicators for 1996–2004', *World Bank Policy Research Working Papers No. 3630*, World Bank: Washington DC.

Keefer, P. and S. Knack (2005) 'Social Capital, Social Norms and the New Institutional Economics', in C. Menard and M. Shirley (eds), *Handbook of New Institutional Economics*, Springer: New York

Kranton, R. (1996) 'Reciprocal Exchange: A Self-Sustaining System', *American Economic Review*, 86(4): 830–51.

Lamber-Mogiliansky, A., K. Sonin and E. Zhuravskaya (2007). 'Are Russian Commercial Courts Biased? Evidence from a Bankruptcy Law Transplant', *Journal of Comparative Economics*, 35(2): 254–77.

Lambsdorff, J.G. (2002) 'How Confidence Facilitates Illegal Transactions', *American Journal of Economics and Sociology*, 61(4): 829–53.

Lipset, S. (1960) *Political Man: The Social Basis of Modern Politics*, Doubleday: New York.

McGuire, M. and M. Olson (1996) 'The Economics of Autocracy and Majority Rule: The Invisible Hand and the Use of Force', *Journal of Economic Literature*, 34: 72–96.

Mersijanova I. and L. Jakobson (2007) *Social Activity of Population and Citizens' Perception of Conditions for Civil Society Development*, HSE Publishers: Moscow.

Murphy, K., A. Shleifer and R. Vishny (1993) 'Why Is Rent-Seeking So Costly to Growth?' *American Economic Review*, 83(2): 409–14.

North, D. (1990) *Institutions, Institutional Change, and Economic Performance*, Cambridge University Press: Cambridge, MA.

Olson, M. (1965) *The Logic of Collective Action: Public Goods and the Theory of Groups*, Harvard University Press: Cambridge, MA.

Olson, M. (1982) *The Rise and Decline of Nations*, Yale University Press: New Haven.

Pistor, K. (1999) 'Supply and Demand for Law in Russia', *East European Constitutional Review*, 8(4): 105–8.

Pistor, K. and C. Xu (2003) 'Incomplete Law: A Conceptual and Analytical Framework and its Application to the Evolution of Financial Market Regulation', *Journal of International Law and Politics*, 35(4): 931–1013.

Polishchuk, L. (1999) 'Russian Federalism: Decentralization that Failed', *World Economic Affairs*, 2: 69–75.

Polishchuk, L. (2001) 'Legal Initiatives of Russian Regions: Determinants and Effects', in P. Murrell (ed.) *The Value of Law in Transition Economies*, University of Michigan Press: Chicago.

Polishchuk, L. (2004) 'Decentralization in Russia: Impact on Quality of Governance', in M. Kimeney and P. Meagher (eds), *Devolution and Development: Governance Prospects in Decentralizing States*, Ashgate: Aldershot.

Polishchuk, L. (2008a) 'Comparative Advantages of the Non-Profit Sector: Theory, Global Practice, and Russian Realities', in *Non-Profit Sector: Law, Economics, and Management*, Moscow (in Russian).

Polishchuk, L. (2008b) 'Misuse of Institutions: Patterns and Causes', *The Journal of Comparative Economic Studies*, 4: 57–80.

Polishchuk, L. (2009) 'Corporate Social Responsibility vs. Government Regulation: Institutional Analysis with an Application to Russia', *HSE Working Papers*, WP10/2009/01, Higher School of Economics: Moscow.

Polishchuk, L. (2010) 'Collective Reputation in Post-Secondary Education: An Equilibrium Model Analysis' (in Russian), *Journal of the New Economic Association*, 7: 46–69.

Polishchuk, L. and A. Savvateev (2004) 'Spontaneous (Non)emergence of Property Rights', *Economics of Transition*, 12(1): 103–27.

Polishchuk, L., O. Shchetinin and O. Shestoperov (2008) 'Intermediaries Between Private Sector and State: Supporting Business or Abetting Corruption?' (in Russian), *Voprosy Ekonomiki*, 3: 14–27.

Polishchuk, L. and G. Syunyaev (2011) 'Taming the (Not So) Stationary Bandit: Turnover of Ruling Elites and Protection of Property Rights', mimeo.

Polterovich, V. (2001) 'Transplantation of Economic Institutions' (in Russian), *Ekonomicheskaya Nauka Sovremennoj Rossii*, 3: 44–59.

Polterovich, V. (2007). *Elements of Reform Theory* (in Russian), Ekonomika Publishers: Moscow.

Porter, M. (2000) 'Attitudes, Values, Beliefs, and the Microeconomics of Prosperity', in L. Harrison and S. Huntington (eds), *Culture Matters*, Basic Books: New York.

Przeworski, A. (2004) 'The Last Instance: Are Institutions the Primary Cause of Economic Development?', *European Journal of Sociology*, 45(2): 165–88.

Putnam, R. (1993). *Making Democracy Work: Civic Traditions in Modern Italy*, Princeton University Press: Princeton, NJ.

Radygin, A. and Y. Simachev (2005) 'Institution of Bankruptcy in Russia: Evolution, Problems and Prospects' (in Russian), *Rossijskij Zhurnal Menedzhmenta*, 3: 11–23.

Rajan, R. and L. Zingales (2003) *Saving Capitalism from Capitalists*, Crown Business: New York.

Robinson, J., R. Torvik and T. Verdier (2006) 'Political Foundations of the Resource Curse', *Journal of Development Economics*, 79(2): 447–68.

Rodrik, D. (2000) 'Institutions for High Quality Growth: What They Are and How to Acquire Them', *Studies in Comparative International Development*, 35(3): 3–31.

Roland, G. (2000). *Transition and Economics: Politics, Markets, and Firms*, MIT Press: Cambridge, MA.

Roland, G. (2004) 'Understanding Institutional Change: Fast-Moving and Slow-Moving Institutions', *Studies in Comparative International Development*, 38(4): 109–31.

Rose, R. (2000) 'Uses of Social Capital in Russia: Modern, Pre-Modern, and Anti-Modern', *Post-Soviet Affairs*, 16(1): 35–57.

Shirley, M. (2005) 'Institutions and Development', in C. Menard and M. Shirley (eds), *Handbook of New Institutional Economics*, Springer: New York.

Shleifer, A. and R. Vishny (1994) 'Politicians and Firms', *Quarterly Journal of Economics*, 109(4): 995–1025.

Stigler, G. (1971) 'The Theory of Economic Regulation', *Bell Journal of Economics*, 2(1): 3–21.

Tabellini, G. (2008a) 'Institutions and Culture', *Journal of the European Economic Association*, 6(2–3): 255–94.

Tabellini, G. (2008b) 'The Scope of Co-operation: Norms and Incentives', *Quarterly Journal of Economics*, 123(3): 905–50.

VTSIOM (2009) *Press Release No. 1395.*

Weingast, B. (1997) 'The Political Foundations of Democracy and the Rule of Law', *American Political Science Review*, 91(2): 245–63.

Yakovlev, A. (2006) *Agents of Modernization* (in Russian), HSE Publishers: Moscow.

8
Civil Society, Institutional Change, and the Politics of Reform: The Great Transition

László Bruszt, Nauro F. Campos, Jan Fidrmuc, and Gérard Roland

1 Introduction

Nearly two decades after the start of economic and political reforms in the former communist countries, the economic and political outcomes are very diverse. On the one hand, the countries of Central Europe and the Baltics were able, for the most part, to stabilize their economies after a few years of output fall and to recover their pre-1989 output levels. On the other hand, the former Soviet Union (FSU) and former Yugoslavia (with the exception of Slovenia) experienced a much more severe and protracted output drop and, subsequently, also slower recovery (Figure 8.1). Furthermore, market reforms were faster and deeper in the former group of countries while the countries of the FSU lagged behind (EBRD 2007; Kaufmann et al. 2003). The progress with respect to political liberalization was similar. Some post-communist countries, again mostly those in Central Europe and the Baltics, quickly introduced free elections and political freedoms, and stabilized their democracies. In contrast, former Yugoslavia went through a horrible war experience before any substantial democratization could be observed, while most countries of the FSU underwent a period of limited democratization before drifting towards autocratic rule (Figure 8.2).

The widely diverging outcomes of the post-communist transition on the economic or political front gave rise to a large literature on the determinants of transition success. There is by now a consensus that proximate causes, such as the outcomes of the very first democratic elections, or differences in economic policies alone (speed and sequencing of reforms, type of privatization policies, conduct of stabilization policies, and so on), cannot fully explain the observed divergence and that differences in the institutional set-ups provide a better explanation (see, among others, Johnson et al. 1999; Ekiert and Kubik 1998; Møller 2009). However, how do we explain the differences in the institutional evolution in different countries? Taking

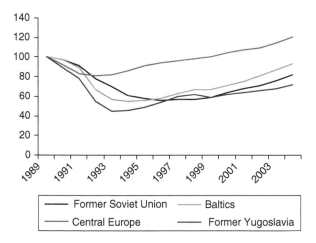

Figure 8.1 Evolution of real GDP index (1989 = 100)

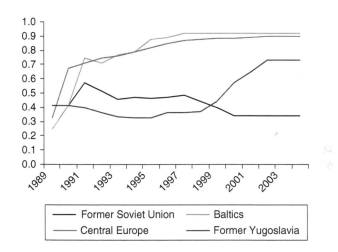

Figure 8.2 Evolution of democracy index (Freedom House)
Note: The index represents the simple average of political rights and civil liberties indicators compiled by Freedom House (www.freedomhouse.org/).

institutions as exogenous cannot be a satisfactory answer, as all transition countries have been undergoing rapid and profound institutional change since the end of communism.

Various explanations for the institutional divergence in Central and Eastern Europe (CEE) have been proposed, stressing geopolitical and accession effects (see Roland and Verdier 2003; Berglöf and Roland 1997), or highlighting the differences in economic, political, or cultural lega-cies (Kitschelt 2003: 49-86; Kitschelt and Malesky 2000; Møller 2009). Surprisingly, a potentially important causal channel has been neglected—differences in the development of civil society and in the patterns of interaction between civil activists and the power-holders, prior to the fall of communism. The analysis provided in this study fills the gap. We construct an original dataset measuring the breadth and depth of the pre-transition civil society. We then proceed to investigate the impact of civil society on subsequent institutional, economic and political developments. We expect the pre-transition civil society to have played an important role for a num-ber of reasons. In countries where a more active civil society has exploited the political opportunity of communist collapse, the demand for imple-menting and consolidating institutional checks and balances, and limits to executive powers, was certainly stronger than in those countries where civil society developments were weaker. And in countries with a more vibrant civil society, incentives for the incumbents to introduce encompassing and sustainable economic reforms were different from those of incumbents who faced a silenced civil society.

We use the political concept of civil society in the same manner as it is used in the 'transitology' literature to refer to the presence of organized actors who are independent of the state and are ready and capable to politicize issues of change (see O'Donnell and Schmitter 1986; Linz and Stepan 1996). Note that in this conceptualization the stress is on contentious action and not on the representation of specific values. The concept encom-passes contentious actors and actions that aim to advance the more general, universal values, like democratization or the extension of human rights. It also includes actions directed at advancing more particularistic issues, like diverse economic goals or nationalistic values. During the downfall of the state-socialist regimes, civil societies differed not only with respect to their strengths or vibrancy but also with respect to the goals motivating civic action. From a dynamic and relational perspective they have also differed in their capacity to carve out autonomous space for contentious political action. In some of these countries, civil societies were in ascendancy at the start of regime change, while in others they were in retreat, weakened by growing state repression.

Our data cover the period between the start of *glasnost* and the fall of com-munism (i.e. during 1985–9) for the 27 former centrally planned economies of CEE and Central Asia. The data collected from the Open Society Archives in Budapest provide information about various aspects of political oppo-sition events. These events were reported by Radio Free Europe (RFE) and other news sources that specialized in reporting on dissident activities. Our database contains quantitative information—the number of events, dates, and participants—as well as qualitative information about the types of event (e.g. strikes and demonstrations), motivation for the event, and whether and how severely the government reacted. While these data obviously only measure very partial civil society developments, they nevertheless have several advantages. First, they contain some of the most relevant facts relating to our specific interest, namely the level, form, and content of dissident activity. Indeed, we expect a stronger level of dissident activity to be associated with greater citizen involvement in the shaping of new democratic institutions and thus with stronger checks and balances later on. On the other hand, while mobilization for human rights and political change might have positive effects on the characteristics of the new institutions, we do not expect the same from large-scale mobilization demanding direct economic or nationalistic change.

A second advantage of our data is that we measure civil society by observing actual actions rather than organizational membership or the density of inter-organizational ties (the latter are assumed to determine the propensity to act for change). Our study thus deviates from the neo-Tocquevillian approach that would define and measure civil society by the density of civic ties and participation in diverse non-political associations (e.g. Leonardi et al. 1993). Our concept and measure are closer to the way the social movement literature defines contentious action (della Porta et al. 1999; Tarrow 1989). We study political action in authoritarian state-socialist regimes that had no freedom of association and assembly, and no guaranteed political rights. In such regimes, any non-licensed gathering of people or non-authorized public speech could be construed as contentious, illegal action. As we will demonstrate, before the regime change, countries differed greatly in the propensity of their citizens to enter into any type of contentious action and engage in political confrontation.

The cross-country comparison could be biased if the data sources we used were biased towards reporting more activities from some countries than others (on the problems of data reliability in protest event analysis, see Koopmans and Rucht 1999). We have good reason to believe this is not the case. News agencies like RFE were closely related to the Central Intelligence Agency (CIA) and, given the context of the Cold War, had no interest in reporting fewer dissident activities from specific countries. To overcome any problem of potential bias, RFE used numerous sources ranging from newspaper accounts or news smuggled through borders by dissident activists to reports by various human rights organizations. Dissident organizations also often had close contacts in the West so that their protest activities could be reported; it was this publicity that would occasionally give them some protection from harsher forms of repression. This incentive existed even for the dissident organizations—such as nationalist or religious extremist groups—that did not necessarily share Western political values. We are thus quite confident that the data we put together allow for a meaningful comparison across countries.

We find that political opposition before 1989 was much more intense in Central Europe than in the Soviet republics. This is true even for a country like Czechoslovakia, where the regime was much more repressive than in Poland or Hungary. Moreover, the lower level of dissident activity in the FSU was accompanied by greater repression; not only was the probability of government reaction greater there but so was the probability that the government would resort to physical violence. Further, we note that differences in civil society development in the 1980s played an important role in explaining whether the country adopted a political regime based on distributed power with checks and balances or a political regime with high power concentration. Moreover, our findings support the claim that having a more vibrant and organized civil society at the start of economic reforms was an asset both for launching and for implementing these reforms.

This chapter is organized as follows. The next section provides a discussion of the construction of our dataset, and that is followed by a section that discusses the stylized facts revealed by the data. A later section presents our main econometric results on the link between civil society development and institutional change, with a final concluding section.

2   Data collection and documentation

Our analysis is based on the long tradition in history, political sociology, and the study of social movements of using event catalogues to trace the evolution of diverse forms of collective/contentious action and their effects (for an excellent overview, see Tilly 2002). Such event catalogues and datasets on multiple social and/or political interactions are used, in the first place, to describe more formally the characteristics of general phenomena, such as the evolution of civil society or patterns of state-society interactions. These allow for the quantification of various properties of contentious actions (timing, frequency, size, forms and goals) as well as the immediate reactions of the repressive apparatus of the state (Koopmans and Rucht 1999). In addition to descriptions, event catalogues are also used to account for the causes and long-term effects of the phenomena traced in this manner (see, e.g., Tilly 2002.) Although an extensive literature already exists on protest event analysis in the more established democracies (see, e.g., Tarrow 1989; Tilly 2002; McAdam et al. 2001; Rucht and Koopmans 1999; della Porta et al. 1999), there is only a handful of studies on the forms and effects of contentious civic action in the pre- or post-transition CEE countries. The most encompassing studies that deal with this part of the world either discuss a single country or compare some characteristically different cases. Ekiert and Kubik, pioneers in the comparative event analysis in the post-communist world, use data from just four Central European countries (Ekiert and Kubik

1998). Several other excellent studies focus on the evolution of contentious action in a single country (e.g. Szabo 1996; Ekiert and Kubik 1998). As yet, no one has undertaken cross-country data collection as comprehensive as ours.[1]

Building on the concepts and methods of this research tradition, we focused our data collection on tracing different patterns of interactions between civil society and the socialist regime. We collected detailed data about various aspects of civil society action: their size, frequency, timing, type, form and content. We were interested, however, in more than just a comparison of the differences in the strength of the various civil societies and the patterns of civic activities across these countries. In addition to a comparison of civil societies, we wanted to trace the evolution of the balance of power between states and civil societies in the period leading to regime change. Thus, in order to be able to compare countries from this perspective, we collected data on the frequency, form and content of the reaction of the state. Data collection was based on the sources of the Open Society Archives, which were created by the Information Resources Department of RFE/the Radio Liberty Research Institute (East European Archives). This collects comprehensive information about political, economic, religious, media, social, and cultural issues occurring during 1945–94 in the former socialist bloc countries. The archive records include news agency releases (mostly from Reuters, the Associated Press, United Press International, Agence France Press, Deutsche Presse-Agentur and other national agencies), excerpts from the foreign and national press, transcripts of national radio broadcasts, abstracts of media reports about the countries, and copies of articles from scientific publications. Importantly, they also contain the RFE's research reports (background and situation reports), which elaborate on a specific topic (e.g. village razing in Romania), with several references to news agency releases and their own research work, interviews, and so on.

In order to capture political dissident activities, a selection was first made according to a list of archival boxes (container list), which listed all the available records in alphabetical order (e.g. from 'agriculture' to 'youth'). Quite often the record 'dissident(s)' or 'opposition', for example, was not available as a distinct category. In such cases, we selected and processed boxes that could have contained events relevant to the researchers' interest (like parties, persecution and purges, ethnic minorities, terrorism, exile, resistance to and criticism of the regime, and so forth). The container list is available on the internet at www.osa.ceu.hu.[2] The selected countries include Albania, Bulgaria, former Czechoslovakia, Hungary, Poland, Romania, the 15 Republics of the FSU and the by-now independent states of former Yugoslavia. The timespan for the CEE countries covers the years 1985–9, and 1985–91 for the FSU. The period for the latter is longer in order to account for the fact that political and economic changes were initiated later in these countries. Importantly, in the case of former Czechoslovakia, former

Yugoslavia and the FSU, the data were collected separately for the various constituent republics even before independence. If a record was identified as 'dissident activity' (or repression induced by the state against dissidents or dissident activity—see later), the following variables to help characterize this event were identified, collected and coded:

- *Date of event:* In most cases it was possible to identify the exact date of the event (day/month/year). However, sometimes only the year or the month was available. In a few cases, we only had the date when the news of the event was published. In other instances, we had only the year in which the event took place.
- *Source of information:* This is the name of the news agency (or agencies as quite often more than one reported the event) or any other source (RFE's situation reports, Amnesty International, Helsinki Watch, or the country's domestic and/or exile dissident source/samizdat/news agency). Furthermore, the person(s) who informed the agencies (or any other body), if available, was recorded (but this was rather rare as it was dangerous to publish the name of the informant).
- *Actor(s):* This is the name(s) (or ethnicity, in the case of minorities) of the person(s) involved (and their profession(s), if available). At times, the name list was incomplete or names simply were not available, in which case at least their 'party' affiliation (their interest) was indicated (e.g. member of Charter 77). This information allowed us to measure the density of associational activity, proxied by the number of distinct organizations observed for each country.
- *Location of event:* This is the region/city/village or, if available, the street or square or the name of the owner of an apartment/house.
- *The number of participants:* If the number of persons involved in a certain activity (e.g. street demonstration) was unknown or if reports gave conflicting figures, a range (or an estimate) was used.
- *Types of activity:* These could be (i) demonstrations or rallies, (ii) meetings, (iii) the setting-up of organizations, clubs, and so on, (iv) mass disorder, disturbances, (v) strikes, (vi) hunger strikes, (vii) terrorist activities, (viii) emigration, (ix) dissident literature (publishing or distribution), and (x) petitions (appeals, statements, open letters). Quite often a record contained several types of activities because a dissident gathering with the aim of establishing a protest organization involved various stages, such as meeting, setting up an organization, and drafting of a petition or declaration for publication in a dissident newsletter. These were coded as an event with multiple aspects.
- *Motivation:* In order to clarify the reasons of a particular activity, motives were recorded if available. Recording the motivation made it possible to get a clearer picture about the intentions of dissident activity (religious,

ethnic, cultural, ecological or human rights concerns). Some events had multiple motives, and this was recorded by our data as well.

- *Reactions of the authorities:* Immediate and ultimate reactions were recorded (e.g. detention or prison sentences), including the severity of the response. It is worth mentioning that often the 'reaction' was first publicized by foreign news agencies and only after days or months, if ever, was the 'action'—or to be precise, the circumstances and details of the 'action'—identified by the local news agencies.
- *Counter-reaction:* This is the response from the side of the 'punished' (the dissidents) generated by the reaction of the state authorities.
- Separately, repression, induced by government authorities against dissidents, was also recorded by identifying the time, place, intensity, type and motives.

3 Depth and nature of civil society: what do the data say?

There are stark differences between the three main groups of countries; Central Europe, former Yugoslavia, and FSU. In some cases, data from the Baltic countries are different from those from the FSU countries in other important aspects as well. We present the main trends observed from our data for these different country groups, isolating the Baltic states from the other FSU countries, when relevant.

The average number of dissident events (Figure 8.3) shows these to be substantially higher in Central Europe and former Yugoslavia than in the FSU (including the Baltics). Only in 1988, at the height of the *glasnost* period under Gorbachev, was there a slight increase in the number of events in the FSU. There is no reason to think that this could be due to a reporting bias in the archive sources. Most sources had a keen interest in reporting any dissident activity taking place in the Soviet Union. In contrast with the FSU,

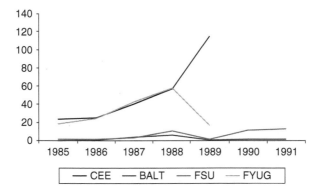

Figure 8.3 Average number of dissident events

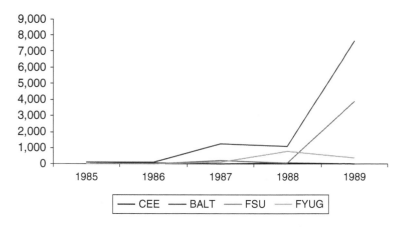

Figure 8.4   Median number of participants

there is a very strong upward trend in dissident activities in the Baltics and former Yugoslavia. As can be seen from Figure 8.4, the median number of participants was higher in the Baltics and former Yugoslavia than in other countries. Median participation in the FSU spiked in 1988 but was lower for the other years than elsewhere.

Table 8.1 gives the composition of dissident activities in the different country groups. Specifically, it shows the overall average number of dissident events per country over the 1985–9 period, revealing both the absolute number and the relative importance of different types of activities. These in the FSU were mainly demonstrations, marches and rallies (on average accounting for 12 out of 19 events per country). Demonstrations constituted the second most common category in CEE, albeit in absolute numbers dwarfing the events (62 out of 256 incidents) recorded in the FSU. The most common type of dissent episode in CEE was the issuing of statements, declarations and petitions (82 incidents on average per country), and meetings (33 occurrences). Demonstrations, marches and rallies were foremost in the Baltic countries (on average accounting for 10 out of 11 episodes per country). Note that the Baltic republics almost paralleled the FSU countries in this category despite the former's much smaller average size.

Finally, the most important category of dissident activities in former Yugoslavia was strikes (45 out of 137 events per country), followed by demonstrations (43) and petitions (29). Central Europe had the more politicized form of protest, as is evident in the prevalence of its political declarations and meetings. In the former Yugoslavia, on the other hand, dissent was largely driven by labour market disputes. The motives for dissident activity varied considerably across the three regions as well, although human

Table 8.1   Summary statistics on pre-transition civil society

	CEE	Baltic States	FSU	Former Yugoslavia
Summary				
Events per year	52.0	2.3	3.6	31.8
Participants per event	20	2043	828	265
Government response (%)	29.0	17	23	14
Government repression (%)	5	15	9	2
Unique organizations	33.9	3	10.6	4
Motives (%)				
Human rights	53	45	22	21
Political change	18	15	3	13
Economic	7	0	2	44
Environmental	3	9	2	1
Nationalistic	8	10	8	11
Religious	8	0	2	3
No. of events by type (overall, 1985–9)				
Demonstrations	62	10	12	43
Strikes	19	0	0	45
Hunger strikes	10	0	1	4
Petitions	82	1	1	29
Meetings	33	0	1	2
New organizations	18	0	1	3
Published dissident literature	17	0	2	10
Terrorism/sabotage	1	0	1	1
Granting interviews to press	9	0	0	0
Emigration	5	0	0	0

Source: See text.

rights concerns were very important in all countries. Furthermore, political change played an important role in CEE, the Baltic countries, and former Yugoslavia. These motives, however, displayed different dynamics. While the importance of human rights tended to decline over time (Figure 8.5), the demand for political change increased (Figure 8.6). This suggests that as protests intensified, the concern for human rights was gradually replaced by direct demands for political change. In contrast, economic motivation

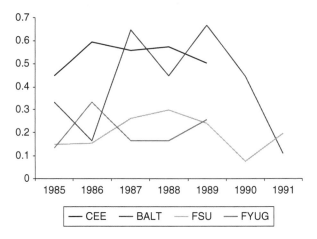

Figure 8.5   Human rights motive

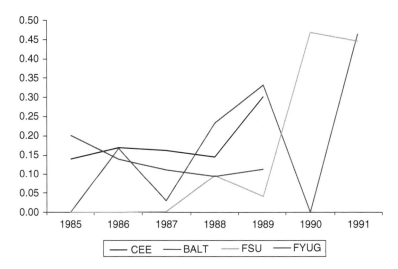

Figure 8.6   Political change motive

was by far the strongest in former Yugoslavia, especially towards the end of the 1980s (Figure 8.7). This is consistent with the prevalence of strikes as the main form of protest activity. Nationalist aspirations were the second most important motive in former Yugoslavia (Figure 8.8). It was prominent also in the Baltics where it took the form of pro-independence movements, while in Central Europe its importance was relatively minor. Figure 8.9 charts religious motives for dissident activities.

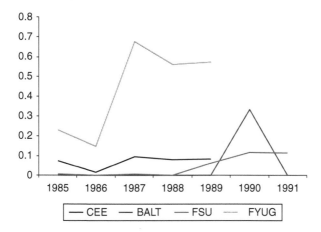

Figure 8.7 Economic motive

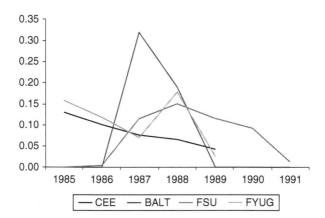

Figure 8.8 Nationalistic motive

Government reaction to dissident incidents was not uniform either. Figure 8.10 shows the percentage of events that triggered government repression. One sees clearly that government reaction was small and diminishing in Central Europe, decreasing from around 40 per cent in 1985 to 20 per cent in 1989. In contrast, repression in the FSU (including the Baltics) showed an increasing trend for the same period, although declining subsequently in 1990–1. Figure 8.11 shows the percentage of events that were met with violent government reaction. Again, repression was stronger in the FSU and the Baltics than in Central Europe and former Yugoslavia. Note in particular the dramatic increase in violent repression in the Baltics. Not surprisingly, there seems to be a negative correlation between repression

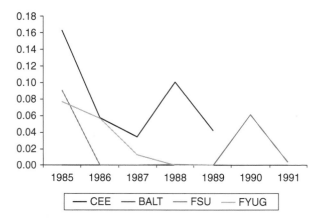

Figure 8.9   Religious motive

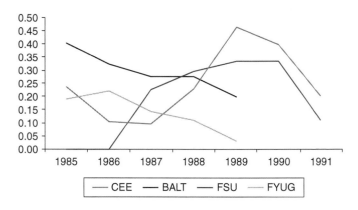

Figure 8.10   Average frequency of government action

and dissident activity; the more repressive countries displayed less dissident activity. Figures 8.12a–d document this pattern for Poland, the Czech Republic, Russia, and Serbia and Montenegro. Note that despite the more repressive character of the Czechoslovak regime, the number of its dissident activities did not greatly surpass those of Poland. Note, however, that repression was still much stronger in Gorbachev's Russia than in Husak's Czechoslovakia.

A consistent picture emerges from these data. Central Europe exhibited a relatively high level of dissident activity and somewhat less repressive governments. Protest activity in Central Europe was more politicized, directly striving for political change. There was considerable dissent in the former Yugoslavia as well, and the country was also less repressive. Yet, protest was mostly in form of strikes with a clear economic motivation. Nationalism

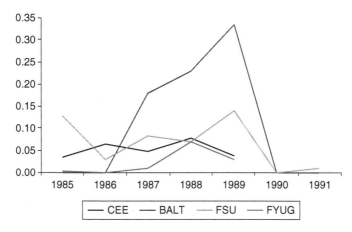

Figure 8.11 Government reaction violent

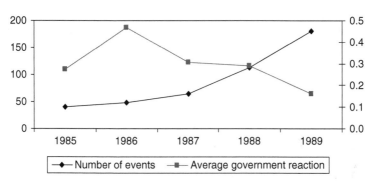

Figure 8.12a Patterns of interaction between dissident activity and government reaction, Poland, 1985–9

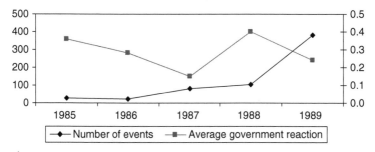

Figure 8.12b Patterns of interaction between dissident activity and government reaction, Czech Republic, 1985–9

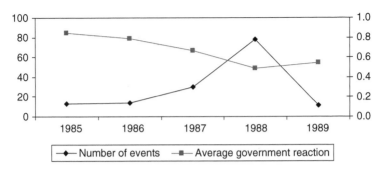

Figure 8.12c Patterns of interaction between dissident activity and government reaction, Russia, 1985–9

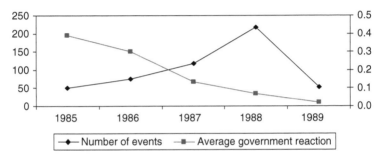

Figure 8.12d Patterns of interaction between dissident activity and government reaction, Yugoslavia (Serbia and Montenegro), 1985–9

was also important. There were fewer dissident events and greater repression in the FSU, where protest manifested as demonstrations defending human rights. These became more politicized only later on. An exception was the Baltics, where very strong and massive nationalist (pro-independence) activities were evident in the late 1980s. Given these differences, we expect civil society to have contributed to shaping the process and pace of institutional change.

Up to now, we have considered the pre-transition civil society to be more or less exogenously given. However, the different historical legacies and cultural factors characterizing these countries are likely to have played a role in shaping the nature and intensity of the civil society. Therefore, we regress in Table 8.2 the average number of dissident events on a number of plausible country-specific indicators. The analysis suggests that countries exposed to a shorter term of communist regime and those closer to Western Europe experienced more dissident activity. More liberal political conditions before 1989 were also a factor. Interestingly enough, large countries did not necessarily report a greater number of dissident episodes than small countries.

Table 8.2 Determinants of pre-transition civil society

	(1)	(2)	(3)	(4)	(5)	(6)	(7)	(8)	(9)	(10)
GNP per capita, 1989	0.001 (0.003)	0.004 (0.003)								
Years under communism	-3.293 (1.328)*		-1.238 (0.447)*							
Distance from Vienna	0.011 (0.009)			-0.015 (0.005)*						
Average liberalization, 1989	-620.225 (216.64)*				149.966 (103.28)					
Average democracy, 1989	173.977 (34.91)**					63.488 (49.516)				
EBRD initial conditions index	7.427 (6.061)						7.854 (2.807)*			
Polity IV score, average during 1918-8	-2.251 (1.765)							3.046 (2.080)		
Independent state during 1918-8	-37.859 (27.986)								24.336 (13.688)	
Population, 1985 (thousands)	0.001 (0.000)**									0 (0.000)
Constant	160.751 (83.843)	-3.133 (14.263)	88.757 (30.10)**	33.353 (11.00)**	15.326 (6.562)*	3.993 (14.992)	18.016 (5.151)**	32.457 (12.464)*	12.224 (7.24)	18.58 (6.872)*
Observations	24	24	25	25	27	27	25	27	27	27
R^2	0.71	0.07	0.28	0.2	0.1	0.07	0.35	0.17	0.12	0.02

Note: The dependent variable is the average number of events per country per year. Standard errors are in parentheses. Significance levels: *significant at 5%; ** significant at 1%.
Source: See text.

Moreover, favourable economic conditions, measured by indexes of initial liberalization, did not play a robustly significant role.

4   Institutional and economic impact of pre-transition civil society

Next we turn to the regression analysis of the impact of civil society on institutional and economic outcomes during transition. We assume that the nature and depth of the pre-transition dissident movement laid an important foundation for subsequent political and institutional changes as well as for policy choices. Table 8.3 considers the choice between presidential and parliamentary systems. Given that an electoral regime rarely changes, the analysis is carried out in a cross-sectional framework. We see important differences in regime choices: all countries in Central Europe opted for a parliamentary regime, whereas most of those in the FSU, apart from the Baltics, opted for a presidential regime. Presidential regimes can come in different guises and some feature a very good system of checks and balances. However, in the FSU, presidential regimes tended to concentrate considerable power in the hands of the president and to have few checks and balances. In Table 8.3 we see a clear and significant negative association between the number of dissident activities and the choice of a presidential regime (the number of events is significant at least at the 10 per cent level in all columns except in the last). The repression rate and the frequency of violent repression, in some specifications, also correlate positively with the dependent variable. The protest motive seems to have played a minor role: the only statistically significant variable is 'economic motivation', which carries a negative sign.

A similar exercise is performed in Table 8.4, albeit with a more refined measure of the strength of the executive obtained from the Polity database. This ranges between 1 and 4, with higher values indicating a stronger executive or greater centralization of power in the hands of the president. Estimated as an ordered logit, the regression results are very similar: the number of events is negatively associated with a strong executive; and government repression and violent repression increased the probability of having a strong executive (the last two effects are not significant, however).

Finally, Table 8.5 represents the determinants of presidential powers, based on Timothy Frye's index of presidential powers, which also reflects the degree of concentration of presidential powers. This index, identifying 29 executive powers that are maintained with the president or the legislature, ranges between 0 (very weak presidency) and 29 (strong presidential system with highly centralized power). The actual range represented in our data is between 3 (Slovenia) and 19 (Azerbaijan and, from 1996 onwards, Belarus). Since a few countries (Albania, Belarus, Croatia, and Moldova) amended

Table 8.3 Determinants of presidential system

	(1)	(2)	(3)	(4)	(5)
No. of events	−0.083(0.064)	−0.124(0.064)	−0.179(0.087)*	−0.343(0.181)§	−0.03(0.040)
Frequency of government reaction		3.883(3.087)	6.676(4.145)	5.267(3.964)	
Median no. of participants			00.000	−0.001(0.001)	
Frequency of violent reaction				17.813(13.634)	
Motives					
Human rights					−0.437(2.366)
Political change					−14.461(9.801)
Economical					−9.141(3.624)*
Nationalistic					2.412(5.021)
Religious					−8.464(7.695)
Constant	0.574(0.530)	0.015(0.734)	0.116(0.706)	0.449(0.830)	1.89(1.139)§
Wald χ^2 (*p*-value)	1.69(0.19)	4.53(0.10)	4.86(0.18)	4.40(0.35)	12.6(0.05)
Observations	25	25	25	25	25

Note: Estimated with logit. Standard errors in parentheses. The dependent variable takes a value of 1 if the country has a presidential system of government and 0 if a parliamentary system. Significance levels: § significant at 10%, * significant at 5%.
Source: See text.

Table 8.4 Determinants of political system

	(1)	(2)	(3)	(4)	(5)
No. of events	−0.07(0.032)*	−0.076(0.029)**	−0.109(0.037)**	−0.113(0.044)**	−0.019(0.017)
Frequency of government reaction		0.914(2.664)	2.989(2.791)	2.323(3.572)	
Median no. of participants			0(0)	−0.001(0)	
Frequency of violent reaction				2.173(5.710)	
Motives					
Human rights					−3.861(3.218)
Political change					−15.595(6.934)*
Economical					−10.966(4.266)*
Nationalistic					−4.446(4.546)
Religious					11.036(8.697)
Wald χ^2 (p-value)	4.73(0.03)	6.74(0.03)	8.95(0.03)	6.99(0.14)	30.3(0.00)
Observations	25	25	25	25	25

Note: Estimated with ordered logit. Standard errors in parentheses. The dependent variable takes a value of 1 if the country has a parliamentary system of government, 2 in the case of a mixed system, 3 for a weak presidential system and 4 for a strong presidential system. Significance levels: significant at 10%, * significant at 5%; ** significant at 1%.
Source: See text.

Table 8.5 Determinants of presidential system (using Tim Frye's index of presidential powers)

	(1)	(2)	(3)	(4)	(5)
No. of events	−0.016(0.008)*	−0.019(0.008)*	−0.023(0.009)**	−0.023(0.009)**	0.002(0.011)
Frequency of government reaction		2.63(2.441)	3.48(2.236)	4.331(4.286)	
Median no. of participants			0(0)	0(0)	
Frequency of violent reaction				−2.299(8.557)	
Human rights					−6.121(4.227)
Political change					−2.3(5.293)
Economic					−6.216(5.804)
Nationalistic					2.421(2.887)
Religious					10.946(8.884)
Wald χ^2 (*p*-value)	4.06(0.04)	6.07(0.05)	8.42(0.04)	7.86(0.10)	14.3(0.03)
Observations	25	25	25	25	25

Note: Estimated with ordered logit. Standard errors in parentheses. The dependent variable is increasing in the strengths of the president's authority. The possible range of the index is between 0 and 29. The regressions are estimated with the index reflecting the first post-communist constitution; results with the last post-communist constitution are very similar (the constitutionally mandated presidential powers have changed only in Albania, Belarus, Croatia, and Moldova during the period we consider). Significance levels: § significant at 10%; *significant at 5%; **significant at 1%.
Source: See text.

their constitution during the period covered by the analysis, we considered both the index value corresponding to the first post-communist constitution and its final value. The results are essentially the same and we therefore only report the former. Again, a familiar pattern emerges: countries with a greater number of events were less likely to adopt a strongly centralized political system whereas government repression increased the probability of adopting such a regime.

In summary, these results suggest that the countries with a broad, active civil society, and where governments engaged in relatively low levels of repression, were subsequently more likely to espouse broadly representative regimes. On the other hand, countries lacking pre-transition civil society or faced with a high level of repression tended to implement strongly centralized presidential regimes.

Next, to consider the impact of civil society on policy choices, we specifically looked at the progress of implementing market-oriented economic reform as well as political liberalization. We proxied economic reform by the eight progress-in-transition indicators compiled and published annually by the European Bank for Reconstruction and Development (EBRD) for 27 post-communist countries. These indicators measure economic reform in the following areas: price liberalization, trade and foreign exchange, competition policy, small-scale privatization, large-scale privatization, governance and enterprise restructuring, banking reform and interest-rate liberalization, and securities markets and non-bank financial institutions. The indicators range between 1 (unreformed centrally planned economy) and 4.33 (fully liberalized market economy). Our dependent variable is the average value of these indicators. We used the Freedom House indicators of political freedoms and civil liberties to measure political liberalization. These range from 1 (completely free) to 7 (not free). To make the interpretation easier and to facilitate the comparison with economic liberalization, these indicators are inverted so that higher values indicate greater freedom. We again use the average of these two sub-indicators as a composite index of democracy.

Unlike the political-regime variables used above, progress in economic and political liberalization varied from year to year, at times substantially. We can therefore carry out our analysis in a panel-data framework. However, by definition, our measures of pre-transition civil society are time-invariant. We therefore combined cross-sectional analysis with panel-data analysis, with the latter allowing for the time-varying effects of civil society. Specifically, we interacted civil society with time trend (including a quadratic time term in some regressions) defined so that 1989, the last year of the communist regime, is set as year 0. This effectively allowed for the effect of dissident activity to vary (to diminish or strengthen) over time, whereas the time-invariant impact of civil society, if any, is captured by the country-fixed effects in these regressions.

The cross-section results are reported in Table 8.6: economic reform in columns (1–5) and democracy in columns (6–10). We regressed the level of each index on civil society at five-year intervals—1990, 1995, 2000, and 2005—as well as for 2007 (the last year in our data). This allowed us to determine whether the pre-transition civil society has had an impact on the economic reform process and democratization at five discrete points spanning the entire transition period. Obtaining statistically significant results was necessarily an uphill struggle in this case as we had a multitude of civil society indicators but altogether only 25 observations. Indeed, we found no statistically significant effect of the number of events, participation or government repression. Nevertheless, the motives for dissident activity appeared to be important. In particular, we observed that countries where dissident activity was motivated mainly by the desire for political change tended to progress further in terms of both economic and political liberalization (the effect on economic reform, however, was only significant for 1990, although it remained positive throughout). The effect of human rights and economic motivation is similar, albeit less consistently significant. Finally, the greater the number of distinct dissident organizations, the greater the level of reform implemented in 1990, although this effect ceased to be significant in subsequent years. Hence, it appears that it was not only the extent of the dissident activity and its motives but also the density of the pre-transition civil society (measured by the number of organizations) that mattered for subsequent policy choices.[3]

In Table 8.7 we present the results obtained in a panel framework. Here the initial effect of pre-transition civil society, along with other time-invariant factors, is captured by the country-specific fixed effect. Nevertheless, using the interaction effects described above, the regressions include the time-varying effects of civil society. In analysing the determinants of economic reform, we also included the democracy index in column (1). This is in line with Fidrmuc's (2003) finding that democratization fosters economic liberalization in post-communist countries. For comparison, however, column (2) presents the regression results obtained by omitting the democratization index. These two sets of results are very similar. We find that countries with numerous dissident episodes tended to experience sustained economic liberalization and democratization: the interaction term between the number of events and time trend is positive (although only marginally significant). Hence, dissident activity appears to leave a legacy that is long-lasting and becomes translated into policy gradually. Government response to such events reinforces this effect: the fraction of events that induced government reaction also had a positive effect on economic and political reforms (and this effect may be non-linear, levelling off with the passing of time). Violent repression of dissident activity had the opposite effect on democratization—the fraction of repressed dissident events makes political liberalization decelerate over time (note that this effect is only marginally significant). Similarly,

Table 8.6 Determinants of progress in market-oriented reform and democratization, cross-section model

	(1)	(2)	(3)	(4)	(5)	(6)	(7)	(8)	(9)	(10)
	Reform					Democracy				
	1990	1995	2000	2005	2007	1990	1995	2000	2005	2007
Events	-0.004 (0.004)	0 (0.007)	0.006 (0.008)	0.007 (0.010)	0.007 (0.010)	0.016 (0.012)	0.018 (0.022)	0.025 (0.023)	0.03 (0.021)	0.03 (0.024)
Participants	0.000 (0.000)	0.000 (0.000)	0.000 (0.000)	0.000 (0.000)	0.000 (0.000)	0.000 (0.000)	0.000 (0.000)	0.000 (0.000)	0.000 (0.000)	0.000 (0.000)
Government reaction	-0.733 (0.796)	-0.987 (1.568)	0.023 (1.796)	-0.305 (2.028)	-0.189 (2.046)	0.73 (2.660)	-5.666 (4.648)	-1.539 (4.883)	-0.787 (4.442)	-0.932 (5.216)
Government repression	-1.001 (1.244)	-0.616 (2.449)	-1.008 (2.805)	0.51 (3.168)	0.558 (3.195)	-2.312 (4.154)	5.459 (7.260)	0.929 (7.627)	-1.57 (6.937)	-0.403 (8.146)
Motives										
Human rights	-0.248 (0.275)	0.66 (0.542)	0.679 (0.621)	0.859 (0.701)	0.882 (0.707)	-1.523 (0.919)	5.384 (1.607)**	3.475 (1.688)	4.165 (1.535)*	4.57 (1.803)*
Political change	1.561 (0.631)*	1.894 (1.242)§	2.695 (1.422)§	3.039 (1.606)§	3.011 (1.620)§	5.296 (2.106)*	6.144 (3.681)	9.686 (3.867)*	9.542 (3.517)*	10.803 (4.130)*
Economical	1.518 (0.346)**	0.901 (0.682)	0.601 (0.781)	0.323 (0.882)	0.384 (0.890)	-1.666 (1.157)	1.302 (2.022)	1.602 (2.124)	2.483 (1.932)	1.467 (2.268)
Environmental	0.539 (1.53)	3.789 (3.00)	3.224 (3.44)	2.042 (3.89)	2.132 (3.919)	1.76 (5.095)	-4.183 (8.904)	2.078 (9.355)	5.769 (8.508)	0.822 (9.992)

	(1)	(2)	(3)	(4)	(5)	(6)	(7)	(8)	(9)	(10)
Nationalistic	0.297	−0.9	−0.019	0.91	0.974	1.016	5.75	3.761	2.942	3.989
	(0.676)	(1.331)	(1.524)	(1.722)	(1.736)	(2.257)	(3.946)	(4.145)	(3.770)	(4.427)
Religious	−0.033	0.663	−0.627	−0.976	−1.080	−6.227	−4.392	−4.977	−4.662	−7.344
	(1.441)	(2.838)	(3.249)	(3.670)	(3.701)	(4.812)	(8.410)	(8.835)	(8.036)	(9.437)
No. of distinct dissident groups	0.014	0.009	−0.004	−0.008	−0.009	0.013	−0.015	−0.036	−0.044	−0.052
	(0.006)*	(0.013)	(0.015)	(0.016)	(0.017)	(0.022)	(0.038)	(0.040)	(0.036)	(0.042)
Constant	1.044	2.199	2.382	2.532	2.556	3.623	2.598	2.561	2.445	2.686
	(0.096)**	(0.188)**	(0.216)**	(0.244)**	(0.246)**	(0.319)**	(0.558)**	(0.586)**	(0.533)**	(0.626)**
Observations	25	25	25	25	25	25	25	25	25	25
R^2	0.81	0.68	0.65	0.61	0.61	0.75	0.73	0.73	0.81	0.75

Notes: Estimated with OLS. Standard errors in parentheses. Significance levels: § significant at 10%, * significant at 5%, ** significant at 1%. The dependent variable is the average of EBRD progress-in-transition indicators (reform) and the average of Freedom House indicators of political rights and civil liberties (democracy), inverted so that higher values correspond to greater freedom.
Source: See text.

Table 8.7 Determinants of progress in market-oriented reform and democratization, panel fixed effects model with time-varying effects of civil society

	(1)	(2)	(3)
	Reform		Democracy
Democracy (log)	0.128(0.020)**		-0.113(0.037)**
Time	0.28(0.015)**	0.266(0.016)**	0.003(0.002)§
Time squared	-0.01(0.001)**	-0.01(0.001)**	1.251(0.842)§
Events/1000	0.477(0.335)	0.637(0.351)	0.000(0.038)
Events squared/1000	-0.011(0.015)	-0.011(0.016)	
Government reaction/1000	73.472(63.895)	143.141(66.111)*	544.726(158.665)**
Government reaction squared/1000	-0.368(2.699)	-2.623(2.809)	-17.629(6.742)**
Government repression/1000	48.668(58.276)	13.656(60.897)	-273.749(146.152)
Participants/1000	-0.008(0.003)**	-0.008(0.003)**	-0.003(0.008)
Human rights motive/1000	15.78(13.053)	30.778(13.484)*	117.262(32.362)**
Political change motive/1000	14.037(30.379)	63.007(30.892)*	382.881(74.141)**
Economic motive/1000	-72.525(16.359)**	-55.962(16.959)**	129.497(40.702)**
Environmental motive/1000	5.555(71.538)	50.544(74.726)	351.758(179.341)
Nationalistic motive/1000	79.187(31.550)*	77.889(33.109)*	-10.147(79.461)
Religious motive/1000	-157.523(67.289)*	-173.96(70.567)*	-128.517(169.359)
No. of distinct dissident groups/1000	-0.817(0.310)**	-1.291(0.317)**	-3.7(0.760)**
Constant	0.472(0.088)**	0.993(0.038)**	4.075(0.090)**
Observations	450	450	450
No. of countries	25	25	25
R^2	0.89	0.88	0.40

Notes: Standard errors in parentheses. Significance levels: § significant at 10%; * significant at 5%; **significant at 1%. The dependent variable is the average of EBRD progress-in-transition indicators (reform) and the average of Freedom House indicators of political rights and civil liberties (democracy), rescaled so that higher values correspond to greater freedom. Civil society characteristics are interacted with time trend (and quadratic time trend, where indicated), to make them time-varying.

Source: See text.

countries where dissident events were attended by large numbers of people experience a slowing down of economic liberalization over time. Note, however, that this says nothing about the effects of these aspects of pre-transition civil society on the initial economic liberalization. In Table 8.6, none of the preceding indicators has a statistically significant effect on market-oriented reforms.

The effect of the motives for dissident activity changed over time as well. Countries where protests were driven mainly by human rights concerns and the desire for political change experienced sustained economic and political liberalization. Again, we can combine this result with our findings from the cross-section analysis above—human rights and political change concerns led to rapid initial liberalization followed by further improvements over time. Economic motives affected economic and political liberalization differently. Economic concerns were associated with extensive initial economic liberalization (with little effect on initial political change), subsequently followed by slower economic reform but faster democratization. The effect of nationalistic motives appeared positive only for economic reform while religious motives tended to suppress the pace of subsequent market-oriented reform. Finally, the associational density (reflected in the number of distinct dissident organizations) had a positive effect on the initial level of economic reform but translated into a slower pace of economic and political liberalization over time. Hence, while civil society density may help to cement the initial consensus on the need for change, it may later make it more difficult to maintain sustained progress in reform. In summary, we find strong evidence that the level and nature of civil society as measured by dissident activity during the late 1980s had an impact on institutional developments and policy choices, including the speed of economic and political reform, during transition.

5 Conclusions

The demise of communism did not adhere to a uniform scenario all across the FSU. In some countries, communism collapsed amid widespread public protests and was replaced by broadly based dissident groups. Elsewhere, the former regimes ceased to pay lip service to the communist ideology but otherwise remained largely in place. In documenting the variations in the depth and breadth of the pre-transition civil society in the communist countries of Eastern Europe and the Soviet Union, we utilized these data to explain the diversity of outcomes in terms of institutional change as well as policy choices. Our results suggest that the emergence of strong presidential regimes in the FSU—which subsequently proved to have a poorer record on human rights than the parliamentary and more genuinely democratic regimes in Central Europe and the Baltics—can be directly related to the lower frequency of political opposition in the pre-transition period, to its nature, and to the nature of government repression. Similarly, we find that the pre-transition civil society also had an effect on the subsequent nature and pace of market-oriented reform and democratization. These results suggest that the differences in civil society development and collective action processes in societies before the beginning of the post-communist transition process have had a long-lasting and important legacy. The success or failure of institutional change, reform and political liberalization was strongly linked to the political events that unfolded during the last years of communism. Countries with a vibrant pre-transition civil society have embarked on a path towards sound political institutions, economic reforms, and democratization. Countries that had little by way of civil society and/or whose governments repressed it have, in turn, introduced more authoritarian regimes or, at best, dragged their feet on economic and political liberalization.

Acknowledgements

We thank Daniel Berkowitz, Horst Feldmann, Dennis Mueller, Martin Paldam, Mark Schaeffer and seminar participants at the International Monetary Fund, Columbia University, the European Center for Advanced Research in Economics and Statistics (ECARES) (Brussels), ASSA 2007 (Chicago), the First World Meeting of the Public Choice Society (Amsterdam), and participants of the United Nations University's World Institute for Development Economics Research conference Reflections on Transition: Twenty Years after the Fall of the Berlin Wall, in Helsinki in September 2009, for valuable comments. Roman Horvath, Dana Popa and Aitalina Azarova provided excellent research assistance. This research was partly supported by a Global Development Network grant 'Explaining the Dynamics of Institutional Change, Policy Choices and Economic Outcomes during Post-communist Transition'. Nauro Campos acknowledges financial support from the Economic and Social Research Council (grant RES-000-22-0550). Jan Fidrmuc was a Marie Curie Fellow at ECARES, Université Libre de Bruxelles, when this research was initiated; the financial support of the European Commission is gratefully acknowledged. The usual disclaimer applies.

Notes

1. The by-now classic work of Beissinger (2002), using 150 different sources, provides the deepest event dataset on the FSU. A recent contribution is the volume edited by Roberts and Garton Ash (2009).
2. The processed materials are in English.
3. This echoes with the argument put forward by Leonardi et al. (1993) about the importance of social capital for economic and political outcomes.

References

Beissinger, M.M. (2002) *Nationalist Mobilization and the Collapse of the Soviet State*, Cambridge University Press: Cambridge.

Berglöf, E. and G. Roland (1997) 'The EU as an "Outside Anchor" for Transition Reforms', in *A Bigger and Better Europe?*, final report to the Swedish Government from the Committee on the Economic Effects of EU Enlargement, Stockholm.

della Porta, D., H. Kriesi and D. Rucht (eds) (1999) *Social Movements in a Globalizing World*, Macmillan: Basingstoke.

EBRD (European Bank for Reconstruction and Development) (2007) *Transition Report Update*, available at: www.ebrd.com/pubs/econo/tru07.htm.

Ekiert, G., and J. Kubik (1998) 'Contentious Politics in the New Democracies: East Germany, Hungary, Poland and Slovakia, 1989–93', *World Politics*, 50(4): 547–81.

Fidrmuc, J. (2003) 'Economic Reform, Democracy and Growth during Post-Communist Transition', *European Journal of Political Economy*, 19(3): 583–604.

Kaufmann, D., A. Kraay and M. Mastruzzi (2003) 'Governance Matters III: Governance Indicators for 1996–2002', *World Bank Policy Research Working Paper No. 3106*.

Kitschelt, H.P. (2003) 'Accounting for Post-Communist Regime Diversity: What Counts as a Good Cause?', in G. Ekiert and S. Hanson (eds) *Legacies of Communism*, Cambridge University Press: Cambridge.

Kitschelt, H. and E. Malesky (2000) 'Constitutional Design and Postcommunist Economic Reform', paper presented at the Midwest Political Science Conference (Panel on Institutions and Transition) 28 April, Chicago, available at www//irps.ucsd.edu/assets/003/5283.pdf.

Koopmans, R. and D. Rucht (1999) 'Protest Event Analysis: Where to Now?', *Mobilization*, 4(2): 123–30.

Leonardi, R., R.Y. Nanetti and R.D. Putnam (1993) *Making Democracy Work: Civic Traditions in Modern Italy*, Princeton University Press: Princeton.

Linz, J. and A. Stepan (1996) *Problems of Democratic Transition and Consolidation: Southern Europe, South America, and Post Communist Europe*, Johns Hopkins University Press: Baltimore.

McAdam, D., S. Tarrow and C. Tilly (2001) *Dynamics of Contention*, Cambridge University Press: Cambridge.

Møller, J. (2009) *Post-Communist Regime Change: A Comparative Study*, Routledge: London.

O'Donnell, G. and P. Schmitter (1986) *Transitions From Authoritarian Rule: Tentative Conclusions about Uncertain Democracies*, Vol. 4, Johns Hopkins University Press: Baltimore.

Roberts, A. and T. Garton Ash (eds) (2009) *Civil Resistance and Power Politics: The Experience of Non-violent Action from Gandhi to the Present*, Oxford University Press: Oxford.

Roland, G. and T. Verdier (2003) 'Law Enforcement and Transition', *European Economic Review*, 47(4): 669–85.

Rucht, D. and R. Koopmans (eds) (1999) 'Protest Event Analysis', *Mobilization*, 4(2): 123–30.

Szabo, M. (1996) 'Politischer Protest in Postkommunistischen Ungarn 1989–1994', *Berliner Journal für Soziologie*, 6(4): 501–17.

Tarrow, S. (1989) *Democracy and Disorder: Protest and Politics in Italy, 1965–1975*, Oxford University Press: Oxford.

Tilly, C. (2002) 'Event Catalogs as Theories'. *Sociological Theory*, 20(2): 248–54.

9
Twenty Years Later and the Socialist Heritage is Still Kicking: The Case of Russia

Gur Ofer

1 Introduction

It took almost two decades for Russia to regain the level of its production (GDP) achieved in the late 1980s.[1] That production level, attained during the final years of the old regime, reflects the long-term inefficiencies of the communist economic system, the declining rates of growth and productivity during the last two decades of the old regime, and the productivity losses of the failed attempts of partial reforms under Gorbachev during the second half of the 1980s. On the basis of these, one could have expected a much faster growth after 1992 to reflect a recovery of productivity levels based on the gradual elimination of the old regime's distortions and the introduction of mechanisms and institutions of a market economy. Instead, there was a period of steep decline in output and a sequence of crises. Only since 2000 has significant growth resumed, a trend that continued until the 2008 world financial crisis, which caused a sharp drop in output in 2009 and a very slow recovery in 2010 (as projected). The period of impressive growth since 2000 has resulted from a series of market reforms, as well as the disorganization of the Yeltsin term being replaced by a more orderly regime under Putin. But foremost, growth can be attributed to the much higher energy and material prices, riding on the wave of the global economic boom; and a number of other short-term factors (OECD 2009; Aslund 2009).

A 'more orderly' regime under Putin, and then Medvedev and Putin, is a mixed bag of better order, and some continuation of reforms and improvements in the functioning of the government and the economy, most of which ended by 2002. At the same time, it meant a recentralization of power and increased regulation, a rise in the level of government intervention (mostly as 'command and control'), and quite a significant renationalization of 'strategic' industries (especially in the spheres of energy and natural resources, media and defence), increased protectionism and more limited openness, a retreat in democracy and freedoms, and increased tension with the West (OECD 2009; EBRD 2008). Based on the above, it is difficult to give tribute for the recent (pre-crisis) high rates of growth. It is not impossible that some of what may be considered as the retreat of reforms had a positive, if only temporary, impact on growth.[2] It is, however, agreed by most that the short-term growth factors are running out of steam and that growth rates will go down unless there is a serious resumption of structural and institutional reforms (EBRD 2008; OECD 2009; Aslund 2009) or a return of high energy and resource prices.

Yet, even if most of the growth in Russia during the last decade can be attributed to positive transition reforms, the achievements must be evaluated as modest, achieving at best a recovery to the initial, pre-transition GDP level. Bergson estimates the productivity loss of central planning for 1975 at about a third as compared to a market economy at a similar level of economic development (Ofer 2005: 250–3). Berliner (1993: 388–9) estimates the Soviet efficiency gap as higher, at 55 per cent, to which the effect of the elements mentioned above needs to be added. The recovery of these productivity gaps is still pending. Moreover, the old regime bestowed on its successor a number of assets that should, or at least could, have contributed under favourable policies to higher growth. The most important was the significant stock of human capital, a relatively advanced educational system, research capacity, and innovation potential. Taking advantage of these assets has been conditional on establishing the proper institutional setting for a market economy, an endeavour that so far has been accomplished only partially.

Total GDP, as discussed above, represents the production capacity of the Russian economy. It should be mentioned that during the same period of the last two decades, private household consumption grew much faster than GDP. This was due mainly to a significant structural shift in GDP from defence, investment, and other public services to private household consumption (Popov 2009: 8–12). It also reflects a somewhat faster growth of GDP per capita than total GDP because of Russia's slowly declining population. As a result, consumption per capita declined less than output during transition's early years and grew faster than output once growth resumed (EBRD, various years). The material welfare of households increased even faster after the disappearance of shortages and queues, the improvement in variety and quality of goods and services (including in particular the supply of housing, cars, telephones and computers), imported goods, foreign travel, and media access—all in great demand and short supply under the old regime (Guriev and Zhuravskaya 2009: Table 1; Aslund 2009: Chapter 3). Welfare was also enhanced by personal freedom expanding in many directions. True, structural changes in the production mix entailed short-run costs in terms of growth, but these were later partly resolved and contributed to growth.

The transition and growth experience of Russia was shared by the other transition economies, albeit at a different pace. The group of transition economies in Central and Eastern Europe and the Baltic States (CEB) generally managed higher growth rates during the last two decades (relative to their initial GDP levels), and by 2007 they had reached, as a group, 150 per cent of their last socialist level; Poland, with nearly 175 per cent, took first place. Another group of transition economies in the Balkans and former Yugoslavia is on average very close to Russia (attaining around 110 per cent) but most countries are below full recovery. Internal conflicts in some successor states have postponed recovery. The growth record among the transition economies of the Commonwealth of Independent States (CIS) group ranges from just above 50 per cent (Georgia and Moldova) to a high of nearly 200 per cent in Turkmenistan, the highest among all transition economies (EBRD 2008: 13).

The differences in the growth record among the transition economies are explained by a number of factors. With the exclusion of countries faced with the vicious circle of poverty, growth is typically higher for the low-income countries, reflecting their greater technological convergence potential. Growth is also higher among countries that are resource-rich, such as Turkmenistan (boosted by high energy prices); that have shorter periods of communist rule (thus benefiting from a degree of modern institutional legacy); that can benefit from geopolitical advantages (such as proximity to Western Europe); that joined, or are about to join, the European Union (EU); or that are free from internal and external conflicts. Growth is higher also in countries that had inherited (and further developed) human capital and innovation capabilities and, last but not least, in those that implemented better policies, economic reforms, and institution building. Many of these factors have benefited the CEB countries and hence contributed to their growth recovery as a group. At the same time, a number of the reform laggers (Turkmenistan, Uzbekistan and Belarus) have also exhibited quite high growth and GDP recovery records (EBRD 2008: Chapters 1–3; Sinitsina et al. 2008). Is it a question of these countries merely postponing the transition crisis, or will they be able to benefit from the 'advantage of being backward' and learn from the mistakes of their predecessors (see Popov 2009)?

This study concentrates on the impact that the 'socialist heritage' had on the Russian transition process and its record of growth. From a list of many potential factors, it focuses on two: first, the nature of institutions inherited from the old regime and its transformation; and second, the inherited human capital and its innovation potential. Both are major factors that affected the transition, and they are at the same time considered to be the key determinants and leading growth engines of the present era. A short but thorough recent survey on the role of institutions in the transition process is given in Murrell (2008). The institutional approach to transition, dubbed 'evolutionary institutionalist perspective', which replaced the earlier 'gradualism', is embedded in the extensive theoretical framework by Roland (2000).

The choice of Russia as the case study for this investigation is based, first of all, on its leading role as the architect of the communist system. The system was tailored in many ways to fit (at least in the eyes of its creators) the economic character and aspirations of a large country, rich in natural resources, and on the verge of an industrialization take-off and modernization. Russia is where authoritarianism and coercion, and the centrally planned and directed economic system, reached near perfection and lasted the longest. It also lacked significant experience of modern institutions until the 1917 revolution. Efforts by the Soviet Union to become a leading military superpower correlated closely with the system and made the Soviet model even more oppressive. The demise of the Russian-designed system and regime, as well as the break-up of the Soviet Union and its empire, and its decline in global status, inflicted a severe moral blow to the people and leaders. Even though most of the population had suffered under the old regime and many opposed it, there was resistance to change. At the same time, the change was embraced by the majority in other transition economies as an act of independence from a hated, oppressive colonial power, despite the difficulties of the early transition years. Thus while other transition economies rushed to join the West, Russia developed strong sentiments of resentment and suspicion towards it, affecting its international relations, the level of openness and, of late, its transition strategy. Russia is the largest transition country in Europe, still claiming to be a world power and imposing great economic and political influence on the other transition economies in the CIS. It is therefore of special interest and a showcase for the transition process (see Roland 2000: 338–9).

The writings of Douglass North (1990, 1999) on the relationship between institutions and development are used as the main conceptual framework of the discussion on institutions. He looks at the various aspects and qualities of institutions and the mutual relationship between them as the tools and mechanisms to expand markets and reduce transaction costs, and thus contribute to growth. This study also looks at the more recent theory by North et al. (2005, 2006, 2007, 2009) on the major transition from a 'closed state' or a 'natural state'—a category that includes most of the developing countries as well as the former communist countries—to an 'open state', implying the developed markets and democratic countries. Finally, the analysis also incorporates the recent work of Aghion et al. (2010) for an alternative theory of institutional transition and corruption, in which the outcome is quite similar to those of North and colleagues.

The empirical relationship between the quality of institutions and governance, and economic growth, is well covered in the literature (La Porta et al. 1999; EBRD 2008; Barro and Sala-i-Martin 2004). In earlier papers (Ofer

2003; Keren and Ofer 2008) we extensively used the material presented in *Governance Matters* (various years) by Kaufman et al. (2009) and the accompanying World Bank governance indicators database. This study extends the empirical analysis to a number of other surveys: the global competitiveness index (GCI) of the World Economic Forum, and the Knowledge Assessment Methodology (KAM) survey of the World Bank's Knowledge for Development (K4D) programme, which presents information about the level and quality of education, innovation, and information and communication technology (ICT), and how they contribute to economic growth, as well as about institutional quality (World Bank 2009d). These and the other surveys used here evaluate the quality of many individual indicators, which are then aggregated into clusters representing the fields under investigation. The contribution of the elements of the 'knowledge economy' to growth in the present era is discussed extensively in the literature and there is a growing emphasis on the key role of higher education in this process, even in the developing and transitional economies.[3]

The recent extensive study by Sinitsina et al. (2008) contains a systematic analysis of the many factors contributing to the above-mentioned 'divide' and makes an attempt to quantify it. Using methodologies similar to ours, the study, on the basis of a long list of indicators, compares performance within the different groups of the transitional economies as well as with the performance of various EU country-groups. Therefore, the present study concentrates mostly on a comparison of the performance of Russia with groups of countries at similar or lower (or, at times, higher) levels of economic development. The main focus of the analysis here is to compare Russia's institutional and human capital performance with that of non-former communist countries and to subsequently study the particular character of the communist transition.[4]

The main proposition of this chapter is that the past institutional framework of socialism created serious obstacles to the introduction of market institutions, to their effective performance, and to proper enforcement, and that these brought about weak government capabilities and misguided policies. The outcome so far has been only partially successful in taking full advantage of the valuable assets inherited from the old regime and utilizing them for economic growth. Finally, these obstacles still persist today, after two decades, caused among other things by the slowdown and retreat of the reforms that may continue to slow economic growth in the future.

The chapter is structured as follows. The next section provides a conceptual discussion of the contradictions between the institutional structure of central planning and the requirements of rapid economic growth under authoritarian socialism, and the institutional requirements and structure needed to lead to a market economy under democracy. It concentrates on the nature and role of institutions in different economic and political regimes, on the distinction between formal and informal institutions and the sources of tension between them, and on the resulting levels of mistrust and corruption. That discussion is followed by a section that surveys the institutional levels reached by Russia by the end of the second decade of transition and their impact on its economic performance. The penultimate section discusses the ability of modern Russia to develop and productively utilize the 'knowledge assets' bestowed by the old regime, and it followed by a concluding section.

2 Institutions under Soviet socialism, market systems, and the transition

2.1 The basic theory of institutions

How well economies function is, to a large extent, a reflection of the quality of their institutions. Well-designed rules that are properly enforced, supplemented by consistent and supporting informal norms of behaviour, reduce transaction costs and enhance the scope and efficiency of the market. Institutions consist of three main elements: formal institutions, the rules of the transactions game, and the legal infrastructure; informal institutions, the behavioural norms of the bureaucracy and the public, and their mutual trust and operating 'culture'; and a system of enforcement. Formal institutions are normally embedded in organizations that are designed to implement the goals and missions of the institutions (North 1990, 1999). A major decline in transaction costs is facilitated by a shift from transactions that depend on personal relationships to impersonal transactions based on universal rules that are enforced effectively by a third party. This can be the legal system and the government, but also members of society, based on mutual trust and confidence in the proper behaviour of others. Such trust depends on the accumulation of social capital, a series of civic institutions and networks that provide for common cultural norms, social solidarity and cohesiveness. The quality of government is determined, to a large extent, by its success in creating good institutions, while proper informal behavioural rules complement the formal structure and further reduce transaction costs. Finally, since external conditions change all the time, institutions must also be able to evolve flexibly in order to accommodate the needed changes. Institutions with a higher level of adaptive efficiency are better prepared for such changes. One problem here is that informal institutions are, in many cases, dependent on history and tradition and therefore respond with a lag to changes in formal institutions. This conflict creates tensions, raises transaction costs, and delays the effective functioning of newly introduced or adjusted institutions.

In recent works, North et al. (2005, 2006, 2007, 2009) expand the institutional theory by dividing all countries into two types (three, actually, but we will concentrate on two): the 'closed access' or 'natural state', which includes most of the developing and transitional economies; and the second type—'open access'—which encompasses the developed and democratic market economies. Limited access countries or 'natural states' are characterized by autocratic or non-democratic rule, by a coalition of elites that control (military) power and collect rents by limiting entry of the rest of the society to productive activities, and distributing these among the different elites, thereby establishing order and stability. It is dominated by personal relationships that also limit the potential for specialization and expanding markets and therefore also economic growth. According to North et al. (2009: 27), the transition from a state of limited access to that of open access is a discontinuing process of relatively short duration, typically around 50 years. It is triggered by incentives to the elite to expand access in various dimensions in order to increase its incomes, expanding markets through impersonal exchanges, collecting (higher) taxes instead of (lower) rents, creating other open access types of institutions but with limited access that can later open up and expand entry, responding to external challenges, and so on. Such moves are intended to increase revenue, but they may cause unintended changes in other complementary spheres that could snowball into a systemic change. The risk of accompanied disorganization, and therefore failure, is always present (North et al. 2006: 47–70, 2007: 17, 2009: Chapter 5).

North's observations on the institutional situation in developing countries and transitional economies, all considered as limited access states, are rather bleak. The combination of a lack of knowledge, improper policies and formal rules, and the conflict between new formal rules and fragile enforcement on one side, and strongly rooted traditional informal rules on the other, produces a weak institutional environment for proper market development. These result in a weak rule of law and they account for the high level of corruption, and dysfunctional behaviour and policies by principals and agents of the public sector (North 1999; North et al. 2007). The sad truth is that while both developing and transitional economies suffer from a greater incidence of market failures, which would warrant better government intervention, their institutions are faced with serious government failure, and this questions the merits of such intervention. In his book on globalization, Stiglitz (2002) makes a strong case with respect to the developing and transitional economies for more government intervention in a number of areas, including, among others, trade restrictions as part of industrial policy, control over the financial sector and financial flows, more limited, delayed and gradual privatization, and larger budgets and more attention to public and welfare services. Unfortunately the dilemma is that there may be an overestimation of the ability of these governments to pursue such policies in an effective and non-corrupt way. This dilemma and the possibility that transition will induce greater disorder are both embedded in a model of transition developed by Aghion et al. (2009). High levels of social capital and trust (SC&T) reduce transaction costs and save on regulation and law enforcement, and also facilitate more impersonal transactions and thus larger markets and more specialization. Low levels of SC&T, manifested in negative (social) externalities by the private sector, encourage people to support more regulation and government intervention, even by a corrupt government. The cost of government corruption is deemed lower than the cost of the negative externalities inflicted by the business sector. The model produces a case of dual equilibrium and the dynamics depend on the specific starting point; low initial levels of SC&T may deteriorate into high levels of corruption and regulation while a higher level of initial SC&T may gravitate to regulation-free and honest government and markets.

2.2 Institutions and social capital in Russia before transition

The task of institution-building in the economies under transition was especially burdensome and difficult for three reasons. First, the formal institutional structure under the old regime was diametrically opposite to the one aimed for through transition. It is difficult to imagine any other situation with such extreme contradictions between two institutional systems. Second, the transition was a major non-continuous process where changes had to take place over a short period of time, whether under a shock therapy approach or even under so called gradualism. During the transition, the conflict between new formal institutions and informal norms of behaviour widens, causing higher transaction costs and hence lower efficiency (Murrell 2008). The conflict between government and the people under conditions of the 'natural state' produces mutual mistrust and cynicism that when carried over to the transition period develops into a major barrier to sound institutional functioning. Russia (and a few other former Soviet states) provides an extreme example for such a development (see Ledeneva 2006). Third, the main responsibility of implementing reforms falls on the government, which is often unprepared, unmotivated, and weak. The government itself is confronted with similar problems at a time when it is needed the most and can become a major part of the problem rather than the solution.

Enforcement under a democratic and developed market system, while strict, is based on social consent, an impartial and independent legal system, and a general culture of abiding by and following informal behavioural norms. The bulk of the informal institutions operate in this manner in support of, and as complements to, formal institutions, and therefore reinforce and improve the institutional infrastructure of the economy. Under authoritarian central planning, enforcement is achieved through strict discipline, harsh sanctions and intimidation, controlled by the communist party. The 'legal' system, devoid of real legality, is arbitrary but always sides with the regime (Litwack 1991).

The command and bureaucratic nature of central planning, and complete government control of the economy, its assets and transactions, opened the door for corruption that could be restrained only partly with very harsh sanctions, fear and intimidation. The limited relaxation of discipline and of sanctions, both intentional and unintentional, after the death of Stalin, introduced more opportunities for corruption and other anti-system activities. Taut plans and tight supply channels encouraged unlawful action even in efforts to meet official production targets. Corruption subsequently became more common in the production sector as well as in public services, such as education and health, where school certificates, examinations, university degrees, medical treatment, and lucrative jobs were all quite freely bought like any other commodity. The same applied to law enforcement, legal and court services: officials, judges, managers and accountants considered themselves part-owners, or at least legitimate stakeholders, of the assets and the rents they provided.

The gully between formal and informal institutions was further widened by the hypocritical behaviour of the leadership. This manifested over time as an increasing contrast between the declared goals and values of the regime and its hidden agenda. Cynicism increased as larger segments of the population recognized the growing gap between the declared benevolent goals of the regime and the narrow self-serving behaviour of the elite. The response to such hypocrisy was evasion, a growing sense of despair, and strong mistrust, which further encouraged unlawful 'informal' behaviour. Likewise, shirking became the response to the non-existent sharing of the national product among the people. All these contributed to the development of informal norms that were based on personal relationships and were antagonistic to the regime. As put by Ledeneva cited in Sinitsina et al. 2008: 45):

> Social capital in the USSR took a very much specific form of the so-called *blat*, the reputation-based interpersonal networks of informal reciprocal exchange with favours of access to scarce goods and services penetrated the whole Soviet society.[5]

Informal institutions develop in societies in the context of social and civil society organizations. In this respect, the communist regime left the Soviet Union, as well as other transitional economies, a scorched land. It eroded all genuine institutions of civil society, decimated any remnants of social capital and positive social networking, and destroyed the basis for solidarity and voluntary compliance with the law.

2.3 And under transition

After transition and the resulting collapse of central planning, and of most of the related operating tools and *raisons d'être* of the old institutions, new institutions had to be created. Void of domestic experience or traditions, these had to be built on the basis of international experience, and were indeed 'imported' from abroad. Even with the best advisers, design of the new formal institutions must have been hindered by the lack of foreign and domestic expertise, particularly given the difficulties of applying foreign designs to local conditions and of co-ordinating their dynamic and interactive development over time. Even with the best design, implementation faced more serious problems: the new imported rules were *terra incognita* to the officials implementing them but even more so to the public. Implementation was also hampered by the resistance of the existing bureaucracy assigned to the task. In some cases the new institutions were manipulated to perform unintended functions that contradicted their reform mission (Polishchuk, Chapter 7 in this volume; see also Ledeneva 2006). The radical change of formal institutions left informal behaviour patterns lagging behind. On the one hand, the legacy of opposing the government and circumventing its orders was now directed at the new government and unfamiliar institutions. The lure of, and incentives for, illegal action were much stronger given the huge stock of public assets available for redistribution. Paradoxically, the 'winds of freedom' (*glasnost*) were often translated into, and interpreted as, an extreme version of *laissez-faire* and the exaggerated freedom of action. At the same time, the erosion in discipline from above was not compensated by greater interpersonal trust and social cohesion. Tension between the newly introduced formal institutions and the old established informal ones hampered the transition progress.

The tension between the old and new can best be seen in the context of a number of important public institutions that are the key to successful change. The legal system needed to introduce and enforce a completely new body of private property rights and protection, especially in connection with the privatization of public enterprises and the new regime of corporate governance. It also needed to adopt the role of an honest enforcer of contracts and arbiter between governmental agencies and the public. The police and other law-enforcement agencies had to change in the same direction. The financial and banking sector had to reinvent itself completely from a virtual government agency into the main vehicle of financing according to sound economic criteria. This implied a revolutionary new role for the central bank. The government had to establish, almost from scratch, a new tax system that included an effective tax-collection mechanism, becoming an organization able to overcome strong resistance from the newly created business sector to paying taxes. After privatization, the government had to change its role as top manager and owner of the production sector to that of a regulator 'at arm's length', applying measures such as material incentives and the imposition of hard budget constraint. Together with the central bank, it became responsible for macroeconomic stabilization and had to keep a balanced budget. Its budget had to be reduced to a new level consistent with its new capacity to collect taxes. Budget reduction was achieved by reducing or eliminating direct support to, and investment in, the production sector, cutting defence expenditure, and concentrating public funding on social services (education and health), infrastructure and social safety nets to soften the negative impact of the reforms. The newly elected parliaments should have resisted the temptation to use their newly acquired powers and should have refrained from populist measures. Kornai has coined the term 'premature welfare state' to underline the government's burden in the transition process. Other researchers show that larger social budgets seem to be correlated with a more successful transition.[6]

A weak government with limited implementation and enforcement capacities opens the door to corruption and 'state capture' (Hellman et al. 2000), and the growth of substitute private contract-enforcement organizations. The large volumes of assets waiting to be privatized, and of legislation to be enacted, in a context of antagonistic informal institutions and behaviour by the government bureaucracy and by the production managers, provided ample opportunities for such behaviour (La Porta et al. 1999: 17, 28–9). A strong government, which could be a democratic one, can avoid the low-level and corrupt equilibrium described above, and can aim towards a reform- and growth-oriented high-level equilibrium. The capacity of the government to act in this manner may depend, to some extent, also on the size of its budget and the initial pressures to initiate sharp budgetary cuts (Popov 2000, 2009).

3   Russia's transition record: building new institutions

In this section, information is collected from a number of surveys on the quality of governance and the institutional development of various country-groups in order to evaluate the extent of institution building in Russia during transition thus far. The study compares Russia's success in this sphere with that of a group of countries at a similar GDP per capita level; that is, the 'upper middle-income' countries (UMI) according to the World Bank classification.[7] Comparisons with other groups of developing countries are also used, although comparisons with other groups of transitional economies are limited since much of these data have recently been analysed in great detail (EBRD 2008; Sinitsina et al. 2008). A consistent finding of this literature is the 'great divide' with respect to the transition performance between the CEB and CIS countries, including Russia. Despite the foregoing, the earlier draft of the study (Ofer 2010: 11–12) included a section that summarized quantitatively, based on EBRD 2008, the gaps between Russia and a few countries in Eastern Europe in the (institutional) achievements of the transition.

3.1 The World Bank and worldwide governance indicators

The worldwide governance indicators (WGI), well-known and extensively used, consist of six clusters of different aspects of governance at the national level for 212 countries (World Bank 2009c). The clusters are calculated as the aggregation of an extensive list of available studies and surveys relevant to each particular governance cluster. This is the most comprehensive, albeit aggregated, assessment of the levels of broad institutional categories. The institutional levels are given in two forms: as percentile ranks among all the countries, and on a scale of absolute score ranging between −2.5 and +2.5. See Table 9.1 and Figure 9.1 for the list of clusters and levels for Russia for the period 1996–2008. The table and the figure depict a gloomy picture in two respects. First, all scores are negative and, according to the most recent survey, are below the 25th percentile, the bottom quartile among all countries.

Table 9.1 Russia's governance indicators (WGI)

Governance indicator	Year	Percentile rank (0–100)	Governance score (−2.5 to +2.5)	Standard error
Voice and accountability	2008	21.6	−0.97	0.11
	2003	33.7	−0.57	0.15
	2000	33.7	−0.46	0.21
	1996	34.9	−0.43	0.23
Political stability	2008	23.9	−0.62	0.2
	2003	23.1	−0.80	0.23
	2000	23.1	−0.72	0.23
	1996	15.4	−1.04	0.32
Government effectiveness	2008	45.0	−0.32	0.17
	2003	50.7	−0.21	0.15
	2000	33.2	−0.58	0.17
	1996	34.6	−0.51	0.23
Regulatory quality	2008	31.4	−0.56	0.16
	2003	40.5	−0.37	0.16
	2000	19.0	−0.78	0.19
	1996	28.3	−0.39	0.23
Rule of law	2008	19.6	−0.91	0.12
	2003	19.5	−0.92	0.13
	2000	14.8	−1.06	0.13
	1996	28.6	−0.67	0.18
Control of corruption	2008	15.5	−0.98	0.12
	2003	28.2	−0.76	0.13
	2000	13.6	−0.99	0.15
	1996	23.3	−0.80	0.21

Source: World Bank (2009c).

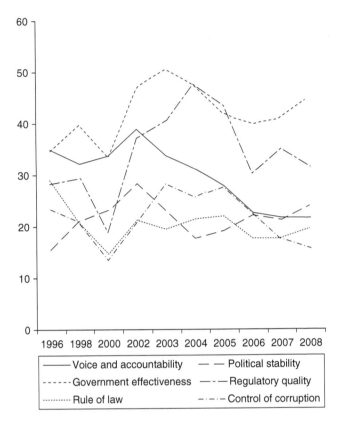

Figure 9.1   Governance indicators for Russia, 1996–2008 (percentiles)

Note: The governance indicators presented here aggregate the views on the quality of governance provided by a large number of survey respondents in industrial and developing countries. These data are gathered from a number of survey institutes, think tanks, non-governmental organizations, and international organizations.

Source: Based on data from Kaufman et al. (2009).

Second, there is no significant positive trend (beyond the statistical confidence limits) except perhaps for one indicator. Indeed, there are a few recent setbacks from the higher levels achieved during Putin's early years. The first two clusters—'voice' and 'political stability'—denote the quality of democracy and political institutions, and the main point to note here is the significant retreat of voice since the early 2000s, in both the level of democracy and the range of civic freedoms. Can this be the flip side of the significant increase in the measure of government effectiveness since the early 2000s? At the same time the levels of the rule of law, regulatory quality, and the control of corruption are currently very similar to their respective

Table 9.2 Governance indicators (WDI), Russia, and UMIs, 2008

Governance indicator	Percentile rank, Russia (0–100)	Income average, percentile rank, UMI countries	Governance score, Russia (−2.5 to +2.5)	Standard error
Voice and accountability	21.6	62.8	−0.97	0.11
Political stability	23.9	61.7	−0.62	0.20
Government effectiveness	45.0	61.2	−0.32	0.17
Regulatory quality	31.4	60.0	−0.56	0.16
Rule of law	19.6	59.9	−0.91	0.12
Control of corruption	15.5	59.9	−0.98	0.12

Source: World Bank (2009c).

1996 levels, with the first two exhibiting some improvement during the early 2000s but then, in recent years, a retreat.

How does the institutional level of Russia compare with other countries at the same level of economic development? Russia is classified by the World Bank as an UMI country.[8] A comparison of the UMI country-group for 2008 is given in Table 9.2, which shows that the average UMI levels converge around the 60th percentile for all six clusters. This is, by a wide margin, significantly higher than for Russia, where the best result is for government effectiveness but still trails behind the UMI level. Russia's institutional level is also lower than the average of the lower middle-income (LMI) country-group and parallels the average of the low-income (LI) countries, located between the 20th and the 30th percentile points. Even here only two of Russia's indicators—government effectiveness and regulatory quality—are above the LI levels. According to these measures, Russia is still in the early stages of institution building and has a long way to go to overcome the institutional barriers imposed by its inheritance.

3.2 The global competitiveness index and the knowledge economy index

As mentioned above, the WGI is composed of data provided by various individual surveys that examine the institutional and other attributes of countries around the world. Two of these are presented here. The GCI is compiled by the World Economic Forum, with special emphasis on the competitive capabilities of countries as gauged by many indicators, including institutional quality. The knowledge economy index (KEI)—created by the World Bank using the KAM of its K4D programme—evaluates the contribution of knowledge and innovation capabilities of a country to its growth potential. Institutional indicators are included in both surveys as the major determinants of competitiveness and of knowledge, respectively, and their contribution to growth. In what follows, we do two things: first, with the GCI supplemented with the K4D, we study Russia's detailed institutional position in a comparative context. Next, in the following section, we use the K4D survey to estimate and compare the levels of its knowledge and innovation indicators. Here, K4D leads and GCI supports. The GCI is composed of 12 pillars indicating competitiveness, among which only one is labelled 'institutions', but institutions are present in the other pillars; that is, those capturing aspects such as the efficiency of various markets (for goods, labour and financing), business sophistication, and so forth. The indicator levels are identified according to their ranking position among the 134 countries and according to a grade (or score) ranging between 1 and 7, from worst to best. Table 9.3 presents a detailed account of the institutions pillar and Table 9.4 the GCI overall rank position and scores for all 12 pillars.

Table 9.3 GCI first pillar: institutions, Russia

		Rank (out of 134 countries)	Score (ranging from 1 to 7)
1.01	Property rights	122	3.3
1.02	Intellectual property protection	98	2.9
1.03	Diversion of public funds	102	2.9
1.04	Public trust of politicians	111	1.9
1.05	Judicial independence	109	2.9
1.06	Favouritism in decisions of government officials	88	2.8
1.07	Wastefulness of government spending	82	3.2
1.08	Burden of government regulation	118	2.5
1.09	Efficiency of legal framework	107	2.9
1.10	Transparency of government policy-making	119	3.2
1.11	Business costs of terrorism	100	5.1
1.12	Business costs of crime and violence	80	4.5
1.13	Organized crime	105	4.3
1.14	Reliability of police services	105	3.2
1.15	Ethical behaviour of firms	112	3.5
1.16	Strength of auditing and reporting standards	108	3.8
1.17	Efficacy of corporate boards	35	5.1
1.18	Protection of minority shareholders' interests	128	3.3

Source: GCI database, available at www.weforum.org.

Table 9.4 Russia 2008 GCI, 12 pillars

		Rank (out of 134 countries)	Score (1–7)
GCI 2008–9		51	4.3
GCI 2007–8 (out of 134)		58	4.2
GCI 2006–7 (out of 122)		59	4.1
Basic requirements		56	4.5
First pillar	institutions	110	3.3
Second pillar	infrastructure	59	3.7
Third pillar	macroeconomic stability	29	5.6
Fourth pillar	health and primary education	59	5.6
Efficiency enhancers		50	4.3
Fifth pillar	higher education and training	46	4.4
Sixth pillar	goods market efficiency	99	3.9
Seventh pillar	labour market efficiency	27	4.7
Eighth pillar	financial market sophistication	112	3.6
Ninth pillar	technological readiness	67	3.4
Tenth pillar	market size	8	5.7
Innovation and sophistication factors		73	3.6
Eleventh pillar	business sophistication	91	3.7
Twelfth pillar	innovation	48	3.4

Source: GCI database; available at www.weforum.org.

A quick glimpse at Table 9.4 demonstrates that the pillars with large institutional content assign the lowest ranks for Russia, far below the corresponding ranks of countries at Russia's income level. Russia is ranked 110th (out of 134) on the institutions pillar with a score of 3.3 out of 7.0. The pillar of 'financial markets' ranks the country even lower, at 112th place, with a score of 3.6. Also, the pillar of 'goods market efficiency' assesses Russia in 99th place and that of 'business sophistication' 91st. All these ranks are characteristic of the range of 42 LI countries.[9] The first pillar—institutional competitiveness—includes 18 indicators covering most spheres of economic and government activities (Table 9.3). Here, Russia is ranked 122nd for the definition and protection of property rights, the cornerstone of a market system and a free society, and 98th regarding intellectual property. Positioned near or below Russia on property rights are a few Central Asian transitional economies as well as countries at much lower economic development levels in Africa, South Asia and Latin America.

A number of indicators explore the quality performance of the government—public corruption (diversion of public funds), state capture (favouritism in decisions of government officials) and trust of politicians. Here, Russia's scores reduce its rankings to, or below, 100. The same is obvious with respect to the (bureaucratic) burden of regulation, ranked 118th, the efficiency of budget allocations, ranked 82nd, and the transparency of policy-making, ranked 119th. With respect to enforcement, the GCI evaluates the judicial system as being highly influenced by politicians and business, and the legal system's enforcement of contracts as extremely inefficient. Likewise, the police are found to be unreliable in upholding law and order (ranked 105th). The conduct of firms, also part of the first pillar (Table 9.3), is no better: the level of ethical behaviour is ranked 112th, with a score of 3.5, auditing and reporting standards are low, ranked 108th with a score of 3.8, and minority stockholders' rights are poorly protected, ranked 128th with a score of 3.3.[10] These are also supported by the rather poor showing of the Russian business sector in a World Bank (2009b) business survey. On the total costs of doing business, a concept similar to transaction costs, Russia is ranked 120th out of the total of 181 countries, of which 104 are either LI or LMI countries; 32nd out of 35 UMI countries; and 22nd among the 25 transitional economies. Russia's ranking is especially poor with regard to construction permits (180th), payment of taxes (134th), and cross-border trading (161st), but it is doing better in enforcing contracts (18th) and registering property (49th).

In the following, we survey the institutional showing (CGI) in three major markets: financial, goods, and labour. As we have seen, Russia ranks 112th among 134 countries in the eighth pillar of financial market sophistication. The modern structure of the Russian industry, consisting mostly of large enterprises and elaborate input–output networks, called for early privatization and restructuring of the financial sector. The particular importance of an early transition of the financial sector is due also to the early need to replace the government as it existed under central planning and to provide financial services for a fast recovery of orderly production, supply, and economic growth. Unlike most of the transitional economies in Central and Eastern Europe, Russia did not invite Western banks to take over the bulk of its banking sector. Thus, despite some recent improvements (establishment of deposit insurance, expansion of consumer credits, and better functioning of the central bank), Russia's financial services in 2008 were at the level of the sub-Saharan African countries. Russia ranks 107th on the soundness of its banks, 110th on the quality of regulations of securities and exchanges, 125th on restrictions on capital flows, 86th on the ease of getting loans, and so on (see also Aslund 2009; OECD 2009: 97–124). Four groups of indicators demonstrate the weak competitiveness of the goods markets in Russia: its high concentration (limited dominance), poor competition, weak antimonopoly policy, and a high burden of support to agriculture, ranking 79th, 108th, 95th, and 104th, respectively. Likewise, obstacles created by the tax system are ranked in the 90s range, and barriers to international trade rank Russia above 100, as high as the 129th position. The levels of customer orientation by businesses and of customer sophistication are also low, ranked in the 70s range. The amount of time that it takes to start a business is still somewhat long, but the number of steps required to obtain a licence are relatively few (44th rank).[11]

Russia is ranked high (27th position) on the contribution of its labour market to competitiveness. This surprising evaluation is due, in the first instance, to considerable flexibility in hiring and firing (ranked 23rd), to the low cost of firing (28th), and to high correspondence of wages to productivity (11th on a global scale). The main factor that pulls Russia's ranking down is the high level of non-wage social costs, a direct remnant of the old regime (at 31 per cent of wages, ranked 112th). Also contributing to a lower ranking are poor co-operation in labour–employer relations (82nd) and relatively high rigidity of employment (87th), which apparently contradicts the high ranking for hiring and firing above. The competitive features of the labour market in Russia (and other CIS countries) reflect mostly the failure to replace the command nature of the old regime's labour market with a more co-operative form of these relations, as in many market economies (e.g. creation of unions and of collective bargaining), and the pro-labour legislation that imposes constraints and limits free competition in labour markets in developed economies, especially in Western Europe. This is not the place to discuss what might constitute optimal competitiveness in the labour market; it well may lie somewhat to the 'left' of the present 'free' market situation in Russia. The point to be made here is that after 20 years into the transition, the Russian labour market has failed so far to reorganize itself for market conditions. On the other hand, the heritage of the old regime also includes the relatively large burden of non-wage social costs (that many employers still try to evade), as well as the high participation rate of women in the labour force, a clear advantage, and the relatively low level of brain drain (ranking 44th), thus testifying to some extent to the relatively good quality of the educational and research infrastructure.

3.3   Formal and informal institutions: corruption and (dis)trust

Most of the institutional indicators in the first pillar, as well as those included in other pillars, reflect their formal structure, in terms of new laws and policies and the establishment of proper organizations, and so on, as well as their informal side, reflecting the quality of behaviour of the relevant agents and consistence with the requirements of the new formal institutions. It is clear from the low ranking and scores that whatever the state of the formal institutions, the required informal behaviour frequently did not fully follow. Moreover, in view of the lag in the establishment of new formal institutions, it is no wonder that informal behaviour followed a negative and opposing stance towards them. The visible conflict between formal and informal institutions is apparent, for example, in the first pillar, where the efficacy of corporate boards received high marks at a time when minority rights were poorly protected and the ethical behaviour of firms was ranked 112th. The most explicit manifestation of poor-quality and non-co-operative informal institutions is the low level of social capital, expressed as the overall lack of trust, corrupt behaviour, and state capture. Some of this may be the outcome of the unfamiliar nature of the new institutions, many of which were imported, and of the new and unfamiliar roles played by entrepreneurs, employers and 'businessmen', bureaucrats, and fellow citizens. Much of this negative reaction and lack of trust were relics of the old regime's behaviour patterns and the cynical approach of the population toward the government. We have already seen the very poor position of Russia, with respect to the control of corruption, in the WGI indicators, as well as the GCI ranking of Russia in positions 102nd, 111th, and 88th regarding the diversion of public funds, public trust of politicians, and organized crime, respectively (Table 9.3). According to the GCI survey, corruption is also the most serious problem with respect to conducting business in Russia, as indicated by 19.4 per cent of the respondents. A detailed account of the 'informal' and antagonistic behaviour of businessmen and other players during the first transition decade is presented by Ledeneva (2006). A full edifice of 'informal institutions' has been put in place to enable the newly created markets to operate.

Transparency International's corruption perception index (CPI) grades Russia with a score of 2.1 out of 10, placing it 147th out of 180 countries, on a par with Kenya, Bangladesh, and Syria. Transparency International's bribe payers index (BPI) positions Russia as last (first among paying bribes in other countries) out of the 22 countries included (Transparency International 2009). More evidence of the corruption and low levels of trust and of social capital is provided by Sinitsina et al. (2008), Ledeneva (2006) and others. This, plus evidence of the increased support for more government regulation and intervention, is discussed in Aghion et al. (2010) and Denisova et al. (2009), two studies that also show evidence of an increase in the level of corruption since 1989 in the transitional economies, particularly Russia (Denisova et al. 2009). It is claimed that this trend represents a shift towards a bad 'uncivil' equilibrium where people demand greater government intervention even while recognizing that the government itself is highly corrupt. People resent the negative externalities and bad behaviour of the new business entrepreneurs. The rationale is that increased government intervention limiting the negative behaviour of the business community, even at the cost of more corruption, is the lesser of two evils. Note that according to the model, greater government intervention and regulation will intensify the level of corruption and further erode trust and social capital. All that it takes in order to start such a process is a sufficiently high initial level of distrust and corruption, a condition easily characterizing Russia. The weak institutional base and considerable corruption during the last two decades of the new regime offered minimal opportunity to change courses. It takes a very bold move by a (new) government to reverse this trend.

A similar story can be told using the recent conceptual framework developed by North et al. (2005, 2006, 2007, 2009). The move by Gorbachev to introduce partial reforms intended to expand entrance to the existing state of limited access got out of control, spilled over to other spheres, and brought about a much broader systemic change. The many obstacles to the creation of new institutions, some of them particularly relevant for Russia, created disorganization, prolonged the process of transition, and increased the risks of failure. Measures taken to ascertain that the changes were irreversible, like privatization, later backfired and encouraged the government to partly reverse the process. In a way, it was a return to limiting access on this score, foreign investors included. Weak formal institutions and enforcement, and a high level of corruption, encouraged antagonistic informal institutional behaviour and made things worse. North et al. (2009) believe it will take 50 years or so to accomplish a transition to open access. In Russia, the transition may have to use most of this time.

In two papers on corruption, Treisman claims, first, that the level of corruption in transition economies can be explained by universal variables (2000) that apply in all countries and, second, a corollary of the first, that similar variables, all existing before the transition, also determine the differences in the level of corruption between transition states (2005). The most relevant variables to our discussion here are the levels of GDP per capita, the time under the communist regime (for the study of corruption in transition countries), and the (partially correlated) length of time with the absence of a democratic regime. The discussion of corruption in this study, so we claim, describes the processes and mechanisms that emerge from the last two variables. In addition we believe that the structures of the economies and societies of most transition countries, Russia in particular, are much more advanced and modern than other countries of similar income levels, therefore calling for a lower level of corruption. Yet, Russia's level of corruption is higher than expected (there is a large remaining residual) in Treisman's analysis of transition countries (Treisman 2005: 221–3; see also Denisova et al. 2009: Figure 1). This study also investigates the reasons for such a residual.

4 Human capital, education, and innovation

The Soviet Union was a world power with regard to research and development (R&D) and innovation, even though the majority of this effort was directed to the military at the expense of the civilian sector. Innovation effort was supported by an excellent educational system at all levels and a network of top research institutes, made up of the largest number of scientists and engineers in the world and very generous R&D budgets. The military innovation network was promoted through top research centres that were favoured with the best in scientists and engineers, materials, and other inputs, as well as priority status in planning and supply. This priority treatment partly compensated for the basic systemic defect and many other obstacles to innovation that characterized the centrally planned system.[12]

The role of human capital in economic development and growth has long been recognized. Under the acknowledged view, developing countries devote most of their innovation effort to the importation and absorption of existing technologies for the production of goods at the lower end of the product cycle, and hence their main educational efforts should be focused on elementary and secondary schools. Developed countries, positioned at the technological frontiers, concentrate more on pushing these frontiers outwards and onwards to top-level production and new products. Thus, they concentrate on higher education and top research centres (Acemoglu et al. 2006; Aghion et al. 2009). However, lately the importance of high-level tertiary centres of excellence has been recognized also in connection with developing countries. Their active involvement in frontline innovation is considered important for growth as well as for limiting the brain drain of the best scientists and for engaging the scientific diasporas in 'brain circulation'.[13] This is considered relevant for countries such as India, China, and Brazil, thus Russia should, and can, definitely aspire to become a frontrunner among the transitional and developing countries on the education and innovation frontiers. In order to achieve this, Russia needs (i) to provide the budgets required to preserve and strengthen its education and research capacities inherited from the old regime, but at the same time (ii) to replace the old institutional and structural settings with those that complement a market economy and a democratic society. These include transforming the incentive structure, the forms of governance, and the modes of operation to open—internally and globally—more flexible systems; adjusting the curricula contents and changing the methods of study and of doing research; refocusing innovation efforts from military to civilian targets, and designing better methods of disseminating innovations to the production sector; and engaging the private sector as a partner to the innovation effort. Adequate budgets are necessary but without the required institutional changes, more money will not do the job.

The GCI ranks Russia's overall competitiveness level in 2008–9 in 51st place out of 134 countries, much above the institutional ranks and scores indicated above (see Table 9.4 and GCI). This higher performance is explained by a number of other features (like the size of the economy and its macroeconomic policy), and also as expected, by factors related to human capital, education, research, and innovation. A similar contrast is apparent in the World Bank assessment of its K4D indexes of the KEI and the knowledge index (KI). The K4D indexes assess the development (growth) potential of countries on the basis of three knowledge pillars: level of education, innovative capacity, and level of ICT. These three knowledge pillars are aggregated into KI. An additional pillar, economic incentive regime (EIR), is combined with the KI to create the overall index: the KEI—the potential contribution of knowledge of growth. The EIR includes, among others, many general institutional indicators that make up the system tools that enable the knowledge indicators to contribute to economic growth.

Table 9.5 includes data about Russia's rankings according to each of the six indexes mentioned above. Here too, as before, Russia's recent rank with respect to the incentives (institutional) pillar, EIR, is 124th out of 134 countries, with a score of 1.55 (lower than in 1995), while its KI rank is 41st, indicative of its good relative performance in both the education and innovation pillars. The overall KEI index, however, pushes Russia down to 61st position, 20 steps lower. The most significant observation in the two surveys is the high ranking and scores for the knowledge indicators. In the K4D study, Russia stands 37th on education and 38th on innovation, but lower, at 55th, with regard to its ICT level. These levels and the corresponding scores (over a range of 1–10; see Figure 9.2 and Annexe 9.1), are above for education and on a par for innovation and ICT compared with the average levels of the UMI country-group, and also with the transitional country-group of Eastern Europe and Central Asia (EECA). The great divide is much narrower as far as Russia's knowledge indicators are concerned. Yet Russia's knowledge indexes are still significantly below those of the high-income countries, somewhat less so with respect to education (Figure 9.2 and Annexe 9.1). This may be surprising, given the priority granted to research and education under the old regime. It may reflect some retreat that has taken place during the transition years.

Table 9.5 Russia's ranking, KAM indexes, 1995 and recent

	KEI	KI	Economic incentive regime	Innovation	Education	ICT
Recent	61	41	124	38	37	55
1995	56	—	112	55	25	—

Note: Innovation indicators weighted by population, 140 countries; recent = 2007 or nearest year.
Source: World Bank's KAM database.

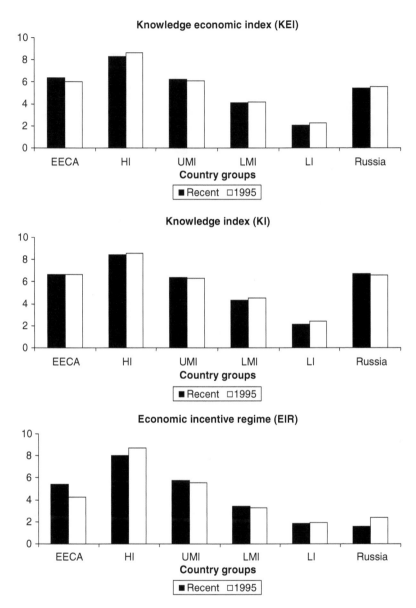

Figure 9.2 Knowledge scores for Russia and various country-groups, recent and 1995
Note: Innovation indicators weighted by population size; recent = 2007, or the nearest year.
Source: Based on data from the World Bank's KAM database and Appendix Table.

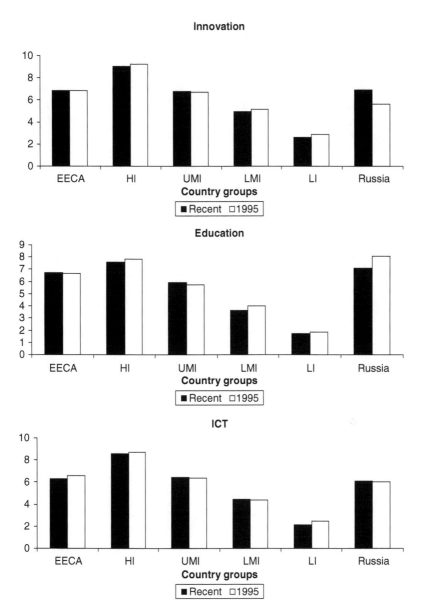

Figure 9.2   (Continued)

Similar results, albeit somewhat less positive, are observed for Russia in the GCI survey (Table 9.4), in which it is ranked 46th on the higher education and training pillar and 48th on innovation, both just marginally above its overall rank of 51.[14] Russia is ranked just 67th on technological readiness and 91st with respect to business sophistication, the institutional underpinning for innovation. Based on the GCI, Russia is positioned somewhere near the bottom of the UMI group, an adequate position but far from outstanding, and yet considerably above its institutional ranking.[15]

5 Discussion and conclusions

As seen above, the overall ranking of Russia with respect to the KEI at 61st place is 20 steps below the 'pure' KI index, all due to internal (inside the sector) and general institutional weaknesses. This is one example of how weak institutions and high levels of corruption reduce the potential contribution, in this case, of the knowledge assets to a country's economic development. This pattern repeats itself in other spheres where productive assets inherited from the old regime cannot be utilized to their full potential because of internal and general institutional weaknesses. Other examples are the governance and the industrial structure of public utilities and infrastructure, the functioning of the financial sector, the low competitive level of the market for goods and services, and so on. Sinitsina et al. (2008: 192–7) highlight this 'imbalance in the levels of development' among the various pillars and call for a policy to balance them. The emphasis, in my view, should be on bringing up the institutional level to bridge the gap with the other growth engines as soon as possible— in this case, the knowledge assets. A more balanced institutional growth in tandem with economic development is, indeed, a great advantage for other developing economies that are progressing along an evolutionary path and gradually establishing new institutions as the need for them arises (Ofer 2004).

The difficulties in the establishment of the appropriate institutional infrastructure originate first of all from the extreme contradiction between the institutional structure inherited from a regime of central planning and authoritarian rule and the structure needed for a market economy and a democracy. Special attention has to be given to the rigidity, high cost, and aversion to changes that are embedded in the old system, and to the resulting and growing gap between formal and informal institutions. This gap, in turn, results (to a large extent) from the lack of social capital, and the culture of cynical approach and distrust (of the people in their government under the old regime) carried over to the transition period. This gap required strong enforcement, which the new regime was unable or unwilling to provide.[16]

In a recent study, Popov (2009) comes back to a discussion that took place throughout the transition and has been mentioned above, namely the desired level of the government budget during transition. The claim is that given the difficulties of creating new institutional infrastructure, governments needed more resources—first of all for effective institutions and enforcement, but also for preserving the stock of human capital and innovation capacity, as well as health care and other safety-net services. I fully agree. Prudent use of Russia's energy revenues should make this feasible. There is no doubt that the fact that only 3.6 per cent of GDP is being devoted to education during the transition period contributes to the decline in its quality and ranking, and that the rise over the same period in the financing of R&D and innovation up to 1 per cent of GDP contributes to its modest rise in ranking. However, additional resources should be strictly and effectively conditioned upon the implementation of the needed structural institutional reforms. As Popov concludes—and is confirmed by many—the allocation of energy revenues so far has not been adequate for this purpose, and the abundance of natural resources was more of a curse than a blessing in more ways than one (Polterovich et al. 2008), indeed, facilitating and encouraging the recent retreat of reforms. This demonstrates that while more money is essential, the crucial issue is guaranteeing its proper use. This is illustrated in the following excerpts from a report on the quality of higher education in recent years in Russia:

> Fifteen years into independence, the universal problem in Russia remains the need for good management and good governance (of universities). A poor governance and incentive structure at universities threatens to skew the Russian state's now-ambitious plans for and major new investments in higher education.
>
> (Kotkin 2007: 6)
>
> Amid all the rhetoric about 'disintegration', the university system (like many other subunits) did not disintegrate. On the contrary, the state system proved it could absorb fantastic sums of grant money and more or less continue on its merry way.
>
> (ibid.: 8)

What is true for higher education is also valid for many other spheres where old institutions need to be replaced by new (see Murrell 2008). The consequences were the entrepreneurs and bureaucrats capitalizing on the disorganization and weak enforcement, and the disappointment of many people (and some leaders?) in the virtues of the new system. All this leads towards low-level equilibrium, as identified by Aghion et al. (2010), or to renewed efforts by powerful groups to revert to limiting access, à la North et al. (2009) to collect rents through the (re)creation of (new) barriers on ownership, trade, free information, power, or just rent-grabbing activity related to the Dutch disease created by the oil boom. This trend became more visible in recent years when the government grew much stronger (and even more 'efficient', as we have seen) but diverted its efforts away from the badly needed structural reforms (Aslund 2009; OECD 2009). Even Murrell (2008), who lauds the fast institutional advances in the transitional economies of the CEB group, acknowledges the slow pace, and even the retreat in institutional reforms in Russia and other CIS countries. The recent withdrawal from reforms need not become permanent. Any of the three conceptual frameworks mentioned above provides for a reversal by forces within the present or future regime. They may all still occur within the 50-year timeframe suggested by North et al. (2009).

Dmitry Medvedev fully recognizes the transition problems existing in Russia today, which can and should be addressed by his version of modernization. According to his prognosis of the problem, it is a question of 'should a primitive economy based on raw materials and endemic corruption accompany us into the future?' To change this situation, he proposes replacing the 'humiliating dependence on raw materials' with knowledge- and innovation-based production and growth (dubbed by many as 'diversification'), founded on both inherited and imported scientific infrastructure; honest (non-corrupt) markets and democratic institutions; less paternalistic government intervention and more private entrepreneurship; and an active civic society (Medvedev 2009a, 2009b). Medvedev is at present the leading westernizer in Russia, while Putin is leaning more towards a Slavophile stance, supporting a strategy labelled 'conservative modernization' (OSC 2009). Time will tell which approach will prevail and to what extent rhetoric can be translated into action. It is interesting to note how the quest for knowledge-based 'intensive growth' that haunted the Soviet Union for decades is still present, although the culprit now is the above-mentioned 'humiliating dependence on raw materials'.

The difficulties and the costs involved in attempts to jump over the gulf separating the two contrasting institutional edifices of central planning and the market raise the issue of whether the entire communist episode has paid off in terms of a faster pace of modernization and growth.[17] A comparison by this author (Ofer 2004, 2008b) of the long-term economic growth of the Soviet Union and Russia with a counterfactual alternative gives a negative answer. In this study we have shown in greater detail the impact of the difficulties of institutional transition to this outcome.

Annexe

Annexe 9.1 Scores for Russia, EECA, and UMI, recent and 1995

	KEI		KI		EIR		Innovation		Education		ICT	
	Recent	1995	Recent	1995	Recent	1995	Recent	1995	Recent	1995	Recent	1995
EECA	6.35	6.06	6.65	6.67	5.44	4.22	6.88	6.82	6.74	6.65	6.33	6.55
HI	8.31	8.61	8.41	8.58	8.03	8.70	9.05	9.22	7.60	7.81	8.58	8.72
UMI	6.21	6.11	6.35	6.29	5.78	5.57	6.76	6.69	5.89	5.76	6.41	6.40
LMI	4.10	4.18	4.33	4.49	3.41	3.26	4.95	5.11	3.61	4.02	4.43	4.35
LI	2.08	2.29	2.15	2.41	1.88	1.95	2.63	2.90	1.71	1.87	2.10	2.46
Russia	5.40	5.54	6.69	6.57	1.55	2.43	6.89	5.62	7.09	8.05	6.08	6.05

Note: Innovation indicators weighted by population; recent = 2007 or nearest.
Source: World Bank's KAM database.

Notes

1. Russia's GDP level in 2007 was estimated at 102 per cent of the 1989 level (EBRD 2008: Table A.1), and at 108 per cent a year later. However, in 2009, Russia's GDP was projected to decline by 8.5 per cent (EBRD 2009: Table 1.1). See also Popov (Chapter 12 in this volume).
2. Some of the great laggers in terms of market reforms and democracy, like Belarus and Turkmenistan, experienced relatively high growth rates.
3. See, for example, Aghion et al. (2010); Aghion et al. (2007); Barro and Sala-i-Martin (2004); EBRD (2008: Chapter 3); Kuznetsov (2007, 2009); Kuznetsov and Sable (2009); *The Economist* (2005); and Ofer (2008a).
4. See Sinitsina et al. (2008) for an extensive literature survey on most of the relevant topics discussed here.
5. A study by Denisova et al. (2009: 8–9) based on the Russia Longitudinal Monitoring Survey (RLMS) reports a high level of 'trust in most other people' in 1991, just before the fall of the Soviet Union. The authors themselves doubt that this was really the case.
6. See, among others, Popov (2000, 2009); La Porta et al. (1999); EBRD (2008: Chapter 3).
7. There are 42 UMI countries, ten of which are transitional economies in Eastern Europe, the Baltics, Kazakhstan and Russia (World Bank 2009a: 351). Back-of-the-envelope calculations showed that the impact of transition economies on the averages of the UMIs is not significant.
8. See endnote 7.
9. Based on the assumption of a close correlation between the income level and the quality of institutions among the developing economies.
10. In view of this, it is rather surprising that the survey finds the efficacy of corporate boards high and ranks Russia 35th with a score of 5.1 out of 7 (investors and boards exert strong supervision of management decisions).
11. A detailed discussion of the high level of regulation and intervention by the Russian government in the goods market is included in OECD (2009, Chapter 5, Annexe 5.A1).
12. See Kornai (Chapter 1 in this volume) for a recent detailed account of the innovation deficiencies under central planning. See also Ofer (1987).
13. World Bank (2002); Chawla et al. (2007, Chapter 6); Kuznetsov (2007, 2009); Kuznetsov and Sable (2009); Aghion et al. (2007); *The Economist* (2005); Ofer (2008a).
14. Russia's overall rank of 51st in the GCI is due to other favourable factors: its market size (8th), a natural advantage, its labour market efficiency (27th) (discussed above), its success in achieving macroeconomic stability (29th), due to a considerable extent to oil and gas revenues (OECD 2009: Chapter 2), and in spite of its poor position (109th) with regard to high inflation rate. The level of infrastructure, ranked 59th, pushes Russia's overall ranking somewhat down, mostly due to bad roads (104th), and quality of air transport and port facilities (88th and 76th, respectively).
15. A more detailed discussion of the levels and time trends of the various KI indexes and their structure is included in an earlier version of this study (Ofer 2010: 22–4). Among others, the data reveal a decline over time (since 1995) in the ranking and score of the educational pillar, a slow rise in the levels of the innovation pillar,

a static trend in the ICT pillar, and, as we have seen, a decline over time in the institutional index.

16. The GCI for 2009–10 has just been issued as this study is being published. Over the last year, Russia has continued to retreat along the competitiveness scale, moving back 12 places on the overall GC index from 51st to 63rd position. Almost all the relevant indicators discussed in this study have retreated.

17. On the cost of switching growth strategies and institutions, see Aghion and Howitt (2009: Chapter 11) and Acemoglu et al. (2006).

References

Acemoglu, D., P. Aghion and F. Zilibotti (2006) 'Distance to Frontier, Selection and Economic Growth', *Journal of the European Economic Association*, 4(1): 37–74.

Aghion, P., M. Dewatripont, C. Hoxby and A. Mas-Colell (2007) 'Why Reform Europe's Universities?', *Bruegel Policy Brief*, Bruegel.

Aghion, P., D. Hemous, E. Kharroubi (2009) 'Credit Constraints, Cyclical Fiscal Policy and Industry Growth'. NBER Working Paper No. 15119.

Aghion, P. and P. Howitt (2009) *The Economics of Growth*, MIT Press: Cambridge, MA.

Aghion, P., Y. Algan, P. Cahuc and A. Shleifer (2010) 'Regulation and Distrust', *Quarterly Journal of Economics*, 125(3): 1015–49.

Aslund, A. (2009) 'Russia's Economic Revival: Past Recovery, Future Challenges', in A. Aslund and A. Kuchins (eds), *The Russia Balance Sheet*, Peterson Institute for International Economics: Washington, DC.

Barro, R. and X. Sala-i-Martin (2004) *Economic Growth*, MIT Press: Cambridge, MA.

Berliner, J. (1993) 'Perestroika and the Chinese Model', mimeo. Brandeis University: Waltham MA.

Chawla, M., G. Betcherman and A. Benerji (2007) *From Red to Gray: The 'Third Transition' of Aging Populations in Eastern Europe and the Former Soviet Union*, World Bank: Washington, DC.

Denisova, I., M. Eller and E. Zhuravskaya (2009) 'What Do Russians Think about Transition? Evidence from the RLMS Survey', *Economics of Transition*, 18(2): 249–80.

EBRD (European Bank for Reconstruction and Development) (2008) *Transition Report 2008: Growth in Transition*, EBRD: London.

EBRD (2009) *EBRD Database*, EBRD: London.

Guriev, S. and E. Zhuravskaya (2009) '(Un)happiness in Transition', *Journal of Economic Perspectives*, 23(2): 143–68.

Hellman, J.S., G. Jones, D. Kaufman and M. Schenkerman (2000) 'Measuring Governance, Corruption and State Capture: How Firms and Bureaucrats Shape the Business Environment in Transition Economies', *World Bank Policy Research Working Paper No. 2312*, World Bank: Washington, DC.

Kaufman, D., A. Kraay and M. Mastruzzi (2009) 'Governance Matters VIII: Aggregate and Individual Governance Indicators, 1996–2008', *World Bank Policy Research Working Paper No. 4978*, World Bank: Washington, DC.

Keren, M. and G. Ofer (2008) 'Are Transition Economies Normal Developing Countries? The Burden of the Socialist Past', in S. Estrin, G.W. Kolodko and M. Uvalic (eds) *Transition and Beyond*, Palgrave Macmillan: Basingstoke.

Kotkin, S. (2007) 'Academic Innovation: Individuals, Networks, Patronage: An Evaluation of Higher Education Support in Russia', prepared for the Ford Foundation, Moscow Office.

Kuznetsov, E. (2007) 'Radical Reform Step by Step: India in Light of China', mimeo. World Bank: Washington, DC.

Kuznetsov, E. (ed.) (2009) *Diaspora Networks and the International Migration of Skills: How Countries can draw on their Talent Abroad*, World Bank: Washington, DC.

Kuznetsov Y., and C. Sabel (2009)' International Migration of Talent, Diaspora Networks, and Development: Overview of Main Issues', in E. Kuznetsov (ed.), *Diaspora Networks and the International Migration of Skills: How Countries can draw on their Talent Abroad*, World Bank: Washington DC.

La Porta, R., F. Lopez-de-Salines, A. Shleifer and R. Vishny (1999) 'The Quality of Government', *Journal of Law, Economics and Organization*, 15(1): 22–32.

Ledeneva, A.V. (2006) *How Russia Really Works*, Cornell University Press: Ithaca and London.

Litwack, J. (1991) 'Legality and Market Reform in Soviet-Type Economies', *Journal of Economic Perspectives*, 5(4): 77–90.

Medvedev, D. (2009a) Presidential Address to the Federal Assembly of the Russian Federation, 12 November, The Kremlin: Moscow, provided by Johnson's Russia List, available at www.cdi.org/Russia/johnson/default.cfm.

Medvedev, D. (2009b) 'Go Russia', 10 September, The Kremlin: Moscow, provided by Johnson's Russia List, available at www.cdi.org/Russia/johnson/default.cfm.

Murrell, P. (2008) 'Speculation on the Path of Institutional Development in the Transition Economies', in S.N. Durlauf and L.E. Blume (eds), *The New Palgrave Dictionary of Economics*, 2nd edn, Palgrave McMillan: Basingstoke.

North, D.C. (1990) *Institutions, Institutional Change and Economic Performance*, Cambridge University Press: Cambridge, MA.

North, D.C. (1999) 'Dealing with a Non-Ergodic World: Institutional Economics, Property Rights, and the Global Environment', *Duke Environmental Law and Policy Forum*, 10(1): 15–27.

North, D., J.J. Wallis and B.R. Weingast (2005) 'The Natural State: The Political-Economy of Non-Development', UCLA International Institute: Los Angeles, available at www.international.ucla.edu/research/article.asp?parentid=22899.

North, D., J.J. Wallis and B.R. Weingast (2006) 'A Conceptual Framework for Interpreting Recorded Human History', *NBER Working Paper No. 12795*, National Bureau of Economic Research: Cambridge, MA.

North, D., J.J. Wallis, S.B. Webb and B.R. Weingast (2007) 'Limited Access Orders in the Developing World: A New Approach to the Problems of Development', *World Bank Policy Research Paper No. 4359*, World Bank: Washington, DC.

North, D., J.J. Wallis and B.R. Weingast (2009) *Violence and Social Order: A Conceptual Framework for Interpreting Recorded Human History*, Cambridge University Press: Cambridge, MA.

OECD (2009) 'Russian Federation', *OECD Economic Surveys*, July, OECD: Paris.

Ofer, G. (1987) 'Soviet Economic Growth: 1928–1935', *Journal of Economic Literature*, 25(4): 1767–833.

Ofer, G. (2003) 'Transition and Developing Economies: Comparing the Quality of Governments', in N.F. Campos and J. Fidrmuc (eds), *Political Economy of Transition and Development: Institutions, Politics and Policies*, Kluwer Academic Publishers: London.

Ofer, G. (2004) 'Switching Development Strategies and the Costs of Transition: the Case of the Soviet Union and Russia', paper presented at the *AEA Meetings 3–5 January, San Diego*.

Ofer, G. (2005) 'Abram Bergson: The Life of a Comparativist', *Comparative Economic Studies*, 47(2): 240–58.

Ofer, G. (2008a) 'From "Brain Drain" to "Brain Circulation": The Case of NES and Modern Economics in Russia', paper presented at the 10th EACES Conference, August, Moscow.

Ofer, G. (2008b) 'Soviet Growth Record', in S.N. Durlauf and L.E. Blume (eds), *The New Palgrave Dictionary of Economics*, 2nd edn, Palgrave McMillan: Basingstoke.

Ofer, G. (2010) 'Twenty Years Later and the Socialist Heritage is still kicking: The Case of Russia', *WIDER Working Paper No. 2010/59*, UNU-WIDER: Helsinki.

OSC (US Open Source Center) BBC Monitoring (2009) 'Analysis: Putin, Medvedev Speeches Suggest Differences on Modernization, Other Issues', 10 December, Johnson's Russia List, available at www.cdi.org/Russia/johnson/default.cfm.

Polterovich, V., V. Popov and A. Tonis (2008) 'Mechanisms of Resource Curse, Economic Policy and Growth', *NES Working Paper No. 2008/000*, New Economic School: Moscow.

Popov, V. (2000) 'Shock Therapy versus Gradualism, the End of the Debate (Explaining the Magnitude of Transformational Recession)', *Comparative Economic Studies*, 42(1): 1–57.

Popov, V. (2009) 'Lessons from the Transition Economies: Putting the Success Stories of the Postcommunist World into a Broader Perspective', *WIDER Research Paper No. 2009/15*, UNU-WIDER: Helsinki.

Roland, G. (2000) *Transition and Economics: Politics, Markets, and Firms*, MIT Press: Cambridge, MA.

Sinitsina, I., A. Atamanov, A. Chubrik, I. Denisova, V. Dubrovskiy, M. Kartseva, I. Lukashova, I. Makenbaeva, M. Rokicka and M. Tokmazishvili (2008) 'The Development Gap between the CIS and the EU', *CASE Network Report No. 81*, CASE: Warsaw.

Stiglitz, J.E. (2002) *Globalization and its Discontents*, Norton: New York.

The Economist (2005) 'Survey: Higher Education', 8 September.

Transparency International (2009) '2008 Corruption Perceptions Index' and 'Bribe Paying Index', available at www.transparency.org.

Treisman, D. (2000) 'The Causes of Corruption: A Cross-national Study', *Journal of Public Economics*, 76: 399–457.

Treisman, D. (2005) 'Postcommunist Corruption', in N.F. Campos and J. Fidrmuc (eds), *Political Economy of Transition and Development: Institutions, Politics and Policies*, Kluwer: Boston, MA.

World Bank (2002) *Constructing Knowledge Societies: New Challenges for Tertiary Education*, World Bank: Washington, DC.

World Bank (2009a) *World Development Report 2009*, World Bank: Washington, DC.

World Bank (2009b) *Doing Business*, World Bank: Washington, DC, available at www.doingbusiness.org.

World Bank (2009c) Governance Matters: Worldwide Governance Indicators Database (WGI), available at info.worldbank.org/governance/wgi.

World Bank (2009d) *Knowledge Assessment Methodology (KAM) of the Knowledge for Development Programme*, World Bank: Washington, DC, available at www.info.worldbank.org/etools/kam2/KAM.

World Economic Forum (2009) *Global Competitive Index (GCI), 2008–2009*, WEF: Geneva, available at www.weforum.org.

10
European Transition at Twenty: Assessing Progress in Countries and Sectors

Erik Berglöf, Lise Bruynooghe, Heike Harmgart, Peter Sanfey,
Helena Schweiger, and Jeromin Zettelmeyer

1 Introduction

As Central and Eastern Europe are marking the end of communism and the commencement of the process of transition towards democracy and market economy, it is natural to ask how far they have progressed relative to the objectives set at the time. How different is the transition region still from that of other countries at comparable levels of economic prosperity? Are there major differences within the transition region in this regard? In which countries and sectors, in particular, does the transition agenda remain incomplete? What should be the main priorities for future reforms?

An initial answer to these questions is provided by the European Bank for Reconstruction and Development (EBRD) transition indicators; see Figure 10.1 for the aggregate indicators (including upgrades in 2009) and Table 10.5 for sector indicators. These assess the progress towards a defined well-functioning market economy. The problem is that the understanding of what is a well-functioning market economy, and how to measure progress towards this objective, has evolved. Moreover, the availability and quality of data, particularly at the micro level, has improved tremendously. This study complements the assessment of the transition indicators in three important respects. First, it takes a broad view of transition objectives that emphasises not only market mechanisms and private sector development but also complementarities between the state and the private sector, and the role and quality of state institutions. Second, as far as the data allow, the analysis emphasises comparisons with countries outside the transition region (the transition indicators are only available for the transition countries in the EBRD region). Finally, and most importantly, the study draws on several new data sources and studies at the sector and firm levels.

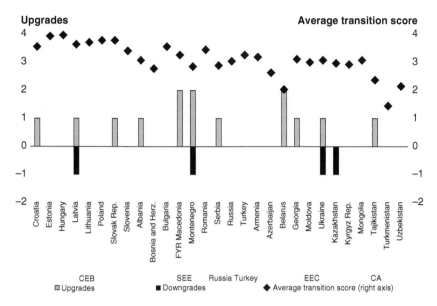

Figure 10.1 EBRD transition indicators
Source: Based on EBRD transition indicators.

The analysis begins with a summary of how the concept of transition has evolved since the mid-1990s, and what this implies for transition measurement. It then reviews transition from four perspectives:

- the latest (2008/09) Business Environment and Enterprise Performance Survey (BEEPS IV), which the EBRD and World Bank jointly undertake every three to four years;
- a new EBRD-World Bank survey of management practices;
- a sector-level comparison of competition across countries;
- a comprehensive analysis of remaining transition challenges across 13 specific sectors.

The concluding section considers whether the transition region is still different from other countries at comparable stages of development and indicates priorities for future reform.

2 Transition to where?

Since the early 1990s, the word 'transition' has been used to describe the evolution from a planned economy to a well-functioning market economy. In the light of the overwhelming role of the state at the start of the process, the questions of what exactly constitutes a well-functioning market economy and what part the state should play in it were initially given less attention. The imperatives were to reduce state ownership, direct state intervention and build market mechanisms. However, as the transition process and economic thought evolved during the decade, it became increasingly clear that this approach was too simplistic—to the point where it could be misleading as a yardstick for reforms—for two reasons.

First, moving from central planning to an 'optimal' role of the state is not just a matter of reducing state interference and control but also involves developing certain state activities. Transition is not just (and perhaps not even primarily) about the size of the state's 'footprint' in the economy but about where and how the state treads—that is, what the state does to affect economic outcomes and how it attempts to do so. The consensus in the early 1990s was that it was not the business of the state to set prices, or directly control or interfere with production and allocation decisions. That remains the overwhelming view. However, in order to function properly, the private sector needs market-supporting public institutions and policies.[1] These include a functioning legal system to enforce contractual obligations; regulation to deal with external effects and incentive problems; safety nets to allay concerns about social cohesion; physical and intellectual property rights protection; and competition policy.

Second, the quality of institutions emerged as a critical dimension of transition. State institutions with similar objectives—for example, enforcing laws, collecting taxes, or supervising the financial sector—can have vastly different impacts in terms of their effectiveness (whether laws are actually enforced and taxes collected) and the burden that state activities impose on the private sector. The effectiveness of institutions depends on two factors: technical capacity, which is related to information and human capital, and incentives. The latter will depend not only on the design of economic institutions but also on the political structure, and on complementary civil society institutions that promote transparency and accountability.

The quality dimension is also important with respect to non-state institutions. Markets do not function well if they are not competitive or there are barriers to entry. Corporations do not function well if corporate governance is poor and minority investors are not protected. In large part, these quality differences are driven by the presence (or absence) and effectiveness of supporting state institutions, such as legal frameworks and competition authorities. However, the functioning of market institutions may also depend on such factors as values, attitudes, and practices. Unwritten rules— for example, on what constitutes acceptable behaviour within a firm or in the political arena by government officials—may be as important in practice as explicit rules.

Transition should therefore be about redefining the state as opposed to simply minimizing it, and about improving the quality of state and private institutions and ensuring that they work together well. Defining transition in this way poses significant challenges—or, rather, it makes challenges that are hidden in simpler definitions of transition explicit.

- If the objective is to redefine the role of the state rather than simply maximize the scope of private activity, there must be a clear idea of what that role should be. Beyond some general principles (identified previously), this is likely to be possible mainly at the level of specific sectors.
- Even at the sector level, it will rarely be possible to define a uniquely 'optimal' role of the state. This is due partly to differences in political cultures and traditions. In addition, the desirable role of the state could depend on the quality of state and market institutions. For example, poor state performance in the provision of certain public goods could be an argument for a greater private sector input. Conversely, lack of competition or high barriers to entry could justify a temporarily greater or more heavy-handed role of the state in certain markets.

These challenges both confront a policy maker who is weighing reforms and complicate any attempt to take stock of transition. The following analysis tries to address them in three ways: by characterizing two critical dimensions of institutional quality—the business environment and the quality of managerial practices—that cut across sectors; by taking the analysis to the sector level, focusing on competition, market structure, and institutions; and through the methodology of this sector analysis, which accommodates a range of visions of what the sector-level goal of transition should be. Together, these building blocks give a reasonably complete and consistent picture of the status of transition and the challenges ahead.

3 Business environment

One way in which the state can enable markets to function properly is by creating a favourable business environment. To understand how far the transition region has come in this respect, and where it stands compared with other countries, this section presents the main results of the BEEPS IV—a survey of perceptions and enterprise operations based on face-to-face interviews with the owners or senior managers of randomly chosen companies.[2] Comparisons are drawn with earlier rounds of the survey and with similar recent surveys carried out elsewhere.

3.1 Main obstacles

The main purpose of the BEEPS is to identify problems that affect the operations of enterprises. Many questions in the survey asked respondents to rate the severity of different obstacles to doing business on a five-point scale—0 (no obstacle), 1 (minor obstacle), 2 (moderate obstacle), 3 (major obstacle) or

4 (very severe obstacle)—thereby allowing the construction of simple averages across firms for each obstacle. In addition, owners or managers were given a list of 15 different obstacles in the business environment and asked to identify the biggest one faced by their firm.

Table 10.1 presents the average score for the 15 obstacles for the whole transition region, as well as for the sub-regions (including Russia and Turkey). It also shows the percentage of firms that consider a given obstacle as the 'most serious' facing their operations (using the same regional breakdown). Three obstacles stand out for the region as a whole and across almost all sub-regions. 'Tax rates' is the only obstacle with an average score above 2.0, and it also ranks highest among the 'most serious' obstacles. While it is not surprising that businesses complain about taxes being too high, it is striking that this outweighs any other obstacle in importance. 'Political instability' is the next highest-ranked obstacle according to average score. Unsurprisingly, this features in countries such as Bosnia and Herzegovina, Georgia, Serbia, Turkey, and Ukraine, but also in some less-likely countries, such as Hungary and Lithuania. The sub-region that emphasises this obstacle the least is Central Asia, which perhaps reflects the authoritarian nature of the prevailing regimes. 'Access to finance' is also a significant obstacle, with more than 15 per cent of firms identifying it as their biggest problem—even though most firms were surveyed before the full effects of the global financial crisis were felt.

In other cases, there are larger differences in obstacle ratings across countries and sub-regions. For the transition region as a whole, 'corruption' is viewed as fairly serious (1.7), but more so in Russia (2.2) than in Central and Eastern Europe and the Baltic states (CEB, 1.4). Only in Russia do more than 10 per cent of respondents regard 'corruption' as the 'most serious' obstacle.[3] In contrast, 'competition from the informal sector' is viewed as a relatively minor problem in Russia, but as more serious in most other regions. Lack of 'education' in the workforce is perceived as a major problem in countries that have grown rapidly in recent years, such as Estonia, Romania and Russia.[4]

For most obstacles—'access to finance', 'access to land', 'business licensing and permits', 'corruption', 'courts', 'crime', 'theft and disorder', 'electricity', 'workforce', 'education', and 'transport infrastructure'—Russia, Eastern Europe and the Caucasus (EEC) and Central Asia tend to have higher average obstacle scores than in CEB and South-Eastern Europe (SEE). Since all of these sub-regions contain fast- and slower-growing economies, this finding is likely to reflect broad differences in the quality of infrastructure and institutions rather than differences in the importance that firms attach to particular obstacles. This is confirmed by more objective measures of business obstacles, based on the BEEPS itself[5] and on the World Bank's Doing Business survey (some of the indicators of which overlap conceptually with BEEPS).[6]

Table 10.1 BEEPS IV (2008/9) summary results, by region

	Average obstacle score							Per cent identifying constraint as 'most serious'						
	All transition countries	CEB	SEE	EEC	Russia	Central Asia	Turkey	All transition countries	CEB	SEE	EEC	Russia	Central Asia	Turkey
Access to finance	1.5	1.3	1.6	1.7	1.9	1.7	1.0	14.7	11.2	18.5	10.1	16.9	17.6	25.9
Access to land	1.2	0.9	1.0	1.7	2.0	1.3	0.4	2.5	1.7	2.1	4.0	5.7	1.7	0.4
Business licensing and permits	1.3	1.1	1.2	1.3	1.5	1.3	1.4	4.7	3.3	3.4	8.0	8.0	6.7	2.5
Corruption	1.8	1.4	1.8	1.9	2.2	1.8	2.0	6.6	4.6	7.1	8.9	11.2	9.9	2.0
Crime, theft and disorder	1.4	1.3	1.2	1.7	1.9	1.7	0.7	2.8	3.3	3.0	3.7	1.7	1.6	1.0
Customs and trade regulations	0.9	0.6	0.9	1.2	1.0	1.1	0.8	1.9	1.7	1.1	4.5	0.9	2.2	2.0
Electricity	1.6	1.4	1.3	1.7	2.0	1.9	1.1	2.9	3.5	1.6	2.1	2.0	6.7	3.0
Functioning of the judiciary	1.3	1.2	1.4	1.3	1.3	1.2	1.1	2.1	3.7	1.3	1.9	0.2	0.6	0.2
Inadequately educated workforce	1.7	1.5	1.3	1.7	2.4	1.8	1.5	12.0	12.3	14.0	8.0	15.4	9.1	9.1
Labour regulations	0.9	1.2	1.0	0.8	0.9	0.6	0.9	4.2	6.0	4.1	0.9	4.4	1.4	2.0
Political instability	1.9	1.8	1.9	2.0	2.0	1.6	2.5	10.7	9.8	10.0	15.7	8.1	3.0	17.5
Practices of competitors (informal sector)	1.6	1.4	1.6	1.7	1.3	1.5	1.7	10.5	12.5	8.6	9.2	6.1	9.1	14.7
Tax administration	1.5	1.5	1.5	1.5	1.5	1.4	1.4	4.2	5.8	4.3	3.0	2.2	6.0	0.3
Tax rates	2.2	2.2	1.9	2.2	2.4	2.1	2.4	19.1	19.3	19.3	19.2	17.2	23.3	18.2
Transport	1.2	1.0	0.9	1.3	1.6	1.3	0.9	1.2	1.3	1.7	1.0	0.1	1.2	1.1

Source: Based on BEEPS IV survey, EBRD and World Bank, and World Bank Enterprise Surveys; see text for explanation.

3.2   Comparison over time

How have perceptions of obstacles to doing business changed over time? Figure 10.2 shows how responses to 11 business environment elements have changed on average since 1999 by plotting the percentage of firms in the latest and previous BEEPS rounds that reported a non-zero score for each obstacle—that is, those seeing the problem as being of at least minor importance for their operations.[7] Three interesting findings emerge.

First, there are several categories—'customs and trade regulations', 'functioning of the judiciary', and 'tax administration'—where there appears to be a consistent improvement over time. Second, some obstacles—such as 'tax rates', 'access to finance', and 'corruption'—recorded a significant drop between 1999 and 2002 but have remained more or less the same since then. Lastly, perceived obstacles related to infrastructure—'transport', 'telecommunications', and 'electricity'—significantly increased in the latest round compared with the previous two rounds.[8]

The infrastructure findings may seem surprising, as the EBRD infrastructure reform indicators suggest that there has been continued progress in these areas in recent years. However, a heightened perception of problems could be an indication of a growing economy where firms wishing to expand their operations have run into difficulties that were not binding constraints beforehand. Given the strong growth that the transition region experienced

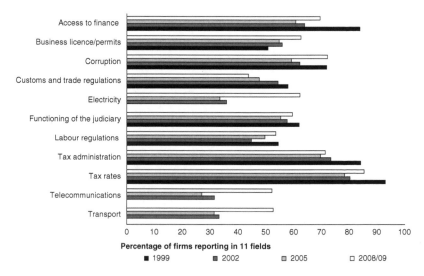

Figure 10.2 Business obstacles across time (percentage of respondents reporting obstacles in 11 areas)

Source: Based on BEEPS IV survey, EBRD and World Bank; see text for explanation.

between 2005 and early 2009, it is likely that the demands on infrastructure services grew more rapidly than the supply (even when improving) could cope with.[9] This demonstrates the need for continued investment and upgrading of these services across the board.

3.3 Comparison across countries

In recent years the World Bank (sometimes in collaboration with other international organizations) has sponsored a wide range of business environment surveys around the world. These differ to some extent from BEEPS, and the timing also varies across countries. However, there is sufficient overlap to allow some comparison to be made with regard to how perceptions of the business climate differ between the transition region and other emerging markets.

Is the business environment worse in the transition region than in other regions of similar GDP per capita? Indicators based on subjective perceptions are not well suited to answer this question as there may be systematic differences in the propensity of firms to report obstacles across countries.[10] Nonetheless, it is possible to come up with a worldwide ranking by constructing an average obstacle score for each country. This suggests that the transition group is not very different, on average, from non-transition developing countries. However, the variation within the transition group is very wide.[11] If the transition countries are separated along geographical lines into CEB, SEE, and Turkey on the one hand and EEC, Russia, and Central Asia on the other, it turns out that there are statistically significant differences across these two groups. On average, business obstacles in the former are as low as, or lower than, in any other developing country region, while in the latter they are higher than in most regions (see Table 10.2).

Aside from the overall rankings, does the nature of perceived business obstacles still differ between the transition region and non-transition countries? Figures 10.3 (A) and (B) plot country mean obstacle scores against

Table 10.2 BEEPS rankings and mean obstacle score, by country group

Group	Number of countries	Mean rank	Mean score
CEB + SEE + Turkey	17	33	1.27
EEC + Russia + Central Asia	12	49	1.50
Latin America	14	50	1.50
Africa	27	33	1.29
Other[1]	8	44	1.47

[1] Consists of a group of Asian and Middle Eastern countries.
Source: Based on BEEPS IV survey, EBRD and World Bank, and World Bank Enterprise Surveys; see text for explanation.

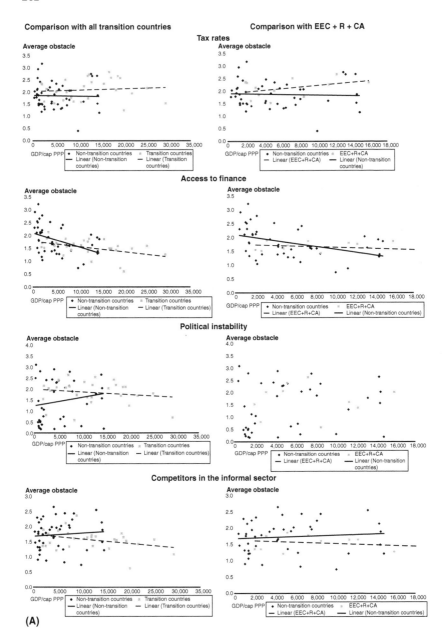

Figure 10.3 Business obstacles: comparison between transition and non-transition countries

Source: See text for explanation.

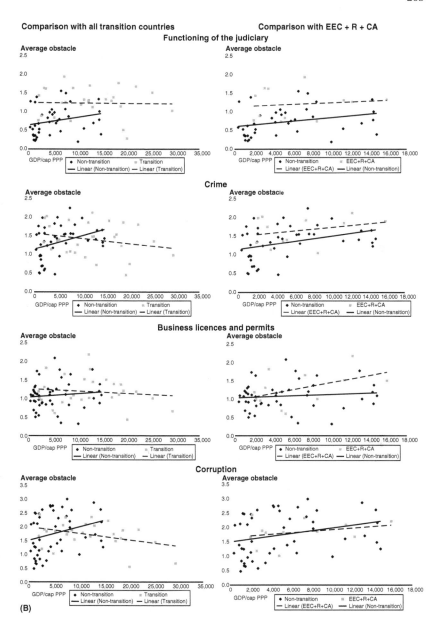

Figure 10.3 (Continued)

purchasing power-adjusted per capita income for eight selected obstacle categories. Transition and non-transition countries are coloured differently, and each group is fitted with a line that shows the relationship between the obstacle score and the per capita income. If the obstacle plays a bigger role in the transition region, the line fitted to the transition group will be shifted up from the non-transition line. In the light of the results in Tables 10.1 and 10.2, comparisons with non-transition countries are shown for the entire transition group in BEEPS IV—left-hand column—and for the EEC countries, Russia, and Central Asian countries (EEC+R+CA) only—right-hand column.

Two facts are worth noting at the outset. First, as expected, the dispersion within the transition economy group is generally quite high—for the most part as high as, or higher than, the dispersion within the 45 non-transition developing countries in the sample. Second, in the transition group as a whole, the average obstacle scores are generally negatively correlated with per capita income, although this relationship is reversed in the EEC, Russia, and Central Asia group. Richer countries in this group tend to have higher perceived business obstacles. One possible interpretation for this is that the richer EEC+R+CA countries are large commodity exporters, which tend to have weaker institutions (see EBRD 2009: Chapter 4).

Figure 10.3(A) plots four categories of business obstacle scores—'tax rates', 'access to finance', 'political instability', and 'competitors in the informal sector'—for which there is no statistically significant difference between the non-transition and transition groups (either as a whole or just EEC+R+CA). (The same is true for the categories of 'transport', 'customs and trade regulations', and 'tax administration', which are not shown in the figure.) This suggests that in some areas that reflected high state interference—particularly 'tax rates', 'tax administration', and 'customs and trade regulations'—the transition region has indeed converged. 'Tax rates' continue to receive a higher average obstacle score in the transition region, particularly in EEC+R+CA, but the difference is no longer statistically significant.

Figure 10.3(B) shows four categories for which there *are* statistically significant differences with respect to non-transition countries. In the 'functioning of the judiciary' and 'crime' categories, this is true for the comparison with the transition group as a whole, but the figure indicates that the differences are driven by higher obstacles in the poorer transition countries, and particularly in EEC+R+CA. (The same pattern arises for the 'telecommunications', 'access to land', and 'workforce education' categories, which are not shown in the figure.) In the case of 'business licences and permits', only the EEC+R+CA group does significantly worse, on average, than non-transition economies. Lastly, the transition region overall scores significantly better than the non-transition sample for 'corruption', but there is no statistical difference between the non-transition group and EEC+R+CA. The same is true for 'electricity' as an obstacle (not shown in the figure).

To conclude, for the transition region as a whole, the business environment appears to be no worse than in other developing countries. However, there is large heterogeneity within the region. CEB countries tend to have a better business environment than other emerging market regions, while Russia and countries in EEC and Central Asia tend to have weaker environments (despite their lower per capita incomes). In some categories—such as 'access to land', some infrastructure constraints, and 'workforce education'—comparatively high average obstacle scores are a new phenomenon and are likely to reflect fast recent growth rather than the legacy of central planning. For the most part, however, the weaknesses are in areas in which the transition economies have traditionally lagged, and in which the EEC+R+CA countries continue to lag.

4 Management practices

The previous section focused on the environment that firms face in their daily operations, but how well are firms managed and organized in the transition region, and how do they compare in this respect to firms in non-transition countries? Recent research suggests that management practices have a strong effect on firm performance. A study of 7000 medium-sized manufacturing firms across Asia, Europe, and North and South America found that there are large differences in management practices across firms as well as countries, and that these are strongly associated with firm-level productivity and other performance measures, such as profitability and survival rates.[12] The USA had the best overall management practices, although Germany, Japan, and Sweden did better in operations management. Multinational firms tended to be well run everywhere, even in developing countries. Importantly, differences in management practices were found to be larger between firms in the same country than across countries, suggesting that firm- and sector-specific factors are at least as important as the general business environment in shaping managerial performance. Differences in management practices were found to be related to competition, labour market flexibility, education, and ownership structure (with dispersed ownership being associated with better performance than state- or family-run firms).

This section reports on the results of a new Management, Organization and Innovation (MOI) survey that applies this line of research to transition economies for the first time. It focuses on practices in four core management areas—'operations', 'monitoring', 'targets' and 'incentives' (see Berglöf et al. 2010: Annexe 1)—conducting 1669 face-to-face interviews with factory managers in ten transition countries (Belarus, Bulgaria, Kazakhstan, Lithuania, Poland, Romania, Russia, Serbia, Ukraine, and Uzbekistan) as well as Germany as an advanced country benchmark. It therefore covered a geographically diverse sample that includes the largest transition countries, with a wide variation in transition progress.

4.1   How different is the transition region?

Like previous studies performed in non-transition countries, the MOI survey suggests a strong positive link between management scores and firm performance, as measured by labour productivity, size, sales growth and innovation (e.g. the introduction of new products). The magnitude of the link can be estimated with econometric techniques: an improvement in an average firm's management practices from the mid-point (or median) to the top 10 per cent is associated with an 18.3 per cent increase in labour productivity when differences in the country where the firm is located, the firm's sector and the size of the firm are controlled for.[13] The effect is smaller, but still significant, when a range of other factors are accounted for.

The ranking in Figure 10.4 of surveyed countries in terms of average management practices shows Germany on top and Uzbekistan at the bottom (although this does not mean that Germany has no firms with bad management practices or that Uzbekistan has no good ones). Figure 10.5 shows that there is a wide spread of management scores in every country. Because of the overlaps in the distribution of management scores across countries, the differences in average scores shown in Figure 10.5 are often small. Indeed, the average scores of Belarus, Bulgaria, Lithuania, Poland, Serbia, and Ukraine are not statistically significantly different from each other; nor are there statistically significant differences between the average scores of Kazakhstan, Romania, Russia, and Ukraine.

Figure 10.6 shows country rankings for each of the four sub-components of management practices ('operations', 'monitoring', 'targets',

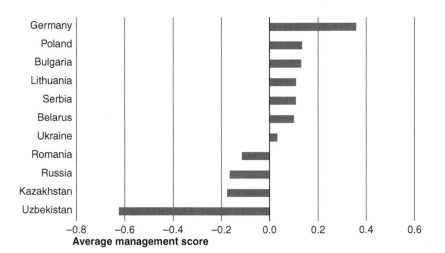

Figure 10.4   Average management scores across countries
Source: Based on the MOI survey; see text for explanation.

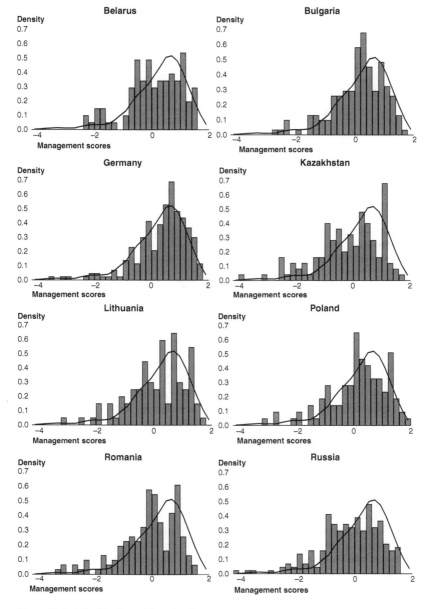

Figure 10.5 Distribution of firm-level management scores
Source: Based on the MOI survey; see text for explanation.

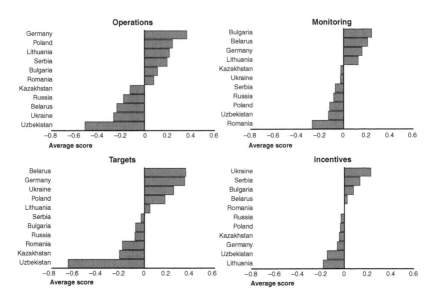

Figure 10.6   Average management scores by sub-component
Source: Based on the MOI survey; see text for explanation.

and 'incentives'). In line with the overall rankings, Germany is in the top three in three out of the four categories, while Uzbekistan is consistently in the bottom two. However, there are also some interesting differences across categories. While many firms interviewed in Belarus and Bulgaria, for example, excel at monitoring—that is, frequently collecting data on several production performance indicators, showing it to factory managers and workers, and regularly reviewing the production performance indicators— they are less adept at translating monitoring into operations. Firms in Belarus also tend to be good at target management (which is perhaps a legacy of meeting planned production targets). However, this is not the case in Kazakhstan and Uzbekistan.[14] The most eclectic ranking emerges on incentives management, although differences across countries are smaller in this category than in others and often not statistically significant. It is never- theless striking that Germany and Lithuania join Uzbekistan in the bottom three, perhaps reflecting a continental European management culture that de-emphasizes high-powered incentives.

4.2   How different is the transition region?

Although the MOI survey did not include non-transition countries (except for Germany), a broader international comparison is possible using aver- age management scores from related studies of non-transition countries (see Figure 10.7).[15] Two facts are striking. First, six out of the ten

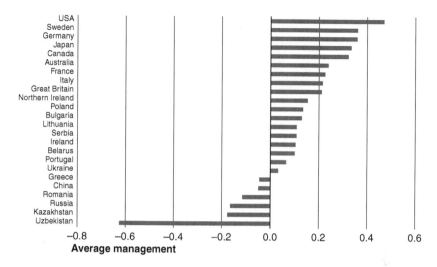

Figure 10.7 Management scores across countries
Source: Based on the MOI survey; see text for explanation.

transition economies studied in the MOI—Belarus, Bulgaria, Lithuania, Poland, Serbia, and Ukraine—are statistically indistinguishable in terms of average scores from more advanced European Union (EU) countries, such as Greece, Ireland, and Portugal. Second, the remaining transition countries—Kazakhstan, Romania, Russia, and Uzbekistan—are at the bottom of the ranking (and below China).

Like the MOI economies, China was a centrally planned economy during most of its post-war history. However, it started the process of transition to a market-based system at least ten years earlier than those countries in the MOI sample (beginning with an initial set of economic reforms in 1978, followed by a second phase in 1982 aiming to introduce market institutions). China's better management practices could also be related to foreign direct investment (FDI) and foreign ownership. Previous research[16] shows that foreign-owned firms tend to have better management practices than domestically owned enterprises. While Kazakhstan and Russia (but not Uzbekistan) enjoy considerable FDI, it is mostly concentrated in the 'natural resources' sector rather than in manufacturing. In contrast, FDI in China has targeted the manufacturing industry, potentially benefiting the management practices of a larger set of firms.

4.3 Explaining differences across firms

Three factors may help to explain the differences in firm-level management scores.[17] First, managers' self-reported measure of the number of competitors is positively and significantly related to management practices. The importance of competitive intensity in improving productivity and management is a robust finding from a wide range of economic studies. Stronger competition can drive out poorly managed firms but can also change the behaviour of incumbent managers who have to lift their performance in order to survive and prosper. (Lack of competition may partly explain the relative paucity of well-managed firms in Uzbekistan.)

Second, ownership matters. Firms belonging to foreign owners from non-transition countries have the best management practices (suggesting that openness to foreign investment is key to spreading best practice) while state-owned firms tend to have the worst. There are at least two possible explanations for this: managers of state-owned firms might have been selected because of political or bureaucratic connections rather than managerial ability; and state-owned firms need to worry less about surviving in the market.[18]

Lastly, privatized (formerly state-owned) firms have similar management practices to enterprises that were privately owned from the beginning, suggesting that privatization is an effective medium-term means of improvement. Given the importance of privatization in transition countries, this is an encouraging result. Furthermore, the quality of management practices is not significantly associated with the number of years since privatization. This suggests that, while privatization does tend to improve management, the magnitude of improvement over the years probably depends on the new owners.

5   Competition

Having highlighted cross-country differences in the business environment and managerial practices, both within the transition region and compared with benchmarks outside, the remainder of this study focuses on cross-country differences at the sector level, beginning with competition. Previous EBRD research has shown that levels of product market competition in transition economies (measured in terms of average profit mark-up) have increased substantially since the beginning of the 1990s. However, they remain below the Organisation for Economic Co-operation and Development (OECD) average, and there is generally less competition in the EEC+R+CA and SEE countries than in the CEB region.[19] However, these cross-country differences cannot necessarily be interpreted in terms of product market regulation or barriers to entry. Some sectors, such as commodities or pharmaceuticals, tend to have intrinsically higher profit mark-up, and so a proportion of the differences in observed average mark-up could reflect differences in sector composition. It is therefore important to compare competition measures at the sector level.

Table 10.3 gives a comparison of mark-up across defined manufacturing sectors based on data from 2005–7 for 25,000 firms in ten transition

Table 10.3 Competition in the 'manufacturing' sector

Sector	Sector average[1]	Central Europe and the Baltic states					Bosnia and Herz.	SEE		Other		Comparator countries			
		Estonia	Hungary	Latvia	Poland	Slovenia		Romania	Serbia	Turkey	Ukraine	India	Indonesia	Germany	UK
Food	0.08	0.09	0.08	0.07	0.08	0.08	0.18	0.09	0.09	0.09	0.07	0.09	0.08	0.07	0.08
Beverages	0.12	0.15	0.14	n.a.	0.11	n.a.	0.20	0.12	0.14	n.a.	0.09	0.09	n.a.	0.14	0.15
Tobacco	0.10	n.a.	N.a.	n.a.	0.08	n.a.	n.a.	0.10	0.13	n.a.	0.13	0.10	0.07	0.02	0.10
Textiles	0.12	0.11	0.11	n.a.	0.11	0.07	0.19	0.14	0.13	n.a.	0.09	0.13	0.10	0.08	0.08
Wearing apparel	0.11	0.10	0.09	n.a.	0.08	0.08	0.29	0.14	0.12	n.a.	0.08	0.10	0.07	0.06	0.06
Leather	0.11	0.08	0.10	n.a.	0.10	0.06	0.24	0.13	0.11	n.a.	0.06	0.11	0.06	0.07	0.08
Wood	0.11	0.11	0.13	0.10	0.10	0.10	0.15	0.13	0.10	n.a.	0.08	0.11	0.06	0.08	0.07
Paper	0.10	0.11	0.09	n.a.	0.10	0.10	0.20	0.11	0.11	n.a.	0.10	0.11	0.15	0.09	0.09
Printing	0.13	0.15	0.13	0.16	0.13	0.12	0.24	0.18	0.14	n.a.	0.10	0.17	n.a.	0.12	0.10
Petroleum refineries	0.10	n.a.	N.a.	n.a.	0.14	n.a.	0.08	0.09	0.11	n.a.	0.05	0.09	n.a.	0.07	0.14
Chemicals	0.11	0.11	0.09	n.a.	0.11	0.10	0.13	0.15	0.11	n.a.	0.06	0.12	0.05	0.09	0.11
Pharmaceutical products	0.14	0.30	0.16	n.a.	0.14	n.a.	0.24	0.17	0.16	n.a.	0.12	0.13	0.06	0.12	0.14
Rubber and plastic	0.11	0.10	0.10	n.a.	0.11	0.14	0.21	0.12	0.11	n.a.	0.08	0.12	0.11	0.08	0.09
Other mineral	0.13	0.16	0.12	n.a.	0.15	0.10	0.22	0.14	0.12	0.15	0.10	0.14	0.19	0.10	0.13
Basic metals	0.09	n.a.	0.09	n.a.	0.08	n.a.	0.13	0.10	0.10	n.a.	0.07	0.10	0.04	0.08	0.09
Fabricated metal	0.11	0.11	0.11	n.a.	0.10	0.14	0.23	0.13	0.13	n.a.	0.08	0.12	0.09	0.09	0.10
Furniture	0.10	0.11	0.08	0.10	0.08	0.15	0.21	0.11	0.11	n.a.	0.08	n.a.	0.09	0.07	0.07
Other manufacturing	0.12	0.17	0.08	n.a.	0.13	0.11	0.30	0.17	0.15	n.a.	0.12	0.11	n.a.	0.10	0.11
Mean	0.11	0.11	0.10	0.10	0.10	0.11	0.19	0.12	0.11	0.12	0.08	0.11	0.09	0.09	0.10
standard deviation	0.10	0.09	0.09	0.06	0.08	0.09	0.18	0.10	0.10	0.08	0.07	0.11	0.07	0.08	0.09

[1]Indicates the difference between value added and the total wage bill expressed as a share of gross output. The index varies between 0 and 1 with higher values indicating less competition.

Source: EBRD staff calculations based on Orbis data.

countries as well as Germany, India, Indonesia, and the UK.[20] The table shows that manufacturing firms in transition economies—even in CEB countries—generally have rather higher profit margins, indicating a lower degree of competition than for firms in Germany or the UK. However, the differences between the CEB countries (and Ukraine) on the one hand and non-transition countries on the other disappear when the comparison is extended to emerging markets, such as India. In contrast, profit margins in the three SEE countries (Bosnia and Herzegovina, Romania, and Serbia) are generally higher. There is significant heterogeneity in this comparison: in some sectors, such as pharmaceuticals or rubber and plastics, profit margins are substantially higher in transition countries, while in other sectors, such as food, they are in line with Germany or the UK (except in the case of Bosnia and Herzegovina).

Apart from cross-country differences in average profit margins, Table 10.3 also shows substantial variation in the degree of competition between manufacturing sectors within a country. Companies operating in Poland face tougher competition if they operate in the food industry than if they produce refined petroleum products. This may reflect differences in barriers to entry, the degree of specialization or research and development (R&D) intensity between these sectors. There are also significant differences in mark-up in the same sector across countries—from very low in basic metals manufacturing to large in beverage production—suggesting that incumbent market power may play a role in this respect.

Research shows that cross-country differences in mark-up reflect a variety of factors,[21] including stages of development of certain industries. The relatively lower degree of competition in the pharmaceutical industry, for example, might be explained by the comparatively low level of development of this high-technology sector in transition countries (as also evidenced by the small number of registered patents or R&D investments). Differences in tariffs and trade regimes—including World Trade Organization (WTO) pre-accession reforms—and changes in corporate tax levels also matter, as they influence barriers to entry and therefore competitive pressure on incumbents. A further important determinant of actual product market competition is the efficiency and effectiveness of competition policy. Figure 10.8 shows that countries that rank higher on the EBRD competition policy indicator do indeed seem to have lower firm mark-ups. This relationship holds true across virtually all manufacturing sectors in the transition region (with the exception of pharmaceuticals, which are not very competitive even if the overall policy environment is conducive to competition).

6   Remaining transition challenges: a sector approach

This section moves from cross-country comparisons to perhaps the most important question posed at the beginning of this study: What are the

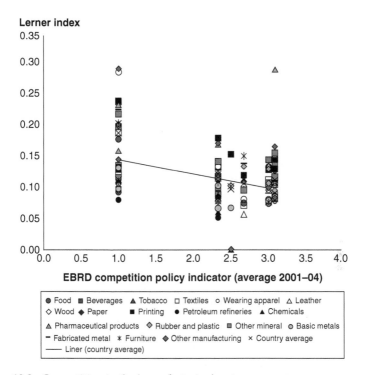

Figure 10.8 Competition in the 'manufacturing' sector
Source: Based on EBRD data.

principal reform and institutional development challenges that remain in transition countries? This can be considered at the sector level using the summary findings of a detailed internal EBRD study, the *2009 Assessment of Remaining Transition Challenges*, encompassing 13 specific sectors in 29 countries.[22] The study defines a set of transition benchmarks and measures the gap between where countries stand to date and the 'end-zone' of transition in terms of two components:

- market structure—the balance between the private sector and the state and the extent of competition;
- market-supporting institutions and policies—the regulatory and policy framework underpinning the functioning of the market in a given sector.

6.1 Report methodology

For every country, each of the 13 sectors was rated on a four-point scale (negligible, small, medium, or large remaining transition challenges) for the two components, and also given an overall rating. Rating the transition challenge in each sector and country involved a four-step process:

- First, for each sector, EBRD economists defined a broad vision of what constitutes good market structure and strong market-supporting institutions. Each was typically defined in terms of three or four criteria related to principles such as efficiency, competition, accountability, transparency and competence.
- Second, a set of indicators was identified to help rate countries on each of these criteria (typically on a ten-point scale), based where possible on data from publicly available sources.
- Third, a scoring and weighting scheme was applied at three levels in order to generate scores for each of the main three to four criteria underlying the market structure and market-supporting institutions categories; weight these criteria to establish overall market structure and market-supporting institution ratings; and average these two main components (usually applying 50:50 weights, but with variations—e.g. 45:55 or 60:40—in some cases).
- Fourth, a judgmental check was applied to ensure that the interaction between market structure and institutions was appropriately reflected. In some cases this led to modifications in the final rating, particularly where there was a large discrepancy between the two component ratings. When the institution rating was below the market structure rating, the final score was usually adjusted downward on the presumption that a good supporting institutional framework is critical for the proper functioning of markets.

Table 10.4 shows an example of the full methodology (except for the judgmental step) in the 'general industry' sector. The weights assigned to the components and criteria are indicated in square brackets.

A consequence of this approach is that two countries may have similar gaps or challenges, as measured by the value of the overall index, as a result of very different combinations of strengths and weaknesses in market structure and market-supporting institutions and policies. This supports the perception that there is not a unique transition path and that countries can embrace different market models and institutions that deliver outcomes of comparable quality.

6.2 Results

Table 10.5 shows the assessments made for transition gaps for all sectors and countries. Out of a total of 377 sector/country ratings, there are 284 medium or large challenges as against 93 small or negligible ones. There are just three negligible ratings overall (in 'general industry' in CEB).

Table 10.4 Rating transition challenges in the 'general industry' sector

Components	Criteria	Data
Market structure [60%]	Market determined prices [20%]	Price liberalization (*EBRD Transition Report 2008*)
	Competitive business environment [40%]	Subsidies in per cent of GDP (CEIC database, data for 2007)[1]
		Energy intensity (Enerdata database, data for 2007)[2]
		MFN trade weighted tariff (World Bank Doing Business Database, data for 2008)
		Lerner index (EBRD calculation from UNIDO statistical database, data for 2006)[3]
		Large-scale privatization (*EBRD Transition Report 2008*)
	Productivity and efficiency [40%]	R&D in per cent of GDP (UNESCO database report on science and technology, data for 2007 and 2006)[4]
		Value added per employee (UNIDO statistical database, data for 2006)[3]; (CEIC database, data for 2007)[1]
		Knowledge Index on Knowledge Economy (World Bank, data for 2008)[5]
Market-supporting institutions and policies [40%]	Facilitation of market entry and exit [40%]	Doing Business—starting a business (World Bank Doing Business Database, data for 2008)
		Doing Business—closing a business (World Bank Doing Business Database, data for 2008)
		Enterprise surveys—percentage of firms identifying permits and licences as major constraint[6]
	Enforcement of competition policy [30%]	Competition index (*EBRD Transition Report 2008*)
	Corporate governance and business standards [30%]	Quality of legislation in corporate governance (EBRD Legal Transition Team survey 2007)
		ISO 9001 and ISO 14001 (ISO survey 2007)[7]

[1] http://www.ceicdata.com/; [2] http://www.enerdata.net/enerdatauk/; [3] http://www.unido.org/index.php?id=1000309; [4] http://stats.uis.unesco.org/unesco/TableViewer/tableView.aspx?ReportId=1782; [5] http://info.worldbank.org/etools/kam2/KAM_page5.asp; [6] https://www.enterprisesurveys.org/; [7] http://www.iso.org/iso/about/iso_members/iso_member_participation_tc.htm?member_id=1597.

Source: Based on EBRD data, see text for explanation.

Table 10.5 Assessment of transition challenges by country and sector: summary of results

	Corporate					Energy and infrastructure				Financial institutions			
	Agribusiness	General industry	Property and tourism	Telecoms	Municipal and environmental infrastructure	Natural resources	Power	Sustainable energy	Transport	Banking	Non-bank financial institutions	MSMEs	Private equity and capital markets
Central Europe and the Baltic states	2.00	1.63	2.13	2.00	2.13	2.13	2.13	2.50	2.63	2.13	2.13	2.88	2.75
Croatia	2	2	3	2	3	2	3	3	3	2	2	3	3
Estonia	2	1	2	2	2	2	2	3	2	2	2	3	3
Hungary	2	1	2	2	2	2	2	2	2	2	2	3	2
Latvia	2	2	2	2	2	2	2	3	3	3	2	3	3
Lithuania	2	2	2	2	2	2	2	2	3	2	2	3	3
Poland	2	2	2	2	2	3	2	2	2	2	2	3	2
Slovak Republic	2	1	2	2	2	2	2	3	3	2	2	2	3
Slovenia	2	2	2	2	2	2	2	2	3	2	3	3	3
South-Eastern Europe	3.00	3.00	3.29	2.71	3.00	2.71	3.14	3.14	3.14	2.86	3.00	3.00	3.57
Albania	3	3	3	3	4	3	3	3	4	3	4	3	4
Bosnia and Herzegovina	3	4	4	3	4	3	4	4	3	3	3	3	4
Bulgaria	3	2	3	2	2	2	2	2	3	2	2	3	3
FYR Macedonia	3	3	3	3	3	3	3	3	3	3	3	3	4
Montenegro	3	4	4	3	3	3	4	4	3	3	4	3	3
Romania	3	2	3	2	2	2	2	2	3	3	2	3	3
Serbia	3	3	3	3	3	3	4	4	3	3	3	3	3
Turkey	3	3	2	3	3	3	3	3	3	3	3	3	2

Eastern Europe and the Caucasus	3.17	3.50	3.67	3.33	3.83	3.50	3.50	3.67	3.50	3.50	3.83	3.50	4.00
Armenia	3	3	3	3	3	3	3	3	3	3	4	3	4
Azerbaijan	3	4	4	4	4	3	4	4	4	4	4	4	4
Belarus	4	4	4	4	4	4	4	4	4	4	4	4	4
Georgia	3	3	3	3	4	3	3	3	3	3	4	3	4
Moldova	3	4	4	3	4	3	3	4	4	4	4	3	4
Ukraine	3	3	4	3	3	4	4	4	4	3	3	4	4
Russia	3	3	3	3	4	4	4	4	3	3	3	3	3
Central Asia	3.50	4.00	3.83	3.50	4.00	3.83	3.83	4.00	3.83	3.83	3.83	4.00	3.83
Kazakhstan	3	4	3	3	4	4	3	4	3	3	3	4	3
Kyrgyz Republic	3	4	4	3	4	3	4	4	4	4	4	4	4
Mongolia	3	4	4	3	4	4	4	4	4	4	4	4	4
Tajikistan	4	4	4	4	4	4	4	4	4	4	4	4	4
Turkmenistan	4	4	4	4	4	4	4	4	4	4	4	4	4
Uzbekistan	4	4	4	4	4	4	4	4	4	4	4	4	4
EBRD region	2.96	3.04	3.21	2.93	3.25	3.11	3.18	3.39	3.32	3.11	3.21	3.43	3.54

Note: 1 = negligible challenge; 2 = small challenge; 3 = medium challenge; 4 = large challenge.
Source: Based on EBRD data.

- In Central Asia there are large transition gaps in nearly all sectors, while large or medium gaps dominate in EEC, Russia and Turkey. Market development in these countries is seriously hampered by state interference in various sectors, the lack of an adequate legal framework (or its effective implementation) and an unfavourable business environment.
- In SEE there is a mixture of small, medium and large challenges (with small challenges prevalent in the two EU countries of Bulgaria and Romania). Despite a gradual alignment of regulation with EU standards, further work is needed in most countries to implement international best practice and strengthen the implementation capacity of regulatory authorities.
- In CEB, transition gaps are mainly small, with the exception of 'sustainable energy', 'transport' and 'financial institutions', where medium challenges remain. All countries have aligned their institutional frameworks with EU norms, and the remaining challenges relate mainly to improving efficiency, productivity and competition.

At the sector level, transition gaps are smallest in the 'corporate' group of sectors, with 'agribusiness', 'general industry' and 'telecommunications' having the highest concentration of small and/or negligible ratings. Within the 'energy and infrastructure' group, the challenges are greatest in 'sustainable energy' and 'transport', where 23 and 26 countries face medium and large challenges, respectively. In the 'financial institutions' group, 28 and 26 countries have medium and large challenges in the 'small business finance' and 'private equity and capital markets' sectors, respectively. The sections below summarize the results for each of the three broad groups of sectors.

6.3 Corporate sectors

The remaining transition challenges in the corporate group of sectors— 'agribusiness', 'general industry', 'telecommunications' and 'property and tourism'—are smaller than in the other groups, but medium and large transition gaps remain in all sub-regions other than CEB (see Figure 10.9).

'General industry' still faces issues related to the restructuring of sensitive industries (such as shipbuilding in Croatia and chemicals in Poland) and a continued high level of state involvement, which have hampered improvements in efficiency and competition. Hurdles remain particularly in business start-up and bankruptcy procedures, and corporate governance and business standards remain weak. Ukraine's accession to the WTO should give further impetus to enterprise reform, although close links between business and politics, weak governance and transparency, and significant barriers to market entry and exit remain key challenges for the country.

In the 'telecommunications' sector, lack of competition and inadequate tariffs (pricing) have led to an investment backlog in many countries, and, in many cases, deterioration in infrastructure. In the CEB countries the main

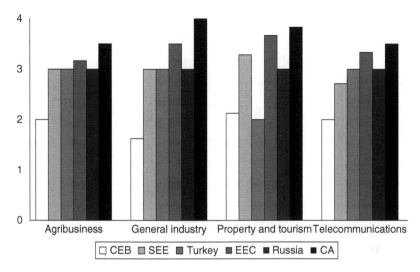

Figure 10.9 Transition challenges in the 'corporate' sector
Source: Based on EBRD data.

outstanding challenges relate to the legal framework (e.g. intellectual property rights), regulatory capacity and infrastructure. In Central Asia and most EEC countries, challenges are much larger. Many countries still need to liberalize their markets, and penetration rates are generally low. State-owned incumbents hamper competition and commercial incentives, and regulation suffers from strong political influence.

In the 'agribusiness' sector the development of efficient private farms remains a challenge, particularly in Central Asia and EEC, due to unclear property rights, land fragmentation and the lack of active land markets. State support measures in the meat, dairy products, sugar, and tobacco segments distort the market, while lack of infrastructure contributes to lower yields and prevents countries from realizing their full agricultural potential. Quality and hygiene standards also need to be improved.

Clearer ownership rights and simpler procedures for land registration and building permits are critical for a balanced longer-term development of the 'property and tourism' sector. Although this sector has witnessed rapid growth in recent years in many countries, investments have been concentrated in the capital cities, leaving regional centres underfunded. With the exception of Georgia, the property sectors of nearly all Central Asian and EEC countries remain underdeveloped, endure a difficult business environment, and need further regulatory reform.

6.4 Energy and infrastructure sectors

Remaining transition challenges are concentrated in Central Asia and EEC, particularly in the infrastructure sectors. In CEB and SEE regions the process

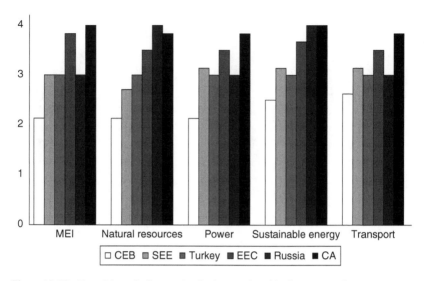

Figure 10.10   Transition challenges in the 'energy' and 'infrastructure' sectors
Source: Based on EBRD data.

(or prospect) of EU accession (involving the harmonization of legislation and regulations) has been a key driver of reforms in these countries, leading to greater market conformity and stronger institutions. In Russia, large challenges remain in the 'natural resources' and 'sustainable energy' sectors, which are increasingly dominated by state-owned, energy-intensive enterprises (see Figure 10.10).

Key challenges in 'municipal and environmental infrastructure' include improving tariff systems, promoting contractual arrangements that foster commercialization, and widening regulatory autonomy. This is applicable particularly to non-EU countries in SEE, where municipal services have been decentralized and corporative but financial performance is still generally weak and private sector participation limited. In Central Asia and EEC, financial and operational performance remains poor. There needs to be tariff reform (as water and district heating tariffs barely cover operating costs) and improvements in governance, regulation, and transparency of contractual arrangements.

In the 'transport' sector the implementation of successful public–private partnerships remains a challenge in CEB, although new efforts are underway in Latvia and the Slovak Republic. Transport operation and policy functions have been separated in the CEB and SEE regions, and road construction and maintenance have generally been contracted out. However, full commercialization of the railways has yet to be achieved, and road concession policies and financing arrangements generally remain below EU standards. In Russia, the private sector has played an increasing role in transport services accounting for a major part of port terminal expansion and rail fleet renewal, but the restructuring and commercialization of state-owned entities needs to be addressed. In the Central Asian countries, core railway businesses continue to operate under state control (except in Kazakhstan), and the road sector remains largely unreformed with no private sector participation, limited commercial financing, and a rudimentary institutional framework.

In the 'natural resources' sector, breaking the monopoly of largely unreformed and non-transparent state-owned oil and gas companies and improving corporate governance and environmental conduct are key challenges in countries like Azerbaijan, Kazakhstan, Russia, Turkmenistan, and Uzbekistan. In the CEB, SEE and resource-importing EEC countries, remaining challenges include diversifying energy sources and suppliers, granting third-party access to transmission networks, and promoting greater competition and entry into the downstream power supply industry. Coal sector reform is an important outstanding issue in those countries with substantial reserves, such as Poland, where a medium transition gap remains.

In the 'power' sector, low energy tariffs and slow progress in enterprise restructuring have hampered progress towards energy efficiency across the transition region. In many countries, domestic gas and electricity prices are not cost-reflective and do not provide incentives to use energy efficiently and invest in renewable sources. With the exception of the new EU member states (where liberalization, private sector participation and regulation have advanced), transition challenges in the rest of the EBRD countries of operation remain formidable. The 'power' sectors are still vertically integrated, state-owned, and only partially unbundled. Transmission and distribution losses are high, regulators are not fully independent, there are affordability constraints on tariff reform, and the legal and institutional capacity for implementing sustainable energy initiatives is low.

In the light of the implications of global climate change, measuring progress towards meeting energy efficiency targets for countries in the transition region (in terms of institutions, policies and outputs) is increasingly important. The EBRD's Index of Sustainable Energy suggests that 23 transition countries still face medium or large challenges in this area.[23] The legacy of central planning in terms of inefficient use of resources is still prevalent, and much remains to be done to improve market structures and supporting institutions to secure energy sustainability.

6.5 Financial institutions sectors

Transition challenges in these sectors reflect unfinished financial deepening and capital market development reforms, particularly in Central Asia and EEC. In addition, shortcomings in supervisory and regulatory institutions

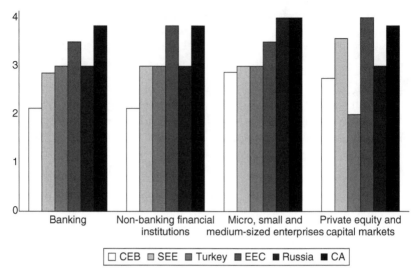

Figure 10.11 Transition challenges in the 'financial institutions' sectors
Source: Based on EBRD data.

have been exposed by the global financial crisis, even in CEB countries (see Figure 10.11).

In the 'banking' sector, the credit boom over the period 2004–8 widened access to finance for many borrowers and broadened the range of available products and services. However, the crisis that engulfed the region from late 2008 revealed the full extent of the remaining transition challenges in terms of supervision, internal bank governance and risk management. With a few exceptions, such as in Poland and the Slovak Republic, bank supervision generally did not effectively address excessive credit growth or foreign currency exposures by unhedged borrowers. In addition, the crisis exposed an excessive concentration of bank assets in a limited number of areas (e.g. construction, and real estate and mortgage lending), suggesting that the risk management of banks was less sophisticated than previously thought. In some countries, notably Kazakhstan, the crisis highlighted an over-reliance on wholesale funding. Russia's fragmented 'banking' sector (with its under-developed segments, such as mortgages and lending in the more remote regions) was also exposed—although the authorities have initiated a number of regulatory reforms to facilitate mergers and raise capital requirements.

For the 'micro, small and medium enterprise' (MSME) sector, the crisis has shown that the improved access to funding was to some extent the product of the credit boom, and it remains to be seen how the sector recovers after the crisis recedes. In many Central Asian and EEC countries and in Russia, small business lending continues to be hampered by structural impediments. Improved credit information services, better enforcement of bankruptcy laws and the establishment of a central collateral registry are necessary to strengthen lending on a sustainable basis.

The 'non-bank financial institutions' sector (incorporating services such as leasing, insurance and asset management) remains under-developed. Given the demographic make-up of the transition region, the establishment of privately funded and managed pension systems based on capital accumulation is a central challenge. The problems arising both from cross-border wholesale lending and foreign exchange bank funding (see EBRD 2009: Chapters 2 and 3) have underlined the importance of developing local currency money and bond markets. Only Hungary, Poland, Russia and Turkey have such markets, but there remains scope for making these deeper and more liquid, particularly at longer maturities.

Regarding the 'private equity and capital markets' sector, domestic equity markets are generally small and relatively illiquid (with the exception of Hungary, Poland, Russia, and Turkey). In many Central Asian, EEC, and some smaller SEE countries, regional financial integration may make more sense than building domestic securities markets—a strategy already adopted by many of the smaller CEB countries. Private equity has played an important role in firm restructuring and as a source of risk-oriented capital in more advanced transition countries. It could also be an important substitute for public equity markets in less advanced transition countries, but this will require stronger shareholder rights and better corporate governance and accounting practices.

7 Conclusion

This chapter has analysed the status of transition from four perspectives: the business environment, competition, managerial practices, and an examination of 13 specific sectors. Although quite different in emphasis, they give rise to a consistent picture. The most striking finding in all four analyses is the heterogeneity of the transition region. This impression arises not only when the region is considered on its own, as in the sector assessment of transition challenges, but also in comparison with other regions. In terms of business environment, competition and managerial practices, countries in the CEB region appear at about the same level as large emerging market countries such as China. However, this is not true for transition countries in other regions.

- On average, firms in EEC, Russia, and Central Asia rate their business environment as worse than in other emerging market regions (or about the same as that reported by Latin American firms).
- The nature of the main reported obstacles in the EEC+R+CA region is also different, with more complaints about the 'judiciary', 'crime', 'business permits', and 'workforce education' compared with the CEB, SEE and non-transition developing countries. In contrast, the only obstacle that is rated higher in CEB compared to other regions is 'labour regulations'.
- With respect to managerial practices, the Central Asian countries and Russia lag behind not only Western benchmarks but also China, while the CEB countries rate similarly with countries such as Greece, Ireland, and Portugal.
- Regarding competition, lack of data precludes sector-level comparisons that include most EEC+R+CA countries. However, data for three SEE countries for the 2001–4 period suggest that these countries lagged behind CEB, Ukraine, and other developing country benchmarks.
- Sector-level analyses show small transition gaps in a majority of sectors in CEB countries, medium gaps in Armenia, Georgia, Kazakhstan, Russia, and most SEE countries (except Bulgaria and Romania) and predominantly large gaps elsewhere.

In light of these results, the question at the start of this chapter—of how different the transition region still is from other countries—has no clear-cut answer. It may be more useful to ask how large the group of transition countries still is. The answer will depend on the sector and the aspect of transition that is emphasized. In general, the analysis of this chapter indicates that most countries in Central Asia, EEC and SEE still face challenges that distinguish them from other countries at comparable income levels. In contrast, most new EU member states now appear to have more in common with non-transition emerging market countries (or even other EU countries) than with the less advanced transition economies. Even within the group of new EU member states, however, significant transition challenges remain in some sectors. This is particularly so in respect of 'sustainable energy' and 'energy efficiency', and also the 'financial sector', where regulatory and supervisory regimes require strengthening, small business finance needs to be further improved, and local capital markets need to be developed.

The large transition gaps in most Central Asian and EEC countries beg the question of why these countries have failed to catch up. EBRD (2009: Chapters 3 and 4) suggests partial answers. Integration into the EU—a powerful motor of reform—has not been an option for some more distant countries. In addition, institutional reform (which facilitates reform more generally) is much more difficult in resource-rich countries. These points may help to explain why the Central Asia-EEC group as a whole has reformed less vigorously and why some countries within the group—such as Armenia or Georgia—have done better. Nonetheless, it remains a puzzle as to why progress in reform in some other countries that do not suffer from a resource curse has remained slow, and why some resource-rich countries have advanced much less than other equally resource-rich peers. A better understanding of these questions will be critical in determining how countries can avoid the 'low reform trap' that may compromise their prospects for development far into the future.

Appendix 1: Management practices in Eastern Europe and Central Asia

To estimate how firm management practices relate to performance in the MOI survey sample, the following firm-level production function has been devised,

$$y_{itc} = \alpha_l l_{itc} + \alpha_k k_{itc} + \alpha_n n_{itc} + \beta M_i + \gamma' Z_{itc} + u_{itc},$$

where y is the natural logarithm of sales, l the natural logarithm of labour, k the natural logarithm of capital, and n the natural logarithm of intermediate inputs (materials) of firm i in country c at time t. The Zs are a number of other controls that will affect productivity, such as workforce characteristics (employees with a completed university degree and the average weekly hours worked), firm characteristics (firm age and whether it is listed on the stock market), a set of three-digit industry dummies, and country-year (or only country) dummies.

M is the variable of interest, average management quality. It is calculated based on a scoring of each of 13 individual management practices, averaged over the variables included in each of the four core areas of management practices, and finally averaged over these four areas.

Table 10.A1 summarizes the findings. Column 1 reports an *OLS* specification with only labour, three-digit industry and country-time dummies as controls. The management score is strongly and statistically significantly associated with higher labour productivity. The magnitude of the effect is comparable to the one reported in previous research.[24] Adding further controls—such as workforce, and firm and interviewer characteristics—reduces the coefficient only slightly (column 2). Adding a measure of materials in column 4 almost halves the management coefficient, along with reducing the sample size, but it remains statistically and economically significant. An improvement in an average firm's management practices from the mid-point (or median) to the top 10 per cent is associated with an increase in productivity of between 6.9 per cent (column 4) and 18.3 per cent (column 1).[25]

Better management practices are also positively and significantly associated with the likelihood both of introducing new products or services

Table 10.A1 Firm performance and management practices

	(1)	(2)	(3)	(4)	(5)	(6)	(7)
Estimation method	OLS	OLS	OLS	OLS	OLS	Probit	Probit
Firms	All	All	All	All	All	All	All
Dependent variable	Ln(Y) labour productivity	Ln(Y) labour productivity	Ln(Y) labour productivity	Ln(Y) labour productivity	Ln(Y) Sales	New products in last three years?	R&D activities in 2007?
Management z-score	0.1831***	0.1400***	0.1263***	0.0688**	0.1383***	0.0462***	0.0709***
	(0.0338)	(0.0362)	(0.0355)	(0.0281)	(0.0384)	(0.0112)	(0.0123)
Ln(N) labour	0.0999***	0.1571***	−0.0004	−0.2916***	0.9623***	0.0379**	0.0783***
	(0.0335)	(0.0400)	(0.0466)	(0.0440)	(0.0524)	(0.0152)	(0.0146)
Ln(N) capital			0.1524***	−0.0583**			
			(0.0244)	(0.0236)			
Ln(N) Materials				0.4939***			
				(0.0271)			
Country*time effects	yes	yes	yes	yes	yes	no	No
Country effects	no	no	no	no	no	yes	Yes
Industry effects	yes	yes	yes	yes	yes	yes	Yes
Firm controls	no	yes	yes	yes	yes	yes	yes
Firms	834	763	761	627	776	1,458	1,405
Observations	3,469	3,193	3,179	2,590	3,321	1,458	1,405

Notes: ***significant at 1 per cent level; **significant at 5 per cent level; *significant at 10 per cent level. In all columns, standard errors are in parentheses under coefficient estimates and allow for heteroscedasticity and serial correlation. Firm controls include natural logs of firm age, average hours worked by production/non-production workers, share of production/non-production workers with a university degree; a dummy variable for stock exchange listing; and a series of 'noise controls' that capture differences across managers who responded to the interview and the interview setting. All regressions include a full set of three-digit industry dummies and country dummies interacted with a full set of time dummies (except columns 6 and 7, which use cross-sectional data). The dependent variables in columns 6 and 7 are dummy variables that take the value 1 if the firm answers 'yes' to the relevant question and 0 otherwise.

Source: Estimations based on MOI survey; see text.

(column 6) and of incidence of spending on R&D (column 7). Nonetheless, little or no evidence was found of a link between management practices and either the percentage of annual sales accounted for by new products and services, or the amount of R&D spending (results not shown). This could reflect greater measurement error in these variables, which are harder for the manager to estimate than incidence.

Appendix 2: Management, Organization and Innovation survey

From October 2008 to March 2009, the EBRD conducted the first MOI survey in collaboration with the World Bank. The survey covered almost 1700 manufacturing firms with between 50 and 5000 employees in ten transition countries—Belarus, Bulgaria, Kazakhstan, Lithuania, Poland, Romania, Russia, Serbia, Ukraine, and Uzbekistan—and Germany (see Table 10.A2). The sampling frame, from which these firms were picked randomly with equal probability, was based on Bureau Van Dijk's Orbis database (as available in August 2008) with the exception of Kazakhstan and Uzbekistan, which Orbis did not cover at the time. The sampling frame in Kazakhstan was the official list of establishments obtained from the Agency of Statistics of the Republic of Kazakhstan, and in Uzbekistan the Uniform State Register of Enterprises and Organizations published by the State Department of Statistics of the Republic of Uzbekistan. In Poland and Germany, several establishments that participated in a previous survey on management practices[26] were re-interviewed as well. All regions within a country had to be covered (with the exception of the far east in Russia), and the percentage

Table 10.A2 MOI firms by country

Country	Total number of firms participating in MOI survey	Panel firms participating in MOI and previous management practices survey
Belarus	102	—
Bulgaria	154	—
Germany	219	97
Kazakhstan	125	—
Lithuania	101	—
Poland	190	108
Romania	154	—
Russia	*216*	—
Serbia	135	—
Ukraine	148	—
Uzbekistan	125	—
Total	1,669	205

Source: Based on MOI survey; see text.

Table 10.A3 Firms participating in the MOI survey

Characteristics	Percentage
Establishment size (number of employees)	
Small and medium (under 249)	72.0
Large (249–5000)	28.0
Largest owner	
Multiple owners	17.4
Foreign	14.8
Domestic private—individual	42.0
Domestic private—family	11.0
State	11.1
Other	3.7
Privatization status	
State-owned	8.7
Privatized	30.8
Always private	60.6
Location	
Capital city	26.5
Large cities (excluding the capital)	35.1
Small cites	26.0
Rural areas	12.3

Note: Largest owner is defined as owner of the largest share of the firm but owning at least 25 per cent. Privatized firms are formerly state-controlled firms whose largest owner is no longer the state.
Source: Based on MOI survey; see text.

of the sample in each region was required to be equal to at least a half of the percentage of the sample frame population in each region. The types of firm taking part in the survey are described in detail in Table 10.A3.

The survey was targeted at factory, production or operations managers, who are close to the day-to-day operations of the firm but are at the same time senior enough to have an overview of management practices.[27] Interviews were conducted face to face in the manager's native language by interviewers employed by the market research companies hired to implement the MOI survey. Each interview took, on average, 50 minutes.

The average response rate to the survey was 44 per cent and this appeared to be uncorrelated with productivity or profitability. There was some evidence that larger firms were more likely to respond, which is why the regressions typically control for this variable to offset any potential sample selection bias. In the initial contact with the firm, the interview was introduced as part of a study that would not discuss the firm's financial position or its accounts, making it relatively non-controversial for managers to participate.

The questionnaire comprised seven sections organized by topic. The first asked questions about the characteristics of the firm, such as legal status, ownership, and number of years in operation. This was followed by sections on management practices, organization of the firm, innovation and R&D, degree of competition, and also labour. Data on the location and size of the firm, interview start and end times, and interviewer and interviewee characteristics were also collected. The MOI questionnaire was developed and tested in two pilot surveys prior to its implementation in the field.

The concept of 'good' or 'bad' management needs to be translated into a measure applicable to different firms across the 'manufacturing' sector. In contrast to previous questionnaires on management practices, the MOI survey consisted mostly of closed questions,[28] in which the options offered to interviewees were based on the most common responses from previous surveys. Management practices were grouped into four areas: 'operations' (one question), 'monitoring' (seven questions), 'targets' (two questions), and 'incentives' (three questions). The 'operations' question focused on how the establishment handled a process problem, such as machinery breakdown. The 'monitoring' questions covered collection, monitoring, revision, and use of production performance indicators. The 'targets' questions focused on the timescale and realism of production targets, and the 'incentives' questions covered promotion criteria, practices for addressing poor employee performance, and rewarding production target achievement.

As the scaling varied across management practices, the scores were converted to z-scores by normalizing each practice (i.e. question) to mean zero and standard deviation 1. To avoid putting the most emphasis on the 'monitoring' aspect of management practices, the unweighted average was first calculated across z-scores for a particular area of the four management practices. An unweighted average was then taken across the scores for the four practices, and finally a z-score of the measure obtained was calculated.[29] This means that the average management practices across all firms in all countries in the sample are equal to zero, and the actual management practices of the firm deviate from zero either to the left ('bad' practices) or to the right ('good' practices).

Firm-level performance data—balance sheets, and income and loss statements—were obtained from Bureau Van Dijk's Orbis database for the countries covered and matched to the sample of completed interviews.

The MOI questionnaire and full dataset are published on the EBRD's web site at www.ebrd.com.

Acknowledgements

This study is an adaptation of Chapter 5 of the 2009 *Transition Report* (EBRD 2009). The authors gratefully acknowledge contributions from Elisabetta Falcetti, Utku Teksoz, Stephen Jeffrey, and Natalie Weisshaar.

Notes

1. See Besley et al. (2009).
2. Earlier rounds of the BEEPS were conducted in 1999, 2002 and 2005, and have been analysed in the EBRD *Transition Reports* published in those years. BEEPS IV is the most ambitious round to date, covering nearly 12,000 firms in 29 countries of the transition region (compared with around 9000 firms in 27 countries in 2005). Most interviews were carried out in 2008 or early 2009. Unlike in previous survey rounds, which concentrated mainly on small and medium-sized enterprises, the aim has been to construct a representative sample of all types of company. About 25 per cent of the enterprises in BEEPS IV are large. Virtually all firms in the sample are privately owned (and mostly private from their inception rather than privatized) with only just over 1 per cent still majority state-owned. Firms that were 100 per cent state-owned were not eligible for inclusion in the survey.
3. The ranking of countries on the 'corruption' score is fairly similar to that of Transparency International (rank correlation coefficient: 0.65).
4. The average scores reported in Table 10.1 are not adjusted for firm or country characteristics; in particular, whether or not firms or countries have been growing in recent years. As a result, differences in reported obstacles could reflect differences in demand for certain public goods, such as education, in addition to a lack of supply of such goods. See Carlin et al. (2007).
5. Within the BEEPS, there are a number of questions about infrastructure services. For example, respondents are asked about the number of power outages they experienced, and their severity in terms of length and extent of losses caused by them. These answers can then be related to the subjective perceptions as a cross-check on the validity of the latter.
6. This statement applies to the comparison of EEC, Russia and Central Asia on the one hand and CEB and SEE on the other. The correlation of corresponding BEEPS and Doing Business indicators on a country-by-country basis is lower, albeit positive (depending on the indicator, between 0 and 0.5). For the relative merits of objective and subjective indicators of the business environment, see Bertrand and Mullainathan (2001), Gelb et al. (2007), and Gaelle and Scarpetta (2004).
7. Focusing on the percentage of firms reporting a non-zero score avoids having to rescale the scores of surveys to achieve comparability over time, in the light of changes in the scale. A rescaled average score would give broadly similar results. The main exception is the variable 'functioning of the judiciary', which rises, rather than falls, in the 2008/09 BEEPS round if an average score is used.
8. Questions about perceived obstacles to infrastructure were not asked in the 1999 BEEPS round.
9. This conclusion is supported by a detailed analysis by Carlin and Schaffer (2009), summarized in World Bank (2009: Chapter 5).
10. In particular, firms in a generally bad business environment may take a more restrictive view on when to call an obstacle 'very serious' compared with those in a generally good environment, so that average obstacle scores may understate differences across countries.
11. This ranges from Estonia (ranked 3rd worldwide) to Ukraine (ranked 73rd out of 76).
12. See Bloom and Van Reenen (2007, 2010).
13. An increase of this magnitude represents approximately 1 standard deviation in the estimated sample.

14. Among the former Soviet Union (FSU) countries, Belarus's overall management scores are fairly close to Ukraine's but differ significantly from Kazakhstan, Russia, and Uzbekistan. Compared with these countries, the higher overall average management scores in Belarus are driven by the fact that many firms in Belarus excel at monitoring and targets management. This could be attributed to the fact that state planning has been dismantled to a lesser degree in Belarus than in other FSU countries that were included in the MOI, and monitoring and targeting are a legacy from that period.

15. See Bloom and Van Reenen (2010). This is a rough and ready comparison as there are methodological differences between the Bloom and Van Reenen (2007, 2010) studies and the MOI survey. The comparison exploits the fact that some of the firms in Germany and Poland participated in both surveys, with relatively high and statistically significant correlations between the management scores across both. The scores from the surveys in non-transition countries were benchmarked to these firms.

16. See Bloom and Van Reenen (2007, 2010).

17. See Bloom et al. (2011).

18. Previous research found that family-owned firms with non-professional managers were the most poorly managed on average. Interestingly, this does not appear to be the case in transition countries, perhaps because family-owned firms tend to be relatively young and do not carry the legacy of central planning.

19. See Aghion et al. (2008).

20. Unfortunately, data coverage precludes most CIS countries—either firm-level data are not available or information about sales and costs is missing.

21. See Aghion et al. (2008, 2010).

22. See Table 10.5 for a full list of countries and sectors.

23. See EBRD (2008).

24. Bloom and Van Reenen (2007).

25. The performance of firms is also positively and significantly associated with most of the underlying 13 management practices as well as all of the four subcomponents of management practices ('operations', 'monitoring', 'targets' and 'incentives'). See Bloom et al. (2011).

26. See Bloom and Van Reenen (2010).

27. Factory managers are usually responsible for the efficient operation, maintenance, and budgetary control of production. Production/operations managers ensure that goods are produced efficiently, at the right quality, quantity, and cost, and that they are produced on time.

28. Closed-ended questions have a finite number of answers (e.g. 'Are employees promoted on merit?' [yes/no]), while an open-ended question has no set of predefined answers (e.g. 'How are employees promoted?').

29. This is an accepted way of calculating index numbers (see Bresnahan et al. 2002).

References

Aghion, P., H. Harmgart and N. Weisshaar (2008) 'Fostering Growth in Transition Economies', *EBRD Transition Report 2008*: Chapter 3, 49–63, European Bank for Reconstruction and Development: London.

Aghion, P., H. Harmgart and N. Weisshaar (2010) 'Competition and Growth in Emerging Markets: Firm-Level Evidence', mimeo.

Bertrand, M. and S. Mullainathan (2001) 'Do People Mean What They Say? Implications for Subjective Survey Data', *American Economic Review*, 91(2): 67–72.

Berglöf, E., L. Bruynooghe, H. Harmgart, P. Sanfey, H. Schweiger, and J. Zettelmeyer (2010). 'European Transition at Twenty: Assessing Progress in Countries and Sectors', WIDER Working Paper 2010/91, UNU-WIDER: Helsinki.

Besley, T., M. Dewatripont and S. Guriev (2009) *Transition and Transition Impact. A Review of the Concept and Implications for the EBRD*, report prepared for the European Bank for Reconstruction and Development, available at http://www.ebrd.com/pages/research/publications/essay/besley.shtml.

Bloom, N. and J. Van Reenen (2007) 'Measuring and Explaining Management Practices Across Firms and Countries', *Quarterly Journal of Economics*, 122(4): 1351–408.

Bloom, N. and J. Van Reenen (2010) 'Why Do Management Practices Differ Across Firms and Countries?', *Journal of Economic Perspectives*, 24(1): 203–24.

Bloom, N., H. Schweiger and J. Van Reenen (2011) The Land that Lean Manufacturing Forgot? 'Management Practices in Transition Countries', EBRD Working Paper No. 131, European Bank for Reconstruction and Development: London.

Bresnahan, T., E. Brynjolfsson and L. Hitt (2002) 'Information Technology, Workplace Organisation, and the Demand for Skilled Labor: Firm-Level Evidence', *Quarterly Journal of Economics*, 117(1): 339–76.

Carlin, W., M. Schaffer and P. Seabright (2007) 'Where are the Real Bottlenecks? Evidence from 20,000 Firms in 60 Countries about the Shadow Costs of Constraints to Firm Performance', *Institute for the Study of Labor Discussion Paper No. 3059*.

Carlin, W. and M. Schaffer (2009) 'Public Infrastructure Constraints on Growth in the Transition Economies: The Legacy of Communism and Evidence from Enterprise Surveys 1999–2008', Background Paper, World Bank: Washington, DC.

EBRD (2008) *Securing Sustainable Energy in Transition Economies*, European Bank for Reconstruction and Development: London.

EBRD (2009) *Transition Report 2009: Transition in Crisis?*, European Bank for Reconstruction and Development: London.

Gaelle, P. and S. Scarpetta (2004) 'Employment Regulations Through the Eyes of Employers: Do They Matter and How Do Firms Respond To Them?', *World Bank Policy Research Working Paper No. 3463*, World Bank: Washington, DC.

Gelb, A., V. Ramachandran, M. Kedia-Shah and G. Turner (2007) 'What Matters to African Firms? The Relevance of Perceptions Data', *World Bank Policy Research Working Papers No. 4446*, World Bank: Washington, DC.

World Bank (2009) *Turmoil at Twenty: Recession, Recovery and Reform in Central and Eastern Europe and the Former Soviet Union*, World Bank: Washington, DC.

11
Transition, Structural Divergence, and Performance: Eastern Europe and the Former Soviet Union during 2000–7

Giovanni Andrea Cornia

1 Introduction: transition and divergence in Eastern Europe and the former Soviet Union

The countries in transition that have emerged from the socialist bloc of Eastern Europe and the former Soviet Union (EE-FSU)[1] have always been very different. Their heterogeneity has distant origins and finds its roots in dissimilar endowments of natural resources, geographies and cultural developments over several centuries. Yet, during the socialist era, public policy explicitly attempted to reduce differentials in levels of development among states, regions within states, and social classes. Such an 'equalization of outcomes' agenda was pursued by compressing the wage distribution, socializing the profits of state-owned enterprises, subsidizing key consumption items, and providing universal pensions, family benefits, and free *de jure* (if not *de facto*) health and education.[2] In turn, cross-country differences were reduced by the use of 'socialist prices' (often equal to one tenth of world prices) in trade among the socialist economies, generous transfers from the USSR budget to poorer Soviet republics (equal, for instance, to a third of Uzbekistan's GDP in 1991), and the funding of major infrastructural projects directly from Moscow. The development pattern was also very similar. While differences in natural endowments affected somewhat the division of labour among the socialist economies (by emphasizing, for instance, manufacturing in Central Europe, oil extraction in Siberia and cotton cultivation in Central Asia), everywhere the emphasis was placed on industry, large enterprises (*kombinati*), and science and technology.

The evidence for convergence in economic and social outcomes during the socialist era points to a complex picture. In a study covering 1945–95, Cornia and Danziger (1997) find a clear convergence in infant mortality rates (IMR) across socialist countries between 1950 and 1970 and a more limited one in the subsequent years. Convergence in levels of life expectancy at birth (LEB) was achieved in the region till the late 1960s, after which the rate of improvement diminished sharply and the speed of convergence declined. Considerable convergence in the quantity (if not in the quality) of schooling was also observed. In the economic field there was a strong similarity in the growth rates of the net material product (NMP) till the end of the 1970s, as all countries grew at planned rates of 4–5 per cent. By definition, however, convergence in growth rates was not accompanied by convergence in the levels of NMP per capita (ibid.). During the last decade of the socialist experiment, the situation was reversed as there was divergence in NMP growth rates, as the richer Central European countries (Hungary, Czechoslovakia, and Poland) grew more slowly than the poorer states of the USSR. However, a study testing for a common growth path in the ex-communist bloc (Estrin et al. 2001) finds little evidence of convergence in NMP per capita within the region, a result that questions the effectiveness of policies to reduce differentials during the socialist era.

Since the onset of the transition, public policy has been inspired by the liberal ideology that attributes a central role to the market in the allocation of resources and limits state intervention in the economy. Such a new policy approach promoted price and trade liberalization, the dismantling of within- and cross-country equalization mechanisms, the adoption of wage policies emphasizing human capital, merit and effort, decentralization, and a shift in welfare policy from the principle of 'equalizing outcomes' to that of 'equalizing opportunities'.

Despite a common emphasis on price liberalization, privatization of housing and small businesses, reorientation of foreign trade and other policies, and some common changes in economic structure (de-agrarization, dismantling of heavy industry, and development of services) in the initial phase of the transition, policy approaches differed markedly across countries. Some nations (e.g. Poland) relied on a shock therapy; others opted for a gradual approach; while post-soviet countries (such as Belarus and Turkmenistan) introduced hardly any reform. Thus, the transition represents a large-scale natural experiment, similar in extent and impact only to the decolonization of the 1950s, in which differences in initial conditions, policy approaches, institutional development and external financing led to vastly different economic and social outcomes. Indeed, output and social conditions deteriorated only up to 1991 in Poland, 1995–6 in most other countries, and 1999 in Moldova and Ukraine. While these initial policy differences affected the level of output and well-being, they did not lead to a visible differentiation in economic structures. In contrast, with a region-wide recovery that started in around 2000, the economic structure of the countries in transition began to diverge. The transition has therefore led to a double differentiation among states sharing similar initial conditions, the first in the 'rate of growth' (over 1989–99) and the second in the 'pattern of growth' (over 2000–7).

2   Evidence of divergence among EE-FSU countries, 1989–2007

2.1   Increasingly similar approaches to the transition since the mid- to late 1990s

In the initial years, the approach to transition differed substantially. Most countries of Central Europe and the Baltics opted for shock therapy, rapidly stabilized their macroeconomy, and swiftly liberalized domestic markets and external transactions. In contrast, other countries (e.g. Uzbekistan) staggered their economic reforms over several years. As a result, till the mid-1990s, the increase in the mean regional value of the European Bank for Reconstruction and Development (EBRD) 'overall reform index' was accompanied by an increase in its coefficient of variation (CV) and standard deviation (SD)[3] (Table 11.1). Since then, the countries that had initially adopted a gradual approach intensified their reform efforts, leading in this way to a gradual convergence in reform approaches—as indicated by the fall of the CV of this variable since 1995. Thus, with the exception of 'post-soviet' Belarus and Turkmenistan, and 'gradualist' Uzbekistan, from the middle–late 1990s, most countries of the region appear to have adopted similar economic policies.

This convergence in reform approaches leads to similar macroeconomic outcomes. While these differed substantially in the early phase of the transition (with most Central European and Baltic economies recording better results than the countries of South Eastern Europe and the Commonwealth of Independent States (CIS)), during the medium term, performance in this area has slowly converged, as the laggards gradually have improved their indicators since the mid-1990s, possibly as a result of the emphasis placed by governments and the International Monetary Fund (IMF) on stabilization and of the requirements to be fulfilled by countries aspiring to enter

Table 11.1   Descriptive statistics of the distribution of the EBRD 'overall economic reform index'

Year	Number of countries	Mean	Median	Min	Max	SD	CV
1989	25	1.13	1.00	1.00	1.78	0.27	0.24
1990	25	1.24	1.00	1.00	2.62	0.46	0.37
1995	25	2.80	2.83	1.40	3.72	0.58	0.21
2000	25	3.12	3.27	1.57	3.87	0.60	0.19
2005	25	3.29	3.43	1.45	3.98	0.64	0.19
2007	25	3.32	3.48	1.45	4.05	0.64	0.19

Source: Author's elaboration on EBRD data. The overall reform index varies between 1 (no reform) and 5 (full reform).

the European Union (EU). As a result, the average budget deficit/GDP, government debt/GDP, and inflation declined steadily from 1995,[4] while their cross-country variability diminished (Cornia 2010, Table 2).

2.2 Economic performance: cross-country divergence followed by hysteresis

Despite increasingly similar policy approaches adopted since the mid- to late 1990s and the convergence observed for most indicators of macroeconomic stabilization, the economic performance of the EE-FSU countries diverged sharply in the initial part of transition (roughly 1989–95 or 1989–9),[5] as the transformational recession affected the Central European countries and Uzbekistan less severely than those of the FSU. During this period the GDP per capita, its annual growth rate, the investment rate and the Gini index of income inequality deteriorated sharply but at different speeds and for different durations, thus causing a clear divergence in economic performance (Figure 11.1). Such differences in income growth, growth volatility, and income inequality increased the sense of insecurity and unfairness, and affected the level and cross-country variability in indicators of unhappiness in the European transition economies (Guriev and Zhuravskaya 2009).

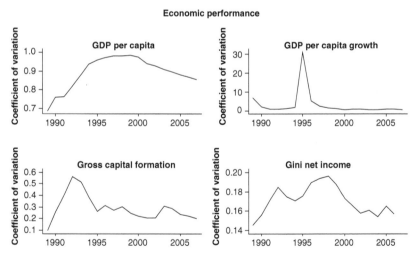

Figure 11.1 1989–2007 trend in the coefficient of variation of GDP per capita, its growth rate, the investment rate, and the Gini coefficient of disposable income, 25 countries, 1989–2007

Note: The sharp rise in the CV of the growth rate of GDP per capita is due to the fact that its 1995 regional mean was close to zero (−0.2). Yet, an increase in its dispersion is confirmed also by the SD, which rose from 5 to 7.2 between 1990 and 1995, to decline to 4.0 in 2000.

Source: Author's elaboration on WDI data.

There is a huge literature on the factors explaining the differences in the extent and duration of the transformational recession. The initial analyses suggested that countries that adopted a shock therapy and quickly liberalized domestic and external transactions performed better than those following a gradual reform path. This view is best summarized in the 1996 *World Development Report*, which notes that 'Consistent policies, combining liberalization of markets, trade and new business entry with reasonable price stability, can achieve a great deal even in countries lacking clear property rights and strong market institutions' (World Bank 1996: 142). Yet, subsequent analyses (Roland 2000; Cornia and Popov 2001; Popov 2005) emphasize the role of initial distortions, wars, the collapse of state institutions, and the supply shocks entailed by too rapid changes in relative prices following price liberalization in highly distorted economies.[6] Indeed, a large share of the variation in the extent of output collapse appears to be explained by the magnitude of the distortions in industrial structure and trade patterns inherited from the socialist era; that is, by the weight of the military sector, extent of overindustrialization, under-development of the service sector, lack of openness of the economy, and share of exports to socialist countries. This explanation emphasizes the difficulties caused by market imperfections (e.g. limited capital and labour mobility, and poorly developed banking and housing market) in restructuring the supply side of the economy and reallocating labour from the declining to the competitive sector during a period of depressed investments. According to this view, the divergence in growth rates was due also to differences in institutional capacity of the state; that is, its ability to collect taxes to fund 'a minimum state' capable of ensuring law and order, protection of property rights, contract enforcement, and basic social services.

Since the late 1990s, the entire region experienced a considerable growth rebound that lasted till the onset of the food–fuel–financial crisis of 2007–09. Such a rebound was driven by factors other than those that influenced performance during the transition, and can thus be analyzed with the usual tools of conventional growth theory. Indeed, it could be expected that several years of economic liberalization led to efficiency gains and a better economic performance, while the impact of pre-transition distortions faded away, institutional capacity improved and macroeconomic policy remained reasonable. During this period, all countries of the region recorded, with rare exceptions, fast rates of growth. As a result there was considerable 'σ-convergence' (i.e. in growth rates) but not, as predicted by most growth models, 'β-convergence' (i.e. in levels of GDP per capita). In this case, the available evidence suggests the presence of hysteresis as the relative and absolute difference in GDP per capita declined only modestly from the peak reached between 1995 and 2000. In many countries, the recovery recorded since the late 1990s was to a large extent a 'growth rebound' that made use of unused capacity rather than of an increase in the capital stock, as suggested by the only limited convergence in gross fixed capital formation

(Figure 11.1). In other words, investments recovered in some countries but not in others, and their cross-country distribution in the mid- to late 2000s remained more polarized than in the early to mid-1990s (ibid.). Similar considerations apply to the Gini coefficient of the distribution of net household income per capita, which rose by about ten points during the first decade of transition, to stabilize since then at the same level, while its CV declined only in part.

2.3   Demographic changes and long-term growth

Long-term growth in the economies in transition will be influenced by population ageing, as proxied by the old age dependency rate, and the future labour supply (which depends on birth, death, and migration rates). As many economies of the region are at the moment net exporters of labour, or are those (e.g. Russia) where their net immigration balance will be unable to solve their population problem by further increases in immigration, long-term growth will increasingly depend on trends in births and deaths. In this regard, Table 11.2 shows that until 1995 the decline in fertility rate affected only part of the region (as shown by the rise in the CV). The decline in fertility spread subsequently to all other countries, as shown by the decline in the CV. During the last three to four years, the fertility rate has climbed imperceptibly in several countries. Yet the birth losses recorded between 1989 and 2005 will reduce labour supply over the next 15 years and beyond in the entire region, with the exception of Central Asia. In part of the region, the initial phase of the transition was also characterized by a surge in male mortality rates (especially for the 25–39 age group), which, starting from 1995, however, slowly returned to its 1989 level (Table 11.2). Yet, as indicated by the rapid rise in the CV and SD, adult mortality in the region increasingly diverged, as several countries of the FSU (e.g. Russia, Ukraine, and Belarus) continued exhibiting abnormally high adult mortality rates while the Eastern European countries showed steady improvements. Finally, with the exception of the countries of Central Asia, most economies in transition recorded a rise in average old-age dependency ratio and in their cross-country variance (ibid).

2.4   Divergence and hysteresis in human well-being

It is well known that transition entailed deterioration in several aspects of human well-being during the years of the transformational recession. Yet, since the mid- to late 1990s, the regional LEB, other social indicators, and indexes of happiness recorded a clear rebound, though remaining well below the level of other middle-income countries (Guriev and Zhuravskaya 2009). However, such improvements resulted from two mutually offsetting trends; that is, gains in Eastern Europe and the Caucasus and losses or continued stagnation in the rest of the CIS. As a result, the LEB and the mortality rate of the 15–19-year-old age group diverged during the first years of transition,

Table 11.2 Descriptive statistics of the cross-country distribution of key demographic indicators, 1990–2007

Variable	Year	Number of countries	Mean	Median	Min	Max	SD	CV
Fertility rate	1989	18	2.27	2.04	1.52	4.18	0.72	0.32
	1990	25	2.42	2.04	1.46	5.09	0.91	0.38
	1995	25	1.96	1.58	1.23	4.52	0.88	0.45
	2000	25	1.70	1.39	1.10	4.00	0.68	0.40
	2005	25	1.66	1.42	1.20	3.53	0.58	0.35
	2007	25	1.70	1.42	1.20	3.35	0.55	0.32
Mortality rate for population 25–39 (per 100,000)	1989	25	188	193	98	264	47	0.25
	1990	25	193	189	104	276	50	0.26
	1995	25	239	213	105	484	105	0.44
	2000	25	201	177	90	457	100	0.50
	2005	25	198	148	77	514	120	0.60
	2007	⋮	⋮	⋮	⋮	⋮	⋮	⋮
Old-age dependency ratio (60+/15−59)	1989	25	21.8	24.2	11.4	30.9	6.6	0.30
	1990	25	22.3	24.6	11.5	31.7	6.7	0.30
	1995	25	23.6	26.6	10.7	34.7	7.3	0.31
	2000	25	24.7	27.9	10.4	34.7	8.1	0.33
	2005	25	24.7	25.8	9.1	35.9	8.9	0.36
	2007	25	24.4	26.4	8.5	36.8	9.2	0.38

Source: Author's elaboration on Transmonee data.

and such a gap either remained high or increased further in the following years (Figure 11.2). In contrast, an initial cross-country divergence followed by hysteresis is evident in the case of the IMR, enrolment rates in tertiary education, and the overall crime rate. All in all, there was a systematic divergence during 1989–2007 in all the aspects of human well-being considered, and a large rise in the cross-country dispersion of several indicators of well-being during the transformational recession, followed by further divergence or hysteresis during the growth years of the last decade. Such a trend is contrary to what is suggested by economic theory in countries experiencing rapid growth, and it runs counter to the trends observed between 1950 and 1989.

2.5   Divergence in political structures

Many indexes are used to measure the extent of democracy. They all suffer from various types of measurement bias. As yet, they offer some information about the evolution of political systems in the countries considered. The indicator selected for this chapter is 'the rule of law index', which ranges between −2.5 (no rule of law) and 2.5 (complete rule of law) and is available from 1996 onwards. In this regard, the data in Table 11.3 show a slow improvement in this index for the region as a whole between 1996 and 2007. However, it also shows a steady increase in its CV from 2000 to 2007, suggesting that after a generalized improvement in the rule of law, political institutions in the region diverged. The Central European countries built democratic regimes characterized by fair and free elections, rule of law, and state institutions able to collect taxes, ensure property rights, enforce contracts, and take responsibility for the universal provision of basic social services. A second group (some of the states of the FSU and the Balkans) evolved into 'illiberal democracies' (Zakaria 1997); that is, regimes characterized by partially free and fair elections, limited rule of law, scant protection of individual rights, and a weak administration unable to ensure the respect of property rights, contracts enforcement, and more than a modicum of social welfare. Finally, Central Asia and Belarus can be characterized as authoritarian regimes lacking genuinely free elections, with no rule of law, and frequent recourse to arbitrary measures by the executive. Given the emphasis placed by the literature on the importance of good governance for economic and social development, the divergence in political institutions observed since 2000 might have affected negatively the investment climate, output, and human well-being in part of EE-FSU.

All in all, it appears that while the EBRD overall policy reform index converged, starting from the mid- to late 1990s (meaning that the policy approaches to the transition became increasingly similar), during 2000–7 there was either hysteresis or further divergence in 11 of the 13 economic and social indicators discussed above (Cornia 2010: Table 5). This increasing regional heterogeneity does not deny that some club convergence

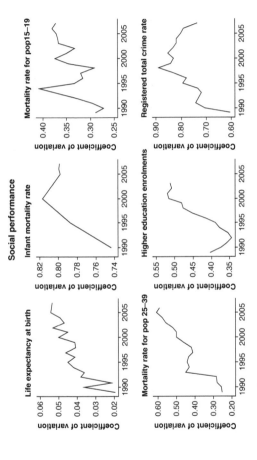

Figure 11.2 1989–2007 trend in the CV of selected social indicators

Source: Author's elaboration on Transmonee data.

Table 11.3 Descriptive statistics of the cross-country distribution of the rule of law index, 1996–2007

Year	Number of countries	Mean	Median	Min	Max	SD	CV
1996	25	−0.24	−0.21	−1.23	0.87	0.65	2.68
2000	25	−0.36	−0.60	−1.40	1.00	0.75	2.10
2005	25	−0.30	−0.50	−1.40	0.81	0.72	2.43
2007	25	−0.27	−0.50	−1.28	1.00	0.72	2.63

Source: Author's elaboration on Worldwide Governance Indicators.

might have taken place within homogeneous clusters (see next section). For instance, Matkowski and Prochniak (2006) found β-convergence over both 1993–9 and 1999–2005 among the EU accession countries (five Central European and the Baltics). The convergence was particularly marked during the latter period. According to these authors, this was the result not only of decreasing return to capital in richer economies but also of structural and regional policy introduced by the EU to reduce the development gap in the region. Yet, while club convergence might have occurred in some cases, the overall regional picture is one of widespread divergence.

3 Structural change and the birth of structurally different country clusters

3.1 Broad trends in structural change in the region

With systemic changes in asset ownership, price formation, allocation of resources, and external economic relationships, all transition economies experienced radical structural change. Gone was the emphasis on state agriculture, forced industrialization, heavy industry, large *kombinati*, limited labour mobility and uniform approaches to development. Five major structural changes occurred in all transition countries, regardless of their initial level of income,[7] factors endowment, and geographical location. The first was 'de-agrarization' (Landesmann 2000); that is, a decline in employment, and the share of agricultural value added, to levels similar to or lower than those of market economies with similar GDP per capita (Table 11.4). It must be noted, however, that over 1991–3, Albania, Armenia, Azerbaijan, Bulgaria, Georgia, Kyrgyzstan, Romania, Tajikistan, Turkmenistan, and Uzbekistan—all countries with a low GDP per capita—experienced a process of 're-agrarization', as agricultural output declined less markedly than in manufacturing and labour moved from urban to rural areas in countries that carried out egalitarian land reforms. This phenomenon was, however, transitory. As a result, from the mid-1990s, agricultural output and employment also fell in the low-income countries in transition, as well as

Table 11.4 Changes in selected structural economic indicators, 1991/2–2006

Country Groups*	Years	Share of VA in agriculture	Share of VA in manufacturing	Share of VA in transport and communication	Share of VA in 'other services'	Energy consumption per capita
Group 1. 8 countries with a 1989 GDP per capita < $1250 (2000 prices)	1991/2	32.5	26.3	4.7	16.4	1560
	1995	35.2	18.8	6.8	17.2	1242
	2000	27.2	15.4	8.2	20.7	1201
	2006	21.9	13.7	9.0	20.3	1320
Group 2. 8 countries with a 1989 GDP per capita > $1250 and < 3,000 $ (2000 prices)	1991/2	21.9	25.5	7.3	20.6	3221
	1995	18.0	20.2	10.0	23.2	2518
	2000	13.2	19.7	11.9	26.2	2266
	2006	9.8	18.4	11.6	30.2	2661
Group 3. 9 countries with a 1989 GDP per capita > $3000 (2000 prices)	1991/2	8.5	26.6	9.7	29.9	2884
	1995	7.6	22.6	9.5	34.2	2721
	2000	5.3	21.4	10.3	37.0	2660
	2006	4.4	20.6	10.3	37.5	3006

Note: *The three groups include the following countries: group 1: Albania, Armenia, Azerbaijan, Kyrgyzstan, Moldova, Tajikistan, Turkmenistan, and Uzbekistan; group 2: Belarus, Bulgaria, Georgia, Kazakhstan, Macedonia, Romania, Russia, and Ukraine; group 3: Croatia, Czech Republic, Estonia, Hungary, Latvia, Lithuania, Poland, Slovakia, and Slovenia. VA = value added.

Source: Author's elaboration on UNCTAD's data.

in countries such as Moldova, Ukraine, Russia, and Kazakhstan, which can count on a strong comparative advantage in agriculture. The second common structural transformation was 'deindustrialization'. All industrial branches, particularly manufacturing and energy generation, suffered a severe reduction in employment and output levels, particularly in countries where the initial distortions (a large share of employment and output in heavy industry and the armament sector) were greatest. Here too there were exceptions to the general rule, particularly in countries of group 3 (Table 11.4), where the share of manufacturing value added remained broadly constant or even rose. Indeed, after a modest drop during 1989–92, the output and employment share of manufacturing remained constant in Hungary, Slovenia, and the Czech Republic, while it rose in Slovakia, which has become a major production platform for multinationals operating in the automotive and other manufacturing sectors. These economies have also shown important structural changes in the field of foreign trade, as suggested by the type of goods exported, countries of destination, and export/GDP ratios.[8] This sub-group appears to have relied on its old expertise in manufacturing production. In contrast, in the rest of group 3, the share of manufacturing declined sharply; for instance from 23 to 16 per cent in Estonia and from 28 to 11 per cent in Latvia.

The third structural change—related to the decline in heavy industry and the change in the relative price of energy—is a substantial decline in energy consumption per capita (Table 11.4), falling by roughly a third in groups 1 and 2 and by a tenth in group 3. While this was expected during the first years of transition, it then also continued over subsequent years, though a modest trend reversal took place in 2006. Fourthly, in all economies in transition there was a substantial expansion of services. This catching-up was, however, partially due to statistical reclassifications and outsourcing of service activities previously undertaken within the industrial sectors (Landesmann 2000). The sub-sectors that caught up most rapidly were 'transport and telecommunication' and 'other services', the latter including banks and other financial institutions, real estate, business services (e.g. accounting, legal, software and consulting), personal services (e.g. private health, nursing and entertainment), and tourism. This was true in particular in countries lacking an established manufacturing tradition, such as the Baltic and South Eastern European countries. Particularly here, the employment and output gains in 'other services' almost completely compensated for the employment and output losses in industry and agriculture.

Finally, the liberalization of the labour market led to a substantial transfer of labour across sectors, informal employment, fast job turnover, and—with the liberalization of labour movements and a reduction in work opportunities during the 1990s—mass emigration, first towards Russia and subsequently towards the EU. In some of the group 1 countries, labour migration reached substantial proportions. Though the literature suggests that migration does not lead to long-term growth (IMF 2005)—in this case also because of the low fertility rates of the countries from which it originated (e.g. Moldova and Ukraine)—in several EE-FSU countries, migrant remittances have become a key source of subsistence and short-term growth. For instance, in 2006–7, migrant remittances accounted for 13–25 per cent of GDP in Albania, Armenia, Kyrgyzstan, and Moldova, and for a staggering 36 per cent in Tajikistan.

3.2 Cluster analysis

As suggested above, different patterns of specialization emerged in the region during the last decade. Particularly during the recovery and growth phase of the late 1990s and 2000s, there was substantial structural diversification within the region, a trend opposite to the structural convergence observed during the socialist era. Thus, though all EE-FSU countries during this period recorded growth of GDP of 5–10 per cent, the drivers of such growth differed remarkably. To identify the groups of economies that have emerged in the region since the onset of transition, a hierarchical cluster analysis was carried out for 1996 (the first year with complete data), 2000 (midway into the transition), and 2006[9] (the last year with complete data) using four scale-unstandardized clustering variables (CLVs) little correlated with each other; that is, (a) 'net manufacturing exports/GDP', which identifies the economies characterized by a dominant manufacturing sector; (b) 'share of 'other services'/GDP', which identifies economies that developed an advanced or informal services sector;[10] (c) 'net exports of fuels and ores/GDP', which characterizes the primary commodities exporters; and (d) the 'sum of Official Development Assistance (ODA) and migrant remittances on GDP'. As noted, in the initial phase of transition, some of the poorest countries relied in a major way on ODA, while from the end of the 1990s increased labour mobility raised substantially their share of migrant remittances on GDP.

The analysis identified four country clusters with dissimilar factor endowments, institutions, and growth drivers (Table 11.5). The first includes several Central European nations (the Czech Republic, Hungary, Poland, Slovenia, and Slovakia) plus Belarus and Ukraine; that is, countries dependent on the export of manufactured goods, supported in most cases by large inflows of foreign direct investment (FDI) and foreign finance. The second, which includes mixed and predominantly tertiarized economies (the three Baltics, Bulgaria, Romania, Macedonia, and Georgia), is somewhat more heterogeneous. The third cluster comprises primary commodities exporters (Russia, Azerbaijan, Turkmenistan, and Kazakhstan), while the fourth (Albania, Armenia, Kyrgyzstan, Moldova, Tajikistan, and Uzbekistan) includes nations initially dependent on foreign aid that later became suppliers of migrants, thus developing dependence for their growth on the inflows of remittances.[11]

Table 11.5 Descriptive statistics of CLVs for four groups of economies in transition, 2006

		Net exports of fuel and ores/GDP	(ODA and remittances)/GDP	Net exports of manufactured goods/GDP	'Other services'/GDP
Cluster 1: Manufacturing exporters: Belarus, Czech Republic, Hungary, Poland, Slovak Republic, Slovenia, Ukraine	Minimum	−7.9	0.6	−2.2	26.6
	Mean	−4.7	1.6	2.3	35.4
	Maximum	−1.3	3.3	7.3	45.3
	CV	0.5	0.6	1.3	0.2
Cluster 2: tertiarized mixed economies: Bulgaria, Croatia, Estonia, Georgia, Latvia, Lithuania, Romania, Macedonia	Minimum	−8.8	1.8	−20.8	28.8
	Mean	−3.5	5.1	−16.2	34.2
	Maximum	4.1	9.1	−10.1	40.0
	CV	1.0	0.6	0.3	0.1
Cluster 3: Oil-ores exporters: Azerbaijan, Kazakhstan, Russia, Turkmenistan	Minimum	21.1	−3.3	−27.0	10.4
	Mean	34.1	0.5	−17.1	23.1
	Maximum	54.4	4.3	−4.5	28.7
	CV	0.5	6.0*	0.5	0.4
Cluster 4: aid-remittances recipient economies: Albania, Armenia, Kyrgyz Republic, Moldova, Tajikistan, Uzbekistan	Minimum	−17.5	9.0	−33.6	15.1
	Mean	−2.7	19.5	−18.2	21.1
	Maximum	5.9	35.8	−10.6	32.3
	CV	3.2	0.5	0.5	0.3
Entire region (25 countries)	Minimum	−17.5	−3.3	−33.6	10.4
	Mean	2.4	6.8	−11.7	29.6
	Maximum	54.4	35.8	7.3	45.3
	CV	6.7	1.3	0.9	0.3

Note: *This value is artificially high as the mean tends to zero. In all these cases the CV is of little use.
Source: Author's calculation on official data.

Country-groups 1, 3 and 4 are unambiguously identified, as the minimum, mean, and maximum of the relevant CLVs differ substantially from those of the other groups while their CV is lower than those of the entire region and of the other groups. The only partial exception is cluster 2 ('tertiarized-mixed economies'). While its CV is lower than that of the other groups, its mean is similar to that of cluster 1. The attribution of the 25 countries to the four clusters seems in most cases in line with what is known about these economies.

The composition of the clusters changed over time following shifts in economic specialization (Table 11.6). Indeed, in 1996 (four to seven years after the onset of the transition) the 'industrial–manufacturing model' inherited from the socialist era was still dominant in 15 of the 25 countries analysed. With the recovery that began in mid-1990s, the growth bonanza of the 2000–7 period, and the rise in world commodity prices, there was, however, an increasing divergence in growth patterns. As a result, seven countries (identified with one or two stars in Table 11.6) changed cluster between 1996 and 2000, while 11 did so between 2000 and 2006. Only nine countries from a total of 25 retained in 2006 their initial economic specialization. All in all, Table 11.6 confirms that during 1996–2007 there were many changes in economic specialization, away from the uniform socialist pattern of heavy industrialization and towards more diversified patterns of growth.

Table 11.6 Evolution over time of four clusters of 25 European countries in transition, 1996, 2000, 2006

	1996	2000	2006
Cluster 1: manufacturing exporters	BLR, BGR, CZ, EST, HRV, HU, LTU, LVA, MDA, MKD, PL, ROM, SVK, SVN, UKR	BGR, CZ, EST, HRV, HU, LTU, LVA, MKD, PL, ROM, SVK, SVN,	BEL**, CZ, HU, PL, SVK, SVN, UKR**
Cluster 2: tertiarized mixed economies	AZE, KAZ, RUS, UZB	BLR*, UKR*	BGR*, EST*, GEO**, HRV*, LTU*, LVA*, MKD*, ROM*
Cluster 3: fuel-ore exporters economies	TKM	AZE*, KAZ*, TKM, RUS*, TJK**	AZE, KAZ, TKM, RUS,
Cluster 4: aid-remittances recipient economies	ALB, ARM,GEO, KGZ, TJK	ALB, ARM,GEO, KGZ, MDA*, UZB*	ALB, ARM, KGZ, MDA, TJK*, UZB

Note: *Indicates the shift over time to a cluster with a lower average GDP per capita; **a shift to a cluster with a higher GDP per capita.
Source: Author's calculations on official data.

4   Economic and social performance by cluster, 2000–7

Sections 2 and 3 argued that the transition led to a marked divergence among the countries of EE-FSU in practically all economic and social fields, and that with domestic and external liberalization, these countries have become increasingly heterogeneous. These four clusters differ not only in terms of economic structures and engines of growth but also in terms of the economic and social indicators (Table 11.3). Cluster 1 ('manufacturing exporters') displays the best indicators in practically all areas: it has the highest GDP per capita, the lowest inequality, the highest public spending (a possible proxy of institutional strength), the best rule of law, the highest LEB, and the lowest mortality rates, old-age dependency ratios, and crime rates. Strangely enough, however, it also has the lowest growth rate of GDP during 2000–7 and the second lowest investment rate. In turn, cluster 3 ('fuel-ore exporters') has the worst indicators in practically all areas but the highest investment and GDP growth rates. In view of all this, this section tests formally whether belonging to a given cluster affects economic performance (measured by the growth rate of GDP per capita) and social performance (measured by LEB).

4.1   Country clusters and growth of GDP per capita

Despite their less pronounced progress in terms of economic and institutional reforms, and contrary to the expectations of most analysts (Åslund and Jenish 2006), from 2000 to 2007 the CIS countries (coinciding with clusters 3 and 4) recorded faster growth than those of Eastern Europe (cluster 1). How can this growth paradox be explained? Why did growth lag behind in the fast reformers? More generally, what explains the growth performance of the countries of the region since 2000? To answer these questions, an 'eclectic growth regression' was estimated, including among the explanatory variables four sets of factors.

(a) First is the stock of production factors; that is, the physical capital (computed by means of the permanent inventory method, i.e. summing up the investment/GDP ratios during the previous eight years, and assuming an amortization rate of 12.5 per cent), public expenditure/GDP (a proxy of the stock of available public goods or, alternatively, a measure of labour supply disincentives), and the rule of law (a proxy of the stock of 'institutional capital').[12]

(b) Next is the initial level of development of each country (measured by the GDP per capita of 1990–3). As suggested by Solow's unconditional convergence, countries with an initial lower level of development grow, *ceteris paribus*, faster than the more advanced ones. This means that the countries of clusters 3 and 4 are expected *ex ante* to grow faster than those of cluster

1. However, Solow's unconditional convergence is expected to occur in the long term while the period analysed here covers only eight years.

(c) Since the period analysed was preceded by a catastrophic, if varying, decline in GDP per capita, a 'growth rebound effect' was also included among the regressors using as a proxy of this phenomenon the growth rate recorded during the difficult years of 1990–3. Thus, a possible explanation of the variation in growth rates during 2000–7 might be simply that GDP rebounded faster in the FSU countries that had recorded a much larger output contraction in the earlier part of the transition and could therefore count on greater unused capacity.

(d) The final factor is the diverging specialization of each country. Thus, four dummy variables were introduced, each of them identifying the four clusters discussed in section 3. This allows us to test whether—in addition to growth factors, growth convergence, and growth rebound—the new economic specializations affected growth during 2000–7.

The regression was carried out on a panel of 25 countries and eight years (from 2000 to 2007), for a total of 200 observations, though lack of data for some countries/years reduced the size of the panel to 168–193 observations, depending on the model tested (Table 11.7). The Haussmann test indicates that the random effect (RE) estimation procedure is the most suitable for this dataset, as this procedure is consistent with the use of time-invariant variables, such as the average GDP per capita during 1990–3, and the growth rate of GDP per capita during the same period.

The results of model 1 (as well as 4, 5, 7 and 8; i.e. five specifications out of nine) suggest that there was β-convergence, as poorer countries grew faster than richer ones. Second, the 'growth rebound' effect was successfully tested in five specifications out of the eight in which such a variable appears, though this effect was always verified at a probability level of only 12–18 per cent. As for the standard growth variables, the results show four things. First, the proxy of the capital stock is always strongly significant (except in model 9 where it is interacted with the cluster dummies). Second, the government expenditure/GDP ratio is always significantly and negatively associated with the growth of GDP, suggesting that the disincentive effect of high taxation associated with high public expenditure prevails on the positive effects of public goods on growth, and that a ten point rise in public expenditure/GDP reduced the rate of growth by 0.9–1.0 per cent. This may suggest not so much a negative effect of providing public goods (infrastructure, health, and education) but rather the 'crowding out' effect that large income transfers may have on investment. This is only a supposition—more detailed tests are needed to confirm it. Third, the parameter of the variable 'rule of law' is almost never significant, possibly because measurement errors do not permit it to proxy this phenomenon

Table 11.7 RE-GLS regression results (dependent variable: growth rate of GDP per capita) 2000–7

Regressors	Model 1	Model 2	Model 3	Model 4	Model 5	Model 6	Model 7	Model 8	Model 9
Constant	0.0861**	0.0590*	0.0173	0.0347	0.0177	0.0989	0.0770**	0.0231	0.1790*
1. GDP per capita 1990–3	-7.90 (e-06)**	-4.12 (e-06)	-5.75 (e-06)	-9.09 (e-06)*	-6.26 (e-06)*	-4.29 (e-06)	-0.00001*	-6.53 (e-06)*	-5.24 (e-06)
2. G.r. GDP per capita 1990–3		– 0.1795***^^^	-0.0731	– 0.1141*^^	-0.1566**	-0.1810*	-0.2316***	-0.1050	-0.1043
3. Σ Investment/GDP (t–8)–t			0.0007***	0.0006***	0.0006***	…	…	0.0006***	-0.0004
4. Gov expenditure/GDP			-0.0010**	-0.0009*	…	-0.0009*	…	-0.0009*	-0.0010**
5. Rule of law			-0.0004	0.0071	…	…	0.0196*	…	0.0047
6. Dummy Manufactures exporters				Pivot	Pivot	Pivot	Pivot	Pivot	Pivot
7. Dummy Mixed economies				-0.0093	-0.0032	-0.0116	-0.0154	-0.0052	-0.1524**
8. Dummy fuel-ore exporters				0.0218	0.0312**	0.0285*^^	0.0467**	0.0204	-0.2108***
9. Dummy recipients of aid-remittances				-0.0164	-0.0052	-0.0295*^	-0.0215	-0.0135	-0.1246*
15. Dummy7 × Σ investment/GDP									0.0010**
16. Dummy8 × Σ investment/GDP									0.0017***
17. Dummy9 × Σ investment/GDP									0.0007*^^
R^2	0.084	0.164	0.364	0.435	0.408	0.328	0.370	0.409	0.481
No. of observations	193	193	168	168	192	193	169	192	168
No. of countries in panel	25	25	24	24	24	25	25	24	24

Notes: ***, **, *, ^, ^^^ indicate that the parameters are not significantly different from zero at the 1%, 5%, 10%, 14%, and 18% probability level.
Source: Author's calculations.

adequately. Fourth and central to the analysis carried out in this chapter, the introduction of cluster dummies (models 4–8) suggests that belonging to the cluster of 'oil-ore exporters' raises in a statistically significant way the rate of growth of GDP per capita by between 2.1 and 4.6 per cent a year in relation to the pivot cluster of 'manufacturing exporters'. This is a large effect that is at odds, however, with the theoretical literature, which suggests that 'Dutch disease' and distributive distortions tend to reduce the long-term growth of commodity exporters. This result should thus be interpreted as a reflection of the short-term effect of high world prices of metals and energy during 2000–7, not as a predictor of sustained long-term growth.

The results in Table 11.7 also show that belonging to the clusters of 'tertiarized-mixed economies' and 'aid-remittances recipient economies' worsens the rate of growth of GDP per capita in relation to the group of 'manufacturing exporters', though this effect is less marked (0.5–2.9 per cent for the first group and 0.3–1.5 per cent for the second, depending on the regression model considered) and statistically non-significant. All in all, it appears that after controlling for the usual growth factors, β-convergence, and growth rebound effects, divergence in economic specialization among originally fairly similar countries did affect growth performance in the medium term. The longer-term effects are, however, not clear because countries endowed with abundant natural resources rarely experience faster growth than countries with other types of specialization (Sachs and Warner 1997).

4.2   Country clusters and changes in LEB

A second test was carried out to ascertain whether the divergence in economic specialization observed since 2000 affected human well-being, proxied here by LEB. As, *ceteris paribus*, GDP per capita affects favourably LEB in middle-income economies, one would expect that the oil-ore exporters also performed better in this area during the last decade. The opposite should be true for the countries of the clusters of tertiarized-mixed economies and 'aid-remittances recipient economies' because the parameters of their dummies (Table 11.7) suggested that belonging to these groups had a negative effect on the growth of GDP per capita.

To test these hypotheses a 'basic LEB regression' was carried out, including several of the usual regressors; that is, log GDP per capita, year-to-year changes in the level of the Gini coefficient of the distribution of household income, public health expenditure/GDP, enrolment rates in secondary education[13] (a proxy of the human capital and health knowledge of the families), and child dependency ratio (which is expected to affect LEB negatively). In addition, the four cluster dummies mentioned above were also introduced, while, as an alternative, they were replaced by the yearly values of the CLVs; that is, net exports of manufactured products/GDP (CLV1), the share of 'other services on GDP' (CLV2), net exports of fuel and ores/GDP (CLV3), and aid plus inward remittances/GDP (CLV4). These variables allow to test whether belonging to a given cluster improves or worsens the LEB of a country, suggesting in this way whether, *ceteris paribus*, the recent shifts in economic specialization affected its health performance. The results presented in Table 11.8 confirm the positive and statistically significant relation between LEB and log GDP per capita. They also suggest a weakly significant but important negative relation between LEB and increases in the Gini coefficient of income inequality. In turn, public health expenditure/GDP affects LEB favourably in the basic model but becomes statistically non-significant when introducing the cluster dummies (models 2–5) or CLV1–CLV4 (model 6). The enrolment rate in upper secondary education does not appear to be significant, possibly for the reasons given in endnote 14, while the child dependency ratio has the expected negative sign (models 4 and 5) but is not significantly different from zero, and becomes inexplicably positive and significant in model 6, contrary to all predictions of economic theory.

The above variables were introduced as controls, and the main objective of the test was to assess the impact of diverging economic specializations on human well-being, which is proxied in this chapter by LEB. In this regard, the results of Table 11.8 show unambiguously that despite a better growth performance, belonging to the cluster of 'oil-ore exporters' entails a cost in terms of lower LEB of 4.2–4.6 years in relation to the pivot cluster of 'manufacturing exporters'. In turn, belonging to the cluster of the mixed economies entails no change in LEB in relation to the pivot cluster, while belonging to that of 'aid-remittances recipient economies' entails a statistically non-significant but positive advantage of 0.5–1.3 years. Finally, the regression using the yearly values of the CLVs instead of the cluster dummies (model 6) broadly confirms the results just mentioned.

5 Concluding remarks

This chapter has argued that contrary to the trends observed during the 45 years of socialist rule (or at least the first 30), and in spite of an increasing convergence in EBRD reform indicators, transitional recession and economic and political liberalization in EE-FSU led in the initial years of transition to a marked cross-country divergence in practically all economic, social, and political dimensions. Limited reconvergence or hysteresis was instead observed during the years of the widespread recovery of the 2000s. As a result, the countries of the region are by now far more heterogeneous than they were twenty years ago.

The chapter has also shown that with the internal and external liberalization of the last two decades, countries with similar economic structures at the beginning of the transition evolved into four main clusters of countries with similar structures, resource endowments, institutions, and growth drivers within each cluster but with major differences across clusters. Thus,

Table 11.8 RE-GLS regression results, dependent variable: LEB, 2000–7

Regressor	Model 1	Model 2	Model 3	Model 4	Model 5	Model 6
Constant	53.7***	54.4***	56.1***	56.3***	56.1***	50.0***
1. Log GDP per capita	2.01***	2.11***	2.12***	2.10***	2.09***	2.24***
2. Δ Gini 2000–7	−0.0587^^	−0.0595^^	−0.0590^^	−0.0589^^	−0.0579*^^	−0.0680*^^
3. Public health Exp/GDP	0.485^^	0.0654			0.0100	0.441
4. Enrolm. rate in upper 2ary		:::	−0.0167	:::	−0.124	−0.0059
5. Child dependency ratio			:::	−0.332	−0.0159	0.0739**
6. DummyC1 (manufacturing export)		Pivot	Pivot	Pivot	Pivot	:::
7. DummyC2 (mixed economics)		0.0654	−0.063	−0.0386	0.0468	:::
8. DummyC3 (fuel-ore exporters)		−4.63***	−4.59***	−4.61***	−4.19**	:::
9. DummyC4 (aid+remittances)		1.067	0.578	1.317	1.171	:::
10. CV 1 manufacturing exports/GDP						0.0264*
11. CV 2 other services/GDP						0.0119
12. CV 3 (oil-ore exports/GDP)						−0.0297*
13. CV 4 (aid and remittances/GDP)						0.0020
R^2	0.560	0.796	0.793	0.782	0.791	0.642
No. of obs.	135	134	134	134	134	134
No. of countries in panel	25	24	24	24	24	24

Notes: ***, **, *, *^^ indicate that the parameters are not significantly different from zero at the 1%, 5%, 10%, 14%, and 18% probability level.
Source: Author's calculations.

as liberal policies grew more similar, the countries grew more dissimilar. This suggests that the similarity of economic structures under socialism was due to an undifferentiated development model being forced upon countries with different resource endowments and institutions. It is therefore not paradoxical that despite increasingly similar EBRD reform indicators (which signal the fact that more freedom to develop has been created), countries showed their intrinsic dissimilarity.

A paradox emerges, however, from the subsequent regression analysis. Indeed, after controlling for a host of factors, the cluster with the fastest growth was not the one that recorded the fastest progress in reforming its institutions (as originally suggested by the World Bank 1996) or with the lowest initial GDP per capita (as suggested by convergence theory) but that of oil-ore exporters. This advantage has been observed, however, over a relatively short period of time, while economic theory suggests that primary commodity exporters generally grow more slowly over the long term than other types of economies. In addition, the better economic performance of this cluster was accompanied by a large and statistically significant loss of LEB in relation to the countries specialized in the export of manufactured goods.

Acknowledgements

I should like to thank Jim Hughes for helpful discussions on a prior version of this paper, Bruno Martorano for compiling the data used in the analysis, and Stefano Rosignoli for his support in carrying out the convergence, cluster, and regression analyses. None of the remaining errors are, however, theirs.

Notes

1. The 25 countries analysed include Albania, Armenia, Azerbaijan, Belarus, Bulgaria, Croatia, the Czech Republic, Estonia, Georgia, Hungary, Kazakhstan, the Kyrgyz Republic, Latvia, Lithuania, Macedonia, Moldova, Poland, Romania, the Russian Federation, Slovakia, Slovenia, Tajikistan, Turkmenistan, Ukraine, and Uzbekistan. Lack of data did not allow the inclusion of Bosnia and Herzegovina, Serbia, and Montenegro. All regional or cluster averages are unweighted.
2. Access to goods and services varied across regions, particularly in the FSU, as the urban areas and towns along the main rail lines were better covered than remote towns and rural areas were. Also, access to health and higher education often entailed the payment of 'voluntary contributions' that discriminated against the poor and less well connected.
3. The measures used here to test σ-divergence are the standard deviation; that is, the square root of the sum of the differences between the values of a variable and its regional mean to the second power, divided by the number of country observations at time t, i.e. $SD = \sqrt{1/n} \, \Sigma \, (x_i - \mu)^2$ (where the first symbol on the RHS is the square root). When the values of x_i change considerably upward or downward over time, comparisons based on SD are biased. In this case it is better

to use the coefficient of variation $CV = SD/\mu$. However, the usefulness of CV disappears when the mean (μ) tends to zero. In this case it is better to use the SD.

4. The data for 1990 refer to a small number of countries and cannot be compared with those of the following years.

5. In Eastern Europe the duration of the transformational recession that began in 1989 varied from a minimum of two years in Poland to three or four in most of the rest, and between eight and ten years in Bulgaria and Romania. In the countries of the FSU the transformational recession started mostly in 1990 (except for Latvia, Kyrgyzstan, Turkmenistan, and Uzbekistan, where it began in 1991), while the recession generally ended in 1996–8, though the Baltic and Caucasus countries, Belarus and Uzbekistan, returned to growth in 1993–5. In contrast, Moldova and Ukraine bottomed out only in 1999.

6. There are several explanations for why a gradual transition may lead to a better performance than a shock therapy; see Roland (2000) for a survey. These explanations emphasize, among others, the weakening of the state and its inability to enforce production quotas under the system of dual pricing; the absence of competitive product markets due to the monopolistic nature of privatized state-owned enterprises; and the 'disorganization' entailed by the disruption of the supplier–producer and producer–retailer linkages inherited from the socialist era, and the high costs or rebuilding these linkages (Blanchard and Kremer 1997). In turn, Popov (2005) argues that with rapid price liberalization, the ability to reallocate resources from the 'non-competitive sector' (i.e. that with the highest price distortions during socialism) to the 'competitive sector' is limited by the low saving and investment capacity of the country, as a rapid contraction of former sector reduces the overall output, saving, and investment capacity. The upper limit to the speed of reallocating resources from non-competitive to competitive industries is thus basically determined by the net investment/GDP ratio.

7. In 1989 GDP per capita (2000 prices) varied from US$500 in Tajikistan to around US$8000 in Slovenia.

8. During 1989–2007, export/GDP ratios rose, respectively, from 45 to 80 per cent in the Czech Republic, from 36 to 80 per cent in Hungary, from 20 to 40 per cent in Poland and from 28 to a staggering 86 per cent in Slovakia.

9. To reduce noise, the 1996 value of the variables is set equal to the average of 1995, 1996, and 1997, that of 2000 to the average of 1999, 2000, and 2001, and that of 2006 to the average of 2005 and 2006.

10. See Section 3.1.

11. In a few cases, the official value of migrant remittances was corrected on the basis of information available to the author. In Armenia, most migrant remittances are recorded as foreign direct investment (FDI), because part of this money is used to purchase houses. To correct for this bias, half of the value of FDI was treated as migrant remittances. A similar approach was followed in Georgia and Ukraine. Likewise, the 2006/7 value of remittances in Uzbekistan was estimated at 10 per cent of GDP on the basis of unofficial data communicated to the author in 2008 by the local Chamber of Commerce. In Uzbekistan the rate of outmigration rose exponentially in the aftermath of the land reform of 2004–7, which expelled two million peasants from privatized *shirkats* (collective farms). Finally, in countries with no data about remittances but that are known to have low rates of migration (e.g. oil producers, the Czech Republic and Slovakia), this variable was assigned the value of 0.1 per cent.

12. The stock of human capital was not included as this variable shows little variation across the countries of the region.
13. The appropriate variable to proxy the level of education and health knowledge of households should be the level of education of adult women, but this was not readily available. However, as the stock of education in the region is distributed very equally, improvements in health scores are evident only for those who completed tertiary education. This information, however, is readily available in the Transmonee database only until 2005 and, furthermore, these data suffer from comparability problems. This is why it was decided to use data about upper-secondary enrolments instead.

References

Åslund, A. and N. Jenish (2006) 'The Eurasian Growth Paradox', *Institute of International Economics Working Paper No. 06-5*, Institute of International Economics: Washington, DC.

Blanchard, O. and M. Kremer (1997) 'Disorganization', *Quarterly Journal of Economics*, 112(4): 1091–126.

Cornia, G.A. (2010) 'Transition, Structural Divergence, and Performance: Eastern Europe and the Former Soviet Union over 2000–2007', *UNU/WIDER Research Paper No. 2010/32*, UNU-WIDER: Helsinki.

Cornia, G.A. and S. Danziger (1997) *Child Poverty and Deprivation in Industrialized Countries: 1945–1995*, Clarendon Press: Oxford.

Cornia, G.A. and V. Popov (2001) '*Transition and Institutions*', Oxford University Press: Oxford.

Estrin, S., G. Urga and S. Lazarova (2001) 'Testing for Ongoing Convergence in Transition Economies: Central and Eastern Europe, 1970–1998', *Journal of Comparative Economics*, 29(4): 677–91.

Guriev S. and E. Zhuravskaya (2009) '(Un)happiness in Transition', *Journal of Economic Perspectives*, 23(2): 143–68.

IMF (2005) 'Globalization and External Imbalances', *World Economic Outlook*, April, IMF: Washington, DC.

Landesmann, M. (2000) 'Structural Change in the Transition Economies, 1989–1999', *Vienna Institute for International Economic Studies Research Report No. 269*, Vienna Institute for International Economic Studies: Vienna.

Matkowski, Z. and M. Prochniak (2006) 'Real Economic Convergence in the EU Accession Countries', paper presented to the 9th Biannual Conference of EACES, available from www.bus.bton.ac.uk/eaces/papers/5e3.pdf.

Popov, V. (2005) 'Shock Therapy Versus Gradualism Reconsidered', *CEFIR/New Economic School Working Paper No. 68*, New Economic School: Moscow.

Roland, G. (2000) '*Transition and Economics: Politics, Markets and Firms*', MIT Press: Cambridge, MA.

Sachs, J. and A. Warner (1997) 'Natural Resource Abundance and Economic Growth', mimeo, Centre for International Development and Harvard Institute for International Development, available from www.cid.harvard.edu/ciddata/warner_files/natresf5.pdf.

World Bank (1996) 'From Plan to Market', *World Development Report*, World Bank: Washington, DC.

Zakaria, F. (1997) 'The Rise of Illiberal Democracies', *Foreign Affairs*, 76(6): 22–43.

12
The Long Road to Normality: Where Russia Now Stands

Vladimir Popov

1 Introduction

The goal of this study is to reveal the long-term trajectory of Russian economic development and to make predictions for the future. We start with a much discussed question: Why did Russia do worse economically during transition than most other countries in Europe and Asia? It is argued that it was caused partly by objective circumstances before transition (distortions in industrial structure and in trade patterns accumulated during the era of central planning), but mostly by the weakening of the institutional capacity of the state during transition.

The second issue deals with the reasons for the institutional collapse that was more pronounced in Russia than either in democratic Eastern Europe (EE) or in authoritarian China and Vietnam. These reasons are partly associated with democratization carried out in a poor rule of law environment (in EE countries the rule of law was stronger, whereas in China and Vietnam democratization was delayed). A possibly more important reason is the long-term trajectory of institutional development; that is, the historical path from traditional collectivist institutions to the modern individual responsibility type. Whereas EE more or less adopted Western institutions, and China preserved the institutional continuity (traditional 'Asian values' institutions), Russia and some other former Soviet Union (FSU) states found themselves in a 'no-man's land'—collectivist institutions were destroyed, but Western law and order institutions did not take root. Russian trajectory of economic development is placed into the comparative context. It is argued that developing regions that preserved institutional continuity (Middle East, East Asia, and North Africa (MENA), and India) offer better conditions for growth than regions where traditional institutions were largely destroyed (sub-Saharan Africa (SSA), Latin America (LA), and the FSU). If this interpretation is correct, the new growth miracles will happen in MENA countries like Turkey, Iran, and Egypt, whereas Russia (together with LA and SSA) will remain a 'normal' developing country with poor institutions, and mediocre and highly volatile growth.

2 A 'normal' country?

The world economic recession of 2008–9 hit Russia harder than it did other countries. Russia's GDP for 2009 fell by about 8 per cent due to the collapse of oil prices and the outflow of capital caused by world recession—more than US, European, and Japanese GDP (2, 4, and 5 per cent, respectively) and considerably more than the GDP in most emerging market economies that did not experience a recession (China registered growth of 8 per cent, India 6 per cent, the Middle East 2 per cent, and SSA 2 per cent). From 1989 to 1998, Russia experienced a transformational recession—its GDP fell to 55 per cent of the pre-recession 1989 level. In 1999–2008 its economy was recovering at a rate of about 7 per cent a year and barely reached the pre-recession peak of 1989 (see Figure 12.1).[1] Now, with some luck, after 4 per cent growth in 2010, its pre-recession 1989 GDP will be surpassed in the period 2011–12. In sum, therefore, for two 'lost decades' there has been no increase in output.

In 2005, Shleifer and Treisman (2005) published an article entitled 'A Normal Country: Russia after Communism'. They compared Russia with Brazil, China, India, Turkey, and other developing countries, and argued that in terms of crime, income inequalities, corruption, macroeconomic instability, and other curses typical of the Third World, Russia is by far not the worst—indeed, it appears somewhere in the middle of the list, better than Nigeria, although worse than China. In short, Russia is a normal developing country.

The USSR was an abnormal developing country. The Soviet Union put the first man into space and had about 20 Nobel Prize winners in science and literature. Out of about 40 living laureates of the Fields Medal (awarded since 1936 and recognized as the 'Nobel Prize for mathematics'), eight come from the FSU (which had about 5 per cent of the world's population). The USSR had universal free health care and education (the best among developing countries), low income inequality, and relatively low crime and corruption. By 1965, Soviet life expectancy had increased to 70 years—only two years less than in the USA, even though per capita income was only 20–25 per cent of the US level (see Ofer: Chapter 9 in this volume; Goskomstat (various)).

The transition to a market economy in the 1990s brought about the dismantling of the Soviet state: the provision of all public goods, from health care to law and order, fell dramatically. The shadow economy, which the most generous estimates place at 10–15 per cent of the GDP under Brezhnev, grew to 50 per cent of the GDP by the mid-1990s (Kaufmann and Kaliberda 1996; Johnson et al. 1997). In 1980–5, the Soviet Union was placed in the middle of a list of 54 countries rated according to their level of corruption,

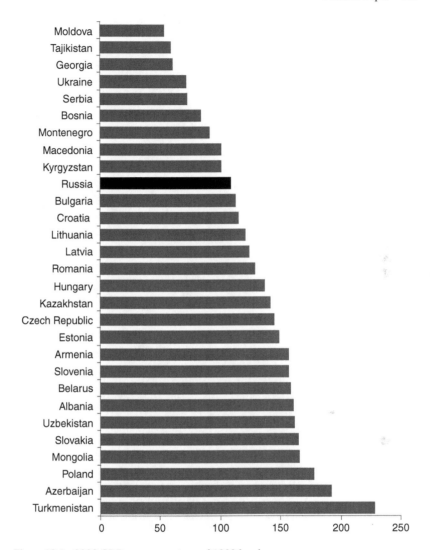

Figure 12.1   2008 GDP as a percentage of 1989 level
Source: Based on EBRD Transition Report 2009 data.

with a bureaucracy cleaner than that of Italy, Greece, Portugal, South Korea, and practically all the developing countries. In 1996, after the establishment of a market economy and the victory of democracy, Russia came in 48th in the same 54-country list, between India and Venezuela.[2]

Income inequalities increased greatly—the Gini coefficient increased from 26 per cent in 1986 to 40 per cent in 2000, and then 42 per cent in 2007

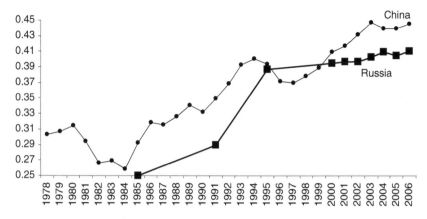

Figure 12.2   Gini coefficient of income distribution in China and Russia, 1978–2006
Source: Based on Chen et al. (2008) and Goskomstat (various) data.

(Figure 12.2). The decile coefficient—the ratio of incomes of the wealthiest 10 per cent of the population to the incomes of the poorest 10 per cent—increased from 8 in 1992 to 14 in 2000, and then to 17 in 2007 (Goskomstat (various)). But the inequalities at the very top increased much faster. In 1995 there was no one in Russia worth over US$1 billion; in 2007, according to *Forbes*, Russia had 53 billionaires, which propelled the country to second or third place in the world in this regard after the USA (415) and Germany (55). Indeed, Russia had two fewer billionaires than Germany, but Russia's were worth a total of US$282 billion (US$37 billion more than Germany's richest). In 2008, right before the recession, the number of billionaires in Russia increased to 86, with a total worth of over US$500 billion—a full third of national GDP. In March 2011, when Russian GDP had not yet recovered to the pre-recession 2008 level, the number of billionaires exceeded 100. Whereas China surpassed Russia in the billionaire headcount (116), it was still behind Russia in terms of the total wealth of billionaires.[3] The Soviet Union was an abnormal developing country: there were no billionaires at all and there were hardly even dollar millionaires (perhaps only a dozen in the shadow economy).

Worst of all, the criminalization of Russian society grew dramatically in the 1990s. Crime had been rising gradually in the Soviet Union since the mid-1960s, but after the collapse of the USSR there was an unprecedented surge—in just a few years in the early 1990s, crime and murder rates doubled and reached one of the highest levels in the world (Figure 12.3). By the mid-1990s, the murder rate stood at over 30 people per 100,000 inhabitants against one to two people in Western Europe (WE) and EE, Canada, China, Japan, Mauritius, and Israel. Only two countries in the world (not counting some war-torn, collapsed states in the developing world) had higher

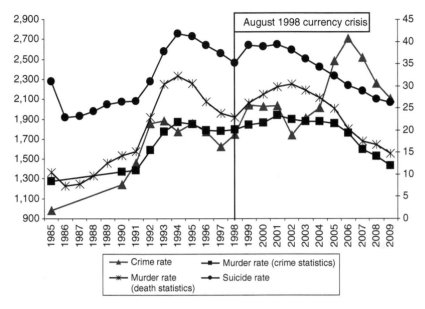

Figure 12.3 Crime rate (left scale), murder rate, and suicide rate (right scale) per 100,000 inhabitants
Source: Based on Goskomstat (various) data.

murder rates—South Africa and Colombia—whereas in countries like Brazil or Mexico it was half the rate. Even the US murder rate, the highest in the developed world—six to seven people per 100,000 inhabitants—pales in comparison with that of Russia.

The Russian rate of deaths from external causes (accidents, murders, and suicides) had, by the beginning of the twenty-first century, skyrocketed to 245 per 100,000 inhabitants. It was higher than in any of the 187 countries covered by World Health Organization (WHO) estimates in 2002, equivalent to 2.45 deaths per 1000 a year (Popov 2007b), or 159 per 1000 over 65 years, which was the average life expectancy in Russia in 2002. Put differently, if these rates were to continue to hold, one out of six Russians born in 2002 would have an 'unnatural' death. To be sure, in the 1980s, murder, suicide, and accidental death rates were already quite high in Russia, Ukraine, Belarus, Latvia, Estonia, Moldova, and Kazakhstan—several times higher than in other former Soviet republics and in the countries of EE. However, they were roughly comparable to those of other countries with the same level of development. In the 1990s, these rates rapidly increased, far outstripping those in the rest of the world. The mortality rate grew from 10 per 1000 in 1990 to 16 per 1000 in 1994, and stayed at a level of 14–16 per 1000 thereafter (Figure 12.4). This was a true mortality crisis—a unique case

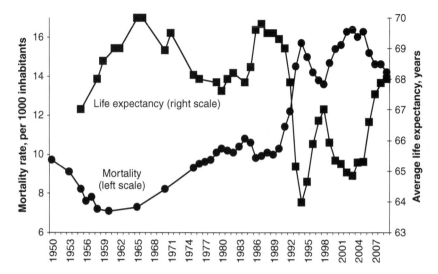

Figure 12.4   Mortality rate (per 1,000, left scale) and average life expectancy (years, right scale)

Source: Based on Goskomstat (various) data.

in history where mortality rates increased by 60 per cent in just five years without any wars, epidemics, or catastrophic volcanic eruptions. Russia had never, in the post-war period, had mortality rates as high as those of the 1990s. Even in 1950–3, during the last years of Stalin's regime, with the high death rates in the labour camps and the consequences of the wartime malnutrition and wounds, the mortality rate was only 9–10 per 1000, as compared with 14–16 in 1994–2008.

Russia became a typical 'petrostate'. Few specialists would call the USSR a resource-based economy, but Russia's industrial structure changed considerably after the transition to the market. For all intents and purposes, the 1990s were the period of rapid deindustrialization and 'resourcialization' of the Russian economy, and the growth of world fuel prices since 1999 seems to have reinforced this trend. The share of output of the major resource industries (fuel, energy, and metals) in total Russian industrial output increased from about 25 per cent to over 50 per cent by the mid-1990s and stayed at this high level thereafter. This was partly the result of changing price ratios (greater price increases in resource industries), but also due to the fact that the real growth rates of output were lower in the non-resource sector. The share of mineral products, metals, and diamonds in Russian exports increased from 52 per cent in 1990 (USSR) to 67 per cent in 1995, and to 81 per cent in 2007, whereas the share of machinery and equipment in exports fell from 18 per cent in 1990 (USSR) to 10 per cent in 1995, and then to below 6 per cent in 2007. The share of spending in research and development was 3.5 per cent of GDP in the late 1980s in the USSR. It fell to 1.1 per cent in Russia by 2007 (compared with 1.3 per cent in China; 2–3 per cent in the USA, Korea, and Japan; 4 per cent in Finland; and 5 per cent in Israel). So today's Russia really looks like a 'normal' resource-abundant developing country.

To understand contemporary Russia, one has to evaluate the record of the last 20 years. In the late 1980s, during Gorbachev's *perestroika* (restructuring), the Soviet Union was aspiring to join the club of rich democratic nations, but instead degraded in the next decade to a position of a normal developing country that is considered neither democratic nor capable of engineering a growth miracle. For some outsiders a 'normal developing country' may look better than the ominous superpower posing a threat to Western values, but the insiders feel differently. Most Russians want to find a way to modernize the country so as to make it prosperous and democratic. However, they also feel that something went very wrong during the transition—the policies and political leaders of the 1990s are totally discredited. To understand the popularity of Putin in 2000–8 and later of Putin–Medvedev in tandem, one has to bear in mind that Putin's policy is the *de facto* denial of the across-the-board-liberalization policies of Yeltsin, his predecessor. It is in essence a modernization project intended to put a halt to the degradation of the 1990s. The actual achievements of 2000–8 may have been modest but they were real: nearly a decade of economic growth; increases in government revenues and spending; accumulation of foreign exchange reserves; decreases in mortality, murder, and suicide rates; and prevention of the disintegration of the country. When Putin was elected president for the first time in 2000, he received 53 per cent of the votes. In 2004 he was elected with 71 per cent of the votes, and over 60 per cent said they would vote for him in September 2007, never mind if he was not going to run. Even in 2009, in the midst of economic recession, Putin–Medvedev policy was getting a 50 per cent-plus approval rate.

3 Short-term perspective: why Russia did worse than other post-communist economies during transition

The debates of the 1990s juxtaposed shock therapy strategy to gradualism. The question of why Russia had to pay a greater price for economic transition was answered differently by those who advocated shock therapy and those who supported gradual piecemeal reforms. Shock therapists argued that much of the costs of the reforms should be attributed to the inconsistencies of the policies followed, namely to slow economic liberalization, and to the inability of the governments and the central banks to fight inflation in the first half of the 1990s. In contrast, the supporters of gradual transition stated exactly the opposite, blaming the attempt to introduce a conventional shock therapy package for all the disasters and misfortunes.

In Popov (2000, 2007a) various explanations of the transformational reces-sion are discussed and the alternative explanation is suggested—the collapse of output was caused primarily by several groups of factors. First were the greater distortions in the industrial structure and external trade patterns on the eve of the transition. Second was the collapse of state and non-state insti-tutions, which occurred in the late 1980s and early 1990s, which resulted in chaotic transformation through crisis management instead of organized and manageable transition. Third were poor economic policies, which basically consisted of bad macroeconomic policy and import substitution industrial policy. Finally, the speed of reforms (economic liberalization) affected perfor-mance negatively at the stage of the reduction in output because enterprises were forced to restructure faster than they possibly could (due to limited investment potential), but positively at the recovery stage.

(1) In the first approximation, economic recession that occurred in FSU states was associated with the need to reallocate resources in order to correct the inefficiencies in industrial structure inherited from a centrally planned economy (CPE). These distortions included overmili-tarization and overindustrialization, perverted trade flows among former Soviet republics and Comecon (CMEA: the Council for Mutual Economic Assistance) countries, and excessively large and poor specialization of industrial enterprises and agricultural farms. In most cases these distor-tions were more pronounced in Russia than in EE—not to speak of China and Vietnam. Thus the larger the distortions, the greater the reduction in output. The transformational recession, to put it in economic terms, was caused by an adverse supply shock similar to that experienced by Western countries after the oil price hikes in 1973 and 1979, and similar to post-war recessions caused by conversion of the defence industries.

As Figure 12.5 shows, the reduction in output in Russia during the transformational recession was to a large extent structural in nature—industries such as light industry, with the greatest adverse supply shock (deteriorating terms of trade, and relative price ratios for outputs and inputs), experienced the largest reduction in output. The evidence for all transition economies is in Table 12.1. Here the reduction in output by coun-try is well explained by the indicator of distortions in industrial structure and trade patterns (it remains statistically significant no matter what con-trol variables are added). The magnitude of distortions, in turn, determines the change in relative prices, when they are deregulated.

The nature of the recession was basically an adverse supply shock caused by the change in relative prices. There was a limit to the speed of reallo-cating capital from non-competitive to competitive industries, which was determined basically by the net investment/GDP ratio (gross investment minus retirement of capital stock in the competitive industries, since in

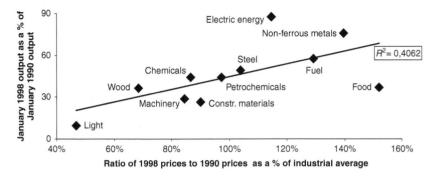

Figure 12.5 Change in relative prices and output in 1990–8 in Russian industry
Source: Popov (2007a).

non-competitive industries the retiring capital stock should not be replaced anyway). It was not reasonable to wipe away output in non-competitive industries faster than capital was being transferred to more efficient industries. Market-type reforms in many post-communist economies created exactly this kind of bottleneck. Countries that followed the shock therapy path found themselves in a supply-side recession that is likely to become a textbook example: an excessive speed of change in relative prices required the magnitude of restructuring that was simply non-achievable with the limited pool of investment. Up to half of their economies was made non-competitive overnight, output in these non-competitive industries was falling for several years and fell in some cases to virtually zero, whereas the growth of output in competitive industries was constrained by, among other factors, the limited investment potential and was not enough to compensate for the output loss in the inefficient sectors (Popov 2000, 2007a).

Hence at least one general conclusion from the study of the experience of transition economies appears to be relevant for the reform process in all countries: provided that reforms create a need for restructuring (reallocation of resources), the speed of those reforms should be such that the magnitude of the required restructuring does not exceed the investment potential of the economy. In short, the speed of adjustment and restructuring in every economy is limited, if only due to the limited investment potential needed to reallocate capital stock. This is the main rationale for gradual, rather than instant, phasing-out of tariff and non-tariff barriers, of subsidies, and of other forms of government support of particular sectors (it took nearly ten years for the European Economic Community or the North American Free Trade Agreement to abolish tariffs). This is a powerful argument against shock therapy, especially when the reforms involved result in a sizeable reallocation of resources. For Western countries with low trade barriers, low subsidies, a low degree of price controls, and so forth, even fast,

Table 12.1 Regression of change in GDP in 1989–96 on initial conditions, policy factors, rule of law, and democracy indexes (robust estimates)

Equations, no. of observations/variables	1, N = 28	2, N = 28	3, N = 28	4, N = 28	5, N = 28	6, N = 28	7, N = 28
Constant	5.3***	5.4***	5.2***	5.4***	5.4***	5.5***	5.7***
Distortions, % of GDP[a]	−0.005**	−0.005**	−0.003	−0.006**	−0.007***	−0.007***	−0.007***
1987 PPP GDP per capita, % of US level	−0.009***	−0.006*	−0.007**	−0.007**	−0.009***	−0.008***	−0.008***
War dummy[b]				−0.19[c]	−0.36***	−0.37***	−0.45***
Decline in government revenues as % of GDP from 1989–91 to 1993–6					−0.011***	−0.011***	−0.011***
Liberalization index			0.05			−0.02	0.03
Log (inflation, % a year, 1990–5, geometric average)	−0.16***	−0.20***	−0.18***	−0.17***	−0.13***	−0.13***	−0.14***
Rule of law index, average for 1989–97, %	0.008***						
Democracy index, average for 1990–8, %	−0.005***						−0.003**
Ratio of rule of law to democracy index		0.07***	0.07***	0.06***	0.05***	0.05***	
Adjusted R^2 %	82	83	83	85	91	91	90

Note: *, **, *** significant at 10, 5 and 1% levels, respectively.

[a] Cumulative measure of distortions as a percentage of GDP equal to the sum of defence expenditure (minus 3% regarded as the 'normal' level), deviations in industrial structure and trade openness from the 'normal' level, the share of heavily distorted trade (among the FSU republics) and lightly distorted trade (with socialist countries) taken with a 33% weight (see Popov 2000 for details).

[b] Equals 1 for Armenia, Azerbaijan, Croatia, Georgia, Macedonia, and Tajikistan, and 0 for all other countries.

[c] Significant at the 13% level. Dependent variable = log (1996 GDP as a percentage of 1989 GDP). For China, all indicators are for the period 1979–86 or similar.

Source: Based on Popov (2000).

radical reforms are not likely to require restructuring that would exceed the limit of investment potential. But for less developed countries with a lot of distortions in their economies supported by explicit and implicit subsidies, fast removal of these subsidies could easily result in such a need for restructuring that is beyond the ability of the economy due to investment and other constraints. However, such a reduction in output due to the inability of the economy to adjust rapidly to new price ratios is by no means inevitable if the deregulation of prices proceeds gradually (or if losses from deteriorating terms of trade for most affected industries are compensated by subsidies). The pace of liberalization has to be no faster than the ability of the economy to move resources from non-competitive (under the new market price ratios) to competitive industries. Therefore, it should be expected that there is a negative relationship between performance and the speed of liberalization. It should also be expected that the larger magnitude of distortions in industrial structure and trade patterns would lead to a greater reduction of output during the transformational recession, but would not have much of an impact on performance during the recovery stage (after the non-competitive sector is shut down completely).

(2) The additional reason for the extreme depth of the transformational recession was associated with the institutional collapse. Here, differences between EE countries and the FSU are striking. The adverse supply shock in this case came from the inability of the state to perform its traditional functions—to collect taxes and to constrain the shadow economy, to ensure property and contract rights, and to uphold law and order in general. Naturally, a poor ability to enforce rules and regulations did not create a business climate conducive to growth and resulted in the increased costs for companies.

The measure of institutional strength is the dynamics of government expenditure during transition. This factor seems to have been far more important than the speed of reforms. In Kolodko's (2004: 259) words, 'there can be no doubt that during the early transition there was a causal relationship between the rapid shrinkage in the size of government and the significant fall in output'. Keeping the government big does not guarantee favourable dynamics of output, since government spending has to be efficient as well. However, the sharp decline in government spending, especially for the 'ordinary government', is a sure recipe to ensure the collapse of institutions and the fall in output accompanied by the growing social inequalities and populist policies.

When real government expenditure falls by 50 per cent and more—as happened in most countries of the Commonwealth of Independent States and Southeast European states in the short period of time under discussion—there is practically no chance to compensate the decrease in the volume of financing by an increase in the efficiency of institutions. As a result, the ability of the state to enforce contracts and property rights, to fight criminalization, and to ensure law and order in general, falls dramatically (Popov 2009a). Thus, the story of the successes and failures of transition is not really the story of consistent shock therapy and inconsistent gradualism. The major plot of the post-socialist transformation 'novel' is the preservation of strong institutions in some countries—from Central Europe (CE) and Estonia to China, Uzbekistan, and Belarus[4]—and the collapse of these institutions in others. At least 90 per cent of this story is about the government failure (strength of state institutions), not about the market failure (liberalization).

It is precisely this strong institutional framework that should be held responsible for both—for the success of gradual reforms in China and shock therapy in Vietnam, where strong authoritarian regimes were preserved and CPE institutions were not dismantled before new market institutions were created; and for the relative success of radical reforms in EE countries, especially in CE countries, where strong democratic regimes and new market institutions emerged quickly. And it is precisely the collapse of the strong state and institutions, which began with the USSR in the late 1980s and continued in the successor states in the 1990s, that explains the extreme length, if not the extreme depth, of the FSU transformational recession.

To put it differently, Gorbachev's reforms of 1985–91 failed not because they were gradual but due to the weakening of the state institutional capacity leading to the inability of the government to control the flow of events. Similarly, Yeltsin's reforms in Russia, as well as economic reforms in most other FSU states, were so costly, not because of the shock therapy, but due to the collapse of the institutions needed to enforce law and order and carry out manageable transition. It turns out that the FSU transition model (with partial exemption of Uzbekistan, Belarus, and Estonia) is based on a most unfortunate combination of unfavourable initial conditions, institutional degradation, and inefficient economic policies, such as macroeconomic populism and import substitution.

What led to the institutional collapse and could it have been prevented? Using the terminology of political science, it is appropriate to distinguish between strong authoritarian regimes (China and Vietnam, and, to an extent, Belarus and Uzbekistan), strong democratic regimes (CE countries), and weak democratic regimes (most FSU and Balkan states). The former two are politically liberal or liberalizing—that is, they protect individual rights, including those of property and contracts, and create a framework of law and administration—while the latter regimes, though democratic, are politically not so liberal since they lack strong institutions and the ability to enforce law and order (Zakaria 1997). This gives rise to the phenomenon of 'illiberal democracies'—countries where competitive elections are introduced before the rule of law is established. While EE countries and East Asian countries recently moved from first establishing the rule of law to gradually introducing democratic elections (Hong Kong is the most obvious example of the rule of law without democracy), in Latin America, Africa, and CIS countries, democratic political systems were introduced into societies without the firm rule of law.

Authoritarian regimes (including communist ones), while gradually building property rights and institutions, were filling the vacuum in the rule of law via authoritarian means. After democratization occurred and illiberal democracies emerged, they found themselves deprived of old authoritarian instruments to ensure law and order, but without the newly developed democratic mechanisms needed to guarantee property rights, contracts, and law and order in general. It is no surprise that this had a devastating impact on the investment climate and output. There is a clear relationship between the ratio of rule of law index on the eve of transition to democratization index, on the one hand, and economic performance during transition, on the other. To put it differently, democratization without strong rule of law, whether one likes it or not, usually leads to the collapse of output. There is a price to pay for early democratization; that is, the introduction of competitive elections of government under conditions when major liberal rights (personal freedom and safety, property, contracts, fair trial in court, and so on) are not well established.

If Russia would take the Chinese way—gradual economic liberalization under an authoritarian regime establishing firm rule of law before democratization—the results of the Russian transition would not be so disappointing. Borrowing Gérard Roland's expression, one can say that 'if Putin would have come before Yeltsin', Russian transition could have been more successful.

(3) Finally, performance was of course affected by economic policy. Given the weak institutional capacity of the state—that is, its poor ability to enforce its own regulations—economic policies could hardly be 'good'. Weak state institutions usually imply populist macroeconomic policies (budget deficits resulting in high indebtedness and/or inflation, and over-valued exchange rates), which have a devastating impact on output. On the other hand, strong institutional capacity does not lead automatically to responsible economic policies. Examples range from the USSR before it collapsed (periodic outburst of open or hidden inflation) to such post-Soviet states as Uzbekistan and Belarus, which seem to have stronger institutional potential than other FSU states but do not demonstrate greater macroeconomic stability.

Regressions tracing the impact of all mentioned factors are reported in Table 12.1 (Popov 2000). Some 80–90 per cent of the variations in the dynamics of GDP in 1989–96 could be explained by the initial conditions (distortions and initial GDP per capita), institutional capacity of the state (decline in government revenues, and rule of law and democracy indexes), and macroeconomic stability (inflation). If the rule of law and democracy indexes are included in the basic regression equation, they have predicted signs (positive impact of the rule of law and negative impact of democracy) and are statistically significant (equation 1), which is consistent with the results obtained for a larger sample of countries.[5] The best explanatory power, however, is exhibited by the index that is computed as the ratio of the rule of law index to the democracy index: 83 per cent of all variations in output can be explained by only three factors: pre-transition distortions, inflation, and the rule-of-law-to-democracy index (Table 12.1, equation 2). If a liberalization variable is added, it turns out to be statistically insignificant and does not improve the goodness of fit (equation 3). At the same time, the ratio of the rule of law to the democracy index and the decline in government revenues are not substitutes but rather complement each other in explaining the process of the institutional decay. These two variables are not correlated and improve the goodness of fit when included together in the same regression: R^2 increases to 91 per cent (equation 5)— a better result than in regressions with either one of these variables. The liberalization index, when added to the same equation, is not statistically significant and has the 'wrong' sign.

To test the robustness of the results, another year, 1998, for the end of the transformational recession was chosen so that the period considered was 1989–98 (by the end of 1998 the absolute trough was reached in 24 out of 26 countries that experienced the recession). The adjusted R^2 is slightly lower but the statistical significance of the coefficients remains high (with the exception of the initial GDP per capita). The best equation is

$$Log(Y98/89) = 5.8 - .006DIST - 0.005Ycap87 - 0.39WAR$$
$$(-2.48)\qquad (-0.09)\qquad (-3.22)$$
$$- 0.01GOVREVdecline - 0.17logINFL - .003DEM$$
$$(-2.94)\qquad\qquad (-4.60)\qquad\quad (-1.74)$$

N = 28, adjusted R^2 = 82%, T-statistics in brackets, and all variables are shown in the same order as in equation 7 from Table 12.1 (liberalization variable is omitted).

Once again, if the liberalization variable is introduced in this equation, it turns out to be insignificant.

(4) Finally, to deal with the endogeneity problem (liberalization affects performance but is also affected by performance; if output falls, liberalization is very likely to be halted), the liberalization variable was instrumented with the democracy level variable (Popov 2007a). The results are in Table 12.2. The main difference from Table 12.1 is that liberalization now affects performance significantly and negatively.

Table 12.2 2SLS robust estimates: regression of change in GDP in 1989–96 on initial conditions, institutional capacity, liberalization, rule of law, and democracy indexes (liberalization index instrumented with the democracy level variable)

Equations, no. of observations/variables	1, $N = 28$	2, $N = 28$	3, $N = 17$	4, $N = 17$
Constant	6.4***	6.3***	6.0***	6.0***
Pre-transition distortions, % of GDP	−0.01***	−0.02***		−0.004
1987 PPP GDP per capita, % of the US level	−0.007**	−0.01***		
War dummy[a]	−0.45***	−0.29[b]		
Liberalization index in 1995	−0.18**	−0.39*	−0.19***	−0.19***
Decline in government revenues as % of GDP from 1989–91 to 1993–6	−0.02***	−0.02***		
Log (inflation, % a year, 1990–5, geometric average)	−1.7***	−0.22***	−0.22***	−0.19***
Rule of law index, average for 1989–97, %		−0.01[c]		
Increase in share of shadow economy in GDP in 1989–94, pp			−0.02***	−0.015***
R2 %	86	77	88	90

Note: *, **, *** significant at 1, 5, and 10% levels, respectively.
[a]Equals 1 for Armenia, Azerbaijan, Croatia, Georgia, Macedonia, and Tajikistan and 0 for all other countries.
[b]Significant at 12% level.
[c]Significant at 16% level. Dependent variable = log (1996 GDP as a percentage of 1989 GDP). For China, all indicators are for the period 1979–86 or similar.
Source: See text for explanation.

As argued by Popov (2007a), at the recovery stage (1998–2005), the impact of distortions on performance disappears but the influence of institutions persists, and the impact of the speed of liberalization (increment increase in liberalization index) becomes positive and significant. This is very much in line with the intuition—after the non-competitive sector is eradicated at the stage of transformation recession, further liberalization (which inevitably becomes gradual at this point) cannot do much harm, whereas institutional capacity always affects growth. We end up with a matrix that summarizes the factors affecting performance during transition (Table 12.3). The FSU in general (there are some exceptions), and Russia in particular, had poor initial conditions—allocation of resources by industries and regions under central planning was very different from market type so when prices were deregulated, and allowed to govern the allocation of capital and labour, sizeable restructuring occurred, leading to a recession. To add insult to injury, there was a dramatic decline in the institutional capacity of the state.

Table 12.3   Initial conditions (distortions) and institutions: classification of countries

Distortions / Institutional capacity	Low	High
High	China, Vietnam	Eastern Europe
Low	Albania, Mongolia	FSU

Source: See text for explanation.

4   The mystery of the genesis of institutions

The matrix leaves us with a frustrating conclusion that the bulk of the recession of the 1990s was inevitable (initial conditions and institutions are exogenous, given by preceding developments) and economic policy (fast liberalization at early stages of development and poor macroeconomic policy) more often than not aggravated the recession. Besides, today, after the transformational recession, the prospects for the future seem to depend mostly on institutional capacity, which is the binding constraint for growth. With respect to distortions, gradual liberalization should have allowed the avoidance of the collapse of output. But would it have been possible to preserve strong institutions, as happened in EE and China?

Manufacturing growth is like cooking a good dish—all the ingredients need to be in the right proportions; if only one is under- or over-represented, the 'chemistry of growth' will not happen. Fast economic growth can materialize in practice only if several necessary conditions are met simultaneously. In particular, rapid growth requires a number of crucial inputs: infrastructure, human capital, even land distribution in agrarian countries, strong state institutions, and economic stimuli, among other things. Once one of these crucial necessary ingredients is missing, the growth simply does not take off. Rodrik et al. (2005) talk about 'binding constraints' that hold back economic growth; finding these constraints is the task of 'growth diagnostics'. In some cases, these constraints are associated with the lack of market liberalization; in others, with the lack of state capacity, or human capital or infrastructure.

By the end of the 1970s, China had virtually everything that was needed for growth except for the liberalization of some markets (a much more easily introduced ingredient than human capital or institutional capacity). But even the seemingly simple task of economic liberalization required careful management. The USSR was in a similar position in the late 1980s. True, the Soviet system lost its economic and social dynamism, the growth rates in the 1960s to 1980s were falling, life expectancy was not rising, and crime rates were slowly growing, but institutions were generally strong and human capital was large, which provided good starting conditions for reform. Nevertheless, economic liberalization in China (since 1979) and in the USSR, and later Russia (since 1989), produced markedly different outcomes (Popov 2000, 2007a). Why did economic liberalization work in CE but not in SSA and LA? The answer, according to the outlined approach, would be that in CE the missing ingredient was economic liberalization, whereas in SSA and LA there was a lack of state capacity, not a lack of market liberalization. Why did liberalization work in China and CE but not in the CIS? It was because in the CIS it was carried out in such a way as to undermine state capacity—the precious heritage of socialist past—whereas in CE, and even more so in China, state capacity did not decline substantially during transition. The trick of transition, as is evident *post factum*, was not simply to carry out economic liberalization but to carry it out in such a way as to not throw the baby away with the bath water—not to squander the precious achievements of the previous communist period in the form of strong institutions. China generally did not squander this heritage (even though government spending fell, income inequalities rose, and crime rates increased), whereas Russia and most other CIS states did.

Here lies a crucial question How did some former communist countries retain their strong institutions during reforms, whereas in other countries institutional capacity, even if previously high, deteriorated? How did EE and China manage to preserve relatively strong institutions during economic liberalization, whereas in Russia state institutions collapsed? Part of the answer is the impact of democratization on the quality of institutions. As argued in previous studies (Polterovich and Popov 2007; Polterovich et al. 2007, 2008; Zakaria 1997), democratization carried out in a poor rule of law environment (weak state institutions) is associated with further weakening of institutions and with worsening of macroeconomic policy, which has a negative impact on growth and does not allow for the creation of a stable democratic regime, especially in resource-rich countries.[6] This is only part of the answer, however, because there are few examples of fast catch-up development under democratic regimes (Japan after the Second World War, and Botswana and Mauritius after gaining independence in the 1960s). Besides, democracy is an institution by itself, and it remains to be explained why some countries adopted it at earlier stages of development whereas others stayed authoritarian, or returned to authoritarianism, after short-lived experiments with democracy. And finally, differences in the institutional capacity of the state in countries with authoritarian regimes (e.g. China, USSR, and Russia) are huge and need to be explained.

5 Long-term perspective: institutional continuity versus transplantation of foreign institution

A possible interpretation of the genesis of the institutions in colonized and non-colonized countries is the continuity perspective (Popov 2009b). All countries had traditional community structures in the past: everywhere before the Reformation, under the Malthusian growth regime, the law of the land was what we now call 'Asian values'—the superiority of the interests of the community over the interests of the individuals.

Colonization of SSA, South America, and, to a lesser extent, South Asia led to complete or near-complete destruction of traditional (community) structures that were only partially replaced by the new Western-style institutions. Among large geographical regions, only East Asia, MENA, and, to an extent, South Asia managed to retain traditional community institutions despite colonialism. It could be hypothesized that those countries and regions that preserved traditional institutions in difficult times of colonialism and imposition of Western values retained a better chance in the catch-up development than the less fortunate regions of the world's periphery, where the continuity of traditional structures was interrupted. Transplantation of institutions is a tricky business that works well only when tailored to the local traditions so that it does not interrupt the institutional continuity (Polterovich 2001). Otherwise it leads either to complete elimination of the local structures (the USA, Canada, and Australia) or to a non-viable mixture of old and new institutions that is not very conducive to growth (SSA and LA). The 'misuse of institutions' discussed by Polishchuk (Chapter 7 in this volume) is more likely to occur when institutional continuity is violated.

If the institutional capacity of the state is defined as the ability of the government to enforce rules and regulations, one of the natural measurement indicators is the murder rate. Crimes are registered differently in different countries: higher crime rates in developed countries seem to be the result of better registration of crimes. But grave crimes, like murder, appear to be registered pretty accurately even in developing countries, so international comparison of the murder rates is well warranted. Among countries in transition, Russia experienced the greatest increase in the murder rate: it quadrupled during 1987–2002, increasing from 8 to 33 per 100,000 inhabitants (Figure 12.6). In EE countries and most FSU states, the increases were much less pronounced. China during 1979–2009 also managed to better preserve the strong state institutions, and its murder rate is still below 3 per 100,000 inhabitants compared with about 30 in Russia in 2002, and about 20 in 2008 (Popov 2007b). The national statistics on murders under the Mao regime are not available, but there are data for some provinces. In the 1970s the murder rate in the Shandong province was less than 1 (Shandong 2009), and in 1987 it was estimated at 1.5 for the whole of China (WHO 2004). The WHO reported ratio for 2004 is 2.1 (WHO site), whereas the United Nations Office on Drugs and Crime reports a murder rate of 1.2 to 2.6 in 2003–07 (UNODC Homicide Statistics Trends, 2003–8). A two- to threefold increase in the murder rate during the market reforms is comparable with the Russian increase, but the Chinese levels are nowhere near those of Russia.

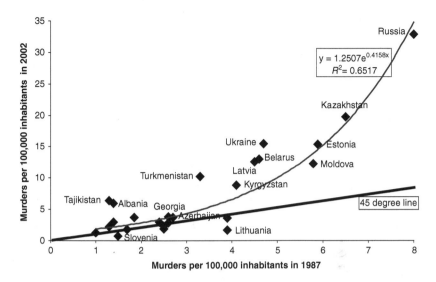

Figure 12.6 Murder rate before and after transition in EE countries and FSU
Source: WHO (2004) data.

It took Western countries 500 years to bring the murder rates from about 100 to just a few (1–3) per 100,000 inhabitants (Figure 12.7). Even in the seventeenth century the murder rates in WE were generally exceeding 10 per 100,000 inhabitants—more than in many developing countries with similar levels of GDP per capita today. In fact among developing countries today we find two major patterns: low murder rates (1–3 per 100,000 inhabitants) in EE, China, and MENA countries; and high murder rates (15–75 murders per 100,000 inhabitants) in FSU, LA, and SSA. India (5.5), and South East Asian countries (about 10, with the exception of Philippines where the rate is 21) fall in between the two groups. The argument is that countries that preserved collectivist institutions (East Asia, MENA countries, and India) were able to retain the institutional capacity of the state, whereas countries that eliminated these institutions while only partly replacing them with an individual responsibility system (the FSU, LA, and SSA) paid a high price in terms of diminished institutional capacity. EE (with the exception of FSU states) could be the exception that proves the rule: it went through a period of low institutional capacity with high murder rates, as did WE between the fifteenth and seventeenth centuries. Although direct evidence here is lacking, all observations for Figure 12.8 are from WE (England, Belgium, Netherlands, Scandinavia, and Italy).[7] By European standards at the time, Russia had a very high murder rate (up to 10 or more per 100,000 inhabitants) at the beginning of the twentieth century, before the first (1905–7) and second (1917) Russian revolutions (Figure 12.9). By the 1960s it was

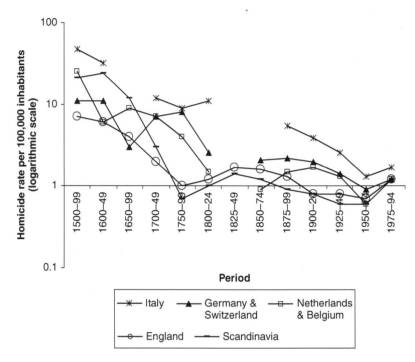

Figure 12.7   Long-term homicide rates in Europe per 100,000 inhabitants
Note: Overall trend in homicide rates, all pre-modern local estimates and four national series. All 398 local estimates from the History of Homicide Database; national series for Sweden, England and Wales, Switzerland, and Italy.
Source: Based on Eisner (2003).

down to 5–7 murders per 100,000 inhabitants, even though mortality from other external causes increased markedly. By the mid-1960s, however, it was on the rise, approaching early twentieth-century levels by the mid-1980s at about 10 murders per 100,000 inhabitants.

Further evidence of the cost of breakdown in institutional continuity comes from data on income inequality in pre-modern societies. The destruction of communal, collectivist institutions that was first carried out in Western countries during the sixteenth to nineteenth centuries was accompanied by an increase in income inequalities. The available data (Milanovic et al. 2007) suggest that in England, Holland, and Spain in the eighteenth century the Gini coefficient of income distribution was at a level of 50 or even 60 per cent[8]—extremely high compared with today's standards and, most probably, compared with the standards of the distant past (about 40 per cent in Rome in the first century and in Byzantium in the eleventh century).[9]

The income inequality story for developing countries is quite consistent with the dynamics of the institutional capacity—in SSA, LA, FSU, where institutional continuity was interrupted and institutional capacity

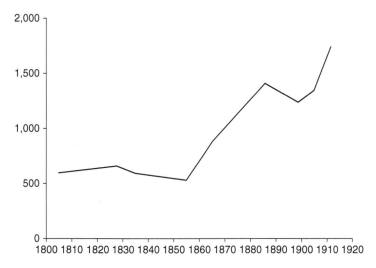

Figure 12.8   Number of all crimes per 100,000 persons in Russia in 1800–1920
Source: Based on Turchin and Nefedov (2009: 285); reproduced with the permission of Princeton University Press.

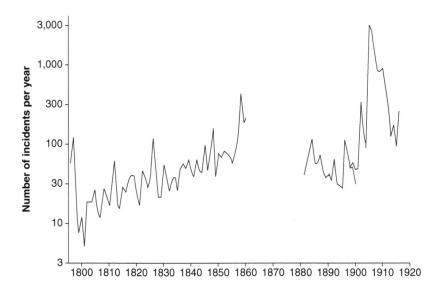

Figure 12.9   Dynamics of peasant disturbances
Source: Turchin and Nefedov (2009: 285); reproduced with the permission of Princeton University Press.

weakened, inequalities increased and still remain high today. Regressions, linking pre-statistical Gini coefficients of income distribution to per capita GDP, population density, urbanization, and colonial status (plus some variables to control for the different quality of the data), suggest that colonialism increased inequalities greatly: colonies had Gini coefficients nearly 13 percentage points higher than non-colonies. In LA, as a whole, inequalities increased from 22.5 per cent in 1491 to over 60 per cent in 1929 (Williamson 2009). In contrast, India, China, and Japan in the eighteenth and nineteenth centuries had a more balanced income distribution (Pomeranz 2000; Saito 2009; Popov 2009b).[10] In MENA, EE, India, and East Asia (especially until the 1990s), inequalities were noticeably lower. Income inequalities, of course, go together with weak institutional capacity, as measured by the murder rate (Popov 2009b).

To summarize, there are two ways to escape the Malthusian trap: (1) by eliminating collectivist institutions and allowing for the costly increase in income inequalities and savings/investment rate at the very early stage of development, at the expense of the consumption of the masses; and (2) by maintaining collectivist institutions and keeping the income inequalities relatively low until slow technological progress and a rise in productivity allows a state to begin accumulating capital at a pace surpassing population growth rates. The first route was adopted by countries that are now called Western and was associated with dramatic social costs between the sixteenth and eighteenth centuries. Moreover, it was imposed on part of the developing world in the nineteenth and twentieth centuries during an era of colonialism. In the developing world this westernization attempt created an institutional vacuum—traditional, collectivist structures were destroyed, whereas the new modern institutions did not take root, which led to even greater costs than several centuries before in the West.

In contrast, those developing countries that managed to resist the westernization of their institutions and to preserve institutional continuity as well as relatively low inequalities (East Asia, MENA countries, and India) did not gain much in terms of economic growth before the mid-1900s, but they were better positioned to take advantage of growth opportunities as soon as natural increases in productivity allowed them to exit the Malthusian trap. The other countries that destroyed their egalitarian institutions prematurely (replicating the Western path) experienced a tremendous decline in institutional capacity and an increase in inequalities. In India, China, and SSA, this path was associated with periodic mass famines, which did not happen before colonialism due to the even distribution of limited food resources by the community institutions.[11] In more developed LA countries the growth rates in the twentieth century did not allow for the gap with the West to be narrowed (Argentina, a developed country in between the two world wars, even fell out of the club after the Second World War). In short, premature dismantling of collectivist institutions, even when allowing countries to overcome the Malthusian trap, did not allow for healthy growth:

> The frequent claim that inequality promotes accumulation and growth does not get much support from history. On the contrary, great economic inequality has always been correlated with extreme concentration of political power, and that power has always been used to widen the income gaps through rent-seeking and rent-keeping, forces that demonstrably retard economic growth.
>
> (Milanovic et al. 2007)

This explains differences in the long-term development trajectory of institutions in China and Russia. The Chinese 1949 Liberation was similar to the Russian revolution of 1917, not only because communists came to power in both countries but because traditional collectivist institutions, ruined by preceding westernization, were re-established and strengthened. However, in Russia between 1917 and 1991 the communist regime just interrupted the process of transplantation of Western institutions that had been going on since at least the seventeenth century, whereas in China the Liberation of 1949 just returned the country to a long-term institutional trajectory that was briefly (and only partly) interrupted after the Opium Wars.

In Russia, capitalist development speeded up after the Emancipation Act of 1861 (elimination of serfdom). Income inequalities (Table 12.4), crime rates, and the number of peasant disturbances all increased sharply in the late nineteenth to early twentieth century. By 1917, Russia was on a Latin American track of reaching income inequalities with Gini coefficients of over 60 per cent and murder rates of several dozen per 100,000 inhabitants.

To put it differently, Russia had already been westernized before 1917, and collectivist institutions that were introduced in Russia as a result of the 1917 revolution had been largely alien to previous long-term institutional development. China, on the other hand, aborted the unsuccessful westernization attempt (1840s to 1949) and returned to collectivist (Asian values) institutions. What was a passing episode and deviation from the trend in Russia was

Table 12.4 Increase in inequalities in Russia, 1600–1900 (social structure of Russian peasantry, percentage of total)

Years	Wealthy	Middle	Poor
1600–1750	15	53	32
1751–1800	10	48	42
1801–60	16	56 ↓	30
1896–1900	18	23	59

Source: Turchin and Nefedov (2009: 277); reproduced with the permission of Princeton University Press.

a return to mainstream development and a restoration of a long-term trend in China. Hence, economic liberalization from 1979 onwards in China, even though accompanied by growing income inequalities, and crime and murder rates, has not resulted so far in institutional collapse.

6   Conclusions

After allowing for differing initial conditions, it turns out that the fall in output in transition economies was associated mostly with poor business environment, resulting from institutional collapse. Liberalization alone, when it is not complemented with strong institutions, cannot ensure good performance. Institutional capacities in turn depend to a large extent on the combination of the rule of law and democracy. The data seem to suggest that both authoritarian and democratic regimes can have strong rule of law and can deliver efficient institutions, whereas under a weak rule of law authoritarian regimes do a better job of maintaining efficient institutions than democracies. To put it in a shorter form, the record of illiberal democracies in ensuring institutional capacities is the worst, which predictably has a devastating impact on output.

Why do illiberal democracies emerge and why did Russia become one of them? It has been argued that the group of developing countries that willingly and unwillingly (via colonialism) transplanted Western institutions (LA, the FSU, and SSA) ended up with high income inequalities and an apparent lack of institutional capacity. In contrast, the other group of developing countries—regions that have never really departed from the collectivist institutions and preserved institutional continuity (EA, India, and MENA)—succeeded in maintaining low income and wealth inequalities. This second group of countries may have stayed in the Malthusian growth regime longer than others but, once technical progress allowed them to exit from the Malthusian trap, their starting conditions for economic growth in terms of institutional capacity turned out to be better than in the first group. If this interpretation is correct, the next large regions of successful catch-up development will be MENA Islamic countries (Turkey, Iran, Egypt, and so forth) and South Asia (India), whereas LA, SSA, and Russia will fall behind.

Acknowledgements

My gratitude for their most helpful comments goes to Perry Anderson, Jack Goldstone, Gérard Roland, Osamu Saito, Yoshikazu Suzuki, Harry Wu, two anonymous referees, and the participants of the UNU-WIDER conference Reflections on Transition: Twenty Years after the Fall of The Berlin Wall in September 2009 in Helsinki, where this study was first presented. The usual disclaimers apply.

Notes

1. Figure 12.1 is based on GDP indexes (2008 as a percentage of 1989) reported in the *EBRD Transition Report 2009*, whereas Figure 12.2 reports chain indexes (based on annual growth rates) from the same source. The discrepancies are not that substantial.
2. Transparency International http://www.icgg.org/corruption.cpi_olderindices_overview.html.
3. Forbes website: http://www.forbes.com/wealth/billionaires
4. Countries like Belarus and Uzbekistan fall into the same group with CE countries and Estonia—with a small reduction of state expenditure as a percentage of GDP during transition, good quality of governance, little bribery, a small shadow economy, and a low state capture index (Hellman et al. 2000). In 2005, Belarus and the Slovak Republic were the only two countries out of 25 surveyed in EE and the FSU (Business Environment and Economic Performance Survey) where significant improvement was registered in 2002–5 in all seven areas of economic governance (judiciary, fighting crime and corruption, customs and trade, business licensing and permits, labour regulations, tax administration); EBRD (2005).
5. For a larger sample of countries (all developing and developed countries, not only transition economies), the result is that there is a threshold level of the rule of law index: if it is higher than a certain level, democratization affects growth positively; if lower, democratization impedes growth (Polterovich and Popov 2007). For the regressions reported in Table 12.1 (to explain changes in output in 1989–96), averages of rule of law and democracy indexes were used for the longer period (1989–98) to account for the fact that business agents often anticipate changes in business climate that are captured in experts' estimates only later.
6. When growth of GDP per capita in 1975–99, y, is regressed on the usual control variables (initial income levels, population growth rates, population density, and investment/GDP ratios) and various indicators of institutional quality (share of shadow economy, World Bank indexes of rule of law, government effectiveness, and so on, corruption perception indexes from Transparency International, investment risk indexes) and democratization (increase in democratic ratings from Freedom House), the best result is usually the threshold equation, like

$$y = \text{CONST.} + \text{CONTR. VAR.} + 0.18\Delta(RL - 0.72),$$

where Δ = democratization (change in index of political rights in 1970–2000), and RL = rule of law index (one of the indicators of the institutional capacity).
7. Other anecdotal evidence of the strength of the collective institutions in East Asia, South Asia, and MENA countries is the virtual absence of urban slums (Pomeranz 2008) and homeless children, which are found in abundance in LA, SSA, and the FSU.
8. In England and Wales the Gini coefficient increased from 46 per cent in 1688 to 53 per cent in the 1860s (Saito 2009).
9. Very high income inequalities in low-income countries mean that a lot of people find themselves in extreme poverty, below subsistence level, which leads to high mortality.

10. In Japan the Gini coefficient allegedly increased from 34 per cent in 1860 to 56 per cent in 1940, but then fell to 30–40 per cent in the period 1960 to the 1990s (Saito 2009).
11. 'Even before the onset of the Victorian famines, warning signals were in place: C. Walford showed in 1878 that the number of famines in the first century of British rule had already exceeded the total recorded cases in the previous two thousand years. But the grim reality behind claims to "good governance" truly came to light in the very decades that Ferguson trumpets. According to the most reliable estimates, the deaths from the 1876–78 famine were in the range of *six to eight million*, and in the double-barrelled famine of 1896–97 and 1899–1900, they probably totalled somewhere in the range of *17 to 20 million*. So in the quarter century that marks the pinnacle of colonial good governance, famine deaths average at least a million per year.' (Chibber 2005). In China, famines claimed 8000 lives a year in 1644–1795, 92,000 lives in 1796–1871, 260,000 lives in 1871–1911, and 583,000 lives in 1911–47. The 1876–9 famine alone took at least 10 million lives—more than all preceding famines since 1644 (Xia Mingfang calculations cited in Pomeranz 2008).

References

Chen, J., W. Hou and S. Jin (2008) 'The Effects of Population on Income Disparity in a Dual Society: Evidence from China', Economic Association annual conference in Cambridge, UK, and the Hong Kong Economic Association Fifth Biennial Conference, Chengdu, China.

Chibber, V. (2005) 'The Good Empire: Should We Pick Up where the British Left Off?', *Boston Review*, February/March 2005.

Eisner, M. (2003) 'Long-Term Historical Trends in Violent Crime', mimeo, University of Chicago.

Goskomstat (various) Federal State Statistics Service of RF (http://www.gks.ru/wps/portal/english), Goskomstat: Moscow.

Hellman, J., G. Jones and D. Kaufmann (2000) 'How Profitable Is Buying the State Officials in Transition Economies?', *Transition: The Newsletter About Reforming Economies*, April: 8–11.

Johnson, S., D. Kaufmann and A. Shleifer (1997) 'The Unofficial Economy in Transition', Brookings Papers on Economic Activity, Fall.

Kaufmann, D. and A. Kaliberda (1996) 'Integrating the Unofficial Economy into the Dynamics of Post-Socialist Economies', *World Bank Policy Research Working Paper No. 1691*.

Kolodko, G.W. (2004) *From Shock to Therapy. Political Economy of Postsocialist Transformation*, Oxford University Press for UNU-WIDER: New York.

Milanovic, B., P.H. Lindert and J.G. Williamson (2007) 'Pre-industrial Inequality: An Early Conjectural Map', mimeo, 23 August.

Polterovich, V. (2001) 'Transplantation of Economic Institutions', *Economics of Contemporary Russia*, 3: 24–50, in Russian, Полтерович В.М. Трансплантация экономических институтов // *Экономическая наука современной России*.

Polterovich, V. and V. Popov (2007) 'Democratization, Quality of Institutions and Economic Growth', in N. Dinello and V. Popov (eds) *Political Institutions and Development: Failed Expectations and Renewed Hopes*, Edward Elgar: Cheltenham.

Polterovich, V., V. Popov and A. Tonis (2007) 'Resource Abundance, Political Corruption, and Instability of Democracy', *NES Working Paper WP/2007/73*.

Polterovich, V., V. Popov and A. Tonis (2008) 'Mechanisms of Resource Curse, Economic Policy and Growth', *NES Working Paper WP/2008/082*.

Pomeranz, K. (2000) *The Great Divergence: Europe, China, and the Making of the Modern World Economy*, Princeton University Press: Princeton, NJ.

Pomeranz, K. (2008) 'Chinese Development in Long-Run Perspective', *Proceedings of the American Philosophical Society*, 152(1): 57–82.

Popov, V. (2000) 'Shock Therapy versus Gradualism: The End of the Debate (Explaining the Magnitude of the Transformational Recession)', *Comparative Economic Studies*, 42(1): 1–57.

Popov, V. (2007a) 'Shock Therapy versus Gradualism Reconsidered: Lessons from Transition Economies after 15 Years of Reforms', *Comparative Economic Studies*, 49(1): 1–31.

Popov, V. (2007b) 'China's Rise, Russia's Fall: Medium-Term Perspective', *TIGER Working Paper No. 99*, TIGER: Warsaw, published subsequently in *História e Economia Revista Interdisciplinar*, 3(1–2).

Popov, V. (2009a) 'Lessons from the Transition Economies: Putting the Success Stories of the Postcommunist World into a Broader Perspective', *WIDER Research Paper No. 2009/15*, UNU-WIDER: Helsinki.

Popov, V. (2009b) 'Why the West Became Rich before China and Why China Has Been Catching Up with the West Since 1949: Another Explanation of the "Great Divergence" and "Great Convergence" Stories', *NES/CEFIR Working Paper No. 132*.

Rodrik, D., R. Hausmann and A. Velasco (2005) 'Growth Diagnostics', mimeo, John F. Kennedy School of Government, Harvard University.

Saito, O. (2009) 'Income Growth and Inequality over the Very Long Run: England, India and Japan Compared', paper presented at the *First International Symposium of Comparative Research on Major Regional Powers in Eurasia 10 July, Sapporo*.

Shandong (2009) Shandong Province database (Shandong sheng shengqing ziliaoku), available at http://www.infobase.gov.cn/bin/mse.exe?seachword=&K=a&A=16&rec=42&run=13 http://bbs.tiexue.net/post_1207004_1.html.

Turchin, P. and S. Nefedov (2009) *Secular Cycles*, Princeton University Press: Princeton, NJ.

Shleifer, A. and D. Triesman (2005) 'A Normal Country: Russia after Communism', *Journal of Economic Perspectives*, 19(1): 151–74.

WHO (2004) *Health for All Database*, available at http://www.euro.who.int/en/what-we-do/data-and-evidence/databases/european-health-for-all-database-hfa-db2.

Williamson, J.G. (2009) 'History without Evidence: Latin American Inequality since 1491', *Georg-August-Universität Göttingen Discussion Paper No. 3*.

Zakaria, F. (1997) 'The Rise of Illiberal Democracies', *Foreign Affairs*, 76(6): 22–43.

13
The Travails of Unification: East Germany's Economic Transition since 1989

Charles S. Maier

1 Introduction

It might have been thought that, at least in economic terms, no post-1989 transition should have been easier than that in East Germany. An economy that was an industrial powerhouse for the Comecon (CMEA: the Council for Mutual Economic Assistance) states fell into the lap of the most powerful West European economy in 1990. It thereby acquired a highly developed legal regime for private property, which other East European economies had to develop from a more rudimentary base. Within a couple of years, perhaps the most highly developed and detailed regime of social welfare and protection in the west was extended to its citizens.[1] And yet the former German Democratic Republic (GDR) had (and has had continuing) difficulties, and even today seems to lag behind West German standards. I write 'seems to lag' because the most recent assessment proposes that the results are really stronger than usually depicted.[2] Nonetheless, as of 2008, before the current crisis really hit, the East German unemployment rate was 13.1 per cent compared with 6.4 per cent in the west. Although the East German population is approximately 20 per cent of Germany's as a whole, labour market expedients were needed far more in the east. A third of those workers in job retraining, and a half of those in various short-term job-creation schemes, which the unemployed had to accept to retain long-term benefits, were in the east. And even the most optimistic assessment must take into account the fact that the stabilization of living conditions involved the continuing emigration of Germans, especially younger ones, from east to west. Politically the transition proved relatively easy, although right-radical outbursts against immigrant workers sullied civic life for several years. Economically, transition proved far more difficult than was expected at the outset. Any serious inquiry must explain this disappointment.

As with most phenomena in economic history, several explanations can be (and have been) proposed. Indeed, the outcome might be thought of as over-determined. Alleged factors have included East Germany's long-standing failure to match the productivity growth of the West German economy; the currency settlement at the time of unification; the possibly misconceived policies of the agency given control of the GDR's state enterprises, the Treuhandanstalt; and even the lack of entrepreneurial vigour among the East German populace. Let us consider these in turn.

The stark fact is that the GDR economy had a lower productivity growth than the Federal Republic of Germany (FRG) at the end of the 1940s and never caught up, although per capita growth probably outpaced the FRG during the 1970s when many Western economies suffered prolonged stagflation.[3] However, GDR total factor productivity fell behind again sharply in the 1980s. As of 1987, value added per person employed in East German manufacturing seems to have been 30.5 per cent of the West German level and 21.4 per cent of the US level (Van Ark 1995: 89). Overall productivity in manufacturing at least continues to lag in the east, and it does so across firm sizes and ages as well. Even a comparison of firms with equivalent knowledge assets (patents) confirms a productivity gap. The only factor that lowers the differential is ownership by a West German company. Becoming a subsidiary makes East German firms shape up, or perhaps the East German firms that have performed better are the ones to have attracted West German purchasers (Czarnitzky 2005: 211–31). Recent investigations have suggested that the federal government may even have subsidized too much innovation among the small and medium-sized East German manufacturing firms for their own good (Czarnitzky and Kraft 2006). Whereas in the west, research and development (R&D) expenditures (as a percentage of sales) had a linear positive impact on credit ratings and thus expectations of future firm performance, this relationship did not hold in the east. Rather, R&D, provided in large measure by government subsidies, was thought to overburden a firm's prospects. The harder you try, in effect, the less profitable you are expected to be. Still, it cannot be the utilization of available R&D that has contributed to the overall gloom. While all these factors have been present, I think it makes most sense to attribute the lagging economic results to what might be described as the failed recontextualization of East German economic life. In effect, the former GDR (the new *Bundesländer*: federated states) was assigned an economic role that had little purpose and no real market demand. Whatever strengths its economy did offer—networks of productive capacity within the frameworks of state-owned *Kombinate*—may have been effectively dismembered by the strategy of selling industrial components individually.

2 Economic difficulties of the GDR

Let us consider more closely the difficulties or challenges that afflicted the GDR before its collapse in 1989–90. Stolper and Nettl outlined early on the difficulties afflicting the period of Soviet occupation and the 1950s, which ended with considerable loss of labour-age population to the west (Buchheim 1995a, 1995b). The erection of the Berlin Wall in 1961 staunched this flow, and the 1960s began with an effort to institute reforms known as the 'new economic system' (NÖS). These gave primacy to investment goods and encouraged, in line with Walter Ulbricht's enthusiasm, cybernetics and the technological enthusiasm that motivated many capitalist states of the period (recall Harold Wilson's invocation of the 'white heat of technology'). As Kopstein (1997: 111–18) points out, the rhetoric of technocracy exceeded its real effects, and by the late 1960s 'retreat from technocracy' was already underway.[4] Like the other economies of the Eastern bloc, the GDR also experimented with a partial introduction of market criteria by which firms could retain profits and would supposedly bear the real costs of losses within the framework of a national plan.[5] The ministries of industry were displaced by a *Vereinigung Volkseigenen Betriebe* (a council of self-governing state enterprises). But as was the case with Czech reforms associated with Otto Sik or with so-called *khozrashchet* in the Soviet Union (individual firm accounting of profits and losses, sometimes associated with the tepid pro-market views of Evsei Lieberman in the Soviet Union), the GDR experiment revealed that a partial dismantling of central planning was very difficult. Independent firms tended to bid against each other, and they provoked unanticipated shortages and bottlenecks and often disappointing results. The new approach also seemed to stimulate unacceptable demands for political liberalization, such as characterized the Prague Spring, and thus was further discredited.

In place of the new economic system, the GDR leadership thus introduced at the VIIth Party Congress of the *Sozialistische Einheitspartei Deutschlands* (SED: the Socialist Unity Party of Germany, the communist-led ruling party of the GDR) in 1971 the supposed 'unity of economy and society', a policy mix associated with the growing influence of Günter Mittag. The unity of economy and society meant an effort to combine economic growth with a relatively high degree of social welfare spending and satisfaction of consumer needs. It was in line with the policies that Edward Gierek adopted in Poland after the explosion of worker dissatisfaction in 1970 and the tendencies toward 'goulash communism', associated with the later phases of Janos Kadar's administration in Hungary. Ritschl, certainly a clear-sighted critic of the planned economy, admits that vis-à-vis the difficulties in the west, the GDR enjoyed relative success, which accompanied its growing political recognition both by the Brandt government in the west and the international community (Ritschl 1995: 32).

Such policies, however, were unsustainable without subsidies or credits from abroad, that is from either the Soviet Union or, more plausibly, from the non-socialist Western economies. The Soviet Union's per capita income was no higher than its satellites, but it could provide oil and other raw materials at a price below world-market levels. Oil price subsidies made a difference after the members of the Organization of the Petroleum Exporting Countries (OPEC) tripled the price of oil they charged Western countries in early 1974. East Germany could buy Soviet oil, refine it further, and sell it at a mark-up to the West. Inexpensive oil also provided the basis for a major chemical industry, as did the earlier development of synthetic oil that had been expanded in preparation for fighting the Second World War. But by the 1980s the Soviets had started raising their oil prices to world-market levels, and in 1985 the Gorbachev administration asked further for payment in convertible currencies. This made the cost of consumer socialism in Poland and the GDR even more dependent on the credits provided by West Germany. Since the new 'Ostpolitik' (eastern policy) of the Sozialdemokratische Partei Deutschlands-Freie Demokratische Partei (SPD-FDP) governments in the FRG specifically sought to moderate East German communist policies by conciliation (*Wandel durch Annäherung*, 'change through rapprochement'), economic assistance and credits formed part of the package. This would lead to substantial indebtedness on the part of the East German economy, especially since the Christian Democratic governments after 1982 essentially continued the policies, indeed with Franz Josef Strauss's efforts at personal diplomacy extending even greater assistance in the late 1980s.

Indebtedness to the West, moreover, played an accentuated role given the policies of the CMEA as a whole. By the 1980s, CMEA trade and exchange was taking place within a complex pattern of bargaining. In theory the CMEA was designed to facilitate an Eastern trade zone and an interdependence that would make for the enhanced efficiency of the socialist world and minimize dependency on the West. But in fact Western dependency had only grown, and in each bargaining session the game became to try to detach one's economy from the reciprocal obligations inside the Comecon. The East European countries wanted as many Western goods as possible, which meant they wanted to minimize their obligations to produce for the Eastern bloc and to find customers in the West. It was easy enough to sell folkloric items such as Russian Matrushka dolls, or Polish carpets and hams, to the West, but these, of course, comprised only trivial items in the balance of accounts. Tourism was under-developed because personal service occupations hardly existed according to Western standards. By dint of sharp discounting, some industrial goods could be sold to the West and to the East Germans, but what the GDR did relatively well was produce industrial goods for the Soviet Union. Its major specializations—heavy industry, machine tools, and chemicals—were oriented toward the CMEA markets where they played an important role. But the CMEA was being prised apart as a zone of economic exchange, with each of its European components being left to make its own arrangements with the West. And what East Germany could offer no longer had a role for Western producers or markets. What East Germany produced, moreover, brought with it particular ecological vulnerabilities since the country's major domestic fuel was lignite or brown coal, a particularly sooty fuel with two-sevenths the thermal output of equivalent weights of hard coal. Moreover, as part of the CMEA as a whole, the GDR lagged in such technological sectors as copiers and computers, and indeed post-industrial services and consumer items in general. Since the FRG was also a machine-tool producer, the East Germans did not have a ready market for these tools in the West. Essentially the East Germans became the industrial machine-tool producer for the socialist world, and it depended on credits, and outright subsidies and personal remittances, from West German relatives for Western consumer goods. These it distributed first through inter-shops for Western currency and then in *exquisit* and *delikat* stores at premium prices, a system that created a network of privilege that naturally undermined the socialist ideology that the regime propagated (Zatlin 2007; Landsman 2005). East Germany was vulnerable to the continuing flow of credits from the West and, above all, from West Germany. In the event of reunification, these were not really likely to halt (and, of course, they did not, having amounted by 2009 to over a trillion euros), and the dependency meant that the vanishing state was in no position to suggest alternatives to the economic reorganization that was decreed after 1990.

Structurally the system was revised in 1979 to group suppliers and producers into so-called *Kombinate* ('combine'), which meant large aggregated production units with their own internal logic—a close approximation to vertically integrated firms. As of 1986 there were 132 centrally managed *Kombinate* with an average of 25,000 employees each, and another 90 or so district *Kombinate* with 2000 employees each. The *Kombinate* models integrated East German engineering expertise, and productivity arrived at certain efficiencies but often at the cost of developing regionally vigorous economies. As in other socialist countries, management of these enterprises involved the pre-emptive purchase of raw materials and continued negotiation with state planners and workers.[6] Although such modifications of central planning can be viewed as undermining economic performance, they also constituted the social learning of East German enterprise, and it was these networks and links that were rudely ruptured by the great sell-off of constituent firm units during 1990–4.

The country had woefully neglected infrastructure in housing and buildings. The 'unity of economy and society' meant that consumer goods might be sought alongside the production of exports to the CMEA or the West, if possible. Investment in the physical plant of GDR cities was sacrificed. What is more, during the 1980s the regime devoted much of its scarce resources for urban development to projects in the capital. As a stake in the Cold War, Berlin-Hauptstadt der DDR received the lion's share of urban development funds. In 1987 the competitive preening for the fifth centennial of Martin Luther's birth in 1983 provided only a final episode. Still, within the overall structure set by these political constraints, the East German economy still satisfied a modicum of welfare. A consumer had to wait a year or more and pay a far larger price in terms of their work time for an inferior automobile, and housing was dilapidated and run down, but within their little republic they made do with a certain shabby cosiness. As of 1980 the per capita income of East Germany (based on purchasing power equivalents) was 45 per cent of the average in the wealthy FRG, France, Sweden, Belgium, Holland, and Switzerland.[7] The next wealthiest socialist economy, Czechoslovakia, achieved 36 per cent.

With the fall of the Berlin Wall on 9 November 1989, however, a new perspective opened up—the possibility of individual entry into a far richer state. In retrospect, one can see a basic inconsistency developing in the East German population: the vision of a higher standard of living and the preservation of all the social guarantees they associated with their own socialist state. Kohl's Ten Point Programme for progressive merger, presented to the Bundestag (national parliament) on 25 November 1989, was a masterly stroke that spoke of progress towards confederative structures without foreclosing what these might be or openly disturbing French and British concern about rapid political unification.

3 Unequal equals

German unification was formalized through two treaties. The State Treaty of 18 May 1990 between the two German states created a 'currency, economic and social union' (*Währungs = Wirtschaft = und Sozialunion*), and came into effect on 1 July of that year. The Unification Treaty (negotiated in the 'two plus four' process) provided for constitutional adhesion of the East German federal states (*Länder*) to the existing FRG by virtue of Article 23 of its basic law. It effectively substituted for a formal peace treaty concluding the Second World War, defined the boundaries of the new united Germany and was ratified by the European nations that had signed the Helsinki Accords in the mid-1970s. It came into effect on 3 October 1990.[8]

The path to this dual settlement was both delicate and turbulent, but was largely foreordained by the weakness of the East German authorities during the merger period. Inside East Germany during the winter of 1990, two authorities contended—the Modrow government of 'national responsibility' and the non-official 'round table'. The five months between the replacement of Erich Honecker in October 1989 and the East German parliamentary (Volkskammer) elections of 18 March, which returned an overwhelming Christian Democratic Union (CDU) majority, was a period of dissipating illusions. The Modrow government's backsliding about dissolving the Ministry for State Security (Stasi) led to angry public demonstrations in January 1990. The clumsy move and the bitter protests made clear the political fragility of the GDR government and undercut any possibility that it might confront the West German negotiators as an equal partner. The official government was still playing with concepts of a transition to a market economy with a large state role (although how one made this transition was not really addressed), while the round table picked up on the ideas of the national trusteeship. On 1 February 1990 the Modrow government—its authority rapidly waning and finding no real support at the time of the premier's Moscow visit at the end of January—announced its plan for a federation of the two Germany, *Deutschland einig Vaterland*, and broadened its party base beyond the SED and the block parties a few days later. It also requested 10–15 billion credits from Bonn, which were refused in mid-February. By this time, Bonn had little interest in any bailout, although it also had to guard against a total rapid collapse in the east. Some 350,000 East Germans had already moved west in the last quarter of 1989 and the budget deficit was growing rapidly. The first (and last) free multi-party Volkskammer elections of 18 March 1990 changed the unification situation with the dramatic victory of the East German CDU led by lawyer (and viola player) Lothar de Maizière. Essentially, the new government saw its task as preparing the most rapid and frictionless union possible. Although the committee pondering a new East German constitution hoped to create the basis of a state that would be democratized but would retain its autonomy for negotiations, the new Volkskammer rejected these projects and pushed through instead an administrative restructuring that recreated six new (or renewed) German *Länder* that would be able to merge into the federal structure of the West German Basic Law according to the provisions of Article 26.

Two issues emerged as critical for the impending economic unification. One was structural: how to continue or dispose of the GDR's collective property. Still, in this period a whole bunch of economic reform proposals emerged that shared the notion that somehow there was a middle or third way between the old planned economy and what was feared to be a ruthless competitive capitalism. The other was how to value GDR monetary assets and ongoing wages, prices and earnings in the transition to a single currency. These were crucially interrelated, because whatever conversion factor was chosen would determine the burden of wages and debts that the GDR's industry would have to shoulder. Among the concepts, most of which remained rather nebulous, the idea that Wolfgang Ullman's *Freie Forschungsgemeinschaft* (later Kollegium) within the movement *Demokratie Jetzt* had the most success. It envisaged a trusteeship institution or holding company (*Treuhandanstalt*) that would take over the state property of the GDR and provide a substantial asset with which to confront the West (Seibel 2005; Kemmler 1994: 69–82; Fischer and Schröter 1993). For a brief while the *Treuhand* ('trust agency') was one of the largest property owners of the world and employed 4 million workers. It took over 8000 units, reorganized them for sale into 12,350, sold about 8400, liquidated 3700, and transferred the remaining hard-to-dispose-of firms into a successor agency (Nativel 2004: 50–1). But what its properties were worth and how they might be utilized were the key issues. Early estimates of the socialist patrimony's value were based on assessments of physical property and took little account of the fact that the whole demand structure was transformed with unification.

The Treuhand would have a tremendous task: it had to find buyers for the nationalized industries of the east who were willing to take on the tasks of rehabilitating their acquisitions. The agency itself did not take on the task of working through the old debts but, according to the terms of the currency union worked out in the spring, assigned these a value in deutschmarks at half their east-mark value. Retaining this burden of debt on Treuhand properties meant that the sums that purchasers offered were correspondingly lower than might have been expected. (In effect, East German properties came with a burden somewhat akin to the 'toxic assets' that vastly reduced the repurchase value of Lehman Brothers or Bear Stearns and other US financial firms in the autumn of 2008—a recent capitalist example of the need for vast write-downs of value. Whereas the United States Treasury stepped in quickly to keep some of these assets afloat, the FRG would find itself required to sustain transfers over the next decade.) Western purchasers expected allowances to be made for the investments needed, above all when an environmental clean-up had to follow. Prospective purchasers could also calculate that employee compensation levels in the east were also likely to rise, as indeed they did from under a third to half the real wages of the west between January 1990 and October 1991, as the West German-based labour unions extracted large pay increases from the Treuhand. The impact of Treuhand sales on the ownership of former GDR property is hard to determine. Some 90 per cent of the buyers were West German firms that wanted essentially to set up 'extended work benches', or factory subsidiaries in the east, with access to markets in East Central Europe, but retain control in the west. On the other hand, the same source reports that three-quarters of East German businesses have East German owners (Nativel 2004: 51).

Treuhand problems became visible once political unification was complete. More attention during the negotiation process was focused on the setting of the exchange rate of the two German currencies at a ratio of 1:1, at a time when the East German currency had an international exchange value of perhaps a quarter or a fifth of the West German deutschmark, although its purchasing parity within the GDR was significantly higher. Overarching the entire settlement was the promise that the deutschmark was to become the new currency of united Germany, and that ongoing obligations in the east, such as wages, pensions, rents and interest payments, would be valued at a parity of 1:1. The basic idea of a currency union was floated by the SPD parliamentarian Ingrid Matthäus-Maier in early 1990, and the Kohl government largely took the idea over in an announcement on 7 February. This decision, which was politically motivated and for which many good reasons can be given, supposedly made the wage costs of GDR industries unsustainable.

In addition, West German unions, which largely took over the wage bargaining in the east, pressed for a rapid convergence of East German pay scales, which far exceeded the convergence of labour productivity rates. Although the Council of Economic Advisers (*Sachverständigenrat*) warned publicly against the implications of the 1:1 currency union two days after the chancellor made it his own, the Scientific Council (*Wissenschaftlicher Beirat*) of the finance ministry gave precedence early on to preventing rapid mass-migration westward. Partially softening the Scientific Council's plan to evaluate existing GDR liabilities and assets at 1:2 and future income streams at 1:1, the new currency and Economic Union provided that personal savings accounts or company balances in GDR marks would be converted at par up to a total of DM 2000 and at 1:2 for amounts higher than 2000 (or up to DM 4000 for senior citizens). In terms of the monetary claims the FRG was adding to its money supply, and the reserves required to cover them, the federal government did not pose an exceptional strain on currency stability. But where the 'mark equals mark' conversion would have graver consequences was in the continuing burden of pay scales. The Bundesbank monthly report of July 1990 (*Die Währungsunion mit der deutschen Demokratischen Republik*) estimated that East German productivity was only 40 per cent of FRG levels. Nonetheless, West German unions insisted that wages in the east converge on western levels. There was a good political argument for this policy. Aside from concerns about massive population transfers, the ideology of unification assumed that the new Germany was to share social burdens and provide equal opportunities. This premise was important in keeping both major West German political parties behind the terms of unification. Nonetheless, the resulting hike in East German real wage costs put new firms under tremendous pressure (see Ritschl 1995: 39–41).

4   Economic landscapes: blossoming or bleeding—*blühend oder blutend*?

By 1992–3, even Chancellor Kohl, who had spoken blithely of 'blossoming landscapes', was compelled to recognize that the economic situation was grave. The mid-1990s probably represented the worst years of transition. Different estimates, which are hard to reconcile, suggest that 70 per cent of the country's employees would lose their jobs, or that 2.5 million workers lost industry jobs during the years of Treuhand transition—approximately 60 per cent of those who had been employed in the industrial sector. From 1990 to 1991, East German industry cut back work time (*Kurzarbeit*) for 900,000 employees. The unemployment rolls hit a million (after many hundreds of thousands had already moved west), and after 1992 early retirement at age 55 went into effect for perhaps 800,000 workers; and job retraining would occupy another 400,000—in effect, massive underemployment. All in all, unemployment reached 15 per cent and the total unemployed, early retired, employed in state-created jobs, or in retraining, were perhaps a third of the potentially employable—a total comparable to the Great Depression of the 1930s.[9] Federal Labour Office statistics show unemployment rising to a million by mid-1991 and then continuing to between 1.2 and 1.5 million through the 1990s. By 1993, agriculture and forestry had fallen to a fourth of its 1989 size (10 per cent of the active population), and industrial employment to a third (of the almost half of the labour force it comprised originally) (Ritter 2007: 122–6). A rise in construction employment of 50 per cent and of services by 40 per cent (although of a reduced overall workforce) partially offset the losses. However, the gains included youth entering the labour market while the losses counted a high proportion of the middle-aged, 50 and older. Women in particular proved vulnerable to unemployment. The GDR had brought most women into the workforce, although it did not place them in high-status positions. Nonetheless, nurseries and child care were extensively available. With unification, the employment pattern reverted towards that of West Germany with fewer women working, and child care facilities more fragmentary.

Only massive transfers made this bloodletting of jobs bearable. Unemployment support, standardized along West German lines, provided about two-thirds of the most recent net pay for a limited period and thereafter about half the salary, at least until the so-called Hartz IV reforms of 2004 tightened benefits. The West German old-age pension insurance system, based on accrued contributions over the years of employment, was also extended to the east in August 1991. The result was to make East German pensions on average 15 per cent bigger than those in the west, in part because GDR workers had experienced virtually no unemployment and far more continuous female employment. Pensions constituted about 18 per cent of East German aggregate income, but only 9–11 per cent in the west. Moreover, it can be estimated that of the East German pensions, about €21 billion are derived from West German fiscal sources. This amounted to about 7.4 per cent of the East German GDP (using this term for that portion of national output generated in the east)—perhaps two-thirds of today's yearly net transfers. Despite these large sums, individual pension entitlements remained less in the east than in the west (57 per cent in 1992, rising to 88 per cent in 2002).

Insofar as productive activity helped to ameliorate the depressed conditions in the east, it was the construction industry that provided a major motor, at least at first. Whereas construction contributed about 5 per cent of the West German GDP, it amounted to about 12 per cent of East German GDP in 1991 and rose to about 17 per cent in 1995, but then fell steadily through 2006. The result of all this building and urban renewal was that whereas the housing stock of East German cities was renewed, and the shabby buildings spruced up, the number of empty residences reached 13 per cent by 1998, twice as high as in the west. As of 2006 the figure was still 12.6 per cent (versus 6.8 per cent in the west). Housing prices had fallen by 15–20 per cent and office space by 30–40 per cent between 1995 and 2005 (Pacqué 2009: 103–5). Of those employed in this sector, 600,000 had lost their jobs, and perhaps for a second time. But they left behind urban neighbourhoods that were restored and attractive. Yet I can testify to the somewhat spectral appearance of beautifully restored city centres (as, e.g., in Gorlitz), with relatively few commercial tenants and space claimed by public agencies.

The challenges of the world market did not hit East Germany alone. The mid-1990s compelled a reconsideration of the costs of the German *Sozialstaat* in general as the impact of globalization really began to strike home. The extensive German social insurance system rested on high costs that employers had to cover, such that the overall cost of hiring a worker with all the 'fringe benefits' might amount to twice their wage. But while the hourly or weekly costs of labour (per worker) remained high on an international scale of comparison, labour was sufficiently productive that the cost per unit of output remained globally competitive. This reflected both the extensive capital equipment that West German labour could work with and the high degree of social investment in training skilled workers. German goods thus retained a reputation for superior quality that also allegedly preserved their market share. Unions and works councils bargained closely with employer associations and provided high-quality labour in return for wage and social guarantees. This social compact, combined with an extensive network of apprenticeship training, constituted what had been admired as *Modell Deutschland* (the German model) in the 1980s and 1990s. By the end of the last century, however, this cosy equilibrium came to be seen by critics as too costly and inflexible as emerging markets provided strong competition. The enviable apprenticeship system produced lifetime workers with high qualifications in diverse branches of industry, but not a labour force that might be moved with alacrity to new sectors. The system in the USA of turning out mass products with less investment in employee skills seemed to be yielding a higher rate of employment and job creation in a more internationally competitive milieu. With respect to East Germany in particular, recent investigations, as noted above, have suggested that the federal government may even have subsidized too much innovation among small and medium-sized East German manufacturing firms for their own good. The whole notion of Germany as a territory on which German products were produced, investment took place, and the economy was territorially based (*Standort Deutschland*) came into question.

'Reform', as might be expected, would have to come at the expense of this humane but stodgy labour partnership, and as usual at the cost of labour union concessions. Given the strength of the unions and the Social Democratic Party, resistance from the Left was to be anticipated but resistance derived, too, from the socially minded wing of the CDU under Norbert Blum, who was strikingly successful in winning continued social payments for the east. By the late 1990s one talked of the *Reformstau* in Germany—the blocked reforms or the 'gridlock' that Americans refer to.

Nonetheless, with the present century, a different sort of German labour market started to emerge—in part because the growing number of immigrant workers offered a more disposable labour force. By the early years of the first decade, the long-term unemployment insurance was cut back (Hartz IV) and layoffs became more possible. German constitutional court decisions made strikes riskier not only for the union delegates represented in a given factory but also for those representing the wider industrial sector that included the factory, who could be assigned the financial costs of factory closures if the owners responded to a strike by a lock-out. The upshot, as it tended to be in many economies, would be a segmentation of the labour force. Migrants and low-wage workers increasingly formed the 'disposable' sector that could be expanded or contracted, while the core skilled workers, who formed the core of the SPD, remained relatively protected.

Looking back at the experience of German labour as a whole during the two decades since 1989, the East German workforce might be deemed to have served as the avant-garde of the newly insecure. They experienced early on and with greater severity the pressures on employment and welfare that would overtake the united country as a whole. Given this overall transition, East German production found it difficult to catch up. In effect, the new *Bundesländer* were too protected to serve as a site for outsourcing from the west, the way in which Slovak and Hungarian factories might serve, but neither were they so efficient as easily to become part of the productive German core that still ran along the Rhine from Baden Wurttemberg north towards a restructured Ruhr and with a new centre of gravity in Bavaria. Ultimately the safety net of the West German economic system may have contributed to East Germany's prolonged laggardness. West German firms seeking to outsource industrial assembly, for instance, did not find it profitable to settle in East German factories, which had become as expensive as their own. It made more sense to establish their suppliers in Hungary or Slovakia, which they could rapidly reach by rail and road, and whose wage costs were lower. East Germany was too costly to become a land of Maquiladoras. On the other hand, it has remained a low-wage area by German comparison. In 2007, 460,000 East German workers were eligible for supplementary wage support, while in the west, with five times the population, the number was 760,000.[10]

5 Conclusion

The concept of transition exerts a curious perspective. It suggests a beginning point and an end point, which can look relatively benign. It tends to make the observer de-emphasize the pain of the process, because ultimately the pain diminishes. Those forced out of the labour market at age 55 in 1995 would have reached normal retirement age by 2005. University professors—to take the sector I know personally—whose faculties were shut down in the early 1990s would have long since become emeriti. A new generation comes to adulthood, and while some remain long-term unemployed or short-term workers with little stability, many find their niche in the new social profile. But to assess the impact on the East German transition we must keep in mind the distress of the years in between. They left a lot of bitterness and disillusion. They contributed to the ongoing support for the heirs of the old communist party or SED, renamed the Party of Democratic Socialism and now merged with the left of the old SPD as *die Linke*. In East Berlin a certain culture of socialist regret (*Ostalgie*) persisted. And even more harmful, the distress augmented a new 'skins' culture of intolerance on the Right.

East Germans had taken their political future in their hands in the autumn of 1989. They could be proud of having finally contributed to the downfall of the regime that walled them in. But unlike the other countries of Eastern Europe, they did not have the same responsibility for their economic future. They had landed in the lap of their wealthy compatriots, who, they felt, often treated them with contempt. Were they not being treated as a colonial land where the westerners were taking over the leading positions in the universities, the public administration, and the reconstructed firms? Was not their own tradition and achievement being consigned to oblivion? Street names were changed; university faculties were shut down; industries were prised apart; and jobs were lost. The euphoria of getting rid of the Berlin Wall and the Stasi quickly dissipated. Many East Germans, far more than those directly impacted, shared a feeling that they had been badly treated; that they had thought they would enter a united Germany as one of two national units but in fact had been marginalized and indeed colonized by what American southerners after 1865 called 'carpetbaggers', who had in this case travelled east to take over their administration, their economic units, their university professorships, and their judgeships.

East Germans sometimes developed a schizophrenic view of what they went through. On the one hand, they suggested that their former state had exerted a degree of totalitarian surveillance through the Stasi that was as evil as the Third Reich. On the other hand, they spoke warmly of the cosy collective mentality that they had enjoyed, their associative life, and the absence of an 'elbow society', and they threw a warm veil of sentiment over the old days. Their more ambitious young people, however, understood that they now enjoyed opportunities and freedoms their parents had never had during the two generations of state socialism. The grounds for mutual reproach were strong. Westerners felt that unification was costly—a 'solidarity tax' that Chancellor Kohl finally imposed to cover some of the costs was finally legislated in 1993 as the impact of transition became clear. But westerners sometimes forgot that they had benefited from the Marshall Plan and US assistance while the East Germans had seen many of their plants shipped east by the Soviets.[11] And had one asked West Germans before 1989 what they might have paid to secure unification, most would have pledged a significant amount.

Two comparisons may help us understand the transition. One was offered by sceptics from the early 1990s on (although I initially resisted it), and that was the idea of the former GDR as a sort of German *Mezzogiorno* without a mafia, as former Chancellor Helmut Scmidt termed the territory—that is, a region afflicted with long-term low productivity, no matter how much investment was provided, and achieving a comparable living standard only by virtue of continuous subsidies. There are some similarities—primarily the fact that in both the Italian south and the German east, income levels have been raised while innovation lags. Despite certain vigorous enclaves around Dresden, Leipzig and Jena, such a bleak assessment can be defended. The Italian south, despite hopeful signs and half a century of continuous investment projects and transfers, still lags behind the north, as does the former GDR. Autonomous vigour is hard to sustain. Nonetheless, there are important differences that limit the value of the comparison. The 'backwardness' of the Italian south dates back centuries: it was a land of barons living at the rim of one distant state after another (Greek, Roman, Arab, Angevin, Spanish, Bourbon, and Piedmontese) and also a land of undercapitalized estates in an arid climate. The *meridionalisti* of the nineteenth century diagnosed difficulties that had taken root long before. The industrial regions of East Germany, in contrast, were traditionally and are of vigorous mid-size and diverse industries and had a long history of development (see Herrigel 1996). But whether in the chemical sector or the textile sector, they are hit hard by globalization. It is clear that when one examines such 'backward' regions (or conversely such regional success stories, say, as Baden Württemberg or, outside Germany, parts of northern Italy, Flanders, Catalonia, or Silicon Valley, and, of course, now, parts of southern Asia), aggregate national economic indexes do not provide enough explanatory power. Somehow the regional *Gestalt*—its culture and geographical embeddedness, the resourcefulness of its local government as well as entrepreneurs, and the mentalities that a regional consciousness inculcates—needs to be brought into play. Where these produce a commitment to regional innovation and co-operation across classes, centres of development can make the transition from one technological basis to another with striking success. Where local elites remain distrustful of state power, jealous of class prerogatives, and heedless of education, we have regions of long-term disappointment and stagnation. That does not mean that such apparently long-term laggardness cannot change. The American south seemed doomed to remain a backward region after 1865 but advanced dynamically from the 1960s onward; Ireland forged ahead in the 1980s and 1990s; and Flanders prospered while Wallonia lagged. The key to such advances is not necessarily extraction of minerals or fossil fuels; it is the potential to create high value added through social capital and a well-educated workforce. The replanted Zeiss concern in Jena promised some local success in the 1990s, and the Dresden region was generating a regional base for computers and software development. But such development is fragile, and it is never clear in advance what combination of factors encourages these rapid changes.

The other comparison, oddly enough, is provided by the current or recent financial crisis. That demonstrated the insubstantial nature of 'worth' or value. Under capitalism, but even more under socialism, the illusion of intrinsic asset values persisted. But value arises only from the intersection of demand with supply. The rapid collapse of derivatives in 2008 revealed that values could be fictitious. The truth is that such fictitiousness can apply to hardware, real machines and buildings as well as to paper assets. No matter what the cost of producing a good, it has no value if no one wants it. East Germans and others believed that their factories, which had a demand within the structures of the socialist economic order, the CMEA, had far less of one within the frameworks of international capitalism. In classical terms, the market clearing price of the assets and what they might produce was lower than the imposed costs of labour or environmental clean-up. Like an old car, which might still serve well in a Third World milieu, the GDR assets had value only as salvage and cannibalized parts within the Western economy.

East Germans are said to have faced a dual transition: one to capitalism, the second to the post-industrial economy that had taken hold in the non-socialist world while they remained in their collectivist CMEA cocoon. Ultimately, the East Germans had to undergo transition from an old industrial society to a post-industrial society in a far more compressed time period than other sections of Western Europe. The Ruhr was deindustrialized over a long generation. Perhaps northern Britain revealed the most similar difficulties—job losses and the shutting-down of industry, but again over a longer period. The coal and iron that had testified to industrial vigour in Europe through the 1950s became its liability from the 1960s on. So, too, for the rust belt of the USA. Sheltered under state socialism, its soft budget policies, and its Marxist idealization of a heroic proletariat, these industries had persisted in the East without their governments reckoning the opportunity costs of preserving them, once they had achieved their function of industrializing formerly agrarian societies, such as Poland, Romania, or Slovakia.

If one looks at Eastern Europe, the results are revealing. As of 2007, labour productivity in East Germany was about 77 per cent of West Germany, whereas in the Czech Republic it was only 33 per cent. And in the latter the contribution of industry to the GDP was 33 per cent whereas in united Germany it was 23 per cent and in the east it was 20 per cent. In general, industrial production clung to its earlier role in Central and Eastern Europe more than in East Germany, where the country had been radically deindustrialized. This came at a cost: industrial wages in Western Germany as of 2006 were about €3270 per month, in Eastern Germany they were €2370, and in the Czech Republic they were roughly €670. Taking the Czech-German comparisons again, East German GDP per capita in 2007 was 72 per cent of united Germany, while the Czech Republic was 42 per cent (Pacqué 2009: 201–5). Still, East European societies could enjoy the sensation of being autonomous actors and determining their own future. And they had not undergone the same degree of unemployment. Only Russia in the 1990s had a more catastrophic depression, uncushioned by the transfers from the west that the East Germans could draw on. Nonetheless, the East Germans often felt demoralized by the rapidity of the changes and the fact that their living standards depended on subsidies and transfers.

The legacy of state socialism in general was to retard the processes of so-called post-industrial development that transformed the West between the 1960s and the 1990s. Did this have to be the case? The Soviet Union, after all, had developed an aerospace sector that rivalled that of the West. Why could it not also have forged informatics and electronic sectors that kept apace? It had the mathematicians. Certainly the closed economic zone of the socialist bloc also limited innovation. Without market price signals, the costs of persisting in ageing industrial sectors could not really be measured. (Conversely, the absence of market signals sometimes allowed, or encouraged, costly efforts at technological emulation that consumed far more resources than in the West or Japan. East German planners did press to develop a modern computer chip industry. They were proud of their 256-bit processor and perhaps gained valuable technological skills in producing it. But from the criterion of international production, it came too slowly and too late, as did such similar ventures as the Walkman they finally manufactured in the late 1980s.)[12] But I think that the answer is ultimately a political one. The heroic images of socialism derived from nineteenth-century industrial society. Read George Orwell on the coal miners of Wigan Pier, and one can see the industrial romanticism that motivated even a non-communist British leftist intellectual. Communism remained wedded to this image of the heroic proletarian, and in the case of the Soviet Union's communist party, or the Italian Resistance tradition, the image of heroic labour was augmented by the military heroism of the Second World War. The ideology of the future became frozen in a vision of the past. The 1960s revealed the forces that would corrode this world view, whether manifested by the Beatles or later by the Xerox machine, and, by the 1980s, the Walkman. The goods that the Eastern bloc celebrated and the strengths it sought to perpetuate, whether in Eisenhüttenstadt or Nowa Huta, would be increasingly provided by producers in Asia, who would also turn out the jeans, the shoes, the T-shirts and the consumer electronics that East Germans craved. Where there were exceptions—highly specialized construction material or optics—there was a future. But it is a painful process to arrive at the future.

It was painful in the West for afflicted regions for a generation, and it would be proportionally even more painful when packed into a decade. Moreover, the world that the East Germans had contracted to join was not the one they found. Bärbel Bohley, a dissident leader, had said: 'We wanted justice and got the *Rechtsstaat.*' The East German population had similarly wanted welfare capitalism but got what they saw as neoliberalism. In fact they got a lot of welfare as well. It was not necessarily a bad deal but they found it a disquieting one.

6   Postscript: another transition through unification?

Not surprisingly, the German economic experience of unification has attracted the interest, and even the unease, of the other country that was divided by ideology and the Cold War in the aftermath of 1945, namely Korea. Reunification has remained a steadfast aim of South Korea throughout that period, and there have been moments where a sudden collapse of the North Korean regime appeared a possibility. I was part of a delegation that discussed this contingency with President Kim Dae-jung of South Korea, the official author of the Sunshine Policy in the late 1990s, which in effect switched Seoul's policy from one of waiting to absorb North Korea into one of softening the Pyongyang regime through economic and other blandishments—an analogue of Willy Brandt's Ostpolitik inaugurated in the late 1960s.

Nonetheless, the economic condition of North Korea has seemed so precarious at moments since that period, verging occasionally on famine, in fact, that Seoul policy makers have asked what the impact of a sudden collapse of the North Korean state would be. Such a contingency would confront the south with the daunting task of absorbing a country that today has a population of almost 24 million inhabitants with a GDP of approximately $20 billion (about $1900 per capita), by a country with close to 50 million inhabitants and a GDP of almost $1000 billion ($30,000 per capita). These economic discrepancies dwarf the German differentials of 1989, and the population to absorb, perhaps a third of a united Korea, would be larger than the (roughly) quarter of the united German population that the FRG was required to subsidize. By the mid-point of the last decade, China had become a major supplier of aid in food, oil, and fertilizer, and unification would mean that South Korea would have to replace this major source of assistance just to sustain the current rate of North Korean income, not to mention bringing that income anywhere close to that of South Korea. Among other estimates, Goldman Sachs in 2000 calculated that economic unification would cost the South Koreans US$2.7–3.9 billion, perhaps twice the level of transfers that post-1990 Germany had to contribute to the new *Bundesländer.*[13] No surprise that the South Korean consensus envisages as desirable not a German-style rapid absorption but a slow rapprochement of the two systems.

In any case, North Korea has proved immensely resilient—it runs a far more successfully repressive regime than the East Germans could manage in the years before 1989. It has no visible group of dissenters; no intellectuals managing to get to the south; a population inured to living at bleak and subsistence levels; and a nuclear programme that continues to lurk as an unpredictable factor in preserving a regime that combines personal dictatorship and perhaps the harshest communist party (and military) rule in the world. History, however, as 1989 taught, comes with surprises. If there were a regime crisis and China abandoned its protection, it is possible that unification might present itself, welcome or not. It would arrive, as in the case of Germany, with an opportunity to realize a national goal that neither North nor South Korea has ever renounced. For all the difficulties, there is little doubt that if the political will materialized, the economic means to carry it through would be found. South Koreans could insist that the upgrading of northern standards of living must take place at a slower pace over a couple of decades than the West Germans felt they had to concede the East Germans. The very frozen backwardness of North Korea, economically and politically, means that many of the pressures for a rapid convergence (as expressed in the currency parity decision and the trade union pressure for wage equalization) would not be present. East Germany was still a sovereign entity after the collapse of the Berlin Wall, and while its negotiating assets dwindled quickly, it brought to negotiations a far more modern civil society than presumably a catastrophically imploded North Korea would, even given its nuclear and missile programmes. If there were a crisis and the will arose, the economic difficulties could be surmounted. Meanwhile, however, the North Korean regime wants to preserve its autonomy, while Beijing probably relishes having a North Korea in place that it can use to irritate the USA, so long as the Americans preserve their implicit umbrella over Taiwan. And apparently, South Koreans feel about a reunified homeland what the young St. Augustine said about chastity: 'Give me unification, O Lord, but not yet."

Notes

1. For a recent account of this process, see Ritter (2007).
2. See Pacqué (2009). Because his is the latest synthesis, I have relied on Pacqué for much of the statistical comparisons cited. The east–west comparison of retraining and work-creation employed comes from p. 119. I use West German and East German (or western Germany and eastern Germany) to refer to the former territories of the FRG and GDR, respectively.
3. See Ritschl's overview (1995/2: 11–46), which provides ranges of estimates for key parameters, from the implausibly high official statistics of the GDR to pessimistic

values and what he deems the most plausible mid-level figures. See also Van Ark (1995: 75–100).

4. For a general survey of the 1950s and 1960s, see Hoffmann (2003).
5. Steiner (2004) outlines the evolution of the GDR economy across its history and provides a detailed bibliography of the monographic literature.
6. For examples of *Kombinate* transactions with their workforce, see Wilczek (2004).
7. See Kopstein (1997: 198) and Janos (1994: 4).
8. For a comprehensive treatment of all the legal and constitutional issues connected with unification, see Quint (1997).
9. Pacqué (2009: 61) for the Treuhand figure; pp. 116–7 for the aggregates. For 2008 the corresponding totals were 13 per cent unemployed, and 16 per cent 'underemployed'; still massive, but half of the early 1990s.
10. Pacqué (2009), citing Bundesagentur für Arbeit, *Arbeitsmarkt 2007*: 141–3.
11. Ritschl (1995: 20–2) argues that the discrepancy between Soviet and western treatment of their respective zones in the late 1940s made little difference, since West Germany had to absorb a greater number of displaced countrymen expelled from Czechoslovakia or the territories occupied by Poles after 1945 as well as those migrating westward. On the other hand, it can be argued that the downward wage pressure exerted by the new arrivals actually served the West German recovery well.
12. See Ritschl (1995) and Maier (1997: 39–107).
13. I draw the basic economic data from the entries in Central Intelligence Agency (2011). I am providing the exchange rate equivalents; purchasing parity estimates would provide a more favorable picture for the south. For estimates of Chinese aid to North Korea, see Choo (2008); and for discussions of evolving South Korean policy toward the North, see Bae (2010: 346), with the estimates of South Korean aid required after unification.

References

Bae, J-Y. (2010) 'South Korean Strategic Thinking toward North Korea: The Evolution of the Engagement Policy and its Impact upon U.S.-ROK Relations', *Asian Survey*, 50: 335–55.

Buchheim, C. (1995a) 'Kriegsfolgen und Witrschaftswachstum in der SBZ/DDR', *Geschichte und Gesellschaft*, 25: 515–29.

Buchheim, C. (ed.) (1995b) *Wirschaftliche Folgelasten des Krieges in der SBZ/DDR*, Nomos: Baden-Baden.

Choo, J. (2008) 'Mirroring North Korea's Growing Economic Dependence on China: Political Ramification', *Asian Survey*, 48: 343–72.

Central Intelligence Agency (2011) entries for North Korea and South Korea, *The World Factbook* (updated 16 March 2011).

Czarnitzky, D. (2005) 'The Extent and Evolution of Productivity Deficiency in Eastern Germany', *Journal of Productivity Analysis*, 24: 211–31.

Czarnitzky, D. and K. Kraft (2006) 'R & D and Firm Performance in a Transition Economy', *KYKLOS*, 59(4): 481–96.

Fischer, W. and H. Schröter (1993) 'Die Entsteung der Treuhandanstalt', in W. Fischer, H. Has and H.K. Schneider (eds), *Treuhandanstalt–Das Unmögliche wagen, Forschungsberichte*, Akademie Verlag: Berlin.

Herrigel, G. (1996) *Industrial Constructions: The Sources of German Industrial Power*, Cambridge University Press: Cambridge, MA.

Hoffmann, D. (2003) *Die DDR unter Ulbricht: Gewaltsame Neuordnung und gescheiterte Modernisierung*, Pendo: Zurich.

Janos, A. (1994) 'Continuity and Change in Eastern Europe: Strategies of Post-Communist Politics', *East European Politics and Societies*, 8(1): 1–32.

Kemmler, M. (1994) *Die Entstehung der Treuhandanstalt. Von der Wahrung zur Privatisierung des DDR-Volkseigentums*, Campus: Frankfurt.

Kopstein, J. (1997) *The Politics of Economic Decline in East Germany, 1945–1989*, University of North Carolina Press: Chapel Hill, NC.

Landsman, M. (2005) *Dictatorship and Demand: The Politics of Consumerism in East Germany*, Harvard University Press: Cambridge, MA.

Maier, C.S. (1997) *Dissolution: The Crisis of Communism and the End of East Germany*, Princeton University Press: Princeton, NJ.

Nativel, C. (2004) *Economic Transition, Unemployment and Active Labour Market Policy: Lessons and Perspectives from the East German Bundesländer*, University of Birmingham Press: Birmingham.

Pacqué, K.H. (2009) *Die Bilanz: Eine wirtschaftliche Analyse der Deutschen Einheit*, Carl Hanser Verlag: Munich.

Quint, P.E. (1997) *The Imperfect Union: Constitutional Structures of German Unification*, Princeton University Press: Princeton, NJ.

Ritschl, A. (1995) 'Aufstieg und Niedergang der Wirtschaft der DDR: Ein Zahlenbild 1845–1989', *Jahrbuch für Wirtschattsgeschichte*, 2: 11–46.

Ritter, G.A. (2007) *Der Preis der Einheit: Die Wiedervereinigung und die Krise des Sozialstaates*, 2nd edition, Beck: Munich.

Seibel, W. (2005) *Verwaltete Illusionen: Die Privatisierung der DDR-Wirstchaft durch die Treuhandanstalt und ihre Nachfolger 1990–2000*, Campus: Frankfurt.

Steiner, A. (2004) *Von Plan zu Plan: Eine Wirschaftsgeschichte der DDR*, Deutsche Verlags-Anstalt: Munich.

Van Ark, B. (1995) 'The Manufacturing Sector in East Germany: A Reassessment of Comparative Productivity Performance, 1950–1988', *Jahrbuch für Wirtschattsgeschichte*, 2: 75–100.

Wilczek, A. (2004) *Einkommen—Karriere—Versorgung: Das DDR-Kombinat und die Lebenslage seiner Beschäftigeten*, Metropol: Berlin.

Zatlin, J. (2007) *The Currency of Socialism: Money and Political Culture in East Germany*, German Historical Institute and Cambridge University Press: Washington, DC and Cambridge.

14
Transition in Southeast Europe: Understanding Economic Development and Institutional Change

Milica Uvalic

1 Introduction

Southeast Europe (SEE) is a region where the transition to a market economy and multi-party democracy has evolved under particularly difficult conditions. In comparison with the more advanced countries in Central and Eastern Europe (CEE), most SEE countries today are lagging behind in their level of economic development, economic and institutional reforms, and integration with the European Union (EU). In this chapter, the SEE region is considered in its narrow definition of the Western Balkan states—Albania, Bosnia and Herzegovina, Croatia, the former Yugoslav Republic (FYR) of Macedonia, Montenegro, Serbia, and Kosovo (the last three were part of the same country until recently).[1] In discussing the initial conditions of 1989, however, reference will also be made to the other three countries in the SEE region—Bulgaria, Romania, and Slovenia.[2]

The chapter analyses the 20-year experience with transition in the SEE region in a comparative framework, illustrating how these countries—most of which had some of the best starting conditions in 1989 for implementing a swift transition to a market economy—encountered difficulties in its implementation. We first recall the initial conditions in the SEE region in 1989 (Section 2). We then proceed to analyse macroeconomic performance of the smaller group of Western Balkan countries (Section 3) and the progress achieved in the various transition-related economic and institutional reforms (Section 4). International issues are also addressed, related to the post-2000 integration of these countries into the European Union (EU) and among themselves (Section 5). The chapter ends by reflecting on the principal factors that are responsible for delays in transition in the Western Balkan region (Section 6). A few concluding remarks are made at the end (Section 7).

2 Historical background: initial conditions in SEE

When the Berlin Wall fell in November 1989, the SEE region consisted of only four countries: Albania, Bulgaria, Romania, and the Socialist Federal Republic (SFR) of Yugoslavia. All four started implementing transition-related economic reforms and held their first democratic multiparty elections in 1989–90, in SFR Yugoslavia only at the level of the single republics. At that time, the general situation in SEE was very different from what it is today.

In 1989, SFR Yugoslavia was the most developed and largest country in SEE, in terms of both territory and population. There were major differences among the SEE countries, however, regarding a number of features. One of the main differences was their very different international relations and resulting trade orientation (Uvalic 2001). SFR Yugoslavia in the late 1980s traded mainly with the European Community (EC), as it was not a member of the Council for Mutual Economic Assistance (CMEA) or of the Warsaw Pact but had concluded several trade agreements with the EC, the first dating back to the early 1970s (Uvalic 1992). Bulgaria and Romania had been members of the CMEA and of the Warsaw Pact for several decades, which naturally determined their main trade orientation towards, primarily, other socialist countries within the CMEA, in line with the 'socialist division of labour'. Albania was the most closed economy in Europe—after having abandoned the CMEA in the early 1960s, it had followed its own autarkic development strategy for many years and had limited economic links with the rest of the world, including its closest neighbours.

In 1989 the institutional framework in the SEE countries was also rather different. In comparison with the other communist countries, SFR Yugoslavia had a longer tradition with market-oriented economic reforms. Starting from the early 1950s, a unique system of workers' self-management was introduced, along with opening up to the outside world and gradual decentralization of the economy, particularly in the 1970s. Nevertheless, also in Yugoslavia, some of the main features of the communist economic system were not abandoned until the late 1980s (Uvalic 1992), including the commitment to non-private property and 'state paternalism' (Kornai 1980).[3] More radical economic reforms in SFR Yugoslavia started only in the late 1980s: amendments to the constitution adopted in 1988 raised the limits on private property and encouraged foreign direct investment (FDI). In December 1989, the last Yugoslav government launched a bold macroeconomic stabilization programme based on 'shock therapy' (the first of its kind),[4] together with a privatization law aimed at introducing a private property regime in the bulk of the economy. The macroeconomic stabilization programme was initially successful in halting inflation, but by mid-1990 the mounting political crisis, which led soon after to Yugoslavia's break-up, impeded its further implementation.

In 1989, therefore, the overall economic conditions in SFR Yugoslavia were far better than in the other communist states, primarily due to the country's specific international relations and its longer experience with market-oriented economic reforms. At the time of the break-up of Yugoslavia in mid-June 1991, all its successor states generally had less distorted economies than the centrally planned economies in CEE (Estrin and Uvalic 2008). Unlike the Yugoslav successor states that in 1991 inherited some elements of the market mechanism, there had been no previous experience of a market economy in Albania, Romania had one of the most centralized economies among all CMEA countries, while only very limited reforms had been implemented in Bulgaria.

Kekic (1996: 5–22) has calculated an index of initial conditions in all communist countries in 1989, based on various economic indicators and institutional characteristics (including the extent of previous market-based economic reforms, exports to the CMEA, external debt, energy intensity, economic structure, and so on). The index suggests that all the Yugoslav republics had better overall conditions than the other SEE (but also many CEE) countries. The index of initial conditions was lower for Bulgaria (13), Albania (15), and Romania (15) than for the Yugoslav republics, where it ranged from 19 for Serbia and Montenegro to 24 for Slovenia.

The economic transition in a large part of the SEE region was interrupted by the disintegration of the Yugoslav federation in mid-1991 into five independent states: Bosnia and Herzegovina, Croatia, FYR Macedonia, Slovenia, and FR Yugoslavia (Montenegro and Serbia, with its two provinces Kosovo and Voivodina). After 1991 there was a notable divergence in the transition paths of the single countries, some progressing much faster than others. Despite Yugoslavia's favourable starting conditions regarding the extent of market-related economic reforms undertaken in the past and closeness to the West, transition in its successor states proved to be extremely difficult, Slovenia being the only exception.

Slovenia has had a much smoother transition than the other countries for a number of reasons. It was the most developed post-communist country with probably the best overall starting conditions, and it was only briefly involved in the Balkan military conflicts.[5] Soon after its independence in June 1991, Slovenia continued implementing major transition-related economic reforms and was able to sign an EU Association Agreement in 1996, to benefit from the EU PHARE aid programme (for the countries of CEE) and later from EU pre-accession funds, which prepared the ground for its entry into the EU in May 2004, together with the other seven CEE countries.

In comparison to Slovenia, Bulgaria and Romania have had a slower pace of economic transition and have experienced major economic instability. Both went through a severe economic crisis also in the second half of the 1990s, which brought negative growth in Romania in 1997–9 and in Bulgaria in 1996–7. Nevertheless, similarly to Slovenia, they were able to benefit from EU support from the early 1990s. Bulgaria and Romania signed EU Association Agreements in 1993 and benefited from PHARE and substantial EU pre-accession funding, which facilitated their joining the EU in January 2007.

The remaining SEE countries—the Western Balkan states—have encountered much greater problems. The extreme political instability in the region, which affected most countries for more than a decade, has left very profound and long-lasting economic consequences. There are a number of factors that have very negatively influenced the economic performance of most Western Balkan countries: the disintegration of the Yugoslav federation in mid-1991 and the military conflicts that accompanied it—in Slovenia (1991), Croatia (1990–1), Bosnia and Herzegovina (1992–5), Kosovo (1998–9), and FYR Macedonia (2001); the pursuit of nationalistic and inward-oriented policies by the newly created states; the authoritarian regimes in some key countries, like FR Yugoslavia and Croatia; the 11-week NATO bombing of FR Yugoslavia in 1999; the severe United Nations (UN) sanctions against FR Yugoslavia during most of the decade; and the Greek embargo against FYR Macedonia. The political events of the 1990s have also postponed many of the economic reforms involved in the transition to a market economy. The way in which the legacies of the previous economic system were dealt with after the disintegration of Yugoslavia has had a fundamental impact on the course of the transition and economic performance of its successor states, resulting in very different outcomes (Estrin and Uvalic 2008). As a result of unsettled political questions and/or postponed transition, the Balkan countries have also substantially delayed their integration into the EU. It was only after the end of the Kosovo war in mid-1999 that the EU elaborated a more coherent and long-term strategy for the integration of the Western Balkan states into the EU (see Section 5).

Why did SFR Yugoslavia disintegrate in such a violent manner, whereas the Soviet Union fell apart in a relatively peaceful way? Giving a complete and fully satisfactory answer to this very complex question goes way beyond the scope of this chapter, but some of the key differences can be mentioned (see Vujacic and Zaslavzky 1991; Vujacic 2004). In both the Soviet Union and Yugoslavia, the collapse has been attributed to the unintended long-term consequences of ethno-territorial federalism (Vujacic and Zaslavsky 1991; Bunce 1999), though some scholars have also stressed the independent role of political processes (Gagnon 1997). A purely 'economistic' explanation of the very different political outcomes is not convincing, since Yugoslavia's higher standard of living, open borders, free movement of labour, and greater managerial autonomy at the enterprise level would have led us to expect that its socialist middle classes would have a much greater vested interest in economic prosperity and political stability. The fact that this did not transpire suggests that the answer must be sought elsewhere, most likely in the very different historical, political–cultural, and institutional legacies;

ethnically motivated violence in the Second World War in Yugoslavia; and the very different collective memories that still animated political and intellectual elites at the time of the break-up (Vujacic 2004). The 'selective reactivation' of elements of those legacies by cultural and political elites has played a key role in Yugoslavia's break-up. In some of the Yugoslav successor states, it is only the bitter disappointment with the failure of Yugoslavism that pushed many citizens in the direction of ethnic nationalism (see Vujacic 2004).

3   Macroeconomic performance of the Balkan countries

3.1   From hyperinflation to economic stabilization

The initial measures of transition, as elsewhere in Eastern Europe, had a number of negative economic consequences also in the Western Balkan countries: high inflation, a substantial fall in real GDP, a rise in unemployment, and worsening of other social indicators. In the Balkan region, however, most of these problems have been of much greater scope than in the CEE countries, primarily because of the negative effects of the break-up of the Yugoslav federation, the military conflicts that accompanied it, and the UN embargo against FR Yugoslavia (Uvalic 2003a).

In the early 1990s, all countries except Albania registered hyperinflation (see Table 14.1). The successor states of former Yugoslavia experienced extreme macroeconomic instability as a consequence of the break-up of the Yugoslav political, economic, and monetary union, further fuelled by expansionary economic policies and other country-specific factors. Macroeconomic stabilization was earliest attained in Croatia and FYR Macedonia: thanks to very restrictive monetary policies, these two countries reduced inflationary pressures as early as 1995–6. Thereafter, both countries continued applying very restrictive monetary policy, which ensured that inflation rates were usually well below 5 per cent. FYR Macedonia even had disinflation in 1998–9 and again in 2004. Under the impact of the global economic crisis, however, there was a steep rise in inflation in both countries in 2008, when the rates more than doubled with respect to 2007, but there was a return to low inflation in 2009.

The radical economic reforms introduced by the Albanian government in 1992 were based on a shock therapy stabilization programme, backed by an International Monetary Fund (IMF) stand by arrangement (Bartlett 2008: 31). Although inflation was brought down to a one-digit rate in 1995, the positive trend was interrupted by the 1997 financial crisis caused by pyramid schemes that deprived the Albanian population of their life savings. Only since 1999 has Albania had a low inflation rate, usually well below 5 per cent, which was maintained up to 2009.

Bosnia and Herzegovina experienced hyperinflation in the years immediately after the break-up of the Yugoslav federation and the war on its territory

Table 14.1 Inflation in the Balkan countries, 1992–2009 (percentage change in annual average retail/consumer price levels)

	Albania	Bosnia and Herzegovina	Bosnian Federation	Republika Srpska	Croatia	Macedonia	FRY/S and M	Serbia	Montenegro	Kosovo
1992	226.0		73.1	7,461	665.5	1,664.4	9,237.0			
1993	85.0		44,069	2,233	1,517.5	338.4	116.5 trillion			
1994	22.6		780.0	1,061	97.6	126.5	3.3			
1995	7.8		-4.4	12.9	2.0	16.4	78.6			
1996	12.7		-24.5	16.9	3.5	2.3	94.3			
1997	33.2		14.0	-7.3	3.6	2.6	21.3	18.3	23.4	
1998	20.6		5.1	-14.0	5.7	-0.1	29.5	30.0	32.4	
1999	0.4		-0.9	14.1	4.0	-0.7	37.1	41.1	67.6	
2000	0.1		1.9	14.0	4.6	5.8	60.4	70.0	97.1	
2001	3.1	3.2	1.9	7.0	3.8	5.5	91.3	91.8	22.6	11.7
2002	5.2	0.4	-0.2	1.7	1.7	1.8	21.4	19.5	16.0	3.6
2003	2.4	0.6	0.1	1.8	1.8	1.2	11.3	11.7	6.7	1.2
2004	2.9	0.4	-0.3	1.9	2.1	-0.4	8.5	10.1	2.4	-1.1
2005	2.4	3.8	3.0	5.2	3.3	0.5	14.1	16.5	2.3	-1.4
2006	2.4	6.1	6.0	6.4	3.2	3.2	11.4	12.7	3.0	0.6
2007	2.9	4.9	1.9	1.1	2.9	2.3	—	6.5	4.2	4.4
2008	1.1	8.5	7.7	6.9	6.1	8.3	—	12.4	8.3	9.4
2009	3.4	Na	-2.7	0.5	2.4	-0.8	—	8.1	3.4	-2.4

Source: Based on EBRD data, except for Kosovo (Commission of the EU 2006, 2009b; Central Bank of the Republic of Kosovo 2010).

in 1992–5. A currency board was introduced in 1997 to facilitate monetary stability, with variable results for the two entities. In the federation, inflation since 1995 has occasionally even been negative, but in the Republika Srpska, a one-digit inflation rate was achieved only after 2001. In 2008, similarly to other countries in the region, there was a multifold increase in the inflation rate in both the Bosnian Federation and the Republika Srpska. This trend was discontinued in 2009, when the federation even had disinflation.

The country that experienced the highest and longest inflationary pressures was FR Yugoslavia. In 1992–3, it recorded one of the highest hyperinflations in world history—in 1993 an annual average inflation rate of 116.5 trillion per cent, which at that time was the second highest (after the Hungarian 1945 hyperinflation) and the second longest hyperinflation (after the Russian episode in the 1920s) ever recorded in economic history. The monetary reconstruction programme in January 1994 based on a currency board, implemented by the newly appointed central bank governor, Dragoslav Avramovic, succeeded in bringing down annual average inflation to 3.3 per cent in 1994. The currency board could not be maintained, however, due to insufficient foreign reserves to back up monetary policies, which had already in mid-1994 become expansionary (Uvalic 2010). Moreover, in the absence of more fundamental systemic changes, inflation remained in double-digits also in the second half of the 1990s. It was only after political changes in October 2000 that radical economic reforms also brought more permanent macroeconomic stabilization. Although price liberalization led to an average inflation rate of over 90 per cent in 2001, inflation was gradually reduced thereafter.

Within FR Yugoslavia, Serbia's inflation rate has been similar to that recorded for the whole country—among the highest in the region though gradually declining. After the split between Serbia and Montenegro in June 2006, Serbia's average inflation declined to 6.5 per cent in 2007, jumped to over 12 per cent in 2008, and then fell again to 8.1 per cent in 2009. Montenegro applied very specific measures early on in order to escape inflationary pressures generated by expansionary monetary policies of the National Bank of Yugoslavia. Already in 1998, the Montenegrin government decided to introduce the German mark as legal tender; that was replaced by the euro in 2002. The unilateral adoption of the deutschmark/euro contributed to a substantial reduction in inflation in Montenegro, especially after 2003, though it did not provide more permanent monetary stability, given that in 2008 average inflation again rose to over 8 per cent. In Kosovo, where the euro has also been used as legal tender since mid-1999, inflation was reduced to low levels after 2002–3, but also in this case there was a sharp increase in average inflation to 9.4 per cent in 2008, followed by disinflation in 2009.

Overall, all Western Balkan countries had by 2007 achieved one-digit average inflation rates. Under the impact of the global economic crisis, which

Table 14.2 Exchange rate regimes in the Balkans

Country	Exchange arrangement	Period of adoption	Currency
Albania	Pegged	1990–1	Lek linked to the US$
	Independently floating	1992 onwards	Lek
Bosnia and Herzegovina	No unique regime	1992–6	BiH dinar, new BiH dinar, Croatian dinar (later kuna), Republika Srpska dinar and Yugoslav dinar
	BiH dinar pegged	After August 1994	
	Currency board	1997 onwards	Convertible marka linked to the euro
Croatia	Pegged	1992	Croatian dinar, in 1993 replaced by the kuna
	Managed float	Oct. 1993 onwards	
FYR Macedonia	Pegged	1992–5	Coupons, later replaced by the Macedonian denar
	Conventional peg	1995 onwards	Macedonian denar
FR Yugoslavia	Pegged	1992–9	Yugoslav dinar
Serbia	Pegged	1992	Yugoslav dinar
	Managed float	Dec. 2000 onwards	
Montenegro	Euroization (euro *de jure* legal tender)	1998 onwards	euro
Kosovo	Euroization (euro *de jure* legal tender)	Mid-1999 onwards	euro

Source: Based on Daviddi and Uvalic (2006).

severely hit most Balkan countries in late 2008, the average inflation rate has increased strongly, though only in Serbia did it exceed 10 per cent. The trend was reversed in 2009 when three countries recorded disinflation: Bosnia, Macedonia and Kosovo.

The Balkan countries have adopted a variety of exchange rate regimes in order to sustain their macroeconomic stabilization efforts, from floating regimes to much more rigid arrangements (see Table 14.2). Still, the choice of the regime does not seem to have fundamentally influenced actual monetary policy. Even in countries with more flexible exchange rate regimes (Albania, Croatia, or Serbia), the objective of low inflation has led to restrictive monetary policies and real appreciation of national currencies, bearing close similarities with policies followed by countries under a more rigid regime— the currency board in Bosnia and Herzegovina, or the adoption of the euro in Montenegro and Kosovo (Daviddi and Uvalic 2006: 261–78).

The situation regarding general government balances has been variable in the individual Balkan countries. Some have registered particularly high deficits in the second half or the end of the 1990s—including Albania, Croatia, and FR Yugoslavia. In FYR Macedonia, relatively high fiscal deficits were present only briefly, in 2001–2, due to the civil war, and therefore were an exception rather than the rule. There has been some fiscal consolidation in all Balkan countries, particularly after 2001 (see Table 14.3).

Restrictive budgetary policies have led to fiscal surpluses, sometimes even for several years in a row: in Bosnia and Herzegovina throughout 2003–6; in FYR Macedonia in 2004–5 and again in 2007; in Montenegro during the 2005–7 period; in Serbia in 2004–5, and in Kosovo in 2001–3 and again in 2006–7. The tax systems in all countries have been subject to radical reforms, but the structure of government expenditure has not changed much, confined to a large extent to wages, pensions, and social transfers, with negligible capital investment. In 2008 the share of government expenditure in GDP was considered high, particularly in Bosnia and Herzegovina (48 per cent), Montenegro (44 per cent), Serbia (40 per cent), and Croatia (39 per cent). The size of the government is much smaller in Albania and FYR Macedonia, where public expenditure in 2008 accounted for only 27 per cent and 34 per cent of their respective GDPs.

By 2009, therefore, all Balkan countries had reached substantial monetary stability, though at different times—Croatia and FYR Macedonia earliest, while Serbia only recently. The conduct of monetary policy has been heavily constrained by the requirements of macroeconomic stabilization, in almost all cases codified in conditionality negotiated and agreed with the IMF. Macroeconomic stability has been supported by more restrictive budgetary policy, although weak tax collection and a large informal economy remain characteristic. If not addressed in a coherent way, fiscal problems could endanger long-term stability (see Trumbic and Uvalic 2005).

3.2 From deep recession towards economic recovery

The Balkan countries went through a very deep recession in the early 1990s (see Table 14.4). Albania registered a strong drop in real GDP in 1991–2 but recovered quickly: in 1993 it registered a growth rate close to 10 per cent. The initial economic reforms implemented by the last Yugoslav government in 1990–1 led to a strong fall in output, but the dissolution of the country further deepened its economic collapse (Bartlett 2008: 114). Consequently, the Yugoslav successor states registered a much stronger cumulative fall in production than most other countries. From 1991 to 1993, real GDP in Bosnia and Herzegovina fell by 12 per cent, 80 per cent and 10 per cent, respectively, while in FR Yugoslavia it fell by 12 per cent, 28 per cent and 31 per cent. Industrial production fell even more, contributing to a rapid process of deindustrialization. In Bosnia and Herzegovina, the war brought a complete collapse in industrial capacity, while in FR Yugoslavia industrial

Table 14.3 General government balances in the Balkan countries, 1994–2009 (percentage of GDP)

	Albania	Bosnia and Herzegovina	Croatia	Macedonia	FRY/S and M	Serbia	Montenegro	Kosovo
1995	−10.1	−0.3	−0.7	−1.0	−4.3			
1996	−9.7	−3.9	−0.4	−1.4	−3.8			
1997	−12.7	−0.4	−1.1	−0.4	−7.6			
1998	−12.1	−0.1	−3.0	−1.7	−5.4			
1999	−12.3	−4.0	−8.2	0.0	NA			
2000	−7.6	−4.7	−7.5	2.5	−0.9	−0.09	−4.0	
2001	−6.9	2.2	−6.8	−6.3	−1.3	−6.3	−2.0	3.7
2002	−6.1	−4.2	−4.9	−5.7	−4.5	−3.2	−1.9	4.4
2003	−4.9	2.3	−4.8	−0.6	−4.2	−1.1	−3.1	2.1
2004	−5.1	1.6	−4.0	0.4	−3.4	0.9	−1.9	−4.5
2005	−3.5	2.2	−3.5	0.3	0.9	1.0	2.1	−3.0
2006	−3.3	2.2	−3.1	−0.3	2.3	−1.6	4.2	2.4
2007	−3.5	−0.1	−2.5	0.6	–	−1.9	6.3	7.1
2008	−5.5	−4.2	−1.4	−1.0	–	−2.6	−0.4	−0.2
2009	−7.4	−4.6	−3.3	−2.6	–	−4.2	−3.6	−0.8

Source: Based on EBRD data, except for Kosovo (Commission of the EU 2006, 2009b; IMF 2010).

Table 14.4 Percentage growth in real GDP of the Balkan countries, 1991–2009

	Albania	Bosnia and Herzegovina	Croatia	Macedonia	FRY/S and M	Serbia	Montenegro	Kosovo	Avg. all transition countries
1990	−10.0	−23.2	−7.1	−9.9	−7.9				−7.9
1991	−28.0	−12.1	−21.1	−7.0	−11.6				−9.2
1992	−7.2	−80.0	−11.7	−8.0	−27.9				−4.9
1993	9.6	−10.0	−8.0	−9.1	−30.8				−5.2
1994	8.3	0.0	5.9	−1.8	2.5	2.5	0.7		0.1
1995	13.3	20.8	6.8	−1.1	6.1	6.1	6.2		0.2
1996	9.1	86.0	5.9	1.2	7.8	7.8	13.9		3.5
1997	−10.9	37.0	6.8	1.4	10.1	10.1	4.2		−0.1
1998	8.6	15.6	2.1	3.4	1.9	1.9	4.0		1.8
1999	13.2	9.6	−1.5	4.3	−18.0	−18.0	−6.7		6.3
2000	6.5	5.5	3.0	4.5	5.0	5.2	3.1		1.8
2001	7.9	4.3	3.8	−4.5	5.5	5.1	1.1		4.5
2002	4.2	5.5	5.4	0.9	4.0	4.5	1.9		5.8
2003	5.8	3.0	5.0	2.8	3.0	2.4	2.5	−2.4	7.2
2004	5.7	6.3	4.2	4.1	5.0	9.3	4.4	−0.1	6.3
2005	5.7	3.9	4.2	4.1	5.0	6.3	4.2	3.4	7.2
2006	5.4	6.7	4.7	4.0	5.0	5.5	8.6	3.9	7.0
2007	6.0	6.8	5.5	5.9	–	6.9	10.7	4.0	4.2
2008	7.8	6.0	2.4	4.8	–	5.5	6.9	4.0	−5.2
2009	3.3	−2.8	−5.8	−0.9	–	−3.1	−5.7	5.4	140.0
GDP 2008 (1989=100)	163.0	84.0	111.0	102.0	NA	72.0	92.0	NA	

Source: Based on EBRD data, except for Kosovo (Commission of the EU 2006, 2009b).

production was particularly affected by the introduction of UN sanctions in May 1992 that lasted for over four years. In Albania, the government never managed to introduce effective structural policies capable of rebuilding the industrial capacity that had been lost in the 1990s by the decline of the old state-owned industries (Bartlett 2008: 120–1).

Economic recovery from the deep recession took place at different times— in 1993 in Albania, in 1994 in most other countries, and only in 1996 in FYR Macedonia, where the recession was milder but lasted longer. There was a reversal in the trend of economic recovery in the second half of the 1990s, though for very different reasons, when all countries except Bosnia and Herzegovina again registered negative growth rates. Albania had a serious financial crisis in 1997 caused by the collapse of pyramid schemes. Croatia experienced a financial crisis when several domestic banks collapsed in 1998, due to politically connected lending to unprofitable enterprises (Bartlett 2008). FR Yugoslavia registered an 18 per cent fall in GDP in 1999, caused by the NATO bombing. FYR Macedonia's economic recovery was also interrupted in 2001 by the outbreak of civil war, which caused a fall in output of 4.5 per cent.

After unsatisfactory growth during much of the 1990s, 2008 was the eighth consecutive year of positive real GDP growth for most Balkan countries, on average close to or over 5 per cent. The only exceptions were FYR Macedonia, which in 2001 experienced negative growth due to the civil war, and Kosovo, where positive GDP growth rates were registered only after 2004. Kosovo has had a slow economic recovery due to reduced international assistance, and the failure of the UN Interim Administration Mission in Kosovo (UNMIK) authorities and the provisional government to implement effective economic reforms (Bartlett 2008: 116–17).

The trend of fast economic recovery was interrupted by the global financial and economic crisis that hit most Balkan countries in late 2008. The crisis was transmitted to the Balkan countries, as in most CEE countries, both through the financial sector, namely the sharp reduction in all forms of foreign capital inflows (FDI, foreign loans, and remittances), and through the real sector, caused by the strong fall in export demand in the EU as their main trading partner (see Nuti 2009; Prica and Uvalic 2009). Albania and Kosovo were the only countries in the Balkan region that registered a positive GDP growth rate in 2009, of 3.3 per cent and 4 per cent, respectively. Croatia and Montenegro were the most negatively affected, having registered a drop in real GDP of almost 6 per cent. Although economic recovery is on its way, economic growth so far has been sluggish.

3.3 External imbalances and FDI

By late 2008, all Balkan countries were facing serious external imbalances. After the 1990s, which were characterized by declining or stagnating exports, in the 2000s, exports from the Balkan countries grew quite impressively.

Nevertheless, imports have grown even faster, inducing rising foreign trade deficits. Restrictive monetary policies implemented to combat inflation have frequently led to strong real appreciation of the national currencies, hampering a faster expansion of exports. Despite the trade preferences granted by the EU to all Balkan countries after 2000, many of their products are not sufficiently competitive on foreign markets or face non-tariff barriers, limiting their capacity to increase exports further.

This is another area where the actual outcomes have been strikingly similar across the Balkan countries. Those countries with more flexible exchange rate regimes have not used exchange rate policy to stimulate exports, at least until the appearance of the global crisis. On the contrary, real currency appreciation has constrained export growth and stimulated increasing imports. The export performance has not been any better in those Balkan countries with a currency board or the euro (Bosnia, Kosovo, and Montenegro), due to additional structural deficiencies and country-specific problems. The main consequence in all cases has been a substantial increase in the trade deficit. All countries have also had persistent current account deficits, which reached alarming levels in 2008 (see Figure 14.1). These high deficits were covered by inflows of capital from abroad—donor assistance, emigrants' remittances, foreign loans, and FDI. By late 2008, most countries also had extremely high levels of gross external debt, particularly Croatia (88 per cent of GDP), Montenegro (77 per cent), and Serbia (63 per cent).

Because of their large external financial needs, the Balkan countries have been among the most exposed to the global credit crunch (see Uvalic 2009a; Prica and Uvalic 2009). Several countries turned to the IMF for support in late 2008 and early 2009, including Serbia, and Bosnia and Herzegovina (see IHS Global Insight 2009). The high dependence of the Balkans on foreign capital inflows is not of recent origin. In the 1990s, foreign assistance programmes greatly helped economic recovery in Bosnia and Herzegovina, but they were accompanied by externally imposed reform agendas and inappropriate aid

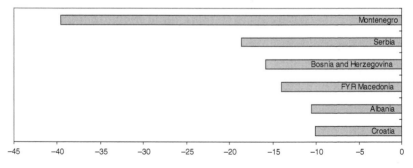

Figure 14.1 Current account deficits in the Balkan countries, 2008 (percentage of GDP)

policies. The phenomenon of 'aid addiction'—transfers of large amounts of international resources without the creation of sound conditions for more permanent economic recovery and self-sustaining growth—became an acute problem, particularly in the international protectorates: Bosnia and Herzegovina, and Kosovo (see Uvalic 2003b: 99–115). However, high dependence on external donors' financial assistance was also present in FR Yugoslavia after the 2000 political changes (see Uvalic 2010). Throughout the 1990s, international assistance packages contributed very marginally to creating conditions for self-sustaining growth in the Balkan region. Until 2000, the prevalent part of foreign aid in the Balkans was used not for investment but for emergency programmes, humanitarian assistance, and food aid (see Uvalic 2001, 2010).

Since 2001, the Balkan countries have finally attracted increasing FDI after a decade of very limited inflows. It is worth recalling that from 1989 to 1996, the cumulative FDI inflows into the four Western Balkan countries (without Bosnia) amounted to less than US$900 million, or 2 per cent of the total invested into 27 transition countries (Uvalic 2003a). Even after 1997, FDI in the Western Balkans remained low, representing only 6 per cent of FDI in all 27 transition economies over the 1989–2001 period. During this initial period, 60 per cent of total FDI in the Western Balkans was concentrated in Croatia.

Along with political stabilization after 2001 and the new EU policy for the Western Balkans launched in mid-1999, FDI has steadily increased, particularly during 2006–8 (see Table 14.5 and Figure 14.2). In 2006, Serbia attracted a record FDI of over US$4 billion, thanks to a few major privatization deals in telecommunications and banking. The recent increase in FDI inflows demonstrates a substantial improvement with respect to the 1990s, but the cumulative FDI of some US$54 billion into the six Western Balkan countries during 1989–2008 is still fairly low: around 8.2 per cent of the total invested into all European Bank for Reconstruction and Development (EBRD) client countries in Eastern Europe. The limited volume of FDI and its inadequate structure, prevalently concentrated in services, is one of the main reasons for the insufficient restructuring of basic industries in the Balkan economies.

Over the whole 1989–2008 period, Croatia remained notably ahead of the other countries in terms of FDI stock, with US$23 billion, but this is still much less than the US$41 billion invested in Bulgaria or the US$58 billion invested in Romania over the same period. The second highest FDI stock is in Serbia (US$15 billion), followed by substantially smaller amounts in Bosnia and Herzegovina (US$6.2 billion), Albania (US$3.5 billion), FYR Macedonia (US$3.2 billion), and Montenegro (US$2.8 billion). Kosovo has so far attracted very little FDI—some €750 million over the 2004–7 period (Commission 2009a). Regarding cumulative FDI inflows per capita, by 2008 Croatia was again ahead (US$5215), followed by Montenegro (US$4229),

Table 14.5 Net inflows of FDI in the Balkan countries, 1989–2008 (US$ millions)

	Albania	Bosnia and Herzegovina	Croatia	Macedonia	Montenegro	Serbia	Total FDI in SEE-6
2000	143	146	1,105	175	NA	50	1,619
2001	207	119	1,398	441	10	165	2,340
2002	135	266	552	105	84	475	1,617
2003	178	382	1,927	117	44	1,365	4,013
2004	324	708	732	322	63	966	3,115
2005	258	608	1,551	94	482	1,550	4,543
2006	315	718	3,194	424	585	4,264	9,500
2007	647	2,088	4,736	700	717	2,523	11,411
2008	844	1,003	4,576	612	805	2,717	10,557
Cumulative net inflows 1989–2008							
US$, million	3,505	6,228	23,164	3,226	2,791	15,040	53,954
Per head US$	1,101	1,639	5,215	1,570	4,229	2,005	–
FDI inflows 2008							
% GDP	6.6	5.3	6.6	6.4	16.7	5.3	–

Source: Based on EBRD data.

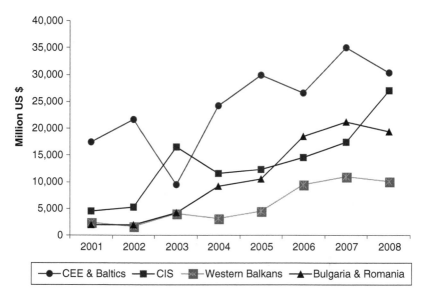

Figure 14.2 FDI in transition countries (net inflows, US$ millions)
Source: Based on EBRD data.

while the other countries have attracted relatively less. The high political risk deriving from the military conflicts in the region was undoubtedly the main barrier for more FDI inflows in the 1990s, but political factors remained important after 2000. Limited inflows of FDI also stem from the smallness of markets of most countries, from uncertain prospects of EU membership, and from the unsatisfactory regulatory environment that has not changed fast enough.

3.4 Slow catching up and 'jobless' growth

Despite strong growth in the Balkans in recent years, economic recovery has not been sufficient to compensate for the very substantial drop in output in the 1990s. As late as 2005, Albania was the only Balkan country that had surpassed its 1989 GDP level, thanks to exceptionally high growth rates throughout most of the 1990s and a very low starting point, while Croatia had just reached its 1989 GDP level. Although there was subsequently some further economic recovery, the situation in the Balkans is still unfavourable for most countries. By 2008, only Albania, Croatia, and Macedonia had surpassed their 1989 GDP levels, while Montenegro was at 92 per cent, Bosnia and Herzegovina at 84 per cent, and Serbia at only 72 per cent (see Table 14.4 and Figure 14.3). For the sake of comparison, real GDP in the nine more advanced countries—the five CEE countries, the three Baltics, and Croatia—by

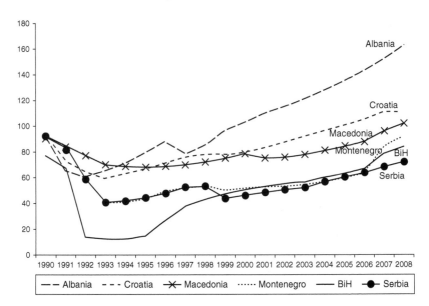

Figure 14.3 Real GDP growth in Serbia and other Balkan countries, 1990–2008 (1989 = 100)

Source: Uvalic (2010: 258), based on EBRD data.

Table 14.6 GDP per head in the Balkan countries and with respect to the EU (US$)

	At market exchange rates		At PPP		GDP per capita in PPS EU 27 = 100	
	2005	2008	2005	2008	2006	2008
Albania	2,690	4,260	5,400	6,920	23	26
Bosnia and Herzegovina	2,850	4,660	6,610	8,650	27	31
Croatia	9,970	13,760	14,940	18,290	57	63
Macedonia	2,820	4,370	7,350	9,140	29	33
Montenegro	3,480	7,850	7,880	10,800	36	43
Serbia	3,500	6,880	8,620	11,160	33	36

Source: Estimates of the Economist Intelligence Unit (June 2009), except for the last two columns, which are Eurostat data (Commission of the EC 2009c).

2008 was 156 per cent of its 1989 level, while in all the 29 EBRD client countries it was 140 per cent.

There are currently large differences among the Balkan countries in the level of economic development, larger than among the CEE countries (see Table 14.6 and Figure 14.4). The richest country by far is Croatia, with a

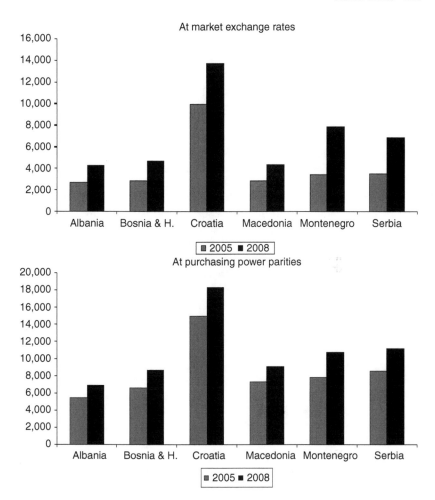

Figure 14.4 GDP per capita of the Balkan countries, 2005 and 2008
Source: Based on Uvalic (2010), and Economist Intelligence Unit data.

GDP per capita (at market exchange rates) in 2008 of over US$13,760, or of US$18,290 at purchasing power parity (PPP), according to estimates of the Economist Intelligence Unit (EIU). In terms of GDP per capita at PPP, the second most developed country is Serbia, but, if we consider market exchange rates, it is Montenegro. The poorer Balkan countries include Albania, FYR Macedonia, and Bosnia and Herzegovina, while the poorest is Kosovo. The EU Commission data show that in 2005 Kosovo had a GDP per capita of only €1105 (at current prices), while that of Croatia was €6643 (see Commission of the EC 2006).

Some catching up has taken place since 2000 with respect to the EU average GDP per capita, both because growth in the Balkans was generally stronger than in the EU and because the EU average has been reduced after the EU 2004–7 enlargements, due to the entry of less developed countries. In 2000 the Balkan countries had a GDP per capita (at purchasing power standards, PPS) of only around 10–30 per cent of the EU-15 average (Uvalic 2003b). By 2008 Croatia had reached 63 per cent of the EU-27 GDP per head at PPS but the other countries were still much further behind— Montenegro was at 43 per cent, Serbia at 36 per cent, Bosnia at 31 per cent, and Albania at 26 per cent of the EU-27 average (Commission of the EU 2009c).

Regarding the structure of the Balkan economies, it has been characterized by a very fast expansion of, primarily, services. Albania is the only country where agriculture still contributes an important proportion of gross value added (21 per cent in 2005). The other countries are less agriculture-oriented: the relative share of agriculture in gross value added had declined by 2006 to 12 per cent in FYR Macedonia, 11 per cent in Kosovo, 10 per cent in both Montenegro and Serbia, and 7 per cent in Croatia. During 2000–7, these changes were accompanied by a decline in the relative share of industry in all countries except Albania, as well as a very strong increase in services. The process of deindustrialization, which was most intense in the Balkan region during the early 1990s, has continued during the more recent period as well. By 2006–7 the contribution of services to gross value added ranged from 57 per cent in FYR Macedonia to 69 per cent in Serbia (Commission of the EC 2009a: 61–2). In comparison with the situation in the EU-27, where in 2007 the services sector contributed 71.6 per cent of gross value added, the Balkan countries' share seems rather high and premature considering their much lower level of economic development. Moreover, recent growth in the Balkan countries—including Bosnia and Herzegovina, Montenegro, Serbia, and Kosovo—has taken place primarily in the non-tradable services, such as retail trade, banking, and telecommunications, and not in the tradeable goods sector. This further explains the poor export performance of most Balkan countries.

The high GDP growth rates in most countries have also been largely insufficient to alleviate the problem of very high unemployment. Though all governments have undertaken measures to create new jobs for laid-off workers, to stimulate private sector development, and to facilitate the entry of new private firms, the unemployment rates remain among the highest in Europe (see Figure 14.5). The Balkan region has been badly hit by the phenomenon of 'jobless growth', much more than the CEE countries in the early years of transition. According to the more realistic statistics provided by labour force surveys (LFS), unemployment in the Balkans has indeed been extremely high—much higher than in CEE

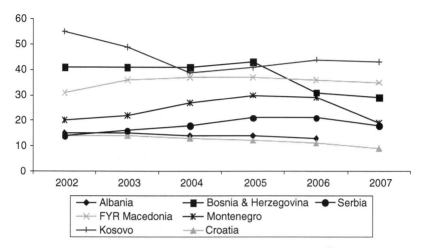

Figure 14.5 Unemployment rates in the Balkan countries (labour force surveys), as a percentage of labour force
Source: Based on Commission of the European Communities (2009a) data.

countries in the 1990s. The LFS unemployment rates in 2007 were particularly high in Bosnia and Herzegovina (29 per cent), FYR Macedonia (35 per cent), and Kosovo (44 per cent). Serbia and Montenegro have also had very high unemployment rates, close to 20 per cent or higher, which started declining in Serbia only in 2007 but again increased in 2009–10. Also, in Bosnia and Herzegovina, FYR Macedonia and Kosovo, unemployment rates have either increased or remained very high over the last six years. Croatia is the only country that has rather substantially reduced its unemployment rate—from 15 per cent in 2002 to less than 10 per cent in 2007—but the global economic crisis has again brought a sharp increase in unemployment.

These very high unemployment rates overestimate the effective number of unemployed workers as they do not take into account people having an activity in the informal economy. According to some estimates of the size of the informal economy in transition economies, it is generally larger in the Balkan than in the CEE countries, ranging on average in 2002 from 32 per cent in Croatia to 45 per cent in FYR Macedonia, though it is smaller than in many Commonwealth of Independent States (CIS) countries (see Schneider 2003). Other estimates suggest that the level of informal activity is highest in Albania (52 per cent of household income), Kosovo and Macedonia (at 45 per cent and 39 per cent, respectively), while the Bosnian Federation, Serbia and Croatia have the lowest levels at 18–19 per cent (Bartlett 2008: 125).

4 Progress with transition-related economic reforms

The economic and institutional reforms of the transition to a market economy have proceeded at variable speed in the individual Balkan countries. Albania, Croatia, and FYR Macedonia initially implemented most reforms at a faster pace than the other countries and have therefore been labelled as the 'early reformers' (Bartlett 2008). Bosnia and Herzegovina, and FR Yugoslavia (Serbia, Montenegro and Kosovo), in contrast, have postponed more radical economic reforms until fairly recently due to military conflicts and other political problems, and they are thus referred to as the 'late reformers'. FR Yugoslavia implemented radical economic reforms only after 2000; at that time, after the political changes, the only areas where some results had been achieved were small-scale privatization and price liberalization. Economic reforms in Bosnia and Herzegovina have been delayed not only by the four-year war but also by serious problems linked to the fragility of its institutions and malfunctioning of the state administration.

Nevertheless, all the Balkan countries have made substantial progress since 2001 in implementing the most important economic reforms, as illustrated by the transition indicators of the EBRD. These indicators evaluate progress in various areas of reform in all EBRD client countries in Eastern Europe, on the basis of scores that range from 1 (no or limited reform) to 4+ (comparable to a developed market economy). Thanks to the acceleration of economic reforms in FR Yugoslavia, and Bosnia and Herzegovina, over the last eight years, these two countries have also achieved excellent results in many areas. The EBRD transition indicators for 2010 show that there are no longer extreme differences between the 'early' and the 'late' reformers (see Table 14.7), as was the case in 2001. Moreover, there are no major differences between the results achieved in CEE and the Balkans regarding price liberalization, the trade and foreign exchange system, or small-scale privatization, since the Balkan countries have also by now practically completed these reforms.

The Balkan countries have successfully implemented price liberalization and have opened up their economies through thorough reforms of the foreign trade regime, the elimination of quantitative restrictions, and substantial lowering of tariff barriers. Small-scale privatization has also been practically completed in all countries except Bosnia and Herzegovina, whereas large-scale privatization, though slower, is on its way (though Albania is forging ahead of the other countries). Progress has been slower in other areas of reform. The most critical indicators relate to enterprise governance and restructuring, competition policies, and the development of securities markets and non-bank institutions. In these three areas, far-reaching reforms have been much more difficult to implement, though these are the areas where changes have been more gradual also in the CEE countries.

Table 14.7 Transition indicator scores for the Balkan countries, mid-2010

	Albania	Bosnia and Herzegovina	Croatia	Macedonia	Montenegro	Serbia
Private sector share of GDP (%) mid-2010	75	60	70	70	65	60
Enterprises						
Large-scale privatization	4–	3	3+	3+	3+	3–
Small-scale privatization	4	3	4+	4	4–	4
Governance and enterprise restructuring	2+	2	3	3–	2	2+
Markets and trade						
Price liberalization	4+	4	4	4+	4	4
Trade and foreign exchange system	4+	4	4+	4+	4	4
Competition policy	2	2	3	2+	2	2+
Financial institutions						
Banking reform and interest rate liberalization	3	3	4	3	3	3
Securities markets and non-bank financial institutions	2–	2–	3	3–	2–	2
Infrastructure reforms	2+	3–	3	3–	2+	2+

Source: Based on EBRD (2009) data.

By 2010 the private sector contributed 60–75 per cent of the Balkan countries' GDP. Albania is the most privatized economy, with a 75 per cent share of the private sector in GDP. The private sector has grown the least in Serbia and in Bosnia and Herzegovina, where it still contributes only 60 per cent of GDP, thus placing these two countries among the six least privatized economies in Eastern Europe. Still, it should be stressed that privatization very often did not improve corporate governance or lead to deep enterprise restructuring. In the privatized sector, microeconomic restructuring has often been delayed due to limited access to credit facilities and insufficient FDI in key industries, ineffective systems of corporate governance or lack of managerial skills. Enterprises were frequently sold under privileged conditions to employed workers and managers, and not to foreign investors having the resources and skills to invest in new technology and modernization.

Another critical area is competition policy. Although most countries have reduced subsidies to large non-privatized enterprises and have adopted laws promoting competition, there have been substantial delays in implementing existing legislation, and the anti-trust authorities have frequently been ineffective. Not surprisingly, in the area of competition policy, all countries except Croatia in 2010 were evaluated by a modest score of 2 (with the addition of a plus or a minus). One of the main factors impeding more competition in the Balkans is the inadequate regulatory business environment, also with regard to firm entry and exit. Although there have been major improvements in easing the conditions for firm entry, there are still substantial barriers, as documented by the World Bank 'Doing Business surveys'.

Another area where developments have been relatively slow is the financial sector. The Balkan countries have also implemented radical banking reforms, including privatization through the sale of majority shares to foreign banks. By 2003, foreign ownership of the banking sector was already very high in Albania (over 95 per cent of total assets), Bosnia and Herzegovina (70 per cent), and Kosovo (61 per cent) (Commission of the EC 2004). In the meantime, foreign ownership has become dominant also in the other countries—in 2007 the asset share of foreign-owned banks in Montenegro was 79 per cent and in Serbia 75 per cent (EBRD 2008: 162, 178). By the end of 2008, Serbia had only one bank, the Komercijalna Banka, in which the Serbian government had a minority (43 per cent) ownership share (Uvalic 2010). Despite positive changes, the loan-to-deposit ratios have generally been lower in the Western Balkans than in the CEE countries, while the net interest spread (the difference between lending and borrowing rates) is still relatively high, particularly in Serbia. Mainly as a consequence of delayed privatization of large enterprises, the stock exchange remains underdeveloped in all countries except Croatia, and little progress has been achieved in creating non-bank financial institutions, such as investment funds.

Infrastructure is another area where the Balkan states are still lagging behind the CEE countries. By 2010, three countries had made notable progress in this area—Bosnia and Herzegovina, Croatia, and FYR Macedonia—while the other countries were still evaluated with a low 2+. Infrastructural reforms are not easy to implement and have taken place very gradually also in the more developed market economies, sometimes not even successfully.

Although progress achieved in transition-related economic reforms within the Balkan region has been variable, the differences today are much less pronounced than in late 2000. Croatia has achieved the best results so far, and has been evaluated by the EBRD as on a par with, or even better than, Bulgaria and Romania. Although the other Balkan countries are lagging behind, even the 'slow' reformers (Bosnia and Herzegovina, Serbia, and Montenegro) have caught up in most areas of reform and are approaching the more advanced countries.

5 International integration of the Western Balkans

A decade of marked political and economic instability in the Balkan region has greatly delayed the economic integration of these countries into the EU. It was only after the end of the Kosovo conflict in mid-1999 that the EU launched the Stabilisation and Association Process (SAP) specifically for the Western Balkan countries. The SAP included various measures to help the transition and integration of the Western Balkans: generous trade preferences, the possibility of establishing contractual relations with the EU through the signing of Stabilisation and Association Agreements (SAAs), and a new programme of financial assistance. Even more important, the Western Balkan countries were offered the prospect of future EU membership for the very first time since 1989. Furthermore, in June 1999 the Stability Pact for South Eastern Europe was adopted by the EU and its member states, other developed countries, and major international organizations, aiming to help the economic reconstruction of the seven SEE countries affected by the 1999 military conflict, in addition to the five Western Balkan countries, Bulgaria, and Romania.

Privileged access to EU markets was assured back in 2000 through EU autonomous trade measures that established a uniform system of trade preferences for all Western Balkan countries (FR Yugoslavia was included somewhat later, on 1 November 2000). These trade preferences provided for the elimination of duties and quantitative restrictions for approximately 95 per cent of products from the Western Balkans entering the EU market, including agricultural and sensitive industrial products, with only a few exceptions. Privileged access to EU markets is provided even before a country signs a SAA. The Balkan-EU trade liberalization process is being implemented on an asymmetric basis, initially envisaging a greater opening of EU markets than those of the Balkan countries. The EU adopted a new programme of financial assistance specifically for the Western Balkans: the Community Assistance to Reconstruction, Development and Stabilisation programme, which ensured some €5 billion over the 2000–6 period.

At the EU-Balkan summit in June 2003 in Thessaloniki, the prospect of EU membership for the Western Balkans was reconfirmed and further steps were undertaken to strengthen the EU-Balkan integration process. One of the novelties was the introduction of European partnerships for the Western Balkan countries, which serve to identify the main priorities and checklists (similar to the earlier partnerships designed for the CEE countries). A new tool for financial assistance was also adopted in July 2006—the Instrument of Pre-Accession Assistance (IPA)—to replace all previous financial assistance programmes. It is through the IPA programme that EU assistance is now delivered to candidate and potential candidate countries—the Western Balkans, but also Turkey and, more recently, Iceland. The total pre-accession funding within the IPA for the current EU financial framework (2007–13) is €11.5 billion.

A more favourable climate was also created to increase trade among the Balkan countries. Thanks to the changed political climate after 2000, one of the most important regional co-operation initiatives of the Stability Pact for SEE is the process of trade liberalization. A Memorandum of Understanding on Trade Liberalization and Facilitation was signed on 27 June 2001 in Brussels by the foreign trade ministers of the then seven SEE countries (the five Western Balkan countries, Bulgaria, and Romania); Kosovo participates as a separate entity, while Moldova has also joined the initiative in the meantime. This led to the conclusion of bilateral free trade agreements (FTA) among the SEE countries, providing for a substantial reduction or elimination of trade barriers. The process has effectively led to the creation of a free trade area in the SEE region (Uvalic 2006; Bartlett 2007). Since Bulgaria and Romania joined the EU in early 2007, EU trade regulations have superseded the FTAs signed with the other Balkan countries. Because these bilateral FTAs concluded by the Balkan states have been criticized as representing a 'spaghetti bowl' of differentiated trade relations, another important agreement was concluded in Bucharest in April 2006, when it was agreed to transform the FTAs into a single agreement, by enlarging and modernizing the current Central European Free Trade Agreement (CEFTA). Known as 'CEFTA 2006', the new single FTA is a modern trade agreement that harmonizes trade rules across the Balkan region and incorporates new provisions, such as trade in services, intellectual property rights, public procurement and investment promotion.

The overall results of the process of trade liberalization in the Balkans, both vis-à-vis the EU and with other countries in the region, have been positive. Since 2001 the Balkan countries have increasingly integrated with the EU economy (Uvalic 2007b: 233–50). EU trade has increased faster with the Balkan countries than with the rest of the world. The EU has become the main trading partner of all countries, accounting in 2008 for 55–80 per cent of the Western Balkan countries' imports and exports. The positive trade effects are particularly evident for countries like Serbia and Montenegro, which had no or limited EU trade preferences before late 2000. However, due to much larger imports than exports, the Balkan economies have experienced growing trade deficits. Insufficient restructuring and modernization of key industries due to delayed privatization, limited FDI, and rigid exchange rate policies leading to the real appreciation of national currencies are among the main reasons for the limited competitiveness of Balkan products in EU markets.

The process of trade liberalization within the SEE region has also had a positive influence on regional trade, at least for the Western Balkan countries. The majority of countries have registered an increase in trade with other countries in the region, although the impact has been extremely uneven across countries (Uvalic 2009b: 176–94). The initiative has had marginal effects in Albania, Bulgaria, and Romania, where the EU's much earlier trade liberalization measures have facilitated a major reorientation of trade primarily towards the EU. In contrast, regional trade for most countries of the former Yugoslavia has remained an important part of their overall trade, and intra-Balkan trade liberalization has further stimulated its expansion.

In 1989 the most integrated part of the SEE region was the Yugoslav economy (Uvalic 2001). Some 18 years later, the successor states of the former Yugoslavia are still the most integrated economies in the region. This may appear to be a paradox, since the break-up of the Yugoslav federation, the imposition of trade and non-trade barriers, the multiple military conflicts of the 1990s, and the economic sanctions imposed on some countries have clearly pushed in the opposite direction. This suggests that historical trade links inherited from the past can be of fundamental importance, which is confirmed in the case of the Western Balkans (Uvalic 2006). Although all Balkan countries have made major efforts to reorient their exports primarily towards EU countries, this has often produced limited results. As a consequence, being able to find alternative, more liberalized markets in the Balkan region has helped their exports grow more than would have been the case otherwise.

The Balkan countries have become more integrated into the EU both through increasing trade and through other channels. The largest part of recent FDI inflows into the Balkan region originates from EU countries. Balkan-EU integration has also taken place through fast integration of financial and capital markets, prompted by the privatization of the banking sector. As mentioned earlier, major EU multinational banks today own 60–95 per cent of the banking assets in Western Balkan countries. Foreign ownership of banks was welcome for the process of bank restructuring and privatization, but more recently it has rendered the Balkan countries more vulnerable to the global financial crisis.

Table 14.8 Stabilization and association agreements signed by the Balkan countries and the EU

Country	Date of signature	Date effective
FYR Macedonia	9 April 2001	1 April 2004
Croatia	29 October 2001	1 February 2005
Albania	12 June 2006	1 April 2009
Montenegro	15 October 2007	Ratification process not complete
Serbia	29 April 2008	Ratification process not complete
Bosnia and Herzegovina	16 June 2008	Ratification process not complete

Source: Based on Uvalic (2010); see text for explanation.

In contrast to fast economic integration, most Balkan countries have been rather slow in establishing contractual relations with the EU. Only two countries were able to sign a SAA with the EU early on: FYR Macedonia in April 2001, and Croatia in October 2001 (see Table 14.8). For the other countries, the process has been substantially delayed, most frequently due to very strict EU political and economic conditionality. Albania concluded its SAA in June 2006 and Montenegro in October 2007. The last two countries to sign a SAA were Serbia (April 2008), and Bosnia and Herzegovina (June 2008). In the case of Serbia, the ratification of the SAA and the application of the interim trade agreement were postponed for more than a year due to the country's non-compliance with political conditions—primarily insufficient collaboration with the International Criminal Tribunal for the former Yugoslavia (the process was unblocked only in mid-2010).

Thus the Balkan countries today are at very different stages of EU integration. Croatia is the only candidate at the time of writing negotiating EU membership, with the objective of joining in 2013. FYR Macedonia and Montenegro have candidate status, but accession negotiations have not yet commenced. Among the potential candidates, Albania and Serbia have applied for candidate status, which yet needs to be approved; Bosnia and Herzegovina remains a potential candidate for now; while Kosovo has a special status under the so-called 'tracking mechanism'.[6] With the exception of Croatia, the prospects of EU membership for the other countries are rather uncertain, despite promises regarding accession being reconfirmed by the EU on various occasions.

6   Understanding delays in transition in the Balkans

The ongoing analysis of macroeconomic performance and transition-related economic reforms in the Balkans suggests that there has been major convergence over the past decade. Although some countries have achieved the desired objectives much earlier, macroeconomic performance after

2001 has also improved in the 'late reformers' that were characterized by extreme economic instability in the 1990s. Similarly, many transition-related reforms have by now been implemented successfully also in countries that were institutionally lagging behind in the 1990s (Bosnia and Herzegovina, Montenegro, and Serbia). Today we observe a notable reduction in the institutional differences among the individual Balkan countries. Nevertheless, most of them still lag behind the CEE countries regarding certain economic reforms, the level of economic development, and the EU integration process. One might have expected that the extent of market-oriented reforms undertaken in the past, which provided all of the Yugoslav successor states with initial conditions that were among the best within the former socialist countries, would have been an important advantage facilitating the transition. However, instead of being the leaders in the transition region, these countries have turned out to be the laggards (Estrin and Uvalic 2008). Why has the success of CEE not been replicated in the Balkans?

There is enormous empirical literature that tries to disentangle the role of various factors responsible for the diverging progress of the individual transition countries, and that considers the importance of initial conditions, policies such as privatization and liberalization, and institutions (see, e.g., Godoy and Stiglitz 2007: 89–117). Over the last two decades, the Balkan countries have experienced very different paths of transition, but in their case it seems even harder to establish the determinants of variable outcomes. This is because there are additional and specific factors in the Balkan region that have crucially influenced the different pace and contents of transition. Three groups of factors seem particularly important for understanding delays in the attainment of transition-related economic objectives in the Western Balkans:

i) political events;
ii) delayed support and integration with the EU;
iii) inappropriate economic policies.

(i) The political events of the early 1990s—the break-up of the Yugoslav federation and the accompanying military conflicts—interrupted the ongoing economic reforms, representing the primary factor responsible for subsequent delays in transition. Objectives on the political agenda became much more important, primarily those related to the building of new nation states. The political objectives were given priority, even at the cost of military conflicts, international isolation, and high economic instability. As a result, the overall political and economic conditions in the Balkan region during the 1990s were fundamentally different from those in CEE. The legacy of the 1990s, a decade marked by extreme political instability, left a heavy burden on most countries, including delicate problems relating to borders, status, return of refugees, property, and minority rights. The political events of the 1990s have also had very profound and long-term economic consequences for the entire Balkan region, not only for those countries that were the most involved. Albania and FYR Macedonia were not active participants in the Balkan military conflicts in the 1990s,[7] but they have also felt the negative effects of political instability in the region, as confirmed by the limited FDI inflows and delayed association with the EU. Major improvements in macroeconomic performance and faster implementation of economic reforms in all Balkan countries after 2001 were not sufficient to fully compensate for the negative trends of the 1990s. Even after 20 years, three countries have still not attained their 1989 GDP levels.

(ii) The second group of factors that explains the slower pace of economic transition in the Western Balkans is delayed integration into the EU. EU policies towards the Western Balkan region, particularly in the 1990s, were very different from those applied towards the CEE countries or even other SEE countries (Bulgaria, Romania, or Slovenia). Due to the outbreak of war in the region in the early 1990s, the EU failed to elaborate a long-term strategy for the Western Balkans, which in turn substantially delayed their integration into the EU. In order to be offered substantial financial support through PHARE and other forms of assistance, in the early 1990s it was sufficient for the CEE countries to declare their desire to implement the transition to multi-party democracy and market economy. EU Association Agreements were concluded soon after, during 1993–6. The Western Balkan countries, in contrast, were not offered more substantial financial assistance and the possibility to conclude EU Association Agreements until 2000. The non-fulfilment of the required EU conditions, which have become even more numerous and more stringent for the Balkan than for the CEE states, have greatly delayed EU-Balkan integration.

(iii) The third factor is inappropriate economic policy. In part this was due to policy choices of the countries themselves, but in part it was the consequence of the transition strategy recommended by foreign advisers and main international organizations, which had been applied throughout most of Eastern Europe earlier on.

Some countries have postponed the attainment of transition-related economic objectives because of exceptional political circumstances (Bosnia and Herzegovina), or because of the deliberate choice of a gradualist transition strategy (FR Yugoslavia). The economic policies implemented in Serbia in the 1990s were often reversals of progressive transition-related economic reforms implemented in 1989–91, or were even a return to practices long abandoned in the former Yugoslavia (Uvalic 2007a). Only more recently have these two countries introduced more radical economic reforms, similar to those implemented in the other Balkan countries some years earlier. The timing of transition-related economic reforms was different, but the contents were rather similar, designed along the lines of the neoliberal approach implemented elsewhere in CEE, based on the recommendations of the 'Washington consensus' (see Williamson 1990). Also in the Balkan countries, government policies gave priority to liberalization, macroeconomic stabilization, and privatization, disregarding many other important reforms. The high level of monetary instability in the region in the early 1990s and the frequent presence of the IMF brought monetary policies intended to minimize inflation, irrespective of their negative effects on growth.

Although the 'post-Washington consensus' developed in the second half of the 1990s had already suggested the very high costs, in terms of slower growth, of excessively restrictive macroeconomic policies (Kolodko and Nuti 1997: 49–52), this was not taken into account in the Balkans. Other important messages of the 'post-Washington consensus' were mostly ignored in the Balkans (ibid.). The new consensus stressed the importance of 'organic' growth of the private sector through the expansion of *de novo* enterprises rather than just privatization of existing firms; the importance of corporate governance as opposed to a mere transfer of property titles; and the recognition of the negative consequences of neglect or discriminatory penalization of the state sector. At a time when the invisible hand of the market continued to be glorified, the 'post-Washington consensus' stressed the new role of the state and active government policies, not just less government but a different role for government. In particular, the importance of industrial policy was pointed out, including measures for promoting investment in certain sectors, improving access to credit for small and medium-sized enterprises, encouraging innovation, or introducing and protecting quality and technical standards.

There was no effective industrial policy in the Balkan countries. As a result, the process of industrial restructuring has been very slow, contributing to limited competitiveness and insufficient export growth. Although the first decade of transition in CEE has produced many important lessons, mistakes from the early years were forgotten only too readily by the countries that embarked on radical reforms much later, like Serbia (see Uvalic 2010). Despite strong growth since 2000, most Balkan countries today are relatively under-developed—only three had by 2008 reached their 1989 GDP levels; they have the highest unemployment rates in Europe; and due to the structural weaknesses of their economies, they face serious external imbalances.

The neoliberal strategy of transition was applied with minor variations in all the Balkan countries, though under different circumstances. The hyper-liberal policies implemented in the early 1990s in Albania and FYR Macedonia, backed by the IMF-supported shock therapy programmes, contained a number of fatal flaws. In particular, the substantial cuts in

government expenditure that reduced the role of the state to a bare minimum had adverse consequences for important sectors, including education
and health. There were probably even greater policy failures in international
protectorates—Bosnia and Herzegovina or Kosovo—where liberalization, stabilization and privatization brought highly disappointing results, a stable
currency being probably the only important exception. Economic recovery of these war-devastated and highly deindustrialized economies has been
very slow, institution-building has taken much longer than expected, and
many solutions imposed externally by international donors have not been
appropriate. One of the most notorious policy mistakes that ought to be
mentioned is the private pension fund in Kosovo, which was invested
entirely in mutual investment funds outside the country (Bartlett 2008:
154), with highly adverse consequences after the outbreak of the global
economic crisis. In FR Yugoslavia (Serbia and Montenegro), the acceleration
of transition-related reforms since late 2000 and strong economic recovery
have not been sufficient to alleviate the negative effects of the earlier decade.
In Serbia, capacity restructuring was expected to take place almost entirely
through privatization—a process that has proceeded very slowly and has not
been accompanied by other important measures, such as improving the regulatory environment for enterprise entry and exit, or increasing competition
through effective anti-trust policy (Uvalic 2010). Croatia has achieved faster
progress with regard to many reform objectives and is the most developed
Balkan country, but it should be recalled that it had among the best starting
conditions, since it was the second most developed Yugoslav republic (after
Slovenia) in 1991. Yet Croatia also has a number of reforms to complete and
its recent growth has been based on heavy borrowing from abroad, making
it the most indebted Balkan country and among the most severely hit by
the global economic crisis (indeed, in 2009, it registered a 5.8 per cent fall
in GDP).

Some of Popov's (2009) reflections about the lessons from the transition
economies seem appropriate also for the Western Balkans. Optimal policies
are context-dependent: they rely on specific backgrounds and are different
for each stage of economic development. There are no universal recipes as
there is more than one route to success. The reforms needed to stimulate
growth are different and crucially depend on the historical legacies. Path
dependency and historical legacies have been extremely important for all
the Balkan countries, yet these features have often been overlooked by the
policy advice offered to the region during the last 20 years, with a number
of adverse consequences.

7 Conclusions

By 2009, most Western Balkan countries had successfully attained many of
the economic objectives of the transition to a market economy. The only

possible exception is Kosovo, which is still in a rather difficult political and economic situation.[8] These countries have become more open market economies with dominant private ownership, they have reformed many key institutions, and they have liberalized their trade with the EU and with their neighbours. Their financial sectors are dominated by foreign-owned EU banks and there is an emerging stock exchange. Since the early 2000s, the Western Balkan states have been among the fastest-growing transition economies. In comparison to their position in the 1990s, the Balkans have attained substantial macroeconomic stability and, until the global economic crisis, had stable or slightly appreciating internally convertible national currencies. Privatization opportunities still abound in most countries and FDI has been on an upward trend, at least until mid-2008. With respect to the beginning of the decade, the gap regarding transition-related economic reforms within the Balkan region, between the early and late reformers, as well as between the Western Balkans and the CEE countries, has been greatly reduced. Strong economic integration of the Balkan countries into the EU has taken place through increasing trade, FDI, and financial flows, even though the establishment of contractual relations with the EU has proceeded at a much slower pace.

Over the past two decades there have been a number of major policy failures as well. Today's low level of output with respect to 1989 in all the Balkan states illustrates how deeply the recessions of the 1990s, greatly amplified by the multiple political events of those times, have affected these countries. Strong economic growth during 2001–8 has not been sufficient to compensate for the rapid economic decline during the 1990s. The history of very high and persistent inflation has led all Balkan countries, some earlier and some later, to subscribe to the safe recipe of very restrictive monetary policies. While these policies were successful in reducing inflation, they have not assured economic development in the longer run and a fast process of catching up with the more developed European countries. The limited restructuring of many industrial sectors and the failure to establish appropriate institutional, regulatory and legal frameworks have resulted in the failure to generate the supply response necessary to reduce unemployment and generate sustained economic development (Daviddi and Uvalic 2006).

Although the EBRD in 1995 made a sharp distinction between the concepts of transition and of economic development—transition being defined as the process of establishing open market economies through institutional change, and development referring to the enhancement of living standards—it is clear that transition to a market economy has been largely motivated by the pursuit of economic development (Kekic 1996). The systemic changes required by the transition to a market economy should, therefore, also have been a major instrument for attaining long-term economic development, but this has proved more difficult to achieve in the Balkan countries. Transition-related institutional changes implemented in a particularly unstable political and economic environment have not favoured fast economic development.

At present, following the strong effects of the global economic crisis of 2008–10, the key issue is what the future model of growth for the Balkan countries should be. Although further integration into the global economy clearly remains the preferable option, among other reasons because the Balkan states are all very small economies, some thought should be given to policies that could facilitate their improved export performance and increase their competitiveness on world markets. After the strong process of deindustrialization in the 1990s, foreign investors have contributed very little to the modernization and restructuring of many industrial sectors in the Balkans, since FDI has gone prevalently into services. In view of the recent sharp drop in FDI and its unlikely recovery over the next few years, the Balkan countries will have to rely much more on their scarce domestic resources and urgently conceptualize what type of policies could reinforce their key industries. As mentioned earlier, some kind of industrial policy would be desirable to achieve these goals.

Despite important economic tasks still to be accomplished by the Balkan governments, the political challenges are just as important. The Balkan states need to make a major effort to resolve the remaining political issues, as this is clearly in the interest of all. The EU should also reconfirm, in a credible way, the prospects of EU membership for the Western Balkans. To accomplish permanent stability in the Balkan region, it is essential to integrate all countries into the EU as soon as possible, not only economically but also politically.

Notes

1. The Federal Republic (FR) of Yugoslavia was constituted in April 1992 and consisted of Serbia with its two provinces, Voivodina and Kosovo, and Montenegro. The country changed its name to the State Union of Serbia and Montenegro on 4 February 2003. Following the May 2006 referendum on independence in Montenegro, Serbia and Montenegro became two independent states in mid-June 2006. According to the UN Security Council Resolution 1244 adopted in mid-1999 Kosovo officially remained part of Serbia, though thereafter it has effectively been governed by UNMIK. In February 2008, Kosovo unilaterally declared its independence, but at the time of writing has still not been recognized by not only Serbia but also the UN and five EU member states (Cyprus, Greece, Romania, Slovakia and Spain). All statistical data after 1999 on FR Yugoslavia/Serbia do not include Kosovo.
2. Although Slovenia is more frequently classified among the CEE countries, since it was one of the Yugoslav republics it is appropriate to consider it as well.
3. Kornai (1980) uses the term 'state paternalism' to describe one of the most fundamental features of the socialist system, namely the paternalistic relationship between the state and the firm, whereby the firm is constantly protected and supported by the state. State paternalism is at the basis of 'soft-budget constraints'

typical of the traditional socialist economy, namely soft terms set in the tax and credit system and toleration by the political authorities of enterprise financial indiscipline.

4. As a response to hyperinflation, the 'shock therapy' was based on the pegging of the exchange rate to the German mark, introduction of resident convertibility, freezing of money wages, strict monetary control, liberalization of 75 per cent of prices (except for public utilities, some metals and pharmaceuticals) and liberalization of 95 per cent of imports.

5. After Slovenia declared independence in June 1991, the Yugoslav army intervened to defend Yugoslavia's territorial integrity, but it withdrew after just ten days.

6. Since 2001, the Kosovo provisional authorities under UNSCR 1244 have prioritized the European agenda and committed to a long-term European integration process. A permanent technical and political dialogue with Kosovan authorities, called the SAP tracking mechanism (STM), has been established to provide sound policy advice and guidance to Kosovo's reform efforts. Since then, regular meetings have been held to assess Kosovo's progress in realizing European partnership objectives.

7. The 2001 civil war additionally destabilized the Macedonian economy, but this happened only ten years after Yugoslavia's break up.

8. Kosovo declared political independence in February 2008, but by mid 2011 it was still not recognized by the UN and a number of countries (as indicated earlier). Kosovo is the least developed of all Balkan countries. In May 2009 it obtained membership in the IMF and some months later in the World Bank.

References

Bartlett, W. (2007) 'Regional Integration and Free-Trade Agreements in the Balkans: Obstacles, Opportunities, and Policy Issues', in S. Bianchini, J. Marko, C. Nation and M. Uvalic (eds) *Regional Co-operation, Peace Enforcement, and the Role of the Treaties in the Balkans*, Angelo Longo Editore: Ravenna.

Bartlett, W. (2008) *Europe's Troubled Region: Economic Development, Institutional Reform and Social Welfare in the Western Balkans*, Routledge: London and New York.

Bunce, V. (1999) *Subversive Institutions: The Design and Destruction of Socialism and the State*, Cambridge University Press: Cambridge.

Central Bank of the Republic of Kosovo (2010) *Monthly Statistical Bulletin*, various issues.

Commission of the European Communities (2004) 'European Economy: Western Balkans in Transition', *Enlargement Paper No. 23*.

Commission of the European Communities (2006) 'European Economy: Western Balkans in Transition', *Enlargement Paper No. 30*.

Commission of the European Communities (2009a) *Pocketbook on Candidate and Potential Candidate Countries*, Eurostat Pocketbooks.

Commission of the European Communities (2009b) 'EU Candidate and Pre-Accession Countries Economic Quarterly', *DG Economic and Financial Affairs*, October.

Commission of the European Communities (2009c) 'GDP per Inhabitant in Purchasing Power Standards', *Eurostat News Release No. 182/2009*.

Daviddi, R. and M. Uvalic (2006) 'Currencies in the Western Balkans on their Way towards EMU', in F. Torres, A. Verdun and H. Zimmermann (eds) *EMU Rules: The*

Political and Economic Consequences of European Monetary Integration, Nomos: Baden-Baden.

Economist Intelligence Unit (2009, various issues) *Economies in Transition: Eastern Europe and the Former Soviet Union: Regional Overview*, EIU: London.

Estrin, S. and M. Uvalic (2008) 'From Illyria towards Capitalism: Did Labour-Management Theory Teach Us Anything about Yugoslavia and Transition in Its Successor States?', *Comparative Economic Studies*, 50th Anniversary Essay, 50: 663–96.

EBRD (European Bank for Reconstruction and Development) (various years) *Transition Report*, EBRD: London.

Gagnon, V. (1997) 'Ethnic Nationalism and International Conflict: The Case of Serbia', in E. Brown, O.R. Coté, Jr., S.M. Lynn-Jones and S. Miller (eds) *Nationalism and Ethnic Conflict*, MIT Press: Cambridge, MA and London.

Godoy, S. and J.E. Stiglitz (2007) 'Growth, Initial Conditions, Law and Speed of Privatization in Transition Countries: 11 Years Later', in S. Estrin, G.W. Kolodko and M. Uvalic (eds) *Transition and Beyond: Essays in Honour of Mario Nuti*, Palgrave Macmillan: Basingstoke.

IHS Global Insight (2009) 'Global Crisis Hits Western Balkan Economies', 5 August, available at www.ihsglobalinsight.com.

IMF (2010) 'Republic of Kosovo: Request for Stand-By Arrangement', *IMF Country Report No. 10/245*, July.

Kekic, L. (1996) 'Assessing and Measuring Progress in the Transition', *Country Forecast: Economies in Transition: Eastern Europe and the Former Soviet Union: Regional Overview*, 2nd quarter, EIU: London.

Kolodko, G.W. and D.M. Nuti (1997) 'The Polish Alternative: Old Myths, Hard Facts and New Strategies in the Successful Polish Economic Transformation', *WIDER Research for Action No. 33*, UNU-WIDER: Helsinki.

Kornai, J. (1980) *The Economics of Shortage*, North-Holland: Amsterdam.

Nuti, D.M. (2009) 'The Impact Of The Global Crisis On Transition Economies', *Economic Annals*, LIV(181): 7–20.

Popov, V. (2009) 'Lessons from the Transition Economies. Putting the Success Stories of the Post-Communist World into a Broader Perspective', *WIDER Research Paper*, 2009/15, UNU-WIDER: Helsinki.

Prica, I. and M. Uvalic (2009) 'The Impact of the Global Economic Crisis on Central and Southeast Europe', in A. Prascevic, B. Cerovic, M. Jaksic (eds) *Economic Policy and Global Recession*, Vol. 1, Faculty of Economics of the University of Belgrade Publishing Centre: Belgrade.

Schneider, F. (2003) 'The Size and Development of the Shadow Economies and Shadow Economy Labour Force of 22 Transition and 21 OECD Countries: What do We Really Know?', in B. Belev (ed.) *The Informal Economy in the EU Accession Countries: Size, Scope, Trends and Challenges to the Process of EU Enlargement*, Center for the Study of Democracy (in co-operation with the Bertelsmann Foundation and the World Bank): Sofia.

Trumbic, T. and M. Uvalic (2005) 'Croatia's Progress towards the European Union: Achievements and Risks', paper presented at the 6th International Conference Enterprise in Transition, 26–28 May, Split.

Uvalic, M. (1992) *Investment and Property Rights in Yugoslavia: The Long Transition to a Market Economy*, Cambridge University Press: Cambridge.

Uvalic, M. (2001) 'Regional Co-operation in Southeast Europe', *Journal of Southeast European and Black Sea Studies*, 1(1): 55–75.

Uvalic, M. (2003a) 'Economic Transition in Southeast Europe', *Southeast European and Black Sea Studies*, 3(1): 63–80.

Uvalic, M. (2003b) 'Southeast European Economies: From International Assistance towards Self-Sustainable Growth', in W. van Meurs (ed.) *Prospects and Risks Beyond EU Enlargement. Southeastern Europe: Weak States and Strong International Support*, Leske & Budrich: Opladen.

Uvalic, M. (2006) 'Trade in Southeast Europe: Recent Trends and Some Policy Implications', *European Journal of Comparative Economics*, 3(2): 171–95.

Uvalic, M. (2007a) 'How Different is Serbia?', in S. Estrin, G.W. Kolodko and M. Uvalic (eds) *Transition and Beyond: Essays in Honour of Mario Nuti*, Palgrave Macmillan: Basingstoke.

Uvalic, M. (2007b) 'Transition and Economic Development in Southeast Europe', in J. Deimel and W. van Meurs (eds) *The Balkan Prism: A Retrospective by Policy Makers and Analysts*, Verlag Otto Sagner: München.

Uvalic, M. (2009a) 'The Impact of the Global Financial Crisis on Eastern Europe', paper presented at the Eighth International Conference of the Faculty of Economics, (University of Split) on the Challenges of Europe, 21–23 May, Bol (Croatia).

Uvalic, M. (2009b) 'Regionalism in Southeast Europe', in P. Della Posta, M. Uvalic and A. Verdun (eds) *Interpreting Globalization: A European Perspective*, Palgrave Macmillan: Basingstoke.

Uvalic, M. (2010) *Serbia's Transition: Towards a Better Future*, Palgrave Macmillan: Basingstoke.

Vujacic, V. (2004) Perceptions of the State in Russia and Serbia: The Role of Ideas in the Soviet and Yugoslav Collapse', *Post-Soviet Affairs*, 20(2): 164–94.

Vujacic, V. and Zaslavsky, V. (1991) 'The Causes of Disintegration in the Soviet Union and Yugoslavia', *Telos*, 88: 120–40.

Williamson, J. (1990) 'What Washington Means by Policy Reform', in J. Williamson (ed.) *Latin American Adjustment: How Much Has Happened?*, Institute for International Relations: Washington, DC.

World Bank Group (n.d.) Doing Business Indicators, available at www.doingbusiness.org.

15
Central Asia after Two Decades of Independence

Richard Pomfret

1 Introduction

A striking feature of the five Central Asian countries is that they followed divergent economic strategies after becoming independent in 1991. Despite similarities in culture, history, geography and economic structure, their transitions from Soviet central planning ranged from the most rapidly liberalizing (the Kyrgyz Republic) to the least-reforming (Turkmenistan) of all former Soviet republics. By the turn of the century, when the transition from central planning was essentially complete, the Central Asian countries had created vastly different economic systems. This chapter analyses the interaction of economic strategy, institutional change, political evolution and external influences, and their consequences for economic performance.

The end of the second decade since the dissolution of the Soviet Union is a good time for reflection because many developments have taken time to work themselves out. Gradual reform in Uzbekistan was associated with the best GDP performance of any Soviet successor state during the 1990s, and a lively debate sought to explain this phenomenon, but the outcome in Uzbekistan has been less positive in the second decade. The other large economy in the region, Kazakhstan, appeared to under-perform in the 1990s, which was ascribed to institutional shortcomings, such as pervasive corruption, but in the second decade Kazakhstan has been one of the best-performing economies in the world. The economic performance of the three smaller economies has been less positive. Tajikistan is now one of the poorest countries in Asia with characteristics of a failed state. The Kyrgyz Republic appears to be descending along a similar path, despite being praised by many economists during the 1990s for introducing market-friendly reforms. Turkmenistan, despite gross mismanagement under its first president, has more options because of its abundant energy resources, but the nature of the regime remains opaque.

Apart from the differences, some commonalities remain, in particular the establishment of super-presidential political systems under autocratic rulers, obstacles to trade posed by geography (landlockedness), and unwillingness to engage in serious regional co-operation. Corruption is also rampant, but comparative measures of corruption do not show common patterns of change. This study aims to balance the impact of unchanging (or hard-to-change) geographical and cultural constraints against the impact of differing (and changeable) national policies to explain these similarities and divergences of outcome over the first two decades, and to draw tentative conclusions about future prospects and general lessons in the relationship between economic systems and performance.

2 Dissolution of the USSR and the transition from central planning

The five Central Asian countries had no history as nation states before 1992, and during the Soviet era economic policy and development strategies were determined in Moscow. None had anticipated the dissolution of the Soviet Union before its final months, and all were unprepared for the severing of Soviet ties. The unexpected challenges of nation-building were superimposed on the transition from a centrally planned economy, which had begun in the late 1980s but had little influence on Central Asia before the Soviet economic system began to unravel in 1991. All five countries suffered serious disruption from the dissolution of the USSR.

Demand and supply networks based on under-valued transport inputs quickly collapsed in the early 1990s. The shift to world prices notionally benefited the energy exporters, Kazakhstan and Turkmenistan (Tarr 1994), but in the 1990s their ability to realize these gains was limited by dependence on Russian pipelines. Falling output and rising prices became much worse after the formal dissolution of the USSR removed residual central control over the Soviet economic space (Tables 15.1 and 15.2). Attempts to maintain economic links by retaining the ruble as a common currency in 1992–3 exacerbated the problem of hyperinflation, and these were abandoned by the end of 1993.[1]

The decade after independence was dominated by nation-building, which was a slow process in countries where the main state institutions and the associated human capital had been controlled from Moscow. The national leaders cemented their personal power by creating super-presidential regimes, in which the balance of power between executive and legislature was overwhelmingly weighted towards the former. In Tajikistan, the only one of the five countries not to evolve peacefully from Soviet republic to independent state under unchanged leadership, the bloody civil war dominated political developments until 1997 and delayed implementation of a serious and consistent economic strategy, but by the end of the decade President Rahmonov had constructed a political system similar to that of his neighbours.

Table 15.1 Percentage growth in real GDP, 1989–2008

	Kazakhstan	Kyrgyz Rep.	Tajikistan	Turkmenistan	Uzbekistan
1989	0	8	-3	−7	4
1990	0	3	−2	2	2
1991	−13	−5	−7	−5	−1
1992	−3	−19	−29	−5	−11
1993	−9	−16	−11	−10	−2
1994	−13	−20	−19	−17	−4
1995	−8	−5	−13	−7	−1
1996	1	7	−4	−7	2
1997	2	10	2	−11	3
1998	−2	2	5	5	4
1999	2	4	4	16	4
1999; 1989 = 100	63	63	44	64	94

Source: EBRD Transition Report Update (April 2001: 15).

	Kazakhstan	Kyrgyz Rep	Tajikistan	Turkmenistan	Uzbekistan
1998	−2	2	5	7	4
1999	3	4	4	17	4
2000	10	5	8	19	4
2001	14	5	10	20	4
2002	10	0	9	16	4
2003	9	7	10	17	4
2004	10	7	11	15	8
2005	10	0	7	13	7
2006	11	3	7	11	7
2007	9	8	8	12	10
2008	3	8	8	11	9
2009	1	2	3	6	8
2010	6	−4	6	11	8

Notes: 2010 = preliminary actual figures from official government sources.
Source: Based on EBRD data at http://www.ebrd.com/pages/research/economics/data/macro.shtml#macro (accessed 16 January 2011).

The five countries' economies gradually became more differentiated as their governments introduced national strategies for transition to a market-based economy. By the early twenty-first century all five countries had essentially completed the process of nation-building and the transition from central planning. However, the typology of market-based economies varied substantially from the comprehensive price and trade liberalization, and extensive privatization introduced in the Kyrgyz Republic between 1993 and 1998 to the non-reform in Turkmenistan.

The Kyrgyz Republic embraced advice from Western institutions and advocates of rapid change and, within limits, President Akayev fostered the emergence of the most liberal regime in the region. Prices and foreign trade

Table 15.2 Percentage inflation (change in consumer price index), 1991–2005

	Kazakhstan	Kyrgyz Rep.	Tajikistan	Turkmenistan	Uzbekistan
1991	79	85	112	103	82
1992	1,381	855	1,157	493	645
1993	1,662	772	2,195	3,102	534
1994	1,892	229	350	1,748	1,568
1995	176	41	609	1,005	305
1996	39	31	418	992	54
1997	17	26	88	84	59
1998	8	36	28	24	29
1999	7	12	43	17	18

Source: EBRD Transition Report Update (April 2001: 16)

	Kazakhstan	Kyrgyz Rep.	Tajikistan	Turkmenistan	Uzbekistan
1998	7	11	43	17	29
1999	8	36	28	24	29
2000	13	19	33	8	25
2001	8	7	39	12	27
2002	6	2	12	9	27
2003	6	3	16	6	12
2004	7	4	7	6	7
2005	8	5	7	11	10
2006	9	6	10	8	14
2007	11	10	13	6	12
2008	17	25	21	15	13
2009	7	7	6	-3	14
2010	7	6	8	5	10

Notes: 2010 = preliminary actual figures from official government sources.
Source: Based on EBRD data at http://www.ebrd.com/pages/research/economics/data/macro.
shtml#macro (accessed 16 January 2011).

were fully liberalized and small-scale privatization was completed. In July 1998, the Kyrgyz Republic became the first Soviet successor state to accede to the World Trade Organization (WTO). The more difficult areas of transition, such as enterprise reform and creation of a market-driven financial sector, were less complete, and controversial infrastructure areas, such as transport and water, remained unreformed (Table 15.3).

At independence, Kazakhstan appeared to be the best placed among the Central Asian countries. Per capita incomes were substantially higher than those of the four southern countries (Table 15.4), and this was reflected in higher education and other human capital indicators. Moreover, the country's substantial energy and mineral resources held great potential; the oil reserves were about to be tapped by the Chevron-Tengiz project under the largest foreign investment agreement in Soviet history. In 1992

Table 15.3 EBRD transition indicators, 1999 and 2008

	Kazakhstan		Kyrgyz Republic		Tajikistan		Turkmenistan		Uzbekistan	
	1999	2008	1999	2008	1999	2008	1999	2008	1999	2008
Large-scale privatization	3	3	3	3.67	2.33	2.33	1.67	1	2.67	2.67
Small-scale privatization	4	4	4	4	3	4	2	2.33	3	3.33
Enterprise restructuring	2	2	2	2	1.67	1.67	1.67	1	2	1.67
Price liberalization	4	4	4.33	4.33	3.67	3.67	2.67	2.67	2.67	2.67
Trade and forex system	3.33	3.67	4.33	4.33	2.67	3.33	1	2	1	2
Competitive policy	2	2	2	2	2	1.67	1	1	2	1.67
Banking reform and interest rate liberalization	2.33	3	2	2.33	1	2.33	1	1	1.67	1.67
Securities markets and non-bank financial institutions	2	2.67	2	2	1	1	1	1	2	2
Overall infrastructure reform	2	2.67	1.33	1.67	1	1.33	1	1	1.33	1.67

Note: Indicators are measured on a scale from 1 (no reform) to 4, with pluses and minuses (e.g. 3+ and 3– are represented by 3.33 and 2.67).
Source: Based on EBRD *Transition Report Update* (May 2009).

Table 15.4 Demographic data, output and income, 1990–1 and 2007

	Kazakhstan	Kyrgyzstan	Tajikistan	Turkmenistan	Uzbekistan
1990–1					
Population (million), mid-1990	16.8	4.4	5.3	3.7	20.5
GDP (US$ billion)	24.9	2.6	2.5	3.2	13.8
GNP per capita	2,600	1,570	1,130	1,690	1,340
Life expectancy (in yrs), 1991	69	68	70	66	69
Adult literacy (%), 1991	98	97	97	98	97
2007					
Population (million)	15.5	5.2	6.7	5	26.9
GDP (US$ billion)	104.9	3.7	3.7	12.9	22.3
GNI per capita (PPP)	9,600	1,980	1,710	4,350*	2,430
Trade/GDP (%)	77	95	106	104	58

Note: *2005.
Source: Based on data from World Bank (1992) and World Bank (n.d.).

Kazakhstan followed Russia's sweeping price reform with fewer exceptions than other Central Asian countries, but, as the 1990s progressed, Kazakhstan also resembled Russia in the way that privatization created powerful private interests that distorted the reform process (Kalyuzhnova 1998; Olcott 2002). By the end of the 1990s Kazakhstan had similar transition indicators to those of the Kyrgyz Republic, with less complete trade liberalization but a better functioning financial sector and more reformed infrastructure. These two countries were the most successful in stabilizing the macroeconomy, bringing inflation below 50 per cent in 1995 and 1996, respectively (Table 15.2).

In Tajikistan the civil war destroyed the planned economy and effectively privatized economic activity without the institutions, such as security of contract, crucial to efficient operation of a market economy. Thus the country scored highly on price liberalization and privatization but poorly on enterprise reform and competition policy, and abysmally on financial sector reform and infrastructure (Table 15.3). After the 1997 peace agreement, Tajikistan was considered to be a delayed reformer with liberalization of trade and financial sector policies, but institutions remain weak.

Uzbekistan and Turkmenistan are usually lumped together with Belarus as the least reforming of the Soviet successor states, but there are significant differences between them. Although cautious, Uzbekistan was not a non reformer. Small-scale privatization and housing reform were undertaken quickly. Macroeconomic stabilization was not an initial priority but, after the collapse of the ruble zone at the end of 1993, the country moved purposefully to reduce inflation. Macroeconomic policy in the two-and-a-half years after January 1994 followed standard International Monetary Fund (IMF) advice, and relations with the international financial institutions improved over this period. In October 1996, however, despite having made commitments to the IMF to adopt current account convertibility, Uzbekistan responded to falling world cotton prices (Figure 15.1) by introducing foreign exchange (forex) controls. These were attractive because, together with the state order system for cotton and wheat, they underpinned a non-transparent but large taxation of the farm sector. Expropriation of agricultural rents allowed Uzbekistan to maintain public expenditures without inflationary financing, and it was instrumental in retaining a credible social safety net and the highest ratio of education spending to GDP in the Commonwealth of Independent States (CIS). Nevertheless, these benefits came at a high cost, as the controls hindered desirable resource reallocation to actual and potential export sectors and the systemic nature of the rent-extraction system underpinned glacially slow progress on economic reforms after 1996. Uzbekistan's financial sector remained dominated by a state-owned bank, and financial repression was severe. In rail transport and in some utilities, the government gradually allowed some market forces to operate. Overall, Uzbekistan became a market-oriented economy, but with substantial

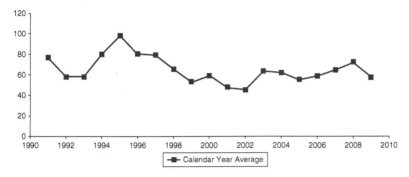

Figure 15.1 World cotton prices (Cotlook A index), annual averages, January 1991 – July 2009 (US cents per pound)

Source: Cotlook A index from data in the public domain, available at http://www.imf.org/external/np/res/commod/index.asp.

government direction (Pomfret 2000). A key distinction between Uzbekistan and the Kyrgyz Republic or Tajikistan is that the former's legislative record is less reformist but its implementation is more effective.

Turkmenistan established the most personalized and autocratic regime in Central Asia, pursuing a policy based on neutrality and economic independence, with minimal economic reform (Ochs 1997; Lubin 1999; Pomfret 2001). The central planning mechanisms, which broke down in the early 1990s, were replaced by a poorly functioning market economy with heavy state influence. President Niyazov (or Turkmenbashi the Great, as he later preferred to be called) retained control over resource allocation decisions, which was relatively easy given the simple structure of the economy with its high dependence on energy and cotton exports, but was very inefficient.[2] Soon after independence he adopted a populist strategy of providing free water, electricity, gas, heating, salt and other necessities up to certain limits intended to include most household consumption, but much of the state revenue went on prestige projects to support a bizarre personality cult and on maintaining internal security. An import-substituting industrialization strategy was designed to increase value-added in the energy and cotton sectors, but the textile mills probably created negative value-added (Pomfret 2001). In sum, the economy was minimally reformed in the transition from central planning, and government intervention was cruder and less developmental than in Uzbekistan.

3 Economic performance during the first decade after independence

The people of Central Asia experienced a huge economic shock in the early 1990s, although measuring the exact size of the economic decline both across countries and over time is difficult. The conceptual measurement issues related to the systemic shift from central planning affect our assessment of the entire decade, because measures of, say, GDP, which relate a year to a stable base year, such as 1989 (as in Table 15.1), are more useful than the volatile annual growth rates. Moreover, gross national expenditure (GNE) probably fell by more than output in the early 1990s, so that the real GDP estimates may fail to capture the decline in living standards when resource flows from the rest of the USSR were cut off.[3] Later in the 1990s there were country-specific gaps between GNE and GDP; the Kyrgyz Republic benefited from substantial capital inflows from multilateral and bilateral official sources, but the other Central Asian countries received little net capital inflow, apart from military assistance to Tajikistan and some direct foreign investment in Kazakhstan.[4]

On top of these general data issues are country-specific measurement problems. Tajikistan was devastated by a civil war, which lasted for much of the 1990s, and even after the 1997 peace agreement the central government did not control all of the national territory. In Turkmenistan, and to a lesser extent in Uzbekistan, old attitudes about information being power, and associated practices of data manipulation or secrecy, persist. The Turkmenistan data have often been queried by the multilateral agencies and are the least reliable in the CIS.[5] Despite this catalogue of problems, the data in Table 15.1 represent the most plausible output estimates and the general patterns correspond with other evidence, including casual observation.[6] The economic decline in Tajikistan was traumatic; by 2000, with a national income per capita of $180, Tajikistan was poorer than most of sub-Saharan Africa or the poorest countries of Asia.[7] Kazakhstan and the Kyrgyz Republic both suffered substantial setbacks during the first half of the 1990s; both economies began growing after 1995, but they were negatively impacted by the 1998 Russian crisis. Uzbekistan's economy suffered a smaller transitional recession than any other former Soviet republic, and, contrary to some predictions, it experienced positive economic growth after the mid-1990s.[8] Turkmenistan's performance is the most controversial, and independent checks on official data are scarce; despite positive GDP figures, the country suffered palpable economic decline and increased poverty, but energy revenues and political stability limited the extent of the decline.

The five countries' economic performance in the 1990s has mostly been analysed in the context of over two dozen countries in Eastern Europe and the former USSR abandoning central planning within a few years of one another. The East European countries as a group outperformed the CIS countries, but whether that reflected superior policies or better initial conditions is difficult to determine.[9] That is not to say that we learned nothing from the econometric studies. Conflict was bad for growth; countries with civil or interstate wars tended to be slow reformers and had a poor growth record. High inflation is bad for growth, although moderate inflation is less clearly harmful. Although there are debates about the threshold, all transition economies quickly recognized the costs of hyperinflation and, whether they were committed to structural reform or not, sooner rather than later they attacked hyperinflation with standard monetary policy weapons.[10] A complement to the econometric work is national case studies.

The Central Asian countries offer a natural experiment, with their fairly similar initial conditions and radically different approaches to creating market-based economies. On more detailed investigation, the situation is less clear than this simplified characterization suggests. Initial conditions did vary; ranking by degree of reform is not as straightforward as simple transition indicators suggest, and policy-making has not always been consistent over time.

3.1 Kazakhstan

Despite its advantages, Kazakhstan faced two serious obstacles. First, it was the only Central Asian country where the titular nationality was not in the majority. In the 1989 census, the population was approximately two-fifths Kazakh, two-fifths Russian and one-fifth other ethnic groups. Following the dissolution of the USSR, most of the substantial German population and many of the Russian population chose to emigrate, and the emigrants tended to come from among the better educated, thus eroding Kazakhstan's human capital advantage. The large remaining Russian population was heavily concentrated in the north and east, close to the Russian border, and posing a potential secessionist threat, which had a powerful political influence. Kazakhstan's president was the major advocate of retaining some form of common economic space with Russia, and the national capital was relocated at great expense from Almaty in the south east to Astana in the centre north.

The second obstacle to fulfilling Kazakhstan's economic potential was connected to the oil sector. The only outlets for the state's oil were pipelines through Russia, and Russia exploited its monopoly position by regulating flows and levying high tariffs. Despite many plans for alternative pipelines, the position a decade after independence was essentially unchanged, with small amounts of oil being shipped across the Caspian Sea but most still being exported through Russia. Oil played a key role in Kazakhstan's economic and political development.

The privatization programme of the mid-1990s led to insiders and politically well-connected people gaining control over the valuable assets. The regime became more autocratic and the system more corrupt. Economic reform stalled in the mid-1990s, and in 1995, Kazakhstan ranked behind both the Kyrgyz Republic and Uzbekistan according to the European Bank for Reconstruction and Development (EBRD) transition indexes.

Explanation of Kazakhstan's disappointing economic performance over the period 1992–5, when estimated GDP fell by almost half, is overdetermined. The initial conditions in terms of resource abundance proved to be negative, because the resources could not be exported at world prices

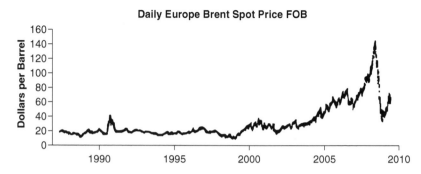

Figure 15.2   Oil prices, 1987–2009 (US$ per barrel)
Source: US Energy Information Administration (in the public domain and not subject to copyright), available at www//tonto.eia.doe.gov/dnav/pet/hist/wtotworldw.htm.

and because of the associated political economy factors. The limited extent of economic reform and crony capitalism also inhibited healthy economic development in the mid-1990s. In 1996–7, Kazakhstan's economy began to grow, but it was hard hit by the 1998 Russian crisis. Although the crisis itself was exogenous, the contagion effect reflected a relative failure to diversify Kazakhstan's international economic relations away from Russia.

After 1999 the economic situation in Kazakhstan turned around (Pomfret 2005). The recovery from the 1998 crisis was driven by market forces and by good fortune. A sharp real depreciation of the currency stimulated exports and helped to validate policy makers' understanding of market mechanisms. Recovery of world oil prices, which had stagnated from 1986 to 1998 (Figure 15.2), reinforced the positive trade developments, while large new offshore oil discoveries and new pipeline routes created unbounded optimism.

3.2   The Kyrgyz Republic

The Kyrgyz Republic was a poor mountainous Soviet republic with few natural resources. Its economy was tightly linked to the union economy and suffered substantially from the dissolution of the USSR.[11] Although the Kyrgyz were in the majority, there was a large Slav minority in the north and a large Uzbek population in the south of the country. The Soviet republic was associated with economic backwardness and conservatism, but a fortuitous combination of events led to the appointment in 1990 of a physics professor as first secretary.

From 1993 to 1998 the country was by far the most reformist of the Central Asian republics. Whether this was because President Akayev was the most liberal leader or whether he had the fewest options is debatable. In May 1993 the Kyrgyz Republic was the first Central Asian country to replace the ruble by a national currency, and unlike the other countries this was explicitly part of an economic reform programme aimed at curbing inflation so that relative prices could direct resource allocation. It received the most support from the international financial institutions, and following their standard policy recommendations it brought annual inflation down below 50 per cent in 1995. Prices were liberalized, the currency made convertible, and tariffs reduced. In July 1998 the Kyrgyz Republic became the first Soviet successor state to accede to the WTO.

Small-scale privatization also progressed rapidly. In other areas, however, reform was less smooth. Land privatization was delayed until 1998 and, even when accepted in principle, a five-year moratorium on transfer of ownership was imposed. Large-scale privatization also proved difficult in practice, partly due to unrealistic pricing of assets. The only large productive enterprise with a positive output record was the Kumtor goldmine, operated as a joint venture with a Canadian company. The mine was accounting for a sixth of GDP by the early 2000s, but front-loading of returns to the foreign investor limited the benefits accruing to Kyrgyz residents.[12] Institutional reforms were often impressive on paper but implementation was poor.

Its economic performance was similar to that of Kazakhstan, with a substantial output decline followed by economic growth in 1996 and 1997. Whether this was a better achievement depends on a comparison of the initial conditions, which many saw as less favourable in the Kyrgyz Republic, and on evaluation of the role of foreign assistance. The country was successful in cutting inflation, and yet it ran large fiscal deficits as tax revenues fell and public expenditures were not reduced in line; the general government budget deficit was reduced from a high of 17 per cent of GDP in 1995 but was still 10–11 per cent of GDP in 1999–2000 (Mogilevsky and Hasanov 2004: 227). The situation was sustained by substantial IMF and World Bank financial aid, which enabled the central bank to limit inflationary financing of the budget deficit but led to a rapid build-up of external debt.

The fragility of the Kyrgyz economy was exposed by the 1998 Russian crisis. Although the economy was less closely linked to Russia than Kazakhstan's was, the contagion effects were strong because the Kyrgyz financial sector was weak. Three of the country's four largest banks were liquidated in 1998/9 and banking sector assets fell from $160 million to $90 million at the end of 2000; that is, from 10 per cent of GDP to 7 per cent. The apparently extensive financial reforms of the mid-1990s were revealed to be fragile, and this was symbolic of much of the reform structure.

One consequence of the financial crisis was to stimulate a rethinking of economic policies. Concerns over the country's rising debt burden also contributed to rethinking of the adherence to the policies recommended by the international financial institutions, whose adoption was now seen as having been costly. After 1998, economic reforms were placed on hold for several years, although they began to move forward again in the early 2000s.

Economic performance in the Kyrgyz Republic in the 1990s is difficult to evaluate. Its role as the reform leader in Central Asia led to anticipation of healthy growth. That this was not realized could be ascribed to poor initial conditions, poor implementation of reforms, or not staying the course after 1998.

3.3 Tajikistan

Tajikistan shared many of the Kyrgyz Republic's disadvantages, but these were compounded by a civil war in which tens of thousands were killed and half a million people were displaced in the first year after independence. The war fluctuated hot and cold over the next five years until the 1997 peace agreement brought opposition parties into the government. Roads, bridges and other infrastructure were destroyed during the fighting, and much has still not been repaired. Many men left the country either for economic reasons or to avoid the draft.

After 1997, government policies appeared to be fairly liberal. The government courted the international financial institutions and largely followed their policy recommendations. Implementation has, however, been poor, especially in the late 1990s when the central government did not have full control over the national territory. After September 2001, President Rahmonov became more assertive in cleansing the government of opposition figures—with the tacit support of the West, which approved of his secular position and mistrusted the Islamic parties—and in establishing government control, but local warlords, outside the formal structure of the government or the pre-1997 opposition, continued to operate on their own account. The years of war and the burgeoning narcotics trade hampered the emergence of civil society.

Economic performance in the 1990s was disastrous. Output fell by two-thirds in the early and mid-1990s. Lack of economic opportunity led many men to migrate to Russia in search of work and, because their remittances were largely brought back as cash and were not reported, it is difficult to estimate how much this contributed to incomes. Foreign assistance, mainly from Russia, was primarily military aid, which contributed little to the economy apart from leaving Tajikistan with the highest debt/GDP ratio of any Soviet successor state. Although the economy began to grow after 1997, growth from the low base was sluggish.

3.4 Turkmenistan

Although Turkmenistan was historically one of the poorest republics in the USSR, its economy was experiencing rapid growth in the final Soviet decades based on cotton and natural gas. The construction of the Karakum Canal, begun in the 1950s, greatly increased the land area under cotton. In the 1980s the natural gas sector was modernized and production expanded rapidly. The shift from Soviet to world prices offered larger terms of trade gains to Turkmenistan than to any other Soviet successor state (Tarr 1994), but the inherited infrastructure directed energy exports exclusively to the CIS and the monopsonistic buyers quickly ran up substantial arrears.[13] Turkmenistan eventually addressed the problem with the drastic measure of cutting off the gas supply to delinquent customers between March 1997 and January 1999. This is reflected in the negative GDP growth in 1997, when other countries had begun to recover (Table 15.1), but Turkmenistan's economic problems run deeper than a simple strategic blip in the late 1990s. The economy remained essentially unreformed. The central planning mechanisms broke down in the early 1990s but were not replaced by a functioning market economy. Retaining centralized control over resource allocation decisions was relatively easy, given the simple structure of the economy and the relative ease of monitoring revenues from cotton and gas exports, but it was very inefficient. The government kept tight control over the farm sector with a system similar to Uzbekistan's state marketing monopoly and with forex controls that were tightened after 1998. Repressive agricultural policies (Pastor and van Rooden 2000) and poor management led to cotton yields falling by much more than in neighbouring Uzbekistan, and export revenues declined sharply over the 1990s (Pomfret 2008a). The energy sector also remained under tight presidential control; production declined drastically during the 1990s and little was done to exploit the potentially large offshore reserves (Table 15.5), but output remained sufficient after 2000 to generate enough export earnings for the president's needs.

The data for Turkmenistan are the least reliable of any economy in transition and are manipulated for political impact. Nevertheless, it was clear to any observer that economic conditions deteriorated substantially after independence, especially outside the capital city.

Table 15.5 Production and exports of natural gas, Turkmenistan 1990–2007 (billion m^3)

	1990	1991	1992	1993	1994	1995
Production	81.9	78.6	56.1	60.9	33.3	30.1
Exports		74.9	46.9	55.7	24.7	22.0
	1996	1997	1998	1999	2000	2001
Production	32.8	16.1	12.4	21.3	43.8	47.9
Exports	24.0	40.0	2.0	10.0	35.7	38.6
	2002	2003	2004	2005	2006	2007
Production	49.9	55.1	54.4	58.8	62.2	67.4
Exports	39.4	43.4				

Source: Based on data from Pomfret (2011: 341–73).

3.5 Uzbekistan

Uzbekistan is the most populous of the Central Asian countries and its record since independence is the most controversial. Initial conditions were at first seen as neutral and its economic reforms were cautious, but during the 1990s Uzbekistan was the most successful of all Soviet successor states—including the rapidly reforming and geographically advantaged Baltic countries—in terms of output performance (Pomfret 2000; Spechler 2000). The Uzbek government had frosty relations with the international financial institutions, and this may have clouded judgements of what became known as the Uzbek puzzle: How could one explain the good economic performance of a lagging economic reformer?

Uzbekistan illustrates the difficulty of determining what are favourable initial conditions. Its major export, cotton, was not under-priced in the USSR, so the country did not have the expected terms of trade gains that energy producers like Kazakhstan or Turkmenistan anticipated. On the other hand, cotton was not restricted to fixed transport modes and it could be fairly easily exported to new markets. Up to 1996 this advantage was enhanced by buoyant world prices for cotton (Figure 15.1). Uzbekistan's second most valuable export, gold, was even easier to export at world prices.

Another favourable initial condition was Tashkent's position as the regional capital of Soviet Central Asia. At a physical level, the principle that the Soviet successor states inherited assets in their territory meant that Uzbekistan gained the biggest air fleet and most military equipment in Central Asia. Less tangibly, but perhaps more important, it inherited the most effective administrators in the region. The physical infrastructure, including both the domestic transport network and the irrigation canals crucial to the cotton economy, was relatively well maintained. Corruption was, and still is, widespread in all of Central Asia, but available evidence suggested lower levels in Uzbekistan than in the other four countries,[14] implying more effective central control and (admittedly by the low standards of the region) a relatively strong sense of public service.

The Uzbek puzzle is partly a matter of overestimating performance, but it has more to do with underestimating reform progress and, especially, failure to recognize the key importance of infrastructure and the institutional setting in which markets function. Uzbekistan is not an open society and this may stifle economic progress, but having a relatively well-managed economy helped to minimize the extent of the transitional recession, and gradual reform was sufficient to provide the basis for modest but reasonably steady growth after the mid-1990s.

This is not to discount the potential cost of Uzbekistan's clearly misguided policies. The history of regional administration contributed to a stronger sense of independence in policy-making. Uzbekistan was sceptical of foreign advice and unwilling to accumulate foreign debt, so its relations with the international financial institutions were poor. The scepticism delayed recognition of the importance of macropolicy measures to contain inflation, but this was not critical for long-term development as the inflation rate was coming down by 1996 (Table 15.2). Much more important was the renunciation of commitments to establish currency convertibility and resort to forex controls after cotton prices declined in 1996. Such controls can have a short-term stabilizing impact, but the substantial long-term resource misallocation costs are familiar from other countries that have relied on similar agricultural taxes (Pomfret 2000, 2008a). Although the government recognized their cost by the end of the 1990s, the forex controls were a stumbling block to reform, even as the government professed a desire to abolish them. An over-valued official exchange rate enabled the state as monopoly buyer of cotton to extract large rents from farmers (effectively the difference between the world price and the domestic price), sheltered domestic producers of import-competing goods from foreign competition, and allowed people with access to foreign currency to profit from the black market. All of these consequences created vested interests that benefited from the regulated system and opposed reforms. And even after the controls were formally abolished in late 2003, many practical limitations on access to foreign exchange remained. Whereas in the 1990s Uzbekistan had jockeyed with Kazakhstan for hegemony in Central Asia, after 2000 it fell behind its regional rival in terms of economic power and political significance.

3.6 Conclusions

The five countries' differing economic performance in the 1990s to some extent reflected policy choices but was also determined by resource endowment and, in Tajikistan's case, by civil war. Attempts to transplant Western institutions into a Central Asian setting did not have the anticipated success in the Kyrgyz Republic because too many other conditions for a successful market economy were lacking. On the other hand, ignoring the advice of economists failed to bring greater economic grief to Turkmenistan and Uzbekistan in the 1990s than to the more reformist Kazakhstan and Kyrgyz Republic. Indeed, good economic management drawing on Soviet-era administrative structures helped Uzbekistan to weather the transitional recession better than other former Soviet republics or most Eastern European countries.

Resource endowment played an important part. Uzbekistan's good performance in the first half of the 1990s was helped by buoyant cotton prices, although the Uzbek government also managed to maintain productivity in the cotton sector better than Turkmenistan or Tajikistan. Turkmenistan also benefited from cotton prices and from large gas exports, although the revenues were largely used to support a highly personalized regime rather than for the public good. Kazakhstan's disappointing performance, compared with perceived potential in 1992, was in part due to stagnant oil prices before 1998. The Kyrgyz Republic and Tajikistan are both resource-poor and became economically poor, although the latter's economic performance was significantly worse due to civil war.

4 Economic performance in the second decade

In prospect, many foreign observers expected the longer-term relative economic performance to reward those countries that had decided to bite the bullet and seriously reform their systems in the 1990s to create effective market economies, while punishing those that had held back on reform. In practice, outcomes in the second decade were primarily determined by whether countries had energy resources or not. Kazakhstan and Turkmenistan both enjoyed rapid growth driven by the rising world price of oil, which had stagnated in the dozen years before 1998, but then increased from under $10 a barrel to $140 in 2008, before plummeting to under $40 (Figure 15.2). Tajikistan enjoyed fairly high growth rates in 2000–4 as domestic peace was established, but this was from a low base and the country remained very poor. A huge percentage of the male population works abroad, mainly in Russia, and remittances are the country's major source of foreign exchange; although data are sketchy, the share of remittances in GDP is perhaps the highest in the world (Kireyev 2006). Uzbekistan and the Kyrgyz Republic had the slowest economic growth (Table 15.1).

A striking feature of the decade 1998–2008 is the lack of further progress in creating an efficient market economy. As measured by the EBRD Transition Indicators (Table 15.3), there was little change apart from Tajikistan completing its price liberalization and small-scale privatization, and some banking reform in Kazakhstan, the Kyrgyz Republic and Tajikistan. Turkmenistan was even downgraded on some indicators of its, very limited, transition in the 1990s. The general impression from Table 15.3 is of a blank slate for reform in the early 1990s to which Central Asian countries responded to differing degrees, but by the turn of the century the type of market economy had been fixed in each country and was then only amenable to limited further change.

4.1 The energy boom

The dominant economic influence in Central Asia from 1999 to 2008 was the boom in energy prices. The oil boom was especially important for Kazakhstan, whose major Caspian oilfields began to produce large quantities of oil after the turn of the century, with the first independent pipeline through Russia opening in 2001 and the first pipeline to Turkey opening in 2005. Thus Kazakhstan benefited from both higher quantity and higher prices, as well as being in a stronger position to negotiate transit fees.

Increased oil prices affected the demand for substitutes. There is no world market for natural gas, but Russian exports to the European

Union (EU) are priced by a formula that includes oil prices, and increases in those prices created pressure to raise the price of Central Asian gas exports to Russia—or for Central Asian exporters to seek alternative pipeline routes with higher long-term price agreements. For Turkmenistan, whose gas reserves are among the world's ten largest, the increase in energy prices was also a boon, even though gas prices were more dependent on long-term contracts with customers on the pipeline network.

Finally, growing energy demand stimulated new projects to harness the huge hydroelectric potential in the mountainous regions of Tajikistan and the Kyrgyz Republic. Any hydro projects are, however, highly controversial because the rivers provide water vital to the irrigated agriculture of Kazakhstan, Uzbekistan and Turkmenistan. In the Soviet era, water resources were managed by Moscow, so that water would be released at appropriate times for downstream agriculture and in return the Kyrgyz and Tajik republics would be provided with energy. Since independence there have been no major new hydro projects and the energy/water swap arrangements continue. Nevertheless, tensions remain. In the severe winter of 2007/8, Uzbekistan failed to supply as much power as Tajikistan needed.[15] In the winter of 2008/9, tensions rose between Uzbekistan and the Kyrgyz Republic, driven in part by Kyrgyz plans to develop the Kambarata complex of hydro power stations despite Uzbek opposition.

For Uzbekistan the direct impact of the oil boom was roughly neutral because the country is more or less self-sufficient in oil and, especially, natural gas. However, the indirect effects were substantial. Tensions with neighbouring Tajikistan and the Kyrgyz Republic escalated over water/energy arrangements as the upstream countries became keener to use their water resources to generate electricity. The economic prosperity of Kazakhstan also posed a challenge to the Uzbek government that had seen itself as the regional leader in the 1990s. Tashkent had been the metropolis of Soviet Central Asia, and Uzbekistan with 21 million people (growing to 27 million in the 2000s) was the most populous of the new independent countries. Kazakhstan with 17 million people, falling to 15 million due to emigration, had higher per capita income in the 1990s, but the gap in overall economic size increased substantially after 2000 (Table 15.4). By the mid-2000s, thousands of Uzbek workers were crossing the border to work as migrant labour in Kazakhstan, underlining the widening gap in living standards.[16]

Relations with external powers were also driven in part by energy geopolitics. The USA championed the Baku–Ceyhan oil pipeline and the Baku–Erzurum gas pipeline, which opened in 2005 and 2006, respectively, and reduced Central Asian energy producers' dependence on Russia for transit.[17] China also became a major presence. Chinese oil companies became more active in Kazakhstan (highlighted by the purchase of PetroKazakhstan from its Canadian owners in 2005) and construction of a pipeline to the Chinese border commenced. President Niyazov, who rarely travelled, made a high-profile trip to Beijing in April 2006, following which the Chinese National Petroleum Corporation was granted drilling rights in Turkmenistan and construction began on a gas pipeline from Turkmenistan to China, which was completed in 2009. Meanwhile, Russia tried to shore up its monopoly position but was hampered by technical and, perhaps, capital shortages, and its announced pipeline projects languished. An important consequence of this confluence of developments was to encourage co-operation among Turkmenistan, Kazakhstan and Uzbekistan in agreeing routes and transit fees on pipelines that ran through the three countries to China and in negotiating jointly on the price of Central Asian gas exports to Russia.

4.2 Domestic political developments

By the early 2000s the presidents had created super-presidential systems and they remained in power by more or less undemocratic means. Opposition was fairly ruthlessly crushed and civil society was slow to emerge. Nevertheless, both the Kyrgyz Republic and Kazakhstan remained relatively open societies, where domestic opposition was vociferous even if operating under duress.

In the former, dissension had a regional dimension as opposition was centred in the south of the country, objecting to a perceived northern bias of President Akayev's government. After disputed elections in February and March 2005, demonstrations initially in the south and then in the national capital led to the resignation of Akayev in April. Following the revolutions in Georgia in 2003 and in Ukraine in 2005, this was the first regime change in Central Asia. However, despite resorting to rule by decree and acquiescing in the enrichment of relatives and friends, Akayev was always the most liberal Central Asian leader. There is doubt over whether the post-Akayev regime truly represents a new political situation or simply the same political system with different leaders.[18]

In Kazakhstan, the regime remains autocratic and dissent is punished, but the president is facing growing pressure for accountability of himself and his entourage. Corruption scandals undermined the government, especially the 'Kazakhgate' affair associated with a concealed Swiss bank account into which President Nazarbayev reportedly deposited over $1 billion in oil revenues and that became the subject of inquiries by US prosecutors. The opposition has been led by powerful political figures who have defected from the government, often in response to the centralization of power in the president's family, and by businessmen, who gained from the 1990s privatization and now want to strengthen the rule of law in order to protect their gains. The 'New Kazakhs' opposition became more open in late 2001, and the government responded harshly in 2002, but the subsequent stand-off reflected the strength of the opposition. After the Ukraine elections of December 2004, the Kazakhstan Government again reacted harshly, closing down one of the main opposition parties, but the situation remained fluid. In the December 2005 election, presidential supporters fixed the ballot to record over 90 per cent support for the incumbent, which was especially disappointing because indicators of public opinion suggested that in the booming economic conditions Nazarbayev would have won a fair election. Nevertheless, despite the undemocratic and ruthless methods used to maintain power, Kazakhstan's political contest has been largely peaceful.

Political opposition has been more violent in Uzbekistan and has accentuated border tensions. After a series of assassinations of public officials in 1997, the Uzbekistan government arrested hundreds of people in a crackdown in 1998. In February 1999, five bombs exploded in downtown Tashkent, killing several people and injuring over a hundred; the biggest one outside the cabinet of ministers building was apparently targeted at the president. In August 1999 some 650 gunmen from the Islamic Movement of Uzbekistan were caught entering Uzbekistan, and attempts to bomb the insurgents' bases hit the wrong targets, killing several Kyrgyz civilians and Tajik cattle, and undermining Uzbekistan's reputation for military effectiveness. Following several sketchily reported episodes of violence in Namangan and Fergana, the most dramatic events in the Ferghana Valley occurred in Andijan in May 2005. The details are disputed, but a large demonstration in the central square was fired upon by troops, leaving hundreds of people dead. These events clearly signalled the will of the Uzbekistan Government to use force to put down dissent.

Turkmenistan, the most repressive regime in the region, faced the first succession due to natural causes when Turkmenbashi died in December 2006. Gurbanguly Berdymukhamedov became acting president and in the February 2007 presidential election he won almost 90 per cent of the vote. In the remainder of 2007 he consolidated his power, operating a super-presidential regime similar to that of his predecessor. Although the change of president fuelled anticipation of policy change, in Berdymukhamedov's first two years, publicized changes were largely cosmetic and serious economic reforms minimal.

5   The international context[19]

Before 1992 Central Asia was part of an integrated economic space. Despite many agreements to strengthen the CIS as an economic zone, there was little implementation and attempts to retain a common currency broke down in 1993. The CIS as an organization floundered in 1992–4 as Russia chose to act unilaterally in regional conflicts in the Caucasus and Moldova, and more or less unilaterally in Tajikistan, and as economic issues were pushed into the background. By 1996 over half of the five Central Asian countries' foreign trade was outside the old Soviet area.

During 1992 the Central Asian leaders were primarily concerned with nation-building. Accession to the United Nations (UN), the IMF and the

World Bank provided an external dimension to national sovereignty. The five countries also joined the Economic Co-operation Organization (ECO) and various non-economic regional organizations in 1992, largely as a statement of their independence from the Soviet Union and as an assertion of their distinctive non-Russian Islamic culture, but they made no substantive concessions of national policy autonomy in participating in any regional organization. ECO, which includes all of the non-Arab Islamic countries in Asia west of India (Pomfret 1999), has been largely ineffective.[20]

During the mid-1990s, Russia attempted to re-establish its influence over Central Asia. Faced with a delicate ethnic balance between Kazakhs and Russians, President Nazarbayev of Kazakhstan tried to deflect the impending Russian dominance into a more co-operative structure by promoting a Eurasian customs union. Tajikistan (which was dependent on Russian military support during the civil war) and the Kyrgyz Republic followed this lead. The latter was, however, more externally oriented, and since its 1998 accession to the WTO with low bound tariff rates, completion of a customs union with Russia seems infeasible.[21]

Uzbekistan and Turkmenistan were resistant both to Russian regional designs and to falling too much under the influence of multilateral organizations. Although nominally a CIS member, Turkmenistan ceased to even provide statistics to the secretariat.[22] With substantial export earnings from natural gas and cotton, it adopted an autarchic political position, seeking UN guarantees of its neutrality.[23] Uzbekistan, by contrast, became more prominent on the international stage as President Karimov first sought to portray himself as the region's leader, and then in 1995–6 his country became the leading regional ally of the USA.[24] Concerns about potential Uzbek hegemony pushed Kazakhstan and the Kyrgyz Republic, which also fears Uzbek irredentist claims to its territory, closer to Russia. Kazakhstan, the Kyrgyz Republic and Tajikistan became members of the Union of Five (with Russia and Belarus) and of the Shanghai Forum (with Russia and China).

The August 1998 Russian financial crisis had strong contagion effects on Kazakhstan and, to a lesser extent, on the Kyrgyz Republic.[25] Uzbekistan was relatively insulated from the Russian crisis. Failing to make much progress in establishing a Central Asian community under its leadership, Uzbekistan formally aligned itself in 1999 with the GUAM (Georgia, Ukraine, Azerbaijan, and Moldova) countries, whose *raison d'être* was collective resistance to Russian influence.[26] The years 1998–9 saw the division of Central Asia into two opposing camps. In October 2000 the Union of Five was renamed the Eurasian Economic Community (EurAsEc).

This division eased during 2000–1, in part due to the incursion of Islamic fighters into the Fergana Valley, presenting a common problem to the three countries whose territory was involved (Uzbekistan, the Kyrgyz Republic and Tajikistan). China played a catalytic role in bringing the Central Asian countries together. In 1997–8, China had been an economic anchor in East Asia and had sought closer relations with the USA, but it gradually came to resent a perceived asymmetry in this rapprochement, which brought little gain to China. After the US bombing of the Chinese embassy in Belgrade in spring 1999, China embraced Japanese proposals for Asian monetary co-operation (which were opposed by the USA) and promoted a more formal successor to the Shanghai Forum. At the June 2001 summit, Uzbekistan became the sixth member and the forum was renamed the Shanghai Co-operation Organization (SCO). Although Russia saw the SCO as a vehicle for its leadership in Central Asia, for the Central Asian leaders, especially Uzbekistan, the SCO was palatable because of China's counterweight. Nevertheless, the regional faultline persisted as Kazakhstan, the Kyrgyz Republic and Tajikistan participated in the Russian-led Collective Security Treaty and Uzbekistan did not.

The events of September 2001 and the overthrow of the Taliban government in Afghanistan provided a major milestone in the region's international relations. The Central Asian leaders, along with those of Russia and China, gave verbal support to the USA-led war on terrorism. Uzbekistan and the Kyrgyz Republic went further by providing material assistance, such as making airbases available to the US military. These developments upped the international perceptions of Central Asia's strategic significance. Russia, although officially supporting the USA, attempted to reassert its own influence.[27]

The USA-led invasion of Iraq in March 2003 provided a second milestone. It highlighted the possibility that the USA might invade a country not only to rid it of religious fanatics like the Taliban but also to remove an autocratic secular regime. Coinciding with growing Western criticism of repression in Uzbekistan (and Turkmenistan), this provided a backdrop to a reversal of allegiances in Central Asia.[28] Uzbekistan ordered the closure of the US base on its territory in July 2005 (Gleason 2006) and moved closer to Russia, joining the Eurasian Community in October 2005. This was accompanied by formal dissolution of the Central Asian Co-operation Organization, to which the four Central Asian EurAsEc members also belonged. Thus after 2005 there was no specifically Central Asian regional institution and the two main active regional organizations had their secretariats in Moscow (EurAsEc) and Beijing (SCO). Symbolic of the resurgence of Russian influence was the agreement signed in May 2007 by Russia, Turkmenistan and Kazakhstan to build a gas pipeline along the eastern coast of the Caspian, feeding into the Russian pipeline network.[29]

Even as the realignment to the authoritarian regimes of Russia and China peaked, there were signs that the Central Asian countries wished to maintain a counter-balance. The Kyrgyz Republic paid lip service to, but failed to comply with, a Russian- and Chinese-inspired bid to eject all US bases from the region.[30] Kazakhstan also appeared to distance itself from the hard-line authoritarian stance, reflecting its renewed independence from Russia as oil prices soared and non-Russian pipeline routes were coming on stream. Both Kazakhstan and Turkmenistan, which made positive statements about the

Nabucco pipeline—intended to reduce Russia's dominance of EU gas supplies to Tajikistan—while becoming more dependent on remittances from migrant workers in Russia's booming economy, grew increasingly upset at the treatment of those workers.[31] Most importantly, the long-term shared interests of Uzbekistan and the USA reasserted themselves, and in October 2008 the former announced its intention to withdraw from the EurAsEc.[32] The USA and EU reciprocated by playing down human rights concerns,[33] and in 2009 the EU removed the last of the economic sanctions imposed in the aftermath of the 2005 Andijan events.

The international economic relations of the five Central Asian countries have evolved since independence. Their trade has increased substantially and has been directed away from former Soviet markets. The long-term counterpart has been the adoption of multilateral trade policies, even though all Central Asian leaders, to varying extents, recognize the desirability of regional co-operation and use regional agreements to signal political allegiance. The most striking features of the changing alignments are the ongoing influence of Russia, the emerging importance of China and other major economic powers, and the very limited development of ties with regional neighbours with a shared cultural heritage. Many commentators in the early 1990s foresaw a battle between Iran and Turkey for the hearts and minds, and markets, of Central Asia. Although both have increased their Central Asian ties relative to the Soviet era, neither Iran nor Turkey has yet established a strong economic or political presence in Central Asia.

International economic relations could be seen as a tug-of-war between Western influences (in favour of more market-driven economies) and Russia (as a *status quo* influence for limited economic reform). In practice, international economic relations were driven by geopolitical interests, and the only significant economic element concerned oil and gas pipelines. The shifting political alignments did, however, have an important indirect economic impact in that they forestalled construction of specifically Central Asian regional institutions, which has been a serious shortcoming. Among the issues needing to be addressed at the regional level are trade and transit, energy and water, and perhaps security (UNDP 2005).

6 Conclusions

When the five Central Asian countries became unexpectedly independent during the second half of 1991, they faced three large negative shocks: the end of central planning, the dissolution of the Soviet Union, and hyperinflation. All experienced a transitional recession; output fell, inequality widened and poverty increased. Their national experiences, however, diverged during the first decade after independence, both with respect to the type of economic system created and with respect to economic performance.

By the turn of the century the national economies had changed substantially from the centrally planned economy of the Soviet era and all were, in one form or another, market-based economies. The Kyrgyz Republic and Kazakhstan had liberalized prices and trade policy, and they moved much further on privatization than the more regulated economies of Uzbekistan or Turkmenistan. In Tajikistan, prices had effectively liberalized and small enterprises were privatized in the chaos of civil war, but enterprise restructuring lagged and reform had scarcely begun in the financial sector or with respect to infrastructure.

Expectations that economic performance would be correlated with the speed and extent of transition were not borne out in the 1990s. The Kyrgyz Republic, Kazakhstan and Turkmenistan had almost identical GDP performance over the decade 1989-9 (Table 15.1), despite the extensive reforms in the Kyrgyz Republic and the absence of reforms in Turkmenistan. Tajikistan's poor performance is readily understandable in terms of the civil war. Despite limited market-friendly reforms, Uzbekistan in the 1990s was economically the most successful of all Soviet successor states, an achievement that can be explained by buoyant world cotton prices up to 1996 and by the country's relatively good economic management in day-to-day matters.

Expectations that long-term growth rates would depend on economic policies have also not been borne out in the second decade since independence. Variations in economic performance during the 2000s were overwhelmingly determined by energy endowments. High energy prices in 1998-2008 powered Kazakhstan's rapid growth, at least until the country ran into a financial crisis in 2008, and also supported high growth rates in Turkmenistan (possibly exaggerated in Table 15.1), despite poor policies. Meanwhile, Uzbekistan's regulated economy slipped into the low growth familiar from many import-substituting countries of the 1950s and 1960s. The more market-friendly, but resource-poor and landlocked, economies of the Kyrgyz Republic and Tajikistan fared even worse.

All five countries have established super-presidential political regimes, although the degrees of repression are palpably different.[34] The post-2000 economic growth may increase pressure for political change, although national security forces still seem to have the situation well under control. Prospects for significant change in economic policies in the near future are limited because the entrenched political regimes have little incentive to sponsor major reforms. In sum, a big unknown with respect to future economic prospects is the domestic political environment, especially in the two largest economies, where the succession to presidents Karimov and Nazarbayev is unclear. Fundamental across Central Asia is the question of whether an autocratic and repressive political regime is consistent with a flourishing market-based economy.

International relations, which were predicted to centre on a new 'great game' among external powers, have been more muted than anticipated. During the 1990s the low profile of other powers perpetuated Russian hegemony in the region, even though Russia's outreach was limited. After 2000, and especially since 2005, external powers' interest increased. This has primarily focused on energy projects and pipeline routes; inflows of non-energy foreign investment have been minimal. The Central Asian countries have managed to balance competing foreign interests and have avoided falling under the dominant influence of a foreign power. An unfortunate consequence of the shifting alignments has been the stalling of economic co-operation within Central Asia, which is essential with respect to water and energy, desirable for trade and transit, and perhaps necessary for regional security.

Notes

1. The situations before independence and the immediate post-independence period (1992–3) are analysed in Pomfret (1995). Islamov (2001), Gleason (2003) and Pomfret (2006) provide alternative accounts of the region's economic development during the 1990s.
2. Cotton was the main source of rents in the 1990s, but heavy-handed intervention led to falling yields (Pomfret 2008a). After 1998, as energy prices began to rise, natural gas exports dominated and provided sufficient revenues to fund the president's grandiose schemes (Garcia 2006; Global Witness 2006).
3. The inter-republic flows in the USSR are difficult to measure because the Soviet economy was treated as a single unit and large flows took place within all-union enterprises. Outsiders estimated the net flow to the Kyrgyz Republic in the late 1980s at around a seventh of the republic's gross product (Pomfret 1995: 72; Griffin 1996: 19), but Central Asian economists have argued that the net inflow was much smaller, or even that Central Asia subsidized the rest of the USSR through Moscow-manipulated transfer pricing (Islamov 2001).
4. Remittances became increasingly important for Tajikistan, but in the 1990s much of the inflow was in cash and not captured in official statistics.
5. The figures in Tables 15.1, 15.2 and 15.4 come from national sources and, while international organizations adjust data for definitional consistency, they have no way of correcting undisclosed collection or reporting biases. One discouraging sign in some of the Central Asian data is the large revisions made to the growth rates within a few years of their initial publication. For example, the EBRD *Transition Report Update* of May 2005 gave Turkmenistan's 2002 growth rate as 8 per cent but by the 2009 edition reported in Table 15.1 this had been changed to 16 per cent.
6. Rapid surveys were used to assess immediate needs in the early 1990s (e.g. Howell 1996 on the southern districts of the Kyrgyz Republic), and qualitative methods have been used to conceptualize interactions between social, economic and psychological elements of changes in living standards (e.g. the chapters by Kuehnast on the Kyrgyz Republic and by Gomart on Tajikistan and Uzbekistan in Dudwick et al. 2003). The small and possibly unrepresentative samples make generalization of the results difficult, but the patterns of traumatic economic decline during the

first half of the 1990s, especially outside the capital cities, are incontrovertible. The household survey data (analysed in Anderson and Pomfret 2003) present a picture of widespread poverty in the mid-1990s.

7. At PPP the Central Asian countries' incomes are higher. By the PPP estimates of Maddison (2001: 183–5), Tajikistan's 1998 per capita GDP of I$830 (international dollars) was about the same as that of Haiti or Bangladesh, only Afghanistan had lower per capita GDP in Asia, and in Africa only 13 of the 42 countries for which Maddison provides estimates had lower per capita GDP than Tajikistan. According to the World Bank's *World Development Indicators 2002*, Tajikistan's 2000 GNI per capita at PPP was $1090; corresponding figures for the Kyrgyz Republic are $270 and $2540 (PPP), for Uzbekistan $360 and $2360 (PPP), for Turkmenistan $750 and $3820 (PPP), and for Kazakhstan $1260 and $5490 (PPP). As emphasized above, care needs to be taken in interpreting the national accounts data, and PPP conversions are even less firmly based.

8. Uzbekistan's relatively good GDP performance during the 1990s may in part be a statistical artefact due to fewer under-reported unofficial activities and some over-valuation of the official economy, but this is not the whole explanation (Taube and Zettelmeyer 1998).

9. The econometric literature is reviewed in Pomfret (2002: 90–3) and in World Bank (2002).

10. The idea of a threshold value beyond which inflation is harmful to growth was popularized by Bruno and Easterly (1998), although their threshold of 40 per cent now appears too high. Focusing only on transition economies, Christoffersen and Doyle (1998) estimate a threshold of 13 per cent. Turkmenistan, and to a lesser extent Uzbekistan, used price controls as well as monetary policy to address hyperinflation.

11. The largest single enterprise, a sugar refinery that accounted for 3 per cent of GNP in 1991, used cane sugar from Cuba as the raw material and this supply link broke down completely. Other large industrial enterprises were part of the Soviet military–industrial complex and also encountered breakdown of their demand and supply chains after 1990.

12. Kumtor accounted for over two-fifths of industrial output and its share of GDP was 16 per cent in the first quarter of 2001; Centre for Social and Economic Research in Kyrgyzstan, *Kyrgyz Economic Outlook* 2/2001, 9.

13. The arrears complicated Turkmenistan's national accounts because gas sales were recorded as exports valued at the contract price. The arrears appeared in the capital account of the balance of payments as capital outflows from Turkmenistan, even though the foreign assets being accumulated were worth far less than their face value. The actual accounts were extremely opaque because revenues received from energy and cotton exports went into off-budget funds under the president's personal control.

14. See, for example, the results of the Business Environment and Enterprise Performance survey (BEEPS) reported in the EBRD's *Transition Report 1999*. Among the 20 transition economies covered by the 1999 BEEPS, Uzbekistan ranked about fourth for lack of corruption, ahead of several East European countries generally considered to be transition leaders.

15. Much of Tajikistan's hydroelectricity is used by a single aluminium smelter that is the country's main source of foreign exchange earnings.

16. The gap was especially clear given that much of the migration was to the cotton-growing region of South Kazakhstan, the poorest part of the country.

17. US opposition thwarted significant energy exports via Iran, despite it having the closest access to ocean transport, and security conditions worked against pipelines via Afghanistan to the booming energy markets of South Asia.

18. Since the 2009 conference in Helsinki, Finland, where this study was first presented, President Bakiyev was overthrown (in April 2010) because the system had not changed.

19. This section draws on Pomfret (2009), and my contribution to the Asian Development Bank project *Institutions for Regionalism: Enhancing Asia's Economic Cooperation and Integration*. Linn (2004) highlights the process of disintegration in Central Asia.

20. The ECO has three founding members—Iran, Pakistan and Turkey—plus Afghanistan, Azerbaijan and the Central Asian countries, which all joined in 1992. The secretariat is in Tehran.

21. A common external tariff at Kyrgyz rates would be unacceptable to Russia, but a tariff structure close to Russia's would impose substantial economic costs on the Kyrgyz Republic and Kazakhstan (Tumbarello 2005), as well as forcing the former to renege on its WTO commitments. Kazakhstan's WTO application has moved slowly; a draft Report of the Working Party, which typically indicates that the endgame of accession negotiations has been reached, was prepared in May 2005, but completion of the negotiations always seems to be expected 'next year'. Uzbekistan and Tajikistan also have WTO applications in process but they are further from completion.

22. Sakwa and Webber (1999) provide a general account of the CIS in the 1990s.

23. The UN General Assembly formally recognized Turkmenistan's neutrality in a resolution of 12 December 1995 (Freitag-Wirminghaus 1998; Werner 2001). On Turkmenistan's neutrality, see Pomfret (2008b).

24. On occasion, only Israel and Uzbekistan voted with the USA at the UN, and at the May 1996 ECO summit, Uzbekistan's denunciation of Iran was so vitriolic that the summit ended a day earlier than planned. In July 1996, President Karimov was warmly received by President Clinton in Washington DC. For more details of Uzbekistan's evolving foreign economic policies, see Bohr (1998), Pomfret (2000) and Spechler (1999).

25. The main impact on the Kyrgyz economy was to destroy the banking system, which subsequently became dominated by Kazakh banks.

26. Uzbekistan formally joined the four GUAM countries in 1999, effectively withdrew from the alliance in 2002 and withdrew *de jure* in May 2005.

27. Especially after the expansion of NATO in Eastern Europe at the November 2002 Prague summit, President Putin tried to obtain recognition of Russian hegemony over Central Asia and the Caucasus as a *quid pro quo* for his acquiescence in the NATO enlargement. President Karimov of Uzbekistan, however, had a fairly high profile at Prague, meeting President Jacques Chirac and Secretary of State Colin Powell, who praised 'the practical actions of Uzbekistan in the international fight against terrorism' (quoted at www.press-service.uz/eng/vizits_eng/ve21112002.htm by the press service of the President of Uzbekistan). President Rahmonov of Tajikistan also publicized improved ties with France and the USA, making visits to the two countries in December 2002 as a signal of displeasure with Russia's deportation of Tajik workers. By contrast, on 18–19 February 2003, President Nazarbayev of Kazakhstan, facing US and EU criticisms of his regime's corruption and human rights record, made an official visit to Russia, where he was not criticized for such things.

28. The EBRD decision to hold its 2003 annual meetings in Tashkent highlighted the gap between commitments to democracy and Central Asian realities. The killing of several hundred demonstrators in Andijan by Uzbek security forces in May 2005 was the final catalyst for a break in relations.
29. The 10 billion m³ a year East Caspian pipeline would be in addition to the 50+ billion m³ a year currently flowing to Russia. As a further incentive for Turkmenistan to sign the pipeline contract, Russia-connected companies provided capital. For example, Itera was a lead investor in the $4 billion development project to turn the area around the Caspian port of Turkmenbashi into a tourist centre. However, the 2007 announcement failed to pre-empt alternative gas pipeline routes such as that begun from Turkmenistan to China a few months later or the proposed Nabucco pipeline through Turkey and Southeast Europe, and the East Caspian project remains a pipe dream.
30. In February 2009 the Kyrgyz government finally gave the USA six months' notice to quit the base, but this appeared to be a bargaining tactic and a new agreement was signed in July 2009 with no apparent disruption of US operations.
31. A sign of antipathy towards Russian influence was President Rahmonov's announcement in March 2007 that he had changed his name to Rahmon, dropping the Russian ending '-ov'. He urged other Tajiks to follow his example and return to their cultural and national roots.
32. Although all sides sought to keep the arrangements low key, by 2009 both Uzbekistan and Turkmenistan allowed refuelling of aircraft and overland transport of supplies for US forces in Afghanistan and humanitarian assistance.
33. The Central Asian countries continued to score poorly on international rankings of democracy and human rights. For example, in the Freedom House *Nations in Transit 2009 Report*, all five rank among the eight 'consolidated authoritarian regimes', together with Belarus, Azerbaijan and Russia. Turkmenistan, with 6.93 out of 7, had the lowest score among the 29 Eastern European and CIS countries surveyed; Uzbekistan scored 6.89, Kazakhstan 6.32, Tajikistan 6.14 and the Kyrgyz Republic 6.04. On Kazakhstan's record, the report observed that 'Notwithstanding its impending takeover of the 2010 chairmanship of the Organization for Security and Co-operation in Europe, the Kazakhstani government has not taken a single convincing step towards promoting democratic rule, aiding political liberalization, establishing genuine tolerance, or creating conditions for the functioning of an independent media and civil society.' Every one of the five had lower democracy scores in 2009 than their 1999/2000 scores of 5.08 (Kyrgyz Republic), 5.50 (Kazakhstan), 5.75 (Tajikistan), 6.38 (Uzbekistan) and 6.75 (Turkmenistan).
34. This may complicate the assessments of economic performance in the previous paragraph. The greater liberty in the Kyrgyz Republic underpins a flourishing market culture, and the two largest bazaars, in Osh and in Bishkek, cater primarily to Uzbeks; lack of consumer choice and extensive bureaucratic allocation in Uzbekistan (and in Turkmenistan) may be associated with lower economic well-being for a given real GDP.

References

Anderson, K.H. and R. Pomfret (2003). *Consequences of Creating a Market Economy: Evidence from Household Surveys in Central Asia*, Edward Elgar: Cheltenham.
Bohr, A. (1998). *Uzbekistan: Politics and Foreign Policy*, Royal Institute of International Affairs: London, and Brookings Institution: Washington, DC.

Bruno, M. and W. Easterly (1998). 'Inflation Crises and Long-Run Growth', *Journal of Monetary Economics*, 41(1): 3–26.

Christoffersen, P. and P. Doyle (1998). 'From Inflation to Growth: Eight Years of Transition', *IMF Working Paper WP/98/100*, International Monetary Fund: Washington, DC.

Dudwick, N., E. Gomart and A. Marc, and K. Kuehnast (2003). *When Things Fall Apart: Qualitative Studies of Poverty in the Former Soviet Union*, World Bank: Washington, DC.

EBRD (European Bank for Reconstruction and Development) (various issues) *Transition Report Update*, EBRD: London, available at /www.ebrd.com.

Freedom House (n.d.) *Nations in Transition 2009 Report*, available at www.freedomhouse.org/template.cfm?page=17&year=2006.

Freitag-Wirminghaus, R. (1998) 'Turkmenistan's Place in Central Asia and the World', in T. Atabaki and J. O'Kane (eds), *Post-Soviet Central Asia*, Tauris Academic Studies: London.

Garcia, D. (2006) *Le Pays où Bouygues est Roi*, Éditions Danger Public: Paris.

Gleason, G. (2003) *Markets and Politics in Central Asia*, Routledge: London.

Gleason, G. (2006) 'The Uzbek Expulsion of US Forces and Realignment in Central Asia', *Problems of Post-Communism*, 53(2): 49–60.

Global Witness (2006) *It's a Gas: Funny Business in the Turkmen-Ukraine Gas Trade*, Global Witness: Washington, DC.

Griffin, K. (ed.) (1996) *Social Policy and Economic Transformation in Uzbekistan*, International Labour Organization: Geneva.

Howell, J. (1996) 'Poverty and Transition in Kyrgyzstan: How Some Households Cope', *Central Asian Survey*, 15(1): 59–73.

Islamov, B. (2001). *The Central Asian States Ten Years After: How to Overcome Traps of Development, Transformation and Globalisation?*, Maruzen: Tokyo.

Kalyuzhnova, Y. (1998) *The Kazakstani Economy: Independence and Transition*, Macmillan: Basingstoke.

Kireyev, A. (2006) 'The Macroeconomics of Remittances: The Case of Tajikistan', *IMF Working Paper No. 06/2*, International Monetary Fund: Washington, DC.

Linn, J. (2004) 'Economic (Dis)Integration Matters: The Soviet Collapse Revisited', mimeo, Brookings Institution: Washington, DC.

Lubin, N. (1999) 'Energy Wealth, Development, and Stability in Turkmenistan', *NBR Analysis*, 10(3): 61–78.

Maddison, A. (2001) *The World Economy: A Millennial Perspective*, OECD Development Centre: Paris.

Mogilevsky, R. and R. Hasanov (2004) 'Economic Growth in Kyrgyzstan', in G. Ofer and R. Pomfret (eds), *The Economic Prospects of the CIS: Sources of Long-Term Growth since 1991*, Edward Elgar: Cheltenham.

National Cotton Council of America (n.d.) Cotlook A(FE) index, available at www.cotton.org/econ/prices/cotlook-a-indices.cfm.

Ochs, M. (1997) 'Turkmenistan: The Quest for Stability and Control', in K. Dawisha and B. Parrott (eds), *Conflict, Cleavage and Change: Central Asia and the Caucasus*, Cambridge University Press: Cambridge.

Olcott, M.B. (2002) *Kazakhstan: A Faint-Hearted Democracy*, Carnegie Endowment for International Peace: Washington, DC.

Pastor, G. and R. van Rooden (2000) 'Turkmenistan: The Burden of Current Agricultural Policies', *IMF Working Paper No. WP/00/98*, International Monetary Fund: Washington, DC.

Pomfret, R. (1995) *The Economies of Central Asia*, Princeton University Press: Princeton, NJ.

Pomfret, R. (1999) *Central Asia Turns South? Trade Relations in Transition*, Royal Institute of International Affairs: London, and Brookings Institution: Washington, DC.

Pomfret, R. (2000) 'The Uzbek Model of Economic Development 1991–99', *Economics of Transition*, 8(3): 733–48.

Pomfret, R. (2001) 'Turkmenistan: From Communism to Nationalism by Gradual Economic Reform', *MOCT-MOST Economic Policy in Transitional Economies*, 11(2): 165–76.

Pomfret, R. (2002) *Constructing a Market Economy: Diverse Paths from Central Planning in Asia and Europe*, Edward Elgar: Cheltenham.

Pomfret, R. (2005) 'Kazakhstan's Economy since Independence: Does the Oil Boom Offer a Second Chance for Sustainable Development?', *Europe-Asia Studies*, 57(6): 859–76.

Pomfret, R. (2006) *The Central Asia Economies since Independence*, Princeton University Press: Princeton, NJ.

Pomfret, R. (2008a) 'Chapters on Kazakhstan and on Tajikistan, Turkmenistan and Uzbekistan', in K. Anderson and J. Swinnen (eds), *Distortions to Agricultural Incentives in Europe's Transition Economies*, World Bank: Washington, DC.

Pomfret, R. (2008b) 'Turkmenistan's Foreign Policy', *The China and Eurasian Forum Quarterly*, 6(4): 9–34.

Pomfret, R. (2009) 'Regional Integration in Central Asia', *Economic Change and Restructuring*, 42(1–2): 47–68.

Pomfret, R. (2011) 'Turkmenistan and EU Gas Supplies', in L. Wylie and P. Winand (eds.), Peter Lang, Brussels.

Sakwa, R. and M. Webber (1999) 'The Commonwealth of Independent States, 1991–1998: Stagnation and Survival', *Europe-Asia Studies*, 51: 379–415.

Spechler, M. (1999) 'Uzbekistan: The Silk Road to Nowhere?', *Contemporary Economic Policy*, 18(3): 295–303.

Spechler, M. (2000) 'Hunting the Central Asian Tiger', *Comparative Economic Studies*, 42(3): 101–20.

Tarr, D. (1994) 'The Terms-of-Trade Effects of Moving to World Prices on Countries of the Former Soviet Union', *Journal of Comparative Economics*, 18(1): 1–24.

Taube, G. and J. Zettelmeyer (1998) 'Output Decline and Recovery in Uzbekistan: Past Performance and Future Prospects', *IMF Working Paper No. WP/98/11*, International Monetary Fund: Washington, DC.

Tumbarello, P. (2005) 'Regional Integration and WTO Accession: Which is the Right Sequencing? An Application to the CIS', *IMF Working Paper No. 05/94*, International Monetary Fund: Washington, DC.

UNDP (2005) 'Bringing Down Barriers: Regional Co-operation for Human Development and Human Society', *Central Asia Human Development Report*, UNDP: Bratislava.

Werner, M. (2001) 'Im Reich des grossen Führers: Turkmenistan: eine zentralasiatische Despotie', *Osteuropa*, 51(2): 127–34.

World Bank (n.d.) *World Development Indicators*, World Bank: Washington, DC, available at www.worldbank.org.

World Bank (1992) 'Measuring the Incomes of Economies of the Former Soviet Union', *World Bank Policy Research Working Paper No. WPS 1057*, World Bank: Washington, DC.

World Bank (2002) *Transition: The First Ten Years*, World Bank: Washington, DC.

Index

Note: Page number in italics represents tables and figures.